PROFESSIONAL HADOOP® SOLUTIONS

PROFESSIONAL

Hadoop® Solutions

Boris Lublinsky
Kevin T. Smith
Alexey Yakubovich

A Wiley Brand

Professional Hadoop® Solutions

Published by
John Wiley & Sons, Inc.
10475 Crosspoint Boulevard
Indianapolis, IN 46256
www.wiley.com

Copyright © 2013 by John Wiley & Sons, Inc., Indianapolis, Indiana

Published simultaneously in Canada

ISBN: 978-1-118-61193-7
ISBN: 978-1-118-61254-5 (ebk)
ISBN: 978-1-118-82418-4 (ebk)

Manufactured in the United States of America

10 9 8 7 6 5 4 3 2 1

For general information on our other products and services please contact our Customer Care Department within the United States at (877) 762-2974, outside the United States at (317) 572-3993 or fax (317) 572-4002.

Wiley publishes in a variety of print and electronic formats and by print-on-demand. Some material included with standard print versions of this book may not be included in e-books or in print-on-demand. If this book refers to media such as a CD or DVD that is not included in the version you purchased, you may download this material at http://booksupport.wiley.com. For more information about Wiley products, visit www.wiley.com.

Library of Congress Control Number: 2013946768

To my late parents, who always encouraged me to try something new and different.

— BORIS LUBLINSKY

To Gwen, Isabella, Emma, and Henry.

— KEVIN T. SMITH

To my family, where I always have support and understanding.

— ALEXEY YAKUBOVICH

CREDITS

EXECUTIVE EDITOR
Robert Elliott

PROJECT EDITOR
Kevin Shafer

TECHNICAL EDITORS
Michael C. Daconta
Ralph Perko
Michael Segel

PRODUCTION EDITOR
Christine Mugnolo

COPY EDITOR
Kimberly A. Cofer

EDITORIAL MANAGER
Mary Beth Wakefield

FREELANCER EDITORIAL MANAGER
Rosemarie Graham

ASSOCIATE DIRECTOR OF MARKETING
David Mayhew

MARKETING MANAGER
Ashley Zurcher

BUSINESS MANAGER
Amy Knies

PRODUCTION MANAGER
Tim Tate

VICE PRESIDENT AND EXECUTIVE GROUP PUBLISHER
Richard Swadley

VICE PRESIDENT AND EXECUTIVE PUBLISHER
Neil Edde

ASSOCIATE PUBLISHER
Jim Minatel

PROJECT COORDINATOR, COVER
Katie Crocker

PROOFREADER
Daniel Aull, Word One New York

INDEXER
John Sleeva

COVER DESIGNER
Ryan Sneed

COVER IMAGE
iStockphoto.com/Tetiana Vitsenko

ABOUT THE AUTHORS

BORIS LUBLINSKY is a principal architect at Nokia, where he actively participates in all phases of the design of numerous enterprise applications focusing on technical architecture, Service-Oriented Architecture (SOA), and integration initiatives. He is also an active member of the Nokia Architectural council. Boris is the author of more than 80 publications in industry magazines, and has co-authored the book *Service-Oriented Architecture and Design Strategies* (Indianapolis: Wiley, 2008). Additionally, he is an *InfoQ* editor on SOA and Big Data, and a frequent speaker at industry conferences. For the past two years, he has participated in the design and implementation of several Hadoop and Amazon Web Services (AWS) based implementations. He is currently an active member, co-organizer, and contributor to the Chicago area Hadoop User Group.

KEVIN T. SMITH is the Director of Technology Solutions and Outreach in the Applied Mission Solutions division of Novetta Solutions, where he provides strategic technology leadership and develops innovative, data-focused, and highly secure solutions for customers. A frequent speaker at technology conferences, he is the author of numerous technology articles related to web services, Cloud computing, Big Data, and cybersecurity. He has written a number of technology books, including *Applied SOA: Service-Oriented Architecture and Design Strategies* (Indianapolis: Wiley, 2008); *The Semantic Web: A Guide to the Future of XML, Web Services, and Knowledge Management* (Indianapolis: Wiley, 2003); *Professional Portal Development with Open Source Tools* (Indianapolis: Wiley, 2004); *More Java Pitfalls* (Indianapolis: Wiley, 2003); and others.

ALEXEY YAKUBOVICH is a system architect with Hortonworks. He worked in the Hadoop/Big Data environment for five years for different companies and projects: petabyte stores, process automation, natural language processing (NLP), data science with data streams from mobile devices, and social media. Earlier, he worked in technology domains of SOA, Java 2 Enterprise Edition (J2EE), distributed applications, and code generation. He earned his Ph.D. in mathematics for solving the final part of the First Hilbert's Problem. He worked as a member of the MDA OMG group, and has participated and presented at the Chicago area Hadoop User Group.

ABOUT THE TECHNICAL EDITORS

MICHAEL C. DACONTA is the Vice President of Advanced Technology for InCadence Strategic Solutions (http://www.incadencecorp.com), where he currently guides multiple advanced technology projects for government and commercial customers. He is a well-known author, lecturer, and columnist who has authored or co-authored 11 technical books (on such subjects as Semantic Web, XML, XUL, Java, C++, and C), numerous magazine articles, and online columns. He also writes the monthly "Reality Check" column for *Government Computer News*. He earned his Master's degree in Computer Science from Nova Southeastern University, and his bachelor's degree in Computer Science from New York University.

MICHAEL SEGEL has been working for more than 20 years in the IT industry. He has been focused on the Big Data space since 2009, and is both MapR and Cloudera certified. Segel founded the Chicago area Hadoop User Group, and is active in the Chicago Big Data community. He has a Bachelor of Science degree in CIS from the College of Engineering, The Ohio State University. When not working, he spends his time walking his dogs.

RALPH PERKO is a software architect and engineer for Pacific Northwest National Laboratory's Visual Analytics group. He is currently involved with several Hadoop projects, where he is helping to invent and develop novel ways to process and visualize massive data sets. He has 16 years of software development experience.

ACKNOWLEDGMENTS

TO THE MANY PEOPLE that I have worked with. They always have been pushing me to the limit, questioning my solutions, and consequently making them better. A lot of their ideas are used in this book, and hopefully made the book better.

Many thanks to Dean Wampler, who has contributed Hadoop domain-specific languages content for Chapter 13.

To my co-authors, Kevin and Alexey, who brought their own perspective on Hadoop to the book's coverage, and made it better and more balanced.

To the technical editors for many valuable suggestions on the book's content.

To the Wiley editorial staff — Bob Elliott, for deciding to publish this book; our editor, Kevin Shafer, for relentlessly working to fix any inconsistencies; and many others, for creating the final product that you are reading.

— BORIS LUBLINSKY

FIRST OF ALL, I would like to thank my co-authors and the great team at Wrox Press for this effort. As this is my seventh book project, I would like to especially thank my wonderful wife, Gwen, and my sweet children, Isabella, Emma, and Henry, for putting up with the long days, nights, and weekends where I was camped out in front of my computer.

A sincere thanks to the many people who read the early drafts of these chapters, and provided comments, edits, insights, and ideas — specifically Mike Daconta, Ralph Perko, Praveena Raavichara, Frank Tyler, and Brian Uri. I am grateful to my company, Novetta Solutions, and I would especially like to thank Joe Pantella and the rest of the Novetta executive team for being supportive of me in writing this book.

There were several things that could have interfered with my book writing this year. For a while, the Washington Redskins seemed unstoppable, and if they had actually made it to the Super Bowl, this would have put my book deadlines in jeopardy. However, the Redskins' season and another season that I was involved in were abruptly brought to an end. Therefore, we have the Redskins and the POJ to thank for the timeliness of this book.

Finally, special thanks to CiR, Manera, and the One who was, is, and is to come.

— KEVIN T. SMITH

TO MY COLLEAGUES at Nokia, where I was working while writing the book, and whose advice and knowledge created the highly professional context for my chapters.

To my co-authors, Boris and Kevin, who made this book and my participation possible.

To the Wiley editorial staff, for publishing the book, and for providing all the necessary help and guidance to make the book better.

— ALEXEY YAKUBOVICH

CONTENTS

INTRODUCTION

IN THIS FAST-PACED WORLD of ever-changing technology, we have been drowning in information. We are generating and storing massive quantities of data. With the proliferation of devices on our networks, we have seen an amazing growth in a diversity of information formats and data — Big Data.

But let's face it — if we're honest with ourselves, most of our organizations haven't been able to proactively manage massive quantities of this data effectively, and we haven't been able to use this information to our advantage to make better decisions and to do business smarter. We have been overwhelmed with vast amounts of data, while at the same time we have been starved for knowledge. The result for companies is lost productivity, lost opportunities, and lost revenue.

Over the course of the past decade, many technologies have promised to help with the processing and analyzing of the vast amounts of information we have, and most of these technologies have come up short. And we know this because, as programmers focused on data, we have tried it all. Many approaches have been proprietary, resulting in vendor lock-in. Some approaches were promising, but couldn't scale to handle large data sets, and many were hyped up so much that they couldn't meet expectations, or they simply were not ready for prime time.

When Apache Hadoop entered the scene, however, everything was different. Certainly there was hype, but this was an open source project that had already found incredible success in massively scalable commercial applications. Although the learning curve was sometimes steep, for the first time, we were able to easily write programs and perform data analytics on a massive scale — in a way that we haven't been able to do before. Based on a MapReduce algorithm that enables us as developers to bring processing to the data distributed on a scalable cluster of machines, we have found much success in performing complex data analysis in ways that we haven't been able to do in the past.

It's not that there is a lack of books about Hadoop. Quite a few have been written, and many of them are very good. So, why this one? Well, when the authors started working with Hadoop, we wished there was a book that went beyond APIs and explained how the many parts of the Hadoop ecosystem work together and can be used to build enterprise-grade solutions. We were looking for a book that walks the reader through the data design and how it impacts implementation, as well as explains how MapReduce works, and how to reformulate specific business problems in MapReduce. We were looking for answers to the following questions:

➤ What are MapReduce's strengths and weaknesses, and how can you customize it to better suit your needs?

➤ Why do you need an additional orchestration layer on top of MapReduce, and how does Oozie fit the bill?

➤ How can you simplify MapReduce development using domain-specific languages (DSLs)?

➤ What is this real-time Hadoop that everyone is talking about, what can it do, and what can it not do? How does it work?

➤ How do you secure your Hadoop applications, what do you need to consider, what security vulnerabilities must you consider, and what are the approaches for dealing with them?

➤ How do you transition your Hadoop application to the cloud, and what are important considerations when doing so?

When the authors started their Hadoop adventure, we had to spend long days (and often nights) browsing all over Internet and Hadoop source code, talking to people and experimenting with the code to find answers to these questions. And then we decided to share our findings and experience by writing this book with the goal of giving you, the reader, a head start in understanding and using Hadoop.

WHO THIS BOOK IS FOR

This book was written by programmers for programmers. The authors are technologists who develop enterprise solutions, and our goal with this book is to provide solid, practical advice for other developers using Hadoop. The book is targeted at software architects and developers trying to better understand and leverage Hadoop for performing not only a simple data analysis, but also to use Hadoop as a foundation for enterprise applications.

Because Hadoop is a Java-based framework, this book contains a wealth of code samples that require fluency in Java. Additionally, the authors assume that the readers are somewhat familiar with Hadoop, and have some initial MapReduce knowledge.

Although this book was designed to be read from cover to cover in a building-block approach, some sections may be more applicable to certain groups of people. Data designers who want to understand Hadoop's data storage capabilities will likely benefit from Chapter 2. Programmers getting started with MapReduce will most likely focus on Chapters 3 through 5, and Chapter 13. Developers who have realized the complexity of not using a Workflow system like Oozie will most likely want to focus on Chapters 6 through 8. Those interested in real-time Hadoop will want to focus on Chapter 9. People interested in using the Amazon cloud for their implementations might focus on Chapter 11, and security-minded individuals may want to focus on Chapters 10 and 12.

WHAT THIS BOOK COVERS

Right now, everyone's doing Big Data. Organizations are making the most of massively scalable analytics, and most of them are trying to use Hadoop for this purpose. This book concentrates on the architecture and approaches for building Hadoop-based advanced enterprise applications, and covers the following main Hadoop components used for this purpose:

➤ Blueprint architecture for Hadoop-based enterprise applications

➤ Base Hadoop data storage and organization systems

➤ Hadoop's main execution framework (MapReduce)

➤ Hadoop's Workflow/Coordinator server (Oozie)

➤ Technologies for implementing Hadoop-based real-time systems

➤ Ways to run Hadoop in the cloud environment

➤ Technologies and architecture for securing Hadoop applications

HOW THIS BOOK IS STRUCTURED

The book is organized into 13 chapters.

Chapter 1 ("Big Data and the Hadoop Ecosystem") provides an introduction to Big Data, and the ways Hadoop can be used for Big Data implementations. Here you learn how Hadoop solves Big Data challenges, and which core Hadoop components can work together to create a rich Hadoop ecosystem applicable for solving many real-world problems. You also learn about available Hadoop distributions, and emerging architecture patterns for Big Data applications.

The foundation of any Big Data implementation is data storage design. *Chapter 2 ("Storing Data in Hadoop")* covers distributed data storage provided by Hadoop. It discusses both the architecture and APIs of two main Hadoop data storage mechanisms — HDFS and HBase — and provides some recommendations on when to use each one. Here you learn about the latest developments in both HDFS (federation) and HBase new file formats, and coprocessors. This chapter also covers HCatalog (the Hadoop metadata management solution) and Avro (a serialization/marshaling framework), as well as the roles they play in Hadoop data storage.

As the main Hadoop execution framework, MapReduce is one of the main topics of this book and is covered in Chapters 3, 4, and 5.

Chapter 3 ("Processing Your Data with MapReduce") provides an introduction to the MapReduce framework. It covers the MapReduce architecture, its main components, and the MapReduce programming model. This chapter also focuses on MapReduce application design, design patterns, and general MapReduce "dos" and "don'ts."

Chapter 4 ("Customizing MapReduce Execution") builds on Chapter 3 by covering important approaches for customizing MapReduce execution. You learn about the aspects of MapReduce execution that can be customized, and use the working code examples to discover how this can be done.

Finally, in *Chapter 5 ("Building Reliable MapReduce Apps")* you learn about approaches for building reliable MapReduce applications, including testing and debugging, as well as using built-in MapReduce facilities (for example, logging and counters) for getting insights into the MapReduce execution.

Despite the power of MapReduce itself, practical solutions typically require bringing multiple MapReduce applications together, which involves quite a bit of complexity. This complexity can be significantly simplified by using the Hadoop Workflow/Coordinator engine — Oozie — which is described in Chapters 6, 7, and 8.

Chapter 6 ("Automating Data Processing with Oozie") provides an introduction to Oozie. Here you learn about Oozie's overall architecture, its main components, and the programming language for each component. You also learn about Oozie's overall execution model, and the ways you can interact with the Oozie server.

Chapter 7 ("Using Oozie") builds on the knowledge you gain in Chapter 6 and presents a practical end-to-end example of using Oozie to develop a real-world application. This example demonstrates how different Oozie components are used in a solution, and shows both design and implementation approaches.

Finally, *Chapter 8 ("Advanced Oozie Features")* discusses advanced features, and shows approaches to extending Oozie and integrating it with other enterprise applications. In this chapter, you learn some tips and tricks that developers need to know — for example, how dynamic generation of Oozie code allows developers to overcome some existing Oozie shortcomings that can't be resolved in any other way.

One of the hottest trends related to Big Data today is the capability to perform "real-time analytics." This topic is discussed in *Chapter 9 ("Real-Time Hadoop")*. The chapter begins by providing examples of real-time Hadoop applications used today, and presents the overall architectural requirements for such implementations. You learn about three main approaches to building such implementations — HBase-based applications, real-time queries, and stream-based processing.

This chapter provides two examples of HBase-based, real-time applications — a fictitious picture-management system, and a Lucene-based search engine using HBase as its back end. You also learn about the overall architecture for implementation of a real-time query, and the way two concrete products — Apache Drill and Cloudera's Impala — implement it. This chapter also covers another type of real-time application — complex event processing — including its overall architecture, and the way HFlame and Storm implement this architecture. Finally, this chapter provides a comparison between real-time queries, complex event processing, and MapReduce.

An often skipped topic in Hadoop application development — but one that is crucial to understand — is Hadoop security. *Chapter 10 ("Hadoop Security")* provides an in-depth discussion about security concerns related to Big Data analytics and Hadoop — specifically, Hadoop's security model and best practices. Here you learn about the Project Rhino — a framework that enables developers to extend Hadoop's security capabilities, including encryption, authentication, authorization, Single-Sign-On (SSO), and auditing.

Cloud-based usage of Hadoop requires interesting architectural decisions. *Chapter 11 ("Running Hadoop Applications on AWS")* describes these challenges, and covers different approaches to running Hadoop on the Amazon Web Services (AWS) cloud. This chapter also discusses trade-offs and examines best practices. You learn about Elastic MapReduce (EMR) and additional AWS services (such as S3, CloudWatch, Simple Workflow, and so on) that can be used to supplement Hadoop's functionality.

Apart from securing Hadoop itself, Hadoop implementations often integrate with other enterprise components — data is often imported into Hadoop and also exported. *Chapter 12 ("Building Enterprise Security Solutions for Hadoop Implementations")* covers how enterprise applications that use Hadoop are best secured, and provides examples and best practices.

The last chapter of the book, *Chapter 13 ("Hadoop's Future")*, provides a look at some of the current and future industry trends and initiatives that are happening with Hadoop. Here you learn about availability and use of Hadoop DSLs that simplify MapReduce development, as well as a new MapReduce resource management system (YARN) and MapReduce runtime extension (Tez). You also learn about the most significant Hadoop directions and trends.

WHAT YOU NEED TO USE THIS BOOK

All of the code presented in the book is implemented in Java. So, to use it, you will need a Java compiler and development environment. All development was done in Eclipse, but because every project has a Maven pom file, it should be simple enough to import it into any development environment of your choice.

All the data access and MapReduce code has been tested on both Hadoop 1 (Cloudera CDH 3 distribution and Amazon EMR) and Hadoop 2 (Cloudera CDH 4 distribution). As a result, it should work with any Hadoop distribution. Oozie code was tested on the latest version of Oozie (available, for example, as part of Cloudera CDH 4.1 distribution).

The source code for the samples is organized in Eclipse projects (one per chapter), and is available for download from the Wrox website at:

    www.wrox.com/go/prohadoopsolutions

CONVENTIONS

To help you get the most from the text and keep track of what's happening, we've used a number of conventions throughout the book.

> **NOTE** *This indicates notes, tips, hints, tricks, and/or asides to the current discussion.*

As for styles in the text:

➤   We *highlight* new terms and important words when we introduce them.

➤   We show keyboard strokes like this: Ctrl+A.

➤   We show filenames, URLs, and code within the text like so: persistence.properties.

➤   We present code in two different ways:

We use a monofont type with no highlighting for most code examples.

We use bold to emphasize code that is particularly important in the present context or to show changes from a previous code snippet.

SOURCE CODE

As you work through the examples in this book, you may choose either to type in all the code manually, or to use the source code files that accompany the book. Source code for this book is available for download at www.wrox.com. Specifically, for this book, the code download is on the Download Code tab at:

www.wrox.com/go/prohadoopsolutions

You can also search for the book at www.wrox.com by ISBN (the ISBN for this book is 978-1-118-61193-7) to find the code. And a complete list of code downloads for all current Wrox books is available at www.wrox.com/dynamic/books/download.aspx.

Throughout selected chapters, you'll also find references to the names of code files as needed in listing titles and text.

Most of the code on www.wrox.com is compressed in a .ZIP, .RAR archive, or similar archive format appropriate to the platform. Once you download the code, just decompress it with an appropriate compression tool.

> **NOTE** *Because many books have similar titles, you may find it easiest to search by ISBN; this book's ISBN is 978-1-118-61193-7.*

Alternatively, you can go to the main Wrox code download page at www.wrox.com/dynamic/books/download.aspx to see the code available for this book and all other Wrox books.

ERRATA

We make every effort to ensure that there are no errors in the text or in the code. However, no one is perfect, and mistakes do occur. If you find an error in one of our books, like a spelling mistake or faulty piece of code, we would be very grateful for your feedback. By sending in errata, you may save another reader hours of frustration, and at the same time, you will be helping us provide even higher quality information.

To find the errata page for this book, go to:

www.wrox.com/go/prohadoopsolutions

Click the Errata link. On this page, you can view all errata that has been submitted for this book and posted by Wrox editors.

If you don't spot "your" error on the Book Errata page, go to www.wrox.com/contact/techsupport.shtml and complete the form there to send us the error you have found. We'll check the information and, if appropriate, post a message to the book's errata page and fix the problem in subsequent editions of the book.

P2P.WROX.COM

For author and peer discussion, join the P2P forums at `http://p2p.wrox.com`. The forums are a web-based system for you to post messages relating to Wrox books and related technologies, and to interact with other readers and technology users. The forums offer a subscription feature to e-mail you topics of interest of your choosing when new posts are made to the forums. Wrox authors, editors, other industry experts, and your fellow readers are present on these forums.

At `http://p2p.wrox.com`, you will find a number of different forums that will help you, not only as you read this book, but also as you develop your own applications. To join the forums, just follow these steps:

1. Go to `http://p2p.wrox.com` and click the Register link.

2. Read the terms of use and click Agree.

3. Complete the required information to join, as well as any optional information you wish to provide, and click Submit.

4. You will receive an e-mail with information describing how to verify your account and complete the joining process.

> **NOTE** *You can read messages in the forums without joining P2P, but in order to post your own messages, you must join.*

Once you join, you can post new messages and respond to messages other users post. You can read messages at any time on the web. If you would like to have new messages from a particular forum e-mailed to you, click the Subscribe to this Forum icon by the forum name in the forum listing.

For more information about how to use the Wrox P2P, be sure to read the P2P FAQs for answers to questions about how the forum software works, as well as many common questions specific to P2P and Wrox books. To read the FAQs, click the FAQ link on any P2P page.

1

Big Data and the Hadoop Ecosystem

WHAT'S IN THIS CHAPTER?

➤ Understanding the challenges of Big Data

➤ Getting to know the Hadoop ecosystem

➤ Getting familiar with Hadoop distributions

➤ Using Hadoop-based enterprise applications

Everyone says it — we are living in the era of "Big Data." Chances are that you have heard this phrase. In today's technology-fueled world where computing power has significantly increased, electronic devices are more commonplace, accessibility to the Internet has improved, and users have been able to transmit and collect more data than ever before.

Organizations are producing data at an astounding rate. It is reported that Facebook alone collects 250 terabytes a day. According to Thompson Reuters News Analytics, digital data production has more than doubled from almost 1 million petabytes (equal to about 1 billion terabytes) in 2009 to a projected 7.9 zettabytes (a zettabyte is equal to 1 million petabytes) in 2015, and an estimated 35 zettabytes in 2020. Other research organizations offer even higher estimates!

As organizations have begun to collect and produce massive amounts of data, they have recognized the advantages of data analysis. But they have also struggled to manage the massive amounts of information that they have. This has led to new challenges. How can you effectively store such a massive quantity of data? How can you effectively process it? How can you analyze your data in an efficient manner? Knowing that data will only increase, how can you build a solution that will scale?

These challenges that come with Big Data are not just for academic researchers and data scientists. In a Google+ conversation a few years ago, noted computer book publisher Tim O'Reilly made a point of quoting Alistair Croll, who said that "companies that have massive amounts of data without massive amounts of clue are going to be displaced by startups that have less data but more clue ..." In short, what Croll was saying was that unless your business *understands* the data it has, it will not be able to compete with businesses that do.

Businesses realize that tremendous benefits can be gained in analyzing Big Data related to business competition, situational awareness, productivity, science, and innovation. Because competition is driving the analysis of Big Data, most organizations agree with O'Reilly and Croll. These organizations believe that the survival of today's companies will depend on their capability to store, process, and analyze massive amounts of information, and to master the Big Data challenges.

If you are reading this book, you are most likely familiar with these challenges, you have some familiarity with Apache Hadoop, and you know that Hadoop can be used to solve these problems. This chapter explains the promises and the challenges of Big Data. It also provides a high-level overview of Hadoop and its ecosystem of software components that can be used together to build scalable, distributed data analytics solutions.

BIG DATA MEETS HADOOP

Citing "human capital" as an intangible but crucial element of their success, most organizations will suggest that their employees are their most valuable asset. Another critical asset that is typically not listed on a corporate balance sheet is the *information* that a company has. The power of an organization's information can be enhanced by its trustworthiness, its volume, its accessibility, and the capability of an organization to be able to make sense of it all in a reasonable amount of time in order to empower intelligent decision making.

It is very difficult to comprehend the sheer amount of digital information that organizations produce. IBM states that 90 percent of the digital data in the world was created in the past two years alone. Organizations are collecting, producing, and storing this data, which can be a strategic resource. A book written more than a decade ago, *The Semantic Web: A Guide to the Future of XML, Web Services, and Knowledge Management* by Michael Daconta, Leo Obrst, and Kevin T. Smith (Indianapolis: Wiley, 2004) included a maxim that said, "The organization that has the best information, knows how to find it, and can utilize it the quickest wins."

Knowledge is power. The problem is that with the vast amount of digital information being collected, traditional database tools haven't been able to manage or process this information quickly enough. As a result, organizations have been drowning in data. Organizations haven't been able to use the data well, and haven't been able to "connect the dots" in the data quickly enough to understand the power in the information that the data presents.

The term "Big Data" has been used to describe data sets that are so large that typical and traditional means of data storage, management, search, analytics, and other processing has become a challenge. Big Data is characterized by the magnitude of digital information that can come from many sources and data formats (structured and unstructured), and data that can be processed and analyzed to find insights and patterns used to make informed decisions.

What are the challenges with Big Data? How can you store, process, and analyze such a large amount of data to identify patterns and knowledge from a massive sea of information?

Analyzing Big Data requires lots of storage and large computations that demand a great deal of processing power. As digital information began to increase over the past decade, organizations tried different approaches to solving these problems. At first, focus was placed on giving individual machines more storage, processing power, and memory — only to quickly find that analytical techniques on single machines failed to scale. Over time, many realized the promise of distributed systems (distributing tasks over multiple machines), but data analytic solutions were often complicated, error-prone, or simply not fast enough.

In 2002, while developing a project called Nutch (a search engine project focused on crawling, indexing, and searching Internet web pages), Doug Cutting and Mike Cafarella were struggling with a solution for processing a vast amount of information. Realizing the storage and processing demands for Nutch, they knew that they would need a reliable, distributed computing approach that would scale to the demand of the vast amount of website data that the tool would be collecting.

A year later, Google published papers on the Google File System (GFS) and MapReduce, an algorithm and distributed programming platform for processing large data sets. Recognizing the promise of these approaches used by Google for distributed processing and storage over a cluster of machines, Cutting and Cafarella used this work as the basis of building the distributed platform for Nutch, resulting in what we now know as the Hadoop Distributed File System (HDFS) and Hadoop's implementation of MapReduce.

In 2006, after struggling with the same "Big Data" challenges related to indexing massive amounts of information for its search engine, and after watching the progress of the Nutch project, Yahoo! hired Doug Cutting, and quickly decided to adopt Hadoop as its distributed framework for solving its search engine challenges. Yahoo! spun out the storage and processing parts of Nutch to form Hadoop as an open source Apache project, and the Nutch web crawler remained its own separate project. Shortly thereafter, Yahoo! began rolling out Hadoop as a means to power analytics for various production applications. The platform was so effective that Yahoo! merged its search and advertising into one unit to better leverage Hadoop technology.

In the past 10 years, Hadoop has evolved from its search engine–related origins to one of the most popular general-purpose computing platforms for solving Big Data challenges. It is quickly becoming the foundation for the next generation of data-based applications. The market research firm IDC predicts that Hadoop will be driving a Big Data market that should hit more than $23 billion by 2016. Since the launch of the first Hadoop-centered company, Cloudera, in 2008, dozens of Hadoop-based startups have attracted hundreds of millions of dollars in venture capital investment. Simply put, organizations have found that Hadoop offers a proven approach to Big Data analytics.

Hadoop: Meeting the Big Data Challenge

Apache Hadoop meets the challenges of Big Data by simplifying the implementation of data-intensive, highly parallel distributed applications. Used throughout the world by businesses, universities, and other organizations, it allows analytical tasks to be divided into fragments of work and distributed over thousands of computers, providing fast analytics time and distributed storage of massive amounts of data. Hadoop provides a cost-effective way for storing huge quantities of data. It provides a scalable and reliable mechanism for processing large amounts of data over a cluster of commodity hardware. And it provides new and improved analysis techniques that enable sophisticated analytical processing of multi-structured data.

Hadoop is different from previous distributed approaches in the following ways:

➤   Data is distributed in advance.

➤   Data is replicated throughout a cluster of computers for reliability and availability.

➤   Data processing tries to occur where the data is stored, thus eliminating bandwidth bottlenecks.

In addition, Hadoop provides a simple programming approach that abstracts the complexity evident in previous distributed implementations. As a result, Hadoop provides a powerful mechanism for data analytics, which consists of the following:

➤   **Vast amount of storage** — Hadoop enables applications to work with thousands of computers and petabytes of data. Over the past decade, computer professionals have realized that low-cost "commodity" systems can be used together for high-performance computing applications that once could be handled only by supercomputers. Hundreds of "small" computers may be configured in a cluster to obtain aggregate computing power that can exceed by far that of single supercomputer at a cheaper price. Hadoop can leverage clusters in excess of thousands of machines, providing huge storage and processing power at a price that an enterprise can afford.

➤   **Distributed processing with fast data access** — Hadoop clusters provide the capability to efficiently store vast amounts of data while providing fast data access. Prior to Hadoop, parallel computation applications experienced difficulty distributing execution between machines that were available on the cluster. This was because the cluster execution model creates demand for shared data storage with very high I/O performance. Hadoop moves execution toward the data. Moving the applications to the data alleviates many of the high-performance challenges. In addition, Hadoop applications are typically organized in a way that they process data sequentially. This avoids random data access (disk seek operations), further decreasing I/O load.

➤   **Reliability, failover, and scalability** — In the past, implementers of parallel applications struggled to deal with the issue of reliability when it came to moving to a cluster of machines. Although the reliability of an individual machine is fairly high, the probability of failure grows as the size of the cluster grows. It will not be uncommon to have daily failures in a large (thousands of machines) cluster. Because of the way that Hadoop was designed and implemented, a failure (or set of failures) will not create inconsistent results. Hadoop detects failures and retries execution (by utilizing different nodes). Moreover, the scalability support built into Hadoop's implementation allows for seamlessly bringing additional (repaired) servers into a cluster, and leveraging them for both data storage and execution.

For most Hadoop users, the most important feature of Hadoop is the clean separation between business programming and infrastructure support. For users who want to concentrate on business logic, Hadoop hides infrastructure complexity, and provides an easy-to-use platform for making complex, distributed computations for difficult problems.

Data Science in the Business World

The capability of Hadoop to store and process huge amounts of data is frequently associated with "data science." Although the term was introduced by Peter Naur in the 1960s, it did not get wide acceptance until recently. Jeffrey Stanton of Syracuse University defines it as "an emerging area of work concerned with the collection, preparation, analysis, visualization, management, and preservation of large collections of information."

Unfortunately, in business, the term is often used interchangeably with business analytics. In reality, the two disciplines are quite different.

Business analysts study patterns in existing business operations to improve them.

The goal of data science is to extract meaning from data. The work of data scientists is based on math, statistical analysis, pattern recognition, machine learning, high-performance computing, data warehousing, and much more. They analyze information to look for trends, statistics, and new business possibilities based on collected information.

Over the past few years, many business analysts more familiar with databases and programming have become data scientists, using higher-level SQL-based tools in the Hadoop ecosystem (such as Hive or real-time Hadoop queries), and running analytics to make informed business decisions.

NOT JUST "ONE BIG DATABASE"

You learn more about this a little later in this book, but before getting too far, let's dispel the notion that Hadoop is simply "one big database" meant only for data analysts. Because some of Hadoop's tools (such as Hive and real-time Hadoop queries) provide a low entry barrier to Hadoop for people more familiar with database queries, some people limit their knowledge to only a few database-centric tools in the Hadoop ecosystem.

Moreover, if the problem that you are trying to solve goes beyond data analytics and involves true "data science" problems, data mining SQL is becoming significantly less useful. Most of these problems, for example, require linear algebra, and other complex mathematical applications that are not well-translated into SQL.

This means that, although important, SQL-based tools is only one of the ways to use Hadoop. By utilizing Hadoop's MapReduce programming model, you can not only solve data science problems, but also significantly simplify enterprise application creation and deployment. You have multiple ways to do that — and you can use multiple tools, which often must be combined with other capabilities that require software-development skills. For example, by using Oozie-based application coordination (you will learn more about Oozie later in this book), you can simplify the bringing of multiple applications together, and chaining jobs from multiple tools in a very flexible way. Throughout this book, you will see practical tips for using Hadoop in your enterprise, as well as tips on when to use the right tools for the right situation.

Current Hadoop development is driven by a goal to better support data scientists. Hadoop provides a powerful computational platform, providing highly scalable, parallelizable execution that is well-suited for the creation of a new generation of powerful data science and enterprise applications. Implementers can leverage both scalable distributed storage and MapReduce processing. Businesses are using Hadoop for solving business problems, with a few notable examples:

➤ **Enhancing fraud detection for banks and credit card companies** — Companies are utilizing Hadoop to detect transaction fraud. By providing analytics on large clusters of commodity hardware, banks are using Hadoop, applying analytic models to a full set of transactions for their clients, and providing near-real-time fraud-in-progress detection.

➤ **Social media marketing analysis** — Companies are currently using Hadoop for brand management, marketing campaigns, and brand protection. By monitoring, collecting, and aggregating data from various Internet sources such as blogs, boards, news feeds, tweets, and social media, companies are using Hadoop to extract and aggregate information about their products, services, and competitors, discovering patterns and revealing upcoming trends important for understanding their business.

➤ **Shopping pattern analysis for retail product placement** — Businesses in the retail industry are using Hadoop to determine products most appropriate to sell in a particular store based on the store's location and the shopping patterns of the population around it.

➤ **Traffic pattern recognition for urban development** — Urban development often relies on traffic patterns to determine requirements for road network expansion. By monitoring traffic during different times of the day and discovering patterns, urban developers can determine traffic bottlenecks, which allow them to decide whether additional streets/street lanes are required to avoid traffic congestions during peak hours.

➤ **Content optimization and engagement** — Companies are focusing on optimizing content for rendering on different devices supporting different content formats. Many media companies require that a large amount of content be processed in different formats. Also, content engagement models must be mapped for feedback and enhancements.

➤ **Network analytics and mediation** — Real-time analytics on a large amount of data generated in the form of usage transaction data, network performance data, cell-site information, device-level data, and other forms of back office data is allowing companies to reduce operational expenses, and enhance the user experience on networks.

➤ **Large data transformation** — The *New York Times* needed to generate PDF files for 11 million articles (every article from 1851 to 1980) in the form of images scanned from the original paper. Using Hadoop, the newspaper was able to convert 4 TB of scanned articles to 1.5 TB of PDF documents in 24 hours.

The list of these examples could go on and on. Businesses are using Hadoop for strategic decision making, and they are starting to use their data wisely. As a result, data science has entered the business world.

BIG DATA TOOLS — NOT JUST FOR BUSINESS

Although most of the examples here focus on business, Hadoop is also widely used in the scientific community and in the public sector.

In a recent study by the Tech America Foundation, it was noted that medical researchers have demonstrated that Big Data analytics can be used to aggregate information from cancer patients to increase treatment efficacy. Police departments are using Big Data tools to develop predictive models about when and where crimes are likely to occur, decreasing crime rates. That same survey showed that energy officials are utilizing Big Data tools to analyze data related to energy consumption and potential power grid failure problems.

The bottom line is that Big Data analytics are being used to discover patterns and trends, and are used to increase efficiency and empower decision making in ways never before possible.

THE HADOOP ECOSYSTEM

When architects and developers discuss software, they typically immediately qualify a software tool for its specific usage. For example, they may say that Apache Tomcat is a web server and that MySQL is a database.

When it comes to Hadoop, however, things become a little bit more complicated. Hadoop encompasses a multiplicity of tools that are designed and implemented to work together. As a result, Hadoop can be used for many things, and, consequently, people often define it based on the way they are using it.

For some people, Hadoop is a data management system bringing together massive amounts of structured and unstructured data that touch nearly every layer of the traditional enterprise data stack, positioned to occupy a central place within a data center. For others, it is a massively parallel execution framework bringing the power of supercomputing to the masses, positioned to fuel execution of enterprise applications. Some view Hadoop as an open source community creating tools and software for solving Big Data problems. Because Hadoop provides such a wide array of capabilities that can be adapted to solve many problems, many consider it to be a basic framework.

Certainly, Hadoop provides all of these capabilities, but Hadoop should be classified as an ecosystem comprised of many components that range from data storage, to data integration, to data processing, to specialized tools for data analysts.

HADOOP CORE COMPONENTS

Although the Hadoop ecosystem is certainly growing, Figure 1-1 shows the core components.

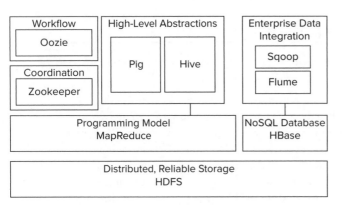

FIGURE 1-1: Core components of the Hadoop ecosystem

Starting from the bottom of the diagram in Figure 1-1, Hadoop's ecosystem consists of the following:

➤ **HDFS** — A foundational component of the Hadoop ecosystem is the Hadoop Distributed File System (HDFS). HDFS is the mechanism by which a large amount of data can be distributed over a cluster of computers, and data is written once, but read many times for analytics. It provides the foundation for other tools, such as HBase.

➤ **MapReduce** — Hadoop's main execution framework is MapReduce, a programming model for distributed, parallel data processing, breaking jobs into *mapping* phases and *reduce* phases (thus the name). Developers write *MapReduce jobs* for Hadoop, using data stored in HDFS for fast data access. Because of the nature of how MapReduce works, Hadoop brings the processing to the data in a parallel fashion, resulting in fast implementation.

➤ **HBase** — A column-oriented NoSQL database built on top of HDFS, HBase is used for fast read/write access to large amounts of data. HBase uses Zookeeper for its management to ensure that all of its components are up and running.

➤ **Zookeeper** — Zookeeper is Hadoop's distributed coordination service. Designed to run over a cluster of machines, it is a highly available service used for the management of Hadoop operations, and many components of Hadoop depend on it.

➤ **Oozie** — A scalable workflow system, Oozie is integrated into the Hadoop stack, and is used to coordinate execution of multiple MapReduce jobs. It is capable of managing a significant amount of complexity, basing execution on external events that include timing and presence of required data.

➤ **Pig** — An abstraction over the complexity of MapReduce programming, the Pig platform includes an execution environment and a scripting language (Pig Latin) used to analyze Hadoop data sets. Its compiler translates Pig Latin into sequences of MapReduce programs.

➤ **Hive** — An SQL-like, high-level language used to run queries on data stored in Hadoop, Hive enables developers not familiar with MapReduce to write data queries that are translated into MapReduce jobs in Hadoop. Like Pig, Hive was developed as an abstraction layer, but geared more toward database analysts more familiar with SQL than Java programming.

The Hadoop ecosystem also contains several frameworks for integration with the rest of the enterprise:

➤ *Sqoop* is a connectivity tool for moving data between relational databases and data warehouses and Hadoop. Sqoop leverages database to describe the schema for the imported/exported data and MapReduce for parallelization operation and fault tolerance.

➤ *Flume* is a distributed, reliable, and highly available service for efficiently collecting, aggregating, and moving large amounts of data from individual machines to HDFS. It is based on a simple and flexible architecture, and provides a streaming of data flows. It leverages a simple extensible data model, allowing you to move data from multiple machines within an enterprise into Hadoop.

Beyond the core components shown in Figure 1-1, Hadoop's ecosystem is growing to provide newer capabilities and components, such as the following:

➤ **Whirr** — This is a set of libraries that allows users to easily spin-up Hadoop clusters on top of Amazon EC2, Rackspace, or any virtual infrastructure.

➤ **Mahout** — This is a machine-learning and data-mining library that provides MapReduce implementations for popular algorithms used for clustering, regression testing, and statistical modeling.

➤ **BigTop** — This is a formal process and framework for packaging and interoperability testing of Hadoop's sub-projects and related components.

➤ **Ambari** — This is a project aimed at simplifying Hadoop management by providing support for provisioning, managing, and monitoring Hadoop clusters.

More members of the Hadoop family are added daily. Just during the writing of this book, three new Apache Hadoop incubator projects were added!

THE EVOLUTION OF PROJECTS INTO APACHE

If you are new to the way that the Apache Software Foundation works, and were wondering about the various projects and their relationships to each other, Apache supports the creation, maturation, and retirement of projects in an organized way. Individuals make up the membership of Apache, and together they make up the governance of the organization.

Projects start as "incubator" projects. The Apache Incubator was created to help new projects join Apache. It provides governance and reviews, and "filters" proposals to create new projects and sub-projects of existing projects. The Incubator aids in the creation of the incubated project, it evaluates the maturity of projects, and is responsible for "graduating" projects from the Incubator into Apache projects or sub-projects. The Incubator also retires projects from incubation for various reasons.

To see a full list of projects in the Incubator (current, graduated, dormant, and retired), see http://incubator.apache.org/projects/index.html.

The majority of Hadoop publications today either concentrate on the description of individual components of this ecosystem, or on the approach for using business analysis tools (such as Pig and Hive) in Hadoop. Although these topics are important, they typically fall short in providing an in-depth picture for helping architects build Hadoop-based enterprise applications or complex analytics applications.

HADOOP DISTRIBUTIONS

Although Hadoop is a set of open source Apache (and now GitHub) projects, a large number of companies are currently emerging with the goal of helping people actually use Hadoop. Most of these companies started with packaging Apache Hadoop distributions, ensuring that all the software worked together, and providing support. And now they are developing additional tools to simplify Hadoop usage and extend its functionality. Some of these extensions are proprietary and serve as differentiation. Some became the foundation of new projects in the Apache Hadoop family. And some are open source GitHub projects with an Apache 2 license. Although all of these companies started from the Apache Hadoop distribution, they all have a slightly different vision of what Hadoop really is, which direction it should take, and how to accomplish it.

One of the biggest differences between these companies is the use of Apache code. With the exception of the MapR, everyone considers Hadoop to be defined by the code produced by Apache projects. In contrast, MapR considers Apache code to be a reference implementation, and produces its own implementation based on the APIs provided by Apache. This approach has allowed MapR to introduce many innovations, especially around HDFS and HBase, making these two fundamental Hadoop storage mechanisms much more reliable and high-performing. Its distribution additionally introduced high-speed Network File System (NFS) access to HDFS that significantly simplifies integration of Hadoop with other enterprise applications.

Two interesting Hadoop distributions were released by Amazon and Microsoft. Both provide a prepackaged version of Hadoop running in the corresponding cloud (Amazon or Azure) as Platform as a Service (PaaS). Both provide extensions that allow developers to utilize not only Hadoop's native HDFS, but also the mapping of HDFS to their own data storage mechanisms (S3 in the case of Amazon, and Windows Azure storage in the case of Azure). Amazon also provides the capability to save and restore HBase content to and from S3.

Table 1-1 shows the main characteristics of major Hadoop distributions.

TABLE 1-1: Different Hadoop Vendors

VENDOR	HADOOP CHARACTERISTICS
Cloudera CDH, Manager, and Enterprise	Based on Hadoop 2, CDH (version 4.1.2 as of this writing) includes HDFS, YARN, HBase, MapReduce, Hive, Pig, Zookeeper, Oozie, Mahout, Hue, and other open source tools (including the real-time query engine — Impala). Cloudera Manager Free Edition includes all of CDH, plus a basic Manager supporting up to 50 cluster nodes. Cloudera Enterprise combines CDH with a more sophisticated Manager supporting an unlimited number of cluster nodes, proactive monitoring, and additional data analysis tools.

Hortonworks Data Platform	Based on Hadoop 2, this distribution (Version 2.0 Alpha as of this writing) includes HDFS, YARN, HBase, MapReduce, Hive, Pig, HCatalog, Zookeeper, Oozie, Mahout, Hue, Ambari, Tez, and a real-time version of Hive (Stinger) and other open source tools. Provides Hortonworks high-availability support, a high-performance Hive ODBC driver, and Talend Open Studio for Big Data.
MapR	Based on Hadoop 1, this distribution (Version M7 as of this writing) includes HDFS, HBase, MapReduce, Hive, Mahout, Oozie, Pig, ZooKeeper, Hue, and other open source tools. It also includes direct NFS access, snapshots, and mirroring for "high availability," a proprietary HBase implementation that is fully compatible with Apache APIs, and a MapR management console.
IBM InfoSphere BigInsights	As of this writing, this is based on Hadoop 1 and available in two editions. The Basic Edition includes HDFS, Hbase, MapReduce, Hive, Mahout, Oozie, Pig, ZooKeeper, Hue, and several other open source tools, as well as a basic version of the IBM installer and data access tools. The Enterprise Edition adds sophisticated job management tools, a data access layer that integrates with major data sources, and BigSheets (a spreadsheet-like interface for manipulating data in the cluster).
GreenPlum's Pivotal HD	As of this writing, this is based on Hadoop 2, and includes HDFS, MapReduce, Hive, Pig, HBase, Zookeeper, Sqoop, Flume, and other open source tools. The proprietary advanced Database Services (ADS) powered by HAWQ extends Pivotal HD Enterprise, adding rich, proven, parallel SQL processing facilities.
Amazon Elastic MapReduce (EMR)	As of this writing, this is based on Hadoop 1. Amazon EMR is a web service that enables users to easily and cost-effectively process vast amounts of data. It utilizes a hosted Hadoop framework running on the web-scale infrastructure of Amazon Elastic Compute Cloud (Amazon EC2) and Amazon Simple Storage Service (Amazon S3). It includes HDFS (with S3 support), HBase (proprietary backup recovery), MapReduce, Hive (added support for Dynamo), Pig, and Zookeeper.
Windows Azure HDInsight	Based on the Hortonworks Data Platform (Hadoop 1), this runs in the Azure cloud. It is integrated with the Microsoft management console for easy deployment and integration with System Center. It can be integrated with Excel through a Hive Excel plug-in. It can be integrated with Microsoft SQL Server Analysis Services (SSAS), PowerPivot, and Power View through the Hive Open Database Connectivity (ODBC) driver. The Azure Marketplace empowers customers to connect to data, smart mining algorithms, and people outside of the users' firewalls. Windows Azure Marketplace offers hundreds of data sets from trusted third-party providers.

Certainly, the abundance of distributions may leave you wondering, "What distribution should I use?" When deciding on a specific distribution for a company/department, you should consider the following:

➤ **Technical details** — This should encompass, for example, the Hadoop version, included components, proprietary functional components, and so on.

➤ **Ease of deployment** — This would be the availability of toolkits to manage deployment, version upgrades, patches, and so on.

➤ **Ease of maintenance** — This would be cluster management, multi-centers support, disaster-recovery support, and so on.

➤ **Cost** — This would include the cost of implementation for a particular distribution, the billing model, and licenses.

➤ **Enterprise integration support** — This would include support for integration of Hadoop applications with the rest of the enterprise.

Your choice of a particular distribution depends on a specific set of problems that you are planning to solve by using Hadoop. The discussions in this book are intended to be distribution-agnostic because the authors realize that each distribution provides value.

DEVELOPING ENTERPRISE APPLICATIONS WITH HADOOP

Meeting the challenges brought on by Big Data requires rethinking the way you build applications for data analytics. Traditional approaches for building applications that are based on storing data in the database typically will not work for Big Data processing. This is because of the following reasons:

➤ The foundation of traditional applications is based on transactional database access, which is not supported by Hadoop.

➤ With the amount of data stored in Hadoop, real-time access is feasible only on a partial data stored on the cluster.

➤ The massive data storage capabilities of Hadoop enable you to store versions of data sets, as opposed to the traditional approach of overwriting data.

As a result, a typical Hadoop-based enterprise application will look similar to the one shown in Figure 1-2. Within such applications, there is a *data storage layer*, a *data processing layer*, a *real-time access layer*, and a *security layer*. Implementation of such an architecture requires understanding not only the APIs for the Hadoop components involved, but also their capabilities and limitations, and the role each component plays in the overall architecture.

As shown in Figure 1-2, the data storage layer is comprised of two partitions of source data and intermediate data. *Source data* is data that can be populated from external data sources, including enterprise applications, external databases, execution logs, and other data sources. *Intermediate data* results from Hadoop execution. It can be used by Hadoop real-time applications, and delivered to other applications and end users.

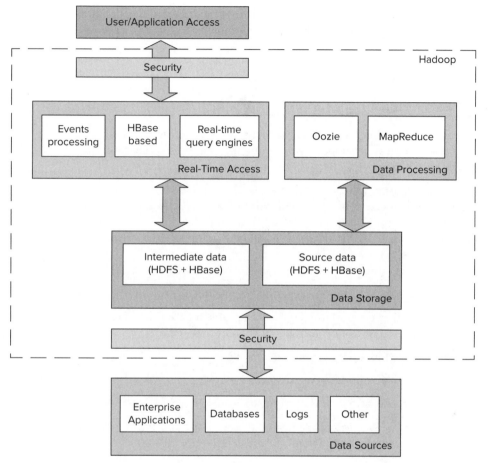

FIGURE 1-2: Notional Hadoop enterprise application

Source data can be transferred to Hadoop using different mechanisms, including Sqoop, Flume, direct mounting of HDFS as a Network File System (NFS), and Hadoop real-time services and applications. In HDFS, new data does not overwrite existing data, but creates a new version of the data. This is important to know because HDFS is a "write-once" filesystem.

For the data processing layer, Oozie is used to combine MapReduce jobs to preprocess source data and convert it to the intermediate data. Unlike the source data, intermediate data is not versioned, but rather overwritten, so there is only a limited amount of intermediate data.

For the real-time access layer, Hadoop real-time applications support both direct access to the data, and execution based on data sets. These applications can be used for reading Hadoop-based intermediate data and storing source data in Hadoop. The applications can also be used for serving users and integration of Hadoop with the rest of the enterprise.

Because of a clean separation of source data used for storage and initial processing, and intermediate data used for delivery and integration, this architecture allows developers to build applications of virtually any complexity without any transactional requirements. It also makes real-time data access feasible by significantly reducing the amount of served data through intermediate preprocessing.

HADOOP EXTENSIBILITY

Although many publications emphasize the fact that Hadoop hides infrastructure complexity from business developers, you should understand that Hadoop extensibility is not publicized enough.

Hadoop's implementation was designed in a way that enables developers to easily and seamlessly incorporate new functionality into Hadoop's execution. By providing the capability to explicitly specify classes responsible for different phases of the MapReduce execution, Hadoop allows developers to adapt its execution to a specific problem's requirement, thus ensuring that every job is executed in the most cost-effective and performant way.

The main customization of Hadoop execution can include the following:

➤ Customizing the ways Hadoop parallelizes problem execution, including the way execution is partitioned and the location of execution

➤ Support for new input data types and locations

➤ Support for new output data types

➤ Customizing the locations of the output data

A significant portion of this book is dedicated to describing approaches to such customizations, as well as practical implementations. These are all based on the results of work performed by the authors.

As you will discover, this book covers all the major layers of Hadoop-based enterprise applications shown in Figure 1-2.

Chapter 2 describes the approaches for building a data layer. There you learn about options for building the data layer, including HDFS and HBase (both architecture and APIs). You will also see some comparative analysis of both, along with some guidelines on how to choose one over the other, or use a combination of both. The chapter also covers Avro — Hadoop's new serialization/marshaling framework — and the role it plays in storing or accessing data. Finally, you learn about HCatalog, and the way it can be used to advertise and access data.

The description of data processing represents the bulk of the discussions throughout this book. For the data-processing portion of applications, you will find that the authors recommend using MapReduce and Oozie.

WHY SUCH A FOCUS ON MAPREDUCE CODE IN THIS BOOK?

You may be asking yourself why so much focus is being placed on MapReduce code throughout this book — versus the use of higher-level languages that can make MapReduce programming simpler. You can find a lot of similar discussions on the web and within the Hadoop community about this subject. An argument given in such discussions is that MapReduce code is typically larger (in terms of lines of code) compared to Pig code providing the same functionality. Although this may be an undisputed fact, you have several additional things to consider:

➤   Not everything can be expressed in a high-level language. Certain things actually require good old-fashioned Java code for their implementation.

➤   If you are writing a piece of code to be executed once, the number of lines of code may be important to you. But if you are writing enterprise applications, you should consider other criteria, including performance, reliability, and security. Typically, these qualities are easier to implement using MapReduce code, which provides significantly more options.

➤   By supporting customization of execution, MapReduce provides users with the capability to further improve performance, reliability, and security of applications.

In Chapter 3, you learn about the MapReduce architecture, its main components, and its programming model. The chapter also covers MapReduce application design, some design patterns, and general MapReduce "dos" and "don'ts." The chapter also describes how MapReduce execution is actually happening. As mentioned, one of the strongest MapReduce features is its capability to customize execution. Chapter 4 covers details of customization options and contains a wealth of real-life examples. Chapter 5 rounds out the MapReduce discussion by demonstrating approaches that can help you build reliable MapReduce applications.

Despite the power of MapReduce itself, practical solutions typically require bringing multiple MapReduce applications together, which involves quite a bit of complexity. Integration of MapReduce applications can be significantly simplified by using Hadoop's Workflow/Coordinator engine.

THE VALUE OF OOZIE

One of the most undervalued components of Hadoop is Oozie. Few (if any) of the available books on Hadoop discuss this extremely valuable component. This book demonstrates not only what Oozie can do, but also provides an end-to-end example that shows you how to leverage Oozie functionality to solve practical problems.

continues

> *continued*
>
> Similar to the rest of Hadoop, Oozie functionality is very extensible. You learn about different approaches to extending Oozie functionality.
>
> Finally, one of the most underappreciated Hadoop challenges is integration of Hadoop execution with the rest of the enterprise processing. By using Oozie to orchestrate MapReduce applications and expose these Hadoop processes using Oozie APIs, you have available to you a very elegant integration approach between Hadoop processing and the rest of the enterprise processing.

Chapter 6 describes what Oozie is, its architecture, main components, programming languages, and an overall Oozie execution model. To better explain the capabilities and roles of each Oozie component, Chapter 7 presents end-to-end, real-world applications using Oozie. Chapter 8 completes the Oozie description by showing some of the advanced Oozie features, including custom Workflow activities, dynamic Workflow generation, and uber-jar support.

The real-time access layer is covered in Chapter 9. That chapter begins by giving examples of real-time Hadoop applications used by the industry, and then presents the overall architectural requirements for such implementations. You then learn about three main approaches to building such implementations — HBase-based applications, real-time queries, and stream-based processing. The chapter covers the overall architecture and provides two complete examples of HBase-based real-time applications. It then describes a real-time query architecture, and discusses two concrete implementations — Apache Drill and Cloudera's Impala. You will also find a comparison of real-time queries to MapReduce. Finally, you learn about Hadoop-based complex event processing, and two concrete implementations — Storm and HFlame.

Developing enterprise applications requires much planning and strategy related to information security. Chapter 10 focuses on Hadoop's security model.

With the advances of cloud computing, many organizations are tempted to run their Hadoop implementations on the cloud. Chapter 11 focuses on running Hadoop applications in Amazon's cloud using the EMR implementation, and discusses additional AWS services (such as S3), which you can use to supplement Hadoop's functionality. It covers different approaches to running Hadoop in the cloud and discusses trade-offs and best practices.

In addition to securing Hadoop itself, Hadoop implementations often integrate with other enterprise components — data is often imported and exported to and from Hadoop. Chapter 12 focuses on how enterprise applications that use Hadoop are best secured, and provides examples and best practices of securing overall enterprise applications leveraging Hadoop.

SUMMARY

This chapter has provided a high-level overview of the relationship between Big Data and Hadoop. You learned about Big Data, its value, and the challenges it creates for enterprises, including data storage and processing. You were also introduced to Hadoop, and learned about a bit of its history.

You were introduced to Hadoop's features, and learned why Hadoop is so well-suited for Big Data processing. This chapter also showed you an overview of the main components of Hadoop, and presented examples of how Hadoop can simplify both data science and the creation of enterprise applications.

You learned a bit about the major Hadoop distributions, and why many organizations tend to choose particular vendor distributions because they do not want to deal with the compatibility of individual Apache projects, or might need vendor support.

Finally, this chapter discussed a layered approach and model for developing Hadoop-based enterprise applications.

Chapter 2 starts diving into the details of using Hadoop, and how to store your data.

2

Storing Data in Hadoop

WHAT'S IN THIS CHAPTER?

➤ Getting to know the Hadoop Distributed File System (HDFS)

➤ Understanding HBase

➤ Choosing the most appropriate data storage for your applications

WROX.COM CODE DOWNLOADS FOR THIS CHAPTER

The wrox.com code downloads for this chapter are found at www.wiley.com/go/ prohadoopsolutions on the Download Code tab. The code is in the Chapter 2 download and individually named according to the names throughout the chapter.

The foundation of efficient data processing in Hadoop is its data storage model. This chapter examines different options for storing data in Hadoop — specifically, in the Hadoop Distributed File System (HDFS) and HBase. This chapter explores the benefits and drawbacks of each option, and outlines a decision tree for picking the best option for a given problem. You also learn about Apache Avro — an Hadoop framework for data serialization, which can be tightly integrated with Hadoop-based storage. This chapter also covers different data access models that can be implemented on top of Hadoop storage.

HDFS

HDFS is Hadoop's implementation of a distributed filesystem. It is designed to hold a large amount of data, and provide access to this data to many clients distributed across a network. To be able to successfully leverage HDFS, you first must understand how it is implemented and how it works.

HDFS Architecture

The HDFS design is based on the design of the Google File System (GFS). Its implementation addresses a number of problems that are present in a number of distributed filesystems such as Network File System (NFS). Specifically, the implementation of HDFS addresses the following:

➤   To be able to store a very large amount of data (terabytes or petabytes), HDFS is designed to spread the data across a large number of machines, and to support much larger file sizes compared to distributed filesystems such as NFS.

➤   To store data reliably, and to cope with the malfunctioning or loss of individual machines in the cluster, HDFS uses data replication.

➤   To better integrate with Hadoop's MapReduce, HDFS allows data to be read and processed locally. (Data locality is discussed in more detail in Chapter 4.)

The scalability and high-performance design of HDFS comes with a price. HDFS is restricted to a particular class of applications — it is not a general-purpose distributed filesystem. A large number of additional decisions and trade-offs govern HDFS architecture and implementation, including the following:

➤   HDFS is optimized to support high-streaming read performance, and this comes at the expense of random seek performance. This means that if an application is reading from HDFS, it should avoid (or at least minimize) the number of seeks. Sequential reads are the preferred way to access HDFS files.

➤   HDFS supports only a limited set of operations on files — writes, deletes, appends, and reads, but not updates. It assumes that the data will be written to the HDFS once, and then read multiple times.

➤   HDFS does not provide a mechanism for local caching of data. The overhead of caching is large enough that data should simply be re-read from the source, which is not a problem for applications that are mostly doing sequential reads of large-sized data files.

HDFS is implemented as a block-structured filesystem. As shown in Figure 2-1, individual files are broken into blocks of a fixed size, which are stored across an Hadoop cluster. A file can be made up of several blocks, which are stored on different *DataNodes* (individual machines in the cluster) chosen randomly on a block-by-block basis. As a result, access to a file usually requires access to multiple DataNodes, which means that HDFS supports file sizes far larger than a single-machine disk capacity.

The DataNode stores each HDFS data block in a separate file on its local filesystem with no knowledge about the HDFS files themselves. To improve throughput even further, the DataNode does not create all files in the same directory. Instead, it uses heuristics to determine the optimal number of files per directory, and creates subdirectories appropriately.

One of the requirements for such a block-structured filesystem is the capability to store, manage, and access file metadata (information about files and blocks) reliably, and to provide fast access to the metadata store. Unlike HDFS files themselves (which are accessed in a write-once and read-many model), the metadata structures can be modified by a large number of clients concurrently. It

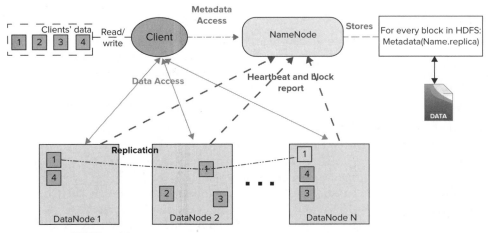

FIGURE 2-1: HDFS architecture

is important that this information never gets out of sync. HDFS solves this problem by introducing a dedicated special machine, called the *NameNode*, which stores all the metadata for the filesystem across the cluster. This means that HDFS implements a *master/slave* architecture. A single NameNode (which is a master server) manages the filesystem namespace and regulates access to files by clients. The existence of a single master in a cluster greatly simplifies the architecture of the system. The NameNode serves as a single arbitrator and repository for all HDFS metadata.

Because of the relatively low amount of metadata per file (it only tracks filenames, permissions, and the locations of each block), the NameNode stores all of the metadata in the main memory, thus allowing for a fast random access. The metadata storage is designed to be compact. As a result, a NameNode with 4 GB of RAM is capable of supporting a huge number of files and directories.

Metadata storage is also persistent. The entire filesystem namespace (including the mapping of blocks to files and filesystem properties) is contained in a file called the FsImage stored as a file in the NameNode's local filesystem. The NameNode also uses a transaction log to persistently record every change that occurs in filesystem metadata (metadata store). This log is stored in the EditLog file on the NameNode's local filesystem.

SECONDARY NAMENODE

As mentioned, the implementation of HDFS is based on master/slave architecture. On the one hand, this approach greatly simplifies the overall HDFS architecture. But on the other hand, it also creates a single point of failure — losing the NameNode effectively means losing HDFS. To somewhat alleviate this problem, Hadoop implements a *Secondary NameNode*.

The Secondary NameNode is not a "backup NameNode." It cannot take over the primary NameNode's function. It serves as a checkpointing mechanism for the

continues

continued

primary NameNode. In addition to storing the state of the HDFS NameNode, it maintains two on-disk data structures that persist the current filesystem state: an *image file* and an *edit log*. The image file represents an HDFS metadata state at a point in time, and the edit log is a transactional log (compare to a log in a database architecture) of every filesystem metadata change since the image file was created.

During the NameNode (re)starts, the current state is reconstructed by reading the image file and then replaying the edit log. Obviously, the larger the edit log is, the longer it takes to replay it and consequently start a NameNode. To improve NameNode startup performance, an edit log is periodically rolled, and a new image file is created by applying an edit log to the existing image. This operation can be fairly resource-intensive. To minimize the impact of checkpoint creation and the NameNode functioning, checkpointing is performed by the Secondary NameNode daemon, often on a separate machine.

As a result of checkpointing, the Secondary NameNode holds a copy (out-of-date) of the primary's persistent state in the form of last image file. In the cases when an edit file is kept relatively small, a secondary node can be used to recover the filesystem's state. In this case, you must be aware of a certain amount of metadata (and corresponding data) loss, because the latest changes stored in the edit log are not available.

There is ongoing work to create a true backup NameNode, which would be able to take over in the event of the primary node failure. HDFS high-availability implementation introduced in Hadoop 2 is discussed later in this chapter.

To keep the memory footprint of the NameNode manageable, the default size of an HDFS block is 64 MB — orders of magnitude larger than the block size of the majority of most other block-structured filesystems. The additional benefit of the large data block is that it allows HDFS to keep large amounts of data stored on the disk sequentially, which supports fast streaming reads of data.

SMALLER BLOCKS ON HDFS

One of the misconceptions about Hadoop is the assumption that smaller blocks (less than the block size) will still use the whole block on the filesystem. This is not the case. The smaller blocks occupy exactly as much disk space as they require.

But this does not mean that having many small files will use HDFS efficiently. Regardless of the block size, its metadata occupies exactly the same amount of memory in the NameNode. As a result, a large number of small HDFS files (smaller than the block size) will use a lot of the NameNode's memory, thus negatively impacting HDFS scalability and performance.

It is virtually impossible to avoid having smaller HDFS blocks in a real system. There is a fairly high probability that a given HDFS file will occupy a number of complete blocks and smaller blocks. Is this a problem? Considering that the majority of HDFS files are fairly large, the number of such smaller blocks in the overall system is going to be relatively small, which is typically fine.

The downside of HDFS file organization is that several DataNodes are involved in the serving of a file, which means that a file can become unavailable in the case where any one of those machines is lost. To avoid this problem, HDFS replicates each block across a number of machines (three, by default).

Data replication in HDFS is implemented as part of a write operation in the form of a *data pipeline*. When a client is writing data to an HDFS file, this data is first written to a local file. When the local file accumulates a full block of data, the client consults the NameNode to get a list of DataNodes that are assigned to host replicas of that block. The client then writes the data block from its local storage to the first DataNode (see Figure 2-1) in 4K portions. The DataNode stores the received blocks in a local filesystem, and forwards that portion of data to the next DataNode in the list. The same operation is repeated by the next receiving DataNode until the last node in the replica set receives data. This DataNode stores data locally without sending it any further.

If one of the DataNodes fails while the block is being written, it is removed from the pipeline. In this case, when the write operation on the current block completes, the NameNode re-replicates it to make up for the missing replica caused by the failed DataNode. When a file is closed, the remaining data in the temporary local file is pipelined to the DataNodes. The client then informs the NameNode that the file is closed. At this point, the NameNode commits the file creation operation into a persistent store. If the NameNode dies before the file is closed, the file is lost.

The default block size and replication factor are specified by Hadoop configuration, but can be overwritten on a per-file basis. An application can specify block size, the number of replicas, and the replication factor for a specific file at its creation time.

One of the most powerful features of HDFS is optimization of replica placement, which is crucial to HDFS reliability and performance. All decisions regarding replication of blocks are made by the NameNode, which periodically (every 3 seconds) receives a heartbeat and a block report from each of the DataNodes. A *heartbeat* is used to ensure proper functioning of DataNodes, and a *block report* allows verifying that a list of blocks on a DataNode corresponds to the NameNode information. One of the first things that a DataNode does on startup is sending a block report to the NameNode. This allows the NameNode to rapidly form a picture of the block distribution across the cluster.

An important characteristic of the data replication in HDFS is *rack awareness*. Large HDFS instances run on a cluster of computers that is commonly spread across many racks. Typically, network bandwidth (and consequently network performance) between machines in the same rack is greater than network bandwidth between machines in different racks.

The NameNode determines the rack ID that each DataNode belongs to via the Hadoop Rack Awareness process. A simple policy is to place replicas on unique racks. This policy prevents losing data when an entire rack is lost, and evenly distributes replicas in the cluster. It also allows using bandwidth from multiple racks when reading data. But because a write must, in this case, transfer blocks to multiple racks, the performance of writes suffers.

An optimization of a Rack Aware policy is to cut inter-rack write traffic (and consequently improve write performance) by using the number of racks that is less than the number of replicas. For example, when a replication factor is three, two replicas are placed on one rack, and the third one is on a different rack.

To minimize global bandwidth consumption and read latency, HDFS tries to satisfy a read request from a replica that is closest to the reader. If a replica exists on the same rack as the reader node, that replica is used to satisfy the read request.

As mentioned, each DataNode periodically sends a heartbeat message to the NameNode (see Figure 2-1), which is used by the NameNode to discover DataNode failures (based on missing heartbeats). The NameNode marks DataNodes without recent heartbeats as dead, and does not dispatch any new I/O requests to them. Because data located at a dead DataNode is no longer available to HDFS, DataNode death may cause the replication factor of some blocks to fall below their specified values. The NameNode constantly tracks which blocks must be re-replicated, and initiates replication whenever necessary.

HDFS supports a traditional hierarchical file organization similar to most other existing filesystems. It supports creation and removal of files within a directory, moving files between directories, and so on. It also supports user's quota and read/write permissions.

Using HDFS Files

Now that you know how HDFS works, this section looks at how to work with HDFS files. User applications access the HDFS filesystem using an HDFS *client*, a library that exposes the HDFS filesystem interface that hides most of the complexities of HDFS implementation described earlier. The user application does not need to know that filesystem metadata and storage are on different servers, or that blocks have multiple replicas.

ACCESSING HDFS

Hadoop provides several ways of accessing HDFS. The FileSystem (FS) shell commands provide a wealth of operations supporting access and manipulation of HDFS files. These operations include viewing HDFS directories, creating files, deleting files, copying files, and so on. Additionally, a typical HDFS install configures a web server to expose the HDFS namespace through a configurable TCP port. This allows a user to navigate the HDFS namespace and view the contents of its files by using a web browser. Because the focus of this book is on writing Hadoop applications, the discussion focuses on HDFS Java APIs.

Access to HDFS is through an instance of the `FileSystem` object. A `FileSystem` class is an abstract base class for a generic filesystem. (In addition to HDFS, Apache provides implementation of `FileSystem` objects for other filesystems, including `KosmosFileSystem`, `NativeS3FileSystem`, `RawLocalFileSystem`, and `S3FileSystem`.) It may be implemented as a distributed filesystem, or as a "local" one that uses the locally connected disk. The local version exists for small Hadoop instances and for testing. All user code that may potentially use HDFS should be written to use a `FileSystem` object.

You can create an instance of the `FileSystem` object by passing a new `Configuration` object into a constructor. Assuming that Hadoop configuration files (`hadoop-default.xml` and `hadoop-site.xml`) are available on the class path, the code snippet shown in Listing 2-1 creates an instance of `FileSystem` object. (Configuration files are always available if the execution is done on one of the Hadoop cluster's nodes. If execution is done on the remote machine, the configuration file must be explicitly added to the application class path.)

LISTING 2-1: Creating a FileSystem object

```
Configuration conf = new Configuration();
FileSystem fs = FileSystem.get(conf);
```

Another important HDFS object is `Path`, which represents names of files or directories in a filesystem. A `Path` object can be created from a string representing the location of the file/directory on the HDFS. A combination of `FileSystem` and `Path` objects allows for many programmatic operations on HDFS files and directories. Listing 2-2 shows an example.

LISTING 2-2: Manipulating HDFS objects

```
Path filePath = new Path(file name);

if(fs.exists(filePath))
    //do something

if(fs.isFile(filePath))
    //do something

Boolean result = fs.createNewFile(filePath);

Boolean result = fs.delete(filePath);

FSDataInputStream in = fs.open(filePath);
FSDataOutputStream out = fs.create(filePath);
```

The last two lines in Listing 2-2 show how to create `FSDataInputStream` and `FSDataOutputStream` objects based on a file path. These two objects are subclasses of `DataInputStream` and `DataOutputStream` from the Java I/O package, which means that they support standard I/O operations.

> **NOTE** *In addition to* `DataInputStream`, `FSDataInputStream` *also implements* `Seekable` *and* `PositionedReadable` *interfaces, and consequently implements methods to seek and read from a given position.*

With this in place, an application can read/write data to/from HDFS the same way data is read/written from the local data system.

> **WRITING LEASES**
>
> When a file is opened for writing, opening client is granted an exclusive writing lease for the file. This means that no other client can write to this file until this client completes the operation. To ensure that no "runaway" clients are holding a lease, the lease periodically expires. The use of leases effectively ensures that no two applications can simultaneously write to a given file (compared to a write lock in the database).
>
> The lease duration is bound by a *soft limit* and a *hard limit*. For the duration of a soft limit, a writer has an exclusive access to the file. If the soft limit expires and the client fails to close the file or renew the lease (by sending a heartbeat to the NameNode), another client can preempt the lease. If the hard limit (one hour) expires and the client has failed to renew the lease, HDFS assumes that the client has quit, and automatically closes the file on behalf of the writer, and then recovers the lease.
>
> The writer's lease does not prevent other clients from reading the file. A file may have many concurrent readers.

Hadoop-Specific File Types

In addition to "ordinary" files, HDFS also introduced several specialized files types (such as `SequenceFile`, `MapFile`, `SetFile`, `ArrayFile`, and `BloomMapFile`) that provide much richer functionality, which often simplifies data processing.

`SequenceFile` provides a persistent data structure for binary key/value pairs. Here, different instances of both key and value must represent the same Java class, but can have different sizes. Similar to other Hadoop files, `SequenceFiles` are append-only.

When using an ordinary file (either text or binary) for storing key/value pairs (typical data structures for MapReduce), data storage is not aware of key and value layout, which must be implemented in the readers on top of generic storage. The use of `SequenceFile` provides a storage mechanism natively supporting key/value structure, thus making implementations using this data layout much simpler.

`SequenceFile` has three available formats: Uncompressed, Record-Compressed, and Block-Compressed. The first two are stored in a record-based format (shown in Figure 2-2), whereas the third one uses block-based format (shown in Figure 2-3).

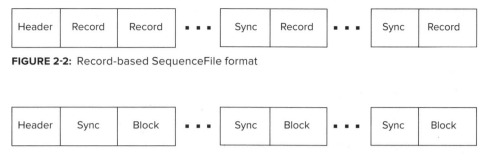

FIGURE 2-2: Record-based SequenceFile format

FIGURE 2-3: Block-based SequenceFile format

The choice of a specific format for a sequence file defines the length of the file on the hard drive. Block-Compressed files typically are the smallest, while Uncompressed are the largest.

In Figure 2-2 and Figure 2-3, the header contains general information about SequenceFiles, as shown in Table 2-1.

TABLE 2-1: SequenceFile Header

FIELD	DESCRIPTION
Version	A 4-byte array containing three letters (SEQ) and a sequence file version number (either 4 or 6). The currently used version is 6. Version 4 is supported for backward compatibility.
Key Class	Name of the key class, which is validated against a name of the key class provided by the reader.
Value class	Name of the value class, which is validated against a name of the key class provided by the reader.
Compression	A key/value compression flag.
Block Compression	A block compression flag.
Compression Codec	CompressionCodec class. This class is used only if either key/value or block compression flag are true. Otherwise, this value is ignored.
Metadata	A metadata (optional) is a list of key/value pairs, which can be used to add user-specific information to the file.
Sync	A sync marker.

> **NOTE** *A* sync *is a specialized marker, which is used for faster search inside* SequenceFiles. *A sync marker also has a special use in MapReduce implementation — data splits are done only on sync boundaries.*

As shown in Table 2-2, a record contains the actual data for keys and values, along with their lengths.

TABLE 2-2: Record Layout

FIELD	DESCRIPTION
Record length	The length of the record (bytes)
Key Length	The length of the key (bytes)
Key	Byte array, containing the record's key
Value	Byte array, containing the record's value

In this case, header and sync are serving the same purpose as in the case of a record-based `SequenceFile` format. The actual data is contained in the blocks, as shown in Table 2-3.

TABLE 2-3: Block Layout

FIELD	DESCRIPTION
Keys lengths length	In this case, all the keys for a given block are stored together. This field specifies compressed key-lengths size (in bytes)
Keys Lengths	Byte array, containing compressed key-lengths block
Keys length	Compressed keys size (in bytes)
Keys	Byte array, containing compressed keys for a block
Values lengths length	In this case, all the values for a given block are stored together. This field specifies compressed value-lengths block size (in bytes)
Values Lengths	Byte array, containing compressed value-lengths block
Values length	Compressed values size (in bytes)
Values	Byte array, containing compressed values for a block

All formats use the same header that contains information allowing the reader to recognize it. The header (see Table 2-1) contains key and value class names that are used by the reader to instantiate those classes, the version number, and compression information. If compression is enabled, the `Compression Codec class name` field is added to the header.

Metadata for the `SequenceFile` is a set of key/value text pairs that can contain additional information about the `SequenceFile` that can be used by the file reader/writer.

Implementation of write operations for Uncompressed and Record-Compressed formats is very similar. Each call to an `append()` method adds a record containing the length of the whole record (key length plus value length), the length of the key, and the raw data of key and value to the SequenceFile. The difference between the compressed and the uncompressed version is whether or not the raw data is compressed, with the specified codec.

The Block-Compressed format applies a more aggressive compression. Data is not written until it reaches a threshold (block size), at which point all keys are compressed together. The same thing happens for the values and the lists of key and value lengths.

A special reader (SequenceFile.Reader) and writer (SequenceFile.Writer) are provided by Hadoop for use with SequenceFiles. Listing 2-3 shows a small snippet of code using SequenceFile.Writer.

LISTING 2-3: Using SequenceFile.Writer

```
Configuration conf = new Configuration();
FileSystem fs = FileSystem.get(conf);
Path path = new Path("fileName");
SequenceFile.Writer sequenceWriter = new SequenceFile.Writer(fs, conf, path,
        Key.class,value.class,fs.getConf().getInt("io.file.buffer.size",
4096),fs.getDefaultReplication(), 1073741824, null,new Metadata());


...............................
sequenceWriter.append(bytesWritable, bytesWritable);
...........................
IOUtils.closeStream(sequenceWriter);
```

A minimal SequenceFile writer constructor (SequenceFile.Writer(FileSystem fs, Configuration conf, Path name, Class keyClass, Class valClass)) requires the specification of the filesystem, Hadoop configuration, path (file location), and definition of both key and value classes. A constructor that is used in the previous example enables you to specify additional file parameters, including the following:

➤ int bufferSize — The default buffer size (4096) is used, if it is not defined.

➤ short replication — Default replication is used.

➤ long blockSize — The value of 1073741824 (1024 MB) is used.

➤ Progressable progress — None is used.

➤ SequenceFile.Metadata metadata — An empty metadata class is used.

Once the writer is created, it can be used to add key/record pairs to the file.

One of the limitations of SequenceFile is the inability to seek based on the key values. Additional Hadoop file types (MapFile, SetFile, ArrayFile, and BloomMapFile) enable you to overcome this limitation by adding a key-based index on top of SequenceFile.

As shown in Figure 2-4, a MapFile is really not a file, but rather a directory containing two files — the data (sequence) file, containing all keys and values in the map, and a smaller index file, containing a fraction of the keys. You create MapFiles by adding entries in order. MapFiles are typically used to enable an efficient search and retrieval of the contents of the file by searching on their index.

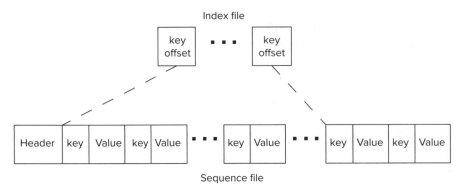

FIGURE 2-4: MapFile

The index file is populated with the key and a `LongWritable` that contains the starting byte position of the record corresponding to this key. An index file does not contain all the keys, but just a fraction of them. You can set the `indexInterval` using `setIndexInterval()` method on the writer. The index is read entirely into memory, so for the large map, it is necessary to set an index skip value that allows making the index file small enough so that it fits in memory completely.

Similar to the `SequenceFile`, a special reader (`MapFile.Reader`) and writer (`MapFile.Writer`) are provided by Hadoop for use with map files.

`SetFile` and `ArrayFile` are variations of `MapFile` for specialized implementations of key/value types. The `SetFile` is a `MapFile` for the data represented as a set of keys with no values (a value is represented by `NullWritable` instance). The `ArrayFile` deals with key/value pairs where keys are just a sequential `long`. It keeps an internal counter, which is incremented as part of every append call. The value of this counter is used as a key.

Both file types are useful for storing keys, not values.

BLOOM FILTERS

A *bloom filter* is a space-efficient, probabilistic data structure that is used to test whether an element is a member of a set. The result of the test is that the element either *definitely is not* in the set or *may be* in the set.

The base data structure of a bloom filter is a bit vector. The probability of false positives depends on the size of the element's set and size of the bit vector.

Although risking false positives, bloom filters have a strong space advantage over other data structures for representing sets, such as self-balancing binary search trees, tries, hash tables, or simple arrays or linked lists of the entries. Most of these require storing at least the data items themselves, which can require anywhere from a small number of bits (for small integers) to an arbitrary number of bits, such as for strings. (Tries are an exception, because they can share storage between elements with equal prefixes.)

This advantage of a bloom filter comes partly from its compactness (inherited from arrays), and partly from its probabilistic nature.

Finally, the `BloomMapFile` extends the `MapFile` implementation by adding a dynamic bloom filter (see the sidebar, "Bloom Filters") that provides a fast membership test for keys. It also offers a fast version of a key search operation, especially in the case of sparsely populated `MapFiles`. A writer's `append()` operation updates a `DynamicBloomFilter`, which is then serialized when the writer is closed. This filter is loaded in memory when a reader is created. A reader's `get()` operation first checks the filter for the key membership, and if the key is absent, it immediately returns `null` without doing any further I/O.

DATA COMPRESSION

An important consideration for storing data in HDFS files is data compression, shifting the computation load in data processing from I/O to CPU. As shown in several publications, providing a systematic evaluation of the compute versus I/O trade-offs when using compression for MapReduce implementation, the benefits of data compression depend on the type of data-processing jobs. For read-heavy (I/O bound) applications (for example, text data processing), compression gives 35 to 60 percent performance savings. On the other hand, for compute-intensive applications (CPU bound), performance gains from data compression are negligible.

This does not mean that data compression is not advantageous for such applications. Hadoop clusters are shared resources, and as a result, a diminishing I/O load for one application increases the capability of other applications to use this I/O.

Does this mean that data compression is always desirable? The answer is "no." For example, if you are using text or custom binary input files, data compression might be undesirable, because compressed files are not splittable (which you learn more about in Chapter 3). On the other hand, in the case of `SequenceFiles` and their derivatives, compression is always desirable. Finally, it always makes sense to compress the intermediate files used for shuffle and sort (which you learn more about in Chapter 3).

Keep in mind that the results of data compression depend greatly on the type of data being compressed and the compression algorithm.

HDFS Federation and High Availability

The main limitation of the current HDFS implementation is a single NameNode. Because all of the file metadata is stored in memory, the amount of memory in the NameNodes defines the number of files that can be available on an Hadoop cluster. To overcome the limitation of a single NameNode memory and being able to scale the name service horizontally, Hadoop 0.23 introduced *HDFS Federation,* which is based on multiple independent NameNodes/namespaces.

Following are the main benefits of HDFS Federation:

➤ **Namespace scalability** — HDFS cluster storage scales horizontally, but the namespace does not. Large deployments (or deployments using a lot of small files) benefit from scaling the namespace by adding more NameNodes to the cluster.

➤ **Performance** — Filesystem operation throughput is limited by a single NameNode. Adding more NameNodes to the cluster scales the filesystem read/write operation's throughput.

➤ **Isolation** — A single NameNode offers no isolation in a multi-user environment. An experimental application can overload the NameNode and slow down production-critical applications. With multiple NameNodes, different categories of applications and users can be isolated to different namespaces.

As shown in Figure 2-5, implementation of HDFS Federation is based on the collection of independent NameNodes that don't require coordination with each other. The DataNodes are used as common storage for blocks by all the NameNodes. Each DataNode registers with all the NameNodes in the cluster. DataNodes send periodic heartbeats and block reports, and handle commands from the NameNodes.

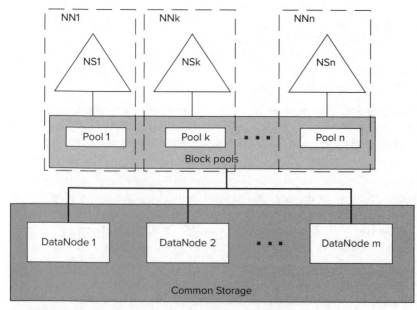

FIGURE 2-5: HDFS Federation NameNode architecture

A namespace operates on a set of blocks — a *block pool*. Although a pool is dedicated to a specific namespace, the actual data can be allocated on any of the DataNodes in the cluster. Each block pool is managed independently, which allows a namespace to generate block IDs for new blocks without the need for coordination with the other namespaces. The failure of a NameNode does not prevent the DataNode from serving other NameNodes in the cluster.

A namespace and its block pool together are called a *namespace volume*. This is a self-contained unit of management. When a NameNode/namespace is deleted, the corresponding block pool at the DataNodes is deleted. Each namespace volume is upgraded as a unit, during cluster upgrade.

HDFS Federation configuration is backward-compatible, and allows existing single NameNode configuration to work without any change. The new configuration is designed such that all the nodes in the cluster have the same configuration without the need for deploying a different configuration based on the type of the node in the cluster.

Although HDFS Federation solves the problem of HDFS scalability, it does not solve the NameNode reliability issue. (In reality, it makes it worse — a probability of one NameNode failure in this case is higher.) Figure 2-6 shows a new HDFS high-availability architecture that contains two separate machines configured as NameNodes with exactly one of them in an active state at any point in time. The active NameNode is responsible for all client operations in the cluster, while the other one (standby) is simply acting as a slave, maintaining enough state to provide a fast failover if necessary. To keep state of both nodes synchronized, the implementation requires that both nodes have access to a directory on a shared storage device.

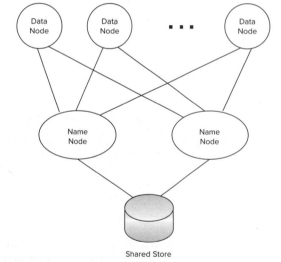

When any namespace modification is performed by the active node, it durably logs a record of the modification to a log file located in the shared directory. The standby node is constantly watching this directory for changes, and applies them to its own namespace. In the event of a failover, the standby ensures that it has read all of the changes before transitioning to the active state.

FIGURE 2-6: HDFS failover architecture

To provide a fast failover, it is also necessary for the standby node to have up-to-date information regarding the location of blocks in the cluster. This is achieved by configuring DataNodes to send block location information and heartbeats to both DataNodes.

Currently, only manual failover is supported. This limitation is eliminated by patches to core Hadoop committed to trunk and branch 1.1 by Hortonworks. This solution is based on a Hortonworks failover controller, which automatically picks an active NameNode.

HDFS provides very powerful and flexible support for storing large amounts of data. Special file types like SequenceFiles are very well suited for supporting MapReduce implementation. MapFiles and their derivatives (Set, Array, and BloomMap) work well for fast data access.

Still, HDFS supports only a limited set of access patterns — write, delete, and append. Although, technically, updates can be implemented as overwrites, the granularity of such an approach (overwrite will work only on the file level) can be cost-prohibitive in most cases. Additionally, HDFS design is geared toward supporting large sequential reads, which means that random access to the data can cause significant performance overhead. And, finally, HDFS is not well suited for a smaller file size. Although, technically, those files are supported by HDFS, their usage creates significant overhead in NameNode memory requirements, thus negatively impacting the upper limit of Hadoop's cluster memory capacity.

To overcome many of these limitations, a more flexible data storage and access model was introduced in the form of HBase.

HBASE

HBase is a distributed, versioned, column-oriented, multidimensional storage system, designed for high performance and high availability. To be able to successfully leverage HBase, you first must understand how it is implemented and how it works.

HBase Architecture

HBase is an open source implementation of Google's BigTable architecture. Similar to traditional relational database management systems (RDBMSs), data in HBase is organized in tables. Unlike RDBMSs, however, HBase supports a very loose schema definition, and does not provide any joins, query language, or SQL.

> **NOTE** *Although HBase does not support real-time joins and queries, batch joins and/or queries via MapReduce can be easily implemented. In fact, they are well-supported by higher-level systems such as Pig and Hive, which use a limited SQL dialect to execute those operations. You learn more about Pig and Hive later in this chapter.*

The main focus of HBase is on Create, Read, Update, and Delete (CRUD) operations on wide sparse tables. Currently, HBase does not support transactions (but provides limited locking support and some atomic operations) and secondary indexing (several community projects are trying to implement this functionality, but they are not part of the core HBase implementation). As a result, most HBase-based implementations are using highly denormalized data.

Similar to HDFS, HBase implements master/slave (HMaster/region server) architecture, as shown in Figure 2-7.

HBase leverages HDFS for its persistent data storage. This allows HBase to leverage all advanced features that HDFS provides, including checksums, replication, and failover. HBase data management is implemented by distributed region servers, which are managed by HBase master (HMaster).

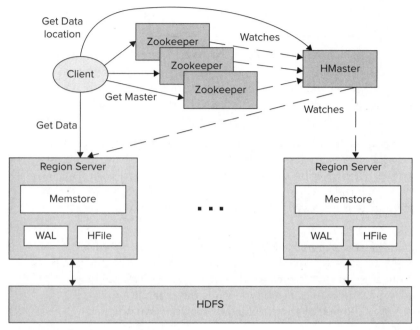

FIGURE 2-7: High-level HBase architecture

A region server's implementation consists of the following major components:

➤ `memstore` is HBase's implementation of in-memory data cache, which allows improving the overall performance of HBase by serving as much data as possible directly from memory. The `memstore` holds in-memory modifications to the store in the form of key/values. A write-ahead-log (WAL) records all changes to the data. This is important in case something happens to the primary storage. If the server crashes, it can effectively replay that log to get everything up to where the server should have been just before the crash. It also means that if writing the record to the WAL fails, the whole operation must be considered a failure.

> **NOTE** *One of the HBase optimization techniques is disabling the writes to the WAL. This represents a trade-off between performance and reliability. Disabling writes to the WAL prevents recovery when a region server fails before a write operation completes. You should use such an optimization with care, and only in cases when either data loss is acceptable, or a write operation can be "replayed" based on an additional data source.*

➤ `HFile` is a specialized HDFS file format for HBase. The implementation of `HFile` in a region server is responsible for reading and writing `HFiles` to and from HDFS.

ZOOKEEPER

Zookeeper is a replicated synchronization service with eventual consistency. It is robust, because the persisted data is distributed between multiple nodes (this set of nodes is called an *ensemble*) and a client that connects to any of them (that is, a specific "server"), migrating if a given server fails. As long as a strict majority of nodes are working, the ensemble of Zookeeper nodes is alive.

Zookeeper's master node is dynamically chosen by consensus within the ensemble. If the master node fails, the remainder of nodes picks a new master. The master is the authority for writes. This guarantees that the writes are persisted in-order (that is, writes are *linear*). Each time a client writes to the ensemble, a majority of nodes persist the information. This means that each write makes the server up-to-date with the master.

A canonical example of Zookeeper usage is distributed-memory computation, where some data is shared between client nodes, and must be accessed/updated in a very careful way to account for synchronization. Zookeeper offers the library to construct custom synchronization primitives, while the capability to run a distributed server avoids the single-point-of-failure issue you have when using a centralized message repository.

A distributed HBase instance depends on a running Zookeeper cluster. (See the sidebar, "Zookeeper," for a description of this service.) All participating nodes and clients must be able to access the running Zookeeper instances. By default, HBase manages a Zookeeper "cluster" — it starts and stops the Zookeeper processes as part of the HBase start/stop process. Because the HBase master may be relocated, clients bootstrap by looking to Zookeeper for the current location of the HBase master and -Root- table.

As shown in Figure 2-8, HBase uses an auto-sharding and distribution approach to cope with a large data size (compared to HDFS block-based design and fast data access).

To store a table of arbitrary length, HBase partitions this table into regions, with every region containing a sorted (by primary key), continuous range of rows. The term "continuous" here does not mean that a region contains all the keys from the given interval. Rather, it means that all keys from an interval are guaranteed to be partitioned to the same region, which can have any number of holes in a key space.

The way regions are split depends not on the key space, but rather on the data size. The size of data partition for a given table can be configured during table creation. These regions are "randomly" spread across region servers. (A single region server can serve any number of regions for a given table.) They can also be moved around for load balancing and failover.

When a new record is inserted in the table, HBase decides which region server it should go to (based on the key value) and inserts it there. If the region's size exceeds the predefined one, the region

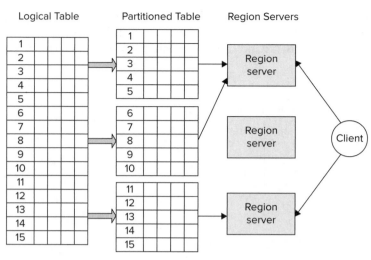

FIGURE 2-8: Table sharding and distribution

automatically splits. The region split is a fairly expensive operation. To avoid some of it, the table can also be pre-split during creation, or manually at any point (more on this later in this chapter).

When a record (or set of records) is read/updated, HBase decides which regions should contain the data, and directs the client to the appropriate ones. From this point, region servers implement the actual read/update operation.

As shown in Figure 2-9, HBase leverages a specialized table (.META.) to resolve a specific key/table pair to the specific region server. This table contains a list of available region servers, and a list of descriptors for user tables. Each descriptor specifies a key range for a given table, contained in a given region.

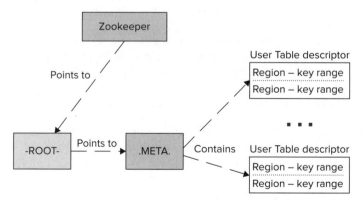

FIGURE 2-9: Region server resolution in HBase

A .META. table is discovered using another specialized HBase table (-ROOT-), which contains a list of descriptors for a .META. table. A location of the -ROOT- table is held in Zookeeper.

As shown in Figure 2-10, an HBase table is a sparse, distributed, persistent multidimensional sorted map. The first map level is a key/row value. As mentioned, row keys are always sorted, which is the foundation of a table's sharding and efficient reads and scans — reading of the key/value pairs in sequence.

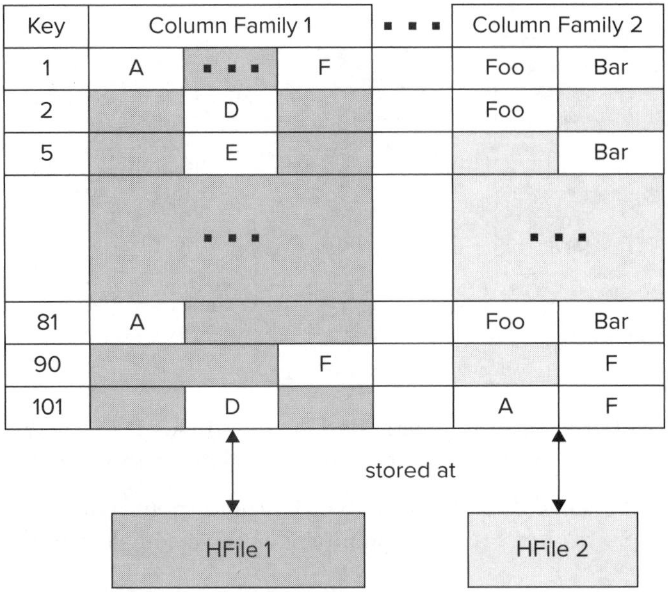

Key	Column Family 1			▪ ▪ ▪	Column Family 2	
1	A	▪ ▪ ▪	F		Foo	Bar
2		D			Foo	
5		E				Bar
		▪ ▪ ▪			▪ ▪ ▪	
81	A				Foo	Bar
90			F			F
101		D			A	F

stored at

HFile 1	HFile 2

FIGURE 2-10: Rows, column families, and columns

> **NOTE** *One thing to be aware of is the fact that HBase operates on byte arrays. All of the components of HBase data — keys, column family names, and column names — are treated by HBase as arrays of uninterpreted bytes. This means that all internal value comparisons and, consequently, sorting, is done in lexicographical order. This is very important to remember, especially for the row keys design to avoid unpleasant surprises. A typical example is usage of integer keys. If they are not left padded to have the same length, then, as a result of HBase sorting, a key 11, for example, will appear before 5.*

The second map level used by HBase is based on a *column family*. (Column families were originally introduced by columnar databases for fast analytical queries. In this case, data is stored not row by row as in a traditional RDBMS, but rather by column families.) Column families are used by HBase for separation of data based on access patterns (and size).

Column families play a special role in HBase implementation. They define how HBase data is stored and accessed. Every column family is stored in a separate HFILE. This is an important consideration to keep in mind during table design. It is recommended that you create a column family per data access type — that is, data typically read/written together should be placed in the same column family.

A set of the column families is defined during table creation (although it can be altered at a later point). Different column families can also use a different compression mechanism, which might be an important factor, for example, when separate column families are created for metadata and data (a common design pattern). In this case, metadata is often relatively small, and does not require compression, whereas data can be sufficiently large, and compression often allows improving HBase throughput.

Because of such a storage organization, HBase implements merged reads. For a given row, it reads all of the files of the column families and combines them together before sending them back to the client. As a result, if the whole row is always processed together, a single column family will typically provide the best performance.

The last map level is based on columns. HBase treats columns as a dynamic map of key/value pairs. This means that columns are not defined during table creation, but are dynamically populated during write/update operations. As a result, every row/column family in the HBase table can contain an arbitrary set of columns. The columns contain the actual values.

Technically, there is one more map level supported by HBase — versioning of every column value. HBase does not distinguish between writes and updates — an update is effectively a write with a new version. By default, HBase stores the last three versions for a given column value (while automatically deleting older versions). The depth of versioning can be controlled during table creation. A default implementation of the version is the timestamp of the data insertion, but it can be easily overwritten by a custom version value.

Following are the four primary data operations supported by HBase:

➤ Get returns values of column families/columns/versions for a specified row (or rows). It can be further narrowed to apply to a specific column family/column/version. It is important to realize that if Get is narrowed to a single column family, HBase would not have to implement a merged read.

➤ Put either adds a new row (or rows) to a table if the key does not exist, or updates an existing row (or rows) if the key already exists. Similar to Get, Put can be limited to apply to a specific column family/column.

➤ Scan allows iteration over multiple rows (a key range) for specified values, which can include the whole row, or any of its subset.

➤ Delete removes a row (or rows), or any part thereof from a table. HBase does not modify data in place, and, as a result, Deletes are handled by creating new markers called *tombstones*. These tombstones, along with the dead values, are cleaned up on major compactions. (You learn more about compactions later in this chapter.)

Get and Scan operations on HBase can be optionally configured with *filters* (filters are described later in this chapter), which are applied on the region server. They provide an HBase read optimization technique, enabling you to improve the performance of Get/Scan operations. Filters are effectively conditions that are applied to the read data on the region server, and only the rows (or parts of the rows) that pass filtering are delivered back to the client.

HBase supports a wide range of filters from row key to column family, and columns to value filters. Additionally, filters can be combined in the chains using boolean operations. Keep in mind that filtering does not reduce the amount of data read (and still often requires a full table scan), but can significantly reduce network traffic. Filter implementations must be deployed on the server, and require its restart.

In addition to general-purpose `Put`/`Get` operations, HBase supports the following specialized operations:

➤ Atomic conditional operations (including atomic compare and set) allow executing a server-side update, guarded by a check and atomic compare and delete (executing a server-side guarded `Delete`).

➤ Atomic "counters" increment operations, which guarantee synchronized operations on them. Synchronization, in this case, is done within a region server, not on the client.

This is the logical view of HBase data. Table 2-4 describes the format that HBase uses to store the table data.

TABLE 2-4: Table Data Layout in the File

KEY	TIMESTAMP	COLUMN FAMILY : COLUMN NAME	VALUE
Row key	Timestamp of the last update	Family:column	Value

This table explains the mechanics used by HBase to deal with sparsely populated tables and arbitrary column names. HBase explicitly stores each column, defined for a specific key in an appropriate column family file.

Because HBase uses HDFS as a persistence mechanism, it never overwrites data. (HDFS does not support updates.) As a result, every time `memstore` is flushed to disk, it does not overwrite an existing store file, but rather creates a new one. To avoid proliferation of the store files, HBase implements a process known as *compaction*.

Two types of compaction exist: minor and major. *Minor compactions* usually pick up a couple of the smaller adjacent store files and rewrite them as one. Minor compactions do not drop `Deletes` or expired cells; only major compactions do this. Sometimes a minor compaction picks up all the store files, in which case it actually promotes itself to being a major compaction.

After a *major compaction* runs, there will be a single store file per store, which usually improves performance. Compactions will not perform region merges.

For faster key search within the files, HBase leverages bloom filters, which enable you to check on row or row/column level, and potentially filter an entire stored file from read. This filtering is especially useful in the case of a population of sparse keys. Bloom filters are generated when a file is persisted, and are stored at the end of each file.

HBase Schema Design

When designing an HBase schema, you should take the following general guidelines into consideration:

➤ The most effective access to HBase data is usage of `Get` or `Scan` operations based on the row key. HBase does not support any secondary keys/indexes. This means that, ideally, a row key should be designed to accommodate all of the access patterns required for a specific table. This often means using the composite row key to accommodate more data access patterns. (Best practices for row key design are discussed later in this chapter.)

➤ A general guideline is to limit the number of column families per table not to exceed 10 to 15. (Remember that every column family is stored by HBase in a separate file, so a large amount of column families are required to read and merge multiple files.) Also, based on the fact that the column family name is stored explicitly with every column name (see Table 2-4), you should minimize the size of the column family. Single-letter names are often recommended, if the amount of data in the column is small.

➤ Although HBase does not impose any limitation on the size of columns in a given row, you should consider the following:

  ➤ Rows are not splittable. As a result, a huge column data size (close to the region size) typically manifests that this type of data should not be stored in HBase.

  ➤ Each column value is stored along with its metadata (row key, column family name, column name), which means that a very small column data size leads to a very inefficient use of storage (that is, more space is occupied with metadata than the actual table data). It also implies that you should not use long column names.

➤ When deciding between tall-narrow (millions of keys with a limited amount of columns) versus flat-wide (a limited number of keys with millions of columns) table design, the former is generally recommended. This is because of the following:

  ➤ In the extreme cases, a flat-wide table might end up with one row per region, which is bad for performance and scalability.

  ➤ Table scans are typically more efficient compared to massive reads. As a result, assuming that only a subset of the row data is needed, a tall-narrow design provides better overall performance.

One of the main strengths of HBase design is the distributed execution of requests between multiple region servers. However, taking advantage of this design and ensuring that there are no "hot" (overloaded) servers during an application's execution might require special design approaches for the row key. A general recommendation is to avoid a monotonically increasing sequence (for example, 1, 2, 3, or timestamps) as the row key for massive `Put` operations. You can mitigate any congestion in a single region brought on by monotonically increasing keys by randomizing the key values so that they are not in sorted order.

Data locality is also an important design consideration for HBase `Get`/`Scan` operations. Rows that are often retrieved together should be co-located, which means that they must have adjacent keys.

A general rule is to use sequential keys in the `Scan`-heavy cases, especially if you can leverage bulk imports for data population. Random keys are recommended for massive parallel writes with random, single key access.

The following are some specific row key design patterns:

➤ **Key "salting"** — This entails prefixing a sequential key with a random value, which allows for "bucketing" sequential keys across multiple regions.

➤ **The swap/promotion of key fields (for example "reverse domains")** — A common design pattern in web analytics is to use a domain name as a row key. Using a reverse domain name as a key helps in this case by keeping information about pages per site close to each other.

➤ **Complete randomization of keys** — An example of this would be to use an MD5 hash.

A final consideration for the key design is the key size. Based on the information shown in Table 2-4, a key value is stored with every column value, which means that a key size should be sufficient for the effective search, but not any longer. Excessive key sizes will have negative impacts on the size of HBase store files.

Programming for HBase

HBase provides native Java, REST, and Thrift APIs. In addition, HBase supports a command-line interface and web access via HBase master web pages, both of which are well described in other HBase books, and are not tackled here. Because this book is aimed at the developers who access HBase from their applications, only the Java interface (which can be split into two major parts — data manipulation and administration) is discussed here.

All programmatic data-manipulation access to HBase is done through either the HTableInterface or the HTable class that implements HTableInterface. Both support all of the HBase major operations described previously, including Get, Scan, Put, and Delete.

Listing 2-4 shows how an instance of the HTable class can be created based on the table name.

LISTING 2-4: Creating an HTable instance

```
Configuration configuration = new Configuration();
HTable table = new HTable(configuration, "Table");
```

One thing to keep in mind is that HTable implementation is single-threaded. If it is necessary to have access to HBase from multiple threads, every thread must create its own instance of the HTable class. One of the ways to solve this problem is to use the HTablePool class. This class serves one purpose — pooling client API (HTableInterface) instances in the HBase cluster. Listing 2-5 shows an example of creating and using HTablePool.

LISTING 2-5: Creating and using an HTablePool instance

```
Configuration configuration = new Configuration();
HTablePool _tPool = new HTablePool(config, mSize);
.................................................................
HTableInterface table = _tPool.getTable("Table");
.................................................................
```

```
_tPool.putTable(table);
..........................................................................
_tPool.closeTablePool("testtable");
```

Once an appropriate class or an interface is obtained, all of the HBase operations, described previously (including Get, Scan, Put, and Delete), are available as its methods.

The small example in Listing 2-6 shows an implementation of the Get operation on the table "table" for key "key".

LISTING 2-6: Implementing a Get operation

```
HTable table = new HTable(configuration, "table");
Get get = new Get(Bytes.toBytes("key"));
Result result = table.get(get);
NavigableMap<byte[], byte[]> familyValues =  result.getFamilyMap(Bytes.toBytes
     "columnFamily"));
for(Map.Entry<byte[], byte[]> entry : familyValues.entrySet()){
     String column = Bytes.toString(entry.getKey);
     Byte[] value = entry.getValue();
     .......................................................................
}
```

Here, after getting the whole raw, only content of the column family "columnFamily" is required. This content is returned by HBase in the form of a navigable map, which can be iterated to get the values of the individual columns with their names.

Put and Delete are implemented by leveraging the same pattern. HBase also provides an important optimization technique in the form of a multi Get/Put, as shown in Listing 2-7.

LISTING 2-7: Implementing a multi-Put operation

```
Map<String, byte[]> rows = ..................;
HTable table = new HTable(configuration, "table");
List<Put> puts = new ArrayList<Put>();
for(Map.Entry<String, byte[]> row : rows.entrySet()){
     byte[] bkey = Bytes.toBytes(row.getKey());
     Put put = new Put(bkey);
put.add(Bytes.toBytes("family"), Bytes.toBytes("column"),row.getValue());
     puts.add(put);
}
table.put(puts);
.......................................................................
```

In this code snippet, it is assumed that input comes in the form of a map containing a key and value, which should be written to a family called "family", column named "column". Instead of sending individual Put requests, a list of Put operations is created, and is sent as a single request. The actual performance improvements from usage of a multi Get/Put can vary significantly, but in general, this approach always seems to lead to better performance.

One of the most powerful operations provided by HBase is `Scan`, which allows iterating over a set of consecutive keys. `Scan` enables you to specify a multiplicity of parameters, including a start and end key, a set of column families and columns that will be retrieved, and a filter that will be applied to the data. Listing 2-8 (code file: `class BoundinBoxFilterExample`) shows an example of how to use `Scan`.

LISTING 2-8: Implementing a Scan operation

```
Put put = new Put(Bytes.toBytes("b"));
put.add(famA, coll1, Bytes.toBytes("0.,0."));
put.add(famA, coll2, Bytes.toBytes("hello world!"));
hTable.put(put);
put = new Put(Bytes.toBytes("d"));
put.add(famA, coll1, Bytes.toBytes("0.,1."));
put.add(famA, coll2, Bytes.toBytes("hello HBase!"));
hTable.put(put);
put = new Put(Bytes.toBytes("f"));
put.add(famA, coll1, Bytes.toBytes("0.,2."));
put.add(famA, coll2, Bytes.toBytes("blahblah"));
hTable.put(put);
// Scan data
Scan scan = new Scan(Bytes.toBytes("a"), Bytes.toBytes("z"));
scan.addColumn(famA, coll1);
scan.addColumn(famA, coll2);
WritableByteArrayComparable customFilter = new BoundingBoxFilter("-1.,-1., 1.5,
        1.5");
SingleColumnValueFilter singleColumnValueFilterA = new SingleColumnValueFilter(
                famA, coll1, CompareOp.EQUAL, customFilter);
singleColumnValueFilterA.setFilterIfMissing(true);
SingleColumnValueFilter singleColumnValueFilterB = new SingleColumnValueFilter(
                famA, coll2, CompareOp.EQUAL, Bytes.toBytes("hello HBase!"));
singleColumnValueFilterB.setFilterIfMissing(true);
FilterList filter = new FilterList(Operator.MUST_PASS_ALL, Arrays
                .asList((Filter) singleColumnValueFilterA,
                singleColumnValueFilterB));
scan.setFilter(filter);
ResultScanner scanner = hTable.getScanner(scan);

for (Result result : scanner) {
    System.out.println(Bytes.toString(result.getValue(famA, coll1)) + " , "
                    + Bytes.toString(result.getValue(famA, coll2)));
}
```

In this code snippet, the table is first populated with the sample data. When this is done, a `Scan` object is created. Then, both start and end keys for the scan are created. The thing to remember here is that the start key is inclusive, whereas an end key is exclusive. Then it is explicitly specified that the scan will read only `coll1` and `coll2` columns from the column family `famA`. Finally, a filter list containing two filters — a custom bounding box filter (Listing 2-9, code file: `class BoundingBoxFilter`) and a "standard" string comparison filter, provided by HBase — are specified. Once all settings are done, the code creates a `ResultScanner`, which can be iterated to `Get` results.

LISTING 2-9: Bounding box filter implementation

```java
public class BoundingBoxFilter extends WritableByteArrayComparable{

    private BoundingBox _bb;
    public BoundingBoxFilter(){}

    public BoundingBoxFilter(byte [] value) throws Exception{

        this(Bytes.toString(value));
    }

    public BoundingBoxFilter(String v) throws Exception{
        _bb = stringToBB(v);
    }

    private BoundingBox stringToBB(String v)throws Exception{

        ..................................................................... .

    }

    @Override
    public void readFields(DataInput in) throws IOException {

        String data = new String(Bytes.readByteArray(in));
        try {
            _bb = stringToBB(data);
        } catch (Exception e) {
            throw new IOException(e);
        }
    }

    private Point bytesToPoint(byte[] bytes){

        ..................................................................... .

    }

    @Override
    public void write(DataOutput out) throws IOException {

        String value = null;
        if(_bb != null)
            value = _bb.getLowerLeft().getLatitude() + "," +
                    _bb.getLowerLeft().getLongitude() +
            "," + _bb.getUpperRight().getLatitude() + "," +
                    _bb.getUpperRight().getLongitude();
        else
            value = "no bb";
        Bytes.writeByteArray(out, value.getBytes());
    }

    @Override
```

continues

LISTING 2-9 *(continued)*

```
public int compareTo(byte[] bytes) {

    Point point = bytesToPoint(bytes);
    return _bb.contains(point) ? 0 : 1;
    }
}
```

> **NOTE** *As shown here, HBase reads can be implemented using* Get, *multi* Get, *and* Scans. Get *is used only if there is truly a single row to be read from the table at a time. Preferred implementations are multi* Get *and* Scan. *When using* Scan, *setting a cache value using* scan.setCaching(HBASECASHING) *(where* HBASECASHING *specifies the number of rows to cache) can significantly increase performance. The size of caching depends significantly on the processing that is done on the data. Timeouts can result (for example,* UnknownScannerException*) if it takes longer to process a batch of records before the client goes back to the region server for the next set of data. If data is processed quickly, the caching can be set higher.*

A custom bounding box filter (Listing 2-9) extends Hadoop's WritableByteArrayComparable class and leverages BoundingBox and Point classes for doing geospatial calculations. Both classes are available from this book's companion website (code file: class BoundingBox and class Point). Following are the main methods of this class that must be implemented by every filter:

➤ The CompareTo method is responsible for a decision on whether to include a record into a result.

➤ The readFields and write methods are responsible for reading filter parameters from the input stream, and writing them to the output stream.

Filtering is a very powerful mechanism, but, as mentioned, it is not as much about improving performance. A scan of a really large table will be slow even with filtering (every record still must be read and tested for the filtering condition). Filtering is more about improving network utilization. Filtering is done in the region server, and, as a result, only records that pass filtering criteria are returned back to the client.

HBase provides quite a few filtering classes that range from a set of column value filters (testing values of a specific column) to column name filters (filtering on the column name) to column family filters (filtering on the column family name) to row key filters (filtering on the row key values or amounts). Listing 2-9 showed how to implement a custom filter for the cases where it is necessary to achieve specific filtering. One thing about custom filters is the fact that they require server deployment. This means that, in order to be used, custom filters (and all supporting classes) must be "jar'ed" together and added to the class path of HBase.

As mentioned, HBase APIs provide support for both data access and HBase administration. For example, you can see how to leverage administrative functionality in the HBase schema manager. Listing 2-10 (code file: class `TableCreator`) shows a table creator class that demonstrates the main capabilities of programmatic HBase administration.

LISTING 2-10: TableCreator class

```java
public class TableCreator {

    public static List<HTable> getTables(TablesType tables, Configuration
        conf)throws Exception{

        HBaseAdmin hBaseAdmin = new HBaseAdmin(conf);
        List<HTable> result = new LinkedList<HTable>();
        for (TableType table : tables.getTable()) {
            HTableDescriptor desc = null;
            if (hBaseAdmin.tableExists(table.getName())) {
                if (tables.isRebuild()) {
                    hBaseAdmin.disableTable(table.getName());
                    hBaseAdmin.deleteTable(table.getName());
                    createTable(hBaseAdmin, table);
                }
                else{
                    byte[] tBytes = Bytes.toBytes(table.getName());
                    desc = hBaseAdmin.getTableDescriptor(tBytes);
                    List<ColumnFamily> columns = table.getColumnFamily();
                        for(ColumnFamily family : columns){
                            boolean exists = false;
                            String name = family.getName();
                            for(HColumnDescriptor fm :
                                desc.getFamilies()){
                            String fmName = Bytes.toString(fm.getName());
                            if(name.equals(fmName)){
                                exists = true;
                                break;
                            }
                        }
                        if(!exists){
                            System.out.println("Adding Family " + name +
" to the table " + table.getName());
                            hBaseAdmin.addColumn(tBytes,
                                buildDescriptor(family));
                        }
                    }
                }
            } else {
                createTable(hBaseAdmin, table);
            }
            result.add( new HTable(conf, Bytes.toBytes(table.getName())) );
        }
        return result;
```

continues

LISTING 2-10 *(continued)*

```
        }

        private static void createTable(HBaseAdmin hBaseAdmin,TableType table)
            throws Exception{
            HTableDescriptor desc = new HTableDescriptor(table.getName());
            if(table.getMaxFileSize() != null){
                Long fs = 1024l * 1024l * table.getMaxFileSize();
                desc.setValue(HTableDescriptor.MAX_FILESIZE, fs.toString());
            }
            List<ColumnFamily> columns = table.getColumnFamily();
                for(ColumnFamily family : columns){
                    desc.addFamily(buildDescriptor(family));
                }
                hBaseAdmin.createTable(desc);
        }

        private static HColumnDescriptor buildDescriptor(ColumnFamily family){

                HColumnDescriptor col = new HColumnDescriptor(family.getName());
                if(family.isBlockCacheEnabled() != null)
                    col.setBlockCacheEnabled(family.isBlockCacheEnabled());
                if(family.isInMemory() != null)
                    col.setInMemory(family.isInMemory());
                if(family.isBloomFilter() != null)
                    col.setBloomFilterType(BloomType.ROWCOL);
                if(family.getMaxBlockSize() != null){
                    int bs = 1024 * 1024 * family.getMaxBlockSize();
                    col.setBlocksize(bs);
                }
                if(family.getMaxVersions() != null)
                    col.setMaxVersions(family.getMaxVersions().intValue());
                if(family.getTimeToLive() != null)
                    col.setTimeToLive(family.getTimeToLive());
                return col;
        }
    }
```

All of the access to administration functionality is done through the HBaseAdmin class, which can be created using a configuration object. This object provides a wide range of APIs, from getting access to the HBase master, to checking whether a specified table exists and is enabled, to creation and deletion of the table.

You can create tables based on HTableDescriptor. This class allows manipulating table-specific parameters, including table name, maximum file size, and so on. It also contains a list of HColumnDescriptor classes — one per column family. This class allows setting column family-specific parameters, including name, maximum number of versions, bloom filter, and so on.

> **NOTE** *As mentioned, a table split is a fairly expensive operation, and, if possible, should be avoided. In the case when the population of keys in a table is known upfront, the* HBaseAdmin *class enables you to create a pre-split table, using the following two methods:*
>
> ```
> admin.createTable(desc, splitKeys);
> admin.createTable(desc, startkey, endkey, nregions);
> ```
>
> *The first method takes the table descriptor and byte array of keys, where every key specifies a start key of the region. The second method takes a table descriptor, start and end key, and the number of regions. Both methods create a table that is pre-split into multiple regions, which can improve performance of this table usage.*

THE ASYNCHRONOUS HBASE API

An alternative HBase API implementation — asynchronous HBase — is available from StumbleUpon. This implementation is quite different from HBase's own client (HTable). The core of asynchronous HBase is an HBaseClient, which is not only thread-safe, but also provides an access to any HBase table (compared to HTable, which is per table).

The implementation allows accessing HBase in a completely asynchronous/non-blocking fashion. This leads to dramatic improvements in throughput, especially for Put operations. The Get/Scan operations do not show such dramatic improvements, but still are quite a bit faster.

In addition, asynchronous HBase generates less lock contention (almost four times less input-heavy workloads), while using less memory and far fewer threads. (The standard HBase client requires a very large number of threads to perform well, and this leads to poor CPU utilization because of excessive context switching.)

Finally, asynchronous HBase also tries hard to work with any version of HBase. With the standard client, your application must use exactly the same HBase jar version as the server. Any minor upgrade requires restarting your applications with the updated jar. Asynchronous HBase supports all currently released versions of HBase since 0.20.6 (and maybe earlier). So far, it has required applications to be updated only once, during the rollout of 0.90 (which introduced backward incompatibility in the Get remote procedure call, or RPC).

Despite all the advantages of asynchronous HBase, it has not yet received wide adoption among the HBase development community for the following reasons:

continues

continued

➤ It is asynchronous. Many programmers still don't feel comfortable with this programming paradigm. Although, technically, these APIs can be used to write synchronous invocations, this must be done on top of fully asynchronous APIs.

➤ There is a very limited documentation on these APIs. As a result, in order to use them, it is necessary to read through the source code.

HBase provides a very powerful data storage mechanism with rich access semantics and a wealth of features. However, it isn't a suitable solution for every problem. When deciding on whether to use HBase or a traditional RDBMS, you should consider the following:

➤ **Data size** — If you have hundreds of millions (or even billions) of rows, HBase is a good candidate. If you have only a few thousand/million rows, using a traditional RDBMS might be a better choice because all of your data might wind up on a single node (or two), and the rest of the cluster may be sitting idle.

➤ **Portability** — Your application may not require all the extra features that an RDBMS provides (for example, typed columns, secondary indexes, transactions, advanced query languages, and so on). An application built against an RDBMS cannot be "ported" to HBase by simply changing a Java Database Connector (JDBC) driver. Moving from an RDBMS to HBase requires a complete redesign of an application.

New HBase Features

The following two notable features have recently been added to HBase:

➤ HFile v2 format

➤ Coprocessors

HFile v2 Format

The problem with the current HFile format is that it causes high memory usage and slow startup times for the region server because of large bloom filters and block index sizes.

In the current HFile format, there is a single index file that always must be stored in memory. This can result in gigabytes of memory per server consumed by block indexes, which has a significant negative impact on region server scalability and performance. Additionally, because a region is not considered opened until all of its block index data is loaded, such block index size can significantly slow up region startup.

To solve this problem, the HFile v2 format breaks a block index into a root index block and leaf blocks. Only the root index (indexing data blocks) must always be kept in memory. A leaf index is stored on the level of blocks, which means that its presence in memory depends on the presence of blocks in memory. A leaf index is loaded in memory only when the block is loaded, and is evicted when the block is evicted from memory. Additionally, leaf-level indexes are structured in a way to allow a binary search on the key without deserializing.

A similar approach is taken by HFile v2 implementers for bloom filters. Every data block effectively uses its own bloom filter, which is being written to disk as soon as a block is filled. At read time, the appropriate bloom filter block is determined using binary search on the key, loaded, cached, and queried. Compound bloom filters do not rely on an estimate of how many keys will be added to the bloom filter, so they can hit the target false positive rate much more precisely.

Following are some additional enhancements of HFile v2:

➤ A unified HFile block format enables you to seek to the previous block efficiently without using a block index.

➤ The HFile refactoring into a reader and writer hierarchy allows for significant improvements in code maintainability.

➤ A sparse lock implementation simplifies synchronization of block operations for hierarchical block index implementation.

An important feature of the current HFile v2 reader implementation is that it is capable of reading both HFile v1 and v2. The writer implementation, on the other hand, only writes HFile v2. This allows for seamless transition of the existing HBase installations from HFile v1 to HFile v2. The use of HFile v2 leads to noticeable improvements in HBase scalability and performance.

There is also currently a proposal for HFile v3 to improve compression.

Coprocessors

HBase coprocessors were inspired by Google's BigTable coprocessors, and are designed to support efficient computational parallelism — beyond what Hadoop MapReduce can provide. In addition, coprocessors can be used for implementation of new features — for example, secondary indexing, complex filtering (push down predicates), and access control.

Although inspired by BigTable, HBase coprocessors diverge in implementation detail. They implement a framework that provides a library and runtime environment for executing user code within the HBase region server (that is, the same Java Virtual Machine, or JVM) and master processes. In contrast, Google coprocessors do not run inside with the tablet server (the equivalent of an HBase region server), but rather outside of its address space. (HBase developers are also considering an option for deployment of coprocessor code external to the server process for future implementations.)

HBase defines two types of coprocessors:

➤ *System coprocessors* are loaded globally on all tables and regions hosted by a region server.

➤ *Table coprocessors* are loaded on all regions for a table on a per-table basis.

The framework for coprocessors is very flexible, and allows implementing two basic coprocessor types:

➤ *Observer* (which is similar to triggers in conventional databases)

➤ *Endpoint* (which is similar to conventional database stored procedures)

Observers allow inserting user's code in the execution of HBase calls. This code is invoked by the core HBase code. The coprocessor framework handles all of the details of invoking the user's code. The coprocessor implementation need only contain the desired functionality. HBase 0.92 provides three observer interfaces:

➤ `RegionObserver` — This provides hooks for data access operations (`Get`, `Put`, `Delete`, `Scan`, and so on), and provides a way for supplementing these operations with custom user's code. An instance of `RegionObserver` coprocessor is loaded to every table region. Its scope is limited to the region in which it is present. A `RegionObserver` needs to be loaded into every HBase region server.

➤ `WALObserver` — This provides hooks for write-ahead log (WAL) operations. This is a way to enhance WAL writing and reconstruction events with custom user's code. A `WALObserver` runs on a region server in the context of WAL processing. A `WALObserver` needs to be loaded into every HBase region server.

➤ `MasterObserver` — This provides hooks for table management operations (that is, create, delete, modify table, and so on) and provides a way for supplementing these operations with custom user's code. The `MasterObserver` runs within the context of the HBase master.

Observers of a given type can be chained together to execute sequentially in order of assigned priorities. Coprocessors in a given chain can additionally communicate with each other by passing information through the execution.

Endpoint is an interface for dynamic remote procedure call (RPC) extension. The endpoint implementation is installed on the server side, and can then be invoked with HBase RPC. The client library provides convenient methods for invoking such dynamic interfaces.

The sequence of steps for building a custom endpoint is as follows:

1. Create a new interface extending `CoprocessorProtocol` and supporting a data exchange required for RPC implementation. Data transfer must be implemented as byte arrays.

2. Implement the endpoint interface using (extending) the abstract class `BaseEndpointCoprocessor`, which hides some internal implementation details (such as coprocessor framework class loading). The implementation must contain all of the required coprocessor functionality, and will be loaded into and executed from the region context. There is nothing that prevents this implementation from issuing HBase operations, which might involve additional region servers.

On the client side, the endpoint can be invoked by new HBase client APIs that allow executing it on either a single region server, or a range of region servers.

The current implementation provides two options for deploying a custom coprocessor:

➤ Load from configuration (which happens when the master or region servers start up)

➤ Load from a table attribute (that is, dynamic loading when the table is (re)opened)

When considering the use of coprocessors for your own development, be aware of the following:

➤ Because, in the current implementation, coprocessors are executed within a region server execution context, badly behaving coprocessors can take down a region server.

➤ Coprocessor execution is non-transactional, which means that if a `Put` coprocessor that is supplementing this `Put` with additional write operations fails, the `Put` is still in place.

Although HBase provides a much richer data access model and typically better data access performance, it has limitations when it comes to the data size per row. The next section discusses how you can use HBase and HDFS together to better organize an application's data.

COMBINING HDFS AND HBASE FOR EFFECTIVE DATA STORAGE

So far in this chapter, you have learned about two basic storage mechanisms (HDFS and HBase), the way they operate, and the way they can be used for data storage. HDFS can be used for storing huge amounts of data with mostly sequential access, whereas the main strength of HBase is fast random access to data. Both have their sweet spots, but neither one alone is capable of solving a common business problem — fast access to large (megabyte or gigabyte size) data items.

Such a problem often occurs when Hadoop is used to store and retrieve large items, such as PDF files, large data samples, images, movies, or other multimedia data. In such cases, the use of straight HBase implementations might be less than optimal because HBase is not well-suited to very large data items (because of splitting, region server memory starvation, and so on). Technically, HDFS provides a mechanism for the fast access of specific data items — map files — but they do not scale well as the key population grows.

The solution for these types of problems lies in combining the best capabilities of both HDFS and HBase.

The approach is based on creation of a `SequenceFile` containing the large data items. At the point of writing data to this file, a pointer to the specific data item (offset from the beginning of the file) is stored, along with all required metadata at HBase. Now, reading data requires retrieving metadata (including a pointer to the data location and a filename) from HBase, which is used to access the actual data. The actual implementation of this approach is examined in more detail in Chapter 9.

Both HDFS and HBase treat data (for the most part) as binary streams. This means that the majority of applications leveraging these storage mechanisms must use some form of binary marshaling. One such marshaling mechanism is Apache Avro.

USING APACHE AVRO

The Hadoop ecosystem includes a new binary data serialization system — *Avro*. Avro defines a data format designed to support data-intensive applications, and provides support for this format in a variety of programming languages. Its functionality is similar to the other marshaling systems such as Thrift, Protocol Buffers, and so on. The main differentiators of Avro include the following:

➤ **Dynamic typing** — The Avro implementation always keeps data and its corresponding schema together. As a result, marshaling/unmarshaling operations do not require either code generation or static data types. This also allows generic data processing.

➤ **Untagged data** — Because it keeps data and schema together, Avro marshaling/unmarshaling does not require type/size information or manually assigned IDs to be encoded in data. As a result, Avro serialization produces a smaller output.

➤ **Enhanced versioning support** — In the case of schema changes, Avro contains both schemas, which enables you to resolve differences symbolically based on the field names.

Because of high performance, a small codebase, and compact resulting data, there is a wide adoption of Avro not only in the Hadoop community, but also by many other NoSQL implementations (including Cassandra).

At the heart of Avro is a data serialization system. Avro can either use reflection to dynamically generate schemas of the existing Java objects, or use an explicit Avro schema — a JavaScript Object Notation (JSON) document describing the data format. Avro schemas can contain both simple and complex types.

Simple data types supported by Avro include `null`, `boolean`, `int`, `long`, `float`, `double`, `bytes`, and `string`. Here, `null` is a special type, corresponding to no data, and can be used in place of any data type.

Complex types supported by Avro include the following:

➤ `Record` — This is roughly equivalent to a C structure. A record has a name and optional namespace, document, and alias. It contains a list of named attributes that can be of any Avro type.

➤ `Enum` — This is an enumeration of values. `Enum` has a name, an optional namespace, document, and alias, and contains a list of symbols (valid JSON strings).

➤ `Array` — This is a collection of items of the same type.

➤ `Map` — This is a map of keys of type `string` and values of the specified type.

➤ `Union` — This represents an `or` option for the value. A common use for unions is to specify nullable values.

SCHEMA EVOLUTION SUPPORT

One of the important considerations for marshaling/unmarshaling frameworks is the support for schema evolution. To simplify dealing with this problem, Avro supports the capability to read data with the schema that is different from the schema that was used for writing data. In Avro, the schema used to write the data is called the *writer's schema*, and the schema that the application expects is called the *reader's schema*. It is an error if the two schemas do not match.

To match, one of the following must hold:

➤ Arrays with matching item types must appear in both schemas.

➤ Maps with matching value types must appear in both schemas.

> ➤ enums with matching names must appear in both schemas.

> ➤ Records with the same name must appear in both schemas.

> ➤ The same primitive type must be contained in both schemas.

> ➤ Either schema can be a union.

> > The data types in the writer's schema may be promoted to the data types in the reader's schema similar to the Java data type promotion rules. Another caveat of Avro schema evolution has to do with the fact that Avro does not support optional fields. As a result, the following is true:

> ➤ If the writer's record contains a field with a name not present in the reader's record, the writer's value for that field is ignored (optional fields in the writer).

> ➤ If the reader's record schema has a field that contains a default value, and the writer's schema does not have a field with the same name, then the reader should use the default value from its field (optional fields in the reader).

> ➤ If the reader's record schema has a field with no default value, and the writer's schema does not have a field with the same name, an error is thrown.

In addition to pure serialization Avro also supports Avro RPCs, allowing you to define Avro Interactive Data Language (IDL), which is based on the Avro schema definitions. According to the Hadoop developers, Avro RPCs are on a path to replacing the existing Hadoop RPC system, which currently is the main Hadoop communications mechanism used by both HDFS and MapReduce.

Finally, the Avro project has done a lot of work integrating Avro with MapReduce. A new `org.apache.avro.mapred` package provides full support for running MapReduce jobs over Avro data, with map and reduce functions written in Java. Avro data files do not contain key/value pairs as expected by Hadoop's MapReduce API, but rather just a sequence of values that provides a layer on top of Hadoop's MapReduce API.

Listing 2-11 shows an example of Avro schema from the Lucene HBase implementation. (This implementation is discussed in detail in Chapter 9.)

LISTING 2-11: Example Avro schema

```
{
  "type" : "record",
  "name" : "TermDocument",
  "namespace" : "com.navteq.lucene.hbase.document",
  "fields" : [ {
    "name" : "docFrequency",
    "type" : "int"
```

continues

LISTING 2-11 *(continued)*

```
    }, {
      "name" : "docPositions",
      "type" : ["null", {
        "type" : "array",
        "items" : "int"
      }]
    } ]
}
```

Once the schema is in place, it can be used by a simple code snippet (shown in Listing 2-12) to generate Avro-specific classes.

LISTING 2-12: Compiling Avro schema

```
inputFile = File.createTempFile("input", "avsc");
fw = new FileWriter(inputFile);
fw.write(getSpatialtermDocumentSchema());
fw.close();
outputFile = new File(javaLocation);
System.out.println( outputFile.getAbsolutePath());
SpecificCompiler.compileSchema(inputFile, outputFile);
```

After Avro classes have been generated, the simple class shown in Listing 2-13 can be used to marshal/unmarshal between Java and binary Avro format.

LISTING 2-13: Avro marshaler/unmarshaler

```
        private static EncoderFactory eFactory = new EncoderFactory();
        private static DecoderFactory dFactory = new DecoderFactory();

        private static SpecificDatumWriter<singleField> fwriter = new
            SpecificDatumWriter<singleField>(singleField.class);
        private static SpecificDatumReader<singleField> freader = new
            SpecificDatumReader<singleField>(singleField.class);
        private static SpecificDatumWriter<FieldsData> fdwriter = new
            SpecificDatumWriter<FieldsData>(FieldsData.class);
        private static SpecificDatumReader<FieldsData> fdreader = new
            SpecificDatumReader<FieldsData>(FieldsData.class);
        private static SpecificDatumWriter<TermDocument> twriter = new
            SpecificDatumWriter<TermDocument>(TermDocument.class);
        private static SpecificDatumReader<TermDocument> treader = new
            SpecificDatumReader<TermDocument>(TermDocument.class);
        private static SpecificDatumWriter<TermDocumentFrequency> dwriter = new
            SpecificDatumWriter<TermDocumentFrequency>
            (TermDocumentFrequency.class);
        private static SpecificDatumReader<TermDocumentFrequency> dreader = new
            SpecificDatumReader<TermDocumentFrequency>
            (TermDocumentFrequency.class);
```

```
private AVRODataConverter(){}

public static byte[] toBytes(singleField fData)throws Exception{

    ByteArrayOutputStream outputStream = new ByteArrayOutputStream();
    Encoder encoder = eFactory.binaryEncoder(outputStream, null);
    fwriter.write(fData, encoder);
    encoder.flush();
    return outputStream.toByteArray();
}

public static byte[] toBytes(FieldsData fData)throws Exception{

    ByteArrayOutputStream outputStream = new ByteArrayOutputStream();
    Encoder encoder = eFactory.binaryEncoder(outputStream, null);
    fdwriter.write(fData, encoder);
    encoder.flush();
    return outputStream.toByteArray();
}

public static byte[] toBytes(TermDocument td)throws Exception{

    ByteArrayOutputStream outputStream = new ByteArrayOutputStream();
    Encoder encoder = eFactory.binaryEncoder(outputStream, null);
    twriter.write(td, encoder);
    encoder.flush();
    return outputStream.toByteArray();
}

public static byte[] toBytes(TermDocumentFrequency tdf)throws Exception{

    ByteArrayOutputStream outputStream = new ByteArrayOutputStream();
    Encoder encoder = eFactory.binaryEncoder(outputStream, null);
    dwriter.write(tdf, encoder);
    encoder.flush();
    return outputStream.toByteArray();
}

public static singleField unmarshallSingleData(byte[] inputStream)throws
         Exception{

    Decoder decoder = dFactory.binaryDecoder(inputStream, null);
    return freader.read(null, decoder);
}

public static FieldsData unmarshallFieldData(byte[] inputStream)throws
         Exception{

    Decoder decoder = dFactory.binaryDecoder(inputStream, null);
    return fdreader.read(null, decoder);
}
```

continues

LISTING 2-13 *(continued)*

```
    public static TermDocument unmarshallTermDocument(byte[]
            inputStream)throws Exception{

        Decoder decoder = dFactory.binaryDecoder(inputStream, null);
        return treader.read(null, decoder);
    }

    public static TermDocumentFrequency unmarshallTermDocumentFrequency(byte[]
            inputStream)throws Exception{

        Decoder decoder = dFactory.binaryDecoder(inputStream, null);
        return dreader.read(null, decoder);
    }
```

One of the complications in current Avro usage is the fact that no tools exist for designing Avro schemas, which might be fairly complex in the case of large, complicated data structures. An interesting approach to solving this problem is leveraging existing XML schema (XSD) design tooling, and then programmatically converting those XSDs into Avro schemas. Considering that, today, XSD is the de facto standard for data definition/design, and a lot of tools are available for XSD design, such an approach enables data designers to use familiar tools and approaches to design Avro schemas.

Many applications running in the Hadoop ecosystem may require access to the same data. HCatalog provides a centralized registry of data definitions that can be leveraged by many applications.

MANAGING METADATA WITH HCATALOG

Between HDFS and HBase, Hadoop provides many ways to store data in a way that it can be accessed by a multiplicity of applications. But storing this data centrally and providing multiple applications access to it have posed a new set of challenges, including the following:

➤ How can you share data that can be stored and processed in any format the user desires?

➤ How can you integrate between different Hadoop applications and with other systems?

One of the common ways of accessing the data is through table abstraction, commonly used for accessing relational databases and, consequently, familiar to (and widely adopted by) many developers. It is also used by such popular Hadoop systems as Hive and Pig. Such an abstraction provides decoupling between how data is stored (HDFS files, HBase tables) from how it is seen by an application (table format). Additionally, it enables you to "filter" data of interest from a larger data corpus.

To support this abstraction, Hive provides a metastore in the form of a relational database that enables you to capture dependencies between actual physical files (and HBase tables) and tables (virtual) used to access this data.

HIVE AND PIG

Traditionally, data has been stored in databases, where SQL has been a main interface for data workers.

A data warehouse system for Hadoop — *Hive* — is aimed at simplifying Hadoop usage for such data workers by providing *HiveQL* — a SQL-like language for accessing and manipulating Hadoop-based data that can be stored in both HDFS and HBase. HiveQL supports ad-hoc queries, joins, summarization, and so on, by transparently converting them into MapReduce execution. As a result, Hive queries are implemented not in real time, but rather as batch tasks.

Pig is another warehouse system for Hadoop that, instead of an SQL-like language, uses Pig's proprietary scripting language — *Pig Latin*. Pig Latin treats data as a set of *tuples* (ordered set of fields), enabling you to convert input tuples into output. Similar to Hive, Pig supports ad-hoc queries, joins, and other operations, converting Pig Latin code into MapReduce execution. Pig also supports substantial parallelism and a slew of optimization techniques, which enables it to tackle very large data sets.

Chapter 13 provides more detail about both Hive and Pig.

A new Apache project (HCatalog) extends the reach of Hive's metastore while preserving components from the Hive DDL for table definition. As a result, Hive's table abstraction (when using HCatalog) is available to Pig and MapReduce applications, which leads to the following major advantages:

➤   It frees data consumers from knowing where or how their data is stored.

➤   It allows data producers to change physical data storage and the data model, while still supporting existing data in the old format so that data consumers do not have to change their processes.

➤   It provides a shared schema and data model for Pig, Hive, and MapReduce.

The HCatalog application's data model is organized in tables, which can be placed in databases. Tables can be hash-partitioned on one or more keys, which enables you to group all the rows with a given value of a key (or set of keys). For example, if a table is partitioned on date with three days of data in the table, there will be three partitions in the table. New partitions can be created and removed from a table dynamically. Partitions are multidimensional and not hierarchical.

Partitions contain records. Once a partition is created, a corresponding record set is fixed and cannot be modified. Records are divided into columns that have a name and a data type. HCatalog supports the same data types as Hive.

HCatalog also provides an API for "storage format developers" to define how to read and write data stored in the actual physical file or HBase tables (compare to Hive serialization/

deserialization — `SerDe`). The default data format for HCatalog is `RCFiles`. But if data is stored in a different format, a user can implement an `HCatInputStorageDriver` and `HCatOutputStorageDriver` to define translation between the underlying data storage and an application's record format. The scope of a `StorageDriver` is a partition, which allows for flexibility of the underlying storage as partition changes, or combining multiple files with different layouts into a single table.

Following are the three basic uses of HCatalog:

➤ **Communication between tools** — The majority of complex Hadoop applications employ multiple tools for processing of the same data. They might use a combination of Pig and MapReduce for extract, transform, load (ETL) implementation; MapReduce for the actual data processing; and Hive for analytic queries. The use of a centralized metadata repository simplifies data sharing, and ensures that the results of execution by one tool will be always available by another tool.

➤ **Data discovery** — A common situation for a large Hadoop cluster is multiplicity of applications and data. Often, data from one application can be used by others, but trying to discover such situations requires a lot of cross-application knowledge. In this case, HCatalog can be used as a data registry available to any application. Publishing data in HCatalog makes it discoverable by other applications.

➤ **Systems integration** — The REST service provided by HCatalog opens up Hadoop data and processing for use within an overall enterprise data and processing infrastructure. An easy interface to Hadoop is provided by simple APIs and an SQL-like language.

This section has outlined several ways of storing data, and how to marshal/unmarshal it. The next section offers some guidelines for how to design a data layout for your specific application.

CHOOSING AN APPROPRIATE HADOOP DATA ORGANIZATION FOR YOUR APPLICATIONS

Choosing appropriate data storage is one of the most important parts of overall application design in Hadoop. To do this correctly, you must understand which applications are going to access the data, and what their access patterns are.

For example, if the data is exclusively accessed by a MapReduce implementation, HDFS is probably your best choice — you need sequential access to the data, and data locality plays an important role in the overall performance. Those are the features that are well-supported by HDFS.

Once you are settled on the data storage mechanism, the next task is to pick the actual file format. Typically, `SequenceFiles` are the best option — their semantics are well-aligned with MapReduce processing, they allow for flexible extensible data models, and they support independent compression of values (which is especially important in the case of significantly sized value data types). Of course, you can use other file types, especially if integration with other applications expecting specific data formats is necessary. However, be aware that using a custom format (especially binary) might lead to additional complexities in reading, splitting, and writing data.

The decision process does not stop here, however. You must also consider the types of calculations that you are doing. If all calculations always use all the data, then you have no additional considerations. But this is a rare case. Typically, a specific calculation uses only a subset of data, which often calls for the data partitioning to avoid unnecessary data reads. The actual partitioning schema depends on the data usage pattern for an application. For example, in the case of spatial applications, a common partitioning schema is tile-based partitioning. For log processing, a common approach is two-level partitioning — by time (day) and server. These two levels can be in different order, depending on calculation requirements. A general approach to creating an appropriate partitioning schema is assessing data requirements for calculations.

This approach for choosing data storage works fairly well, with the exception of situations where new data is created. You should consider a different design when the data should be updated as a result of calculations. The only updatable storage mechanism provided by Hadoop is HBase. So, if MapReduce calculations are updating (rather than creating) data, HBase is typically your best choice for data storage. The caveat for such a decision is data size.

As discussed previously, HBase is not the best choice in cases where the size of the data (column values) is too large. In these cases, a typical solution is to use an HBase/HDFS combination described earlier in this chapter — HDFS for storage of the actual data, and HBase for its indexing. In this case, an application writes out results in a new HDFS file, while simultaneously updating HBase-based metadata (an index). Such implementations typically require custom data compactions (similar to HBase compaction described earlier).

The use of HBase as a data storage mechanism typically does not require application-level data partitioning — HBase partitions data for you. On the other hand, in the case of using an HBase/HDFS combination, partitioning of HDFS data is often required, and can be guided by the same principles as ordinary HDFS data partitioning described earlier.

If the data is used for the real-time access, depending on data size, Hadoop provides several usable solutions. If the data's key space is relatively small, and data does not change often, `SequenceFiles` can be a reasonably good solution. In the cases of larger key spaces and data update requirements, HBase or HBase/HDFS combinations are typically the most appropriate solutions.

Once you have made a data storage decision, you must pick a way to convert your data to a byte stream — that is, the format that is used by Hadoop/HBase to internally store the data. Although different potential options exist for marshaling/unmarshaling application-specific data to the byte stream (ranging from standard Java serialization to custom marshaling approaches), Avro provides a reasonably generic approach that enables you to significantly simplify marshaling, while preserving both performance and compact data size. It also allows for storing a data definition along with the data itself, thus providing powerful support for data versioning.

The last (but certainly not least) consideration for choosing appropriate data storage is security. (Chapter 10 provides an in-depth discussion of Hadoop security.) Both HDFS and HBase have quite a few security risks, and although some of them are currently being fixed, the implementation of the overall security currently requires application/enterprise-specific solutions to ensure data security. For example, these might include the following:

➤ Data encryption, limiting exposure in case it gets to the wrong hands.

➤ Custom firewalls, limiting Hadoop's data and execution access from the rest of the enterprise.

➤ Custom service layer, centralizing access to Hadoop's data and execution, and implementing required security on the level of the service.

As with every software implementation, it is necessary to secure your data when using Hadoop. However, you must implement only as much security as you really need. The more security you introduce, the more complex (and expensive) it will become.

SUMMARY

This chapter discussed options provided by Hadoop for data storage. You learned about the architecture and Java APIs for main data storage options — HDFS and HBase. You also learned how to use Avro for converting arbitrary data structures to and from binary streams that are used for the actual physical storage. Finally, you learned about the main considerations for choosing data storage for specific applications.

Now that you know how to store data in Hadoop, Chapter 3 discusses how to use this data for computations — specifically, MapReduce applications.

3

Processing Your Data with MapReduce

WHAT'S IN THIS CHAPTER?

➤ Understanding MapReduce fundamentals

➤ Getting to know MapReduce application execution

➤ Understanding MapReduce application design

So far in this book, you have learned how to store data in Hadoop. But Hadoop is much more than a highly available, massive data storage engine. One of the main advantages of using Hadoop is that you can combine data storage and processing.

Hadoop's main processing engine is MapReduce, which is currently one of the most popular big-data processing frameworks available. It enables you to seamlessly integrate existing Hadoop data storage into processing, and it provides a unique combination of simplicity and power. Numerous practical problems (ranging from log analysis, to data sorting, to text processing, to pattern-based search, to graph processing, to machine learning, and much more) have been solved using MapReduce. New publications describing new applications for MapReduce seem to appear weekly. In this chapter, you learn about the fundamentals of MapReduce, including its main components, the way MapReduce applications are executed, and how to design MapReduce applications.

GETTING TO KNOW MAPREDUCE

MapReduce is a framework for executing highly parallelizable and distributable algorithms across huge data sets using a large number of commodity computers.

The MapReduce model originates from the map and reduce combinators concept in functional programming languages such as Lisp. In Lisp, a *map* takes as input a function and a sequence of values. It then applies the function to each value in the sequence. A *reduce* combines all the elements of a sequence using a binary operation.

> **NOTE** *A* combinator *is a function that builds program fragments from program fragments. Combinators aid in programming at a higher level of abstraction, and enable you to separate the strategy from the implementation. In functional programming, where combinators are directly supported first-class citizens, their usage enables you to construct most of a program automatically.*

The MapReduce framework was inspired by these concepts and introduced by Google in 2004 to support distributed processing on large data sets distributed over clusters of computers. It was then implemented by many software platforms, and currently is an integral part of the Hadoop ecosystem.

MapReduce was introduced to solve large-data computational problems, and is specifically designed to run on commodity hardware. It is based on *divide-and-conquer* principles — the input data sets are split into independent chunks, which are processed by the mappers in parallel. Additionally, execution of the maps is typically co-located (which you learn more about in Chapter 4 during a discussion on data locality) with the data. The framework then sorts the outputs of the maps, and uses them as an input to the reducers.

The responsibility of the user is to implement *mappers* and *reducers* — classes that extend Hadoop-provided base classes to solve a specific problem. As shown in Figure 3-1, a mapper takes input in a form of key/value pairs (k_1, v_1) and transforms them into another key/value pair (k_2, v_2). The MapReduce framework sorts a mapper's output key/value pairs and combines each unique key with all its values (k_2, {v_2, v_2,...}). These key/ value combinations are delivered to reducers, which translate them into yet another key/value pair (k_3, v_3).

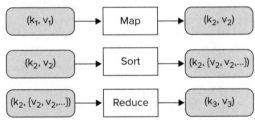

FIGURE 3-1: The functionality of mappers and reducers

A mapper and reducer together constitute a single Hadoop *job*. A mapper is a mandatory part of a job, and can produce zero or more key/value pairs (k_2, v_2). A reducer is an optional part of a job, and can produce zero or more key/value pairs (k_3, v_3). The user is also responsible for the implementation of a *driver* (that is, the main application controlling some of the aspects of the execution).

The responsibility of the MapReduce framework (based on the user-supplied code) is to provide the overall coordination of execution. This includes choosing appropriate machines (nodes) for running mappers; starting and monitoring the mapper's execution; choosing appropriate locations for the reducer's execution; sorting and shuffling output of mappers and delivering the output to reducer nodes; and starting and monitoring the reducer's execution.

Now that you know what MapReduce is, let's take a closer look at how exactly a MapReduce job is executed.

MapReduce Execution Pipeline

Any data stored in Hadoop (including HDFS and HBase) or even outside of Hadoop (for example, in a database) can be used as an input to the MapReduce job. Similarly, output of the job can be stored either in Hadoop (HDFS or HBase) or outside of it. The framework takes care of scheduling tasks, monitoring them, and re-executing failed tasks.

Figure 3-2 shows a high-level view of the MapReduce processing architecture.

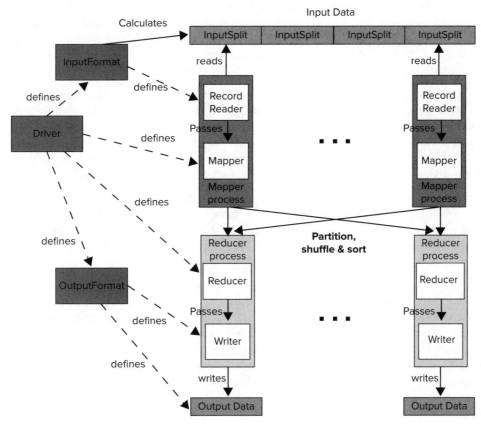

FIGURE 3-2: High-level Hadoop execution architecture

Following are the main components of the MapReduce execution pipeline:

➤ **Driver** — This is the main program that initializes a MapReduce job. It defines job-specific configuration, and specifies all of its components (including input and output formats, mapper and reducer, use of a combiner, use of a custom partitioner, and so on). The driver can also get back the status of the job execution.

➤ **Context** — The driver, mappers, and reducers are executed in different processes, typically on multiple machines. A context object (not shown in Figure 3-2) is available at any point of MapReduce execution. It provides a convenient mechanism for exchanging required system and job-wide information. Keep in mind that context coordination happens only when an appropriate phase (driver, map, reduce) of a MapReduce job starts. This means that, for example, values set by one mapper are not available in another mapper (even if another mapper starts after the first one completes), but is available in any reducer.

➤ **Input data** — This is where the data for a MapReduce task is initially stored. This data can reside in HDFS, HBase, or other storage. Typically, the input data is very large — tens of gigabytes or more.

➤ InputFormat — This defines how input data is read and split. InputFormat is a class that defines the InputSplits that break input data into tasks, and provides a factory for RecordReader objects that read the file. Several InputFormats are provided by Hadoop, and Chapter 4 provides examples of how to implement custom InputFormats. InputFormat is invoked directly by a job's driver to decide (based on the InputSplits) the number and location of the map task execution.

➤ InputSplit — An InputSplit defines a unit of work for a single *map task* in a MapReduce program. A MapReduce program applied to a data set is made up of several (possibly several hundred) map tasks. The InputFormat (invoked directly by a job driver) defines the number of map tasks that make up the mapping phase. Each map task is given a single InputSplit to work on. After the InputSplits are calculated, the MapReduce framework starts the required number of mapper jobs in the desired locations.

➤ RecordReader — Although the InputSplit defines a data subset for a map task, it does not describe how to access the data. The RecordReader class actually reads the data from its source (inside a mapper task), converts it into key/value pairs suitable for processing by the mapper, and delivers them to the map method. The RecordReader class is defined by the InputFormat. Chapter 4 shows examples of how to implement a custom RecordReader.

➤ **Mapper** — The mapper performs the user-defined work of the first phase of the MapReduce program. From the implementation point of view, a mapper implementation takes input data in the form of a series of key/value pairs (k_1, v_1), which are used for individual map execution. The map typically transforms the input pair into an output pair (k_2, v_2), which is used as an input for shuffle and sort. A new instance of a mapper is instantiated in a separate JVM instance for each map task that makes up part of the total job input. The individual mappers are intentionally not provided with a mechanism to communicate with one another in any way. This allows the reliability of each map task to be governed solely by the reliability of the local machine.

➤ **Partition** — A subset of the intermediate key space (k_2, v_2) produced by each individual mapper is assigned to each reducer. These subsets (or *partitions*) are the inputs to the reduce tasks. Each map task may emit key/value pairs to any partition. All values for the same key are always reduced together, regardless of which mapper they originated from. As a result, all of the map nodes must agree on which reducer will process the different pieces of the intermediate data. The Partitioner class determines which reducer a given key/value pair will go to. The default Partitioner computes a hash value for the key, and assigns the partition based on this result. Chapter 4 provides examples on how to implement a custom Partitioner.

➤ **Shuffle** — Each node in a Hadoop cluster might execute several map tasks for a given job. Once at least one map function for a given node is completed, and the keys' space is partitioned, the run time begins moving the intermediate outputs from the map tasks to where they are required by the reducers. This process of moving map outputs to the reducers is known as *shuffling*.

➤ **Sort** — Each reduce task is responsible for processing the values associated with several intermediate keys. The set of intermediate key/value pairs for a given reducer is automatically sorted by Hadoop to form keys/values $(k_2, \{v_2, v_2,...\})$ before they are presented to the reducer.

➤ **Reducer** — A reducer is responsible for an execution of user-provided code for the second phase of job-specific work. For each key assigned to a given reducer, the reducer's `reduce()` method is called once. This method receives a key, along with an iterator over all the values associated with the key. The values associated with a key are returned by the iterator in an undefined order. The reducer typically transforms the input key/value pairs into output pairs (k_3, v_3).

➤ `OutputFormat` — The way that job output (job output can be produced by reducer or mapper, if a reducer is not present) is written is governed by the `OutputFormat`. The responsibility of the `OutputFormat` is to define a location of the output data and `RecordWriter` used for storing the resulting data. Examples in Chapter 4 show how to implement a custom `OutputFormat`.

➤ `RecordWriter` — A `RecordWriter` defines how individual output records are written.

The following are two optional components of MapReduce execution (not shown in Figure 3-2):

➤ **Combiner** — This is an optional processing step that can be used for optimizing MapReduce job execution. If present, a combiner runs after the mapper and before the reducer. An instance of the `Combiner` class runs in every map task and some reduce tasks. The `Combiner` receives all data emitted by mapper instances as input, and tries to combine values with the same key, thus reducing the keys' space, and decreasing the number of keys (not necessarily data) that must be sorted. The output from the `Combiner` is then sorted and sent to the reducers. Chapter 4 provides additional information about combiners.

➤ **Distributed cache** — An additional facility often used in MapReduce jobs is a *distributed cache*. This is a facility that enables the sharing of data globally by all nodes on the cluster. The distributed cache can be a shared library to be accessed by each task, a global lookup file holding key/value pairs, `jar` files (or archives) containing executable code, and so on. The cache copies over the file(s) to the machines where the actual execution occurs, and makes them available for the local usage. Chapter 4 provides examples that show how to use distributed cache for incorporating existing native code in the MapReduce execution.

One of the most important MapReduce features is the fact that it completely hides the complexity of managing a large distributed cluster of machines, and coordination of job execution between these nodes. A developer's programming model is very simple — he or she is responsible only for implementation of mapper and reducer functionality, as well as a driver, bringing them together as a single job and configuring required parameters. All users' code is then packaged into a single `jar` file (in reality, the MapReduce framework can operate on multiple `jar` files), that can be submitted for execution on the MapReduce cluster.

Runtime Coordination and Task Management in MapReduce

Once the job `jar` file is submitted to a cluster, the MapReduce framework takes care of everything else. It transparently handles all of the aspects of distributed code execution on clusters ranging from a single to a few thousand nodes.

The MapReduce framework provides the following support for application development:

➤ **Scheduling** — The framework ensures that multiple tasks from multiple jobs are executed on the cluster. Different schedulers provide different scheduling strategies ranging from "first come, first served," to ensuring that all the jobs from all users get their fair share of a cluster's execution. Another aspect of scheduling is *speculative execution*, which is an optimization that is implemented by MapReduce. If the JobTracker notices that one of the tasks is taking too long to execute, it can start an additional instance of the same task (using a different TaskTracker). The rationale behind speculative execution is ensuring that non-anticipated slowness of a given machine will not slow down execution of the task. Speculative execution is enabled by default, but you can disable it for mappers and reducers by setting the `mapred.map.tasks.speculative.execution` and `mapred.reduce.tasks.speculative.execution` job options to `false`, respectively.

➤ **Synchronization** — MapReduce execution requires synchronization between the map and reduce phases of processing. (The reduce phase cannot start until all of a map's key/value pairs are emitted.) At this point, intermediate key/value pairs are grouped by key, which is accomplished by a large distributed sort involving all the nodes that executed map tasks, and all the nodes that will execute reduce tasks.

➤ **Error and fault handling** — To accomplish job execution in the environment where errors and faults are the norm, the JobTracker attempts to restart failed task executions. (You learn more about writing reliable MapReduce applications in Chapter 5.)

As shown in Figure 3-3, Hadoop MapReduce uses a very simple coordination mechanism. A job driver uses `InputFormat` to partition a map's execution (based on data splits), and initiates a job client, which communicates with the JobTracker and submits the job for the execution. Once the job is submitted, the job client can poll the JobTracker waiting for the job completion. The JobTracker creates one map task for each split and a set of reducer tasks. (The number of created reduce tasks is determined by the job configuration.)

The actual execution of the tasks is controlled by *TaskTrackers*, which are present on every node of the cluster. TaskTrackers start map jobs and run a simple loop that periodically sends a *heartbeat* message to the JobTracker. Heartbeats have a dual function here — they tell the JobTracker that a TaskTracker is alive, and are used as a communication channel. As a part of the heartbeat, a TaskTracker indicates when it is ready to run a new task.

At this point, the JobTracker uses a scheduler to allocate a task for execution on a particular node, and sends its content to the TaskTracker by using the heartbeat return value. Hadoop comes with a range of schedulers (with *fair scheduler* currently being the most widely used one). Once the task is assigned to the TaskTracker, controlling its task slots (currently every node can run several map and reduce tasks, and has several map and reduce slots assigned to it), the next step is for it to run the task.

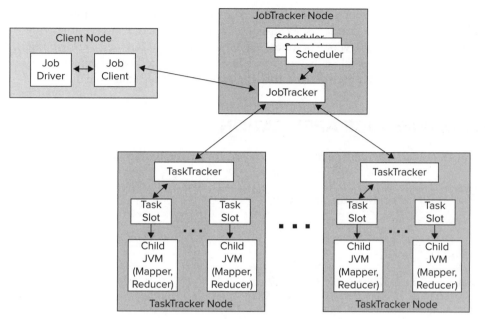

FIGURE 3-3: MapReduce execution

First, it localizes the job `jar` file by copying it to the TaskTracker's filesystem. It also copies any files needed by the application to be on the local disk, and creates an instance of the task runner to run the task. The task runner launches from the distributed cache a new Java virtual machine (JVM) for task execution. The child process (task execution) communicates with its parent (TaskTracker) through the umbilical interface. This way, it informs the parent of the task's progress every few seconds until the task is complete.

When the JobTracker receives a notification that the last task for a job is complete, it changes the status for the job to "completed." The job client discovers job completion by periodically polling for the job's status.

> **NOTE** *By default, Hadoop runs every task in its own JVM to isolate them from each other. The overhead of starting a new JVM is around 1 second, which, in the majority of cases, is insignificant (compare it to several minutes for the execution of the map task itself). In the case of very small, fast-running map tasks (where the order of execution time is in seconds), Hadoop allows you to enable several tasks to reuse JVMs by specifying the job configuration* `mapreduce.job` `.jvm.numtasks`. *If the value is* 1 *(the default), then JVMs are not reused. If it is* -1, *there is no limit to the number of tasks (of the same job) a JVM can run. It is also possible to specify some value greater than* 1 *using the* `Job.getConfigura` `tion().setInt(Job.JVM_NUM_TASKS_TO_RUN, int)` *API.*

Now that you know what MapReduce is and its main components, you next look at how these components are used and interact during the execution of a specific application. The following section uses a word count example, which is functionally quite simple and is well explained in the MapReduce literature. This will preclude having to wade through any additional explanation, and will concentrate on the interaction between the application and the MapReduce pipeline.

YOUR FIRST MAPREDUCE APPLICATION

Listing 3-1 shows a very simple implementation of a word count MapReduce job.

LISTING 3-1: Hadoop word count implementation

```java
import java.io.IOException;
import java.util.Iterator;
import java.util.StringTokenizer;

import org.apache.hadoop.conf.Configuration;
import org.apache.hadoop.conf.Configured;
import org.apache.hadoop.fs.Path;
import org.apache.hadoop.io.IntWritable;
import org.apache.hadoop.io.LongWritable;
import org.apache.hadoop.io.Text;
import org.apache.hadoop.mapreduce.Job;
import org.apache.hadoop.mapreduce.Mapper;
import org.apache.hadoop.mapreduce.Reducer;
import org.apache.hadoop.mapreduce.lib.input.TextInputFormat;
import org.apache.hadoop.mapreduce.lib.output.TextOutputFormat;
import org.apache.hadoop.util.Tool;
import org.apache.hadoop.util.ToolRunner;


public class WordCount extends Configured implements Tool{

    public static class Map extends Mapper<LongWritable, Text, Text,
      IntWritable> {
        private final static IntWritable one = new IntWritable(1);
        private Text word = new Text();
         @Override
        public void map(LongWritable key, Text value, Context context)
throws IOException, InterruptedException {
                String line = value.toString();
                StringTokenizer tokenizer = new StringTokenizer(line);
                while (tokenizer.hasMoreTokens()) {
                    word.set(tokenizer.nextToken());
                    context.write(word, one);
                }
            }
        }
    }
    public static class Reduce extends Reducer<Text, IntWritable, Text,
      IntWritable>{
```

```
        @Override
        public void reduce(Text key, Iterable<IntWritable> val, Context
            context)
throws IOException, InterruptedException {
            int sum = 0;
            Iterator<IntWritable> values = val.iterator();
            while (values.hasNext()) {
                sum += values.next().get();
            }
            context.write(key, new IntWritable(sum));
        }
    }

    public int run(String[] args) throws Exception {
        Configuration conf = new Configuration();
        Job job = new Job(conf, "Word Count");
        job.setJarByClass(WordCount.class);

        // Set up the input
        job.setInputFormatClass(TextInputFormat.class);
        TextInputFormat.addInputPath(job, new Path(args[0]));
        // Mapper
        job.setMapperClass(Map.class);
        // Reducer
        job.setReducerClass(Reduce.class);
        // Output
        job.setOutputFormatClass(TextOutputFormat.class);
        job.setOutputKeyClass(Text.class);
        job.setOutputValueClass(IntWritable.class);
        TextOutputFormat.setOutputPath(job, new Path(args[1]));
        //Execute
        boolean res = job.waitForCompletion(true);
        if (res)
            return 0;
        else
            return -1;
    }

    public static void main(String[] args) throws Exception {
        int res = ToolRunner.run(new WordCount(), args);
        System.exit(res);
    }
}
```

> **NOTE** *Two versions of MapReduce APIs are provided by Hadoop — new (contained in the* `org.apache.hadoop.mapreduce` *package), and old (contained in the* `org.apache.hadoop.mapred` *package). Throughout this book, only the new APIs are used.*

This implementation has two inner classes — `Map` and `Reduce` — that extend Hadoop's `Mapper` and `Reducer` classes, respectively.

The `Mapper` class has three key methods (which you can overwrite): `setup`, `cleanup`, and `map` (the only one that is implemented here). Both `setup` and `cleanup` methods are invoked only once during a specific mapper life cycle — at the beginning and end of mapper execution, respectively. The `setup` method is used to implement the mapper's initialization (for example, reading shared resources, connecting to HBase tables, and so on), whereas `cleanup` is used for cleaning up the mapper's resources and, optionally, if the mapper implements an associative array or counter, to write out the information.

The business functionality (that is, the application-specific logic) of the mapper is implemented in the `map` function. Typically, given a key/value pair, this method processes the pair and writes out (using a `context` object) one or more resulting key/value pairs. A `context` object passed to this method allows the `map` method to get additional information about the execution environment, and report on its execution. An important thing to note is that a map function does not read data. It is invoked (based on the "Hollywood principle") every time a reader reads (and optionally parses) a new record with the data that is passed to it (through `context`) by the reader. If you are curious, take a look at the additional method (not widely advertised) in the base mapper class shown in Listing 3-2.

> **NOTE** *The Hollywood principle — "Don't call us, we'll call you" — is a useful software development technique in which an object's (or component's) initial condition and ongoing life cycle is handled by its environment, rather than by the object itself. This principle is typically used for implementing a class/component that must fit into the constraints of an existing framework.*

LISTING 3-2: Run method of the base mapper class

```
/**
 * Expert users can override this method for more complete control over the
 * execution of the Mapper.
 * @param context
 * @throws IOException
 */
public void run(Context context) throws IOException, InterruptedException {
  setup(context);
  while (context.nextKeyValue()) {
    map(context.getCurrentKey(), context.getCurrentValue(), context);
  }
  cleanup(context);
}
```

This is the method behind most of the magic of the mapper class execution. The MapReduce pipeline first sets up execution — that is, does all necessary initialization (see, for example, Chapter 4 for a description of `RecordReader` initialization). Then, while input records exist for this mapper, the `map` method is invoked with a key and value passed to it. Once all the input records are processed, a `cleanup` is invoked, including invocation of `cleanup` method of the mapper class itself.

Similar to mapper, a reducer class has three key methods — setup, cleanup, and reduce — as well as a run method (similar to the run method of the mapper class shown in Listing 3-2). Functionally, the methods of the reducer class are similar to the methods of the mapper class. The difference is that, unlike a map method that is invoked with a single key/value pair, a reduce method is invoked with a single key and an iterable set of values (remember, a reducer is invoked after execution of shuffle and sort, at which point, all the input key/value pairs are sorted, and all the values for the same key are partitioned to a single reducer and come together). A typical implementation of the reduce method iterates over a set of values, transforms all the key/value pairs in the new ones, and writes them to the output.

> **NOTE** *The Hadoop* Tool *interface is the standard way for implementing any Java MapReduce application driver that supports the handling of generic command-line options. The usage of the* Tool *interface also makes driver implementation more testable by allowing you to inject arbitrary configurations using* Configured's setConf() *method.*

The WordCount class itself implements the Tool interface, which means that it must implement the run method responsible for configuring the MapReduce job. This method first creates a configuration object, which is used to create a job object.

A default configuration object constructor (used in the example code) simply reads the default configuration of the cluster. If some specific configuration is required, it is possible to either overwrite the defaults (once configuration is created), or set additional configuration resources that are used by a configuration constructor to define additional parameters.

A job object represents job submitter's view of the job. It allows the user to configure the job's parameters (they will be stored in the configuration object), submit it, control its execution, and query its state.

Job setup is comprised of the following main sections:

➤ **Input setup** — This is set up as InputFormat, which is responsible for calculation of the job's input split and creation of the data reader. In this example, TextInputFormat is used. This InputFormat leverages its base class (FileInputFormat) to calculate splits (by default, this will be HDFS blocks) and creates a LineRecordReader as its reader. Several additional InputFormats supporting HDFS, HBase, and even databases are provided by Hadoop, covering the majority of scenarios used by MapReduce jobs. Because an InputFormat based on the HDFS file is used in this case, it is necessary to specify the location of the input data. You do this by adding an input path to the TextInputFormat class. It is possible to add multiple paths to the HDFS-based input format, where every path can specify either a specific file or a directory. In the latter case, all files in the directory are included as an input to the job.

➤ **Mapper setup** — This sets up a mapper class that is used by the job.

➤ **Reducer setup** — This sets up `reducer` class that is used by the job. In addition, you can set up the number of reducers that are used by the job. (There is a certain asymmetry in Hadoop setup. The number of mappers depends on the size of the input data and split, whereas the number of reducers is explicitly settable.) If this value is not set up, a job uses a single reducer. For MapReduce applications that specifically do not want to use reducers, the number of reducers must be set to `0`.

➤ **Output setup** — This sets up output format, which is responsible for outputting results of the execution. The main function of this class is to create an `OutputWriter`. In this case, `TextOutputFormat` (which creates a `LineRecordWriter` for outputting data) is used. Several additional `OutputFormats` supporting HDFS, HBase, and even databases are provided with Hadoop, covering the majority of scenarios used by MapReduce jobs. In addition to the output format, it is necessary to specify data types used for output of key/value pairs (`Text` and `IntWritable`, in this case), and the output directory (used by the output writer). Hadoop also defines a special output format — `NullOutputFormat` — which should be used in the case where a job does not use an output (for example, it writes its output to HBase directly from either map or reduce). In this case, you should also use `NullWritable` class for output of key/value pair types.

> **NOTE** *If the output directory specified in the output format already exists, MapReduce execution throws an error. As a result, one of the "best practices" is to remove this directory prior to job execution.*

Finally, when the job object is configured, a job can be submitted for execution. Two main APIs are used for submitting a job using a `Job` object:

➤ The `submit` method submits a job for execution, and returns immediately. In this case, if, at some point, execution must be synchronized with completion of the job, you can use a method `isComplete()` on a `Job` object to check whether the job has completed. Additionally, you can use the `isSuccessful()` method on a `Job` object to check whether a job has completed successfully.

➤ The `waitForCompletion` method submits a job, monitors its execution, and returns only when the job is completed.

Hadoop development is essentially Java development, so you should use your favorite Java IDE. Eclipse usage for Hadoop development is discussed here.

Building and Executing MapReduce Programs

Using Eclipse for developing Hadoop code is really straightforward. Assuming that your instance of Eclipse is configured with Maven, first create a Maven project for your implementation. Because there is no Hadoop Maven archetype, start with the "simple" Maven project and add `pom.xml` manually, similar to what is shown in Listing 3-3.

LISTING 3-3: pom.xml for Hadoop 2.0

```xml
<project xmlns="http://maven.apache.org/POM/4.0.0"
        xmlns:xsi="http://www.w3.org/2001/XMLSchema-instance"
    xsi:schemaLocation="http://maven.apache.org/POM/4.0.0
        http://maven.apache.org/xsd/maven-4.0.0.xsd">
    <modelVersion>4.0.0</modelVersion>
    <groupId>com.nokia.lib</groupId>
    <artifactId>nokia-cgnr-sparse</artifactId>
    <version>0.0.1-SNAPSHOT</version>
    <name>cgnr-sparse</name>
    <properties>
        <hadoop.version>2.0.0-mr1-cdh4.1.0</hadoop.version>
        <hadoop.common.version>2.0.0-cdh4.1.0</hadoop.common.version>
        <hbase.version>0.92.1-cdh4.1.0</hbase.version>
    </properties>
    <repositories>
        <repository>
            <id>CDH Releases and RCs Repositories</id>
            <url>https://repository.cloudera.com/content/groups/cdh-
                releases-rcs</url>
        </repository>
    </repositories>
    <build>
        <plugins>
            <plugin>
                <groupId>org.apache.maven.plugins</groupId>
                <artifactId>maven-compiler-plugin</artifactId>
                <version>2.3.2</version>
                <configuration>
                    <source>1.6</source>
                    <target>1.6</target>
                </configuration>
            </plugin>
        </plugins>
    </build>
    <dependencies>
        <dependency>
            <groupId>org.apache.hadoop</groupId>
            <artifactId>hadoop-core</artifactId>
            <version>${hadoop.version}</version>
            <scope>provided</scope>
        </dependency>
        <dependency>
            <groupId>org.apache.hbase</groupId>
            <artifactId>hbase</artifactId>
            <version>${hbase.version}</version>
            <scope>provided</scope>
        </dependency>
        <dependency>
            <groupId>org.apache.hadoop</groupId>
```

continues

LISTING 3-3 *(continued)*

```
                <artifactId>hadoop-common</artifactId>
                <version>${hadoop.common.version}</version>
                <scope>provided</scope>
            </dependency>
            <dependency>
                <groupId>junit</groupId>
                <artifactId>junit</artifactId>
                <version>4.10</version>
            </dependency>
        </dependencies>
    </project>
```

> **NOTE** *Quite a few versions of Hadoop exist, including different versions of Cloudera distributions (CDH3 and CDH4), Hortonworks distribution, MapR distribution, Amazon EMR, and so on. Some of them are compatible, some are not. You should use different Maven pom files to build a targeted executable for a particular run time. Additionally, Hadoop currently supports only Java version 6, so a Maven compiler plug-in is used here to ensure that the right version is used.*

The pom file shown in Listing 3-3 is for Cloudera CDH 4.1 (note the inclusion of the Cloudera repository in the pom file). It includes a minimal set of dependencies necessary for developing a Hadoop MapReduce job — hadoop-core and hadoop-common. Additionally, if you use HBase for an application, you should include an hbase dependency. It also contains junit for supporting basic unit tests. Also note that all Hadoop-related dependences are specified as provided. This means that they will not be included in the final jar file generated by Maven.

Once the Eclipse Maven project is created, all of the code for your MapReduce implementation goes into this project. Eclipse takes care of loading required libraries, compiling your Java code, and so on.

Now that you know how to write a MapReduce job, take a look at how to execute it. You can use the Maven install command to generate a jar file containing all the required code. Once a jar file is created, you can FTP it to the cluster's edge node, and executed using the command shown in Listing 3-4.

LISTING 3-4: Hadoop execution command

```
hadoop jar your.jar mainClass inputpath outputpath
```

Hadoop provides several JavaServer Pages (JSPs), enabling you to visualize MapReduce execution. The MapReduce administration JSP enables you to view both the overall state of the cluster and details of the particular job execution. The MapReduce administration main page shown in Figure 3-4 displays the overall state of the cluster, as well as a list of currently running, completed, and failed jobs. Every job in every list (running, completed, and failed) is "clickable," which enables you to get additional information about job execution.

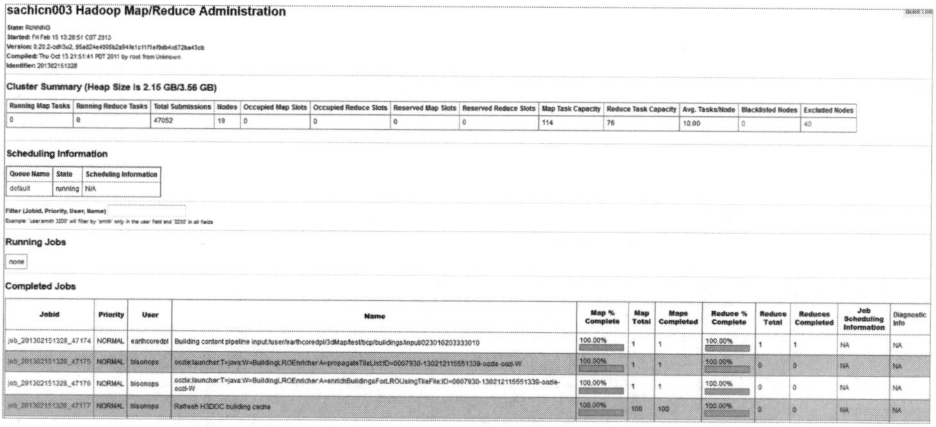

FIGURE 3-4: MapReduce administration main page

The job detail page shown in Figure 3-5 provides (dynamic) information about execution. The page exists starting from the point when the JobTracker accepts the job, and keeps track of all the changes during the job execution. You can also use it for post-mortem analysis of the job execution. This page has the following four main parts (with the fourth one not shown on Figure 3-5):

➤ The first part (top of the page) displays the combined information about the job, including job name, user, submitting host, start and end time, execution time, and so on.

➤ The second part contains summary information about mappers/reducers for a given job. It tells how many mappers and reducers a job has, and splits them by their states — pending, running, complete, and killed.

➤ The third part show jobs counters (for an in-depth discussion on counters, see Chapter 4), which are split by namespaces. Because this example implementation does not use custom counters, only standard ones appear for it.

➤ The fourth part provides nice histograms detailing mapper and reducer execution.

The job detail page provides more information (through the "clickable links"), which helps you to analyze job execution further. Those pages are discussed in detail in Chapter 5 during a discussion about building reliable MapReduce applications.

Next, you look at the design of MapReduce applications.

Hadoop job_201212061101_37666 on sachicn003

User: blublins
Job Name: Word Count
Job File: hdfs://sachicn001/tmp/hadoop-mapred/mapred/staging/blublins/.staging/job_201212061101_37666/job.xml
Submit Host: sachidn003.hq.navteq.com
Submit Host Address: 10.8.120.40
Job-ACLs:
  mapreduce.job.acl-view-job: No users are allowed
  mapreduce.job.acl-modify-job: No users are allowed
Job Setup: Successful
Status: Succeeded
Started at: Thu Dec 27 09:26:02 CST 2012
Finished at: Thu Dec 27 09:26:19 CST 2012
Finished in: 17sec
Job Cleanup: Successful

Kind	% Complete	Num Tasks	Pending	Running	Complete	Killed	Failed/Killed Task Attempts
map	100.00%	1	0	0	1	0	0 / 0
reduce	100.00%	1	0	0	1	0	0 / 0

	Counter	Map	Reduce	Total
	SLOTS_MILLIS_MAPS	0	0	3,796
	Launched reduce tasks	0	0	1
	Total time spent by all reduces waiting after reserving slots (ms)	0	0	0
Job Counters	Rack-local map tasks	0	0	1
	Total time spent by all maps waiting after reserving slots (ms)	0	0	0
	Launched map tasks	0	0	1
	SLOTS_MILLIS_REDUCES	0	0	8,504
	FILE_BYTES_READ	0	337,824	337,824
FileSystemCounters	HDFS_BYTES_READ	189,986	0	189,986
	FILE_BYTES_WRITTEN	388,640	388,536	777,176
	HDFS_BYTES_WRITTEN	0	76,043	76,043
	Reduce input groups	0	5,527	5,527
	Combine output records	0	0	0
	Map input records	2,676	0	2,676
	Reduce shuffle bytes	0	0	0
	Reduce output records	0	5,527	5,527
Map-Reduce Framework	Spilled Records	25,741	25,741	51,482
	Map output bytes	286,336	0	286,336
	SPLIT_RAW_BYTES	111	0	111
	Map output records	25,741	0	25,741
	Combine input records	0	0	0
	Reduce input records	0	25,741	25,741

FIGURE 3-5: WordCount job page

DESIGNING MAPREDUCE IMPLEMENTATIONS

As discussed, the power of MapReduce comes from its simplicity. In addition to preparing the input data, the programmer must only implement the mapper and reducer. Many real-life problems can be solved using this approach.

In the most general case, MapReduce can be thought of as a general-purpose parallel execution framework that can take full advantage of the data locality. But this simplicity comes with a price — a designer must decide how to express his or her business problem in terms of a small number of components that must fit together in very specific ways.

> **NOTE** *Although a lot of publications describe the use of MapReduce APIs, very few describe practical approaches to designing a MapReduce implementation.*

To reformulate the initial problem in terms of MapReduce, it is typically necessary to answer the following questions:

➤ How do you break up a large problem into smaller tasks? More specifically, how do you decompose the problem so that the smaller tasks can be executed in parallel?

➤ Which key/value pairs can you use as inputs/outputs of every task?

➤ How do you bring together all the data required for calculation? More specifically, how do you organize processing the way that all the data necessary for calculation is in memory at the same time?

It is important to realize that many algorithms cannot be easily expressed as a single MapReduce job. It is often necessary to decompose complex algorithms into a sequence of jobs, where data output of one job becomes the input to the next.

This section takes a look at several examples of designing MapReduce applications for different practical problems (from very simple to more complex). All of the examples are described in the same format:

➤ A short description of the problem

➤ A description of the MapReduce job(s), including the following:

    ➤ Mapper description

    ➤ Reducer description

Using MapReduce as a Framework for Parallel Processing

In the simplest case, source data is organized as a set of independent records, and the results can be specified in any order. These classes of problems ("embarrassing parallel" problems) require the same processing to be applied to each data element in a fairly independent way — in other words, there is no need to consolidate or aggregate individual results. A classic example would be processing several thousand PDF files to extract some key text and place into a CSV file for later insertion into a database.

Implementation of MapReduce in this situation is very simple — the only thing that is required is the mapper, processing each record independently and outputting the result. In this case,

MapReduce controls distribution of the mappers, and provides all of the support required for scheduling and error handling. The following example shows how to design this type of application.

Face Recognition Example

Although not often discussed as a Hadoop-related problem, an image-processing implementation fits really well in the MapReduce paradigm. Assume that there is a face-recognition algorithm implementation that takes an image, recognizes a set of desired features, and produces a set of recognition results. Also assume that it is necessary to run face recognition on millions of pictures.

If all the pictures are stored in Hadoop in the form of a sequence file, then you can use a simple map-only job to parallelize execution. A set of input key/value pairs in this case is imageID/Image, and a set of output key/value pairs is imageID/list of recognized features. Additionally, a set of recognizable features must be distributed to all mappers (for example, using the distributed cache).

Table 3-1 shows the implementation of a MapReduce job for this example.

TABLE 3-1: Face Recognition Job

PROCESS PHASE	DESCRIPTION
Mapper	In this job, a mapper is first initialized with the set of recognizable features. For every image, a map function invokes a face-recognition algorithm implementation, passing it an image itself, along with a list of recognizable features. The result of recognition, along with the original imageID, is output from the map.
Result	A result of this job execution is recognition of all the images contained in the original images.

NOTE *To achieve complete independence of the execution of mappers/reducers, every mapper/reducer in a MapReduce implementation creates its own output file. This means that, as a result of the face recognition, the job execution will be a set of files (in the same directory), each containing the output of an individual mapper. If it is necessary to have them in a single file, a single reducer must be added to a face-recognition job. This reducer will be a very simple one. Because, in this case, every input key for reduce will have a single value (assuming here that* imageIDs *are unique), the reducer just writes input key/values directly to the output. An important thing to realize in this example is that although a reducer is extremely simple, its addition to the job can significantly increase the job's overall execution time. This is because the addition of a reducer invokes shuffle and sort (which are not present in map-only jobs), which can take a significant amount of time if the number of images is very large.*

Now take a look at a more complex case, where the results of the map execution must be grouped together (that is, ordered in certain way). Many practical implementations (including filtering, parsing, data conversion, summing, and so on) can be solved with this type of a MapReduce job.

Simple Data Processing with MapReduce

An example of such a case is the building of inverted indexes. These types of problems require a full MapReduce implementation where shuffle and sort are required to bring all results together. The following example shows how to design this type of application.

Inverted Indexes Example

In computer science, an *inverted index* is a data structure that stores a mapping from content (such as words or numbers) to its location in a document or a set of documents, as shown in Figure 3-6. The purpose of an inverted index is to allow fast full-text searches, at a cost of increased processing during a document addition. The inverted index data structure is a central component of a typical search engine, enabling you to optimize the speed of finding the documents in which a certain word occurs.

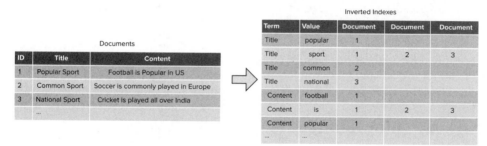

FIGURE 3-6: Inverted index

To build an inverted index, it is possible to feed the mapper each document (or lines within a document). The mapper will parse the words in the document to emit [word, descriptor] pairs. The reducer can simply be an identity function that just writes out the list, or it can perform some statistic aggregation per word.

> **NOTE** *You learn more about how you can use HBase to store inverted indexes in Chapter 9.*

Table 3-2 shows the implementation of a MapReduce job for this example.

TABLE 3-2: Calculation of Inverted Indexes Job

PROCESS PHASE	DESCRIPTION
Mapper	In this job, the role of the mapper is to build a unique record containing a word index, and information describing the word occurrence in the document. It reads every input document, parses it, and, for every unique word in the document, builds an index descriptor. This descriptor contains a document ID, number of times the index occurs in the document, and any additional information (for example, index positions as offset from the beginning of the document). Every index descriptor pair is written out.
Shuffle and Sort	MapReduce's shuffle and sort will sort all the records based on the index value, which guarantees that a reducer will get all the indexes with a given key together.
Reducer	In this job, the role of a reducer is to build an inverted indexes structure. Depending on the system requirements, there can be one or more reducers. A reducer gets all the descriptors for a given index, and builds an index record, which is written to the desired index storage.
Result	A result of this job execution is an inverted index for a set of the original documents.

More complex MapReduce applications require bringing data from the multiple sources (in other words, joining data) for processing. Next you look at how to design, implement, and use data joins using MapReduce.

Building Joins with MapReduce

A generic join problem can be described as follows. Given multiple data sets (S1 through Sn), sharing the same key (a *join key*), you want to build records containing a key and all required data from every record.

Two "standard" implementations exist for joining data in MapReduce: reduce-side join and map-side join.

A most common implementation of a join is a *reduce-side join*. In this case, all data sets are processed by the mapper that emits a join key as the intermediate key, and the value as the intermediate record capable of holding either of the set's values. Because MapReduce guarantees that all values with the same key are brought together, all intermediate records will be grouped by the join key, which is exactly what is necessary to perform the join operation. This works very well in the case of one-to-one joins, where at most one record from every data set has the same key.

Although theoretically this approach will also work in the case of one-to-many and many-to-many joins, these cases can have additional complications. When processing each key in the reducer, there can be an arbitrary number of records with the join key. The obvious solution is to buffer all values in memory, but this can create a scalability bottleneck, because there might not be enough memory to hold all the records with the same join key. This situation typically requires a secondary sort, which can be achieved with the value-to-key conversion design pattern.

VALUE-TO-KEY CONVERSION DESIGN PATTERN

Consider a specific retail example. Assume that there is a product catalog data set containing information about all available products, and a store purchases data set describing all the purchases for a given store. It is necessary to calculate the number of purchases for a given product in a given store.

Product catalog data is structured something like (p, productInfo), where p is a product ID, and productInfo is a data set describing a given product (which might include the product's description, price, and so on). Store purchase data is structured like (s, p, purchaseInfo), where s is the store ID, p is the product ID, and purchaseInfo is information about the purchase (including quantity, date of purchase, and so on).

In this case, you can execute the required calculations using the following algorithm:

```
for every product p:
    for every purchase (p, s):
        sum(productInfo.price * purchaseInfo.quantity)
```

Theoretically, it is possible to join both data sets on the product key, but in this case, the order of the store record cannot be guaranteed — records for the same product from multiple stores can come in any order. Buffering all product sales records from every store does not seem feasible (for a large retailer, depending on the product's popularity, there can be millions of records).

The basic idea behind value-to-key conversion design pattern is to move part of the value into the key to form a *composite key*, and let the MapReduce execution framework handle the sorting. In this example, instead of emitting the product ID as the key, a composite key containing the product ID and the store ID is emitted. With this new composite key in place, MapReduce execution sorts all of the product/store records correctly, ensuring that purchase data is sorted by product/store, and can now be processed sequentially.

But there is still a problem with this solution. Introduction of the composite key leads to the fact that now there will be multiple keys for a given product. Although they will be sorted correctly, the default partitioner will not guarantee that all the keys for a given product will come to the same reducer. So, it is necessary to implement a custom composite key-aware partitioner, which will ensure that all the keys for the same product will be directed to the same reducer. Chapter 4 provides an example that demonstrates how to build such a custom partitioner.

The following example shows how you can use reduce-side joins in a realistic application.

Road Enrichment Example

The heart of a road enrichment algorithm is joining a nodes data set (containing a node ID and some additional information about the node) with a link data set (containing link ID, IDs of the nodes that link connects, and some additional information about the link, including the number of link lanes) based on the node IDs.

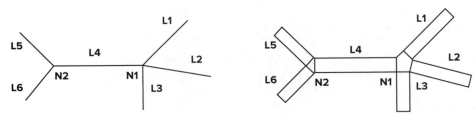

FIGURE 3-7: Road enrichment

A simplified road enrichment algorithm that leverages a reduce-side join might include the following steps:

1. Find all links connected to a given node. For example, as shown in Figure 3-7, node N1 has links L1, L2, L3, and L4, while node N2 has links L4, L5, and L6.

2. Based on the number of lanes for every link at the node, calculate the road width at the intersection.

3. Based on the road width, calculate the intersection geometry.

4. Based on the intersection geometry, move the road's end point to tie it to the intersection geometry.

For the implementation of this algorithm, assume the following:

➤ A node is described with an object N with the key $N_{N1} \ldots N_{Nm}$. For example, node N1 can be described as N_{N1} and N2 as N_{N2}. All nodes are stored in the nodes input file.

➤ A link is described with an object L with the key $L_{L1} \ldots L_{Lm}$. For example, link L1 can be described as L_{L1}, L2 as L_{L2}, and so on. All the links are stored in the links source file.

➤ Also introduce an object of the type link or node (LN), which can have any key.

➤ Finally, it is necessary to define two more types — intersection (S) and road (R).

With this in place, a MapReduce implementation for the road enrichment can consist of two MapReduce jobs.

Table 3-3 shows the implementation of the first MapReduce job for this example.

TABLE 3-3: Calculation of Intersection Geometry and Moving the Road's End Points Job

PROCESS PHASE	DESCRIPTION
Mapper	In this job, the role of the mapper is to build LN_{Ni} records out of the source records — N_{Ni} and L_{Li}. It reads every input record from both source files, and then looks at the object type. If it is a node with the key N_{Ni}, a new record of the type LN_{Ni} is written to the output. If it is a link, keys of both adjacent nodes (N_{Ni} and N_{Nj}) are extracted from the link and two records (LN_{Ni} and LN_{Nj}) are written out.

Shuffle and Sort	MapReduce's shuffle and sort will sort all the records based on the node's keys, which guarantees that every node with all adjacent links will be processed by a single reducer, and that a reducer will get all the LN records for a given key together.
Reducer	In this job, the role of the reducer is to calculate intersection geometry and move the road's ends. It gets all LN records for a given node key and stores them in memory. Once all of them are in memory, the intersection's geometry can be calculated and written out as an intersection record with node key S_{Ni}. At the same time, all the link records connected to a given node can be converted to road records and written out with a link key — R_{Li}.
Result	A result of this job execution is a set of intersection records ready to use, and road records that must be merged together. (Every road is connected to two intersections, and dead ends are typically modeled with a node that has a single link connected to it.) It is necessary to implement the second MapReduce job to merge them. (By default, the output of the MapReduce job writes out the mixture of roads and intersections, which is not ideal. For the purposes here, you would like to separate intersections that are completed, and roads that require additional processing into different files. Chapter 4 examines the way to implement a multi-output format.)

Table 3-4 shows implementation of the second MapReduce job for this example.

TABLE 3-4: Merge Roads Job

PROCESS PHASE	DESCRIPTION
Mapper	The role of the mapper in this job is very simple. It is just a pass-through (or *identity mapper* in Hadoop's terminology). It reads road records and writes them directly to the output.
Shuffle and Sort	MapReduce's shuffle and sort will sort all the records based on the link's keys, which guarantees that both road records with the same key will come to the same reducer together.
Reducer	In this job, the role of the reducer is to merge roads with the same ID. Once the reducer reads both records for a given road, it merges them together, and writes them out as a single road record.
Result	A result of this job execution is a set of road records ready to use.

Now take a look at a special case of a reducer join called a "Bucketing" join. In this case, the data sets might not have common keys, but support the notion of proximity (for example, geographic proximity). In this case, a proximity value can be used as a join key for the data sets. A typical example would be geospatial processing based on the bounding box discussed in the following example.

Links Elevation Example

This problem can be defined as follows. Given a links graph and terrain model, convert two-dimensional (x,y) links into three-dimensional (x, y, z) links. This process is called *link elevation*.

Assume the following:

➤ Every link is specified as two connected points — start and end.

➤ A terrain model is stored in HBase. (Although HDFS has been used in the examples so far, all of the approaches described earlier are relevant to the HBase-stored data as well. There is one serious limitation, though. The current table input format is limited to processing one table. You learn how to implement a table join in Chapter 4.) The model is stored in the form of a height's grids for tiles keyed by the tile ID. (*Tiling* is a partitioning of a space — the whole world in this case — into a finite number of distinct shapes. Here, equal-sized bounding boxes are used as tiles.)

Figure 3-8 shows the model.

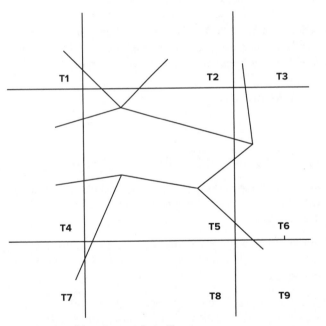

FIGURE 3-8: Mapping roads to tiles

A simplified link elevation algorithm is based on "bucketing" links into tiles, then joining every link's tile with the elevation tile, and processing the complete tile containing both links and elevation data. The algorithm looks as follows:

1. Split every link into fixed-length fragments (for example, 10 meters).

2. For every piece, calculate heights (from the terrain model) for both start and end points of each link.

3. Combine pieces together into original links.

The actual implementation consists of two MapReduce jobs. Table 3-5 shows the implementation of the first MapReduce job for this example.

TABLE 3-5: Split Links into Pieces and Elevate Each Piece Job

PROCESS PHASE	DESCRIPTION
Mapper	In this job, the role of the mapper is to build link pieces, and assign them to the individual tiles. It reads every link record, and splits them into fixed-length fragments, which effectively converts link representation into a set of points. For every point, it calculates a tile to which this point belongs, and produces one or more link piece records, which may be represented as (`tid`, {`lid` `[points array]` }), where `tid` is tile ID, `lid` is the original link ID, and `points array` is an array of points from the original link, which belong to a given tile.
Shuffle and Sort	MapReduce's shuffle and sort will sort all the records based on the tile's IDs, which guarantees that all of the link's pieces belonging to the same tile will be processed by a single reducer.
Reducer	In this job, the role of the reducer is to calculate elevation for every link piece. For every tile ID, it loads terrain information for a given tile from HBase, and then reads all of the link pieces and calculates elevation for every point. It outputs the record (`lid`, `[points array]`), where `lid` is original link ID and `points array` is an array of three-dimensional points.
Result	A result of this job execution contains fully elevated link pieces. It is necessary to implement the second MapReduce job to merge them.

Table 3-6 shows the implementation of the second MapReduce job for this example.

TABLE 3-6: Combine Link's Pieces into Original Links Job

PROCESS PHASE	DESCRIPTION
Mapper	The role of the mapper in this job is very simple. It is an identity mapper. It reads link piece records and writes them directly to the output in the form of (`lid`, `[points array]`) key/value pairs.
Shuffle and Sort	MapReduce's shuffle and sort will sort all the records based on the link's keys, which guarantees that all link piece records with the same key will come to the same reducer together.
Reducer	In this job, the role of the reducer is to merge link pieces with the same ID. Once the reducer reads all of them, it merges them together, and writes them out as a single link record.
Result	A result of this job execution contains elevated links ready to use.

Despite the power of the reducer-side join, its execution can be fairly expensive — shuffle and sort of the large data sets can be very resource-intensive. In the cases when one of the data sets is small enough ("baby" joins) to fit in memory, a map in memory side join can be used. In this case, a small data set is brought into memory in a form of key-based hash providing fast lookups. Now it is possible to iterate over the larger data set, do all the joins in memory, and output the resulting records.

For such an implementation to work, a smaller data set must be distributed to all of the machines where mappers are running. Although it is simple enough to put a smaller data set into HDFS and read it on the mapper startup, Hadoop provides a better solution for this problem — a distributed cache. The native code integration discussion in Chapter 4 provides more details on using the distributed cache.

Problems discussed so far have required implementation of a predefined number of MapReduce jobs. Many practical algorithms (for example, graph processing, or mathematical calculations) are iterative in nature, requiring repeated execution until some convergence criteria is met. Next you look at how to design iterative MapReduce applications.

Building Iterative MapReduce Applications

In the case of iterative MapReduce applications, one or more MapReduce jobs are typically implemented in the loop. This means that such applications can either be implemented using a driver that internally implements an iteration logic and invokes a required MapReduce job(s) inside such an iteration loop, or an external script running MapReduce jobs in a loop and checking conversion criteria. (Another option is using a workflow engine. Chapters 6 through 8 examine Hadoop's workflow engine called Apache Oozie.) Using a driver for execution of iterative logic often provides a more flexible solution, enabling you to leverage both internal variables and the full power of Java for implementation of both iterations and conversion checks.

A typical example of an iterative algorithm is solving a system of linear equations. Next you look at how you can use MapReduce for designing such an algorithm.

Solving Linear Equations Example

Numerous practical problems can be expressed in terms of solving a system of linear equations, or at least reduced to such a system. Following are some examples:

➤ Optimization problems that can be solved with linear programming

➤ Approximation problems (for example, polynomial splines)

> **NOTE** *This example was prepared with the help of Gene Kalmens, a colleague at Nokia.*

Solving linear equations efficiently when the size of the problem is significant — in the ballpark of hundreds of thousands of variables or higher — can be challenging. In this case, the alternative is either to use supercomputers with terabytes of memory, or use the algorithms that allow piecemeal computations and do not require the complete matrix to be brought in memory. The classes of algorithms that adhere to these requirements are iterative methods that provide approximate solutions, with performance tied to the number of iterations necessary to find a solution within a required precision.

With these types of algorithms, the conjugate gradient (CG) method offers the best performance when the system matrix is right. Following is the basic equation in the system of linear equations:

$$Ax = b$$

With CG, you can implement the method of steepest descent applied to the quadratic surface in Rn defined as follows:

$$f(x) = \tfrac{1}{2}x^TAx - x^Tb, x \in R^n$$

Each step improves the solution vector in the direction of the extreme point. Each step's increment is a vector conjugate with respect to A to all vectors found in previous steps.

The CG algorithm includes the following steps:

1. Choose the initial vector x0. It can always be set to 0 for simplicity.

2. Calculate the initial residual vector r0 (for example, $r0 = b - Ax0$).

3. Choose the initial search direction $p0 - r0$.

4. Loop as follows:

   a. Calculate the coefficient: $ak = (r_k^T rk)/(p_k^T Ap_k)$.

   b. Find the next approximation for x: $x_{k+1} = x_k + a_k p_k$.

   c. Calculate the new residual: $r_{k+1} = r_k + a_k Ap_k$.

   d. If $abs(r_k + 1)$ falls within tolerance, exit the loop.

   e. Calculate the scalar to compute the next search direction: $bk = (r_{k+1}^T r_{k+1})/(r_k^T r_k)$

   f. Compute the next search direction: $p_{k+1} = r_{k+1} + b_k p_k$

5. End of loop.

The solution is x_{k+1}.

The only "expensive" operation in this algorithm implementation is the calculation of residual vector (found in steps 2 and 4c), which requires matrix vector multiplication. This operation can be easily implemented using MapReduce.

Assume you have two HBase tables — one for matrix A and one for all the vectors. If matrix A is sparse, then a reasonable HBase data layout is as follows:

➤ Each table row represents a single matrix row.

➤ All elements of a given matrix row are stored in a single column family with a column name corresponding to a column of a given matrix element, and a value corresponding to a matrix value in this row, column value. Considering that the matrix is sparse, the number of columns is going to be significantly smaller than the number of rows.

Although explicit columns for matrix columns are not required for vector multiplication implementation, this table layout might be handy if it is necessary to set/update individual matrix elements.

A reasonable HBase data layout for representing vectors is as follows:

➤ Each table row represents a single vector.

➤ All elements of a given vector are stored in a single column family, with a column name corresponding to a vector index, and a value corresponding to a vector value for an index.

Although, technically, it is possible to use different tables for different vectors using vector indexes as row keys, the proposed layout makes reading/writing vectors significantly faster (single-row reads/writes) and minimizes the amount of HBase connections opened at the same time.

With the HBase table's design in place, a MapReduce matrix vector implementation is fairly straightforward. A single mapper will do the job. Table 3-7 shows the implementation of the matrix vector multiplication MapReduce job.

TABLE 3-7: Matrix Vector Multiplication Job

PROCESS PHASE	DESCRIPTION
Mapper	In this job, a mapper is first initialized with the value of a vector. For every row of the matrix (r), vector multiplication of the source vector and matrix row is calculated. The resulting value (nonzero) is stored at index r of the resulting vector.

In this implementation, the MapReduce driver executes the algorithm described previously, invoking the matrix vector multiplication MapReduce job every time multiplication is required.

Although the algorithm described here is fairly simple and straightforward to implement, in order for CG to work, the following conditions must be met:

➤ Matrix A must be definite-positive. This provides for a convex surface with a single extreme point. It means that the method will converge with any choice of the initial vector x_0.

➤ Matrix A must be symmetric. This ensures the existence of an A-orthogonal vector at each step of the process.

If matrix A is not symmetric, it can be made symmetric by replacing the initial equation with the following one:

$$A^T A x = A^T b$$

$A^T A$ is symmetric and positive. As a result, the previously described algorithm can be applied as is. In this case, the implementation of the original algorithm carries significant performance penalties of calculating the new system matrix $A^T A$. Additionally, convergence of the method will suffer, because $k(A^T A) = k(A)^2$.

Fortunately, you have the choice of not computing $A^T A$ up front, and instead modifying the previous algorithm's steps 2, 4a, and 4c, as shown here:

> **Step 2** — To compute $A^T Ax_0$, perform two matrix vector multiplications: $A^T(Ax_0)$.

> **Step 4a** — To compute the denominator $pk^T A^T Ap_k$, note that it is equal to $(Ap_k)^2$, and its computation comes down to a matrix vector multiplication and an inner product of the result with itself.

> **Step 4c** — Similar to step 2, perform two matrix vector multiplications: $A^T(Ap_k)$.

So, the overall algorithm implementation first must check whether matrix A is symmetric. If it is, then the original algorithm is used; otherwise, the modified algorithm is used.

In addition to the first job, implementation of the overall algorithm requires one more MapReduce job — matrix transposition. Table 3-8 shows the implementation of the matrix transposition MapReduce job.

TABLE 3-8: Matrix Transposition Job

PROCESS PHASE	DESCRIPTION
Mapper	In this job, for every row of matrix (r), each element (r, j) is written to the result matrix as element (j, r).

Note that, in this example, an algorithm conversion criterion is an integral part of the algorithm calculation itself. In the next example, the conversion criterion calculation uses a Hadoop-specific technique.

Stranding Bivalent Links Example

A fairly common mapping problem is stranding bivalent links.

> **NOTE** *This example was prepared with the help of Dmitry Mikhelson, a Nokia colleague.*

Two connected links are called *bivalent* if they are connected via a bivalent node. A *bivalent node* is a node that has only two connections. For example, in Figure 3-9, nodes N6, N7, N8, and N9 are bivalent. Links L5, L6, L7, L8, and L9 are also bivalent. A degenerate case of a bivalent link is link L4.

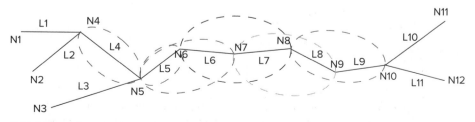

FIGURE 3-9: Example of bivalent links

As shown in Figure 3-9, an algorithm for calculating bivalent link stretches looks very straightforward — any stretch of links between two non-bivalent nodes is a stretch of bivalent links.

For implementation of this algorithm, assume the following:

➤ A node is described with an object N with the key Ni - N^{Ni}. For example, node N1 can be described as N^{N1} and N2 as N^{N2}.

➤ A link is described with an object L with the key Li – L^{Li}. For example, link L1 can be described as L^{L1}, L2 as L^{L2}, and so on. A link object contains references to its start and end nodes (N^{Ni}, N^{Nj}).

➤ Also introduce an object of the type link(s) or node (LN), which can have any key, and can contain either node or one or more links.

➤ Finally, define one more type — a link's strand (S). This data type contains a linked list of links in the strand.

With this in place, an algorithm for stranding of bivalent links looks as follows:

1. Build set of partial bivalent strands.

2. Loop the following:

    a. Combine partial strands.

    b. If no partial strands were combined, exit the loop.

3. End of loop.

The actual implementation consists of two MapReduce jobs. The first one prepares the initial strands, and the second one (executed in the loop) combines partial strands. In this case, the actual combining of the strands is done as part of the MapReduce job execution. As a result, those jobs (not the driver) know how many partial strands were combined during execution. Fortunately, Hadoop provides a simple mechanism for communicating between a driver and MapReduce execution — *counters*.

> **NOTE** *Hadoop provides lightweight objects (counters) to gather job-related metrics/statistics, which can be set and accessed from any place in a MapReduce job. Chapter 5 examines counters in more detail.*

Table 3-9 shows the implementation of the first MapReduce job for this example.

TABLE 3-9: Elimination of Non-Bivalent Nodes Job

PROCESS PHASE	DESCRIPTION
Mapper	In this job, the role of the mapper is to build LN^{Ni} records out of the source records — N^{Ni} and L^{Li}. It reads every input record, and then looks at the object type. If it is a node with the key Ni, a new record of the type LN^{Ni} is written to the output. If it is a link, keys of the both adjacent nodes (Ni and Nj) are extracted from the link, and two records (LN^{Ni} and LN^{Nj}) are written out.

Shuffle and Sort	MapReduce's shuffle and sort will sort all the records based on the node's keys, which guarantees that every node with all adjacent links will be processed by a single reducer, and that a reducer will get all the LN records for a given key together.
Reducer	In this job, the role of the reducer is to eliminate non-bivalent nodes and build partial link strands. It reads all LN records for a given node key and stores them in memory. If the number of links for this node is 2, then this is a bivalent node, and a new strand (combining these two nodes) is written to the output (for example, see pairs L5, L6 or L7, L8). If the number of links is not equal to 2 (it can be either a dead-end or a node at which multiple links intersect), then this is a non-bivalent node. For this type of node, a special strand is created containing a single link, connected to this non-bivalent node (for example, see L4 or L5). The number of strands for such node is equal to the number of links connected to this node.
Result	A result of this job execution contains partial strand records, some of which can be repeated (L4, for example, will appear twice — from processing N4 and N5).

Table 3-10 shows the implementation of the second MapReduce job for this example.

TABLE 3-10: Merging Partial Strands Job

PROCESS PHASE	DESCRIPTION
Mapper	The role of the mapper in this job is to bring together strands sharing the same links. For every strand it reads, it outputs several key/value pairs. The key values are the keys of the links in the strand, and the values are the strands themselves.
Shuffle and Sort	MapReduce's shuffle and sort will sort all the records based on end link keys, which guarantees that all strand records containing the same link ID will come to the same reducer together.
Reducer	➤ In this job, the role of the reducer is to merge strands sharing the same link ID. For every link ID, all strands are loaded in memory and processed based on the strand types: ➤ If two strands contain the same links, the produced strand is complete and can be written directly to the final result directory. ➤ Otherwise, the resulting strand (the strand containing all unique links) is created, and is written to the output for further processing. In this case, the "to be processed" counter is incremented.
Result	A result of this job execution contains all complete strands in a separate directory. It also contains a directory of all bivalent partial strands, along with the value of the "to be processed" counter.

The examples presented here just start to scratch the surface of potential MapReduce usage for solving real-world problems. Next you take a closer look at the situations where MapReduce usage is appropriate, and where it is not.

To MapReduce or Not to MapReduce?

As discussed, MapReduce is a technique used to solve a relatively simple problem in situations where there is a lot of data, and it must be processed in parallel (preferably on multiple machines). The whole idea of the concept is that it makes it possible to do calculations on massive data sets in a realistic time frame.

Alternatively, MapReduce can be used for parallelizing compute-intensive calculations, where it's not necessarily about the amount of data, but rather about the overall calculation time (typically the case of "embarrassingly parallel" computations).

The following must be true in order for MapReduce to be applicable:

➤ The calculations that need to be run must be composable. This means that you should be able run the calculation on a subset of data, and merge partial results.

➤ The data set size is big enough (or the calculations are long enough) that the infrastructure overhead of splitting it up for independent computations and merging results will not hurt overall performance.

➤ The calculation depends mostly on the data set being processed. Additional small data sets can be added using HBase, distributed cache, or some other techniques.

MapReduce is *not* applicable, however, in scenarios when the data set must be accessed randomly to perform the operation (for example, if a given data set record must be combined with additional records to perform the operation). However, in this case, it is sometimes possible to run additional MapReduce jobs to "prepare" data for calculations.

Another set of problems that are not applicable for MapReduce are recursive problems (for example, a Fibonacci problem). MapReduce is not applicable in this case because computation of the current value requires the knowledge of the previous one. This means that you can't break it apart into sub-computations that can be run independently.

If a data size is small enough to fit in a single machine's memory, it is probably going to be faster to process it as a standalone application. Usage of MapReduce, in this case, makes implementation unnecessarily complex and typically slower.

Keep it in mind that, although it is true that a large class of algorithms is not directly applicable to MapReduce implementations, there often exist alternative solutions to the same underlying problems that can be solved by leveraging MapReduce. In this case, usage of MapReduce is typically advantageous, because of the richness of the Hadoop ecosystem in which MapReduce is executed (which supports easier enhancements to the implementation, and integration with other applications).

Finally, you should remember that MapReduce is inherently a batch implementation and should never be used for online computations (for example, real-time calculations for online users' requests).

Common MapReduce Design Gotchas

Following is a list of some things to watch for and avoid when you design your MapReduce implementation:

➤ When splitting data between map tasks, ensure that you do not create too many (typically, the number of mappers should be in hundreds, not thousands) or too few of them. Having the right number of maps has the following advantages for applications:

    ➤ Having too many mappers creates scheduling and infrastructure overhead, and, in extreme cases, can even kill a JobTracker. Also, having too many mappers typically increases overall resource utilization (because of the creation of excessive JVMs) and execution time (because of the limited number of execution slots).

    ➤ Having too few mappers can lead to underutilization of the cluster, and the creation of too much load on some of the nodes (where maps actually run). Additionally, in the case of very large map tasks, retries and speculative execution becomes very expensive and takes longer.

    ➤ A large number of small mappers creates a lot of seeks during shuffle of the map output to the reducers. It also creates too many connections delivering map outputs to the reducers.

➤ The number of reducers configured for the application is another crucial factor. Having too many (typically in thousands) or too few reducers can be anti-productive.

    ➤ In addition to scheduling and infrastructure overhead, having too many reducers results in the creation of too many output files (remember, each reducer creates its own output file), which has a negative impact on a NameNode. It also makes it more complicated to leverage results from this MapReduce job by other jobs.

    ➤ Having too few reducers has the same negative effects as having too few mappers — underutilization of the cluster, and very expensive retries.

➤ Use the job counters appropriately.

    ➤ Counters are appropriate for tracking few, important, global bits of information. (See Chapter 5 for more detail about using counters.) They are definitely not meant to aggregate very fine-grained statistics of applications.

    ➤ Counters are fairly expensive, because the JobTracker must maintain every counter of every map/reduce task for the entire duration of the application.

➤ Consider compressing the application's output with an appropriate compressor (compression speed versus efficiency) to improve write-performance.

➤ Use an appropriate file format for the output of MapReduce jobs. Using `SequenceFiles` is often a best option, because they are both compressable and splittable. (See Chapter 2 for more on compressing files.)

➤ Consider using a larger output block size when the individual input/output files are large (multiple gigabytes).

➤ Try to avoid the creation of new object instances inside `map` and `reduce` methods. These methods are executed many times inside the loop, which means object creation and disposal will increase execution time, and create extra work for a garbage collector. A better approach is to create the majority of your intermediate classes in a corresponding `setup` method, and then repopulate them inside `map`/`reduce` methods.

➤ Do not use distributed cache to move a large number of artifacts and/or very large artifacts (hundreds of megabytes each). The distributed cache is designed to distribute a small number of medium-sized artifacts, ranging from a few megabytes to a few tens of megabytes.

➤ Do not create workflows comprising hundreds or thousands of small jobs processing small amounts of data.

➤ Do not write directly to the user-defined files from either a mapper or reducer. The current implementation of the file writer in Hadoop is single-threaded (see Chapter 2 for more details), which means that execution of multiple mappers/reducers trying to write to this file will be serialized.

➤ Do not create MapReduce implementations scanning one HBase table to create a new HBase table (or write to the same table). `TableInputFormat` used for HBase MapReduce implementation is based on a table scan, which is time-sensitive. On the other hand, HBase writes can cause significant write delays because of HBase table splits. As a result, region servers can hang up, or you could even lose some data. A better solution is to split such a job into two jobs — one scanning a table and writing intermediate results into HDFS, and another reading from HDFS and writing to HBase.

➤ Do not try to re-implement existing Hadoop classes — extend them and explicitly specify your implementation in the configuration. Unlike application servers, a Hadoop command is specifying user classes last, which means that existing Hadoop classes always have precedence.

SUMMARY

This chapter discussed MapReduce fundamentals. You learned about the overall structure of MapReduce and the way the MapReduce pipeline is executed. You also learned how to design MapReduce applications, and the types of problems for which MapReduce is applicable. Finally, you learned how to write and execute a simple MapReduce application, and what happens during the execution.

Now that you know how to design a MapReduce application, as well as write and execute a simple one, Chapter 4 examines customization approaches to different components of the MapReduce pipeline, which enables you to better leverage the MapReduce environment.

4

Customizing MapReduce Execution

WHAT'S IN THIS CHAPTER?

➤ Customizing Hadoop execution to better adhere to requirements of your application

➤ Seamlessly including your non-Java code in the MapReduce executable

WROX.COM CODE DOWNLOADS FOR THIS CHAPTER

The wrox.com code downloads for this chapter are found at www.wiley.com/go/ prohadoopsolutions on the Download Code tab. The code is in the Chapter 4 download and individually named according to the names throughout the chapter.

In Chapter 3, you learned what MapReduce is, its main components, and their roles in MapReduce execution. Each one of these components is implemented as a Java class adhering to a specific interface, defined by a MapReduce framework. Hadoop provides many different implementations of each component, but sometimes you need a specific component to do things slightly differently. One of the most powerful Hadoop features is its extensibility, so you can always roll out your own implementation.

In this chapter, you learn how you can leverage this extensibility for customizing MapReduce execution to better suit the requirements of particular applications. The examples presented in this chapter go through every major MapReduce component, and show how to create its custom implementation to do exactly what you need. Some of the examples can be directly leveraged in your applications; some can just serve as an illustration of how the "magic" happens, and how to approach your own customization.

This chapter starts with a discussion of InputFormat usage for controlling the number of maps and the location of a map's execution.

CONTROLLING MAPREDUCE EXECUTION WITH INPUTFORMAT

As discussed in Chapter 3, the InputFormat class is one of the fundamental classes of the MapReduce framework. It is responsible for defining two main things: InputSplit and RecordReader. InputSplit defines both the size of individual map tasks (and, consequently, the number of map tasks) and its "ideal" execution server (locality). The RecordReader is responsible for actually reading records from the input file, and submitting them (as key/value pairs) to the mapper. RecordReader is discussed in detail later in this chapter. In this section you learn what a split is, and how to implement custom splits and input formats for specific purposes.

A split implementation extends Hadoop's base abstract class — InputSplit — by defining both a split length and its locations. Split locations are a hint for a scheduler to decide where to place a split execution (that is, a particular TaskTracker). A basic JobTracker algorithm operates as follows:

1. Receive heartbeats from the TaskTrackers, reporting map slot availability.

2. Find the queued-up split for which the available node is "local."

3. Submit the split to the TaskTracker for the execution.

> **NOTE** *The algorithm described here is a gross oversimplification aimed only to explain the base mechanics of map allocation. Real scheduler algorithms are significantly more complex, taking into consideration many more parameters than just split locations.*

Split size and locality can mean different things, depending on storage mechanisms and the overall execution strategy. In the case of HDFS, for example, a split typically corresponds to a physical data block, and the location is a set of machines (with the set size defined by a replication factor) where this block is physically located. This is how FileInputFormat calculates splits for a file:

1. Extend InputSplit to capture information about the file location, starting position of the block in the file, and the block length.

2. Get a list of a file's blocks for a file.

3. For every block, create a split with a split length equal to the block size, and split locations equal to locations of a given block. File location, block offset, and length are also saved in a split.

NOTE *Although splitting input files is one of the main techniques for parallelizing the map execution, some of the files cannot be split. For example, compressed text files are nonsplittable in Hadoop. Another example of nonsplittable files would be custom binary files that do not have a marker explicitly separating records. Hadoop's* `FileInputFormat` *(which is a base class for the majority of Hadoop* `InputFormat` *implementations for HDFS files) provides an explicit method allowing to check whether input files are splittable. This method can be overwritten by the* `InputFormat` *classes derived from it. For example,* `TextInputFormat` *overwrites this method by returning* `true` *for uncompressed files and* `false` *for others. Keep in mind that "nonsplittable files" does not mean no parallelization of MapReduce execution. In the case of multi-file input,* `FileInputFormat` *creates a split per block per file. This means that in the case of nonsplittable files, the number of splits will be equal to the number of files.*

EXPLICITLY CONTROLLING SPLIT SIZE FOR HDFS FILES

Although splitting files on the file block boundaries works well in the majority of cases, sometimes such a split might be suboptimal. Fortunately, Hadoop's `FileInputFormat` class (which is a base class for the majority of Hadoop `InputFormat` implementations for HDFS files) supports controlling split size. It provides two methods, `setMinInputSplitSize(Job job,long size)` and `setMaxInputSplitSize(Job job,long size)`, which allow you to explicitly control split size.

This can be useful, for example, when using a default split size leads to the creation of an excessive number of mappers. In this case, increasing a split size can reduce this number. Alternatively, in some cases, a default split size can lead to very few maps with unacceptable execution time. Making a split size smaller, in this case, can lead to a better cluster utilization and shorter execution time.

A different approach is taken by HBase implementers. For HBase, a split corresponds to a set of table keys belonging to a table region, and location is a machine on which a region server is running. No explicit controls exist for the split size in the `TableInputFormat` class. The easiest way to control split size in the case of HBase is to change the way a table is split between regions, such as specifying a table's region file size or pre-splitting a table in a certain way. (See Chapter 2 for more detail on how HBase works.)

NOTE *Do not confuse MapReduce* `InputSplits` *(the way to partition data execution to parallelize it) with HBase's region splits (the way tables are partitioned between region servers for parallelizing access to the data).*

This section examines several examples demonstrating how to build custom `InputFormats` that customize `InputSplit` calculation. The first two examples deal with the custom `InputFormats` for HDFS, and the third deals with HBase.

Implementing InputFormat for Compute-Intensive Applications

A special class of MapReduce applications is compute-intensive applications. (A common example of such applications might be the ones that use MapReduce mostly for parallelization, and employ complex calculation algorithm processing for every key/value, such as the face recognition application example discussed in Chapter 3.) The main characteristic of such applications is that execution of the `map()` function is significantly longer than the data access time (by an order of magnitude, at least).

LONG-RUNNING TASKS IN MAPREDUCE

MapReduce was initially introduced for data-intensive computations, in which `map()` execution times are compatible with the data reading time. As a result, one MapReduce configuration parameter — `mapred.task.timeout` — is, by default, set to 600000 milliseconds (or 600 seconds). This means that if `map` or `reduce` methods do not return or do not write something within 600 seconds, the TaskTracker will consider a corresponding mapper or reducer dead, and will report an error to the JobTracker. A JobTracker, in this case, will kill an attempt, and try to execute it on another node to ensure that the error has not resulted from hardware problems. So, a long-running `map`/`reduce` function must either return within 600 seconds, or let the TaskTracker know that it is healthy every 600 seconds.

The following code shows one of the ways to notify the JobTracker that the job is still alive:

```
public class Heartbeat extends Thread{

    private static final int sleepTime = 400; // time in seconds
    private boolean beating = true;

    private TaskInputOutputContext context = null;

    private Heartbeat(TaskInputOutputContext context){
        this.context = context;
    }

    @Override
    public void run(){
        while (beating){
            try{
                Thread.sleep(sleepTime * 1000); // time in ms
            }
            catch (InterruptedException e){}
            context.setStatus(Long.valueOf
```

```
                            (System.currentTimeMillis()).toString());
            }
    }

    public void stopbeating(){
        beating = false;
    }

    public static Heartbeat createHeartbeat
            (TaskInputOutputContext context){

        Heartbeat heartbeat = new Heartbeat(context);
        Thread heartbeatThread = new Thread(heartbeat);
        heartbeatThread.setPriority(MAX_PRIORITY);
        heartbeatThread.setDaemon(true);
        heartbeatThread.start();
        return heartbeat;
    }
}
```

The `createHeartbeat` method of the `Heartbeat` class creates a new thread that writes into context every `sleepTime` second (400 in the previous code). It is important to set this thread with the highest priority so that it can interrupt mapper/reducer execution. Also, ensure that it is a daemon thread, so that Hadoop (or JVM) can kill it if an execution of the mapper/reducer needs to be killed.

You should invoke this `createHeartbeat` method inside of a mapper/reducer `setup` (preferably in the first line) method, and its `stopbeating` method inside a `cleanup` method.

The other option to achieve the same goal is to increase `mapred.task.timeout` to accommodate prolonged execution. Both approaches achieve the same result, but the `Heartbeat` class implementation does not require a priori knowledge of the calculation duration.

Technically, such applications can still use a "standard" input format implementation. However, this might create a problem by overwhelming the DataNodes where the data resides, and leaving other nodes within the cluster underutilized.

Figure 4-1 (produced by Hadoop's Ganglia monitoring tool) shows that utilization of "standard" data locality for compute-intensive applications can lead to huge variations in the node utilization. The three rows of graphic data at the bottom of the screen show overutilization of some (shown in red on screen, or shaded in this figure) and underutilization of the other ones (shown in yellow and light green on screen, but unshaded in the figure). This means that for compute-intensive applications, the notion of "locality" must be rethought. In this case, the ideal distribution is maximum utilization of compute capabilities of the cluster's machines, and "locality" means even distribution of map execution between all available nodes.

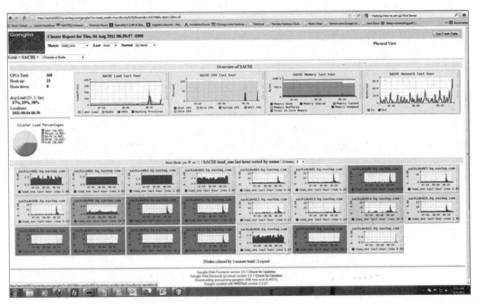

FIGURE 4-1: Nodes utilization in the case of traditional data locality

Listing 4-1 (code file:class `ComputeIntensiveSequenceFileInputFormat`) shows an example of this. Here, a simple `ComputeIntensiveSequenceFileInputFormat` class (which assumes that the source data is available in the form of a set of sequence files) implements the generation of splits, which will be evenly distributed across all servers of the cluster.

LISTING 4-1: ComputeIntensiveSequenceFileInputFormat class

```
public class ComputeIntensiveSequenceFileInputFormat<K, V>
    extends SequenceFileInputFormat<K, V> {

    ................................................................................
    @Override
    public List<InputSplit> getSplits(JobContext job) throws IOException {

        String[] servers = getActiveServersList(job);
        if(servers == null)
            return null;
        List<InputSplit> splits = new ArrayList<InputSplit>();
        List<FileStatus>files = listStatus(job);
        int currentServer = 0;
        for (FileStatus file: files) {
            Path path = file.getPath();
            long length = file.getLen();
            if ((length != 0) && isSplitable(job, path)) {
                long blockSize = file.getBlockSize();
                long splitSize = computeSplitSize(blockSize, minSize, maxSize);

                long bytesRemaining = length;
```

```
                    while (((double) bytesRemaining)/splitSize > SPLIT_SLOP) {
                        splits.add(new FileSplit(path, length-bytesRemaining,
                         splitSize, new String[] {servers[currentServer]}));
                        currentServer = getNextServer(currentServer,
                            servers.length);
                        bytesRemaining -= splitSize;
                    }
                    ..................................................................................
                } else if (length != 0) {
                    splits.add(new FileSplit(path, 0, length,
                            new String[] {servers[currentServer]}));
                    currentServer = getNextServer(currentServer, servers.length);
                }
                    ................................................................................. .
            }

            // Save the number of input files in the job-conf
            job.getConfiguration().setLong(NUM_INPUT_FILES, files.size());

            return splits;
        }

    private String[] getActiveServersList(JobContext context){

            String [] servers = null;
                try {
                JobClient jc = new JobClient((JobConf)context.getConfiguration());
                ClusterStatus status = jc.getClusterStatus(true);
                Collection<String> atc = status.getActiveTrackerNames();
                servers = new String[atc.size()];
                int s = 0;
                for(String serverInfo : atc){
                    StringTokenizer st = new StringTokenizer(serverInfo, ":");
                    String trackerName = st.nextToken();
                    StringTokenizer st1 = new StringTokenizer(trackerName, "_");
                    st1.nextToken();
                    servers[s++] = st1.nextToken();
                }
            } catch (IOException e) {
                e.printStackTrace();
            }

                return servers;
        }

    private static int getNextServer(int current, int max){

            current++;
            if(current >= max)
                current = 0;
            return current;
        }
}
```

> **NOTE** *Extending existing Hadoop classes is a common practice while creating a custom implementation, which is leveraged throughout this chapter. It enables you to reuse an existing implementation, while adding necessary features. For example, extending* SequenceFileInputFormat *and consequently* FileInputFormat *by* ComputeIntensiveSequenceFileInputFormat *significantly simplifies its implementation by leveraging a vast amount of code provided by Hadoop.*

This class extends SequenceFileInputFormat and overwrites the getSplits() method, calculating splits the same way as Hadoop's FileInputFormat. However, it assigns the split's "locality" differently. Instead of using physical location of the block as a "preferred" location of a split execution, locality is assigned here to any of the available servers in the cluster. This implementation leverages two supporting methods:

➤ The getActiveServersList() method queries cluster status to calculate an array of servers (names) currently available in the cluster.

➤ The getNextServer() method is a wraparound iterator over the array of available servers.

> **NOTE** *Although, in some implementations, data locality has no or very little impact on the execution performance, it will always have an impact on the network utilization — more data is transferred over the network if data is not local. When deciding to bypass data locality, ensure that your cluster has this required extra network bandwidth.*

If you want to combine both strategies, you can place as many of the jobs as local to the data as possible, and then distribute the rest of them around the cluster. Listing 4-2 (code file:class ComputeIntensiveLocalizedSequenceFileInputFormat) shows an example of this. You can use this approach if network utilization becomes an issue.

LISTING 4-2: Optimized getSplits method

```java
public List<InputSplit> getSplits(JobContext job) throws IOException {

    List<InputSplit> originalSplits = super.getSplits(job);
    String[] servers = getActiveServersList(job);
    if(servers == null)
        return null;
    List<InputSplit> splits = new
        ArrayList<InputSplit>(originalSplits.size());
    int numSplits = originalSplits.size();
    int currentServer = 0;
    for(int i = 0; i < numSplits; i++, currentServer =
        getNextServer(currentServer,
```

```
                                               servers.length)){
            String server = servers[currentServer]; // Current server
            boolean replaced = false;
            for(InputSplit split : originalSplits){
                FileSplit fs = (FileSplit)split;
                for(String l : fs.getLocations()){
                    if(l.equals(server)){
                        splits.add(new FileSplit(fs.getPath(), fs.getStart(),
    fs.getLength(), new String[] {server}));
                        originalSplits.remove(split);
                        replaced = true;
                        break;
                    }
                }
                if(replaced)
                    break;
            }
            if(!replaced){
                FileSplit fs = (FileSplit)splits.get(0);
                splits.add(new FileSplit(fs.getPath(), fs.getStart(),
                    fs.getLength(),
    new String[] {server}));
                originalSplits.remove(0);
            }
        }
        return splits;
    }
```

This implementation first leverages the superclass (`FileInputFormat`) to get splits with locations calculated to ensure data locality. Then, for every existing server, it tries to assign a split with data local to this server. For the servers that do not have a "local" split, remaining splits are assigned randomly.

HADOOP SCHEDULERS

Several schedulers are available with the Hadoop distribution, with the *fair scheduler* being the most prevalent one. Although the fair scheduler typically works well, it is not very good at guaranteeing data locality. If the data locality is really important, the *delayed fair scheduler* is a better option.

Assuming that the fair scheduler is already set up, add the following block to the `mapred-site.xml` file to enable a delayed fair scheduler. (Note that the delay is in milliseconds, and that after changing the value, it is necessary to restart the JobTracker.)

```
<property>
    <name>mapred.fairscheduler.locality.delay</name>
    <value>360000000</value>
<property>
```

As you can see in Figure 4-2, when you use the `ComputeIntensiveSequenceFileInputFormat` class, you get a much better utilization of the cluster. Processing is distributed much more evenly between the DataNodes, and no CPU hot spots exist.

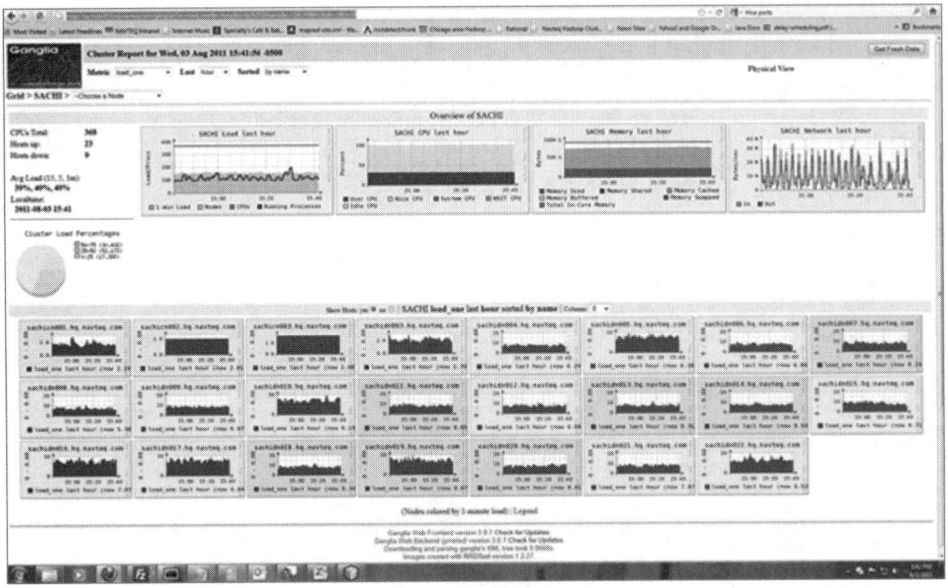

FIGURE 4-2: Node utilization in the case of execution locality

In reality, on a fully loaded cluster, the difference might not be as drastic as shown here, and a "standard" `InputFormat` might work well enough. The purpose of this example is not to propose a different `InputFormat` implementation, but, for the most part, to show the underlying concepts of the inner workings of `InputFormat`, and demonstrate programmatic approaches to its change.

Another common situation in MapReduce implementations is accessing resources (from the map code) outside of an Hadoop cluster (for example, database connections, HTTP connections, and so on). This typically requires explicit controlling of the number of maps.

Implementing InputFormat to Control the Number of Maps

Consider the example of copying a set of files from HDFS to another location, and assume that such copying is done through web services provided by that location. If in this case, you will use a standard `FileInputFormat`, assuming files are nonsplittable, the number of mappers used will be equal to the number of files. If you want to transfer, for example, 1,000 files, this will mean creating 1,000 mappers. This is not the best solution because of the following:

➤ Each mapper execution requires an overhead of creating and destroying a JVM for its execution. This overhead can be significant compared to execution for a single file.

➤ A huge number of splits can start "overwhelming" the JobTracker.

➤ Depending on the scheduler used on a given cluster, such a huge number of map tasks can negatively impact cluster utilization.

Let's start by creating a special InputSplit. Listing 4-3 (code file:class MultiFileSplit) shows a multi-file split that contains both a list of files and information about execution "locality." (This code snippet shows only the implementation of relevant methods.)

LISTING 4-3: MultiFileSplit class

```
public class MultiFileSplit extends InputSplit implements Writable{

        private long length;
        private String[] hosts;
        private List<String> files = null;

        public MultiFileSplit(){

            ........................ . .
        }
        public MultiFileSplit(long l, String[] locations){
            .................................................. . .
        }
        ................................................. . .
    @Override
        public long getLength() throws IOException, InterruptedException {
         return files.size();
    }

    @Override
    public String[] getLocations() throws IOException, InterruptedException {
         return hosts;
    }
        @Override
        public void write(DataOutput out) throws IOException {

            .................................................... .
        }

        @Override
        public void readFields(DataInput in) throws IOException {

            .................................................... .
        }
    }
```

You must derive a custom split class from the InputSplit class and implement the Writable interface. Methods defined in this class and interface must be implemented. Additionally, no arguments constructor (used by the mapper) must be implemented.

> **NOTE** *An* InputSplit *class in Hadoop's implementation is a data container, providing information for the JobTracker — job execution location and input data* RecordReader. *This information is necessary to properly initialize* RecordReader *for a given mapper. As a result, this is the wrong place to add any execution logic. Such logic must be implemented in the* RecordReader.

With the custom split class in place, implementation of the InputFormat is fairly straightforward, as shown in Listing 4-4 (code file:class FileListInputFormat).

LISTING 4-4: FileListInputFormat class

```
public class FileListInputFormat extends FileInputFormat<Text, Text>{

    private static final String MAPCOUNT = "map.reduce.map.count";
    private static final String INPUTPATH = "mapred.input.dir";

    @Override
    public List<InputSplit> getSplits(JobContext context) throws IOException {
        Configuration conf = context.getConfiguration();
        String fileName = conf.get(INPUTPATH, "");
        String[] hosts = getActiveServersList(context);
        Path p = new Path(StringUtils.unEscapeString(fileName));
        List<InputSplit> splits = new LinkedList<InputSplit>();
            FileSystem fs = p.getFileSystem(conf);
        int mappers = 0;
        try{
            mappers = Integer.parseInt(conf.get(MAPCOUNT));
        }
        catch(Exception e){}
        if(mappers == 0)
            throw new IOException("Number of mappers is not specified");
        FileStatus[] files = fs.globStatus(p);
        int nfiles = files.length;
        if(nfiles < mappers)
            mappers = nfiles;
        for(int i = 0; i < mappers; i++)
            splits.add(new MultiFIleSplit(0,hosts));
        Iterator<InputSplit> siter = splits.iterator();
        for(FileStatus f : files){
            if(!siter.hasNext())
                siter = splits.iterator();
            ((MultiFIleSplit)(siter.next())).addFile(f.getPath().toUri()
                .getPath());
        }
        return splits;
    }

    public static void setMapCount(Job job, int mappers){
```

```
                Configuration conf = job.getConfiguration();
                conf.set(MAPCOUNT, new Integer(mappers).toString());
        }

}
```

NUMBER OF LOCATIONS PER SPLIT

In MapReduce, there is a limit on the locations for a single split. The runtime does not control or cap inputs, just cap the maximum number of locations shippable per `InputSplit` object. For a regular file split on a cluster with the default configuration, there will be three input split locations. The default number of locations per split is 10. If this number is exceeded, Hadoop will throw the warning `"Max block location exceeded for split: xxxxxxxxxxxxxxxxxxxxxxxxxx"` and use only the first 10 locations. To get around this limitation, set the `MAX_SPLIT_LOCATIONS` property to your desired number of split locations.

Be aware that the increased number of locations per split increases the size of the `InputSplit` class, and, consequently, the size of network messages. So, you should be sure you really need all of these locations.

The static method `setMapCount` here provides an API for you to set the value of a desired number of maps in the job driver. Its implementation leverages a standard Hadoop approach to pass parameters between distributed Hadoop components — adding a value to the configuration, which is accessible by every component of a given job.

The actual implementation of the `getSplits` method is also fairly straightforward. It first tries to get the number of required mappers, and creates a split for every map. It then goes through all of the available files and adds each of them to one of the splits.

Although `FileListInputFormat` works well when files are about the same size, in the case when file sizes vary significantly, so does the execution time for individual mappers. The problem is that the split is done by the number of the files, not the data size. Moreover, for some of the MapReduce jobs, it is not just the data size itself, but rather the complexity of data (because it is used by map processing). As a result, achieving even-sized (in terms of execution time) splits in the `InputFormat` can be fairly complex.

Figure 4-3 shows how to use queuing as a general approach to evening up execution time for multiple workers (request processors).

In this case, all of the execution requests are written to the queue. Each worker tries to read a new request from the queue, and then executes it. Once execution is complete, a worker tries to read the next request. This type of load balancing is called *worker-driven load balancing*. In this case, the requester does not know anything about execution capabilities, or even the number of workers. A worker reads a new request only after a current one is completed, thus ensuring effective utilization of resources.

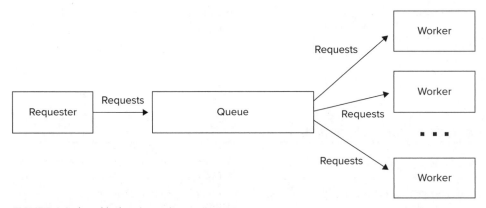

FIGURE 4-3: Load balancing using a queue

Let's see how this approach can be applied to MapReduce job execution. A simple way to create a queue in the Hadoop environment is to use HBase, as shown in Listing 4-5 (code file: class HdQueue).

LISTING 4-5: Implementing a queue using HBase

```java
public class HdQueue {

    ........................................................

    public void enqueue(byte[] data) throws IOException{

        long messageKey = 0;
        // Make sure that the pointer is >= 0
        while ((messageKey = table.incrementColumnValue
(COUNTER_KEY, MESSAGE_FAMILY, COUNTER_COLUMN, 1)) < 0){};
        // Put the message
        String sKey = Long.toString(messageKey);
        Put put = new Put(Bytes.toBytes(sKey));
        put.add(MESSAGE_FAMILY, MESSAGE_COLUMN, data);
        table.put(put);
    }

    public long getCurrentQueueSize() throws IOException{
        return table.incrementColumnValue(COUNTER_KEY, MESSAGE_FAMILY,
            COUNTER_COLUMN, 0);
    }

    ........................................................

    public byte[] dequeue() throws IOException{

        long messageKey =
table.incrementColumnValue(COUNTER_KEY, MESSAGE_FAMILY, COUNTER_COLUMN, -1);
        if (messageKey < 0){
            messageKey = table.incrementColumnValue
(COUNTER_KEY, MESSAGE_FAMILY, COUNTER_COLUMN, 1);
            return null;
```

```
        }
        String sKey = Long.toString(++messageKey);
        Get get = new Get(Bytes.toBytes(sKey));
        get.addColumn(MESSAGE_FAMILY, MESSAGE_COLUMN);
        Result result = table.get(get);
        return result.value();
    }

    ..................................................... .

}
```

In this implementation, a queue is represented by a single table. Implementation is based on an atomic HBase increment operation, applied to a position of the queue pointer. An enqueue operation increments the pointer and uses its current position as a key. A dequeue method decrements the pointer and uses its previous value as a key for retrieving the data. The actual data is stored in the table with the row key equal to a position of the data in a queue. A special row key is dedicated to tracking the queue pointer.

With this simple queuing implementation in place, you can now modify the InputFormat implementation shown in Listing 4-4 to use it.

First, it is necessary to simplify the implementation of the InputSplit class. Because, in this case, a list of files is stored in the queue rather than in the split itself, you can remove a list of files and all methods related to file list processing from the MultiFileSplit class (Listing 4-3). Call this split a SimpleSplit class. With this class in place, your InputFormat implementation will look as shown in Listing 4-6 (code file:class FileListQueueInputFormat).

LISTING 4-6: FileListQueueInputFormat class

```
    public class FileListQueueInputFormat extends FileInputFormat<Text, Text>{

        ..................................................... .
        @Override
        public List<InputSplit> getSplits(JobContext context) throws IOException {
            Configuration conf = context.getConfiguration();
            String fileName = conf.get(INPUTPATH, "");
            String[] hosts = getActiveServersList(context);
            Path p = new Path(StringUtils.unEscapeString(fileName));
            List<InputSplit> splits = new LinkedList<InputSplit>();
               FileSystem fs = p.getFileSystem(conf);
            int mappers = 0;
            try{
                 mappers = Integer.parseInt(conf.get(MAPCOUNT));
            }
            catch(Exception e){}
            if(mappers == 0)
                 throw new IOException("Number of mappers is not specified");
            HdQueue queue = HdQueue.getQueue(conf.get(QUEUE));
            FileStatus[] files = fs.globStatus(p);
            int nfiles = files.length;
            if(nfiles < mappers)
                 mappers = nfiles;
```

continues

LISTING 4-6 *(continued)*

```
            for(FileStatus f : files)
                queue.enqueue(Bytes.toBytes(f.getPath().toUri().getPath()));
            queue.close();
            for(int i = 0; i < mappers; i++)
                splits.add(new SimpleInputSplit(0,hosts));
            return splits;
    }
    public static void setInputQueue(Job job, String queue) throws IOException {
        Configuration conf = job.getConfiguration();
        conf.set(QUEUE, queue);
    }

    public static void setMapCount(Job job, int mappers){
        Configuration conf = job.getConfiguration();
        conf.set(MAPCOUNT, new Integer(mappers).toString());
    }
}
```

This implementation is similar to the one in Listing 4-4, with the exception that instead of storing filenames to the splits, files are stored in the queue. An additional static method is provided in this implementation to provide an input queue name.

Depending on your specific requirements, you can use both `FileListInputFormat` and `FileListQueueInputFormat` to explicitly control the number of maps in a MapReduce job. `FileListInputFormat` is simpler, so if load balancing of map execution is not required, you should use it.

The last example of the custom `InputFormat` discussed here is the one supporting multiple HBase tables.

Implementing InputFormat for Multiple HBase Tables

For MapReduce jobs leveraging HBase-based data sources, Hadoop provides `TableInputFormat`. The limitation of this implementation is that it supports only a single table. Many practical applications such as a table join (compare to joining of MapReduce jobs discussed in Chapter 3) require multiple tables as a job's input. Implementation of such an input format is fairly straightforward.

You must first define a class that can hold information defining an individual table, as shown in Listing 4-7 (code file:class `TableDefinition`). This class enables you to completely identify a table for the MapReduce processing through the table itself, a scan defining which row span of the table you are interested in, and a set of column families (columns relevant for a specific problem).

LISTING 4-7: TableDefinition class

```
    public class TableDefinition implements Writable {

        private Scan _scan = null;
```

```
          private HTable _table = null;
          private String _tableName = null;

          ..................................................................................................
    }
```

Because Hadoop's implementation of `TableInputFormat` supports a single table/scan, all of the information about the table and scan is contained in the `TableInputFormat` implementation, and does not need to be defined in the `InputSplit` class. In this case, different splits can refer to different tables/scan pairs. As a result, you must extend the table split class to contain not only table-related information (name, start and end row, region server location), but also a scan for a given table. Listing 4-8 (code file:class `MultiTableSplit`) shows how to do this.

LISTING 4-8: MultiTableSplit class

```
    public class MultiTableSplit extends TableSplit {

        private Scan scan;

        public MultiTableSplit() {
            .................................................................................
        }

        public MultiTableSplit(byte [] tableName, byte [] startRow, byte [] endRow,
            final String location, Scan scan) {
            .................................................................................
        }
        .................................................................................
    }
```

With these two supporting classes in place, the implementation of the `MultiTableInputFormat` class looks as shown in Listing 4-9 (code file:class `MultiTableInputFormat`).

LISTING 4-9: MultiTableInputFormat class

```
    public class MultiTableInputFormat extends InputFormat<ImmutableBytesWritable,
        Result> implements Configurable{
        ..................................................................................................

        protected void setTableRecordReader(TableRecordReader tableRecordReader) {
            this.tableRecordReader = tableRecordReader;
        }


        @Override
        public List<InputSplit> getSplits(JobContext context) throws IOException,
        InterruptedException {
```

continues

LISTING 4-9 *(continued)*

```
            List<InputSplit> splits = new LinkedList<InputSplit>();
            int count = 0;
            for(TableDefinition t : tables){
                HTable table = t.getTable();
                if (table == null) {
                    continue;
                }
                Pair<byte[][], byte[][]> keys = table.getStartEndKeys();
                if (keys == null || keys.getFirst() == null ||
                        keys.getFirst().length == 0) {
                    continue;
                }
                Scan scan = t.getScan();
                for (int i = 0; i < keys.getFirst().length; i++) {
                    String regionLocation =
                        table.getRegionLocation(keys.getFirst()[i]).
                    getServerAddress().getHostname();
                    byte[] startRow = scan.getStartRow();
                    byte[] stopRow = scan.getStopRow();
                    if ((startRow.length == 0 || keys.getSecond()[i].length == 0 ||
                            Bytes.compareTo(startRow, keys.getSecond()[i]) <
                                0) &&
                            (stopRow.length == 0 ||
                                Bytes.compareTo(stopRow, keys.getFirst()[i])
                                    > 0)) {
                        byte[] splitStart = startRow.length == 0 ||
                        Bytes.compareTo(keys.getFirst()[i], startRow) >= 0 ?
                            keys.getFirst()[i] : startRow;
                        byte[] splitStop = (stopRow.length == 0 ||
                            Bytes.compareTo(keys.getSecond()[i], stopRow) <=
                                0) &&
                                        keys.getSecond()[i].length > 0 ?
                                keys.getSecond()[i] : stopRow;
                        InputSplit split = new
                            MultiTableSplit(table.getTableName(),
                                    splitStart, splitStop, regionLocation,
                                        scan);
                        splits.add(split);
                }
            }
        }
        if(splits.size() == 0){
            throw new IOException("Expecting at least one region.");
        }
        return splits;
    }

    @Override
    public RecordReader<ImmutableBytesWritable, Result> createRecordReader(
            InputSplit split, TaskAttemptContext context) throws IOException,
                InterruptedException {
```

```
                    MultiTableSplit tSplit = (MultiTableSplit) split;
                    TableRecordReader trr = this.tableRecordReader;
                    if (trr == null) {
                        trr = new TableRecordReader();
                    }
                    Scan sc = tSplit.getScan();
                    sc.setStartRow(tSplit.getStartRow());
                    sc.setStopRow(tSplit.getEndRow());
                    trr.setScan(sc);
                    byte[] tName = tSplit.getTableName();
                    trr.setHTable(new HTable(HBaseConfiguration.create(conf), tName));
                        trr.init();
                    return trr;
                }

       ...................................................................
       public static void initTableMapperJob(List<TableDefinition> tables,
                Class<? extends TableMapper> mapper,
                Class<? extends WritableComparable> outputKeyClass,
                Class<? extends Writable> outputValueClass, Job job) throws IOException {
                job.setInputFormatClass(MultiTableInputFormat.class);
                if (outputValueClass != null)
                        job.setMapOutputValueClass(outputValueClass);
                if (outputKeyClass != null) job.setMapOutputKeyClass(outputKeyClass);
                job.setMapperClass(mapper);
                job.getConfiguration().set(INPUT_TABLES, convertTablesToString(tables));
           }
       }
```

This class contains the following key methods:

➤   The getSplits method iterates through the list of tables, and for every table, calculates
    a list of regions with a set of keys inside scan boundaries. For every region, the
    implementation creates a new split and populates the MultitableSplit class with the
    appropriate information.

➤   The createRecordReader method creates a new record reader based on the table and scan
    information. By default, this InputFormat uses the default implementation provided by
    Hadoop — TableRecordReader. Additionally, the setTableRecordReader method allows
    subclasses of this InputFormat class to overwrite RecordReader implementation.

➤   Finally, initTableMapperJob is a helper method that simplifies setting up a MapReduce
    job. It takes a list of table definitions, a mapper class, output keys and values, and a job,
    and sets job parameters correctly. It also "stringifies" a list of table definitions, and sets
    the resulting string to the context object, which makes it available to the InputFormat
    implementation.

Now that you know how to write custom InputFormats to control a mapper's execution, the next
section looks at how to implement a custom RecordReader that enables you to control how input
data is read, processed, and delivered to the mappers.

READING DATA YOUR WAY WITH CUSTOM RECORDREADERS

You can store input data for the MapReduce job in a lot of different (application-dependent) formats. For the job to be able to read a specific data format, it is often necessary to implement a custom `RecordReader`.

> **NOTE** *One of the hallmarks of good development practices is a separation of concerns. Following this principle, mapper implementers should not know the actual data layout. They should operate on the stream of key/value pairs. All of the logic of reading input data and converting it into key/value pairs should be encapsulated in the* `RecordReader`.

Several examples in this section demonstrate how to build custom `RecordReaders`.

Implementing a Queue-Based RecordReader

In the previous section, you learned how to implement a queue-based `InputFormat` that enables you to control the number of mappers and load balance their execution. This `InputFormat` stores filenames in the queue, and requires implementation of a custom queue `RecordReader` for its usage.

Listing 4-10 (code file:class `FileListReader`) shows an implementation of such a custom `RecordReader`. The implementation is based on the assumption that the `map` method of the mapper receives both a key and value as `Text`, where the key is not used, and the value containing filename.

LISTING 4-10: Queue data reader class

```
public class FileListReader extends RecordReader<Text, Text> {

    private HdQueue _queue;
    private Configuration _conf;
    private Text key = new Text("key");
    private Text value = new Text();

    @Override
    public void initialize(InputSplit split, TaskAttemptContext context)
            throws IOException, InterruptedException {
        _conf = context.getConfiguration();
        _queue = HdQueue.getQueue(_conf.get(QUEUE));
    }

    @Override
    public boolean nextKeyValue() throws IOException, InterruptedException {
        return getNextFile();
    }

    @Override
    public Text getCurrentKey() throws IOException, InterruptedException {
        return key;
    }
```

```java
    @Override
    public Text getCurrentValue() throws IOException, InterruptedException {
        return value;
    }

    @Override
    public float getProgress() throws IOException, InterruptedException {
        return 0;
    }

    @Override
    public void close() throws IOException {
        _queue.close();

    }
    private boolean getNextFile(){

        byte[] f = null;
        try {
            f = _queue.dequeue();
        } catch (IOException e) {
            e.printStackTrace();
        }
        if(f == null)
            return true;
        value.set(new String(f));
        return false;
    }
}
```

Following are the key methods implemented in this code:

➤ initialize — This method implements all of the initialization required for proper RecordReader functioning. In this case, initialization amounts to connecting to the queue.

➤ nextKeyValue — This method is called by the mapper to check if there is more data to process. In this implementation, you are invoking a separate method — getNextFile — which stores the filename in the value class variable, and returns true if there is a file in the queue, or false otherwise. The result of the invocation is returned back to the mapper.

➤ getCurrentKey and getCurrentValue — These two methods are used for accessing the current key and value. In this implementation, you just return values, which are stored in the class. You pre-allocate those values at the class creation, and update the value every time you read a new filename from the queue. This approach can significantly save on memory allocation/deallocation, which is an important optimization technique in the MapReduce implementation discussed in Chapter 3.

➤ getProgress — This method is used by Hadoop to report on progress of the mapper execution. Because, in this case, you do not know how many files are still in the queue for you to process, you are always returning 0 here.

➤ close — This method is used to clean up resources at the end of the RecordReader execution. In this case, you are closing the queue.

Depending on the functionality of the mapper, the implementation shown in Listing 4-10 might have a problem. If a mapper instance is killed by Hadoop for any reason, the queue elements processed by this instance are lost. To avoid this situation, you must do the following:

➤ Run a job using this `RecordReader` with speculative execution disabled (see Chapter 3 for a definition of speculative execution and the ways to disable it).

➤ Implement an appropriate shutdown hook to ensure that if a job is killed for any reason, queue elements are restored (enqueued back to the queue). The implementation can store dequeued filenames in memory and enqueue them back to the queue inside of the shutdown hook implementation. The fact that the mapper `cleanup` method is invoked can be used, in this case, as an indicator that the mapper step has been completed successfully, and the list of dequeued filenames can be cleaned up.

USING A JAVA SHUTDOWN HOOK IN HADOOP

A *shutdown hook* is simply an initialized thread. When the virtual machine begins its shutdown sequence, it starts all registered shutdown hooks in some unspecified order, and lets them run concurrently.

You should code shutdown hooks defensively (remember that their sequence is undefined, and several of them can be running concurrently). Following are the basic requirements for shutdown hook implementations:

➤ Their implementation must be thread-safe.

➤ They should not blindly rely upon services that may have registered their own shutdown hooks.

➤ The execution time of shutdown hooks is typically limited. When JVM is terminated because of a user logoff or system shutdown, the underlying operating system may only allow a fixed amount of time in which to shut down and exit. This means that when an `exit` method is invoked, it is expected that the virtual machine will shut down and exit within a fixed time interval.

➤ There is no special behavior for handling uncaught exceptions in shutdown hooks. The default implementation is to print the exception's stack trace, and terminate the thread. It does not cause the virtual machine to exit or halt.

When implementing a shutdown hook in the Hadoop environment, remember that Hadoop's filesystem is using a JVM shutdown hook so that it can clean up the filesystem cache. This means that you cannot implement your own shutdown hook that performs filesystem operations, because this will cause a `java.lang .IllegalStateException: Shutdown in progress` exception. Fortunately, Hadoop allows you to disable a filesystem shutdown hook by using the API `Configuration.setBoolean("fs.automatic.close", false)`. If you do this, you can use a custom shutdown hook to implement filesystem operations.

One of the common formats for the MapReduce input files is XML. Unfortunately, Hadoop does not provide a standard XML `RecordReader`. An implementation presented next demonstrates how such a `RecordReader` can work.

XML TERMINOLOGY

The following XML terminology is used here:

➤ An *XML document* is typically represented by a complete file. Although, technically, a single file can contain multiple XML documents, the assumption here is a one-to-one correspondence between a file and an XML document.

➤ An XML document contains markup and content. *Markup* consists of tags, where every tag starts with < and ends with >. XML defines three types of tags: *start tags* (defining the beginning of the content), *end tags* (defining the end of content), and *empty element tags* (all the content is contained inside a tag itself).

➤ An *XML element* is a logical component of the document located between start and end tags, or inside an empty tag. A *tag name* is an element name.

➤ XML elements can have *attributes*. Attributes provide additional information about an element.

Implementing RecordReader for XML Data

Several examples of XML `RecordReader` implementations are available on the Internet, but most of them suffer from several shortcomings, including the following:

➤ They typically support only a single tag, whereas in real life, a user can be interested in getting XML snippets for multiple tags.

➤ They typically do not support empty XML tags.

➤ They typically do not support zipped/gzipped files. Compression is a common technique to reduce a file size, and although a few reasons exist not to use zipped files for MapReduce processing (files can't be split in this case), compressed files are still commonly used in the case of multi-file MapReduce jobs.

➤ In some applications, you may want to process only a starting tag (in order to get its attributes). A typical case is a starting tag of the document containing the document's metadata in the form of attributes. If this snippet is processed as a whole, it will subsume all of the document's content, and, consequently, no other tags will be found in the document.

Listing 4-11 (code file:class `XMLReader`) shows an implementation that is free of these shortcomings. The `XMLReader` class extends the `RecordReader` class provided by the Hadoop framework.

LISTING 4-11: **XMLReader**

```java
public class XMLReader extends RecordReader<Text, Text> {

    @Override
    public void initialize(InputSplit inputSplit, TaskAttemptContext context)
throws IOException, InterruptedException {

        FileSplit split = (FileSplit) inputSplit;
        Configuration configuration = context.getConfiguration();
        String key = configuration.get(ELEMENT_NAME);

        long s = split.getStart();
        long e = s + split.getLength();
        final Path file = split.getPath();
        CompressionCodecFactory compressionCodecs = new
                            CompressionCodecFactory(configuration);
            final CompressionCodec codec = compressionCodecs.getCodec(file);

        // open the file and seek to the start of the split
        final FileSystem fs = file.getFileSystem(configuration);
        FSDataInputStream fileIn = fs.open(file);
        if (codec != null)
            init(0, Long.MAX_VALUE, key, codec.createInputStream(fileIn));
        else
            init(s, e, key, fileIn);
    }

    @Override
    public void close() throws IOException {

        if(_fileIn != null)
            _fileIn.close();
    }

    @Override
    public Text getCurrentKey() throws IOException, InterruptedException {

        return _key;
    }

    @Override
    public Text getCurrentValue() throws IOException, InterruptedException {

        return new Text( _value);
    }

    @Override
    public float getProgress() throws IOException, InterruptedException {

        if (_start == _end)
            return 0.0f;
        else
```

```java
                    return Math.min(1.0f, (_current - _start) / (float)(_end - _start));
    }

    @Override
    public boolean nextKeyValue() throws IOException, InterruptedException {

        if((_eof) || (_current >= _end))
            return false;

        _firstOnly = false;
        if (readUntilMatch(_startTag, _matchingStartTag, false))
            return true;

        if(_eof)
            return false;

        String endtag = "</" + _key.toString() + ">";
        if(_firstOnly){
            _value += endtag;
            return true;
        }

        _endTag[0] = endtag.getBytes();
        readUntilMatch(_endTag, _matchingEndTag, true);
        if(_eof)
                return false;
        return true;
    }

    private boolean readUntilMatch(byte[][] match, int[] matchingTag,boolean
        withinBlock)
throws IOException {

        ..................................................................
    }

    private void init(long s, long e, String keys, InputStream in) throws
        IOException {

        ..................................................................
    }

    public static void main(String[] args) throws Exception {

        DataInputStream in = new DataInputStream(new FileInputStream(new
            File(args[0])));
        long start = Long.parseLong(args[2]);
        long end = Long.parseLong(args[3]);
        XMLReader reader = new XMLReader();
        reader.init(start, end, args[1], in);
        Map<String, Integer> occurences = new HashMap<String, Integer>();
        while(reader.nextKeyValue()){
            String key = reader.getCurrentKey().toString();
```

continues

LISTING 4-11 *(continued)*

```
                System.out.println("key " + key);
                Integer count = occurences.get(key);
                if(count == null)
                    count = 1;
                else
                    count++;
                occurences.put(key, count);
        }
        for(Map.Entry<String, Integer> entry: occurences.entrySet())
            System.out.println("key " + entry.getKey() + " found " +
                entry.getValue() + " times");

    }
}
```

The `initialize` method is invoked by Hadoop and is responsible for initialization of the reader. To allow testing of the implementation outside of Hadoop, it is split into two methods — `initialize` (which is implementing Hadoop-specific things) and `init` (which you can invoke either by initializing a Java `main` or `Junit` for testing).

The `initialize` method gets a `FileSplit` class that is passed in by Hadoop and extracts an input filename, as well as start and end bytes of the file block passed to this mapper. Additionally, it extracts a list of keys (a comma-separated list of tags) that are of interest to the user. Finally, the `initialize` method gets a compression codec, and, if one already exists, overwrites the start and end bytes. (Remember, zipped files are not splittable and, consequently, their start byte is always 0, and the actual length of an unzipped file is not known. Thus, the end byte is set to a very large number, `Long.MAX_VALUE`.) The `initialize` method uses the input stream from the codec (unzipper) instead of the input stream from the original file. The `initialize` method then invokes the `init` method, which does additional initialization for tag detection.

The set of tags for detection is passed in as a comma-separated list of strings, containing all of the tags of interest. Individual tags are extracted using `stringTokenizer` class. If the string starts with "+", it means the reader will return not the full XML fragment, but only the content of the opening tag itself (including all the attributes contained in the tag). The information describing each tag of interest is stored in the `KeyString` class shown in Listing 4-12 (code file:class `KeyString`). Note how this contains both the tag string and `firstOnly` flag.

LISTING 4-12: KeyString class

```
public class KeyString {

    private String _string;
    private boolean _firstOnly;

    ...........................................................

}
```

The start tag always starts with <, but can end either with either > or a space. Consequently, in the implementation code shown in Listing 4-11, for every tag, the method builds two byte arrays (one for each option) to check against tag completion. Because a closing tag is always searched for a corresponding opening tag, you do not populate the end tags byte array upfront — you are doing this just in time in the readUntilMatch method. Finally, the init method creates counter arrays for matching.

The close method is very simple — it just closes the input stream.

The GetCurrentKey and getCurrentValue methods return corresponding values pre-calculated by the nextKeyValue method.

The getProgress method first checks if the source file was zipped. Because the size of data is unknown upfront in the case of zipped input files, progress is reported as 0. Otherwise, map progress to this point is calculated based on the number of bytes read.

The nextKeyValue method is trying to prepare values for the next invocations of getKey and getValue methods. It returns true if these values are prepared and false otherwise. This method first checks if you must continue (that is, the end of the file has been detected, or you have advanced past the end byte) and returns false if you do not. It then tries to find one of the specified opening tags using the readUntilMatch method. If this method returns true it means that a complete tag is found. If the end of file flag was set during the tag search, the method returns false. Otherwise, it sets up a closing tag (based on a found opening tag). It then checks if you need only an opening tag for the given tag. If that is the case, it adds a closing tag to it and returns true. Finally, it uses the readUntilMatch method to find a closing tag and either returns false (if the end of file flag is set during the search) or true otherwise.

Now that you know how to split input data and read it, the next section takes a look at how to customize the way the results of execution are written out.

ORGANIZING OUTPUT DATA WITH CUSTOM OUTPUT FORMATS

As discussed in Chapter 3, the OutputFormat interface determines where and how (using a writer) the results of a MapReduce job are persisted. Hadoop comes with a collection of classes and interfaces for different types of output formats, but sometimes those implementations are not sufficient for the problem at hand. Two main reasons why you might want to create a custom OutputFormat class are to change where the data is stored, and how the data is written. This section demonstrates how to control where the data is stored.

Before you delve into specific implementation details, take a look at how the MapReduce framework writes output files to HDFS and components involved in the process. (If you are writing to HBase or custom data storage, the components are slightly different.)

As you can see from Figure 4-4, once the job is split into multiple tasks, a task controller starts an "attempt" of task execution. An execution also creates one of the subclasses of FileOutputFormat, which, in turn, creates a FileCommitter class, creating a temporary directory in the output directory specified by FileOutputFormat. This allows multiple tasks and multiple attempts of each task to write their output independently from each other. Once an attempt is complete, a

`FileOutputCommitter` is invoked again. If an attempt fails, the corresponding temporary directory is removed. If it succeeds, output is copied from the temporary directory to the main one, and the temporary directory is removed. When the whole job is completed, a `FileCommitter` is invoked yet again to finalize output data.

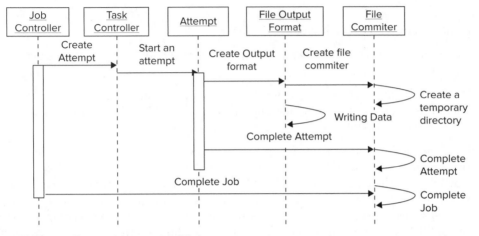

FIGURE 4-4: Processing output in Hadoop

The following example demonstrates how to implement a custom `OutputFormat`.

Implementing OutputFormat for Splitting MapReduce Job's Output into Multiple Directories

In this section, you learn how to implement `OutputFormat` to split a MapReduce job's output into multiple directories, and use different `RecordWriter`s for different directories. This can be useful, for example, when you want to separate a successfully processed record from the ones requiring manual interventions, or geographically splitting processing results.

Hadoop already provides the `MultipleOutputs` class, which enables you to split output into multiple file (in the same directory) with different `RecordWriter` types. If such split is sufficient, you can use this class. Otherwise, you must create a subclass of this class to do both a name change and a directory change, as shown in Listing 4-13 (code file:class `MultipleOutputsDirectories`).

LISTING 4-13: MultipleOutputsDirectories class

```
public class MultipleOutputsDirectories<KEYOUT, VALUEOUT> extends
    MultipleOutputs<KEYOUT, VALUEOUT> {

    .....................................................................

    @Override
    public <K, V> void write(String namedOutput, K key, V value,
```

```
                String baseOutputPath) throws IOException, InterruptedException {
        checkNamedOutputName(context, namedOutput, false);
        checkBaseOutputPath(baseOutputPath);
        if (!namedOutputs.contains(namedOutput)) {
            throw new IllegalArgumentException("Undefined named output '" +
                    namedOutput + "'");
        }
        TaskAttemptContext taskContext = getContext(namedOutput);
        getRecordWriter(taskContext, baseOutputPath).write(key, value);
    }

    private TaskAttemptContext getContext(String nameOutput) throws IOException {

        TaskAttemptContext taskContext = taskContexts.get(nameOutput);
        if (taskContext != null) {
            return taskContext;
        }

        Job job = new Job(context.getConfiguration());
        job.setOutputFormatClass(getNamedOutputFormatClass(context, nameOutput));
        job.setOutputKeyClass(getNamedOutputKeyClass(context, nameOutput));
        job.setOutputValueClass(getNamedOutputValueClass(context, nameOutput));
        String location = FileOutputFormat.getOutputPath(job).toString();
        Path jobOutputPath = new Path(location + "/" + nameOutput);
        FileOutputFormat.setOutputPath(job, jobOutputPath);
        taskContext = new TaskAttemptContext(
                job.getConfiguration(), context.getTaskAttemptID());

        taskContexts.put(nameOutput, taskContext);
        return taskContext;
    }

    private synchronized RecordWriter getRecordWriter(TaskAttemptContext
        taskContext,
String baseFileName) throws IOException, InterruptedException {

        RecordWriter writer = recordWriters.get(baseFileName);

        if (writer == null) {
            FileOutputFormat.setOutputName(taskContext, baseFileName);
            try {
                writer = ((OutputFormat) ReflectionUtils.newInstance(
                taskContext.getOutputFormatClass(),
                    taskContext.getConfiguration()))
                        .getRecordWriter(taskContext);
            } catch (ClassNotFoundException e) {
                throw new IOException(e);
            }

            recordWriters.put(baseFileName, writer);
        }
        return writer;
    }
```

continues

LISTING 4-13 *(continued)*

```
@SuppressWarnings("unchecked")
public void close() throws IOException, InterruptedException {
        for (RecordWriter writer : recordWriters.values()) {
                writer.close(context);
        }
}
@SuppressWarnings("unchecked")
private static Class<? extends OutputFormat<?, ?>> getNamedOutputFormatClass(
        JobContext job, String namedOutput) {
    return (Class<? extends OutputFormat<?, ?>>)
        job.getConfiguration().getClass(MO_PREFIX + namedOutput + FORMAT, null,
            OutputFormat.class);
}
```
....
```
}
```

The most important method in this class is the `write` method. It takes not only a key and value,
but also a name for the output. When obtaining execution context, the class overwrites the output
directory with a new value — concatenation of the base output with the output name. (This creates
a new desired folder in the base output directory.) It then obtains a directory name corresponding to
this directory, and writes both the key and value using this writer.

The `getRecordWriter` method first checks whether a writer already exists, and, if it does not,
creates a new one, based on the current context. Finally, the `close` method closes all currently
opened writers.

Because, in this implementation, a signature of the `write` method is different from the signature
defined in the base `OutputFormat` class, both the Apache `MultipleOutput` class and the
implementation shown in Listing 4-13 are not derived from the `OutputFormat` class. Consequently,
they cannot be directly associated with the MapReduce execution pipeline. As a result, you must use
a slightly more complex implementation of the job driver, as shown in Listing 4-14 (code file:class
`Executor`).

LISTING 4-14: Driver class for using MultipleOutputsDirectories

```
public class Executor extends Configured implements Tool{

    @Override
    public int run(String[] arg0) throws Exception {
        Configuration conf = ConfigManager.getCofiguration(CONFIGFILE);
        Job job = new Job(conf, "Test Multiple Outputs");

        ....................................................................
            job.setOutputFormatClass(MultiTextOutputFormat.class);
        Path jobOutputPath = new Path(OUTPUTPATH);
        MultiFileOutputFormat.setOutputPath(job, jobOutputPath);
        MultipleOutputsDirectories.addNamedOutput(job, "even",
                MultiTextOutputFormat.class,
```

```
                    Text.class,IntWritable.class);
        MultipleOutputsDirectories.addNamedOutput(job, "odd",
                MultiTextOutputFormat.class,
                Text.class,IntWritable.class);

    .............................................................................. . .

    }
}
```

In Listing 4-14, the job is set up with the "normal" OutputFormat class, which is configured with the output directory. This is the directory that will be stored in the job context, and used as a base output directory. Then, the MultipleOutputsDirectories class is configured by adding desired subdirectories with the corresponding OutputFormat for every directory.

Once you have configured your job to use the MultipleOutputsDirectories class, using it for writing data is straightforward. You can do this in the reducer or mapper in the case of a map-only job. Listing 4-15 (code file class: ExecutorMapper) demonstrates how you can do this in a reducer.

LISTING 4-15: Using the MultipleOutputsDirectories class to write data

```
        @Override
        protected void setup(Context context){
          mos = new MultipleOutputsDirectories(context);
          }

        @Override
        public void reduce(LongWritable key, Iterable<Text> lines, Context context)
            throws IOException, InterruptedException {

          .......................................................................
            if (number == 0) {
                  mos.write("even", new Text(tokenizer.nextToken()),new
                    IntWritable(number));
            } else {
                mos.write("odd", new Text(tokenizer.nextToken()),new
                    IntWritable(number));
            }
          ........................................................................
        }
        @Override
        protected void cleanup(Context context){
          try {
              mos.close();
          } catch (Exception e) {
              e.printStackTrace();
          }
        }
```

Here, notice that, instead of writing data to the context class, the MultipleOutputsDirectories class is used directly to write data.

For the OutputFormat code in Listing 4-13, Listing 4-14, and Listing 4-15 to work, you must also implement a custom FileOutputCommitter, as shown in Listing 4-16 (code file:class FileOutputCommitter).

LISTING 4-16: FileOutputCommitter class

```
public class FileOutputCommitter extends
    org.apache.hadoop.mapreduce.lib.output.FileOutputCommitter {
    ........................................................................................ . .

    public FileOutputCommitter(Path outputPath, TaskAttemptContext context)
            throws IOException {
        Job job = new Job(context.getConfiguration());
        String outputDirectories =
            job.getConfiguration().get(MULTIPLE_OUTPUTS, "");
        if (outputDirectories != null) {
            StringTokenizer st = new StringTokenizer(outputDirectories, " ");
            while (st.hasMoreTokens()) {
                pathNames.add(st.nextToken());
            }
        }
        if (outputPath != null) {
            this.outputPath = outputPath;
            outputFileSystem =
                outputPath.getFileSystem(context.getConfiguration());
            workPath = new Path(outputPath,
                    (FileOutputCommitter.TEMP_DIR_NAME + Path.SEPARATOR +
                            "_" + context.getTaskAttemptID().toString()
                    )).makeQualified(outputFileSystem);
            for(String p : pathNames){
                if(outputPath.toString().endsWith(p)){
                    committers.put(p, this);
                    fake = false;
                    break;
                }
            }
        }
    }

    public void setupJob(JobContext context) throws IOException {
        if (outputPath != null) {
            Path tmpDir = new Path(outputPath,
                FileOutputCommitter.TEMP_DIR_NAME);
            FileSystem fileSys =
                tmpDir.getFileSystem(context.getConfiguration());
        }
    }

    private static boolean shouldMarkOutputDir(Configuration conf) {
        return conf.getBoolean(SUCCESSFUL_JOB_OUTPUT_DIR_MARKER, true);
```

```
        }

    private void markOutputDirSuccessful(JobContext context, String path)
            throws IOException {
        if (outputPath != null) {
            Path p = (path == null) ? outputPath : new Path(outputPath, path);
            FileSystem fileSys =
                outputPath.getFileSystem(context.getConfiguration());
            if (fileSys.exists(outputPath)) {
                Path filePath = new Path(p, SUCCEEDED_FILE_NAME);
                fileSys.create(filePath).close();
            }
        }
    }

    public void commitJob(JobContext context) throws IOException {
        pathNames.add(null);
        for (String path : pathNames) {
            cleanupJob(context, path);
            if (shouldMarkOutputDir(context.getConfiguration())) {
                markOutputDirSuccessful(context, path);
            }
        }
    }

    public void cleanupJob(JobContext context, String path) throws IOException {
        if (outputPath != null) {
            Path p = (path == null) ? outputPath : new Path(outputPath, path);
            Path tmpDir = new Path(p, FileOutputCommitter.TEMP_DIR_NAME);
            FileSystem fileSys =
                tmpDir.getFileSystem(context.getConfiguration());
            if (fileSys.exists(tmpDir)) {
                fileSys.delete(tmpDir, true);
            }
        ..........................................................................................
    }

    @Override
    public void abortJob(JobContext context, JobStatus.State state) throws
        IOException {
        pathNames.add(null);
        for (String path : pathNames) {
            cleanupJob(context, path);
        }
    }

    public void commitTask(TaskAttemptContext context) throws IOException {
        if (!fake || (committers.size() == 0)) {
            TaskAttemptID attemptId = context.getTaskAttemptID();
            if (workPath != null) {
                context.progress();
                if (outputFileSystem.exists(workPath)) {
                    // Move the task outputs to their final place
```

continues

LISTING 4-16 *(continued)*

```java
                        moveTaskOutputs(context, outputFileSystem, outputPath,
                            workPath);
                    }
                }
            }
            else{
                for(FileOutputCommitter c : committers.values()){
                    c.commitTask(context);
                }
            }
        }

        private void moveTaskOutputs(TaskAttemptContext context,
                FileSystem fs,Path jobOutputDir,Path taskOutput) throws
                    IOException {
            TaskAttemptID attemptId = context.getTaskAttemptID();
            context.progress();
            if (fs.isFile(taskOutput)) {
                Path finalOutputPath = getFinalPath(jobOutputDir, taskOutput,
                    workPath);
                if (!fs.rename(taskOutput, finalOutputPath)) {
                    if (!fs.delete(finalOutputPath, true)) {
                        throw new IOException("Failed to delete earlier output
                            of task: " +
                                attemptId);
                    }
                    if (!fs.rename(taskOutput, finalOutputPath)) {
                        throw new IOException("Failed to save output of task: " +
                                attemptId);
                    }
                }
            } else if(fs.getFileStatus(taskOutput).isDir()) {
                FileStatus[] paths = fs.listStatus(taskOutput);
                Path finalOutputPath = getFinalPath(jobOutputDir, taskOutput,
                    workPath);
                fs.mkdirs(finalOutputPath);
                if (paths != null) {
                    for (FileStatus path : paths) {
                        moveTaskOutputs(context, fs, jobOutputDir,
                            path.getPath());
                    }
                }
            }
        }

        @Override
        public void abortTask(TaskAttemptContext context) {
            if (!fake || (committers.size() == 0)) {
```

```
                    try {
                        if (workPath != null) {
                            context.progress();
                            outputFileSystem.delete(workPath, true);
                        }
                    } catch (IOException ie) {
                    }
                }
                else{
                    for(FileOutputCommitter c : committers.values()){
                        c.abortTask(context);
                    }
                }
            }
        }
    }
```

The complexity of this class implementation stems from the complexity of its life cycle (Figure 4-4). Additionally, Figure 4-5 shows the actual HDFS layout used in this case.

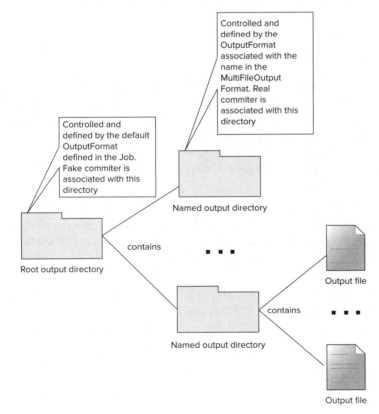

Controlled and defined by the OutputFormat associated with the name in the MultiFileOutput Format. Real commiter is associated with this directory

Controlled and defined by the default OutputFormat defined in the Job. Fake commiter is associated with this directory

Named output directory

contains

Root output directory

Output file

contains

Named output directory

Output file

FIGURE 4-5: Directories layout when using the MultipleOutputsDirectories class

The root output directory is defined by the initial `OutputFormat` class (`MultiTextOutputFormat` in Listing 4-14). This directory is using a `FileOutputCommitter` defined by this `OutputFormat`. The named directories are defined by the `MultiTextOutputFormat` (odd and even in Listing 4-14). These directories are using `OutputCommitters` defined by the corresponding `OutputFormats` specified in `MultiTextOutputFormat` definition (`MultiTextOutputFormat` in Listing 4-14).

Assuming that all directories are using same `FileOutputCommitter` class, it is created and invoked several times in several different Java processes. It is used by the job runner to execute task-related activities (setup, commit, and abort) and by the task runner to set up, commit, or abort the job.

Additionally, the task runner creates several instances of `FileOutputCommitter`. The first instance is created for the `OutputFormat` defined for the job (`MultiTextOutput` format in Listing 4-14), and then for every output format used by `MultiOutputFormatDirectories`. Though multiple instances are available in the task runner, only the first one is used to perform all the task-related activities. That is why this implementation keeps track of all `FileOutputCommitters` currently in use, so that appropriate actions can be taken on every used directory (Figure 4-5).

The constructor of this class checks whether the class was created for the named directory:

➤ **Real** — This `FileOutputCommitter` instance operates on the "true" output directories, or the root one (the default output format).

➤ **Fake** — This `FileOutputCommitter` instance operates on the root output directory that does not contain data — just the real named output directory.

All the real `FileOutputCommitter` instances are stored in the static map, so that operations on the default instance can invoke appropriate operations on the real ones. As a result, both task commit and abort operations check the committer type, and either execute an appropriate operation (for real ones), or loop through all the real ones invoking the operation (for fake ones). For the task commit operation, an implementation moves the result's file for a given task attempt from a temporary directory into the desired directory, and deletes the temporary directory. In the case of abort, the temporary directory (along with its content) is deleted.

An additional method — `getWorkPath()` — returns a work path used by a given committer to store output information. This information can be used by the MapReduce task to determine the output path of the current attempt (for example, to implement custom writes to the same directory). This is the only "safe" way of writing output data directly from MapReduce code bypassing the output format class.

A different approach is used for implementing job functionality. A job cleanup is a separate process, creating a single instance of a committer — the default one. Because, during committer creation, a `mapreduce.multipleoutputs` variable is available, a committer constructor can still create a list of used directories, which is used to calculate how many times an appropriate job-level function should be executed. Each job-related function is executed N+1 times, where N is the number of output formats participating in `MultiOutputFormatDirectories`. The job `commit` method checks whether any of the temporary directories still exist, and deletes them. It also marks the output directory as successful. An `abort` method just does the cleanup.

As a final step, you set up execution with a new custom `FileOutputCommitter`. In the old MapReduce APIs, you did this by setting a `FileOutputCommitter` on the `job` object. In the new APIs, this support is deprecated. The only way to set a custom `FileOutputCommitter` is to overwrite the output format class, as shown in Listing 4-17 (code file:class `MultiTextOutputFormat`).

LISTING 4-17: Setting up a custom FileOutputCommitter

```
public class MultiTextOutputFormat<K, V> extends TextOutputFormat<K, V> {

    private FileOutputCommitter committer = null;

    @Override
    public synchronized
    OutputCommitter getOutputCommitter(TaskAttemptContext context) throws
            IOException {
        if (committer == null) {
            Path output = getOutputPath(context);
            committer = new FileOutputCommitter(output, context);
        }
        return committer;
    }

}
```

This example shows how to modify location of the output, but not its format. Next, you learn how to change the way data is written using a custom writer.

WRITING DATA YOUR WAY WITH CUSTOM RECORDWRITERS

There is certain symmetry in the MapReduce implementation of input and output support. For example, an `OutputFormat` serves as a factory for custom `RecordWriters` (similar to the `InputFormat` creating a `RecordReader`). Another similarity is separation of concerns — a reducer (or mapper) outputs key/value pairs, while it is the responsibility of the custom `RecordWriter` to massage these key/value pairs and output them in the form that is required.

Hadoop provides quite a few implementations of `RecordWriter` that support writing data to HDFS (in different formats), HBase, and even some external systems. But if you need to have output data in some specific proprietary format, you must implement a custom `RecordWriter`. You see how to implement a custom `RecordWriter` in the next section.

Implementing a RecordWriter to Produce Output tar Files

Assume that you have a mapper that generates a complete output file in every map function invocation. Writing this file directly to HDFS will create a lot of fairly small files. So, a better option is to combine all these files. A typical approach to this is to create a sequence file, storing every map's output as a value, and using a key generated by a map as a key. Further assume that the application processing the results of this job cannot read a sequence file, but can consume, for example, tar files.

> **NOTE** tar *(derived from* tape archive*) is a file format that was created in the early days of UNIX. It was standardized by POSIX.1-1988 and later POSIX.1-2001.* tar *files are often used for data archiving and distribution.*

Listing 4-18 (code file:class TarOutputWriter) shows a custom RecordWriter creating a tar output file that extends Hadoop's abstract RecordWriter class, and implements all required methods.

LISTING 4-18: Custom tar output writer

```
class TarOutputWriter extends RecordWriter<BytesWritable, Text> {

    ..................................................... .

    public TarOutputWriter(Configuration conf, Path output) throws
        FileNotFoundException,
            IOException {
        FileSystem fs = output.getFileSystem(conf);
        FSDataOutputStream fsOutStream = fs.create(output, REWRITE_FILES,
            BUFFER_SIZE);
        tarOutStream = new TarArchiveOutputStream(fsOutStream);
    }

    @Override
    public void write(BytesWritable key, Text value) throws IOException {

        if (key == null || value == null ) {
            return;
        }
        TarArchiveEntry mtd = new TarArchiveEntry(key.toString());
        mtd.setSize(value.getLength());
        tarOutStream.putArchiveEntry(mtd);
        IOUtils.copy(new ByteArrayInputStream(value.getBytes()), tarOutStream);
        ..................................................... . .
    }

    @Override
    public void close(TaskAttemptContext context) throws IOException {
        if (tarOutStream != null) {
            tarOutStream.flush();
            tarOutStream.close();
        }
    }
}
```

The workhorse of this class is the `write` method, which creates a `tar` entry out of keys and values. This entry is then added to the `OutputStream` created by the reader's constructor. The `close` method flushes the output stream and closes it.

To use this custom writer, you must create a custom `OutputFormat` that creates your `RecordWriter`. Because, in this case, the only thing you need is to create a custom `RecordWriter` (in other words, you do not need to change where the file is stored, just its format), the simplest way to implement a custom `OutputFormat` is to extend Hadoop's `FileOutputFormat` and overwrite the `getRecordWriter` method, as shown in Listing 4-19.

LISTING 4-19: tar output format using custom tar RecordWriter

```
public class TarOutputFormat extends FileOutputFormat<BytesWritable, Text> {

    public static final String EXTENSION = ".tar";


    @Override
    public RecordWriter<BytesWritable, Text> getRecordWriter(TaskAttemptContext
        job)
            throws IOException, InterruptedException {

        Path outpath = getDefaultWorkFile(job, EXTENSION);
        return new TarOutputWriter(job.getConfiguration(), outpath);
    }
}
```

An important part of this implementation is invoking the `getDefaultWorkFile` method (implemented by a super class) to get the location of output. In this case, the location will be in the temporary directory corresponding to a given attempt.

Now that you know how to customize the processing of input and output data, take a look at some of the optimization techniques that can be introduced into MapReduce execution.

OPTIMIZING YOUR MAPREDUCE EXECUTION WITH A COMBINER

As discussed in Chapter 3, using the combiner is an important Hadoop optimization technique. The primary goal of combiners is to save as much bandwidth as possible by minimizing the number of key/value pairs that will be shuffled across the network between mappers and reducers. Figure 4-6 shows the extended Hadoop's processing pipeline, including combiner and partitioner. (You learn more about the partitioner later in this chapter.)

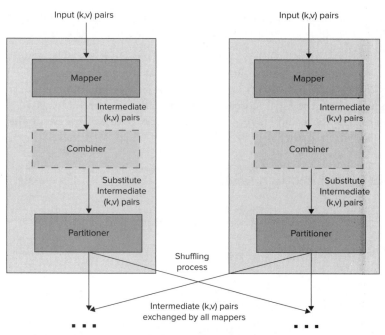

FIGURE 4-6: Additional MapReduce components — combiner and partitioner

NOTE *In the Hadoop implementation, partitioners are actually executed before combiners, so although Figure 4-6 is conceptually accurate, it doesn't precisely describe the Hadoop implementation.*

In Chapter 3, you learned about a link elevation example. Table 4-1 breaks down the first MapReduce job, where the mapper is generating key/value pairs — (tid, {lid [points array]}).

TABLE 4-1: Split Links into Pieces and Elevate Each Piece Job

PROCESS PHASE	DESCRIPTION
Mapper	In this job, the role of the mapper is to build link pieces and assign them to the individual tiles. It reads every link record and splits them into fixed-length fragments, which effectively converts link representation into a set of points. For every point, it calculates a tile to which this point belongs, and produces one or more link piece records, which look as follows (tid, {lid [points array]}), where tid is tile ID, lid is the original link ID, and points array is an array of points (from the original link) that belong to a given tile.
Shuffle and Sort	MapReduce's shuffle and sort will sort all the records based on the tile IDs, which will guarantee that all of the link's pieces belonging to the same tile will be processed by a single reducer.

Reducer	In this job, the role of the reducer is to calculate elevation for every link piece. For every tile ID, it loads terrain information for a given tile from HBase, and then reads all of the link pieces and calculates elevation for every point. It outputs the record (`lid, [points array]`), where `lid` is original link ID and `points array` is an array of three-dimensional points.
Result	A result of this job execution contains fully elevated link pieces. It is necessary to implement the second map reduce job to merge them.

If several million link processed, the map step will produce even more pairs. (Remember, a single link can belong to several tiles.) With combiners, it will potentially send much fewer key/value pairs of the form (`tid, {lid [points access]}, ... , {lid [points access]}`).

> **NOTE** *Be aware that introducing of a combiner typically requires changes to the reducer's interface. Key/value pairs produced by combiners are often different from ones produced by mappers.*

A combiner can be considered a "mini reducer" that is applied to an individual map output during the map phase before sending a new (hopefully reduced) set of key/value pairs to the reducer(s). This is why a combiner's implementation must extend the reducer class.

Quite a few examples of combiners are available elsewhere (such as the MapReduce tutorial at `http://hadoop.apache.org/docs/r1.0.4/mapred_tutorial.html`), so one is not included in the book.

Combiner usage is explicitly configured through a setting on the job class, as shown in Listing 4-20.

LISTING 4-20: Configuring an application to use a combiner

```
job.setCombinerClass(Reduce.class);
```

IN-MAPPER COMBINER DESIGN PATTERN

Whereas combiners provide a general mechanism within the MapReduce framework to reduce the amount of intermediate data generated by the mappers, an *in-mapper combiner* is another popular design pattern that can often be used to serve the same purpose.

This pattern is implemented by using an in-memory hash map to accumulate intermediate results. Instead of emitting a key/value pair for each mapper input, an in-mapper combiner emits a key/value list pair (similar to a "standard" combiner) for each unique output key.

continues

continued

In a nutshell, this pattern incorporates combiner functionality directly into a mapper. This removes the necessity of running a separate combiner, because the local aggregation is already implemented by the mapper.

The two main advantages to using this design pattern are as follows:

➤ It provides more precise control over when local aggregation occurs.

➤ An implementation can exploit different, application-specific aggregation techniques.

Using an in-mapper combiner is more efficient than using actual combiners — there is no additional overhead of reading and instantiation of key/value pairs. The following are also benefits of using an in-mapper combiner:

➤ No read/write of the intermediate data

➤ No additional object creation and destruction (garbage collection)

➤ No serialization or deserialization of objects (both memory and processing)

However, several drawbacks are associated with this pattern. It violates the functional programming model of MapReduce by preserving state across multiple input key/value pairs, which implies that the algorithm's behavior might depend on execution order. It also introduces a fundamental scalability bottleneck associated with storing additional (potentially significant) amounts of data in memory. It critically depends on having sufficient memory to store intermediate results until the mapper has completely processed all key/value pairs in an input split.

One common solution to limiting memory usage when using the in-mapper combiner is to "flush" in-memory data structures periodically (after processing every *n* key/value pairs), instead of emitting data only after all key/value pairs have been processed. Alternatively, the mapper can keep track of its own memory utilization and "flush" intermediate key/value pairs once memory usage has crossed a certain threshold. In both approaches, either the block size or the memory usage threshold must be determined empirically. With too large a value, the mapper may run out of memory, but with too small a value, opportunities for local aggregation may be lost.

Although combiners can often improve both performance and scalability of MapReduce applications, if not used correctly, they can have a negative impact on the application performance.

Let's return to the link elevation example from Chapter 3 and look at the second map reduce job, as shown in Table 4-2. Here, a mapper emits a set of (lid, [points array]) pairs.

TABLE 4-2: Combine Links Pieces into Original Links Job

PROCESS PHASE	DESCRIPTION
Mapper	The role of mapper in this job is very simple. It is an identity mapper in Hadoop. It reads link piece records and writes them directly to the output in the form of (lid, [points access]) key/value pairs.
Shuffle and Sort	MapReduce's shuffle and sort will sort all the records based on the link's keys, which guarantees that all link piece records with the same key will come to the same reducer together.
Reducer	In this job, the role of the reducer is to merge link pieces with same ID. Once the reducer reads all of them, it merges them together and writes them out as a single link record.
Result	A result of this job execution contains elevated links ready to use.

However, because the probability of having more than one key processed by a single mapper is low, in this case, the combiner will not produce any significant reduction in the number of key/value pairs, while additional combiner processing time can negatively impact the overall execution time.

A simple rule for deciding on the combiner usage can be as follows. If the probability of having multiple key/value pairs with the same key is high, combiners can improve performance. Otherwise, their usage will not provide any benefits.

Earlier in this chapter, you learned how you can use InputFormat to control the number and preferred location of mapper tasks. When it comes to the reducers, there is no way to control their number or location (their number is explicitly specified in the job configuration, and the JobTracker decides on their placement). One thing that is controllable in the behavior of reducers is data distribution between reducers. The next section shows how you can do this with custom partitioners.

CONTROLLING REDUCER EXECUTION WITH PARTITIONERS

As defined in Chapter 3, partitioning is the process of dividing up the intermediate key space, and determining which reducer instance will receive which intermediate keys and values. The important part of Hadoop architecture is that mappers are able to partition data independently (see Figure 4-6). They never need to exchange information with one another to determine the partition for a particular key.

This approach improves the overall performance and allows mappers to operate completely independently. For all of its output key/value pairs, each mapper determines which reducer will receive them. Because all the mappers are using the same partitioning for any key, regardless of which mapper instance generated it, the destination partition is the same.

Hadoop uses an interface called Partitioner to determine which partition a key/value pair will go to. A single partition refers to all key/value pairs that will be sent to a single reduce task. You can configure the number of reducers in a job driver by setting a number of reducers on the job object (`job.setNumReduceTasks`).

Hadoop comes with a default partitioner implementation (`HashPartitioner`), which partitions the keys based on their hash code. This is good enough for many applications with evenly distributed keys. In the case of non-even key distribution, using `HashPartitioner` can lead to surprising results. For example, assume that the following integer values are the keys:

> 12, 22, 32, 42, 52, 62, 72, 82, 92, 102

Also assume that you are running your job with 10 reducers using the default `HashPartitioner`. If you look at the result of the execution, you will see that the second reducer is processing all 10 keys, while the other nine reducers are idle. The reason is that `HashPartitioner` calculates a partition as MOD of key value divided by the number of reducers, which in this example is 10. This example shows that even in the case of simple keys, depending on their distribution, it might be necessary to write a custom partitioner to ensure even distribution of load between reducers.

Another case that often requires a specialized implementation of a partitioner is when you use a composite key, such as the implementation of the value-to-key conversion pattern described in Chapter 3.

Implementing a Custom Partitioner for One-to-Many Joins

As described in Chapter 3, the basic idea behind the value-to-key conversion design pattern is to move part of the value into the key to form a composite key, and let the MapReduce execution framework handle the sorting.

This means that the key emitted by the mapper is a composite key. In the value-to-key example presented in Chapter 3, the purchase ID part of the key is the natural key, and the product ID is a group key (created by promoting the product ID value to the key). The group key is used by the partitioner and the group comparator. When you add a group key to a natural key, you get a composite key, as shown in Listing 4-21 (code file:class `CompositeKey`).

LISTING 4-21: CompositeKey

```java
public class CompositeKey implements WritableComparable<CompositeKey> {

    private long productID;
    private long purchaseID;

    ...........................................................................

    @Override
    public int compareTo(CompositeKey key) {
        int result = new Long(productID).compareTo(new Long(key.getProductID()));
        if(result != 0)
            return result;
        return new Long(purchaseID).compareTo(new Long(key.getPurchaseID()));
    }
}
```

The `CompositeGroupComparator` class shown in Listing 4-22 (code file:class `CompositeGroupComparator`) is used to determine to which reducer the mapper output row should go. This comparator does not sort a reducer's value iterator. Instead, it sorts a reducer's input, so that the reducer knows when a new grouping starts. In this example, the value-grouping comparator sorts by the product ID.

LISTING 4-22: CompositeGroupComparator class

```
public class CompositeGroupComparator implements RawComparator<CompositeKey> {

    @Override
    public int compare(CompositeKey k1, CompositeKey k2) {
        return new Long(k1.getProductID()).compareTo(new
            Long(k2.getProductID()));
    }

    @Override
    public int compare(byte[] key1, int start1, int length1, byte[] key2, int
            start2, int length2) {
        DataInput in1 = new DataInputStream(new ByteArrayInputStream(key1));
        CompositeKey k1 = new CompositeKey();
        DataInput in2 = new DataInputStream(new ByteArrayInputStream(key2));
        CompositeKey k2 = new CompositeKey();
        try{
            k1.readFields(in1);
            k2.readFields(in2);
            return compare(k1, k2);
        }
        catch(Exception e){
            return -1;
        }
    }
}
```

The values of the iterator that the reducer gets are sorted by a `CompositeKeyComparator`, as shown in Listing 4-23 (code file:class `CompositeKeyComparator`). An important thing to note is that the key comparator must also enforce the value-grouping comparator's rules. In this example, this means that it must first check if the product IDs are equal. If they are not equal, it should return the same values as the group comparator. Only if the product IDs are equal should you apply value-level sorting (comparing the purchase ID). Because this is the way the comparison method in the composite key class (Listing 4-21) is implemented, that implementation can be used here directly.

LISTING 4-23: CompositeKeyComparator

```
public class CompositeKeyComparator implements RawComparator<CompositeKey> {

    @Override
    public int compare(CompositeKey k1, CompositeKey k2) {
```

continues

LISTING 4-23 *(continued)*

```
            return k1.compareTo(k2);
    }

    @Override
    public int compare(byte[] key1, int start1, int length1, byte[] key2, int
            start2, int length2) {
        DataInput in1 = new DataInputStream(new ByteArrayInputStream(key1));
        CompositeKey k1 = new CompositeKey();
        DataInput in2 = new DataInputStream(new ByteArrayInputStream(key2));
        CompositeKey k2 = new CompositeKey();
        try{
            k1.readFields(in1);
            k2.readFields(in2);
            return k1.compareTo(k2);
        }
        catch(Exception e){
            return -1;
        }
    }
}
```

The partitioner class shown in Listing 4-24 (code file:class `CompositePartitioner`) has a single method that determines to which partition map output should go. In this implementation, it gets the product ID portion of the key and MODs it by the number of reducers.

LISTING 4-24: CompositeKeyPartitioner

```
public class CompositePartitioner extends Partitioner<CompositeKey, ByteWritable> {

    @Override
    public int getPartition(CompositeKey key, ByteWritable value,int
            numPartitions) {
        return (int)key.getProductID()% numPartitions;
    }
}
```

Finally, for the MapReduce run time to use the classes, you must set them in the job's driver, as shown in Listing 4-25.

LISTING 4-25: Setting a custom partitioner

```
........................................................ . .
job.setSortComparatorClass(CompositeKeyComparator.class);
job.setGroupingComparatorClass(CompositeGroupComparator.class);
job.setPartitionerClass(CompositePartitioner.class);
........................................................ . .
```

Although Hadoop is implemented in Java (at least the Apache version — other implementations such as MapR leverage a lot of C++ code), you can implement both a mapper and reducer in a multiplicity of languages. Take a look at the ways non-Java code can take advantage of the Hadoop ecosystem.

> **NOTE** *Technically, inclusion of non-Java code does not constitute a customization of MapReduce execution in Hadoop, but rather the way Hadoop's application code (including mapper and reducer) can be implemented.*

USING NON-JAVA CODE WITH HADOOP

Hadoop itself is written in Java, and, thus, accepts Java code natively for implementation of mappers and reducers. But this does not mean that code written in other languages can't be used with Hadoop. (You have many reasons to use non-Java code with Hadoop, ranging from your existing skill set to legacy code and libraries for more performant implementations, thus leveraging native code.) You can include non-Java code in Hadoop in three basic ways:

➤ Using `Pipes`

➤ Using Hadoop `Streaming`

➤ Using the Java Native Interface (JNI)

Pipes

`Pipes` is a library that enables you to use C++ source code for mapper and reducer implementation. Both key and value inputs to `Pipes` programs are provided as STL strings (`std::string`). An implementation must still define an instance of a mapper and reducer. Unlike the classes of the same names in Hadoop itself, the map and reduce functions take in a single argument that is a reference to an object of type `MapContext` and `ReduceContext`, respectively. The most important methods contained in each of these context objects enable you to get input keys and values (as strings), and emit keys and values.

You implement a program using `Pipes` by writing classes that extend `Mapper` and `Reducer` (and, optionally, `Partitioner`), and then configuring the Hadoop run time (similar to a driver) so that it knows which classes to use to run the job. An instance of appropriate C++ program will be started by the `Pipes` framework on each machine.

The `main` method of these programs should perform any initialization required by the task, then invoke a factory to create mapper and reducer instances as necessary, and run the job by calling the `runTask` method.

Hadoop Streaming

Unlike `Pipes`, which is tailored specifically to running C++ application code in the Hadoop environment, `Streaming` is a generic API that allows programs written in virtually any language to be used as Hadoop mapper and reducer implementations. Both mappers and reducers receive their input on `stdin` and emit output (key/value pairs) to `stdout`.

In a `Streaming` implementation, input and output are always represented textually. The input (key/value) pairs are written to `stdin` for a mapper or reducer, with a tab character separating the key from the value. The `Streaming` programs should split the input on the first tab character on the line to obtain both keys and values. `Streaming` programs write their output to `stdout` in the same format: key and value separated by a tab, and pairs separated by a carriage return. The inputs to the reducer are sorted so that while each line contains only a single key/value pair, all the values for the same key are adjacent to one another.

You can use any Linux program or tool as the mapper or reducer when using `Streaming`, assuming it can handle its input in the text format described here. In this case, you can implement the mapper/reducer in any language of your choice (including bash, Python, Perl, and so on), provided that the necessary interpreter is present on all nodes in your cluster.

Using JNI

JNI is a programming framework that allows Java code running in a JVM to call and to be called by native applications. It enables you to include native methods in the Java program to handle situations in which an application cannot be written entirely in Java (for example, when the standard Java class library does not support the platform-specific features or program libraries). It is also used to modify an existing application — written in another programming language — to be accessible from Java applications. Including performance- and platform-sensitive API implementations in the standard library allows all Java applications to access this functionality in a safe and platform-independent manner.

Using JNI allows "standard" MapReduce implementations to include non-Java code to execute some of the functionality of the mapper and/or reducer.

One of the issues that must be addressed to make the JNI approach work is the distribution of `*.so` libraries. The two mechanisms that you can use for native code distribution are distributed cache and uber `jars`.

Hadoop's distributed cache provides a convenient mechanism for efficient distribution of application-specific, read-only files. It is a facility provided by the MapReduce framework to cache files (text, archives, `jars`, and so on) needed by applications. Applications specify the files to be cached via URLs (`hdfs://`) in the job. The framework copies the necessary files to the slave node before any tasks for the job are executed on that node. Its efficiency stems from the fact that the files are copied only once per job, and the capability to cache archives that are unarchived on the slaves.

A simple native libraries loader such as the one shown in Listing 4-26 (code file:class `NativeLibrariesLoader`) enables you to store libraries in distributed cache, and then retrieve and load them for the execution.

LISTING 4-26: Native libraries loader

```
public class NativeLibrariesLoader {

    public static void storeLibraries(Configuration conf, String baseDir,
        Collection<String> libraries)
                                    throws Exception{
```

```
                DistributedCache.createSymlink(conf);
                boolean first = true;
        StringBuffer sb = new StringBuffer();
        for(String library : libraries){
                DistributedCache.addCacheFile(new URI(baseDir + library), conf);
                if(first)
                    first = false;
                else
                    sb.append(DELIM);
                    sb.append(library);
        }
        conf.set(LIBRARIES, sb.toString());
}

public static void loadLibraries(Configuration conf) throws IOException{
        Map<String, String> libPaths = new HashMap<String, String>();
        StringTokenizer st = new StringTokenizer(conf.get(LIBRARIES),DELIM);
        Path[] libraries = DistributedCache.getLocalCacheFiles(conf);
        for(Path library : libraries){
            libPaths.put(library.getName(), library.toString());
        }
        while(st.hasMoreTokens()){
            System.load(libPaths.get(st.nextToken()));
        }
    }
}
```

The storeLibraries method is executed during the job preparation phase, and should be invoked from the driver class. This method loads libraries from a specified directory into distributed cache, and builds a list of loaded libraries. The loadLibraries method should be invoked where libraries are actually used (mapper or reducer, or both). It reads the list of available libraries and loads all of them independently.

The important thing to watch for using this class is the order of names of the libraries in the libraries parameter. Because the loadLibraries method loads them sequentially, it is sensitive to loading order. If library A depends on library B, library B should be loaded before library A.

WHAT IS UBER JAR?

Although routinely used, the term *uber* jar is not really defined. A Java archive (jar) file format enables you to bundle multiple files into a single archive file. Typically, a jar file contains the class files and auxiliary resources associated with applications. Based on this definition, an uber jar (or super jar) is a jar that, in addition to normal jar content, can contain other jars that an application depends on.

The advantage is that you can distribute your uber jar and not care at all whether or not dependencies are installed at the destination, because your uber jar has *no* dependencies.

An alternative to using Hadoop distributed cache is using uber `jars`. In this case, the Hadoop execution `jar` (uber `jar`) will contain all of the executable libraries required by map/reduce execution. Because Hadoop distributes an execution `jar` to all nodes where execution happens, no additional library distribution mechanism is required. In this case, the only thing that is required is loading native libraries at mapper/reducer startup. You can do this using simple code, as shown in Listing 4-27 (code file:class `SharedLibraryLoader`).

LISTING 4-27: Loading native libraries from the uber jar

```
public class SharedLibraryLoader {
        private File tempPath;

        public SharedLibraryLoader() {
                tempPath = Files.createTempDir();
        }

        private void loadLibrary(String libraryName) throws IOException {
                URL url =
                        this.getClass().getClassLoader()
                        .getResource(libraryName);
                File library = new File(tempPath, libraryName);
                FileUtils.copyURLToFile(url, library);
                library.setExecutable(true);
                System.load(library.getAbsolutePath());
        }
}
```

Here, similar to the distributed cache approach, the order of libraries to load must be known upfront to the requesting application.

When choosing an approach for including non-Java code in a MapReduce implementation, you should weigh implementation simplicity against execution performance. Several publications show that the performance of Java (and, consequently, JNI) surpasses implementations of both `Pipes` (by roughly a factor of 2) and `Streaming` (by roughly a factor of 4).

SUMMARY

This chapter discussed options for customizing MapReduce implementations to better serve your application needs. You learned how to modify map distribution and executions using custom `InputFormats`, how to access proprietary data using custom `RecordReaders`, how to write data in a form that is most appropriate for your applications using custom `OutputFormats`, how to control reducer execution using custom partitioners, and how to incorporate non-Java code and `RecordWriters` into your application.

Chapter 5 discusses how to build reliable MapReduce applications.

5

Building Reliable MapReduce Apps

By now, you should be familiar with MapReduce architecture, application design, and customizing MapReduce execution. This chapter discusses how to build reliable MapReduce code by leveraging unit testing and Hadoop-provided facilities for testing applications. You also learn about different approaches to defensive programming that allow your code to cope with partially corrupted data.

UNIT TESTING MAPREDUCE APPLICATIONS

Bugs in code are a fact of life — the more code you write, the more bugs you create. Even the greatest programmers rarely write bug-free code. That's why code testing is becoming an integral part of code development, and programmers are moving more and more toward test-driven development (TDD).

> **NOTE** *This discussion on MRUnit and its usage for unit testing MapReduce jobs was inspired by Michael Spicuzza, a Nokia colleague.*

TEST-DRIVEN DEVELOPMENT

Test-driven development (TDD) is a programming technique that requires you to simultaneously write actual code and automated code tests. This ensures that you test your code, and enables you to retest your code quickly and easily, because the process is automated.

TDD revolves around a short, iterative development cycle that goes something like this:

1. Before writing any code, you must first write an automated test for it. While writing the automated tests, you must take into account all possible inputs, errors, and outputs. This way, you design your code behavior before actually writing it.

2. The first time you run your automated test, the test should fail — indicating that the code is not yet ready.

3. Afterward, you can begin programming. Because there's already an automated test, as long as the code fails, it means that it's still not ready. The code can be fixed until it passes all assertions.

4. Once the code passes the test, you can then begin cleaning it up, via refactoring. As long as the code still passes the test, it means that it still works. You no longer have to worry about changes that introduce new bugs.

5. Start the whole thing over again with some other method or program.

One of the cornerstones of TDD is unit testing. Although by using enough mock classes, it is technically possible to test the majority of MapReduce implementations using the JUnit framework, there is an alternative approach that can offer an additional level of coverage. MRUnit is a unit testing framework designed specifically for Hadoop. It began as an open source offering included in Cloudera's distribution for Hadoop, and is now an Apache Incubator project. MRUnit is based on JUnit, and allows for the unit testing of mappers, reducers, and some limited integration testing of the mapper-reducer interaction, along with combiners, custom counters, and partitioners.

As explained in Chapter 3, Eclipse provides a very good development platform for MapReduce applications. During that discussion, you learned how to create a `pom.xml` file containing all of the dependences required for MapReduce applications. Eclipse also provides a good platform for MRUnit-based unit testing.

To use MRUnit, you must extend the standard MapReduce Maven pom file presented in Chapter 3 by adding MRUnit dependency, as shown in Listing 5-1.

LISTING 5-1: MRUnit dependency for Maven pom file

```
<project xmlns="http://maven.apache.org/POM/4.0.0"
        xmlns:xsi="http://www.w3.org/2001/XMLSchema-instance"
    xsi:schemaLocation="http://maven.apache.org/POM/4.0.0
        http://maven.apache.org/xsd/maven-4.0.0.xsd">
    <modelVersion>4.0.0</modelVersion>
    <groupId>com.nokia.lib</groupId>
    <artifactId>nokia-cgnr-sparse</artifactId>
    <version>0.0.1-SNAPSHOT</version>
    <name>cgnr-sparse</name>
    <properties>
        <hadoop.version>2.0.0-mr1-cdh4.1.0</hadoop.version>
        <hadoop.common.version>2.0.0-cdh4.1.0</hadoop.common.version>
        <hbase.version>0.92.1-cdh4.1.0</hbase.version>
    </properties>
    <repositories>
        <repository>
            <id>CDH Releases and RCs Repositories</id>
            <url>https://repository.cloudera.com/content/groups/cdh-
                releases-rcs</url>
        </repository>
    </repositories>
    <build>
        <plugins>
            <plugin>
                <groupId>org.apache.maven.plugins</groupId>
                <artifactId>maven-compiler-plugin</artifactId>
                <version>2.3.2</version>
                <configuration>
                    <source>1.6</source>
                    <target>1.6</target>
                </configuration>
            </plugin>
        </plugins>
    </build>
    <dependencies>
        <dependency>
            <groupId>org.apache.hadoop</groupId>
            <artifactId>hadoop-core</artifactId>
            <version>${hadoop.version}</version>
            <scope>provided</scope>
        </dependency>
        <dependency>
            <groupId>org.apache.hbase</groupId>
            <artifactId>hbase</artifactId>
            <version>${hbase.version}</version>
            <scope>provided</scope>
        </dependency>
        <dependency>
```

continues

LISTING 5-1 *(continued)*

```
                <groupId>org.apache.hadoop</groupId>
                <artifactId>hadoop-common</artifactId>
                <version>${hadoop.common.version}</version>
                <scope>provided</scope>
        </dependency>
        <dependency>
                <groupId>junit</groupId>
                <artifactId>junit</artifactId>
                <version>4.10</version>
        </dependency>
      <dependency>
                <groupId>org.apache.mrunit</groupId>
                <artifactId>mrunit</artifactId>
                <version>0.9.0-incubating</version>
                <classifier>hadoop2</classifier>
        </dependency>
    </dependencies>
</project>
```

> **NOTE** *The MRUnit* jar *file, and, consequently, Maven dependency, comes in two versions.* mrunit-0.9.0-incubating-hadoop1.jar *is for MapReduce version 1 of Hadoop, and* mrunit-0.9.0-incubating-hadoop2.jar *is for working with the new version of Hadoop's MapReduce. The newer version is the* hadoop-2.0 *version from Cloudera's CDH 4.*

With this in place, you can implement unit tests for main elements of MapReduce applications. The word count example from Chapter 3 is used for testing examples here. This means that the mapper and reducer from this example are passed as parameters for testing.

Testing Mappers

The use of MRUnit for testing mappers is very straightforward, and is best explained by looking at the actual code shown in Listing 5-2.

LISTING 5-2: Testing Mapper

```
    @Test
    public void testMapper() throws Exception{
        new MapDriver<LongWritable, Text, Text, IntWritable>()
            .withMapper(new WordCount.Map())
            .withConfiguration(new Configuration())
            .withInput(new LongWritable(1), new Text("cat cat dog"))
            .withOutput(new Text("cat"), new IntWritable(1))
            .withOutput(new Text("cat"), new IntWritable(1))
            .withOutput(new Text("dog"), new IntWritable(1))
            .runTest();
    }
```

> **NOTE** *MRUnit supports both old (from the package* mapred*) and new (from the package* mapreduce*) MapReduce APIs. When testing your code, ensure that you use the appropriate instance of the* MapDriver *object. The same applies to the* ReduceDriver *and* MapReduceDriver *objects, described later in this chapter.*

Writing an MRUnit-based unit test for the mapper is quite simple. This simplicity is significantly enhanced by the fluent API style. To write your test, you would do the following:

1. Instantiate the `MapDriver` class parameterized exactly as the mapper under test.

2. Add an instance of the mapper you are testing by using the `withMapper` call. The mapper from the word count application described in Chapter 3 is used here.

3. You can use an optional `withConfiguration` method to pass in a desired configuration to the mapper.

4. The `withInput` call enables you to pass in a desired key and input value — in this case, a `LongWritable` with an arbitrary value, and a `Text` object that contains the line `"cat cat dog"`.

5. The expected output is specified using the `withOutput` call. The expectation in this example is three `Text` objects with the values of `"cat"`, `"cat"`, and `"dog"` with the corresponding `intWritable` values of occurrences — all equal to `1`.

6. If a mapper is incrementing a counter, an optional `.withCounter(group, name, expectedValue)` (not shown in Listing 5-2) enables you to specify the expected value of the counter.

7. The last call, `runTest`, feeds the specified input values into the mapper, and compares the actual output against the expected output set in the `withOutput` method.

The limitation of the `MapDriver` class is that you end up with a single input and output per test. You can call `withInput` and `withOutput` multiple times if you want, but the `MapDriver` implementation will overwrite the existing values with the new ones, so you will only ever be testing with one input/output at any time. To specify multiple inputs, you must use the `MapReduceDriver` object (covered later in this chapter).

Testing Reducers

Testing the reducer follows the same pattern as the mapper test. Again, look at a code example shown in Listing 5-3.

LISTING 5-3: Testing the reducer

```
@Test
public void testReducer() throws Exception {
    List<IntWritable> values = new ArrayList<IntWritable>();
    values.add(new IntWritable(1));
```

continues

LISTING 5-3 *(continued)*

```
        values.add(new IntWritable(1));
        new ReduceDriver<Text, IntWritable, Text, IntWritable>()
            .withReducer(new WordCount.Reduce())
            .withConfiguration(new Configuration())
            .withInput(new Text("cat"), values)
            .withOutput(new Text("cat"), new IntWritable(2))
            .runTest();
    }
```

Following is a breakdown of what is happening in this code:

1. A list of `IntWritable` objects that are used as the input to the reducer is created.

2. A `ReducerDriver` is instantiated, and like the `MapperDriver`, it is parameterized exactly as the reducer under test.

3. An instance of the reducer you want to test is passed in using the `withReducer` call. The reducer from the word count example described in Chapter 3 is used here.

4. An optional `withConfiguration` method enables you to pass a desired configuration to the reducer.

5. The `withInput` call enables you to pass in input values for a reducer. Here, you pass in the key of `"cat"` and the list created by `IntWritable` at the start of the test.

6. You can specify the expected reducer output using the `withOutput` call. Here, you specify the same key of `"cat"` and an `IntWritable` representing the number of `"cat"` words (2) you expect.

7. If a reducer is incrementing a counter, an optional `withCounter(group, name, expectedValue)` (not shown in the Listing 5-3) enables you to specify the expected value of the counter.

8. Finally, you call `runTest`, which feeds the reducer the inputs specified, and compares the output from the reducer against the expected output.

The `ReducerDriver` has the same limitation as the `MapperDriver` of not accepting more than one input/output pair.

So far, this chapter has shown you how to test the mapper and reducer in isolation, but it may also be necessary to test them together in an integration test. You can do this by using the `MapReduceDriver` class. The `MapReduceDriver` class is also the class to use for testing the use of combiners.

Integration Testing

MRUnit provides the `MapReduceDriver` class that enables you to test how a mapper and reducer are working together. The `MapReduceDriver` class is parameterized differently than `MapperDriver` and `ReducerDriver`.

First, you parameterize the input and output types of the mapper, and the input and output types of the reducer. Because the mapper output types always match the reducer input types, you end up with three pairs of parameterized types. Additionally, you can provide multiple inputs and specify multiple expected outputs. Listing 5-4 shows some sample code.

LISTING 5-4: Testing mapper and reducer together

```
@Test
public void testMapReduce() throws Exception {
    new MapReduceDriver<LongWritable, Text, Text, IntWritable, Text,
        IntWritable>()
      .withMapper(new WordCount.Map())
      .withReducer(new WordCount.Reduce())
      .withConfiguration(new Configuration())
      .withInput(new LongWritable(1), new Text("dog cat dog"))
      .withInput(new LongWritable(2), new Text("cat mouse"))
      .withOutput(new Text("cat"), new IntWritable(2))
      .withOutput(new Text("dog"), new IntWritable(2))
      .withOutput(new Text("mouse"), new IntWritable(1))
      .runTest();
}
```

As you can see from this code, the setup is similar to the one used by MapDriver/ReduceDriver classes. You pass in instances of the mapper and reducer. (The mapper and reducer from the word count example described in Chapter 3 are used here.) Optionally, you can use withConfiguration and withCombiner to test configuration and a combiner if required.

The MapReduceDriver class enables you to pass in multiple inputs that have different keys. Here, you are passing in two records — first with a LongWritable with an arbitrary value and a Text object that contains a line "dog cat dog", and second with a LongWritable with an arbitrary value and a Text object that contains the line "cat mouse".

You also specify the expected output from a reducer using the withOutput method. Here, you specify three keys — "cat", "dog", and "mouse" — with the corresponding counters of 2, 2, and 1. Finally, if mapper/reducer is incrementing a counter, an optional .withCounter(group, name, expectedValue) (not shown in Listing 5-4) enables you to specify the expected value of the counter.

If a test fails, the output of MRUnit produces an output similar to Listing 5-5 that explicitly tells what the error is.

LISTING 5-5: Result of unsuccessful MRUnit execution

```
13/01/05 09:56:30 ERROR mrunit.TestDriver: Missing expected output (mouse, 2)
    at position 2.
13/01/05 09:56:30 ERROR mrunit.TestDriver: Received unexpected output (mouse,
    1) at position 2.
```

If the test is successful, you gain a little more confidence that the mapper and reducer are correctly working together.

Although MRUnit makes unit testing easy for mapper and reducer code, the mapper and reducer examples presented here are fairly simple. If your map and/or reduce code starts to become more complex, it is a good design practice to decouple business (that is, application-specific) processing from the Hadoop framework support, and test business logic on its own. Also, as useful as the `MapReduceDriver` class is for integration testing, it's very easy to get to a point where you are no longer testing your code, but rather the Hadoop framework itself, which has already been done.

The unit testing described here typically does a fairly good job of detecting bugs early, but these tests will not really test your complete MapReduce jobs with Hadoop. The local job runner, described in the next section, enables you to run Hadoop on a local machine, in one JVM, making MapReduce jobs a little easier to debug if a job fails.

LOCAL APPLICATION TESTING WITH ECLIPSE

Using Eclipse for Hadoop development provides the capability to run the complete MapReduce application locally — in a "single instance" mode. The Hadoop distribution (`Hadoop-core`) comes with the local job runner that lets you run Hadoop on a local machine, in a single JVM. In this case, you can set breakpoints inside the `map` or `reduce` methods, using the Eclipse debugger, and "step through" the code to examine programming errors.

Running MapReduce in a local mode in Eclipse does not require any special configuration or setup. Just right-click the main class and choose Run As (or Debug As) ➪ Java Application, as shown in Figure 5-1.

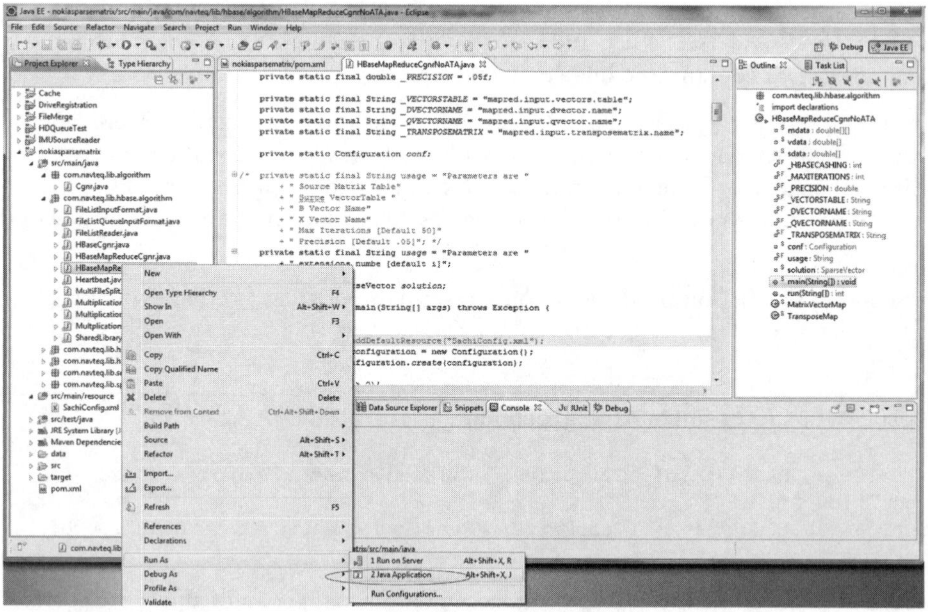

FIGURE 5-1: Running MapReduce applications locally from Eclipse

> **NOTE** *Although a local job runner can run the complete application, it has some limitations. For example, it can't run more than one reducer. (It can support the zero reducer case.) Normally, this is not a problem, because most applications can work with one reducer. The thing to watch out for is that, even if you set the number of reducers to a value of more than one, the local job runner will silently ignore the setting, and use a single reducer. Also, keep in mind that all mappers in the local mode are run sequentially.*

An Eclipse-based "local" execution works on both Linux and Windows. (If you run MapReduce on Windows, you must install Cygwin.) By default, a local job runner uses the local filesystem to read/write data.

Keep in mind that, by default, local Hadoop execution uses the local filesystem. (As described in Chapter 2, HDFS implementation provides support for local data system.) This means that all the data necessary for job testing must be copied locally, and execution results are produced locally.

If this is not an option, you can configure a local job runner to operate on a cluster's data (including HBase). To access an Hadoop cluster during local execution, you must use a configuration file, such as the one shown in Listing 5-6.

LISTING 5-6: Hadoop configuration for accessing cluster data

```xml
<?xml version="1.0" encoding="UTF-8"?>
<configuration>
    <!-- hbase access -->
    <property>
        <name>hbase.zookeeper.quorum</name>
        <value>Comma separated list of zookeeper nodes</value>
    </property>
    <property>
        <name>hbase.zookeeper.property.clientPort</name>
        <value>zookeeper port</value>
    </property>
    <!-- hdfs -->
    <property>
        <name>fs.default.name</name>
        <value>hdfs://<url>/</value>
    </property>
    <!-- impersonation -->
    <property>
        <name>hadoop.job.ugi</name>
        <value>hadoop, hadoop</value>
    </property>
</configuration>
```

This configuration defines three major components — HBase access (defined by referring to the Zookeeper quorum), HDFS access (defined by an HDFS URL), and security impersonation (this is required if your development machine and Hadoop cluster belong to different security domains, or you are using different login names on your local machine and Hadoop cluster). Adding this configuration to the execution is fairly straightforward, as shown in Listing 5-7.

LISTING 5-7: Adding cluster information to configuration

```
Configuration.addDefaultResource("Hadoop properiies");
Configuration conf = new Configuration();
```

Although using the local job runner provides much more thorough testing compared to the unit testing, one important thing that you must remember when testing Hadoop applications is that *size matters*. No matter how many times you run an Hadoop job using a local runner, until the code is tested on the realistic data sample, you can never be sure that it will work correctly.

In fact, a lot of things cannot be verified without testing at scale, including the following:

➤ How many mappers are going to be created during an application run, and how well is data going to be split between them?

➤ What is a realistic timing for shuffle and sort? Is it necessary to implement a combiner? Will an in-memory combiner be a better option?

➤ What kind of hardware/software/network load does an application create? Is it necessary to do additional application/cluster parameter tuning?

This means that to ensure that the application is working correctly, testing with the local job runner must be followed by testing on the real Hadoop cluster with realistic data.

The highly distributed nature of MapReduce execution and its dependency on a huge amount of data makes debugging MapReduce code a challenging job. In the next section, you learn how to use Hadoop's logging to enhance the debugging of Hadoop execution.

USING LOGGING FOR HADOOP TESTING

Logging is widely used in a majority of software projects, and serves many important purposes, including the following:

➤ Creation of an execution audit trail that can be used, for example, for execution analysis, or to identify potential improvements

➤ Collection of execution metrics that can be used for both real-time and postmortem analysis and test automation, error identification, and so on

MapReduce itself keeps logs of all important events during program execution. The location of these files is controlled by Hadoop configuration files. By default, they are stored in the `logs` subdirectory of the Hadoop `version` directory. The most important logs for debugging individual applications are the TaskTracker logs. Any exceptions thrown by a MapReduce job are recorded in those logs.

The `log` directory also has a subdirectory called `userlogs`, which contains a separate subdirectory for every task run. Each task records its `stdout` and `stderr` information to two files in this directory. Any application-specific logging information included in the user's code is stored in these files. On a multi-node Hadoop cluster, these logs are not centrally aggregated — you must check each task node's `logs/userlogs/` directory for their content.

A convenient way of viewing all the logs related to the same task together is by using a JobTracker's web pages, as shown in Figure 5-2. This enables you to display logs for all mappers and reducers produced by this job.

Hadoop job_201212061101_37666 on sachicn003

User: blublins
Job Name: Word Count
Job File: hdfs://sachicn001/tmp/hadoop-mapred/mapred/staging/blublins/.staging/job_201212061101_37666/job.xml
Submit Host: sachicn003.hq.navteq.com
Submit Host Address: 10.8.120.40
Job-ACLs:
   mapreduce.job.acl-view-job: No users are allowed
   mapreduce.job.acl-modify-job: No users are allowed
Job Setup: Successful   Link to the job setup logs
Status: Succeeded
Started at: Thu Dec 27 09:26:02 CST 2012
Finished at: Thu Dec 27 09:26:19 CST 2012
Finished in: 17sec
Job Cleanup: Successful   Link to the job cleanup logs

Link to the job configuration

Link to the maps information

Kind	% Complete	Num Tasks	Pending	Running	Complete	Killed	Failed/Killed Task Attempts
map	100.00%	1	0	0	1	0	0 / 0
reduce	100.00%	1	0	0	1	0	0 / 0

	Counter	Map	Reduce	Total
	SLOTS_MILLIS_MAPS	0	0	3,796
	Launched reduce tasks	0	0	1
	Total time spent by all reduces waiting after reserving slots (ms)	0	0	0
Job Counters	Rack-local map tasks	0	0	1
	Total time spent by all maps waiting after reserving slots (ms)	0	0	0
	Launched map tasks	0	0	1
	SLOTS_MILLIS_REDUCES	0	0	8,504
	FILE_BYTES_READ	0	337,824	337,824
FileSystemCounters	HDFS_BYTES_READ	189,986	0	189,986
	FILE_BYTES_WRITTEN	388,640	388,536	777,176
	HDFS_BYTES_WRITTEN	0	76,043	76,043
	Reduce input groups	0	5,527	5,527
	Combine output records	0	0	0
	Map input records	2,676	0	2,676
	Reduce shuffle bytes	0	0	0
	Reduce output records	0	5,527	5,527
Map-Reduce Framework	Spilled Records	25,741	25,741	51,482
	Map output bytes	286,336	0	286,336
	SPLIT_RAW_BYTES	111	0	111
	Map output records	25,741	0	25,741
	Combine input records	0	0	0
	Reduce input records	0	25,741	25,741

FIGURE 5-2: Job page

All of the job's logging information can be accessed from the TaskTracker's job page (job setup and cleanup logs, as well as mappers' and reducers' pages linked to the corresponding log pages). From this page you can navigate to a job configuration page, as shown in Figure 5-3.

Job Configuration: JobId - job_201212061101_37666

name	
fs.s3n.impl	org.apache.hadoop.fs.s3native.NativeS3FileSystem
dfs.datanode.plugins	org.apache.hadoop.thriftfs.DatanodePlugin
mapred.task.cache.levels	2
hadoop.tmp.dir	/tmp/hadoop-${user.name}
hadoop.native.lib	true
map.sort.class	org.apache.hadoop.util.QuickSort
dfs.namenode.decommission.nodes.per.interval	5
dfs.https.need.client.auth	false
ipc.client.idlethreshold	4000
dfs.datanode.data.dir.perm	700
mapred.system.dir	/hadoop/mapred/system/
mapred.job.tracker.persist.jobstatus.hours	0
dfs.datanode.address	0.0.0.0:50010
dfs.namenode.logging.level	info
dfs.block.access.token.enable	false
io.skip.checksum.errors	false
fs.default.name	hdfs://sachicn001/
mapred.cluster.reduce.memory.mb	-1
mapred.reducer.new-api	true
dfs.thrift.address	0.0.0.0:9090
mapred.child.tmp	./tmp
fs.har.impl.disable.cache	true
dfs.safemode.threshold.pct	0.999f
mapred.skip.reduce.max.skip.groups	0
dfs.namenode.handler.count	50
dfs.blockreport.initialDelay	0
mapred.heartbeats.in.second	100
mapred.jobtracker.instrumentation	org.apache.hadoop.mapred.JobTrackerMetricsInst
mapred.tasktracker.dns.nameserver	default
io.sort.factor	64
mapred.task.timeout	600000
mapred.max.tracker.failures	4

FIGURE 5-3: Job configuration page

The job configuration page contains the content of a configuration object. It is especially important for you to examine this page if you are using a lot of custom configuration (for example, when you pass parameters from your driver to mappers and reducers). This page enables you to confirm that they have the desired values.

Additionally, job setup and cleanup logs, as well as mappers' and reducers' pages, are linked to the corresponding log pages. As shown in Figure 5-4, log pages contain `stdout`, `stderr`, and `syslog` logs.

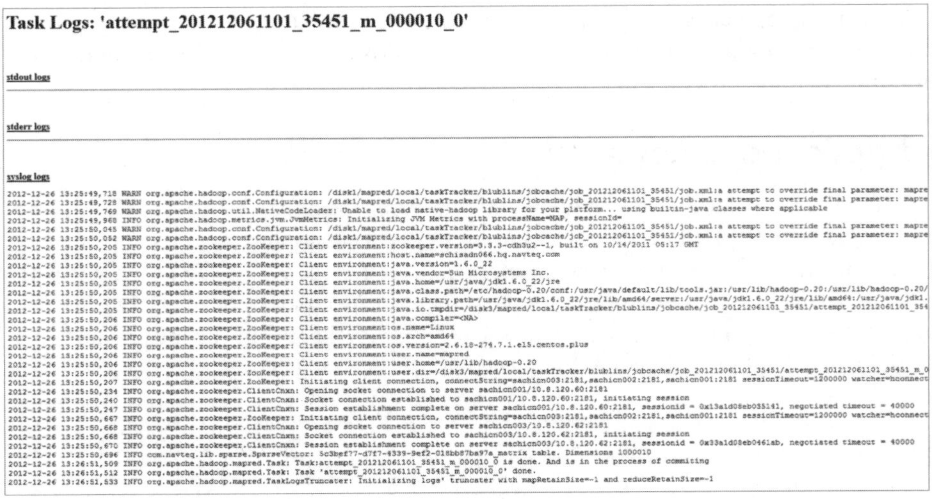

Task Logs: 'attempt_201212061101_35451_m_000010_0'

stdout logs

stderr logs

syslog logs

```
2012-12-26 13:25:49,718 WARN org.apache.hadoop.conf.Configuration: /disk1/mapred/local/taskTracker/blublins/jobcache/job_201212061101_35451/job.xml:a attempt to override final parameter: mapre
2012-12-26 13:25:49,728 WARN org.apache.hadoop.conf.Configuration: /disk1/mapred/local/taskTracker/blublins/jobcache/job_201212061101_35451/job.xml:a attempt to override final parameter: mapre
2012-12-26 13:25:49,769 WARN org.apache.hadoop.util.NativeCodeLoader: Unable to load native-hadoop library for your platform... using builtin-java classes where applicable
2012-12-26 13:25:49,968 INFO org.apache.hadoop.metrics.jvm.JvmMetrics: Initializing JVM Metrics with processName=MAP, sessionId=
2012-12-26 13:25:50,045 WARN org.apache.hadoop.conf.Configuration: /disk1/mapred/local/taskTracker/blublins/jobcache/job_201212061101_35451/job.xml:a attempt to override final parameter: mapre
2012-12-26 13:25:50,052 WARN org.apache.hadoop.conf.Configuration: /disk1/mapred/local/taskTracker/blublins/jobcache/job_201212061101_35451/job.xml:a attempt to override final parameter: mapre
2012-12-26 13:25:50,205 INFO org.apache.zookeeper.ZooKeeper: Client environment:zookeeper.version=3.3.3-cdh3u2--1, built on 10/14/2011 05:17 GMT
2012-12-26 13:25:50,205 INFO org.apache.zookeeper.ZooKeeper: Client environment:host.name=schisadn066.hq.navteq.com
2012-12-26 13:25:50,205 INFO org.apache.zookeeper.ZooKeeper: Client environment:java.version=1.6.0_22
2012-12-26 13:25:50,205 INFO org.apache.zookeeper.ZooKeeper: Client environment:java.vendor=Sun Microsystems Inc.
2012-12-26 13:25:50,205 INFO org.apache.zookeeper.ZooKeeper: Client environment:java.home=/usr/java/jdk1.6.0_22/jre
2012-12-26 13:25:50,205 INFO org.apache.zookeeper.ZooKeeper: Client environment:java.class.path=/etc/hadoop-0.20/conf:/usr/java/default/lib/tools.jar:/usr/lib/hadoop-0.20:/usr/lib/hadoop-0.20/
2012-12-26 13:25:50,205 INFO org.apache.zookeeper.ZooKeeper: Client environment:java.library.path=/usr/java/jdk1.6.0_22/jre/lib/amd64/server:/usr/java/jdk1.6.0_22/jre/lib/amd64:/usr/java/jdk1.
2012-12-26 13:25:50,205 INFO org.apache.zookeeper.ZooKeeper: Client environment:java.io.tmpdir=/disk3/mapred/local/taskTracker/blublins/jobcache/job_201212061101_35451/attempt_201212061101_354
2012-12-26 13:25:50,206 INFO org.apache.zookeeper.ZooKeeper: Client environment:java.compiler=<NA>
2012-12-26 13:25:50,206 INFO org.apache.zookeeper.ZooKeeper: Client environment:os.name=Linux
2012-12-26 13:25:50,206 INFO org.apache.zookeeper.ZooKeeper: Client environment:os.arch=amd64
2012-12-26 13:25:50,206 INFO org.apache.zookeeper.ZooKeeper: Client environment:os.version=2.6.18-274.7.1.el5.centos.plus
2012-12-26 13:25:50,206 INFO org.apache.zookeeper.ZooKeeper: Client environment:user.name=mapred
2012-12-26 13:25:50,206 INFO org.apache.zookeeper.ZooKeeper: Client environment:user.home=/usr/lib/hadoop-0.20
2012-12-26 13:25:50,206 INFO org.apache.zookeeper.ZooKeeper: Client environment:user.dir=/disk3/mapred/local/taskTracker/blublins/jobcache/job_201212061101_35451/attempt_201212061101_35451_m_0
2012-12-26 13:25:50,207 INFO org.apache.zookeeper.ZooKeeper: Initiating client connection, connectString=sachicn003:2181,sachicn002:2181,sachicn001:2181 sessionTimeout=1200000 watcher=hconnect
2012-12-26 13:25:50,234 INFO org.apache.zookeeper.ClientCnxn: Opening socket connection to server sachicn001/10.8.120.60:2181
2012-12-26 13:25:50,240 INFO org.apache.zookeeper.ClientCnxn: Socket connection established to sachicn001/10.8.120.60:2181, initiating session
2012-12-26 13:25:50,247 INFO org.apache.zookeeper.ClientCnxn: Session establishment complete on server sachicn001/10.8.120.60:2181, sessionid = 0x13a1d08eb035141, negotiated timeout = 40000
2012-12-26 13:25:50,667 INFO org.apache.zookeeper.ZooKeeper: Initiating client connection, connectString=sachicn003:2181,sachicn002:2181,sachicn001:2181 sessionTimeout=1200000 watcher=hconnect
2012-12-26 13:25:50,668 INFO org.apache.zookeeper.ClientCnxn: Opening socket connection to server sachicn003/10.8.120.62:2181
2012-12-26 13:25:50,668 INFO org.apache.zookeeper.ClientCnxn: Socket connection established to sachicn003/10.8.120.62:2181, initiating session
2012-12-26 13:25:50,670 INFO org.apache.zookeeper.ClientCnxn: Session establishment complete on server sachicn003/10.8.120.62:2181, sessionid = 0x33a1d08eb0461ab, negotiated timeout = 40000
2012-12-26 13:25:50,696 INFO com.navteq.lib.sparse.SparseVector: 5c3bef77-d7f7-4339-9ef2-018bb87ba97a_matrix table. Dimensions 1000010
2012-12-26 13:26:51,509 INFO org.apache.hadoop.mapred.Task: Task:attempt_201212061101_35451_m_000010_0 is done. And is in the process of commiting
2012-12-26 13:26:51,512 INFO org.apache.hadoop.mapred.Task: Task 'attempt_201212061101_35451_m_000010_0' done.
2012-12-26 13:26:51,533 INFO org.apache.hadoop.mapred.TaskLogsTruncater: Initializing logs' truncater with mapRetainSize=-1 and reduceRetainSize=-1
```

FIGURE 5-4: Map's log

Any application-specific logging should be present in these logs. Because this page can be refreshed in real time, it can be effectively used for watching the progress of an individual execution (assuming that your application is logging appropriate information).

Log processing can be made even more powerful by using a MapReduce framework facility to run user-provided scripts for debugging. These user-defined scripts process output logs to distill information that is most important for an understanding of the problem at hand. The script is allowed to mine data from a task's outputs (`stdout` and `stderr`), `syslog`, and `jobconf`. The outputs from the debug script's `stdout` and `stderr` are available through the job user interface.

You can provide separate scripts for map and reduce task failure. You submit the debug scripts by setting values for the properties `mapred.map.task.debug.script` (for debugging map tasks) and `mapred.reduce.task.debug.script` (for debugging reduce tasks). You can also set these properties by using APIs. The arguments to the script are the task's `stdout`, `stderr`, `syslog`, and `jobconf` files.

When deciding what exactly to log in your MapReduce job, make your decisions in a well-targeted fashion. Here are some recommendations for designing useful logging:

- Exception/error handling code should always log exception information.
- Any unexpected variable's values (for example, `nulls`) should be logged during execution.
- Detection of unexpected execution paths should be logged.
- If execution performance is of a concern, execution timing of the main code blocks should be logged.
- Logging too much makes logging useless. It makes it impossible to find relevant information within a log.

Although the use of a JobTracker can be a convenient option for viewing logs for a specific job, it is not suited for automatic log processing and mining. The following section looks at some of the approaches for automated log processing.

Processing Applications Logs

You can use a wide range of solutions for logging, starting from specialized software (for example, the Splunk App for HadoopOps) and up to a custom log-processing application. To implement custom log processing, all of the log data from all mappers and reducers must be brought together in a single file. You can achieve this by using a simple screen scraper as shown in Listing 5-8 (code file:class `HadoopJobLogScraper`), which enables you to bring together all of the logs related to a particular job, and store them in a single file for subsequent processing.

> **NOTE** *This solution was provided by Dmitry Mikhelson, a Nokia colleague.*

LISTING 5-8: Simple log screen scraper

```
public class HadoopJobLogScraper{
    private String _trackerURL = null;
    public static void main(String[] args) throws IOException{
        if (args.length != 2){
            System.err.println("usage: <JobTracker URL>, <job id>");
        }
        String jobId = args[1];
        String trackerURL = args[0];

        HadoopJobLogScraper scraper = new HadoopJobLogScraper(trackerURL);
        scraper.scrape(jobId, JobType.MAP);
        scraper.scrape(jobId, JobType.REDUCE);
        System.out.println("done");
    }

    public enum JobType{
        MAP("map"), REDUCE("reduce");
        private String urlName;
        private JobType(String urlName){
            this.urlName = urlName;
        }

        public String getUrlName(){
            return urlName;
        }
    }

    private Pattern taskDetailsUrlPattern = Pattern.compile("<a
        href=\"(taskdetails\\.jsp.*?)\">(.*?)</a>");
    private Pattern logUrlPattern = Pattern.compile("<a
        href=\"([^\"]*)\">All</a>");

    public HadoopJobLogScraper (String trackerURL){
```

```
        _trackerURL = trackerURL;
    }

    public void scrape(String jobId, JobType type) throws IOException{
        System.out.println("scraping " + jobId + " - " + type);

String jobTasksUrl = _trackerURL  + "/jobtasks.jsp?jobid=" + jobId +
    "&type=" + type.getUrlName() + "&pagenum=1";
        String jobTasksHtml = IOUtils.toString(new
            URL(jobTasksUrl).openStream());
        Matcher taskDetailsUrlMatcher =
            taskDetailsUrlPattern.matcher(jobTasksHtml);

        File dir = new File(jobId);
        if (!dir.exists()){
            dir.mkdir();
        }

        File outFile = new File(dir, type.getUrlName());
        BufferedWriter out = new BufferedWriter(new FileWriter(outFile));

        while (taskDetailsUrlMatcher.find()){
            out.write(taskDetailsUrlMatcher.group(2) + ":\n");
            String taskDetailsUrl = new String(_trackerURL  + "/" +
                taskDetailsUrlMatcher.group(1));
            String taskDetailsHtml = IOUtils.toString(new
                URL(taskDetailsUrl).openStream());
            Matcher logUrlMatcher = logUrlPattern.matcher(taskDetailsHtml);
            while (logUrlMatcher.find()){
                String logUrl = logUrlMatcher.group(1) +
                    "&plaintext=true&filter=stdout";
                out.write(IOUtils.toString(new URL(logUrl).openStream()));
            }
        }

        out.flush();
        out.close();
    }
}
```

> **NOTE** *This solution is based on the screen scraping and, as such, is inherently unreliable. Any change in the page layout has a potential to "break" this implementation.*

The main method builds a screen scraper for this job from a JobTracker URL and job ID. It then uses this screen scraper to scrape the log information for both mapper and reducer. The scraper method uses regular expressions to locate all mapper/reducer pages, reads the pages, and prints out their content.

Logging is not the only way of getting information about MapReduce execution. Next you look at another option of obtaining an execution's insights — job counters.

REPORTING METRICS WITH JOB COUNTERS

Another Hadoop-specific approach to debugging and testing is the use of a custom metric — *job counters*. As explained in Chapter 3, counters are lightweight objects in Hadoop that enable you to keep track of events of interest in both the map and reduce stages of processing.

MapReduce itself records a set of metric counters for each job that it runs, including the number of input records consumed by mappers and reducers, the number of bytes it reads from or writes to HDFS, and so on. Because the job page (Figure 5-1) updates automatically (by default, every 30 seconds), these counters can be used to track the progress of the execution. These counters can be also used, for example, to verify that all the input records were actually read and processed.

Table 5-1 shows the group names and counter names within those individual groups currently supported by Hadoop.

TABLE 5-1: Hadoop's Built-in Counters

GROUP NAME	COUNTER NAME
org.apache.hadoop.mapred.Task$Counter	MAP_INPUT_RECORDS
org.apache.hadoop.mapred.Task$Counter	MAP_OUTPUT_RECORDS
org.apache.hadoop.mapred.Task$Counter	MAP_SKIPPED_RECORDS
org.apache.hadoop.mapred.Task$Counter	MAP_INPUT_BYTES
org.apache.hadoop.mapred.Task$Counter	MAP_OUTPUT_BYTES
org.apache.hadoop.mapred.Task$Counter	COMBINE_INPUT_RECORDS
org.apache.hadoop.mapred.Task$Counter	COMBINE_OUTPUT_RECORDS
org.apache.hadoop.mapred.Task$Counter	REDUCE_INPUT_GROUPS
org.apache.hadoop.mapred.Task$Counter	REDUCE_SHUFFLE_BYTES
org.apache.hadoop.mapred.Task$Counter	REDUCE_INPUT_RECORDS
org.apache.hadoop.mapred.Task$Counter	REDUCE_OUTPUT_RECORDS
org.apache.hadoop.mapred.Task$Counter	REDUCE_SKIPPED_GROUPS
org.apache.hadoop.mapred.Task$Counter	REDUCE_SKIPPED_RECORDS
org.apache.hadoop.mapred.JobInProgress$Counter	TOTAL_LAUNCHED_MAPS
org.apache.hadoop.mapred.JobInProgress$Counter	RACK_LOCAL_MAPS
org.apache.hadoop.mapred.JobInProgress$Counter	DATA_LOCAL_MAPS
org.apache.hadoop.mapred.JobInProgress$Counter	TOTAL_LAUNCHED_REDUCES
FileSystemCounters	FILE_BYTES_READ
FileSystemCounters	HDFS_BYTES_READ
FileSystemCounters	FILE_BYTES_WRITTEN
FileSystemCounters	HDFS_BYTES_WRITTEN

You can use these counters to get more information about actual task execution — for example, the number of mapper input/output records (`MAP_INPUT_RECORDS`/ `MAP_OUTPUT_RECORDS`), HDFS bytes read and written (`HDFS_BYTES_READ`/ `HDFS_BYTES_WRITTEN`), and so on. Additionally, you can add custom counters for application-specific values — for example, the number of intermediate calculations, or an amount of code branching (which can further aid in application testing and debugging).

The `context` object passed in to mapper and reducer classes can be used to update counters. The same set of counter variables (based on name) is used by all mapper and reducer instances, and is aggregated by the master node of the cluster, so they are "thread-safe" in this manner. Listing 5-9 shows a simple code snippet that demonstrates how to create and use custom counters.

LISTING 5-9: Updating counters

```
private static String COUNTERGROUP = "debugGroup";
private static String DEBUG1 = "debug1";

context.getCounter(COUNTERGROUP, DEBUG1).increment(1);
```

In Listing 5-9, if this is a first usage of the counter, the appropriate counter object will be created with the initial value of `0`.

NUMBER OF COUNTERS PER JOB

Counters are stored in the JobTracker. This means that if a job tries to create millions of counters, the JobTracker will generate an "out of memory" error. (See also the MapReduce design recommendation in Chapter 3.) To avoid this error, the number of counters that can be created per job is limited by the Hadoop framework. Here is a code snippet from the `counters` class in the Hadoop 1.0 release:

```
/** limit on the size of the name of the group **/
private static final int GROUP_NAME_LIMIT = 128;
/** limit on the size of the counter name **/
private static final int COUNTER_NAME_LIMIT = 64;

private static final JobConf conf = new JobConf();
/** limit on counters **/
public static int MAX_COUNTER_LIMIT =
conf.getInt("mapreduce.job.counters.limit", 120);

/** the max groups allowed **/
static final int MAX_GROUP_LIMIT = 50;
```

Note here that the number of counter groups is not configurable, whereas the number of counters is (on a cluster-wide basis).

continues

continued

All of the parameters are made configurable in Hadoop 2.0. Here is a snippet from the `MRJobConfig` class:

```
public static final String COUNTERS_MAX_KEY =
    "mapreduce.job.counters.max";
public static final int COUNTERS_MAX_DEFAULT = 120;

public static final String COUNTER_GROUP_NAME_MAX_KEY =
    "mapreduce.job.counters.group.name.max";
public static final int COUNTER_GROUP_NAME_MAX_DEFAULT = 128;

public static final String COUNTER_NAME_MAX_KEY =
    "mapreduce.job.counters.counter.name.max";
public static final int COUNTER_NAME_MAX_DEFAULT = 64;

public static final String COUNTER_GROUPS_MAX_KEY =
    "mapreduce.job.counters.groups.max";
public static final int COUNTER_GROUPS_MAX_DEFAULT = 50;
```

If a job tries to create more counters than specified in the limit, an exception such as the following will be thrown by the Hadoop run time:

```
org.apache.hadoop.mapred.Counters$CountersExceededException: Error:
Exceeded limits on number of counters - Counters=xxx Limit=xxx
```

Custom counters are available both programmatically and on JobTracker pages related to a specific job (Figure 5-2). Listing 5-10 shows a simple code snippet that demonstrates how to print out the content of the counters of either a completed or running job.

LISTING 5-10: Printing Job's counters

```java
// Now lets get the counters put them in order by job_id and then print
// them out.
Counters c = job.getCounters();
// now walk through counters adding them to a sorted list.
Iterator<CounterGroup> i = c.iterator();
while (i.hasNext()){
    CounterGroup cg = i.next();
    System.out.println("Counter Group =:"+cg.getName());
    Iterator<Counter> j = cg.iterator();
    while (j.hasNext()){
        Counter cnt = j.next();
        System.out.println("\tCounter: "+cnt.getName()+
            "=:"+cnt.getValue());
    }
}
```

Both logs and counters described in this chapter provide ways to get insight into a job's execution. They are useful tools that help you to understand what is going wrong. They help to test and debug execution of the user code. Unfortunately, even an absolutely correct Hadoop implementation can fail because of corrupted data. Defensive programming helps to produce implementations that can cope with partially corrupted code.

DEFENSIVE PROGRAMMING IN MAPREDUCE

Because Hadoop runs on a vast number of input records (some of which can be corrupted), it is often counterproductive to kill a job every time a mapper cannot process an input record either because a record itself is corrupted, or because of bugs in the map function (for example, in third-party libraries, for which the source code is not available). In this case, a "standard" Hadoop retrying mechanism will do you no good. No matter how many times you try to read a "bad" record, the end result is going to be the same — map execution will fail.

If an application can tolerate skipping some of the input data, correctly processing situations like this makes the overall application much more reliable and easier to maintain. Unfortunately, such an implementation is nontrivial. An exception, in this case, can occur either in the reader that is responsible for reading data, or a mapper that is processing this data. Correctly processing these situations requires the following:

➤ Careful error handling in the reader, so that all read errors are correctly processed, and the file pointer is moved to the next record

➤ A mechanism for communicating with the mapper to report reader errors so that the mapper can correctly output information about them

➤ Careful error handling in the mapper, so that all the errors are correctly processed

➤ A custom `OutputFormat` (similar to the one described in the Chapter 4) that writes error data in a dedicated error output directory

Fortunately, Hadoop enables you to avoid such a tedious implementation by providing a feature for skipping over records that it believes to be crashing a task. If this skipping feature is turned on, a task enters into skipping mode after it has been retried several times. Once in skipping mode, the TaskTracker determines which record range is causing the failure. The TaskTracker then restarts the task, but skips over the bad record range.

Applications can control this feature through the `SkipBadRecords` class, which provides several static methods. The job driver must call one or both of the following methods to turn on record skipping for map tasks and reduce tasks:

```
setMapperMaxSkipRecords(Configuration conf, long maxSkipRecs)
setReducerMaxSkipGroups(Configuration conf, long maxSkipGrps)
```

If the maximum skip range size is set to 0 (the default), record skipping is disabled.

The number of records skipped depends on the frequency with which the record counter is incremented by the application. You should increment the counter after every record is processed. If this is not possible (some applications might batch their processing), the framework may skip additional records surrounding the bad one.

Hadoop finds the skip range using a divide-and-conquer approach. It executes the task with the skip range divided by two each time, and determines the half containing the bad record(s). The process iterates until the skip range is within the acceptable size. This is a rather expensive operation, especially if the maximum skip range size is small. It might be necessary to increase the maximum number of task attempts in Hadoop's normal task recovery mechanism to accommodate the extra attempts.

If skipping is enabled, tasks report the records being processed back to the TaskTracker. When the task fails, the TaskTracker retries the task, skipping the records that caused the failure. Because of the extra network traffic and bookkeeping to maintain the failed record ranges, skipping mode is turned on for a task only after it has failed twice.

For a task that consistently fails on a bad record, the TaskTracker runs several task attempts with the following outcomes:

➤ Failed attempt with no special actions (twice)

➤ Failed attempt with failed record is stored by the TaskTracker

➤ New attempt skipping the bad record that has failed in the previous attempt

You can modify the number of task failures needed to trigger skipping mode by using the `setAttemptsToStartSkipping(int attempts)` method on the `SkipBadRecords` class.

Hadoop will log skipped records to HDFS for later analysis. They're written as sequence files in the `_log/skip` directory.

SUMMARY

This chapter discussed options for building reliable MapReduce applications. You have learned how to unit test MapReduce application components by leveraging MRUnit, and how to debug and test complete applications using Hadoop's local job runner. You have also learned how to leverage logging and job counters to get insights into MapReduce execution. Finally, you learned how to use defensive programming to deal with the corrupted data.

Now that you know how to design, implement, and debug MapReduce, Chapter 6 discusses how to orchestrate MapReduce applications using Apache Oozie.

6

Automating Data Processing with Oozie

WHAT'S IN THIS CHAPTER?

➤ Understanding Oozie fundamentals

➤ Getting to know the main Oozie components and programming for them

➤ Understanding the overall Oozie execution model

➤ Understanding Oozie support for a Service Level Agreement

As you have learned in previous chapters, MapReduce jobs constitute the main execution engine of the Hadoop ecosystem. Over the years, solution architects have used Hadoop on complex projects. These architects have learned that utilizing MapReduce jobs without a higher-level framework for orchestration and control of their execution can result in complexities and potential pitfalls because of the following reasons:

➤ Many data processing algorithms require execution of several MapReduce jobs in a certain sequence. (For specific examples of this, see Chapter 3.) For simple tasks, a sequence might be known in advance. Many times, however, a sequence depends on the intermediate execution results of multiple jobs. Without using a higher-level framework for controlling sequence execution, management of these tasks becomes quite difficult.

➤ It is often advantageous to execute a collection of MapReduce jobs based on time, certain events, and the presence of certain resources (for example, HDFS files). Using MapReduce alone typically requires the manual execution of jobs, and the more tasks you have, the more complex this becomes.

You can alleviate these potential difficulties by leveraging the Apache Oozie Workflow engine. Oozie is comprised of the following four main functional components:

➤ **Oozie Workflow** — This component provides support for defining and executing a controlled sequence of MapReduce, Hive, and Pig jobs.

➤ **Oozie Coordinator** — This provides support for the automatic execution of Workflows based on the events and the presence of system resources.

➤ **Oozie Bundles** — This engine enables you to define and execute a "bundle" of applications, thus providing a way to batch together a set of Coordinator applications that can be managed together.

➤ **Oozie Service Level Agreement (SLA)** — This provides support for tracking the execution of Workflow applications.

In this chapter, you learn more about Oozie and its main components. You also learn about languages that are used for programming each component, and how those components work together to provide automation and management of Hadoop jobs. Finally, you learn how to build and parameterize Oozie artifacts (applications) for each component, and how to use support provided by Oozie for SLA tracking. The information in this chapter is the foundation for the Oozie end-to-end example covered in the Chapter 7.

GETTING TO KNOW OOZIE

Oozie is a workflow/coordination system that you can use to manage Apache Hadoop jobs. As shown in Figure 6-1, one of the main components of Oozie is the Oozie server — a web application that runs in a Java servlet container (the standard Oozie distribution is using Tomcat). This server supports reading and executing Workflows, Coordinators, Bundles, and SLA definitions. It implements a set of remote Web Services APIs that can be invoked from Oozie client components and third-party applications.

The execution of the server leverages a customizable database. This database contains Workflow, Coordinator, Bundle, and SLA definitions, as well as execution states and process variables. The list of currently supported databases includes MySQL, Oracle, and Apache Derby. The Oozie shared library component is located in the Oozie HOME directory and contains code used by the Oozie execution.

Finally, Oozie provides a command-line interface (CLI) that is based on a client component, which is a thin Java wrapper around Oozie Web Services APIs. These APIs can also be used from third-party applications that have sufficient permissions.

A single Oozie server implements all four functional Oozie components:

➤ Oozie Workflow

➤ Oozie Coordinator

➤ Oozie Bundle

➤ Oozie SLA

Every functional component of the Oozie server is described in this chapter, starting with what Oozie Workflow is and how you can use it.

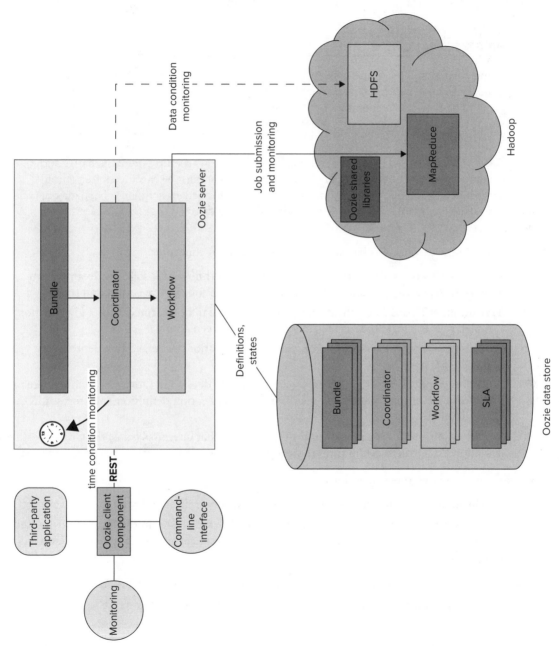

FIGURE 6-1: Main Oozie components

OOZIE WORKFLOW

Oozie *Workflow* supports the design and execution of *Directed Acyclic Graphs* (DAGs) of *actions*.

> ### DIRECTED ACYCLIC GRAPH
>
> In mathematics and computer science, a Directed Acyclic Graph (DAG) is a directed graph with no cycles. DAG is formed by a collection of nodes connected by directed edges. The main characteristic of a DAG is that it does not contain loops — in other words, there is no node N, starting from which there is a sequence of edges that eventually lead back to N.
>
> DAGs are widely used to model several different kinds of structures in mathematics and computer science. For example, a collection of tasks that must be executed in sequence, constrained by the rule that certain tasks must be performed earlier than others, may be represented as a DAG with a node for each task, and a directed edge for each constraint.

An Oozie Workflow definition is based on the following main concepts:

➤ **Action** — This is a specification of an individual Workflow task/step. For example, an action can represent execution of code, a MapReduce job, a Hive script, and so on.

➤ **Transition** — This is a specification of which action can be executed once a given action is completed. It is a way to describe a dependency between actions.

➤ **Workflow** — This is a collection of actions and transitions arranged in a dependency sequence graph.

➤ **Workflow application** — This is an Oozie Workflow defined in Oozie Workflow language. The Oozie server interprets the Oozie Workflow application definition and stores it in the Oozie database.

➤ **Workflow job** — This is a process in the Oozie server that interprets (runs) the Oozie Workflow definition. An Oozie Workflow job controls the sequence and conditions of action submission.

Oozie also supports two types of actions:

➤ **Synchronous** — This action is executed on an execution thread of the Oozie server itself.

➤ **Asynchronous** — This action is executed on an Hadoop cluster in the form of a MapReduce (or Hive/Pig/Sqoop) job. The Oozie server initiates asynchronous action, and then waits for its completion.

Transitions in Oozie Workflow are governed by the following two types of *conditions*:

➤ **Structural conditions** — These are statically defined in a Workflow DAG (transitions and fork-join construct).

➤ **Runtime execution conditions** — These can use results of the execution of previous actions in the form of process variables (switch-case construct) and success/failure paths.

Oozie describes Workflows using the *Hadoop Process Definition Language* (hPDL), which is a dialect of XML inspired by the JBoss Business Process Modeling Language (jBPML). The schema elements shown in Figure 6-2 represent actions supported by hPDL.

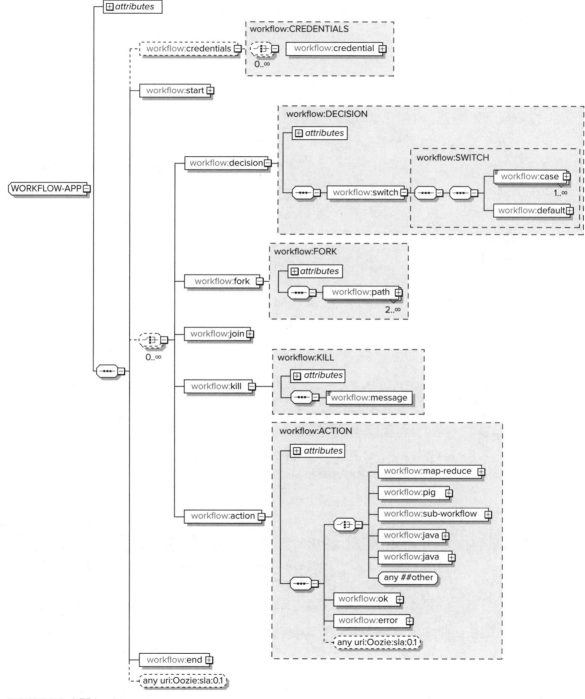

FIGURE 6-2: hPDL schema

hPDL is a fairly compact language, and uses a limited number of flow control and action nodes. Oozie Workflow nodes can be either *flow-control nodes* or *action nodes*.

Flow-control nodes provide a way to control the Workflow execution path. Table 6-1 shows a summary of flow-control nodes.

TABLE 6-1: Flow-Control Nodes

FLOW-CONTROL NODE	XML ELEMENT TYPE	DESCRIPTION
`Start` node	`start`	This specifies a starting point for an Oozie Workflow.
`End` node	`end`	This specifies an end point for an Oozie Workflow.
`Decision` node	`decision`	This expresses the "switch-case" logic.
`Fork` node	`fork`	This splits execution into multiple concurrent paths.
`Join` node	`join`	This specifies that Workflow execution waits until every concurrent execution path of a previous fork node arrives at the join node.
`Sub-workflow` node	`sub-workflow`	This invokes a sub-Workflow.
`Kill` node	`kill`	This forces an Oozie server to kill the current Workflow job.

> **NOTE** *Although the Oozie specification defines* `Sub-workflow` *as an action, the* `Sub-workflow` *functionally plays the role of a special type of flow-control node.*

Action nodes provide a way for a Workflow to initiate the execution of a computation/processing task. Table 6-2 shows the action nodes provided by Oozie.

TABLE 6-2: Action Nodes

ACTION NODE	XML ELEMENT TYPE	DESCRIPTION	TYPE
`Java` action	`java`	This invokes the `main()` method from the specified Java class.	Asynchronous
`Pig` action	`pig`	This runs a Pig job.	Asynchronous
`MapReduce` action	`map-reduce`	This runs an Hadoop MapReduce job (which could be a Java MapReduce job, a streaming job, or a pipe job).	Asynchronous
`Shell` action	`fs`	This enables you to define a sequence of `delete`, `mkdir`, `move`, and `chmod` commands, executed on HDFS.	Synchronous

Oozie additionally supports an extensibility mechanism that enables you to create custom actions (see Chapter 8 for more about Oozie custom actions) that you can use as a new element of the Workflow language. Table 6-3 shows the currently available extension actions.

TABLE 6-3: Oozie Extension Actions

ACTION NODE	XML ELEMENT TYPE	DESCRIPTION	TYPE
Hive action	Hive	This runs a Hive job.	Asynchronous
Email action	Email	This sends an e-mail.	Synchronous
SSH action	Ssh	This invokes an action in a specified shell script located on an Oozie server node (not HDFS).	Synchronous
Sqoop action	Sqoop	This runs a Sqoop job (as a MapReduce job).	Asynchronous
Distcp action	Distcp	This runs a distributed copy job (as a MapReduce job).	Asynchronous

> **NOTE** *Apache Sqoop is a Hadoop tool supporting efficient data transfer between relational databases and Hadoop storage. You can use Sqoop to do a bulk data import from external databases into HDFS and/or HBase. Sqoop can be also used to extract data from Hadoop and export it to external databases.*

As mentioned earlier, Oozie supports two types of actions — synchronous or asynchronous. As indicated in Table 6-2 and Table 6-3, fs, Shell, ssh, and Email are implemented as synchronous actions, whereas the rest are asynchronous. The next section takes a closer look at how Oozie executes asynchronous actions.

Executing Asynchronous Activities in Oozie Workflow

All asynchronous actions are executed on an Hadoop cluster in the form of Hadoop MapReduce jobs. This enables Oozie to leverage the scalability, high-availability, and fault-tolerance benefits of a MapReduce implementation.

If you use Hadoop to execute computation/processing tasks triggered by a Workflow action, the Workflow job must wait until the computation/processing task completes before transitioning to the following node in the Workflow.

Oozie can detect completion of computation/processing tasks by using the following two mechanisms:

➤ **Callback** — When a computation or processing task is started by Oozie, it provides a unique callback URL to the task, and the task should invoke this callback to notify Oozie about its completion.

➤ **Polling** — In situations where the task failed to invoke the callback for any reason (for example, because of a transient network failure), Oozie has a mechanism to poll computation/processing tasks for completion.

Externalizing the execution of resource-intensive computations allows Oozie to conserve its server's resources, ensuring that a single instance of an Oozie server can support thousands of jobs.

Oozie jobs are submitted to the Hadoop cluster using the Action/Executor pattern.

ACTION/EXECUTOR PATTERN

The *Action/Executor pattern* separates what must be done (the action, or the job submission in this case) from how it is done (the execution, or the job execution in this case). The classical example of this pattern is the Java concurrency API (`java .util.concurrent` package).

The Oozie architecture applies the Action/Executor pattern to submission and execution of MapReduce jobs specified with an Oozie application (including Workflow applications). Oozie server components are responsible for the analysis of job dependencies, execution of preconditions, and submission of the asynchronous jobs to the Hadoop cluster. The cluster itself controls job execution, failover, and recovery. If job execution on the Hadoop cluster fails, two pieces of information are returned to the Oozie server: an indicator of success or failure (usually a boolean value), and a user-readable error string (as an out-string parameter).

Each Oozie asynchronous action uses an appropriate Action/Executor pair. The Oozie Executor framework is at the heart of the Oozie server architecture. The examples in this section use the execution of an Oozie `java` action to examine the architecture of the Executor framework, starting with the `Hello World` Workflow example shown in Listing 6-1.

LISTING 6-1: Hello World Workflow

```
<workflow-app name="hello-world-wf" xmlns="uri:oozie:workflow:0.3"
                         xmlns:sla="uri:oozie:sla:0.1">
    <start to="cluster"/>
    <action name="cluster">
        <java>
                <prepare> [PREPARE SECTION] </prepare>
                <main-class>HelloWorld</main-class>
```

```
                <arg>[PROGRAM ARGUMENT]</arg>
                <archive>[ARCHIVE SECTION]</archive>
                <file>[FILE SECTION]</file>
            </java>
        <ok to="end "/>
        <error to="kill "/>
    </action>
    <kill name="fail">
        <message>
            hello-world-wf failed
        </message>
    </kill>
    <end name="end"/>
</workflow-app>
```

This is a very simple Workflow that starts with an execution of the java action (the start node specifies the name of the first node to execute). This java action is implemented using HelloWorld class with specified program arguments. (Oozie will invoke a main method on this class, passing in program arguments.) With the <prepare>, <archive>, and <file> tags, you can specify additional information for class execution (which is described in more detail later in this chapter). If the class execution completes successfully (that is, with an exit code of 0), the transition will progress to an end action. Otherwise, the transition will progress to a kill action, and will produce a "hello-world-wf failed" message. Because a kill action has no explicit transition specified, the next action (end) will be invoked after the execution of the kill action. The end action will stop execution of the process.

> **NOTE** *Although the architecture of the Oozie Executor framework is very stable, code, classes, and method names change from version to version. The description presented here is based on Oozie version 3.20 from the Apache distribution. Also, note that unlike code presented in Chapters 3, 4, and 5, Oozie is using the "old" MapReduce APIs from* org.apache.hadoop.mapred *package.*

As shown in Figure 6-3, processing of the java command starts with the invocation of the call method on the XCommand class. This method starts construction and submission of the MapReduce job for the java action.

The method first obtains the instance of the Instrumentation class from the Services class, which maintains a pool of Instrumentation instances. This instance is used to set up timers, counters, variables, and locks for the job.

It then uses the loadState method of the ActionStartXCommand class to load the job configuration. The implementation of the ActionStartXCommand class achieves this by obtaining the Workflow object wfJob (class WorkflowJobBean) and action object wfAction (class WorkflowActionBean) from the Services class.

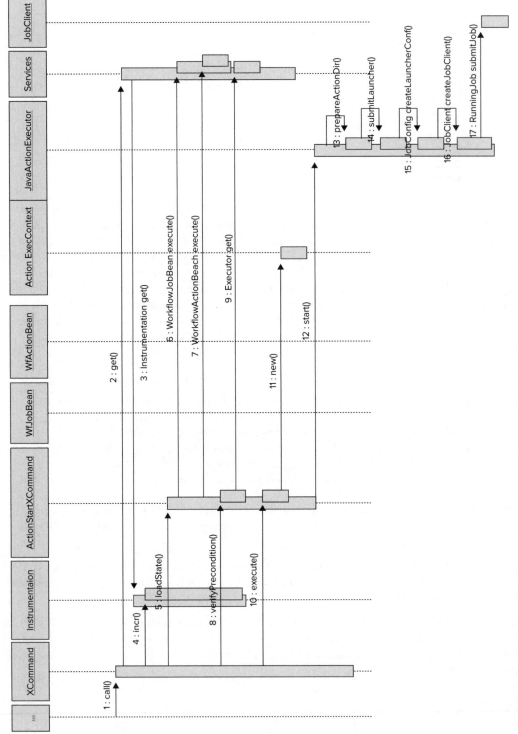

FIGURE 6-3: Submission of a job for the java action in the Oozie Executor framework

Next, the `call` method of `XCommand` uses the `verifyPrecondition` method of the `ActionStartXCommand` class to check the job status and obtain the instance of `ActionExecutor` (`JavaActionExecutor`, in this case) from the `Services` class, which maintains a pool of `ActionExecutor` instances.

Finally, the `call` method of `XCommand` uses the `execute` method of the `ActionStartXCommand` class to do the rest.

This method prepares the Hadoop job configuration, defines the retry policy, and creates the action execution context (class `ActionExecutorContext`), which serves as the container for the job configuration elements. It then invokes a `start` method on `ActionExecutor` (`JavaActionExecutor`, in this case) to complete the invocation.

The `start` method of `ActionExecutor` leverages a set of launchers to implement different steps of the action invocation. These launchers are created during `ActionExecutor` initialization, as shown in Listing 6-2.

LISTING 6-2: Launcher classes in JavaActionExecutor

```
protected List<Class> getLauncherClasses() {
        List<Class> classes = new ArrayList<Class>();
        classes.add(LauncherMapper.class);
        classes.add(LauncherSecurityManager.class);
        classes.add(LauncherException.class);
        classes.add(LauncherMainException.class);
        classes.add(FileSystemActions.class);
        classes.add(PrepareActionsDriver.class);
        classes.add(ActionStats.class);
        classes.add(ActionType.class);
        return classes;
}
```

The launchers are responsible for the following:

➤ The `PrepareActionsDriver` class is used to parse the `<prepare>` XML fragment of the `java` action definition.

➤ The `FileSystemActions` class supports execution of the HDFS operations (`delete`, `mkdir`, and so on) during the preparation phase.

➤ The `ActionType` class is just the enumerator that specifies the type of possible action values (`MAP_REDUCE`, `PIG`, and `HIVE`).

➤ The `LauncherMapper` class is responsible for submitting the `java` action itself to the Hadoop cluster as a MapReduce job with a single mapper and no reducers.

➤ The `LauncherSecurityManager` is used to control security aspects of the Hadoop job.

The `start` method of `ActionStartCommand` first calls the `prepareActionDir` method that moves the launcher's job `jar` from the Oozie server node to the `action` directory on HDFS, and then invokes the `submitLauncher` method.

This method first parses the action XML configuration to create the Hadoop objects `Configuration` and `JobConf` (using the `HadoopAccessorService` class). Once this is done, the `submitLauncher` method configures the `LauncherMapper` object by setting the main class (from the `<java-main>` java action element) and program arguments (from the `<arg>` java action elements).

Then, the `submitLauncher` method specifies the libraries (`<archive>` section) and files (`<file>` section) that will be moved to the Hadoop distributed cache. It sets up the credentials and named parameters, and creates an instance of the Hadoop `JobClient` class. The `JobClient` object is used by the java Executor to submit the Hadoop job to the cluster and implement the retry logic.

Finally, the `submitLauncher` method retrieves the submitted job URL from the `JobConf` instance. This URL is used by the Oozie server to track the job state in the Oozie console (which you learn more about in Chapter 7).

The Java class specified in the Oozie `java` action is actually invoked on the Hadoop cluster from the instance of the `LauncherMapper` class that implements the `org.apache.hadoop.mapred.Mapper` interface. In the `map` method (called only once), it retrieves the class name specified in the Oozie action definition, and invokes the `main` method of that class with the (simplified) code fragment, as shown in Listing 6-3.

LISTING 6-3: Invocation of java action main class on the Hadoop cluster

```
String mainClass = getJobConf().get(CONF_OOZIE_ACTION_MAIN_CLASS);
String[] args = getMainArguments(getJobConf());
Class klass = getJobConf().getClass(CONF_OOZIE_ACTION_MAIN_CLASS,
    Object.class);
Method mainMethod = klass.getMethod("main", String[].class);
mainMethod.invoke(null, (Object) args);
```

The `MapReduceActionExecutor` extends the `JavaActionExecutor` class by overriding several methods. The implementation of the `setupActionConf` method supports `Streaming` and `Pipes` parameters (if the map-reduce action specifies `Pipes` or `Streaming` APIs).

NOTE *Chapter 4 provides more details about* `Pipes` *and* `Streaming`.

The implementation of the `getLauncherClasses` method adds `main` methods for different types of map-reduce invocations, including `Pipes`, `Streaming`, and so on, as shown in Listing 6-4.

LISTING 6-4: Launchers for the map-reduce action

```
protected List<Class> getLauncherClasses() {
    List<Class> classes = super.getLauncherClasses();
    classes.add(LauncherMain.class);
```

```
            classes.add(MapReduceMain.class);
            classes.add(StreamingMain.class);
            classes.add(PipesMain.class);
            return classes;
    }
```

So, when the `jobClient.submitJob(launcherJobConf)` is invoked in the `submitLauncher` method of the `JavaActionExecutor` (base) class, either the `MapReduceMain`, `StreamingMain`, or `PipesMain` launcher is used. As an example, for the Java `map-reduce` action, this would effectively result in running `MapReduceMain.main`, which starts a new MapReduce job on the cluster.

> **NOTE** *As described here, a MapReduce Oozie action effectively creates two MapReduce jobs — an Oozie launcher and the actual job. The launcher job stays around until the actual MapReduce job completes. It's important to remember this when using Oozie on a cluster with a limited number of jobs per user. In this case, using many simultaneous Oozie jobs can lead to a deadlock — launchers occupy all the slots available to the user that prevent actual MapReduce jobs from executing, which results in launcher jobs being "stuck." This situation can be further complicated when* `Pig` *or* `Hive` *actions (which can start multiple MapReduce jobs) are used.*

For `Hive` and `Pig` actions, the invocation steps are similar to the steps described previously, but the main launcher class is specific to each action. As an example, for the `Pig` action, the main launcher class is `PigMain`, which extends the class `LauncherMain`. In the `PigMain` class, the `main`, `run`, and `runPigJob` methods are sequentially invoked on a cluster. The `runPigJob` method invokes the `PigRunner` class (this class is not part of the Oozie distribution — it belongs to the Pig framework). This way, the control over the Workflow job execution is transferred to the Pig framework. That can result in several MapReduce jobs on the Hadoop cluster.

One of the important characteristics of the execution of an action is its retry and recovery implementations. The following section takes a closer look how Oozie retry and recovery works.

Oozie Recovery Capabilities

Oozie provides recovering capabilities for Workflow jobs that are leveraging the Hadoop cluster recovery capabilities. Once an action starts successfully, Oozie relies on MapReduce retry mechanisms. In the case where an action fails to start, Oozie applies different recovery strategies, depending on the nature of the failure. In the case of a transient failure (such as network problems, or a remote system temporarily being unavailable), Oozie sets the maximum retries and retry interval values, and then performs a retry. The number of retries and timer intervals for a type of action can be specified at the Oozie server level, and can be overridden on the Workflow level.

Table 6-4 shows the parameter names and default values.

TABLE 6-4: Oozie Retry Properties

PROPERTY NAME	DEFAULT VALUE	DEFINED IN CLASS
`oozie.wf.action.max.retries`	3	`org.apache.oozie.client` `. OozieClient`
`oozie.wf.action.retry.interval`	60 sec	`org.apache.oozie.client` `. OozieClient`

The Oozie Workflow engine described thus far automates the execution of a group of MapReduce jobs defined as a structured group of Workflow actions. But it does not support the automatic start of Workflow jobs, their repeated execution, analysis of data dependencies between Workflow jobs, and so on. This functionality is supported by the Oozie Coordinator, which you learn more about shortly.

Now that you know what Oozie Workflow is and how it is executed, take a look at a Workflow's life cycle.

Oozie Workflow Job Life Cycle

Once the *Workflow application* is loaded to the Workflow server, it becomes a *Workflow job*. As shown at Figure 6-4, possible states for a Workflow job are PREP, RUNNING, SUSPENDED, SUCCEEDED, KILLED, and FAILED.

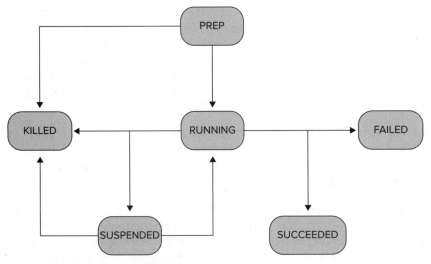

FIGURE 6-4: Workflow job life cycle

A loaded Workflow job is in the PREP state. A job in this state can be started (that is, in the RUNNING state) or deleted (that is, in the KILLED state). A running Workflow can be suspended by the user (SUSPENDED state), succeed (SUCCEEDED state), fail (FAILED state), or it can be killed by the user (KILLED state). A suspended job can be resumed (RUNNING state) or killed (KILLED state).

OOZIE COORDINATOR

The Oozie Coordinator supports the automated starting of Oozie Workflow processes. It is typically used for the design and execution of recurring invocations of Workflow processes triggered by time and/or data availability.

The Coordinator enables you to specify the conditions that trigger Workflow job execution. Those conditions can describe data availability, time, or external events that must be satisfied to initiate a job. The Coordinator also enables you to define dependencies between Workflow jobs that run regularly (including those that run at different time intervals) by defining outputs of multiple subsequent runs of a Workflow as the input to the next Workflow.

The execution of the Oozie Coordinator is based on the following concepts:

- ➤ **Actual time** — This is the time when a Coordinator job is started on a cluster.

- ➤ **Nominal time** — This is the time when a Coordinator job should start on a cluster. Although the nominal time and the actual time should match, in practice, the actual time may occur later than the nominal time because of unforeseen delays.

- ➤ **Data set** — This is the logical collection of data identifiable by a name. Each data instance can be referred to individually using a URI.

- ➤ **Synchronous data set** — This is the data set instance associated with a given time interval (that is, its nominal time).

- ➤ **Input and output events** — These are the definitions of data conditions used in a Coordinator application. The *input event* specifies the data set instance that should exist for a Coordinator action to start execution. The *output event* describes the data set instance that a particular Coordinator action should create on the HDFS.

- ➤ **Coordinator action** — This is a Workflow job associated with a set of conditions. A Coordinator action is created at the time specified in its definition. The action enters a waiting state until all required inputs for execution are satisfied, or until the waiting times out.

- ➤ **Coordinator application** — This is a program that triggers Workflow jobs when a set of conditions is met. An Oozie Coordinator application is defined by using a Coordinator language (which you learn about shortly).

- ➤ **Coordinator job** — This is a running instance of a Coordinator application.

Similar to Oozie Workflow, the Oozie Coordinator language is an XML dialect, as shown in the schema diagram in Figure 6-5.

> **NOTE** *This schema shows only the most important components of the language.*

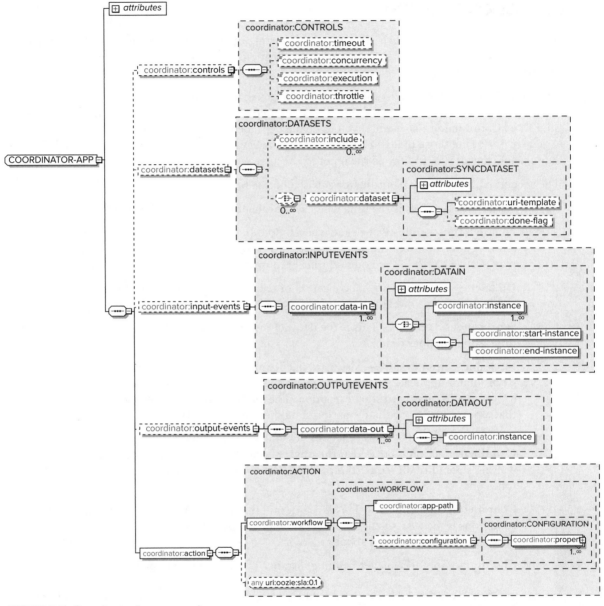

FIGURE 6-5: Coordinator language schema

Table 6-5 summarizes the main elements and attributes of the XML Coordinator language. (Attributes are not shown in Figure 6-5.)

TABLE 6-5: Coordinator Language

ELEMENT TYPE	DESCRIPTION	ATTRIBUTES AND SUB-ELEMENTS
coordinator-app	This is the top-level element of a Coordinator application.	name, frequency, start, end
controls	This specifies the execution policy for a Coordinator job.	timeout, concurrency, execution, throttle
action	This specifies the location of the single Workflow application and properties for that application.	workflow, app-path, configuration
dataset	This represents the collections of data referred to by a logical name. Data sets specify data dependences between Coordinator actions from different Coordinator applications.	name, frequency, initial-instance, uri-template, done-flag
input-events	This specifies the input conditions (in the form of data set instances) that are required to submit a Coordinator action.	name, dataset, start-instance, end-instance
output-events	This specifies the data set that should be produced by a Coordinator action.	name, dataset, instance

The Coordinator `controls` element shown in Figure 6-5 enables you to specify a job's execution policies. This element can contain the following sub-elements:

➤   `timeout` — This is the maximum time that a materialized action will be waiting for all additional conditions before being discarded. The default value of -1 means that the action will wait forever, which is not always the most desirable behavior. In this case, a large number of actions may be in a waiting state, and, at some point, all of them will start executing, which will overwhelm the whole system.

➤   `concurrency` — This is the maximum number of Coordinator jobs that can be running at the same time. The default value is 1.

➤   `execution` — This specifies the execution order for cases when multiple instances of the Coordinator job are simultaneously transitioning from a ready state to an execution state. Valid values include the following:

➤   `FIFO` (the default) — Oldest first

➤   `LIFO` — Newest first

➤   `ONLYLAST` — Discards all older materializations

➤ `throttle` (not shown in Figure 6-5) — This is the maximum number of Coordinator actions that are allowed to be waiting for all additional conditions concurrently.

Data sets are used for specifying input and output events for Coordinator applications. A `dataset` element (described in more detail later in this chapter) may contain the following attributes and sub-elements:

➤ `name` — This is the attribute used for referencing this data set from other Coordinator elements (events). The value of the `name` attribute must be a valid Java identifier.

➤ `frequency` — This is the attribute that represents the rate (in minutes) for creation (periodically) of subsequent instances of a data set. Frequency is commonly indicated using expressions such as `${5 * HOUR}`.

➤ `initial-instance` — This is the attribute that specifies the time when the first instance of the data set should be created (that is, the data set baseline). Instances that follow will be created starting from that baseline using the time intervals specified by the `frequency` element. Each Coordinator application that uses the data set specifies the end time when it stops using the data set.

➤ `uri-template` — This is the sub-element that specifies the base identifier for the data set instances. The `uri-template` is usually constructed using expression language constants and variables. An example of expression language constants used for `uri-template` might be `${YEAR}/${MONTH}/${HOUR}`. An example of variables for `uri-template` might be `${market}/${language}`. Both constants and variables are resolved at run time. The difference is that the expression language constants are resolved by the Oozie server and are Coordinator job-independent, whereas variable values are specific for a given Coordinator job.

➤ `done-flag` — This is the sub-element that specifies the name of the file that is created to mark the completion of data set processing. If `done-flag` is not specified, Hadoop creates a `_SUCCESS` file in the data instance output directory. If the `done-flag` is set to empty, the Coordinator considers it an instance of a data set that is available if the output directory exists.

Listing 6-5 shows a simple example of `dataset`.

LISTING 6-5: Example of using a dataset

```
<dataset name="testDS" frequency="${coord:hours(10)}"
         initial-instance="2013-03-02T08:00Z" timezone="${timezone}">
    <uri-template>
        ${baseURI}/${YEAR}/${MONTH}/${DAY}/${HOUR}/${MINUTE}
    </uri-template>
    <done-flag>READY</done-flag>
</dataset>
```

The dataset defined in Listing 6-5 has the frequency 10 hours (600 minutes). If the variable `baseURI` is defined as `/user/profHdp/sample`, the dataset defines the set of locations for the dataset instances shown in Listing 6-6.

LISTING 6-6: Data set instances directories

```
/user/profHdp/sample/2013/03/02/08/00
/user/profHdp/sample/2013/03/02/18/00
/user/profHdp/sample/2013/03/03/04/00
/user/profHdp/sample/2013/03/03/14/00
/user/profHdp/sample/2013/03/04/00/00
/user/profHdp/sample/2013/03/04/08/00
```

The `input-events` element specifies the input conditions for a Coordinator application. As of this writing, such input conditions are restricted to availability of `dataset` instances. Input events can refer to multiple instances of multiple datasets.

`input-events` is specified with the `<input-events>` element, which can contain one or more `<data-in>` elements, each having the `name` attribute, the `dataset` attribute, and two sub-elements (`<start-instance>` and `<end-instance>`). Alternatively, instead of those two elements, `input-events` can use a single `<instance>` sub-element.

When both `<start-instance>` and `<end-instance>` elements are used, they specify the range of `dataset` instances that should be available to start a Coordinator job. Listing 6-7 shows an example.

LISTING 6-7: Example of the input-events

```
<input-events>
        <data-in name="startLogProc" dataset="systemLog">
                <start-instance>${coord:current(-3)}</start-instance>
                <end-instance>${coord:current(0)}</end-instance>
        </data-in>
        <data-in name="startLogProc" dataset="applicationLog">
                <start-instance>${coord:current(-6)}</start-instance>
                <end-instance>${coord:current(0)}</end-instance>
        </data-in>
    </input-events>
```

The `input-events` `startLogProc` in Listing 6-7 defines a dependency between two data sets: `systemLog` and `applicationLog`. It also specifies that the `startLogProc` event occurs only when three (`-3`) sequential instances of the `systemLog` data set and six (`-6`) instances of the `applicationLog` data set are available.

Figure 6-6 shows a time line for an example in Listing 6-7. If you assume that the Coordinator application A produces an instance of `systemLog` every two hours, and Coordinator application B produces the instance of the `dataset` `applicationLog` every hour, then application C (driven by the input event `startLogProc`) can start every six hours.

`output-events` specifies `datasets` that are produced by Coordinator jobs. Oozie does not enforce `output_events`, but rather allows an output `dataset` to be used in `input_events` for another Coordinator job. At that point, its availability on a cluster will be enforced.

Input and output events enable you to specify the interaction of Coordinator jobs via the `datasets` they produce and consume. That mechanism is referred to as an Oozie *data pipeline*. In Chapter 7, you see an example of Coordinator applications that compose such a data pipeline.

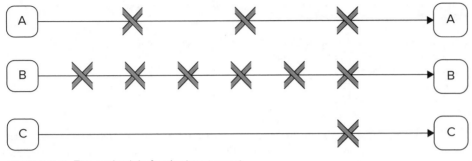

FIGURE 6-6: Time schedule for the input event

The Coordinator job can be in one of the following states: PREP, RUNNING, PREPSUSPENDED, SUSPENDED, PREPPAUSED, PAUSED, SUCCEEDED, DONWITHERROR, KILLED, and FAILED. Figure 6-7 shows all valid transitions between Coordinator job states.

Following are key points to note in Figure 6-7:

➤   A loaded Coordinator job is in the PREP state.

➤   A job in the PREP state can be started (RUNNING state), suspended (PREPSUSPENDED), or reach a pause time (PREPPAUSED state) and deleted (KILLED state). A PREPSUSPENDED job can either resume (PREP state) or be deleted (KILLED state). A PREPPAUSED job can be killed (KILLED state) or a pause time can expire (PREP state).

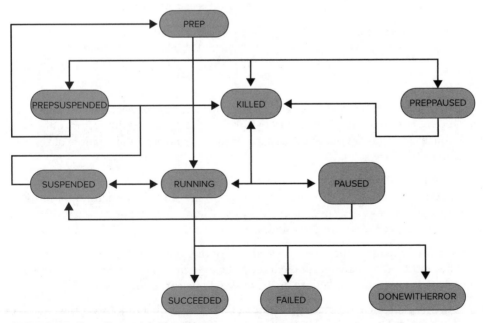

FIGURE 6-7: Coordinator job life cycle

➤ A running Coordinator job can be suspended (SUSPENDED state) or killed (KILLED state) by the user. It can succeed (SUCCEEDED state) or fail (FAILED state). When a user requests to kill a Coordinator job, Oozie sends a kill notification to all submitted Workflow jobs. If any Coordinator action finishes with a status that is not KILLED, Oozie puts the Coordinator job into the DONWITHERROR state. When pause time is reached for a running job, Oozie pauses it (PAUSED state). A suspended job can be resumed (RUNNING state) or killed (KILLED state).

➤ Finally, a paused job can be suspended (SUSPENDED state) or killed (KILLED state), or a pause can expire (RUNNING state).

Although the Oozie Coordinator provides a powerful mechanism for managing Oozie Workflows and defining conditions for their execution, in cases where there are many Coordinator applications, it becomes difficult to manage all of them. Oozie Bundle provides a convenient mechanism for "batching" multiple Coordinator applications, and managing them together.

OOZIE BUNDLE

Oozie Bundle is a top-level abstraction that enables you to group a set of Coordinator applications into a Bundle application (defined earlier in this chapter as a *data pipeline*). Coordinator applications grouped into a Bundle can be controlled (start/stop/suspend/resume/rerun) together as a whole. Bundle does not allow you to specify any explicit dependency among the Coordinator applications. Those dependencies are specified in Coordinator applications themselves through input and output events.

Oozie Bundle uses the following concepts:

➤ kick-off-time — This is the Bundle application starting time.

➤ **Bundle action** — This is a Coordinator job that is started by the Oozie server for a Coordinator application belonging to the Bundle.

➤ **Bundle application** — This is a collection of definitions that specifies a set of Coordinator applications that are included in the Bundle. A Bundle application is defined with the Oozie Bundle language.

➤ **Bundle job** — This is a process in the Oozie server that interprets (runs) an Oozie Bundle application. Before running a Bundle job, the corresponding Bundle application must be deployed to an Oozie server.

A Bundle is defined by using the Bundle language, which is an XML-based language. Figure 6-8 shows a schema for the Bundle language.

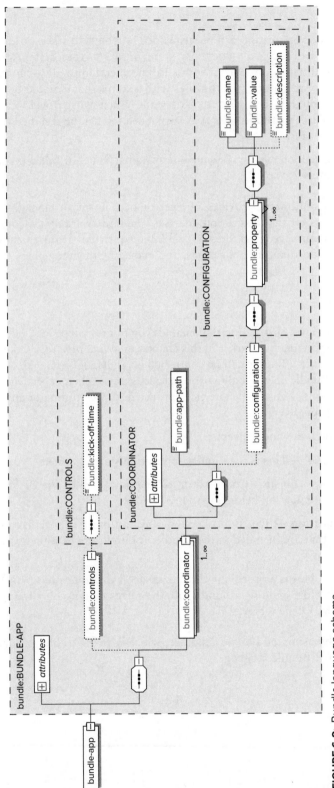

FIGURE 6-8: Bundle language schema

Table 6-6 shows the main top-level elements of the Bundle definition language.

TABLE 6-6: Bundle Language Elements

ELEMENTS AND ATTRIBUTES	DESCRIPTION	ATTRIBUTES AND SUB-ELEMENTS
bundle-app	This is the top-level element of the Bundle application.	name, controls, coordinator
name	This is the attribute that specifies the name for the Bundle. For example, you can use it to refer to the Bundle application in the Hadoop CLI command.	
controls	This is an element that contains only one attribute — kick-off-time. That attribute specifies the start time for a Bundle application.	kick-off-time
coordinator	This element describes a Coordinator application included in the Bundle. A Bundle application can have multiple Coordinator elements.	name, app-path, configuration

Every Bundle is identified by its name. Execution of a Bundle is specified by the controls element, which specifies a Bundle start time (or kick-off-time). A Bundle can contain one or more coordinator elements. For every coordinator element, it requires the following:

➤ name — This is the name of the Coordinator application. It can be used to refer to this application through a Bundle to control such actions as kill, suspend, or rerun.

➤ app-path — This sub-element specifies the location of Coordinator definitions (for example, the coordinator.xml file).

➤ configuration — This is an optional Hadoop configuration to parameterize corresponding Coordinator applications.

Listing 6-8 shows an example of a Bundle application that includes two Coordinator applications.

LISTING 6-8: Example of a Bundle application

```
<bundle-app name='weather-forecast'
    xmlns:xsi='http://www.w3.org/2001/XMLSchema-instance'
    xmlns='uri:oozie:bundle:0.1'>
  <controls>
      <kick-off-time>${kickOffTime}</kick-off-time>
  </controls>
```

continues

LISTING 6-8 *(continued)*

```xml
<coordinator name='monitor-weather-datastream' >
    <app-path>${'monitor-weather-coord-path}</app-path>
        <property>
                <name>monitor-time</name>
                <value>60</value>
        </property>
        <property>
                <name>lang</name>
                <value>${LANG}</value>
        </property>
    <configuration>
</coordinator>
<coordinator name='calc-publish-forecast' >
    <app-path>${'calc-publish-coord-path}</app-path>
    <configuration>
        <property>
                <name>monitor-time</name>
                <value>600</value>
        </property>
        <property>
                <name>client-list</name>
                <value>${LIST}</value>
        </property>
    </configuration>
    </configuration>
    </coordinator>
</bundle-app>
```

The first application in Listing 6-8 monitors and pre-processes raw weather data, and it runs every 60 seconds, as specified in the `<property>` section. The second application calculates and publishes the weather forecast every 10 minutes. It is assumed that the output data sets from the first application are used to pass data to the second application. So, the Bundle groups applications together that create a data pipeline. From this example you can see that it makes perfect sense for operations to control those two applications together as a single unit.

> **NOTE** *In Chapter 7, you see a complete example of a Coordinator application with a pipeline and a Bundle used to manage those applications.*

As shown in Figure 6-9, at any time, a Bundle job can be in one of the following states: PREP, RUNNING, PREPSUSPENDED, SUSPENDED, PREPPAUSED, PAUSED, SUCCEEDED, DONWITHERROR, KILLED, FAILED.

Following are key points to note in Figure 6-9:

➤   A loaded Bundle job is in the PREP state.

➤   A job in this state can be started (RUNNING state), suspended (PREPSUSPENDED state), reach a pause time (PREPPAUSED state), or be deleted (KILLED state). A PREPSUSPENDED job can either be resumed (PREP state) or deleted (KILLED state). A PREPPAUSED job can be killed (KILLED state), or a pause time can expire (PREP state).

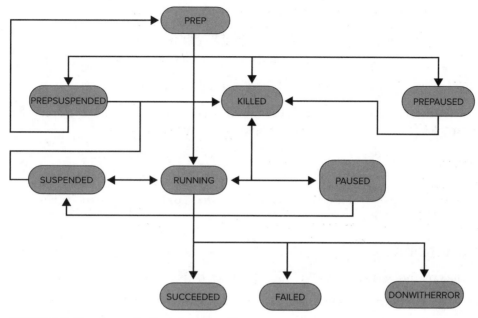

FIGURE 6-9: Bundle application state transition

➤ A running Bundle can be suspended (SUSPENDED state) or killed (KILLED state) by the user.
    It can succeed (SUCCEEDED state) or fail (FAILED state). When a pause time is reached for a
    running job, Oozie pauses the job (PAUSED state). If not all Coordinator jobs finish with the
    same status, Oozie puts the Bundle job into the DONWITHERROR state. A suspended job can
    be resumed (RUNNING state) or killed (KILLED state).

➤ Finally, a paused job can be suspended (SUSPENDED state) or killed (KILLED state), or a pause
    can expire (RUNNING state).

Now that you know the main components of Oozie and the way they are used, the next section
looks at how Oozie's JSP-like Expression Language (EL) can be used to parameterize the definitions
of these components.

OOZIE PARAMETERIZATION WITH EXPRESSION LANGUAGE

All types of Oozie applications (Workflow, Coordinator, and Bundle) can be parameterized with
Oozie Expression Language (EL). In this section, you learn about the most important EL constants
and functions defined by Oozie specifications for Workflow, Coordinator, and Bundle applications.

Basic constants are the simplest elements of EL. Following are some examples:

➤ KB: 1024 — 1 kilobyte

➤ MB: 1024 * KB — 1 megabyte

➤ MINUTE — 1 minute

➤ HOUR — 1 hour

Additional EL constants include Hadoop constants, as in the following examples:

➤   RECORDS — This is the Hadoop record counters group name.

➤   MAP_IN — This is the Hadoop mapper input record counters name.

Some other constants include MAP_OUT, REDUCE_IN, REDUCE_OUT, and GROUPS.

Basic EL functions provide support for operations with string, data, encoding, and access to some configuration parameters. Following are some examples:

➤   concat(String s1, String s2) — This is a string concatenation.

➤   trim(String s) — This returns a trimmed version of a given string.

➤   urlEncode(String s) — This converts a string to the application/x-www-form-urlencoded MIME format.

Workflow Functions

Workflow EL functions provide access to Workflow parameters. Following are some examples:

➤   wf:id() — This returns the Oozie ID of the current Workflow job.

➤   wf:appPath() — This returns the application path of the current Workflow.

➤   wf:conf(String name) — This can be used to obtain the complete content of the configuration for the current Workflow.

➤   wf:callback(String stateVar) — This returns the callback URL for the current Workflow node for a given action. The parameter stateVar specifies the exit state for the action.

➤   wf:transition(String node) — If the node (action) was executed, this function returns the name of the transition node from the specified node.

Some other functions commonly used with Workflow include wf:lastErrorNode(), errorCode(String node), errorMessage(String message), wf:user(), and wf:group().

Coordinator Functions

Coordinator EL functions provide access to Coordinator parameters, as well as parameters of input events and output events. Following are some examples:

➤   coord:current(int n) — This is used to access the name of (n-th) data set instance in input and output events.

➤   coord:nominalTime() — This retrieves the time of the creation of a Coordinator action as specified in the Coordinator application definition.

➤   coord:dataIn(String name) — This resolves to all the URIs for the data set instances specified in an input event dataset section. This EL function is commonly used to pass the URIs of data set instances that will be consumed by a Workflow job triggered by a Coordinator action.

Some other commonly used Coordinator functions include `coord:dataOut(String name)`, `coord:actualTime()`, and `coord:user()`.

Bundle Functions

No specialized EL functions exist for Bundle, but a Bundle definition (along with Workflow and Coordinator definition) can use any of the basic EL functions described earlier.

Other EL Functions

MapReduce EL functions provide access to a MapReduce job's execution statistics (counters). For example, `hadoop:counters(String node)` enables you to obtain the values of the counters for a job submitted by an Hadoop action node.

HDFS EL functions are used to query HDFS for files and directories. Following are some examples:

➤ `fs:exists(String path)` — This checks whether or not the specified path URI exists on HDFS.

➤ `fs: fileSize(String path)` — This returns the size of the specified file in bytes.

Other commonly used HDFS functions include `fs:isDir(String path)`, `fs:dirSize(String path)`, and `fs:blockSize(String path)`.

When you use EL functions, you can significantly simplify access to Oozie and Hadoop functionality and data. You can also externalize most of the Oozie execution parameters. Instead of changing the Oozie application (Workflow/Coordinator/Bundle) every time a parameter (such as file location, timing, and so on) changes, you can externalize these parameters into a configuration file, and change just the configuration file without touching the applications. (Compare this to passing parameters to a Java application.)

Next, you look at the overall Oozie execution model — the way the Oozie server processes Bundle, Coordinator, and Workflow jobs.

OOZIE JOB EXECUTION MODEL

Figure 6-10 shows a simplified model that covers the execution of the Oozie Bundle, Coordinator, Workflow, and Workflow action, including submission of jobs from Oozie to the Hadoop cluster. This model does not show such details as state transition for Coordinator actions, or the difference between a Coordinator job, application, and action (which was discussed earlier in this chapter). Rather, you should concentrate more on the interaction between Oozie components (Bundle, Coordinator, and Workflow) up to the submission of Hadoop jobs (MapReduce, Hive, and Pig jobs) to the Hadoop cluster.

> **NOTE** *The diagram in Figure 6-10 does not show the retirement of any type of objects.*

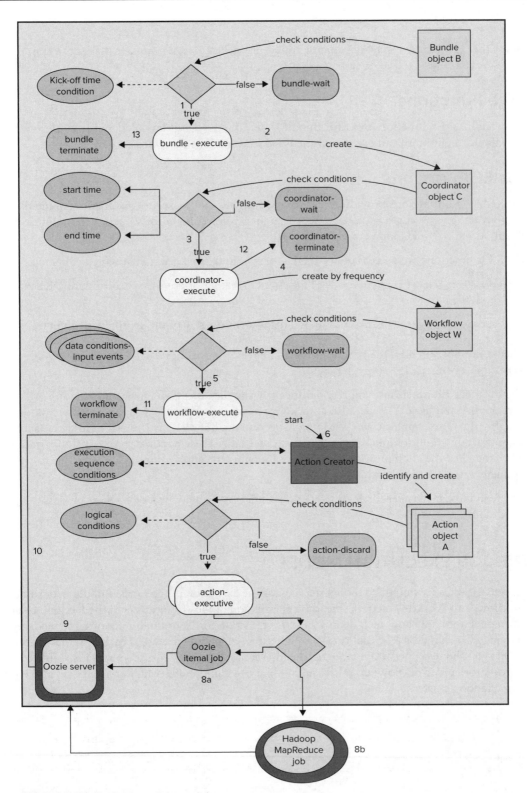

FIGURE 6-10: Oozie execution model

The execution model contains the following types of objects (those objects that represent jobs, not applications):

> Executable objects representing Oozie jobs (actions):

  > Bundle objects

  > Coordinator objects

  > Workflow objects (the complete Workflow DAG)

  > Workflow action objects

> Conditional objects defined in Oozie applications:

  > Data conditions for Coordinator objects (expressed via data sets and input events)

  > Time conditions for Coordinator objects (expressed via start, end, and frequency)

  > Logical conditions for action objects (expressed with data-flow nodes)

  > Execution sequence conditions for action objects (expressed via graph of nodes in Workflow)

  > Concurrency conditions for Coordinator objects

Executable objects can be associated with conditions that are either satisfied or not satisfied. For example, the execution sequence condition for an action is satisfied if and only if all preceding actions in the Workflow DAG have been executed. Each executable object can be in one of two states:

> **Wait state** — It is waiting for conditions to be met before starting execution.

> **Execution state** — It is actually executing.

An object transition from wait state to the execution state occurs when all preconditions associated with that object are satisfied.

Some executable objects are associated with asynchronous actions (such as `java` actions, `map-reduce` actions, `pig` actions, `hive` actions, and `sqoop` actions), and, as a result, are further associated with Hadoop jobs. Other executable objects are associated with synchronous actions (such as `fs` actions, `ssh` actions, and `email` actions), and are executed directly on the Oozie server.

The Oozie execution model has global scope attributes (such as time), Coordinator scope attributes (such as Coordinator action concurrency, start time, and end time), Workflow scope attributes (defined and modified in Workflows), and action scope attributes (defined and modified in actions).

In the execution model, Oozie objects (based on their types) belong to one of the following levels:

> **Bundle objects** — These are nothing more than a set of Coordinator objects without any conditions. Bundle objects are created by the Oozie server from Bundle applications based on conditions specified there (`kick-off-time`).

> **Coordinator objects** — Each Coordinator object references one Workflow object, and it can define conditions for that Workflow object. Coordinator objects are created by the Oozie server from the Coordinator applications based on time conditions (start, end, and frequency). Coordinator objects can be waiting for the data and concurrency conditions to

be satisfied before the appropriate Workflow object will be created. Coordinator objects can be associated with time conditions, data conditions (input events), concurrency conditions, and the Bundle in which they are contained.

➤ **Workflow objects** — A Workflow object contains a complete DAG of action nodes specifying execution and control-flow nodes, which govern the execution sequence and logical conditions. Workflow objects are created by the Oozie server from the standalone Workflow applications or from Bundle objects. Workflow objects can be associated with time conditions, Coordinator objects, or action objects.

➤ **Action objects** — These are created by the Oozie server from the Workflow objects. An action object represents an Oozie Workflow action, and can be associated with a Workflow object, logical conditions, and execution sequence conditions.

➤ **Hadoop jobs** — Hadoop jobs represent a unit of the Hadoop job associated with specific Workflow actions.

As shown in Figure 6-10, the execution model defines the way all these objects interact:

1. The Bundle objects are created and moved to execution state based on specified time condition (`kick-off-time`).

2. When Bundle object B is in the execution state, Coordinator objects specified in Bundle object B are created based on time conditions specified for those objects (start time, end time, and frequency).

3. The Coordinator object C is moved to an execution state when all data and concurrency conditions associated with C are satisfied. (Those can include the presence of specific data set instances and level of concurrency for other instances of the same Coordinator object type.)

4. A Workflow object W is created when the parent Coordinator object is moved to the execution state.

5. Once a Workflow object W is created, the Coordinator waits for all the preconditions for workflow execution to be satisfied.

6. At that moment, the first action object A of the Workflow is created and moved to the execution state.

7. When any action object A is moved to the execution state, the job specified in the action is analyzed.

8. If it is a synchronous action, it is executed directly on the Oozie server. If it is an asynchronous action, a corresponding job is submitted to the Hadoop cluster.

9. The Oozie server waits for completion of the currently executing action. (Under certain conditions such as a `join` activity, a Workflow waits for the completion of several activities before it can proceed.)

10. After action object execution is completed, the Oozie server analyzes the Workflow and takes an appropriate action. In the case of a `fork-join`, the Oozie server can wait until all action objects in the `fork` section complete execution (logical condition). The Oozie server then selects the next action to be executed (sequence condition), creates the action object A, and moves it into the executable state.

11. When a Workflow reaches the end node, a Workflow object W is terminated.

12. When the Workflow object associated with Coordinator C is terminated, Coordinator C is terminated as well.

13. Bundle object B checks whether more Coordinator objects are currently in the execution state. If so, nothing is done; otherwise, Bundle object B terminates.

Knowing Oozie's main components and the way they can be used is necessary for developing Oozie applications, but that is not enough for you to begin using Oozie. You must also know how to access the Oozie server so that you can deploy the components and interact with Oozie jobs that are running. In the next section, you learn what kinds of APIs the Oozie engine provides, and how to view the execution of Oozie jobs by using the Oozie console.

ACCESSING OOZIE

Oozie provides three basic programmatic ways for accessing the Oozie server:

➤ **Oozie Web Services APIs (HTTP, REST, JSON API)** — These provide full administrative and job management capabilities. Oozie Web Services APIs are used by Oozie tools, such as the Oozie execution console (which is examined in more detail later in this chapter).

➤ **Oozie CLI tool** — This is built on top of Web Services APIs and enables you to perform all common Workflow job operations. CLI APIs are typically used by administrators to manage Oozie execution, and by developers to script Oozie invocations.

➤ **Oozie Java Client APIs** — These are built on top of Web Services APIs and enable you to perform all common Workflow job operations. Additionally, the Client API includes a LocalOozie class that you may find useful for testing an Oozie from within an IDE, or for unit testing purposes. Java APIs provide a basis for integrating Oozie with other applications.

In addition to programmatic access, Oozie provides a convenient web application — the Oozie console shown in Figure 6-11.

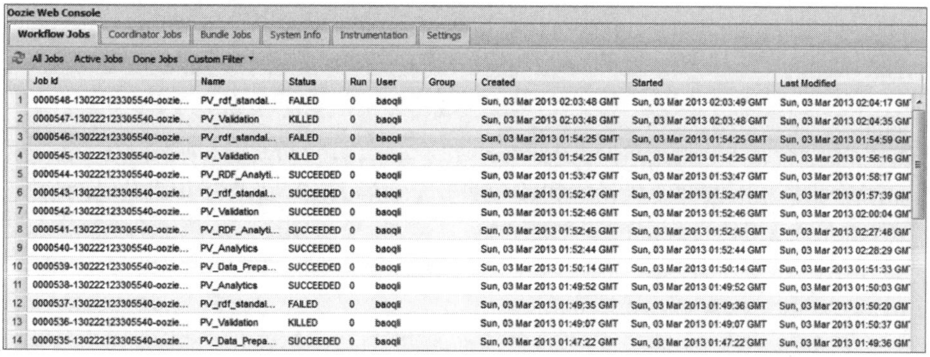

FIGURE 6-11: Oozie console

The basic view of the Oozie console lists currently running and completed Oozie jobs. (Using the tabs at the top of the screen, you can choose to view Workflow, Coordinator, or Bundle jobs.) For every job, you see the job ID, job name, completion status, run number, username, group name, start time, and last modified time. Clicking anywhere on the line for a job brings up a job detail view, as shown at Figure 6-12.

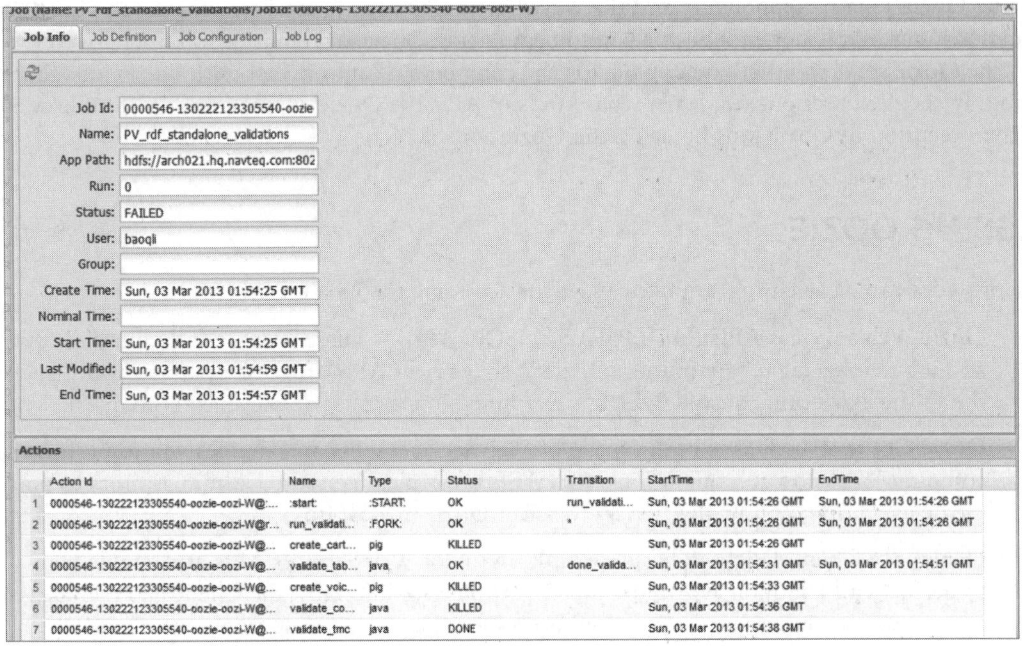

FIGURE 6-12: Oozie job execution details

This view enables you to see all the job-related information, and is generally useful for obtaining information about specific job execution. The top part of the screen contains several tabs that allow you to see overall information about the Oozie job, including job info, definition, configuration, and log. The bottom part of this screen contains information about job actions (specific to Workflow jobs). For every action, it provides basic information that includes action ID, its name, type, status, transition that was taken, start time, and end time.

> **NOTE** *Chapters 7 and 8 provide detailed examples of how these access methods can be used for starting and viewing Oozie jobs, along with the integration of Oozie jobs with the rest of the enterprise system.*

Next you look at another important Oozie component — support for the Oozie Service Level Agreement (SLA).

OOZIE SLA

A *Service Level Agreement* (SLA) is a standard part of a software contract that specifies the quality of the product in measurable terms. More specifically, an SLA is often determined by business requirements, and depends on the nature of the software. For example, for an online web-based application, the SLA may include the average response time, as well as the maximum response time in 99 percent of requests, or system availability (for example, the system is available 95.95 percent of the time).

In an automated and auto-recovering environment such as Oozie, a traditional SLA may not be applicable, whereas some specific SLAs can make sense. Following are some SLA requirements that could be important for jobs running under Oozie control:

➤ Have some of the job instances been delayed (relative to a time specified in the Coordinator), and how long were the delays?

➤ Have some of the job instance execution times been outside specified limits, and how much were the deviations?

➤ What is the frequency and percentage of violating the start time and execution time?

➤ Did some job instances fail?

Oozie SLA provides a way to define, store, and track the desired SLA information for Oozie activities. The term "Oozie activity" here refers to any possible entity that can be tracked in different Oozie functional subsystems (for example, Coordinator and Workflow jobs and actions, Hadoop jobs submitted from Oozie, and so on). Currently, the Bundle specification does not support Oozie SLA.

> **NOTE** *The Oozie SLA subsystem is not a process monitoring tool. It is Oozie's built-in support for tracking SLA. You can implement a process monitoring system external to an Oozie server that leverages Oozie-recorded SLA information.*

Oozie SLA can be specified in the scope of a Coordinator application, Workflow application, and Workflow action. The specification becomes part of (Coordinator or Workflow) application definition, and is expressed as a fragment of an XML document. The SLA language is specified with the XML schema, as shown in Figure 6-13.

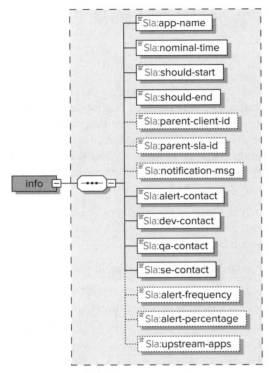

FIGURE 6-13: SLA language schema

Table 6-7 describes the main Oozie SLA elements.

TABLE 6-7: Description of Oozie SLA Elements

ELEMENT NAME	DESCRIPTION
Info	This is the root element of SLA definitions for Workflow or Coordinator.
app-name	This represents logical names with no namespace segregation done. It is up to the application developers to come up with a meaningful naming partition. For example, a package-naming structure similar to that used in Java could be used. The natural way to specify the value of an element in SLA is ${wf:name()}, or with the Coordinator application name.
nominal-time	This is the time specified in coordinator.xml to start a Coordinator action. In many cases, the value used for this element is ${coord:nominalTime()}.
should-start	This is the expected start time for this activity relative to nominal-time. For example, if the actual action is expected to start five minutes after the Coordinator job starts, the value can be specified as <sla:should-start>${5 *MINUTES}</sla:should-start>.

should-end	This is the expected end time for this SLA relative to nominal-time. For example, if an action is normally supposed to end two hours after the Coordinator job starts, the value can be specified as <sla:should-end>${2 * HOURS}</sla:should-end>.
parent-client-id, parent-sla-id	Processing entities (for example, Oozie Coordinator actions) may create/execute processing sub-entities (for example, Oozie Workflow jobs), and processing sub-entities may create/execute smaller processing sub-entities (for example, Oozie Workflow actions). Knowing that a processing sub-entity missed an SLA requirement may help to proactively identify bigger processing entities that may miss SLA requirements. SLAs traversing from a higher entity to a lower sub-entity may help you proactively identify SLA issues. An SLA violation for some processing entity may alert you to what else may be impacted because of the SLA miss.
	The hierarchical information could also be used by any monitoring system to ignore SLA alerts for processing sub-entities if an alert for a higher processing entity has been triggered already. Parent-child relationships of SLA activities can be leveraged by the monitoring system to provide a holistic navigation through SLA activities.
notification-msg, upstream-apps	This is additional information that can be appended to the SLA event.
alert-contact, dev-contact, qa-contact, se-contact	These are elements specifying contact information for each role. By providing the contact as part of the SLA registration event, any monitoring system will not have to deal with any registration/management of applications and e-mails. Applications that want to change the contact information must do this in the application SLA information.

Specifying SLA requirements as part of the definition of activities themselves allows for simpler reading of the overall definition — both execution and SLA information are kept together.

When the SLA is included in Workflow/Coordinator definitions, each invocation of a corresponding action results in recording SLA information into the oozie.SLA_EVENTS table in the Oozie database. Figure 6-14 shows the SLA_EVENTS table definition.

This table contains a field for each SLA XSD element, and some additional fields used for internal bookkeeping. The mapping between XSD elements and corresponding fields is straightforward, with the exceptions noted in Table 6-8.

Column Name	Data Type	Type Name	Column Size
event_id	-5	BIGINT	19
alert_contact	12	VARCHAR	255
alert_frequency	12	VARCHAR	255
alert_percentage	12	VARCHAR	255
app_name	12	VARCHAR	255
dev_contact	12	VARCHAR	255
group_name	12	VARCHAR	255
job_data	-1	TEXT	65535
notification_msg	-1	TEXT	65535
parent_client_id	12	VARCHAR	255
parent_sla_id	12	VARCHAR	255
qa_contact	12	VARCHAR	255
se_contact	12	VARCHAR	255
sla_id	12	VARCHAR	255
upstream_apps	-1	TEXT	65535
user_name	12	VARCHAR	255
bean_type	12	VARCHAR	31
app_type	12	VARCHAR	255
event_type	12	VARCHAR	255
expected_end	93	DATETIME	19
expected_start	93	DATETIME	19
job_status	12	VARCHAR	255
status_timestamp	93	DATETIME	19

FIGURE 6-14: SLA_EVENTS table

TABLE 6-8: Special Mapping between XSD and SLA_EVENTS Table

XSD ELEMENT	TABLE COLUMN
`nominal-time`	No column
`should-start`	`expected_start = nominal-time + should_start`
`should-end`	`expected_end = nominal-time + should_end`

As shown in Table 6-8, the `nominal-time` element is not mapped to any column. Instead, the value written into the `expected_start` column is calculated as a sum of the value specified in the `nominal-time` element, plus an offset specified in the `should-start` element. Similarly, `expected_end` is calculated as `nominal-time` plus `should-end`.

Additionally, the SLA_EVENTS table includes the field `status_timestamp` that contains the timestamp of an SLA recording.

The `sla_id` field contains a foreign key to the tables COORD_JOBS and COORD_ACTIONS. These tables contain all temporal and state information for all Coordinator actions. Additionally, the table COORD_ACTIONS contains the foreign keys to the tables WF_JOBS and WF_ACTIONS, which contain all temporal and state characteristics for Workflow actions. As a result, using the field `sla_id` from the SLA_EVENTS table allows you to link an SLA event with Coordinator and Workflow jobs, as shown in Figure 6-15.

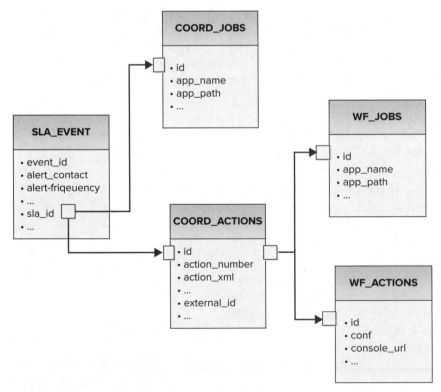

FIGURE 6-15: Oozie ER navigation from SLA_EVENTS table

Table 6-9 shows some of the fields in the SLA_EVENTS table inserted by Oozie.

TABLE 6-9: SLA_EVENTS Fields Populated Automatically by Oozie

FIELD	COMMENT
bean_type	This is the Java class responsible for logging data into the SLA_EVENTS table. The default class is SLAEventBean. It is possible to customize Oozie to use your own class for logging SLA events.
app_type	Possible values for this field include COORDINATOR_ACTION, WORKFLOW_JOB, and WORKFLOW_ACTION.
job_status	Possible values for this field include CREATED, STARTED, and SUCCEEDED. This corresponds to the different life-cycle phases of an Oozie action under SLA. Normally, each action has several records in the SLA_EVENTS table, with each record corresponding to one particular phase of the life cycle.

Other fields include group_name, user_name, and status_timestamp.

Table fields in SLA_EVENTS (which correspond to the SLA XSD elements) are filed by Oozie based on the content of the SLA fragment of the Workfow or Coordinator. You can use Workflow and Coordinator ELs to make this content dynamic.

In addition, Oozie supports access to current SLA information through the Oozie CLI to allow specific SLA queries.

By default, Oozie SLA is disabled. It can be enabled by registering SLA XSD with Oozie. You do this by adding a reference to sla.xsd to oozie-site.xml, as shown in Listing 6-9.

LISTING 6-9: Enabling Oozie SLA

```
<property>
        <name>oozie.service.SchemaService.wf.ext.schemas</name>
        <value>oozie-sla-0.1.xsd </value>
</property>
```

SUMMARY

This chapter has provided a broad overview of the main components of the Oozie server, their capabilities, and the way they interact with each other. The discussion showed the base functionality of Oozie Workflow, Coordinator, and Bundle components, as well as the functionality each provides.

You also learned about the Oozie Expression Language that allows you to parameterize Oozie job definitions with variables, built-in constants, and built-in functions. Additionally, you learned about Oozie APIs that provide both programmatic and manual access to the Oozie engine's functionality, and can be used for starting, controlling, and interacting with Oozie's job executions. Finally, you learned about Oozie SLA and the way it allows you to collect information about Oozie job execution.

This chapter covered a lot of territory. To bring together all this information, and to familiarize you with some programming details not covered in this overview, Chapter 7 provides a concrete example to lead you through a step-by-step description of how to build and execute Oozie Workflow, Coordinator, and SLA applications.

7

Using Oozie

WHAT'S IN THIS CHAPTER?

➤ Designing an Oozie application

➤ Implementing Oozie Workflows

➤ Implementing Oozie Coordinator applications

➤ Implementing an Oozie Bundle

➤ Understanding how to deploy, test, and execute Oozie applications

WROX.COM CODE DOWNLOADS FOR THIS CHAPTER

The wrox.com code downloads for this chapter are found at www.wiley.com/go/
prohadoopsolutions on the Download Code tab. The code is in the Chapter 7 download.
All the downloads for this chapter are provided as a single Eclipse project containing all of the
example's code.

In Chapter 6, you learned about Oozie's main components and their functionality. Oozie is
a large, complicated system, and the simplest way to explain how you use it in real-world
applications is to show an end-to-end example.

In this chapter, you learn how to design and implement all kinds of Oozie jobs (including
Workflow, Coordinator, and Bundle jobs). You learn some implementation approaches for
Oozie Workflow actions, and trade-offs that you must consider. You also learn how to install
and invoke different types of Oozie jobs, and how to interact with them using the Oozie
console.

The end-to-end implementation presented here showcases most of the Oozie capabilities
and explains typical Oozie usage. Throughout the chapter, you build the end-to-end
implementation step-by-step to help solve a real-world problem. Let's start with a description
of the problem that you will be solving.

VALIDATING INFORMATION ABOUT PLACES USING PROBES

The problem discussed in this chapter relates to the validation of information about places by using probes. Before delving into the problem that you will be solving, let's establish a few definitions.

Places or *points of interest* are specific locations that may be important to some people. Those locations are additionally associated with data that explains what is interesting or important about them. These are typically locations where people come for entertainment, interaction, services, education, and other types of social activities. Examples of places include restaurants, museums, theaters, stadiums, hotels, landmarks, and so on. Many companies gather data about places and use this data in their applications.

In the telecommunications industry, *probes* are small packages of information sent from mobile devices. The majority of "smartphones" send probes regularly when the device is active and is running a geographical application (such as maps, navigation, traffic reports, and so on). The probe frequency varies for different providers (from 5 seconds to 30 seconds). Probes are normally directed to phone carriers such as Verizon, Sprint, AT&T, and/or phone manufacturers such as Apple, Nokia, HTC, and so on.

The exact format and set of attributes included in a probe depend on the provider, but the core attributes usually included in each probe are device ID, timestamp, latitude, longitude, speed, direction of movement, and service provider. The device ID randomly changes over a specified time interval (for example, 5 minutes). Probes are widely used for traffic analysis, but, in this chapter, you use probes in connection with places.

The information about places is received from different providers (such as McDonalds, Starbucks, or Marriott hotel chains), or from websites specially designed to gather information from the community. This information can be partially incorrect to start with, or it can change over time. Existing places can move to new locations, close, or change attributes. New places are continuously coming into existence.

Probes can be a useful tool for validation of the information about places. By the very definition of places, people should come there and stay there for some time. Consequently, place locations should correspond to probe *clusters* — that is, congestions of probes around places.

> **NOTE** Clustering *is grouping of a set of objects based on a similarity (similarity can mean different things in different clustering problems). With clustering, objects in a given cluster are more similar to each other than to objects in other clusters.*

Place validation is a complex, multi-step process that requires the coordinated execution of multiple MapReduce jobs, and monitoring the conditions under which they are executed. Additionally, place validation must be executed on a regular basis (preferably without user intervention) — that is, provided the data for execution is ready.

Let's get started with implementation design.

DESIGNING PLACE VALIDATION BASED ON PROBES

Assume that you have a probes repository (such a repository can easily be petabytes in size) and a places repository (such repository can easily be hundreds of terabytes). The following seem to be reasonable steps for implementing a probe-based place validation:

1. Select probes data for a specified time interval, as well as a location from the probes repository.

2. Extract *probes strands*. The idea here is to discover groups of probes from a particular device that belong to an individual who spent some time in one location. More precisely, a usual technique here includes classifying probes strands (such as pedestrians or traffic) and extracting "stay points" from pedestrian strands. However, for the sake of simplicity, those details are not incorporated in this chapter's example.

3. Distribute the strands into geotiles. In practice, it is convenient to use several geotile systems in parallel with different tile sizes (geohash levels).

> **NOTE** Geotiling *is the partitioning of a space into a finite number of distinct shapes. This implementation uses equal-sized bounding boxes. A zoom level defines the size of the tiles. Typically, for the zoom level* n, *the number of tiles for the world is* 2^n.

4. Distribute the places into geotiles.

5. Calculate a *location attendance index*. The location attendance index captures the number of strands located in the proximity of a location, usually associated with a group of places. That enables you to estimate how many people attend places, how long people remain in places, and the distribution of these parameters over time.

6. Cluster stay points by geographical locations, and use clusters not associated with the currently known places for discovery of new place candidates.

Before proceeding with process design, take a look at some additional considerations for this sample implementation:

➤ Information is changing over time — new probes arrive, place information changes, and so on. This means that the overall process should run periodically to be able to use this new information.

➤ Probe and place information is dynamic, and is constantly changing. This means that data preparation typically runs on a different schedule than the actual data processing.

➤ Calculating a place attendance index is a validation function, and is typically more important than clustering strands (which is a predictive operation). Consequently, the two should be calculated with different frequency.

➤ Data preparation processes for both probes and places can be reused in other applications.

➤ Each step should report failure (if it occurs) through e-mail.

> **BEST PRACTICES FOR DESIGNING OOZIE WORKFLOWS**
>
> When designing Oozie Workflows, try to follow best practices for code reuse. Based on these best practices, Workflows should be large enough to encapsulate complete business functionality. On the other hand, similar to any other software development, the larger the process is, the more difficult it is to debug and maintain it.
>
> This means that Oozie Workflow design is a compromise between trying to keep a process as small as possible, and ensuring that it implements a complete business function.
>
> If the business functionality of the process is fairly large, one of the common process design practices is componentization, based on the use of sub-processes (sub-Workflows, in the case of Oozie).

Based on all these requirements, the overall solution to validating places information using probes requires the implementation of three Workflow processes:

➤ Prepare data.

➤ Calculate a place attendance index.

➤ Calculate a cluster strand.

Each of these processes requires its own coordination application to define its execution frequency, as well as input and output events. Finally, a Bundle application can bring the entire execution together in a single data pipeline.

Let's now take a look at Workflow design for this problem.

DESIGNING OOZIE WORKFLOWS

Figure 7-1 shows the first Workflow process. This data preparation Workflow process contains fork and join nodes, thus allowing the data preparation for places and probes to be executed in parallel.

Data preparation for places involves two steps that must be executed sequentially. The first step selects place data for a given area, and is implemented using a Hive query. The second step is geotiling place information, and is a MapReduce job implemented here as a `java` action. (You learn more detail about this decision later in this chapter.)

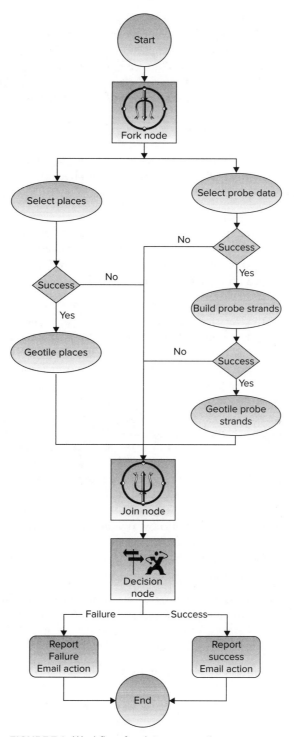

FIGURE 7-1: Workflow for data preparation

> **NOTE** *Although the rest of the book does not cover Hive and Pig (see Chapters 2 and 13) for more information), to show Oozie capabilities here, it is assumed that some of the actions are implemented using Hive and Pig to show how those technologies can be used with Oozie. Because the actual Hive and Pig scripts shown here are very simple, no knowledge of either Hive or Pig is required to follow the example.*

Data preparation for probes contains three steps that must be executed sequentially. The first step selects probe data for a given area, and is implemented as a Hive query. The second step builds probe strands, and is implemented as a Pig script. Finally, the geotiling step is implemented the same way as the probes' geotiling step described previously.

All business steps are happening inside the "fork-join" section, which starts from the Fork node shown in Figure 7-1 and ends with the Join node. At the end of every step, the Workflow checks whether the step has completed successfully. If it has, the control is transferred to the next step. Otherwise, control transferred immediately to the Join node.

After the Join node, the Decision node determines whether any error has happened in any previous step. If an error happened, the Decision node transitions control to the Report Failure node, which sends the error notification via an e-mail. This e-mail would include the exact reason for the failure, as well as details on the step where the failure occurred. Otherwise, the Decision node transitions control to the Report Success node, which sends the success notification e-mail.

> **NOTE** *The majority of actions in the data preparation Workflow are "business actions" — in other words, they implement application functionality as described earlier in this chapter. An exception here is the success/error notification implemented by using an Oozie built-in (extension)* email *action, and the error diagnostics implemented using the Oozie flow-control Decision node.*

As shown in Figure 7-2, the attendance Workflow (which calculates the attendance index) is very simple. Its main action is to calculate the attendance index is implemented as a `pig` action. This Workflow also checks whether or not this action's execution failed. If the action did fail, the Workflow sends an error e-mail to staff; otherwise, it sends a success e-mail.

Figure 7-3 shows the third process for solving this real-world problem. This main activity of the cluster Workflow process is to calculate cluster strands, which is implemented as a MapReduce job with a `java` action node. This process also checks whether execution of this action succeeds (and sends a success e-mail) or fails (and sends an error e-mail).

Now that the Workflow design is complete, you must implement the processes. Unfortunately, Oozie does not provide a graphical process designer, so the translation from process design to an actual implementation must be done manually.

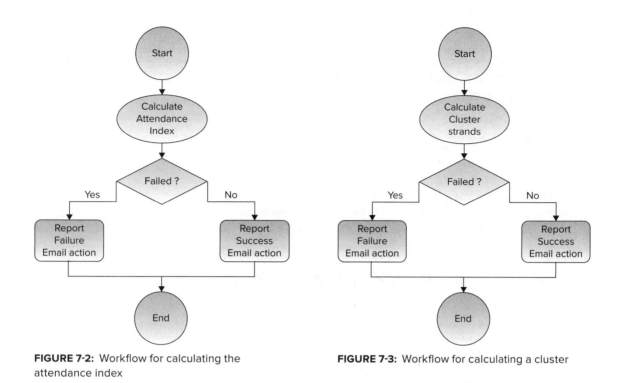

FIGURE 7-2: Workflow for calculating the attendance index

FIGURE 7-3: Workflow for calculating a cluster

IMPLEMENTING OOZIE WORKFLOW APPLICATIONS

Before proceeding to the process implementation, assume that java, hive, and pig actions used in the previously described Workflows are implemented using corresponding Java classes, hdl scripts (Hive), or Pig Latin scripts shown in Table 7-1.

TABLE 7-1: Programming Artifacts for Actions in Workflows

ACTION NAME	TYPE	JAVA CLASS/PIG OR HIVE SCRIPT	MAIN JAR AND ADDITIONAL JARS
select-probes	hive	CLUSTER/selectProbes.hql	
select-places	hive	CLUSTER/selectPlaces.hql	
build strands	pig	CLUSTER/strands.pig	
geotile-strands	java	com.practicalHadoop.geotile. Strands	chapter7*.jar, *.jar
geotile-places	java	com.practicalHadoop.geotile. Places	chapter7*.jar, *.jar

continues

TABLE 7-1 *(continued)*

ACTION NAME	TYPE	JAVA CLASS/PIG OR HIVE SCRIPT	MAIN JAR AND ADDITIONAL JARS
calculate attendance index	pig	CLUSTER/attendInd.pig	
calculate cluster strands	java	com.practicalHadoop.strands. Cluster	chapter7*.jar, *.jar

To keep the code fragments shown in the remainder of this chapter manageable, the example implementation is enhanced incrementally. It starts with complete implementations, omitting many of the details. Then, more implementation details are added iteratively as the discussion (and solution implementation) progresses.

Implementing the Data Preparation Workflow

Start by building the `data-prep-wf` Workflow for the data preparation process shown in Figure 7-1. Listing 7-1 (code file: `dataPrepWf.xml`) shows the skeleton of the `data-prep-wf` Workflow.

LISTING 7-1: Workflow for the data preparation process

```xml
<?xml version="1.0" encoding="UTF-8"?>
<workflow-app name='data-prep-wf' xmlns='uri:oozie:workflow:0.3'
    xmlns:sla="uri:oozie:sla:0.1">
    <start to='prep-fork'/>
    <fork name="prep-fork">
        <path start="select-probes"/>
        <path start="select-places"/>
    </fork>
    <action name='select-probes'>
<hive xmlns="uri:oozie:hive-action:0.2"> [HIVE ACTION BODY] </hive>
        <ok to="build-strands"/>
        <error to="prep-join"/>
    </action>
    <action name='build-strands'>
        <pig> [PIG ACTION BODY] </pig>
        <ok to="geotile-strands"/>
        <error to="prep-join"/>
        <sla:info> [SLA SECTION] </sla:info>
    </action>
    <action name='geotile-strands'>
        <java> [JAVA ACTION BODY] </java>
        <ok to="prep-join"/>
        <error to="prep-join"/>
        <sla:info> [SLA SECTION] </sla:info>
    </action>
    <action name='select-places'>
```

```
    <hive xmlns="uri:oozie:hive-action:0.2"> [HIVE ACTION BODY] </hive>
            <ok to="geotile-places"/>
            <error to="prep-join"/>
        </action>
        <action name='geotile-places'>
            <java> [JAVA ACTION BODY] </java>
            <ok to="prep-join"/>
            <error to="prep-join"/>
            <sla:info> [SLA SECTION] </sla:info>
        </action>
        <join name="prep-join" to="report-success"/>
        <decision name="check-err">
            <switch>
                <case to "report-failure">${wf:lastErrorNode() != null}</case>
                <default to="report-success"/>
            </switch>
        </decision >
        <action name='report-success'>
            <email xmlns="uri:oozie:email-action:0.1"> [EMAIL ACTION BODY] </email>
            <ok to="end"/>
            <error to="fail"/>
        </action>
        <action name='determine-error'>
            <java> [JAVA ACTION BODY] </java>
            <ok to="report-failure"/>
            <error to="fail"/>
        </action>
        <action name='report-failure'>
            <email xmlns="uri:oozie:email-action:0.1"> [EMAIL ACTION BODY] </email>
            <ok to="fail"/>
            <error to="fail"/>
        </action>
        <kill name="fail">
    <message>
    validate-places-wf failed, error message: [${wf:errorMessage(wf:lastErrorNode())}]
    </message>
        </kill>
        <end name="end"/>
        <sla:info> [SLA SECTION] </sla:info>
    </workflow-app>
```

Listing 7-1 shows all the Oozie action nodes and flow-control nodes used in this process. For actions, the listing only shows names and types, flow-control definitions, and placeholders for the action body section. Note several things in this implementation:

➤ A start node points to the name of the first node of the implementation — in this case, a fork action.

➤ In the implementation of the fork action, parallel execution is defined by specifying the execution path for every parallel thread.

➤ Every action contains two tags: ok and error. The ok tag defines transition in the case of a successful execution of an activity. The error tag defines transition in the case of a failed execution.

➤ Implementation of the `join` action contains just a name. The actual joining is done by several actions that specify transition to a `join` action.

➤ `<sla:info>` is included in both individual actions and the Workflow as a whole.

As of this writing, the `hive` action and `email` action are extensions to the main Workflow specification (0.3). To enable the Oozie server to understand those extensions, you should place the action schema definition files in the Oozie `conf` directory. The Oozie `oozie-site.xml` file should include the lines shown in Listing 7-2 (this will also include Oozie SLA support).

LISTING 7-2: Extending Oozie schema with definitions for hive action, email action, and SLA

```
<property>
        <name>oozie.service.SchemaService.wf.ext.schemas</name>
        <value>oozie-sla-0.1.xsd,hive-action-0.2.xsd,email-action-0.1.xsd</value>
</property>
```

> **NOTE** *You can find the schemas for* `hive` *and* `email` *actions in the Apache documentation for Oozie (Action Extensions section), and you can find the schema for SLA in the Apache Coordinator specification.*

The overall data preparation Workflow includes multiple actions, including a `java` action, `pig` action, `hive` action, and `email` action. Listing 7-1 shows only action names and types. In reality, to implement these actions in a Workflow, you would need more configuration information. In the following subsections, you learn how to configure each action type.

java Action

Listing 7-3 (code file: `dataPrepWf.xml`) shows the extended definition of the `geotile-strandsjava` action. (Several omitted sections, including PREPARE, CONFIGURATION, and SLA, are presented shortly.) The `geotile-strandsjava` action uses a driver pattern to submit a MapReduce job on a cluster.

> **NOTE** *A driver pattern in MapReduce is a way to use a* `java` *action for submitting a MapReduce job on a cluster. In a driver pattern, the object (class instance) invoked from the* `java` *action on a cluster configures and submits the Hadoop job programmatically. With Oozie, it is also possible to submit a MapReduce job with the* `map-reduce` *action. (Later in this chapter, you learn more about those two approaches.) With Oozie, it is also possible to configure a* `java` *action that does not start any MapReduce job, but operates directly on HDFS or HBase tables using the Hadoop API.*

LISTING 7-3: Oozie java action

```
<action name='geotile-strands'>
<java>
        <job-tracker>${jobTracker}</job-tracker>
        <name-node>${nameNode}</name-node>
        <prepare> [PREPARE SECTION] </prepare>
        <job-xml>${geotileStrandsProperties}</job-xml>
        <configuration> [CONFIGURATION SECTION] </configuration>
        <main-class> com.practicalHadoop.geotile.Strands</main-class>
        <java-opts>${Dopt_loglevel} ${Xopt_jvm}</java-opts>
        <arg>-tileSize=${tileLevel}</arg>
        <arg>-strandCenter=${strandCenter}</arg>
        <arg>-bBox=${bbox}</arg>
        <arg>-strandCardinality=${cardinality}</arg>
        <arg>-centerMethod=${strandCenterMethod}</arg>
<capture-output/>
    </java>
    <ok to="prep-join"/>
    <error to=" prep-join"/>
    <sla:info> [SLA SECTION] </sla:info>
</action>
```

This Oozie `java` action definition first specifies the JobTracker and the NameNode of the Hadoop cluster. (Remember that a `java` action is executed as a MapReduce job.) You use the `<job-xml>` element to specify a location of the action configuration file on HDFS. Configuration parameters for this Oozie action are discussed later in this chapter.

The `<main-class>` element specifies the Java class with the `main()` method that is used as a starting point for executing the action code in the Hadoop job. The `<java-opts>` element enables you to override JVM options.

In Listing 7-3, the `<java-opts>` element uses an EL expression to define the `logLevel` parameter, and the `java` options. An action definition can contain only one `<java-opts>` element.

The `<arg>` element enables you to specify a parameter for a Java program started with `java` action. In Listing 7-3, the `tileSize` named parameter is defined with the `${tileLevel}` EL expression. Again, this assumes that the value for the property `tileLevel` is already defined. A `java` action can have multiple `<arg>` elements.

The `<capture-output/>` element specifies to Oozie that this `java` action will return some data (name/value pairs of strings) that will be placed in the Workflow execution context. This data becomes a part of Workflow execution context, and is available to the other actions in the same Workflow. This feature is described in more detail later in this chapter.

<prepare> Element

An Oozie action might require some preconditions — for example, that some specific directory structure on HDFS be present. The `<prepare>` element of an action enables you to define the functionality that ensures these preconditions will be fulfilled. For example, remember that the output directory for the MapReduce job should not exist when a MapReduce job starts. You can use the `<prepare>` element to explicitly delete this directory before starting a MapReduce job.

Listing 7-4 demonstrates the content of the `<prepare>` element in the `geotile-strands java` action.

LISTING 7-4: Oozie action `<prepare>` element

```
<prepare>
     <delete path="${strandsTilesPathTmp}"/>
     <delete path="${strandsTilesPathOut}"/>
     <mkdir path="${strandsTilesPathTmp}"/>
</prepare>
```

In this listing, the `<prepare>` element instructs Oozie to delete and then re-create the directory specified by the `${strandsTilesPathTmp}` expression. It then instructs Oozie to delete the directory specified with the `${strandsTilesPathOut}` expression (which is presumed to be the output directory of the MapReduce job).

`<configuration>` Element

This Oozie Workflow enables you to define the execution parameters for individual actions in the `<configuration>` element, as shown in Listing 7-5.

LISTING 7-5: Oozie action `<configuration>` element

```
<configuration>
     <property>
           <name>pool.name</name>
           <value>ARCHITECTURE</value>
     </property>
     <property>
           <name>oozie.launcher.pool.name</name>
           <value>ARCHITECTURE</value>
     </property>
     <property>
           <name>oozie.launcher.mapred.job.priority</name>
           <value>HIGH</value>
     </property>
     <property>
           <name>mapred.job.priority</name>
           <value>HIGH</value>
     </property>
     <property>
           <name>spatial4jVer</name>
           <value>5.2</value>
     </property>
</configuration>
```

In Listing 7-5, the `<configuration>` element specifies the fair scheduler parameters for the `geotile-strands java` action (that is, pool names and priorities). Additionally, it specifies the version of `spatial4j` library for the `geotile-strands` action in the `spatial4jVer` property.

<sla:info> Element

As you learned in Chapter 6, a Service Level Agreement (SLA) is the standard part of a service contract that specifies the quality of service in measurable terms. More specifically, the SLA is determined by business requirements, and depends on the nature of the service.

Oozie jobs and corresponding Hadoop jobs belong to the category of *batch jobs*. The distributed nature of those jobs and highly automated management of resources and failover provided by the Hadoop framework dictate the specifics of the Oozie SLA (as discussed in Chapter 6). Listing 7-6 shows an example SLA definition for the geotile-strands action that leverages all SLA features provided by Oozie.

LISTING 7-6: Oozie action <sla:info> element

```
<sla:info>
     <sla:app-name> geotile-strands </sla:app-name>
     <sla:nominal-time>${startExtract}</sla:nominal-time>
     <sla:should-start>${5 * MINUTES}</sla:should-start>
     <sla:should-end>${15 * MINUTES}</sla:should-end>
     <sla:parent-client-id> data-prep-wf </sla:parent-client-id>
     <sla:parent-sla-id> validate-places </sla:parent-sla-id>
     <sla:notification-msg>
notification for action: geotile-strands</sla:notification-msg>
     <sla:alert-contact>sla.alert@team.com</sla:alert-contact>
     <sla:dev-contact>sla>dev@team.com</sla:dev-contact>
     <sla:qa-contact>sla.qa@team.com</sla:qa-contact>
<sla:se-contact>sla.se@team.com</sla:se-contact>
     <sla:alert-frequency> ${24 * LAST_HOUR} </sla:alert-frequency>
     <sla:alert-percentage>90</sla:alert-percentage>
     <sla:upstream-apps> places </sla:upstream-apps>
</sla:info>
```

The example shown in Listing 7-6 specifies the expected start time (<sla:nominal-time>), delay threshold (<sla:should-start>), and expected completion time (<sla:should-end>). As discussed in Chapter 6, by using information from other Oozie database tables, the monitoring system can control the violations of those conditions.

Other <sla:info> sub-elements here are used to specify the content and addresses for notification about SLA violations. Note that the sla prefix is defined in the xmlns:sla="uri:oozie:sla:0.1" namespace, included as an attribute in the <workflow-app> element in Listing 7-1.

Now that you know how to use and configure the java action, let's take a look at the pig action.

pig Action

As you learned in Chapter 2, Apache Pig is framework (sometimes referred to as a *platform*) that was developed for analyzing large data sets. Pig consists of a high-level language for expressing data analysis in programs, coupled with an infrastructure for executing these programs. Pig offers a high-level language (Pig Latin) to specify highly parallelized data processing on Hadoop clusters, thus leveraging the MapReduce framework.

Oozie provides support for Pig applications in the form of `pig` actions. The Oozie server uses the `pig` action definition to invoke the Pig run time with a specified Pig script and parameters. After that, the Pig run time interprets the script, generates Java code for MapReduce jobs, submits and controls job execution, and eventually returns the status and messages from jobs to the Oozie server.

Listing 7-7 (code file: `dataPrepWf.xml`) shows the definition of the `build-strands` `pig` action. Similar to the `java` action, the `pig` action can use `<prepare>`, `<job-xml>`, `<configuration>`, and `<sla:info>` elements. Those elements play the same role as in the `java` action.

LISTING 7-7: Oozie pig action

```
<action name='build-strands'>
    <pig>
        <job-tracker>${jobTracker}</job-tracker>
        <name-node>${nameNode}</name-node>
        <prepare> [PREPARE SECTION] </prepare>
        <job-xml>${buildStrandsProperties}</job-xml>
        <configuration> [CONFIGURATION SECTION]</configuration>
        <script>/user/practicalHadoop/pig/strands.pig</script>
        <param>-distance=${distance}</param>
        <param>-timeSpan=${timeSpan}</param>
    </pig>
    <ok to="geotile"/>
    <error to="prep-join"/>
    <sla:info> [SLA SECTION] </sla:info>
</action>
```

Following are some differences between the `pig` action and `java` action in this implementation:

➤ Instead of a `<main-class>` element that defines the starting point for the `java` action, the `pig` action contains the `<script>` element that specifies the Pig script on HDFS.

➤ Instead of `<java-opts>` and `<arg>` elements, the `pig` action uses the `<param>` and `<argument>` elements to pass parameters to the Pig script.

➤ The `pig` action cannot return data to the Workflow context, which means that it does not use the `<capture-output/>` element.

hive Action

As you learned in Chapter 2, Hive is a data warehouse system for Hadoop that supports restricted SQL queries against large data sets stored in HDFS and HBase. Hive provides a mechanism to project this data into a table definition, and query the data using a SQL-like language called *HiveQL (HQL)*. Similar to Pig, Hive interprets the HQL script and generates Java code for MapReduce jobs.

Oozie provides support for Hive applications in the form of `hive` actions. The Oozie server uses the `hive` action definition to invoke the Hive run time with the specified HQL script and parameters. After that, the Hive run time interprets the script, generates Java code for MapReduce jobs, submits and controls job execution, and eventually returns the status and messages from jobs to the Oozie server.

Listing 7-8 (code file: `dataPrepWf.xml`) shows the skeleton of the definition of the `select-probes` `hive` action. Similar to a `java` action, a `hive` action can use `<prepare>`, `<job-xml>`, and

`<configuration>` elements. Those elements are used the same way as in the `java` action, and are not examined in detail here for the `hive` action.

LISTING 7-8: Oozie hive action

```
<action name="select-probes">
        <hive xmlns="uri:oozie:hive-action:0.2">
<job-tracker>${jobTracker}</job-tracker>
            <name-node>${nameNode}</name-node>
            <prepare> [PRAPRE SECTION] </prepare>
            <job-xml>${selectProperties}</job-xml>
            <configuration>
            <property>
            <name>oozie.hive.defaults</name>
            <value> ${nameNode}/sharedlib/conf-xml/hive-default.xml </value>
            </property>
[OTHER CONFIGURATION PROPERTIES]
</configuration>
            <script>/user/practicalHadoop/hive/select.hql</script>
            <param>-start=${startTime}</param>
            <param>-end=${endTime}</param>
            <param>-bbox=${bBox}</param>
        </hive>
            <ok to="validate-filter"/>
            <error to="prep-join"/>
</action>
```

The definition of a `hive` action is very similar to the definition of a `pig` action, with the following notable differences:

➤ The `hive` action does not support `<argument>` and `<sla:info>` elements.

➤ The `<configuration>` section of a `hive` action definition should specify the location of the `hive-default.xml` file on HDFS.

> **NOTE** *As of this writing, the* `hive-default.xml` *file (in Hive version 0.7) is not part of the Hive* `jar` *files. So, Oozie needs some way to access it. To accomplish this, Oozie can copy the* `hive-default.xml` *file to the application Workflow directory structure. The location of the file should be specified with the property* `oozie.hive.defaults`. *The path to the file can be absolute, or relative to the application Workflow directory (where the* `workflow.xml` *file is placed). Normally, you can find the original version of the* `hive-default.xml` *file in the* `/usr/hive/conf` *directory on the edge node.*

The Oozie `hive` action is one of Oozie's extension actions. Similar to the case with SLA discussed in Chapter 6, to use `hive` action, you must register the Hive XSD schema definition with the `oozie-site.xml` file (see Listing 7-2 earlier in this chapter). Additionally, you must include the `hive` namespace in the Workflow application, as shown in Listing 7-8 (the `<hive>` element contains the attribute `xmlns="uri:oozie:hive-action:0.2"`).

email Action

You can use Oozie to notify end users about the execution flow of an Oozie job by using an `email`
action. Listing 7-9 (code file: `dataPrepWf.xml`) shows the definition of the `report-failure`
`email` action.

LISTING 7-9: Oozie email action

```xml
<action name="report-failure">
    <email xmlns="uri:oozie:email-action:0.1">
        <to>${EMAIL-ADDRESSES}</to>
        <cc>${EMAIL-CC_ADDRESSES}</cc>
        <subject>validate-places-wf outcome</subject>
        <body>data-prep-wf failed at ${wf:lastErrorNode()} with
            ${wf:errorMessage(wf:lastErrorNode())}</body>
    </email>
    <ok to="fail"/>
    <error to="fail"/>
</action>
```

One interesting detail about the `email` action definition shown in Listing 7-9 is the content of
the `<body>` element. The EL expressions `${wf:lastErrorNode()}` and `${wf:errorMessage
(wf:lastErrorNode())}` use the Oozie native capacity to propagate the error information to all
Workflow nodes.

Similar to the `hive` action, the `email` action is an Oozie extension action. That means that the
`email` action XSD schema definition file should be registered with the `oozie-site.xml` file (see
Listing 7-2 earlier in this chapter), and that the `<email>` element should contain the attribute
`xmlns="uri:oozie:email-action:0.1"`.

Now that you have implemented a data presentation Workflow, you are ready to implement the
other two Workflows to calculate the attendance index and cluster strands.

Implementing Attendance Index
and Cluster Strands Workflows

These two Workflows are very simple and similar to each other. Listing 7-10 (code file:
`attendanceWf.xml`) shows the `attendance-wf` Workflow to calculate the attendance index.

LISTING 7-10: The attendance-wf Workflow application

```xml
<?xml version="1.0" encoding="UTF-8"?>
<workflow-app name="attendance-wf" xmlns="uri:oozie:workflow:0.3"
        xmlns:sla="uri:oozie:sla:0.1">
    <start to="attendance"/>
    <action name="attendance">
        <pig>
            <job-tracker>${jobTracker}</job-tracker>
            <name-node>${nameNode}</name-node>
```

```
            <prepare> [PREPARE SECTION] </prepare>
            <job-xml>${attendanceProperties}</job-xml>
            <configuration> [CONFIGURATION SECTION] </configuration>
            <script>/user/practicalHadoop/pig/attendInd.pig</script>
            <param>-distance=${distance}</param>
            <param>-timeSpan=${timeSpan}</param>
        </pig>
        <ok to="report-success"/>
        <error to="report-failure"/>
        <sla:info> [SLA SECTION] </sla:info>
    </action>
    <action name='report-success'>
        <email xmlns="uri:oozie:email-action:0.1">
            [EMAIL ACTION BODY]
        </email>
        <ok to="end"/>
        <error to="fail"/>
    </action>
    <action name='report-failure'>
        <email xmlns="uri:oozie:email-action:0.1">
            [EMAIL ACTION BODY]
        </email>
        <ok to="fail"/>
        <error to="fail"/>
    </action>
    <kill name="fail">
        <message>
attendance-wf failed, error message: [${wf:errorMessage(wf:lastErrorNode())}]
        </message>
    </kill>
    <end name="end"/>
    <sla:info> [SLA SECTION] </sla:info>
</workflow-app>
```

The `attendance-wf` Workflow application that is shown in Listing 7-10 contains only one asynchronous action — the `attendance pig` action. All elements of this Workflow application are similar to ones discussed earlier in this chapter.

The `cluster-wf` Workflow application shown in Listing 7-11 (code file: `clusterWf.xml`) is very similar to the `attendance-wf` Workflow application.

LISTING 7-11: The cluster-wf Workflow application

```
<workflow-app name="cluster-wf" xmlns="uri:oozie:workflow:0.3"
        xmlns:sla="uri:oozie:sla:0.1">
    <start to="cluster"/>
    <action name="cluster">
        <java>
            <job-tracker>${jobTracker}</job-tracker>
            <name-node>${nameNode}</name-node>
            <prepare> [PRAPRE SECTION] </prepare>
            <job-xml>${clusterProperties}</job-xml>
            <configuration> [CONFIGURATION SECTION] </configuration>
```

continues

LISTING 7-11 *(continued)*

```
                    <main-class>com.practicalHadoop.strand.Cluster</main-class>
                    <java-opts>${Dopt_loglevel} ${Xopt_jvm}</java-opts>
                    <arg>-version=${spatial4jVer}</arg>
                    <arg>-tileSize=${tileLevel}</arg>
                    <arg>-distance=$distance}</arg>
                </java>
                <ok to="report-success"/>
                <error to="report-failure"/>
                <sla:info> [SLA SECTION] </sla:info>
            </action>
            <action name='report-success'>
                <email xmlns="uri:oozie:email-action:0.1">
                    [EMAIL ACTION BODY]
                </email>
                <ok to="end"/>
                <error to="fail"/>
            </action>
            <action name='report-failure'>
                <email xmlns="uri:oozie:email-action:0.1">
                    [EMAIL ACTION BODY]
                </email>
                <ok to="fail"/>
                <error to="fail"/>
            </action>
            <kill name="fail">
                <message>
    cluster-wf failed, error message: [${wf:errorMessage(wf:lastErrorNode())}]
                </message>
            </kill>
            <end name="end"/>
            <sla:info> [SLA SECTION] </sla:info>
        </workflow-app>
```

This Workflow contains only one asynchronous action — the `cluster java` action. All elements of this Workflow application are similar to ones discussed previously in this chapter.

Now that you have seen the implementation of Workflows, let's take a look at the implementation of Workflow activities.

IMPLEMENTING WORKFLOW ACTIVITIES

In general, Oozie does not require special programming for any of the Oozie actions. For example, any existing Pig script or any HQL script can be used as is inside of Oozie actions. The two possible exceptions have to do with Java nodes and MapReduce nodes.

As described earlier in this chapter, Oozie action nodes can consume parameters passed in the form of arguments from the execution context. In addition, Java nodes enable you to pass some of the execution results back to the Workflow execution context for use by other actions.

Let's take a look at how you pass parameters from a `java` action to the execution context.

Populating the Execution Context from a java Action

To enable a `java` action to publish parameters (that is, a map of string name/value pairs), the definition of that action should include the `<capture-output/>` element. Listing 7-12 shows an example of publishing parameters from a `java` action.

LISTING 7-12: Example of publishing parameters from the Oozie java action

```
Properties props = new Properties();
Props. setProperty("height", "7.8");
Props. setProperty("weight", "567");
String oozieProp = System.getProperty("oozie.action.output.properties");
File propFile = new File(oozieProp);
OutputStream os = new FileOutputStream(propFile);
props.store(os, "");
os.close();
```

After this `java` action successfully executes, the parameters `height` and `weight` with the values assigned in the code are available in the Oozie Workflow application, and can be passed to subsequent actions in the form of EL expressions, as shown here:

```
${wf:actionData(troll-recognizer')['height']}
${wf:actionData(troll-recognizer')['weight']}
```

Now, let's discuss options for using MapReduce jobs in Oozie actions.

Using MapReduce Jobs in Oozie Workflows

Oozie provides two different ways of invoking MapReduce jobs — the `java` action implementing a driver pattern, and the `map-reduce` Oozie action.

Invocation of a MapReduce job with a `java` action is somewhat similar to invocation of this job from the edge node using the Hadoop command-line interface (CLI) (as described in Chapter 3). You specify a driver as a class for the Java activity, and Oozie invokes the driver.

On the other hand, using the `map-reduce` action requires a much larger and more complex configuration file, as shown in Listing 7-13.

LISTING 7-13: Oozie map-reduce action

```
<action name='MRSample'>
    <map-reduce>
        <job-tracker>${jobTracker}</job-tracker>
        <name-node>${nameNode}</name-node>
        <prepare>
            <delete path="${prefix}/csv/tmp" />
        </prepare>
        <configuration>
            <property>
```

continues

LISTING 7-13 *(continued)*

```
                    <name>mapred.mapper.new-api</name>
                    <value>true</value>
            </property>
            <property>
                    <name>mapred.reducer.new-api</name>
                    <value>true</value>
            </property>
            <property>
                    <name>mapreduce.map.class</name>
                    <value>[MAPCLASS] </value>
            </property>
            <property>
                    <name>mapreduce.reduce.class</name>
                    <value>[REDUCECLASS] </value>
            </property>
            .......................
        </configuration>
    </map-reduce>
    <ok to="end" />
    <error to="fail" />
</action >
```

The difference between `map-reduce` action and `java` action is that the `map-reduce` action does not include the `<main-class>` element, which does not make sense in this case. Instead, this action's implementation builds the MapReduce job's driver based on the information defined in the action's `configuration` section. This `configuration` section defines all the information typically specified in the MapReduce job's driver (see Chapter 3 for more information), including `mapper` and `reducer` classes, input and output formats, and so on.

When deciding which approach to use, you should consider the normal development cycle from a MapReduce job to an action in an Oozie application, which typically looks like the one shown in Figure 7-4.

At Stages 2 and 3 of the cycle, the driver pattern is the natural option. The driver pattern presumes that the entry point of such an application is some class with the `main()` method. The application is started from the cluster edge node with the `hadoop` command.

At Stage 4 of the cycle (where MapReduce job should be invoked from an Oozie action), it is possible to either use an existing driver as is by using a `java` action, or refactor it for use as an Oozie `map-reduce` action. But that requires development effort, and precludes easily returning to the driver pattern used in Stages 2 and 3. Multiple switches between driver pattern and the `map-reduce` action pattern introduce unnecessary complexity into the development process.

However, by using the driver pattern, you introduce another challenge. The problem with this approach is the fact that Oozie is unaware of the actual MapReduce execution — from its point of view, it just executes a `java` action — which can lead to a "hanging" MapReduce execution. If a Workflow decides to kill a `java` action that invokes a MapReduce job, or the whole Workflow process is killed, it can leave behind MapReduce jobs started by the `java` actions.

You can avoid this problem if you use a Java shutdown hook with the MapReduce driver, as described in Chapter 4.

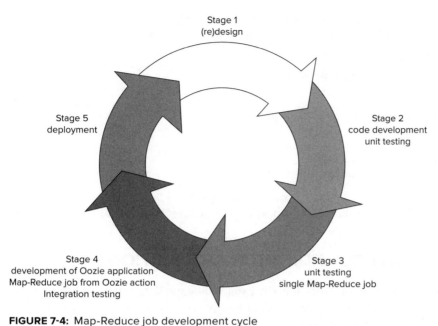

FIGURE 7-4: Map-Reduce job development cycle

Listing 7-14 shows one possible way to implement the shutdown hook with the driver pattern.

LISTING 7-14: Shutdown hook implementation

```
public class DriverHook implements Runnable{
        static public DriverHookNewApi create(Job job){
    return new DriverHookNewApi(job);
      }

        Job job;

        private DriverHookNewApi(Job job){
        this.job = job;
    }

    public void run(){
        System.out.println("Hello from MyHook");
          if(job == null)
              throw new NullPointerException("err msg");
          try{
              JobID hdpJobID = job.getJobID();
              if(!job.isComplete())
                      job.killJob();
      }
        catch (IOException e){
            throw new RuntimeException("err msg");
      }
    }
}
```

When the JVM (containing this hook) shuts down, the `run()` method of the class `DriverHook` is invoked. This method uses the Hadoop API to check whether the job has completed, and kills it if the job is still running.

Listing 7-15 shows how to add a shutdown hook to the driver class.

LISTING 7-15: Adding a shutdown hook to the driver

```
Runnable myHook = DriverHook.create(job);
Thread hookThr = new Thread(myHook);
Runtime.getRuntime().addShutdownHook(hookThr);
```

Now that you are familiar with the details of implementing the Workflow processes to solve the example real-world problem, let's take a look at how to implement Oozie Coordinator applications.

IMPLEMENTING OOZIE COORDINATOR APPLICATIONS

To make the Workflows defined so far work together, you should use data sets and Oozie Coordinator applications. Start by designing two data sets: `probeDataset` and `placeDataset`, as shown in Listing 7-16 (code file: `dataSets.xml`).

LISTING 7-16: Oozie data sets

```
<dataset name="probeDataset" frequency="${coord:hours(4)}"
initial-instance="2013-01-10T80:00Z" timezone="America/Chicago">
    <uri-template>
                ${fullPath}/probes/${YEAR}/${MONTH}/${DAY}/${HOUR}/data
        </uri-template>
    <done-flag/>
</dataset>

<dataset name="placeDataset" frequency="${coord: hours(4)}"
initial-instance="2013-01-10T80:00Z" timezone="America/Chicago">
    <uri-template>
                ${fullPath}/places/${YEAR}/${MONTH}/${DAY}/${HOUR}/data
        </uri-template>
    <done-flag/>
</dataset>
```

The data set `dataSets.xml` specifies data produced by the chain of actions `select-probes`, `build-strands`, and `geotile-strands`. The data set specifies that, every four hours starting from `2013-01-00T80:00Z`, a new data set instance (actual data) should be generated and placed into the location `/user/practicalHadoop/oozie/places//${YEAR}${MONTH}/${DAY}/${HOUR}/data`.

For example, the first three data set instances are placed into the following locations:

```
/user/practicalHadoop/oozie/places/2012/01/01/00/data
/user/practicalHadoop/oozie/places/2012/01/01/04/data
/user/practicalHadoop/oozie/places/2012/01/01/08/data
```

Similarly, the data set `placesDataset` specifies the location of data generated by the chain of actions `select-places` and `geotile-places`. Instances for this data set are also generated every four hours.

You should put each of the three Workflow processes defined thus far in corresponding Coordinator applications. Listing 7-17 (code file: `dataPrepCoord.xml`) shows the definition of the Coordinator application for the `data-prep-wf` Workflow.

LISTING 7-17: Coordinator for the data-prep-wf Workflow

```
<coordinator-app xmlns="uri:oozie:coordinator:0.2" xmlns:sla="uri:oozie:sla:0.1"
        name="data-prep-coord" frequency="${coord:hours(4)}"
        start="2013-01-00T008:00Z" end="2013-06-00T08:00Z"
        timezone="America/Chicago">
    <controls>
        <timeout>60</timeout>
        <concurrency>3</concurrency>
        <execution>LIFO</execution>
        <throttle>4</throttle>
    </controls>
    <datasets>
        <dataset name="probeDataset" frequency="${coord:hours(4)}"
                initial-instance="2013-02-27T08:00Z"
                timezone="America/Chicago">
            <uri-template>${nameNode}/user/ayakubov/data/probes/
            ${YEAR}/${MONTH}/${DAY}/${HOUR}</uri-template>
            <done-flag/>
        </dataset>
        <dataset name="placeDataset" frequency="${coord:hours(4)}"
                initial-instance="2013-02-27T08:00Z"
                timezone="America/Chicago">
            <uri-template>${nameNode}/user/ayakubov/data/places/
                ${YEAR}/${MONTH}/${DAY}/${HOUR}</uri-template>
            <done-flag/>
        </dataset>
    </datasets>
    <output-events>
        <data-out name="output" dataset="probeDataset">
            <instance>${coord:current(1)}</instance>
        </data-out>
        <data-out name="output2" dataset="placeDataset">
            <instance>${coord:current(1)}</instance>
        </data-out>
    </output-events>
    <action>
        <workflow>
            <app-path>${fullPath}/dataPrep</app-path>
            <configuration>
                <property>
                    <name>wfOutput</name>
                    <value>${coord:dataOut('output')}</value>
                </property>
```

continues

LISTING 7-17 *(continued)*

```
                </configuration>
                <property>
                    <name>wfOutput2</name>
                    <value>${coord:dataOut('output2')}</value>
                </property>
            </workflow>
            <sla:info>[SLA SECTION]</sla:info>
        </action>
    </coordinator-app>
```

This Coordinator application defines when the Oozie server can start a Coordinator action (with a Workflow job). The definition describes the initial start time, end time, periodic executions, data conditions, and resource conditions. The attributes of the root element `<coordinator-app>` define the Coordinator name, frequency of the Coordinator actions, start time, and end time of the Coordinator application.

The `<controls>` element specifies the following execution policies:

➤   `concurrency` level — Up to three Coordinator actions are allowed to run concurrently.

➤   `timeout` — How long the Coordinator action will be in `WAITING` or `READY` status (up to 60 seconds) before giving up on its execution.

➤   `execution` — Defines the execution strategy. In this case, it's Last In First Out.

➤   `throttle` — Up to four Coordinator actions are allowed to be in `WAITING` state concurrently.

The `<datasets>` element specifies the data sets important for the data preparation application. The `<outputEvents>` element specifies (indirectly) which data sets should be generated from the Coordinator. In this case, instances of the `probeDataset` and `placeDataset` should be generated every four hours.

The `<action>` element specifies the location of the Workflow application definition (`data-prep-wf` Workflow in the `<app-path>` element) and important configuration parameters (`wfOutput` and `wfOutput2`). Those parameters provide the actions of the `data-prep-wf` Workflow with the name of data set instances that should be generated by the Workflow.

Thus, in the first `data-prep-wf` Workflow invocation, the value of the `wfOutput` parameter will be as follows:

```
/user/ayakubov/data/places/2013/02/27/08
```

During the following `data-prep-wf` Workflow invocation, the value of the `wfOutput` parameter will be as follows:

```
/user/ayakubov/data/places/2013/02/27/12
```

These correspond to the four-hour frequency specified for the `data-prep-coord` Coordinator application.

Additionally, a Coordinator application can use the `<sla:info>` element similar to Workflow application or Workflow action.

In summary, the Coordinator application `data-prep-coord` specifies that the Coordinator action (`data-prep-wf` job) should be submitted every four hours, starting from `2013-01-00T008:00`, and ending at `2013-06-00T08:00` (time conditions). No data dependences are specified in the Coordinator application, but the `<control>` element specifies resource restrictions (`concurrency`, `throttling`).

Listing 7-18 (code file: `attendanceCoord.xml`) shows the definition of the Coordinator application for the `attendance-wf` Workflow.

LISTING 7-18: Coordinator for the attendance-wf Workflow

```
<coordinator-app xmlns="uri:oozie:coordinator:0.1" xmlns:sla="uri:oozie:sla:0.1"
    name="attendance-coord"
    frequency="${coord:endOfDays(1)}"
    start="2013-01-00T008:00Z"
    end="2013-03-00T08:00Z"
    timezone="America/Chicago">
    <controls> [CONTROL SECTION] </controls>
    <datasets>
        <dataset name="probeDataset" frequency="${coord:hours(4)}" initial-
                instance="2013-02-27T08:00Z" timezone="America/Chicago">
            <uri-template>${nameNode}/user/ayakubov/data/probes
                /${YEAR}/${MONTH}/${DAY}/${HOUR}</uri-template>
            <done-flag/>
        </dataset>
        <dataset name="placeDataset" frequency="${coord:hours(4)}"
            initial-instance="2013-02-27T08:00Z"
                timezone="America/Chicago">
            <uri-template>${nameNode}/user/ayakubov/data/places
                /${YEAR}/${MONTH}/${DAY}/${HOUR}</uri-template>
            <done-flag/>
        </dataset>
    </datasets>
    <input-events>
        <data-in name="placeReadyEvent" dataset="placeDataset">
                <instance>${coord:current(-6)}</instance>
        </data-in>
        <data-in name="probeReadyEvent" dataset="probeDataset">
                <instance>${coord:current(-6)}</instance>
        </data-in>
    </input-events>
    <action>
        <workflow>
            <app-path>${fullPath}/attendance</app-path>
            <configuration> [CONFIGURATION SECTION] </configuration>
        </workflow>
        <sla:info> [SLA SECTION] </sla:info>
    </action>
</coordinator-app>
```

The definition of the `attendance-coord` Coordinator action is structurally very similar to the definition of `data-prep-coord`. The frequency of the Coordinator action is one day.

The new elements in the `attendance-coord` Coordinator are input events specified with the `<input-events>` elements. This adds the data conditions that should be met for executing the Coordinator action. Six sequential data instances of both `probesDataset` and `placesDataset` data sets (ending with the data sets for the time of nominal action submission) should exist on HDFS.

Listing 7-19 (code file: `dataPrepCoord.xml`) shows the definition of Coordinator application for the `cluster-wf` Workflow.

LISTING 7-19: Coordinator for the cluster-wf Workflow

```
<coordinator-app xmlns="uri:oozie:coordinator:0.1"
     xmlns:sla="uri:oozie:sla:0.1"
     name="cluster-coord"
     frequency="${coord:weeks(1)}"
     start="2013-01-00T008:00Z"
     end="2013-03-00T08:00Z" timezone="America/Chicago">
       <controls> [CONTROL SECTION]      </controls>
       <datasets>
           <dataset name="probeDataset" frequency="${coord:hours(4)}"
                 initial-instance="2013-02-27T08:00Z"
                 timezone="America/Chicago">
               <uri-template>${nameNode}/user/ayakubov/data/probes
                   /${YEAR}/${MONTH}/${DAY}/${HOUR}</uri-template>
               <done-flag/>
           </dataset>
           <dataset name="placeDataset" frequency="${coord:hours(4)}"
                 initial-instance="2013-02-27T08:00Z"
                 timezone="America/Chicago">
               <uri-template>${nameNode}/user/ayakubov/data/places
                   /${YEAR}/${MONTH}/${DAY}/${HOUR}</uri-template>
               <done-flag/>
           </dataset>
       </datasets>
       <input-events>
           <data-in name="placeReadyEvent" dataset="placeDataset">
                     <instance>${coord:current(-42)}</instance>
           </data-in>
           <data-in name="probeReadyEvent" dataset="probeDataset">
                     <instance>${coord:current(-42)}</instance>
           </data-in>
       </input-events>
       <action>
           <workflow>
               <app-path>${fullPath}/cluster</app-path>
<configuration> [CONFIGURATION SECTION] </configuration>
           </workflow>
           <sla:info> [SLA SECTION] </sla:info>
       </action>
</coordinator-app>
```

In this application, the action frequency is one week, and the `cluster-coord` action should have 42 sequential instances of each of the `probesDataset` and `placesDataset` data sets on HDFS, ending with the data sets for the time of nominal action submission.

Figure 7-5 shows the ideal schedule of submission actions from the `data-prep-coord`, `attendance-coord`, and `cluster-coord` Coordinators.

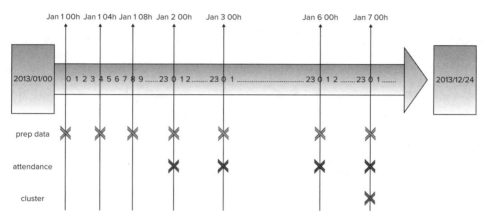

FIGURE 7-5: Scheduling Workflow jobs for the place validation process

As you can see from Figure 7-5, every four hours, the data preparation Coordinator starts the data preparation Workflow. Every 24 hours (daily), the attendance calculation Coordinator starts the attendance calculation Workflow (assuming that all required data files defined in the input events are in place). Finally, once a week, the cluster calculation Coordinator starts the cluster calculation Workflow (also assuming that data sets are in place). So, if all of the Coordinators are started simultaneously and run as expected, they provide the required sequence of task execution.

In the next section, you learn how to ensure that all the Coordinator's executions are synchronized by combining them into a single data pipeline — the Oozie Bundle, which you can use to manage all participating Coordinator applications together.

IMPLEMENTING OOZIE BUNDLE APPLICATIONS

Because the three Coordinator applications just described are coupled with time and data dependencies, you may find it inconvenient to deploy them separately. However, you can use the Oozie Bundle application to bind them together into a single, manageable entity that can be started/ stopped/suspended/resumed/rerun as a whole, thus providing easier operational control.

Listing 7-20 (code file: `bundle.xml`) shows an Oozie Bundle application for the place validation process.

LISTING 7-20: Oozie Bundle application

```
<bundle-app name="place-validation-bl" xmlns='uri:oozie:bundle:0.1'>
    <controls>
        <kick-off-time>2012-12-10T008:00Z</kick-off-time>
    </controls>
<coordinator name="data-prep-coord">
        <app-path>${fullPath}/dataPrep</app-path>
        <configuration>
            </property>
                <name>selectProperties</name>
              <value>${rootPath}/config/select-probs.properties</value>
            </property>
            </property>
                <name>validateFilterProperties</name>
              <value>${rootPath}/config/val-filter.properties</value>
            </property>
                ...
</configuration>
        </coordinator>
        <coordinator name="attendance-coord">
        <app-path>${fullPath}/attendance</app-path>
        <configuration> ... </configuration>
        </coordinator>
    <coordinator name="cluster-coord">
        <app-path>${fullPath}/cluster</app-path>
            <configuration> ...  </configuration>
        </coordinator>
</bundle-app>
```

Implementation of this Bundle application is fairly simple and straightforward. It contains a
<control> element that specifies when to start the Bundle execution, and a set of Coordinator
applications that are included in the Bundle. For every Coordinator application, the Bundle
definition describes where this application is deployed, and provides an optional set of configuration
parameters, which can be passed to corresponding applications.

Now that you have seen how to implement this chapter's sample application, let's take a look at how
you can deploy, test, and execute it.

DEPLOYING, TESTING, AND EXECUTING OOZIE APPLICATIONS

Testing an Oozie application typically starts with the testing of individual actions. You can often
test the java action by running it by itself. Chapter 5 provides details on testing MapReduce
applications. Testing of Pig and Hive scripts is well covered in other literature.

So, let's concentrate on testing Oozie applications. In order to do this, you must first deploy them.

Deploying Oozie Applications

Figure 7-6 shows the suggested location of artifacts (Coordinators, Workflows, jars, Pig and Hive
scripts, as well as configuration files) on HDFS that were developed earlier in this chapter.

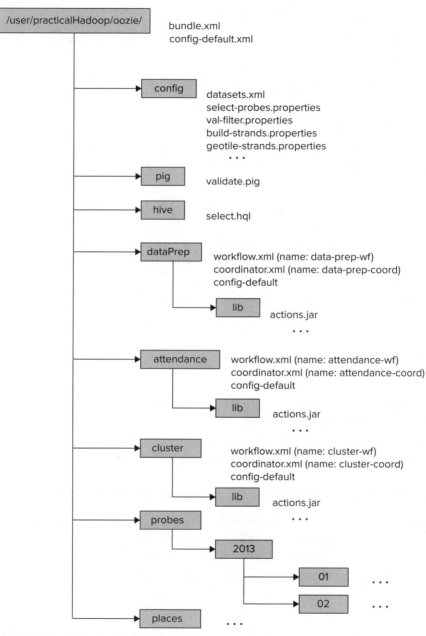

FIGURE 7-6: Deploying Oozie artifacts

For the deployment, an HDFS directory (/user/practicalHadoop/oozie) is chosen. This directory contains both the executable code and data files produced by the applications.

Following are some important things to note about this deployment:

➤ Every Workflow application should be placed in a separate folder, which has the following well-defined layout:

  ➤ It should contain the files `workflow.xml` (Workflow definition) and `config-default.xml` (more about this file later). To keep things together and simplify file layout, you place `coordinator.xml` (Coordinator definition) in the same directory (technically, you could place it in any directory).

  ➤ It should contain the `lib` directory. All the `jar` files required for execution of Workflow activities, along with all the files that they depend on, should be placed in the `lib` directory.

➤ The rest of the directories can be located elsewhere, but in this case, they are brought together to simplify the deployment.

The `config-default.xml` file shown in Figure 7-6 is a configuration file that enables you to specify parameters of the Workflow, Coordinator, or Bundle application. (You learn more about specifying parameters for Oozie execution later in this chapter.)

The deployment file layout shown in Figure 7-6 supports the following execution modes:

➤ Run each Workflow separately with the `oozie` command from the edge node (the first step of integration testing).

➤ Run each Coordinator separately with the `oozie` command from the edge node (the next step of the integration testing).

➤ Run the Oozie Bundle with all three Coordinators with the `oozie` command from the edge node (the last step of the integration testing).

Now that you know how to deploy an Oozie application, let's take a look how to use the Oozie CLI (described in Chapter 6) for Oozie execution of an Oozie application.

Using the Oozie CLI for Execution of an Oozie Application

Oozie provides a command-line interface (CLI) to perform job-related and administrative tasks. All operations are done via sub-commands of the `oozie` CLI command. The `oozie` command requires an Oozie URL as one of its arguments. The Oozie URL points to the RESR endpoint of the Oozie server.

Let's take a closer look at important Oozie sub-commands for the `oozie` command.

submit

The `submit` command is used for submitting a Workflow, Coordinator, or Bundle job. The job will be created, but it will not be started. It will be in the PREP status. Listing 7-21 shows an example.

LISTING 7-21: Submitting an Oozie job with CLI

```
$ oozie job -oozie http://OozieServer:8080/oozie -config job.properties -submit
.
job: 14-20090525161321-oozie-job
```

Here, the argument `-oozie http://OozieServer:8080/oozie` specifies the Oozie URL. The argument `-config job.properties` specifies the job property file (which is explained in detail later in this chapter). The job property file should contain the property that specifies the location of the Oozie application definition on HDFS. The name of the property file that specifies the HDFS location of the application definition depends of the type of Oozie application, as shown in Table 7-2.

TABLE 7-2: Defining Application Location for Different Types of Oozie Applications

TYPE OF OOZIE APPLICATION	NAME OF PROPERTY
Workflow	`oozie.wf.application.path`
Coordinator	`oozie.coord.application.path`
Bundle	`oozie.bundle.application.path`

As shown at Listing 7-21, the `submit` sub-command returns the Oozie job ID.

start

The `start` command starts a previously submitted Workflow job, Coordinator job, or Bundle job that is in PREP status. After the command is executed, the job will be in the RUNNING state. Listing 7-22 shows an example.

LISTING 7-22: Starting an Oozie job with CLI

```
$ oozie job -oozie http://OozieServer:8080/oozie -start 14-20090525161321-oozie-job
```

The argument for the `start` command is the Oozie job ID returned by the `submit` command.

run

The `run` command creates and starts an Oozie job. So, the `run` command is effectively a combination of the `submit` command followed by a `start` command. Listing 7-23 shows an example of the `run` command.

LISTING 7-23: Running an Oozie job with CLI

```
$ oozie job -oozie http://OozieServer:8080/oozie -config job.properties -run

job: 15-20090525161321-oozie-job
```

Similar to the `submit` command, the `run` command returns the Oozie job ID.

kill

The `kill` command enables you to terminate a Workflow, Coordinator, or Bundle job. Listing 7-24 shows an example of the `kill` command.

LISTING 7-24: Terminating an Oozie job with CLI

```
$ oozie job -oozie http://OozieServer:8080/oozie -kill 14-20090525161321-oozie-job
```

sla

The `sla` command enables you to get the status of an SLA event. Listing 7-25 shows an example of this command.

LISTING 7-25: Example of a CLI sla command

```
$ oozie sla -oozie http://OozieServer:11000/oozie -len 2 -offset 0
.
<sla-message>
  <event>
    <sequence-id>1</sequence-id>
    <registration>
      <sla-id>0000573-120615111500653-oozie-oozi-C@1</sla-id>
      <app-type>COORDINATOR_ACTION</app-type>
      <app-name>test-app</app-name>
      <user>ayakubov</user>
      <group>users</group>
      <parent-sla-id>null</parent-sla-id>
      <expected-start>2012-06-28T11:50Z</expected-start>
      <expected-end>2012-06-28T12:15Z</expected-end>
      <status-timestamp>2012-07-02T15:35Z</status-timestamp>
      <notification-msg>Notifying User for 2012-06-28T11:45Z nominal
            time</notification-msg>
      <alert-contact>www@yahoo.com</alert-contact>
      <dev-contact>alexeyy2@yahoo.com</dev-contact>
      <qa-contact>alexeyy2@yahoo.com</qa-contact>
      <se-contact>alexeyy2@yahoo.com</se-contact>
      <alert-percentage>80</alert-percentage>
      <alert-frequency>LAST_HOUR</alert-frequency>
      <upstream-apps />
      <job-status>CREATED</job-status>
      <job-data />
    </registration>
  </event>
  <event>
    <sequence-id>2</sequence-id>
    <status>
      <sla-id>0000573-120615111500653-oozie-oozi-C@1</sla-id>
      <status-timestamp>2012-07-02T15:35Z</status-timestamp>
      <job-status>STARTED</job-status>
      <job-data />
    </status>
  </event>
  <last-sequence-id>2</last-sequence-id>
</sla-message>
```

The command arguments contain the number of required SLA events `len` (2 in this case) and an offset from the first SLA event (`0` in this case). The command execution returns the list of SLA events of the requested length.

That first SLA record in the reply happens to be a `registration` record; the second is a – `status` record. (Those are the only two types of SLA events.)

Some other important CLI commands include `suspend`, `resume`, `change` (parameter), `rerun`, and `info` (check status).

As mentioned previously, the `oozie` CLI is useful for integration testing, but it is also useful for deployment and management of an Oozie application.

As with every application, Oozie jobs are using parameters, which can be passed to Oozie jobs as arguments. Let's now take a look at how to pass arguments to Oozie jobs.

Passing Arguments to Oozie Jobs

As with every application, the reusability of Oozie applications (to a large extent) depends on how arguments are passed to the Oozie job. Several methods exist for specifying parameters (that is, properties or arguments) for Oozie jobs and corresponding Hadoop jobs. This section first examines different methods of passing parameters to Hadoop jobs, and then presents a comparison of different approaches for passing parameters.

Using an Oozie Invocation Command

One of the most obvious ways of passing execution parameters to an Oozie job is as part of the Oozie CLI `run` sub-command. Listing 7-26 shows an example of such an approach.

LISTING 7-26: Oozie CLI invocation command

```
oozie job -oozie ${OOZIE_ENDPOINT} -D country=USA -config job.properties –run
```

Here, the command fragment `-D country=USA` enables you to directly set the parameter `country=USA` in the command line for the Oozie application. That parameter will now be available in the Oozie application execution context, and can be used, for example, as a parameter for `java` action invocation inside the `<arg>` element.

Using an Oozie Job Property File

As shown in the deployment layout in Figure 7-6 and referenced in the discussion about the Oozie `submit` (Listing 7-21) and `run` (Listing 7-23) sub-commands, this Oozie job execution is using the `job.properties` files.

`job.properties` files provide another place where job arguments can be specified. Listing 7-27 shows an example of the property file.

LISTING 7-27: Example of an Oozie job property file

```
<?xml version="1.0" encoding="UTF-8"?>
<configuration>
  <property>
        <name>jobTracker</name>
```

continues

LISTING 7-27 *(continued)*

```
                <value>jtServer:8021</value>
        </property>
        <property>
                <name>nameNode</name>
                <value>hdfs://nnServer:8020</value>
        </property>
        <property>
                <name>rootPath</name>
                <value>/user/practicalHadoop/oozie</value>
        </property>
        <property>
                <name>fullPath</name>
                <value>${nameNode}/${rootPath}</value>
        </property>
        <property>
                <name>tileLevel</name>
                <value>10</value>
        </property>
        <property>
                <name>bbox</name>
                <value>37.71,-122.53,37.93,-122.15</value>
        </property>
        <property>
                <name>geotileStrandsProperties</name>
                <value>${rootPath}/config/geotileStrandsProperties.xml</value>
        </property>
        <property>
                <name>oozie.wf.application.path</name>
                <value>${fullPath}/dataPrep/workflow.xml</value>
        </property>
</configuration>
```

All of the properties specified in this XML file will be available in the job execution context, and consequently can be used throughout the job.

For example, the `java` action definition shown in Listing 7-3 uses the value of the `tileSize` parameter in the expression `tileSize=${tileLevel}`. The value of the `tileLevel` parameter is specified in the job property file. As a result, the parameter `tileSize=10` will be available when the `main()` method of the class `com.practicalHadoop.geotile.Strands` is invoked in the corresponding Hadoop job, as specified in Listing 7-3.

A job property file normally specifies what type of Oozie application should be invoked. To run the Workflow application, you must specify the `oozie.wf.application.path` property. To run the Coordinator application, you specify the `oozie.coord.application.path` property. For the Bundle application, you would use the `oozie.bundle.application.path` property.

Using the config-default.xml File

The `config-default.xml` file is a mandatory file for Oozie Workflow deployment (see Figure 7-6). Listing 7-28 shows a fragment of the `config-default.xml` file for the `data-prep-wf` Workflow application.

LISTING 7-28: Example of config-default file

```xml
<?xml version="1.0" encoding="UTF-8"?>
<configuration>
    ...
    <property>
<name>mapred.input.dir</name>
<value>${rootPath}/dataPrep/strandstiles/input</value>
<description>Input path for the geotile-strands action</description>
    </property>
    <property>
<name>mapred.output.dir</name>
<value>${rootPath}/dataPrep/strandstiles/output</value>
<description>Output path for the geotile-strands action</description>
    </property>
    <property>
<name>strandCenterMethod</name>
<value>median</value>
<description>Method to define strand center</description>
    </property>
...
</configuration>
```

Similar to the property file, the `config-default.xml` file can contain properties, which get populated in the Workflow execution context. For example, the definitions for the `geotile-strands` action uses the `<arg>` element to pass the value of the `strandCenterMethod` variable to the `main()` method.

Using a <configuration> Element in the Action Definition

Arguments specified in `<configuration>` elements have action scope. The property `spatial4jVer` as `5.2` was defined in the example of a `<configuration>` element for the `geotile-strands` action shown in Listing 7-5. That value is available for the `main()` method of the `com.practicalHadoop.geotile.Strands` class through the `<arg>` element in the action definition `<arg>-version=${spatial4jVer}</arg>`.

Using a <job-xml> Element

Similar to the property file and `config-default.xml`, a file pointed to by a `<job-xml>` tag can define properties, as shown in Listing 7-29.

LISTING 7-29: Fragment of a configuration file specified with the element <job-xml>

```xml
<?xml version="1.0" encoding="UTF-8"?>
<configuration>
    ...
    <property>
<name>cardinality</name>
<value>5</value>
<description>Mimimum number of probes in s strand</description>
    </property>
...
<configuration>
```

Properties defined in that file will have the action scope.

Parameters can also be explicitly defined inside an action's `<arg>` tag (if the action supports them).

Deciding How to Pass Arguments to Oozie Jobs

So far, you have learned about several ways to pass parameters to an Oozie job. To help you decide which approach to use, you should first understand how Oozie uses parameters:

➤ Oozie uses parameters explicitly defined inside an action's `<arg>` tag.

➤ If any of the parameters cannot be resolved there, Oozie uses parameters defined in the file specified inside the `<job-xml>` tag.

➤ If any of the parameters cannot be resolved there, Oozie uses parameters defined inside the `<configuration>` tag.

➤ If any of the parameters cannot be resolved there, Oozie uses parameters from the command-line invocation.

➤ If any of the parameters cannot be resolved there, Oozie uses parameters from a job property file.

➤ Once everything else fails, Oozie tries to use `config-default.xml`.

Although documentation does not describe clearly when to use which, the overall recommendation is as follows:

➤ Use `config-default.xml` for defining parameters that never change (for example, cluster configuration).

➤ Use `<arg>`, `<job-xml>`, `<configuration>`, and job property files for the parameters that are common for a given deployment of a job.

➤ Use command-line arguments for the parameters that are specific for a given job invocation.

Now let's see how you can leverage the Oozie console for getting information about Oozie jobs that are running and completed.

USING THE OOZIE CONSOLE TO GET INFORMATION ABOUT OOZIE APPLICATIONS

As described in Chapter 6, Oozie is equipped with an administration console that enables you to visually monitor Bundle jobs, Coordinator jobs, Workflow jobs, and Workflow actions. The console not only presents the status and outcome of jobs and actions, but it also provides in different tabs information about errors, the Workflow XML document, and job configuration parameters. Additionally, the Oozie console supports navigation from an Oozie action to the Hadoop job in the MapReduce Admin console.

Getting to Know the Oozie Console Screens

To demonstrate the Oozie console functionality, first run the Oozie Workflow `data-prep-wf` using the `run` CLI sub-command.

After the command has been executed, the Oozie console will show the front page with the Workflow Jobs tab selected by default. This page shows list of Workflows, including the Workflow you just started, as shown in Figure 7-7.

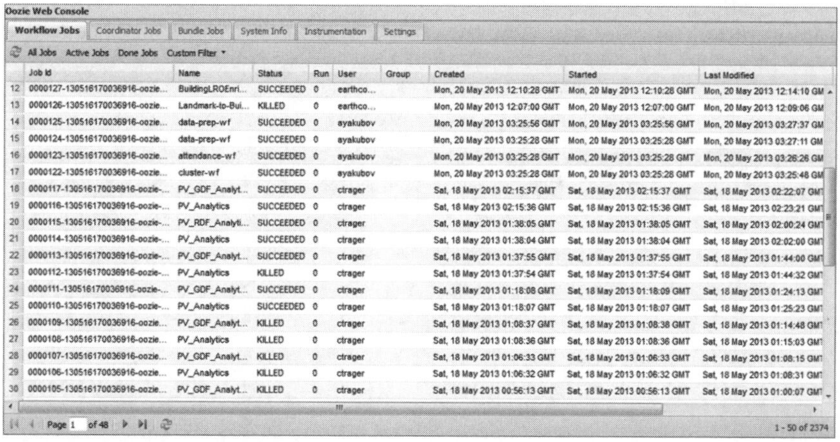

FIGURE 7-7: Workflow jobs

When a particular job is selected, the console will present the job-specific information on the page with four tabs, as shown in Figure 7-8. The default tab, Job Info, presents the job status and current status of all started Workflow actions.

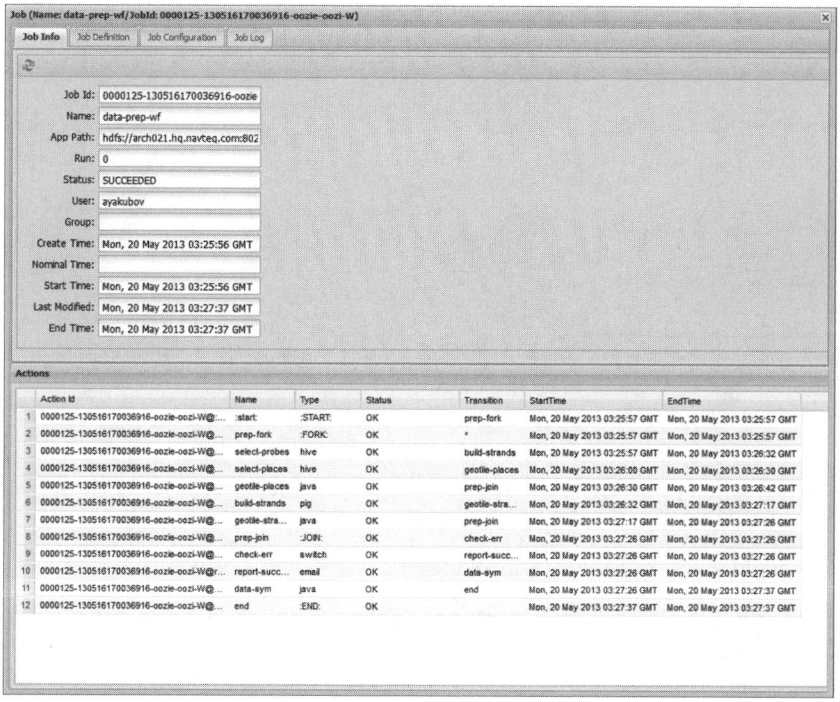

FIGURE 7-8: Job status and action status

This view provides information about the job, including Job ID, Name, its application path, user name, and so on. It also specifies the job's creation time, nominal time, start time, and so on.

Switching to the Job Definition tab enables you to view the complete job definition, as shown in Figure 7-9.

Switching to the Job Configuration tab, you can view the complete job configuration, as shown in Figure 7-10.

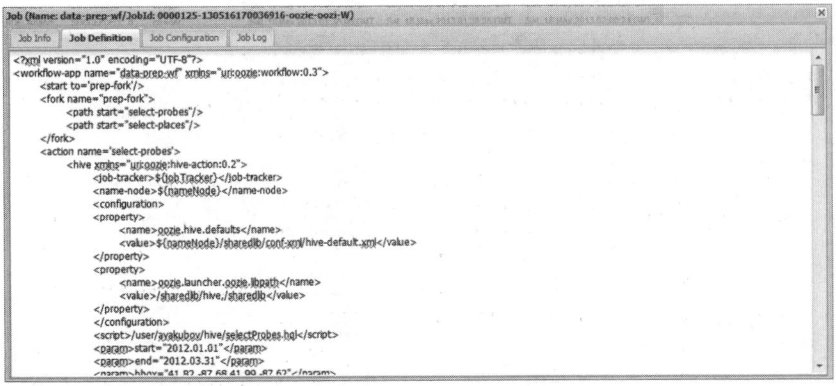

FIGURE 7-9: Job definition

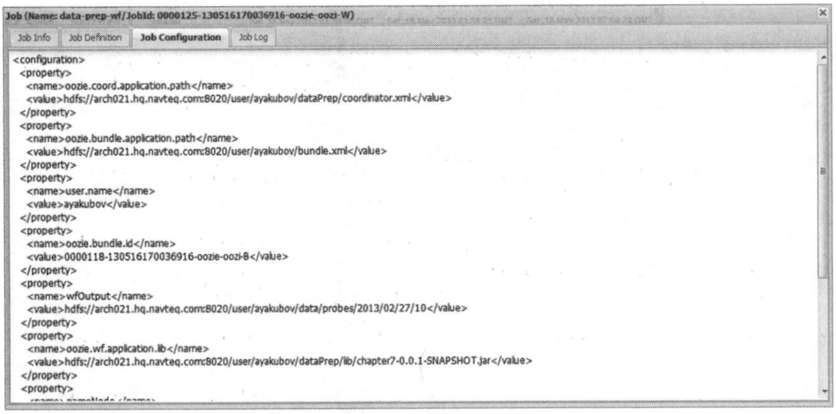

FIGURE 7-10: Job configuration

This view is especially useful when parameters are defined in several places because it brings them all together regardless of where they are actually defined.

Finally, the Job Log pane enables you to browse a job's log file.

In the Job Info tab, if an action is selected (in the lower pane), the Oozie console presents the details of that action. The action details pop-up page has two tabs. As shown in Figure 7-11, the default Action Info tab presents the action status.

The page also contains a Console URL line that enables you to navigate to the Hadoop MapReduce Admin console by clicking the symbol at the end of the field. Figure 7-12 shows the resulting web page. (See Chapter 5 for more information on the MapReduce Admin console.)

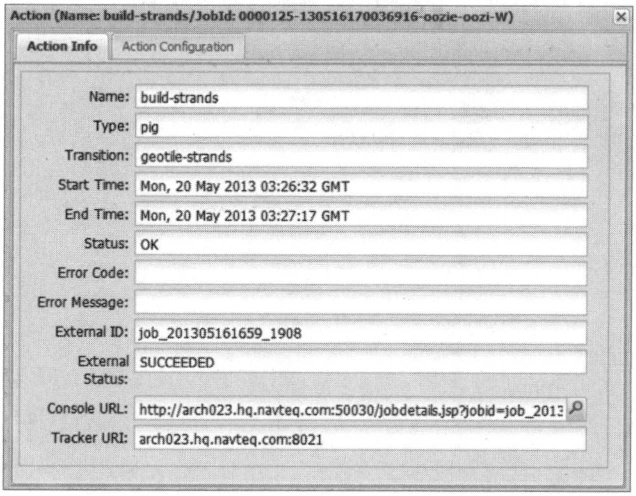

FIGURE 7-11: Workflow action

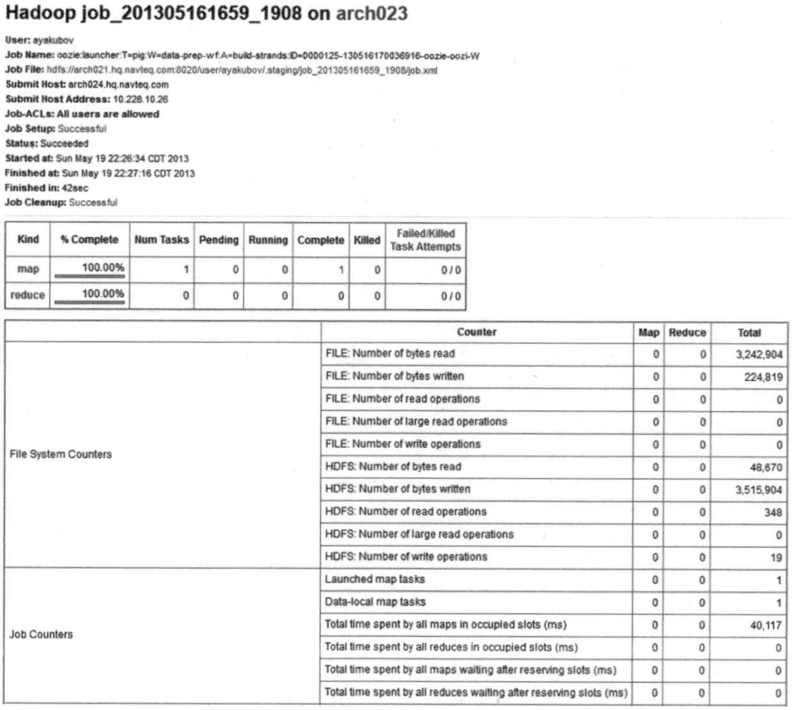

Hadoop job_201305161659_1908 on arch023

User: ayakubov
Job Name: oozie:launcher:T=pig:W=data-prep-wf:A=build-strands:ID=0000125-130516170036916-oozie-oozi-W
Job File: hdfs://arch021.hq.navteq.com:8020/user/ayakubov/.staging/job_201305161659_1908/job.xml
Submit Host: arch024.hq.navteq.com
Submit Host Address: 10.228.10.26
Job-ACLs: All users are allowed
Job Setup: Successful
Status: Succeeded
Started at: Sun May 19 22:26:34 CDT 2013
Finished at: Sun May 19 22:27:16 CDT 2013
Finished in: 42sec
Job Cleanup: Successful

Kind	% Complete	Num Tasks	Pending	Running	Complete	Killed	Failed/Killed Task Attempts
map	100.00%	1	0	0	1	0	0 / 0
reduce	100.00%	0	0	0	0	0	0 / 0

	Counter	Map	Reduce	Total
File System Counters	FILE: Number of bytes read	0	0	3,242,904
	FILE: Number of bytes written	0	0	224,819
	FILE: Number of read operations	0	0	0
	FILE: Number of large read operations	0	0	0
	FILE: Number of write operations	0	0	0
	HDFS: Number of bytes read	0	0	48,670
	HDFS: Number of bytes written	0	0	3,515,904
	HDFS: Number of read operations	0	0	348
	HDFS: Number of large read operations	0	0	0
	HDFS: Number of write operations	0	0	19
Job Counters	Launched map tasks	0	0	1
	Data-local map tasks	0	0	1
	Total time spent by all maps in occupied slots (ms)	0	0	40,117
	Total time spent by all reduces in occupied slots (ms)	0	0	0
	Total time spent by all maps waiting after reserving slots (ms)	0	0	0
	Total time spent by all reduces waiting after reserving slots (ms)	0	0	0

FIGURE 7-12: Navigation from the Oozie console to the Hadoop MapReduce admin console

As shown in Figure 7-13, the other tab on the action details pop-up page, Action Configuration, shows the action definition (a fragment of the Workflow application) with actual action parameters.

You must update the Oozie console page to see the job progress. After the job has successfully ended, the Oozie console will preserve the complete information about the job and each action, as shown in Figure 7-14.

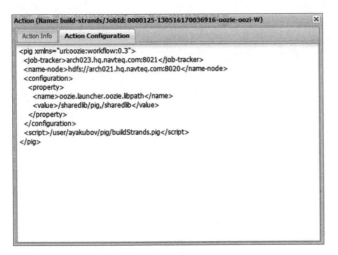

FIGURE 7-13: Action configuration

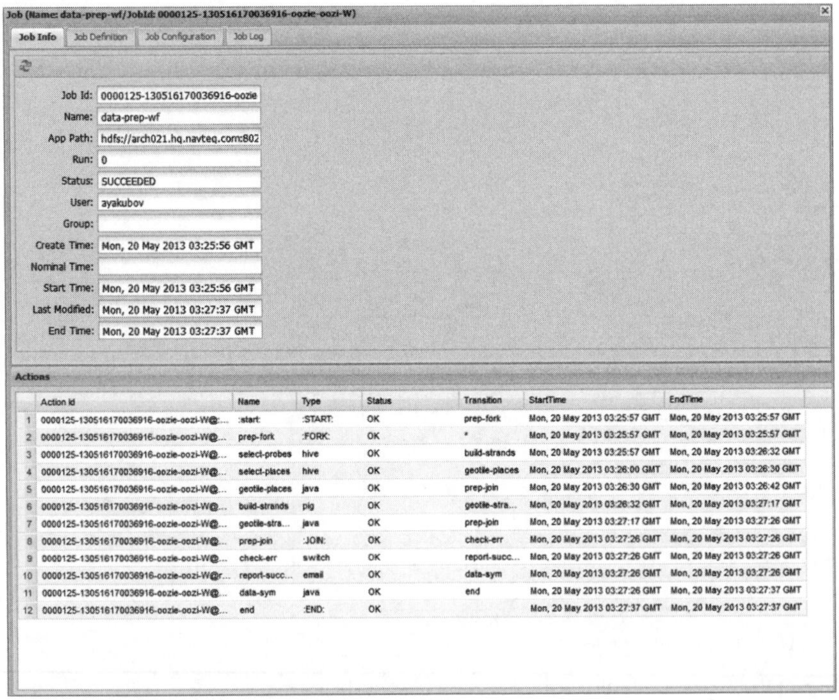

FIGURE 7-14: Workflow job after completion

If any kind of problem happens with the Workflow job or action, in most cases, the sufficient error information can be presented in the Oozie console pages.

Getting Information about a Coordinator Job

You can use the Oozie console to obtain information for a Coordinator job. After starting the Coordinator application `cluster-coord`, select the Coordinator Jobs tab on the front page of the Oozie console web application, as shown in Figure 7-15.

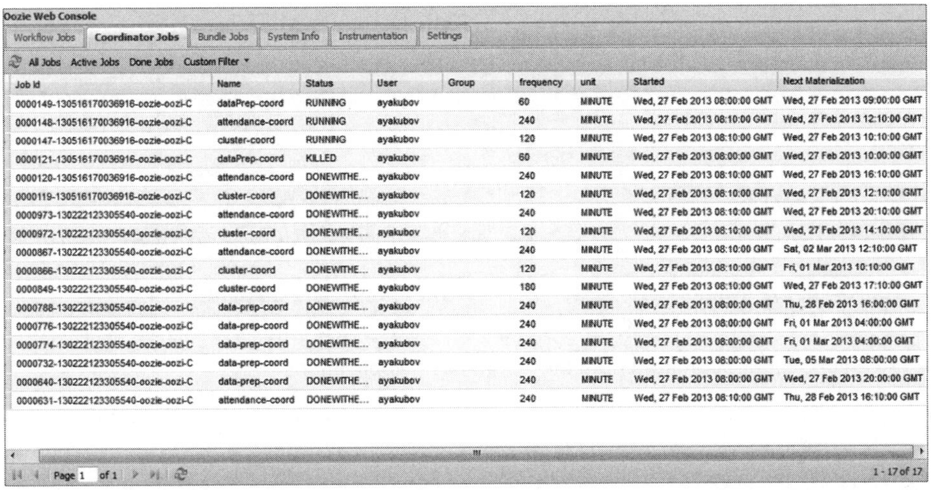

FIGURE 7-15: Coordinator jobs

Here you can see that the Coordinator application `cluster-coord` is in the RUNNING state. It so happens that all of the Coordinator applications are running. The application will be in the RUNNING state until you kill it.

To see details of the `cluster-coord` Coordinator job, you must navigate to the Coord Job Info page (by clicking the Coordinator Jobs tab), which displays information about all Coordinator actions, as shown in Figure 7-16.

Actions IDs for the particular Coordinator application contain suffixes that show the order of action start. For each Coordinator action, the Oozie console shows the ID of the corresponding Workflow action (`Exit Id`). For example, for the Coordinator action with the Action ID `0000147-130516170036916-oozie-oozi-C`, the corresponding Workflow Job ID is shown as `0000150-130516170036916-oozie-oozi-W`. If you navigate to the Workflow Job page (by pressing F5), you can find the Workflow job (the last shown in Figure 7-17).

From here, you can select the Workflow job and look up its actions, navigate to the MapReduce Admin console, and so on.

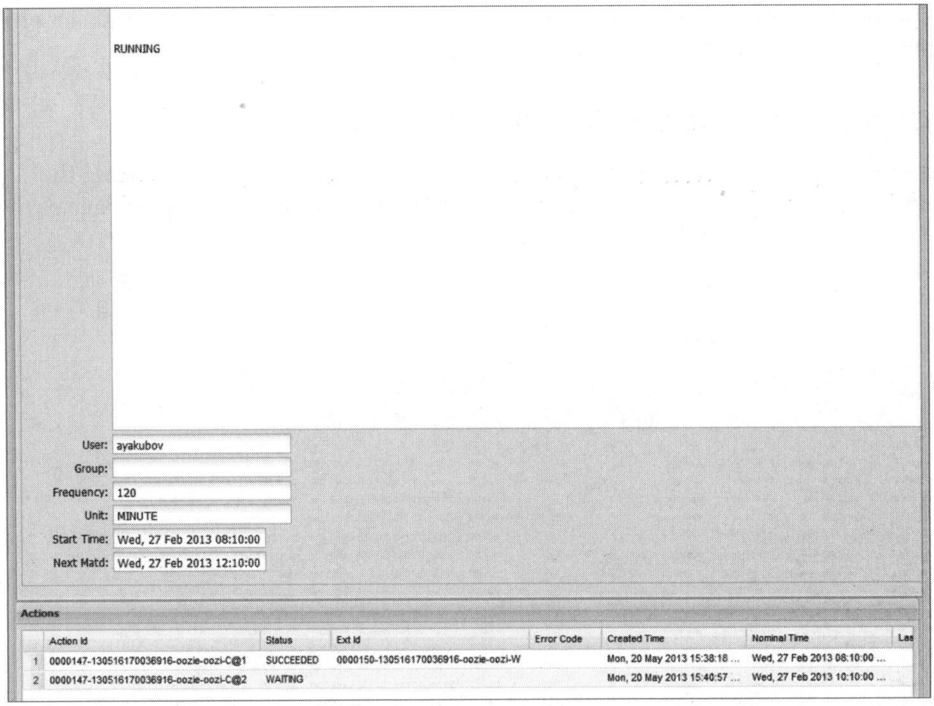

FIGURE 7-16: Coordinator actions submitted from the Coordinator applications

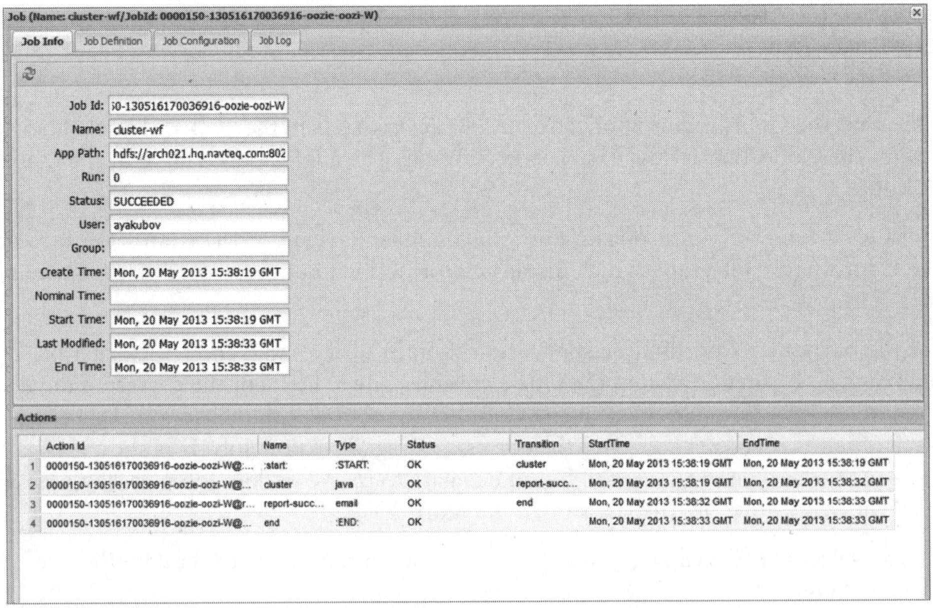

FIGURE 7-17: Navigation from Coordinator pane to Workflow pane

Getting Information about a Bundle Job

Oozie version 3 provides an additional page for Bundle applications. Figure 7-18 shows a page indicating that the `place-validation-bl` Bundle is running.

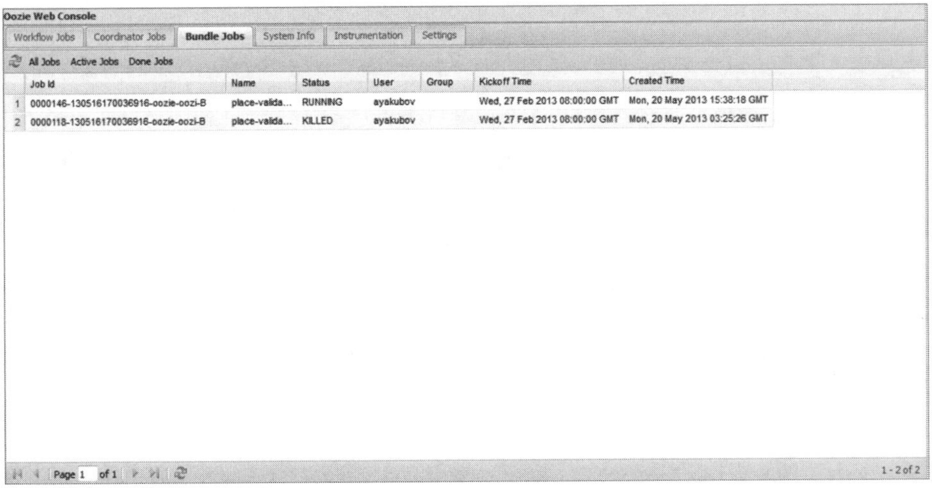

FIGURE 7-18: Bundle jobs

> **NOTE** *Note that Bundle page shows only one bundle running. As you have learned, that Bundle contains three Coordinator applications (and Figure 7-18 shows only those three Coordinator applications are running).*

SUMMARY

This chapter provided a detailed description of Oozie applications designed and implemented to tackle a real-world problem. You learned about best practices for designing Oozie applications with different frequency-repeatable jobs. You also learned about most of the Oozie actions and their configuration parameters. The driver pattern was examined, as well as using a `java` action for MapReduce jobs.

You also learned how to construct a Coordinator application and data pipeline (Bundle) to connect separate Workflows. You learned how to deploy and execute Oozie applications, and how to use the Oozie console to get information about the execution of Oozie applications.

In Chapter 8, you learn about important ways to extend Oozie, including building custom extension actions, working with uber files, code generation for Oozie applications, implementing loops with Oozie, and building reliable custom data pipelines.

8

Advanced Oozie Features

WHAT'S IN THIS CHAPTER?

➤ Building custom Oozie actions

➤ Building a dynamic Workflow

➤ Using the Oozie Java API

➤ Using uber jars with Oozie

➤ Building dynamic data pipelines

WROX.COM CODE DOWNLOADS FOR THIS CHAPTER

The wrox.com code downloads for this chapter are found at `www.wrox.com/remtitle .cgi?isbn=1118611934` on the Download Code tab. The code is in the Chapter 8 download. All downloads for this chapter are provided as a single Eclipse project containing all of the example's code.

By now, you should be familiar with the main components of Oozie and the way they interoperate. You have also learned how to design, build, and deploy Oozie applications, and how to use the Oozie console to view the execution of those applications.

In this chapter, you learn about a number of advanced Oozie topics that, once you understand them, will enable you to extend Oozie functionality and integrate Oozie with other enterprise applications. In this chapter, you learn about the following:

➤ How to build custom Oozie actions

➤ How to build Oozie applications dynamically

➤ How to invoke and control Oozie jobs programmatically through the Java API

➤ How use uber files with Oozie

At the end of the chapter, you will see a custom design for a fully automated data processing pipeline based on Oozie.

Let's start by implementing some custom Oozie Workflow actions.

BUILDING CUSTOM OOZIE WORKFLOW ACTIONS

Out of the box, Oozie offers a minimal number of control and action nodes (described in Chapter 6) that cover the most general features of the Workflow language. In reality, Workflow developers are often faced with the fact that the same activity is useful for many Workflows they are implementing.

Following are some approaches to reusing functionality in Oozie:

➤ **Oozie sub-Workflows** — This approach enables you to reuse partial processes by including them in the main Workflows. Sub-Workflows are a preferred reuse method when a particular sequence of steps is part of several processes.

➤ `java` **action node** — When you want to reuse code libraries that may be useful for many nodes, you can use a `java` action node.

➤ **Custom action nodes** — This approach enables you to reuse a complete node implementation between multiple (sub) processes.

Although similarities exist between the approaches that use the `java` action node and custom action nodes, using the `java` action node has the following limitations:

➤ **Semantic alignment** — Although it supports code reuse, this approach does not provide semantic reuse. The `java` action provides no Workflow semantics (it just says that an action is implemented using Java), which makes it difficult to read a Workflow definition. Adding a custom action node with a well-defined and meaningful business name can significantly improve the overall readability of the process.

➤ **Action's parameters** — A specific action requires a well-defined set of parameters. Unlike the generic `java` action that enables you to specify a generic set of parameters, a custom Oozie action enables you to more precisely define and control the action input parameters.

➤ **Execution locality** — As described in Chapter 6, an Oozie action can be executed either locally (within context of Oozie server), or remotely (that is, on an Hadoop cluster). Both action execution models have their place in Workflow execution. As described in Chapter 6, a `java` action is always executed on one Hadoop DataNode, thus supporting only remote execution.

Based on these considerations, depending on the situation, it might be more advantageous to use custom action nodes, which are described here.

Oozie supports a very elegant extensibility mechanism — an extension of the Oozie language by adding custom nodes. Such an approach enables you to overcome all of the limitations of the `java` action approach. It supports choosing a meaningful business name for an action, defining an action's parameters (using XML schema), and it supports both synchronous (local) and asynchronous (remote) execution modes.

In this section, you learn how to create, deploy, and use a custom action node. This discussion uses an example FTP action, one that enables you to FTP a specified file or a whole directory from HDFS to a specified external location (typically outside of the Hadoop cluster).

Implementing a Custom Oozie Workflow Action

The FTP custom action used as an example in this section can be useful in several processes that are required to move data — for example, the source or result data being moved between an Hadoop cluster and other drives used by the enterprise applications. Here you learn how to build an `ftp` action implementation that is driven by the following arguments:

- ➤ FTP destination server

- ➤ Port

- ➤ User

- ➤ Password

- ➤ Local directory

- ➤ Remote directory

- ➤ `targetFile` (an optional parameter that, if specified, means that only that file is transferred, or else all files from the specified local directory are transferred)

This custom Oozie action implementation must extend the `ActionExecutor` class provided by Oozie and override all of the required methods. The Oozie `ActionExecutor` supports both synchronous and asynchronous actions. Because `ftp` is a relatively lightweight and quick operation, the implementation `ftpExecutor` shown in Listing 8-1 (code file: class `FtpExecutor`) is a synchronous one, meaning that it is executed within the Oozie execution context.

LISTING 8-1: ActionExecutor class for the ftp custom action

```
import org.apache.oozie.ErrorCode;
import org.apache.oozie.action.ActionExecutor;
import org.apache.oozie.action.ActionExecutorException;
import org.apache.oozie.action.ActionExecutorException.ErrorType;
import org.apache.oozie.client.WorkflowAction;
import org.apache.oozie.util.XmlUtils;
import org.jdom.Element;
import org.jdom.Namespace;

import com.practicalHadoop.oozie.ftp.FtpHandle;
import com.practicalHadoop.oozie.ftp.FtpHandleFactory;

public class FtpExecutor extends ActionExecutor
{
    private final static String SERVER_IP = "serverIP";
    private final static String PORT = "port";
    private final static String USER = "user";
```

continues

LISTING 8-1 *(continued)*

```java
    private final static String PASSWORD = "password";
    private final static String TARGET_FILE = "targetFile";
    private final static String REMOTE_DIR = "remoteDir";
    private final static String LOCALE_DIR = "localeDir";

    private static final String NODENAME = "ftp";
    private static final String SUCCEEDED = "OK";
    private static final String FAILED = "FAIL";
    private static final String KILLED = "KILLED";

    FtpExecutor()    {
        super(NODENAME);
    }

    @Override
    public void initActionType() {
        super.initActionType();
    }

    @Override
    public void check(Context arg0, WorkflowAction arg1)
            throws ActionExecutorException {}

    @Override
    public void end(Context context, WorkflowAction action)
            throws ActionExecutorException  {
        String externalStatus = action.getExternalStatus();
        WorkflowAction.Status status = externalStatus.equals(SUCCEEDED) ?
                WorkflowAction.Status.OK : WorkflowAction.Status.ERROR;
        context.setEndData(status, getActionSignal(status));
    }

    @Override
    public boolean isCompleted(String arg0) {
        return true;
    }

    @Override
    public void kill(Context context, WorkflowAction action)
throws ActionExecutorException  {}

    @Override
    public void start(Context context, WorkflowAction action)
            throws ActionExecutorException  {
        try
        {
            Element actionXml = XmlUtils.parseXml(action.getConf());
            validateAndFtp(context, actionXml);
            context.setExecutionData("OK", null);
        }
        catch(Exception ex)
        {
```

```
            context.setExecutionData(FAILED, null);
            throw new ActionExecutorException(ErrorType.FAILED,
                    ErrorCode.E0000.toString(), ex.getMessage());
        }
    }
    …
}
```

The following five methods are defined as `abstract` in the `ActionExecutor` class, and must be overridden by the action executor implementation:

➤ The `check()` method is used by Oozie to check the status of the action. For synchronous actions, this method does not need to be implemented.

➤ The `end()` method is used for any cleanup or processing that may need to be done after the action is completed. It must also set the result of the execution.

➤ The `isCompleted()` method always returns `true` for a synchronous action. This is because the Oozie server thread blocks when it invokes the method, so the thread can be called only after the action is completed.

➤ The `kill()` method is used to kill the running job or action. For synchronous actions, this method does not need to be implemented.

➤ The `start()` method is used to start the execution of the action. With a synchronous action, the whole action is executed here. This method is invoked by Oozie with two parameters:

  ➤ The `Context` object provides access to the Oozie Workflow execution context, which (among other things) contains Workflow variables, and provides very simple APIs (`set`, `get`) for manipulating them.

  ➤ The `WorkflowAction` object provides access to the Oozie definition of the current action.

In this example, two main tasks are performed in the `start()` method: parameter validation and FTP execution. Both tasks are implemented in the `validateAndFtp()` method shown in Listing 8-2 (code file: class `FtpExecutor`), which is called from the `start()` method.

LISTING 8-2: validateAndFtp method

```
private void validateAndFtp(Context context, Element actionXml)
            throws ActionExecutorException {
    Namespace ns = Namespace.getNamespace("uri:oozie:ftp-action:0.1");
    String serverIP = getCheckNotNull(actionXml, SERVER_IP, "FTP001",
        "No server
      IP was specified.");
    int port;
    String sPort = getCheckNotNull(actionXml, PORT, "FTP002", "No port was
specified.");
    try {
        port = Integer.parseInt(sPort);
    }
```

continues

LISTING 8-2 *(continued)*

```java
            catch(NumberFormatException nfe) {
                throw new ActionExecutorException(ErrorType.ERROR, "FTP003", "Invalid
value for port was specified.");
            }

            String userName = getCheckNotNull(actionXml, USER, "FTP004", "No user was
                specified.");
            String password = getCheckNotNull(actionXml, PASSWORD, "FTP005",
                    "No password
was specified.");

            // Optional
            String localFileName;
            try {
                localFileName = actionXml.getChildTextTrim(TARGET_FILE, ns);;
            }
            catch(Exception ex) {
                localFileName = null;
            }

            String remoteDir = getCheckNotNull(actionXml, REMOTE_DIR, "FTP006",
                    "No remote
              directory was specified.");
            String localeDir = getCheckNotNull(actionXml, LOCALE_DIR, "FTP007",
                    "No locale
              directory was specified.");

            try {
                doFtp(serverIP, port, userName, password, localFileName, remoteDir,
                    localeDir, localFileName);
            }
            catch(IOException ioe)
            {
                throw new ActionExecutorException(ErrorType.ERROR, "FTP008",
                        "FTP failse." + ioe);
            }
        }
    }

    private String getCheckNotNull(Element actionXml, String tagName,
            String actionErrID, String actionErrMsg)
                    throws ActionExecutorException
    {
        Namespace ns = Namespace.getNamespace("uri:oozie:ftp-action:0.1");
        String tmp = actionXml.getChildTextTrim(tagName, ns);
        if(tmp == null)
            throw new ActionExecutorException(ErrorType.ERROR, actionErrID,
actionErrMsg);

        return tmp;
    }

    private void doFtp(String serverIP, int port, String userName,
            String password, String targetFileName, String remoteDir,
```

```
            String localeDir, String localFileName)
                throws IOException
{
    FtpHandle ftpHandle = FtpHandleFactory.create(remoteDir, localeDir);
    ftpHandle.doFtpTransaction(serverIP, port, userName, password,
targetFileName);
}
```

The `validateAndFtp()` method, along with the two helper methods, parse the XML action definition, do trivial argument validation, and eventually use the `FtpHandleFactory` and `FtpHandle` classes to implement the FTP transaction.

> **NOTE** *You can find the implementation of those two classes in the Download section for this Chapter of this book's website. Here, you only see how they are using the* `org.apache.commons.net.ftp` *package from the Apache* `commons-net` *project.*

Now that you know how to implement a custom executor, let's take a look at how it can be deployed so that it can be used in the Workflow.

Deploying Oozie Custom Workflow Actions

The first thing you must do to deploy a custom action is to define the XML schema. Listing 8-3 shows how to do this for the example `ftp` action.

LISTING 8-3: XSD for the ftp action, file ftpAction.xsd, in the Oozie conf directory

```xml
<?xml version="1.0" encoding="UTF-8"?>
<xs:schema xmlns:xs="http://www.w3.org/2001/XMLSchema"
        xmlns:ftp ="uri:custom:ftp-action:0.1"
        elementFormDefault="qualified"
        targetNamespace="uri:custom:ftp-action:0.1">
<xs:complexType name="ftpType">
    <xs:sequence>
        <xs:element name="serverIP" type="xs:string" minOccurs="0" maxOccurs="1" />
        <xs:element name="port" type="xs:string" />
        <xs:element name="user" type="xs:string" />
        <xs:element name="password" type="xs:string" />
        <xs:element name="targetFile" type="xs:string" />
        <xs:element name="remoteDir" type="xs:string" />
        <xs:element name="localeFile" type="xs:string" />
    </xs:sequence>
</xs:complexType>
<xs:element name="ftp" type="ftp:ftpType"></xs:element>
</xs:schema>
```

Both the custom action code and XML schema must be packaged in a single `jar` file (for example, `ftpAction.jar`). Listing 8-4 shows the Oozie `oozie-setup.sh` command that you can use to add this (and any other) `jar` file to Oozie's `war` file.

LISTING 8-4: Custom action deployment command

```
$ bin/oozie-setup.sh -jars ftpAction.jar:mail.jar
```

> **NOTE** *Be aware that the* `oozie-setup.sh` *command will rebuild your Oozie* `.war` *file. If you are using the web page to monitor your jobs, you will lose the Java script extensions as well. A simpler approach (which works very well for testing) is to copy the* `jar` *files into* `${CATALINA_BASE}/webapps/oozie/WEB-INF/lib`, *where* `${CATALINA_BASE}` *is* `/var/lib/oozie/oozie-server`.

Additionally, the XML schema for the new actions shown in Listing 8-4 should be added to `oozie-site.xml`, as shown in Listing 8-5.

LISTING 8-5: oozie-site.xml

```
<property>
        <name>oozie.service.SchemaService.wf.ext.schemas</name>
        <value> oozie-sla-0.1.xsd,hive-action-0.2.xsd,email-action-0.1.xsd,
            ftpAction.xsd</value>
</property>
```

Once a custom action has been deployed, it can be used in a Workflow implementation. To demonstrate how to do this, let's extend the cluster workflow (`cluster-wf`) you learned about in Chapter 7 with an `ftp` action that transfers all data from the `cluster` action output directory to the external FTP server. Listing 8-6 shows how to do this.

LISTING 8-6: Custom ftp action in cluster Workflow

```
<workflow-app name="cluster-wf" xmlns="uri:oozie:workflow:0.3"
        xmlns:sla="uri:oozie:sla:0.1">
    <start to="cluster"/>
    <action name="cluster">
        <java>

        ...............................
        </java>
        <ok to="ftp-cluster-results"/>
        <error to="report-failure"/>
    </action>
    <action name="ftp-cluster-results">
        <ftp xlmns="uri:custom:ftp-action:0.1">
          <serverIP>ftpServer.wrox.com</serverIP>
            <port>21</port>
            <user>reader25</user>
            <password>openAccess</password>
            <remoteDir>/home/reader/reader25</remoteDir>
            <localDir>/user/practicalHadoop/chapter7/cluster</localDir>
        </ftp>
```

```
        <ok to="report-success"/>
        <error to="report-failure"/>
    </action>
    <action name='report-success'>
        <email xmlns="uri:oozie:email-action:0.1">
        ***
    <end name="end"/>
</workflow-app>
```

Now, anyone who looks at the Workflow will clearly see that cluster results are transferred through to the external server using FTP.

As described in this section, extensibility can solve many of Oozie's shortcomings with the Workflow programming language. Unfortunately, extensibility does not help with another Oozie shortcoming — the lack of support for dynamic execution. This deficiency includes the absence of support for loops, dynamic fork/joins, and iterative execution, which are often required to implement many practical MapReduce solutions.

In the next section, you learn about some solutions to overcome this limitation.

ADDING DYNAMIC EXECUTION TO OOZIE WORKFLOWS

As defined in Chapter 6, the Oozie Workflow language enables you to define Workflows that can be represented as Directed Acyclic Graphs (DAGs) of actions. In this section, you learn about an approach that enables you to convert many loops and/or dynamic fork/joins to DAG, thus making them applicable for Oozie implementations.

Overall Implementation Approach

Consider the simple example of a Workflow that must produce a variable number of reports, based on certain input parameters. Let's assume that the actual report generation is implemented as a sub-Workflow — ReportGenerator. If those reports are independent, you could have a fork/join construct that spawns the required number of reports. If those reports are interdependent, they must be sequentially invoked using a loop construct. None of these constructs is supported by Oozie.

So, let's consider a different approach. A loop of a fixed (dynamically calculated) length N can be represented as a loop body repeated N times. Such a code transformation would enable you to convert a Directed Cyclic Graph (that is, a loops construct) to a DAG that is supported by Oozie. One simple way to implement such an approach is by using an in-time generation of Oozie Workflow code based on the loop's length N.

> **NOTE** *Although this example describes a loops case, an exact same approach could be used for a dynamic fork/join construct. As described in Chapter 6, a fork construct requires the Oozie code to specify all branches that are executed in parallel. Generation of such a list of branches could be done in the same manner as the generation of the sequence of invocation that represents a loop.*

Figure 8-1 shows the general architecture for such an approach. Here, a main Workflow can create one or more generated controllers and invoke them as sub-Workflows during execution. A generated controller can rely on one or more functional sub-Workflows to implement functionality that is used by the generated controller.

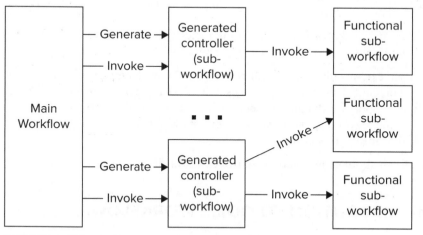

FIGURE 8-1: Using in-time generation

Because the Oozie Workflow language is an XML dialect that is defined by an XML schema, the programmatic generation of a Workflow is fairly straightforward. The simplest way to do this is to use Java Architecture for XML Binding (JAXB) to generate Java binding (based on the Workflow schema), and use these bindings as a Java API to create Oozie Workflows.

You can use the Maven Project Object Model (POM) shown in Listing 8-7 to generate the required Java bindings.

LISTING 8-7: Maven POM to generate JAXB bindings for Oozie Workflow

```
<project xmlns="http://maven.apache.org/POM/4.0.0" xmlns:xsi=
    "http://www.w3.org/2001/XMLSchema-instance"
    xsi:schemaLocation="http://maven.apache.org/POM/4.0.0
    http://maven.apache.org/xsd/maven-4.0.0.xsd">
  <modelVersion>4.0.0</modelVersion>
  <groupId>com.PracticalHadoop</groupId>
  <artifactId>OozieWorkflow</artifactId>
  <version>0.0.1-SNAPSHOT</version>
    <properties>
        <jaxb.version>0.8.0</jaxb.version>
        <jaxb.annotation.version>0.6.0</jaxb.annotation.version>
    </properties>
    <build>
        <plugins>
```

```xml
<plugin>
    <groupId>org.jvnet.jaxb2.maven2</groupId>
    <artifactId>maven-jaxb2-plugin</artifactId>
    <version>${jaxb.version}</version>
    <executions>
        <execution>
          <id>generate-domain</id>
            <phase>generate-sources</phase>
            <goals>
                <goal>generate</goal>
            </goals>
        </execution>
    </executions>
    <configuration>
        <strict>false</strict>
        <schemaDirectory>xml</schemaDirectory>
        <schemaIncludes>
            <value>oozie3.xsd</value>
        </schemaIncludes>
        <bindingIncludes>
            <include>oozie3Bindings.xjb</include>
        </bindingIncludes>
        <extension>true</extension>
        <generateDirectory>src/main/java</generateDirectory>
        <args>
            <arg>-Xannotate</arg>
        </args>
        <plugins>
            <plugin>
                <groupId>org.jvnet.jaxb2_commons</groupId>
                <artifactId>jaxb2-basics-annotate</artifactId>
                <version>${jaxb.annotation.version}</version>
            </plugin>
        </plugins>
    </configuration>
</plugin>

<plugin>
    <groupId>org.apache.maven.plugins</groupId>
    <artifactId>maven-compiler-plugin</artifactId>
    <version>2.3.2</version>
    <configuration>
        <source>1.6</source>
        <target>1.6</target>
    </configuration>
</plugin>
            </plugins>
        </build>
</project>
```

This POM assumes that the Oozie Workflow `.xsd` file (`oozie3.xsd`) is located in the XML directory. It also assumes the JAXB customization file shown in Listing 8-8 is in the same directory.

LISTING 8-8: JAXB customization file

```
<jaxb:bindings
  xmlns:jaxb="http://java.sun.com/xml/ns/jaxb"
       xmlns:xs="http://www.w3.org/2001/XMLSchema"
  xmlns:xjc="http://java.sun.com/xml/ns/jaxb/xjc"
  xmlns:xsi="http://www.w3.org/2001/XMLSchema-instance"
  xmlns:annox="http://annox.dev.java.net"
  xsi:schemaLocation="http://java.sun.com/xml/ns/jaxb
       http://java.sun.com/xml/ns/jaxb/bindingschema_2_0.xsd"
  jaxb:extensionBindingPrefixes="xjc annox"
  version="2.1">

    <jaxb:bindings schemaLocation="oozie3.xsd" node="/xs:schema">
    <jaxb:bindings node="xs:complexType[@name='WORKFLOW-APP']">
      <annox:annotate>
        <annox:annotate annox:class="javax.xml.bind.annotation.XmlRootElement"
            name="WORKFLOW-APP"/>
      </annox:annotate>
    </jaxb:bindings>

    <jaxb:bindings
            node="//xs:complexType[@name='ACTION']/xs:sequence/xs:any
                [@namespace='uri:oozie:sla:0.1']">
            <jaxb:property name="anySLA" />
    </jaxb:bindings>

    </jaxb:bindings>
</jaxb:bindings>
```

Now you can use these bindings as an API for programmatically constructing the Workflow XML.

A more complex use case is with an iterative Workflow, where, for example, the continuation of execution depends on the result of the current iteration. Technically, in this case, the number of iterations is not known upfront. Fortunately, in all practical implementations, the number of iterations is always limited (to ensure the finality of execution). As a result, the same generation approach just described will work.

To better understand this implementation, let's consider a specific example that extends part of the place data validation processes discussed in Chapter 7. After the clusters of stay points are calculated, you want to determine the density of places in the neighborhood (the cluster). You can do this by searching for places around the center point of the cluster latitude and longitude. This is based on calculating "place density" metrics for each cluster.

Rather than going into further implementation details, let's assume that you have a MapReduce application that provides that job. This application additionally classifies (ranges) clusters by a density index, and identifies all clusters with the density index not exceeding the specified threshold. You can interpret those clusters as candidates for potentially discovered new places that you don't know about.

The challenge with this approach is determining the quality of the process for discovering new places. If you knew all unknown places, you could measure this quality as the percentage of discovered places to all unknown places. Another approach (provided by data mining and machine learning techniques) could be to set up an experiment where you estimate the quality.

You could break your collection of places into two parts: places that you treat as *known* (the *basic set*), and places that you will consider *unknown* during the experiment (the *control set*). You can perform all the calculations described in Chapter 7 only with basic set. You would then compare the discovered cluster candidates to the control set. The final measure of quality would be the percentage of places in the control set that were discovered.

Note that the whole process (that is, the set of MapReduce applications controlled from Oozie Workflows, Coordinators, and Bundle) utilizes a number of parameters. For simplicity, let's consider only two parameters: search radius and density threshold. The *search radius* is used in building stay points and clusters of stay points. The *density threshold* is used in selecting clusters — candidates for new places. That can be considered as a computer model with parameters, and raises another question: How can you fine-tune the parameters to improve the quality of the model?

A Machine Learning Model, Parameters, and Algorithm

The approach taken while re-formulating the use case in terms of a computer model, measuring the quality of the model, and tuning the model is very well-known in the realm of machine learning. The natural method to tune the model would be to use a local search (with optimization) — a technique for working with computationally extensive optimization problems. The method suggests refining the solution iteratively.

In this case, the percentage of places in the control set that were discovered can be presented is a function F with two parameters — search radius (r) and density threshold (d), as shown here:

$$F(r,d)$$

The function is not presented analytically. You can only calculate the value for given radius (r) and density threshold (d). To search for a local minimum, you use the Conjugate Gradient method (described in Chapter 3). Let's say you are in the point $p = (r, d)$. You want to calculate the value of F, and you want to continue a local search for a better solution, so you do the following steps.

First, you calculate the value of F in the points:

$$p1 = (r + \Delta r, d)$$

$$p2 = (r + \Delta r, d)$$

$$p3 = (r, d + \Delta d)$$

$$p3 = (r, d + \Delta d)$$

Next, you estimate the derivatives of F(p), or the gradient of the function F(r,d):

$$(\partial F/\partial r) = F(p1) - F(p2))/2\Delta r$$

$$(\partial F/\partial d) = F(p2) - F(p3))/2\Delta r$$

Then you move to the point with a supposedly lower value (in the direction opposite of the gradient vector):

$$Q = (r,d) - \Upsilon (\partial F/\partial r), \partial F/(\partial d))$$

Finally, you calculate the value of function F in the point (r, d), and decide whether you want to continue with the local search.

Figure 8-2 represents the sequence of steps for the Gradient Descent method. Here, the circles represent function values, and the solution trajectory moves from a larger value to a smaller using a gradient.

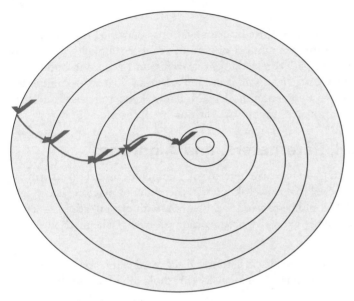

FIGURE 8-2: Local search

That poses a problem, however. How many steps do you want to take before you decide that the parameters of the model are good, or at least you can't find anything better in a reasonable time? You should use the following complex criteria:

➤ The driver class of the MapReduce job will determine if the iteration process should stop because the optimization stops being effective.

➤ In all cases, the number of iterations will be limited with the value specified upfront.

Defining a Workflow for an Iterative Process

To begin defining a Workflow for an iterative process, let's define a functional sub-Workflow that contains the set of unchangeable, repeatedly executed operations, as shown at Listing 8-9 (code file: dynSWF.xml).

LISTING 8-9: Sub-Workflow for model optimization

```xml
<workflow-app name="dyn-swf" xmlns="uri:oozie:workflow:0.3"
    xmlns:sla="uri:oozie:sla:0.1">
    <start to="cluster" />
    <action name="cluster">
```

```xml
        <java>
            <job-tracker>${jobTracker}</job-tracker>
            <name-node>${nameNode}</name-node>
            <job-xml>${clusterProperties}</job-xml>
            <main-class>com.practicalHadoop.strand.Cluster</main-class>
            <arg>-radius=${radius}</arg>
        </java>
        <ok to="range-clusters" />
        <error to="report-failure" />
    </action>
    <action name="range-clusters">
        <java>
            <job-tracker>${jobTracker}</job-tracker>
            <name-node>${nameNode}</name-node>
            <job-xml>${Properties}</job-xml>
            <main-class>com.practicalHadoop.strand.rangeClusters</main-class>
            <arg>-densityThreshold=${densThreshold}</arg>
            <capture-output/>
        </java>
        <ok to="report-success" />
        <error to="report-failure" />
    </action>
    <action name='report-success'>
        <java>
            <job-tracker>${jobTracker}</job-tracker>
            <name-node>${nameNode}</name-node>
            <job-xml>${clusterProperties}</job-xml>
            <main-class>com.practicalHadoop.strand.SaveSFWData</main-class>
        </java>
        <ok to="fail" />
        <error to="end" />
    </action>
    <action name='report-failure'>
        <email xmlns="uri:oozie:email-action:0.1">
            [EMAIL ACTION BODY]
        </email>
        <ok to="end" />
        <error to="fail" />
    </action>
    <kill name="fail">
        <message>
            cluster-wf failed, error message:
                [${wf:errorMessage(wf:lastErrorNode())}]
        </message>
    </kill>
    <end name="end" />
```

The dyn-swf sub-Workflow includes the clustering and ranging actions, and e-mail notification in case of failure. Note, that the range-clusters action definition contains a `<capture-output/>` element that reflects the fact that the action analyzes the progress of the current iteration step and can signal to an external Workflow to exit.

This solution assumes that the value of the function F and the current position (r,d) of the iteration are accumulated in some storage (which could be a table in HBase, or a file in HDFS). Those values are used by the `range-clusters` action to make a decision as to whether the whole iteration process should stop or should continue, as shown in Listing 8-10 (code file: `dynWF.xml`).

LISTING 8-10: The external Workflow for the clustering/ranging process

```
< workflow-app name="dyn-wf" xmlns="uri:oozie:workflow:0.3"
    xmlns:sla="uri:oozie:sla:0.1">
    <start to="call-dyn-wf_1" />
    <action name="call-dyn-wf_1">
        <sub-workflow>
            <app-path>dynWF.xml</app-path>
            <configuration>
                <property>
                    <name>radius</name>
                    <value>0.05</value>
                </property>
                <property>
                    <name>densThreshold</name>
                    <value>10</value>
                </property>
            </configuration>
        </sub-workflow>
        <ok to="check-dynSWF_1" />
        <error to="fail" />
    </action>
    <action name='check-dynSWF_1'>
        <java>
            <job-tracker>${jobTracker}</job-tracker>
            <name-node>${nameNode}</name-node>
            <main-class>com.practicalHadoop.strand.CheckDynSWF</main-class>
            <capture-output />
        </java>
        <ok to="decide-continue" />
        <error to="report-failure" />
    </action>
    <decision name="decide-continue_1">
        <switch>
            <case to="report-success">${wf:actionData('check-dynSWF')['done'
                == "true"]}</case>
            <default to=="call-dyn-wf_2">
        </switch>
    </decision>

    [repeat the group of actions call-dyn-wf_X, check-dynSWF_X and decide-
        continue_X the specified number times ]

    <action name='report-failure'>
        <email xmlns="uri:oozie:email-action:0.1">
            [EMAIL ACTION BODY]
        </email>
        <ok to="fail" />
        <error to="fail" />
    </action>
    <action name='report-success'>
```

```
            <email xmlns="uri:oozie:email-action:0.1">
                  [EMAIL ACTION BODY]
            </email>
            <ok to="end" />
            <error to="fail" />
        </action>
        <kill name="fail">
            <message>
                  cluster-wf failed, error message:
                  [${wf:errorMessage(wf:lastErrorNode())}]
            </message>
        </kill>
        <end name="end" />
    </workflow-app>
```

The dyn-wf Workflow uses the dyn-swf Workflow as a sub-Workflow. It invokes the sub-Workflow, checks the stop signal from the range-clusters action (using the check-dynSWF_X * actions to pick the signal, and the decide-continue_X decision node to check the signal), and stops or continues the iteration. Three actions (call-dyn-wf_X, check-dynSWF_X, and decide-continue_X) represent a group that should be repeated in the Workflow until the process converges. Let's call this group the *iteration control group*. The number of iteration control groups effectively restricts the number of optimization process iterations.

Dynamic Workflow Generation

To generate a dynamic Workflow, you use Java bindings (produced by Maven POM, shown in Listing 8-7) to create a Workflow application shown in Listing 8-10 for the required loop size. Listing 8-11 shows an example of how to do this (code file: class DynWFGen2).

LISTING 8-11: Control group generation

```java
public class DynWfGen2 {
    public static void main(String[] args) throws JAXBException      {
        DynWfGen2 dynWfGen2 = new DynWfGen2("${jobTracker}", "${nameNode}");
        dynWfGen2.createWfApp();

        JAXBContext jc = JAXBContext.newInstance(WORKFLOWAPP.class,
          com.practicalHadoop.oozieEmail.ACTION.class);
        Marshaller m = jc.createMarshaller();
        m.setProperty(Marshaller.JAXB_FORMATTED_OUTPUT, Boolean.TRUE);

        JAXBElement<WORKFLOWAPP> jaxbElem = new JAXBElement<WORKFLOWAPP>(
                new QName("local","workflow-app"),
                WORKFLOWAPP.class,
                dynWfGen2.getWfApp());

        m.marshal(jaxbElem, System.out);
    }

    DynWfGen2(String jobTracker, String nameNode) {
```

continues

LISTING 8-11 *(continued)*

```
            of = new ObjectFactory();
            wfApp = of.createWORKFLOWAPP();
            this.jobTracker = jobTracker;
            this.nameNode = nameNode;
        }

        WORKFLOWAPP getWfApp() {
            return wfApp;
        }

        ObjectFactory of;
        WORKFLOWAPP wfApp;
        String jobTracker;
        String nameNode;
        int totalIter = 2;
        int currentIter = 1;

        void createWfApp() {
            wfApp.setName("dyn-wf");
            addStartNode("call-dyn-wf_1");

            for(currentIter = 1; currentIter <= totalIter; currentIter++) {
                Map<String, String> propMap = new HashMap<String, String>();
                propMap.put("radius", "0.05");
                propMap.put("densThreshold", "10");
                addSunWorkflowAction("call-dyn-wf_" + currentIter, "dynWF.xml",
                        propMap, "check-dynSWF_" + currentIter, "fail");

                propMap = new HashMap<String, String>();
                addJavaAction("check-dynSWF_" + currentIter,
                        "com.practicalHadoop.strand.CheckDynSWF",
                        propMap, "decide-continue_" + currentIter, "fail");

                Map<String, String> cases = new HashMap<String, String>();
                cases.put("report-success", "${wf:actionData('" + "check-dynSWF_"
                        + currentIter + "')['done' == " + "true");

                String sDecisionDefault = "call-dyn-wf_" + (currentIter + 1);
                if(currentIter == totalIter)
                    sDecisionDefault = "report-success";

                addDecisionNode("decide-continue_" + currentIter, cases,
                    sDecisionDefault);
            }
            addEmailAction("report-failure", "fail", "fail",
                    "OoAdmin@company.com", "othersAdmin@company.com",
                    "cluster-wf failed",
                    "cluster-wf failed, error message: /n/t/t
                    [${wf:errorMessage(wf:lastErrorNode())}]");

            addEmailAction("report-success", "end", "fail",
                    "OoAdmin@company.com", "othersAdmin@company.com",
```

```
                    "cluster-wf failed",
                    "cluster-wf finished");
        addKillNode("fail", "cluster-wf failed, error message:
                \n\t[${wf:errorMessage(wf:lastErrorNode())}]");
        addEndNode("end");
    }
```

The number of iterative sections in this code is specified by the value of totalIter. The code uses a number of methods to generate Workflow's nodes and actions.

Listing 8-12 shows two such methods: addDecisionNode and addJavaAction. You can see that those methods are reusable, and after they are created, the generation of a dynamic Workflow becomes a pretty trivial task. Also, it is worth noting that once those helper methods are tested, the chances that a Workflow contains any XML errors are minimal.

LISTING 8-12: Example of helper methods to generate a Workflow

```
    private void addDecisionNode(String name, Map<String, String> cases,
          String defaultElemTo)     {
            DECISION decision = of.createDECISION();
            decision.setName(name);
            wfApp.getDecisionOrForkOrJoin().add(decision);

            SWITCH switchElem = of.createSWITCH();
            decision.setSwitch(switchElem);

            Set<Map.Entry<String, String>> entries = cases.entrySet();
            for(Entry<String, String> entry : entries) {
                CASE caseElem = of.createCASE();
                caseElem.setTo(entry.getKey());
                caseElem.setValue(entry.getValue());
                switchElem.getCase().add(caseElem);
            }

            DEFAULT defaultElem = of.createDEFAULT();
            defaultElem.setTo(defaultElemTo);
            switchElem.setDefault(defaultElem);
    }

    private void addJavaAction(String name, String mainClass, Map<String, String>
        propMap,
              String okNodeName, String failNodeName) {
            ACTION action = of.createACTION();
            action.setName(name);
            JAVA javaAction = of.createJAVA();
            action.setJava(javaAction);

            javaAction.setJobTracker(jobTracker);
            javaAction.setNameNode(nameNode);
            javaAction.setMainClass("com.practicalHadoop.strand.CheckDynSWF");
            javaAction.setCaptureOutput(new FLAG());
```

continues

```
CONFIGURATION callSwfConf = makeConfiguration(propMap);
javaAction.setConfiguration(callSwfConf);

setOkTransition(action, okNodeName);
setFailTransition(action, failNodeName);

wfApp.getDecisionOrForkOrJoin().add(action);
    }
}
```

The generation of a dynamic Workflow, coupled with the general Workflow architecture shown in Figure 8-1, enables you to effectively use Oozie for many Directed Cyclic Graph problems (including loops and dynamic fork/joins).

Now let's look at Oozie's Java APIs, which can be used for programmatically starting and controlling Oozie execution from other applications.

USING THE OOZIE JAVA API

Chapter 7 describes how you can submit and start Oozie jobs from the Hadoop cluster edge node. However, to integrate Hadoop execution into an overall enterprise application, it is often necessary for you to start Oozie jobs programmatically. One possible use case is integrating Oozie with a general-purpose business process management (BPM) engine, where Hadoop applications are only a component of more general business processes, and other components run outside of an Hadoop cluster.

Oozie offers the Java API in the Oozie client component. Actually, the Oozie client includes more than one Oozie Java API in the package org.apache.oozie.client. It also includes the Oozie Command Line Interface (CLI), Oozie REST API, and support for JavaScript Object Notation (JSON). Both the Oozie CLI and Oozie Java API are wrappers around the Oozie REST API.

Listing 8-13 (code file: class WfStarter) shows an example of how to build the Oozie configuration and use it to submit an Oozie Workflow. As described in Chapter 7, Oozie configuration is one of the ways to pass arguments to Oozie jobs. This approach is a preferred option in the case where the Oozie Workflow, Coordinator, or Bundle is submitted through the Java API.

LISTING 8-13: Example of submitting Oozie job through the Oozie Java API

```
package com.practicalHadoop.javaApi;

import java.util.Properties;

import org.slf4j.Logger;
import org.slf4j.LoggerFactory;

import org.apache.oozie.client.OozieClient;
import org.apache.oozie.client.OozieClientException;
```

```
import org.apache.oozie.client.WorkflowJob;
import org.apache.oozie.client.WorkflowJob.Status;

public class WfStarter  {
    final OozieClient oozClient;
    final Properties confProp;

    private static final Logger logger = LoggerFactory.getLogger("WfStarter");

    public static WfStarter createWfStarter(Properties confProp, String
        oozServerURL)
    {
        return new WfStarter(confProp, oozServerURL);
    }

    private WfStarter(Properties confProp, String oozServerURL)  {
        this.confProp = confProp;
        this.oozClient = new OozieClient(oozServerURL);
    }

    public String startJob() throws OozieClientException  {
        logger.info(" ** submitting workflow ");
        String oozJobID = oozClient.run(confProp);
        return oozJobID;
    }


    // returns one of values: PREP, RUNNING, SUCCEEDED, KILLED, FAILED, SUSPENDED
    // (see the enum Status in the class org.apache.oozie.client.WorkflowJob)
    public Status getJobStatus(String jobID) throws OozieClientException  {
        logger.info(" ** submitting job status request ");
        WorkflowJob job = oozClient.getJobInfo(jobID);
        return job.getStatus();
    }
}
```

> **NOTE** *When using java Oozie APIs, be aware that this implementation, by default, utilizes the identity of the user of the machine on which it is running. The following code snippet shows what the Oozie client is doing:*
>
> ```
> public Properties createConfiguration() {
>     Properties conf = new Properties();
>     String userName = USER_NAME_TL.get();
>     if (userName == null) {
>         userName = System.getProperty("user.name");
>     }
>     conf.setProperty(USER_NAME, userName);
>     return conf;
> }
> ```
>
> For a user process to run as a specific user, the userName must be specified in
> Properties.

The main class of the Oozie Java API is the `OozieClient` class. The class is constructed with only one parameter — the Oozie server URL — and provides all communications with an Oozie server. Methods for this class enable you to start an Oozie job, get the job's status (as shown in Listing 8-13), and perform other job-related functionality (including start, submit, resume, suspend, kill Workflow, and more).

A `JUnit` test, `WfStarterTest` shown in Listing 8-14 (code file: class `WfStarterTest`), demonstrates how to use the `WfStarter` class to start a Workflow job and obtain its status.

LISTING 8-14: Test for submitting Workflow with Java API

```
package com.practicalHadoop.javaApi;

import static org.junit.Assert.*;

import java.util.Properties;

import org.apache.oozie.client.OozieClient;
import org.apache.oozie.client.WorkflowJob.Status;
import org.junit.BeforeClass;
import org.junit.Test;
import org.slf4j.Logger;
import org.slf4j.LoggerFactory;

public class WfStarterTest {
    private static final Logger logger = LoggerFactory.getLogger("WfStarterTest");

    static final private String OOZ_URL = "http://arch024:11000/oozie/";
    static final private String JOB_TRACKER = "arch023.hq.navteq.com:8021";
    static final private String NAME_NODE = "hdfs://arch021.hq.navteq.com:8020";
    static final private String WF_LOCATION_URL =
        "${nameNode}/user/ayakubov/dataPrep/workflow.xml";
    static final private String INPUT_DATA = "/user/ayakubov/data/";
    static final private String HIVE_DEFAULT_XML_PATH =
        "${nameNode}/sharedlib/conf-xml/hive-default.xml";
    static final private String WF_APP_LIB =
        ">${nameNode}/user/ayakubov/dataPrep/lib
        /chapter7-0.0.1-SNAPSHOT.jar";

    static WfStarter starter;
    static Properties confProp;

    @BeforeClass
    public static void setUpBeforeClass() throws Exception {
        confProp = new Properties();
        confProp.setProperty(OozieClient.APP_PATH, WF_LOCATION_URL);
        confProp.setProperty("oozie.wf.application.lib", WF_APP_LIB);
        confProp.setProperty("jobTracker", JOB_TRACKER);
        confProp.setProperty("nameNode", NAME_NODE);
        confProp.setProperty("user.name", "ayakubov");
        confProp.setProperty("user.password", "Navteq07");
```

```
        confProp.setProperty("input.data", INPUT_DATA);
        confProp.setProperty("HIVE_DEFAULT_XML_PATH", HIVE_DEFAULT_XML_PATH);
        starter = WfStarter.createWfStarter(confProp, OOZ_URL);
    }

    @Test
    public void testStarter() throws Exception    {
        String jobID = starter.startJob();
        logger.info(" ** started the job: " + jobID);

        Thread.sleep(10 * 1000);

        Status status = starter.getJobStatus(jobID);
        logger.info(" ** job status: " + status);

        while(status == Status.RUNNING)       // can also add the job time threshold
        {
            logger.info(" ** job status: " + status);
            status = starter.getJobStatus(jobID);
        }

        logger.info(" ** job finished with the status: " + status);
        assertEquals(status, Status.SUCCEEDED);
    }
}
```

Note that all the parameters required for running the Workflow job (including the credentials of the user that will be used to run the Workflow) are specified here. Listing 8-15 shows the result of the test execution.

LISTING 8-15: Test for submitting Workflow with Java API

```
6:28.209 [main] INFO  WfStarter -  ** submitting workflow
14:16:28.499 [main] INFO  WfStarterTest -  ** started the job:
     0000192-130325104445038-oozie-oozi-W
14:16:58.501 [main] INFO  WfStarter -  ** submitting job status request
14:16:59.300 [main] INFO  WfStarterTest -  ** job status: RUNNING
14:16:59.300 [main] INFO  WfStarter -  ** submitting job status request
14:17:00.055 [main] INFO  WfStarterTest -  ** job status: RUNNING
***
***
14:17:53.724 [main] INFO  WfStarter -  ** submitting job status request
14:17:55.675 [main] INFO  WfStarterTest -  ** job finished with the status:
     SUCCEDDED
```

As you learned in the Chapter 4, an uber jar file (or super jar) is a jar file that (in addition to normal jar content) can contain whole jar files, as well as native libraries that an application depends on. Hadoop MapReduce jobs accept uber jars. However, as of this writing, you can't use uber jars when submitting Oozie jobs. In the next section, you learn how to overcome this restriction to extend Oozie's functionality.

USING UBER JARS WITH OOZIE APPLICATIONS

Uber `jar` files are quite often used to implement MapReduce applications. So, the fact that Oozie does not support uber `jar` files presents a challenge when using Oozie to orchestrate MapReduce applications.

Before delving into how to meet this challenge, let's first look at how Hadoop MapReduce processes uber `jar` files. When the Hadoop job is invoked using the `hadoop` command, the `main()` method of the `RunJar` class first creates a temporary directory from which resources (including `jar` files) will be distributed to mappers and reducers on cluster nodes. It then invokes the `unJar` method. This method uses the Java API (`java.util.jar.JarFile`) to extract all internal `jar` files from the main `jar` specified in the `hadoop` command, as shown in the (simplified) code (Hadoop-common-2.0.0) shown in Listing 8-16.

LISTING 8-16: Extraction of internal jars in Hadoop

```
JarFile jar = new JarFile(jarFile);
Enumeration<JarEntry> entries = jar.entries();
while (entries.hasMoreElements())
{
    JarEntry entry = (JarEntry)entries.nextElement();
    ........................................
    InputStream in = jar.getInputStream(entry);
    File file = new File(toDir, entry.getName());
    ensureDirectory(file.getParentFile());
    OutputStream out = new FileOutputStream(file);
    IOUtils.copyBytes(in, out, 8192);
    out.close();
    in.close();
}
jar.close();
```

The class `org.apache.hadoop.io.IOUtils` provides actual byte copy for the internal `jar` files. So, when a MapReduce job is started with the `hadoop` command, the extraction of internal `jar` files from the uber `jar` happens on the edge node in the local filesystem. During the job submission steps, `JobClient` copies all those `jar` files to the machines where the mapper and reducer tasks are executed.

As described in Chapter 6, Oozie uses a different mechanism to invoke Hadoop MapReduce jobs (with action executors and launchers). `RunJar`-based uber `jar` processing is not happening in this case, and, consequently, the uber `jar` files are, by default, not supported by the MapReduce job invoked by Oozie.

Figure 8-3 shows a solution. In this case, an intermediate class (`UberLauncher`) is invoked by a `java` action launcher, and this class invokes the actual MapReduce main class. The `UberLauncher` class provides the same functionality for the Oozie `java` action as the class `JarFile` provides for Hadoop jobs that are started with the `hadoop` command.

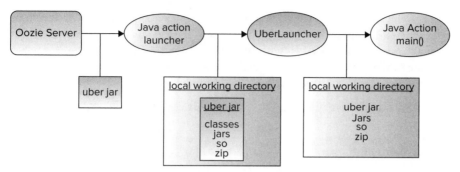

FIGURE 8-3: Using uber jar with the Oozie java action

Here is the sequence of actions provided by the `UberLauncher` class:

1. Identify the `jar` used for MapReduce execution, and find the location of that `jar` (in the local filesystem directory of the mapper task).

2. Un-`jar` (that is, uncompress) all `jar` files (and, optionally, other resources) from the uber `jar` into the same local filesystem directory.

3. Create a new class loader (`PrefUrlClassLoader`), which is a subclass of `java.net.URLClassLoader`. That new class loader adds all `jar` files extracted from the uber `jar` into the class path, and reverses the order of class loading (overriding the method `loadClass()`). The new class loading gives a preference to classes from the uber `jar` and from `jar` files extracted from the uber `jar`.

4. Use reflection to invoke the entry class of a `java` action specified as a parameter (`appMain`).

Listing 8-17 shows the actual `UberLauncher`.

LISTING 8-17: UberLauncher class

```
public static void main(String[] args) throws Exception {
    PropertyMngr propMngr = PropertyMngr.create(args);
    String sAppStart = propMngr.getValue("appMain");
    String sPrefPkg = propMngr.getValue(CLD_PREF_PRG);
    CLDBuilder cldBuilder = new CLDBuilder();
    ClassLoaderNameFilter loadFilter =
        ClassLoaderNameFilter.create(sPrefPkg);
    cldBuilder.buildPrefLoader(loadFilter);

    try {
        cldBuilder.invokeMain(sAppStart, args);
    }
    catch (Throwable e) {
        String errMsg = "………."
        logger.error(errMsg);
        throw new RuntimeException(errMsg);
    }
}
```

The main method obtains the value of the -appMain argument, creates the instance of the CLDBuilder class, invokes the instance first to build and then to deploy a new class loader, and then invokes the entry point of the original java action (specified with the -appMain parameter). The UberLauncher main() method also creates a filter (an instance of the class ClassLoaderNameFilter) that specifies what packages from the uber jar should have preference in loading.

Listing 8-18 shows the new class loader that is created by CLDBuilder (code file: CLDBuilder).

LISTING 8-18: BuildPrefLoader method

```
public ClassLoader buildPrefLoader(ClassLoaderNameFilter loadFilter)
throws Exception {
    CLUtil cldUtil = new CLUtil(prn);
    cldUtil.unpackUberJar(bFlatExtract);
    ClassLoader extLoader = cldUtil.extendClassLoader(loadFilter);
    return extLoader;
}
```

The buildPrefLoader() method orchestrates the building of a new class loader. It uses the unpackUberJar() method to recursively extract jar files from the uber jar, and then calls the method extendClassLoader() from the class CLUtil to finalize the building and to deploy the new class loader.

The PrefUrlClassLoader class extends the URLClassLoader class. It is set up with URLs of all jar files, extracted recursively from the uber jar. This class overrides the loadClass() method of the java.net.URLClassLoader class. The main idea here is to redefine the order of loading — to provide preference loading for the classes from the jar files extracted from the uber jar.

The PrefUrlClassLoader class uses the ClassLoaderNameFilter instance to ensure that only classes from the uber jar will be loaded from jar files. Listing 8-19 (code file: class PrefUrlClassLoader) shows the loadClass method from this class.

LISTING 8-19: Loading classes in PrefUrlClassLoader

```
@Override
public Class<?> loadClass(String name) throws ClassNotFoundException {
    Class<?> cls = null;
    /* for classes from the root of uber jar: they were already loaded with
            parent CL,
     * but we want them with PrefUrlClassLoader, to create "children" with
     * by the same PrefUrlClassLoader
     */
    If(loadFilter.internalLoad(name)) {
        cls = findLoadedClass(name);
        if(cls == null)      {
            try     {
                    cls = findClass(name);
            }
            catch(ClassNotFoundException clnf) {
```

```
                        // never mind, it will try now the parent class loader
                   }
                           catch(Throwable thr) {
                   // never mind, it will try now the parent class loader
                        }
                   }
              }
         }

         if(cls == null) {
         /* this will check both super - URLClassLoader,
          * and parent class loader
          */
              cls = super.findLoadedClass(name);
              if(cls == null) {
              try {
                   cls = getParent().loadClass(name);
              }
              catch(ClassNotFoundException clnf)
    {

                   logger.error(***);
              }
         }
    }
```

As you can see, the `loadClass()` method first checks to see if the class passes the filter for preferential loading (that is, the `internalLoad()` method). If the filter is passed, the `loadClass()` method attempts to find the class in the uber jar (and in jar files extracted from the uber jar). If the filter is not passed, and attempts to find the class fail, the `loadClass()` method resorts to the parent class loader.

The `invokeMain()` method shown in Listing 8-20 (code file: class `CLDBuilder`) loads an instance of the `clazz` class (the entry point of the original java action) with the `PrefUrlClassLoader`. That means that the `clazz` class and all classes created from the `clazz` class will be using `PrefUrlClassLoader`. In fact, that means that whole java action will be using preferential classes from the uber jar and jar files extracted from the uber jar. In particular, this means that all those classes are known to the java action.

LISTING 8-20: Invoking the original java action

```
    public void invokeMain(String clsName, String[] args)
              throws Throwable {
         Thread.currentThread().setContextClassLoader(prefURLClassLoader);
         Class<?> clazz = myCLD.loadClass(clsName);
         Method method = clazz.getMethod("main", new Class<?>[]
                   { String[].class });

         boolean bValidModifiers = false;
         boolean bValidVoid = false;
         if (method != null) {
              // Disable IllegalAccessException
              method.setAccessible(true);
              int nModifiers = method.getModifiers();
```

continues

LISTING 8-20 *(continued)*

```
            bValidModifiers = Modifier.isPublic(nModifiers)
                    && Modifier.isStatic(nModifiers);
            Class<?> clazzRet = method.getReturnType();
                bValidVoid = (clazzRet == void.class);
    }
    if (method == null || !bValidModifiers || !bValidVoid){
        String errMsg = ***
        Logger.error(errMsg);
        throw new NoSuchMethodException(errMsg);
    }
    try {
        method.invoke(null, (Object) args);
    }
    catch (InvocationTargetException e) {
        throw e.getTargetException();
    }
}
```

With the `UberLauncher` class in place, you must now modify the `java` action node definition as shown in Listing 8-21 to specify the `UberLauncher` class as a `main-class` argument and an actual MapReduce `main` class as an invocation argument with the name `appMain`.

LISTING 8-21: Definition of the clustering action for uber jar

```
<action name="cluster">
        <java>
        ..............................................
            <main-class>com.practicalHadoop.uber.UberLauncher</main-class>
            <java-opts>${Dopt_loglevel} ${Xopt_jvm}</java-opts>
            <arg>-appMain=com.practicalHadoop.strand.Cluster</arg>
            <arg>-version=${spatial4jVer}</arg>
            <arg>-tileSize=${tileLevel}</arg>
            <arg>-distance=$distance}</arg>
        </java>
        ..............................
</action>
```

The final discussion in this chapter shows you how many of the advanced Oozie features can be used together to build a data ingestion conveyer.

DATA INGESTION CONVEYER

As mentioned in Chapter 1, a typical use case for the Hadoop platform entails support for a Big Data collection where new data is constantly arriving. In this section, you learn how to utilize that process starting from the point when new data files are transferred to HDFS. A number of tools are used to collect, aggregate, and move large amounts of data to HDFS, including Flume, Scribe, FTP, distcp, and so on.

Figure 8-4 shows the general data life cycle on the Hadoop platform. As you can see, this involves the following steps:

1. Units of data are collected, aggregated, and moved to the Hadoop platform.

2. Data is preprocessed, grouped, and ingested into permanent data repositories. (For example, in Chapter 7, you learned about two such data repositories: the probe data repository and the places data repository.)

3. Data is stored and maintained in data repositories.

4. Data is used by a variety of Hadoop applications.

5. Data can be retired from the data repositories.

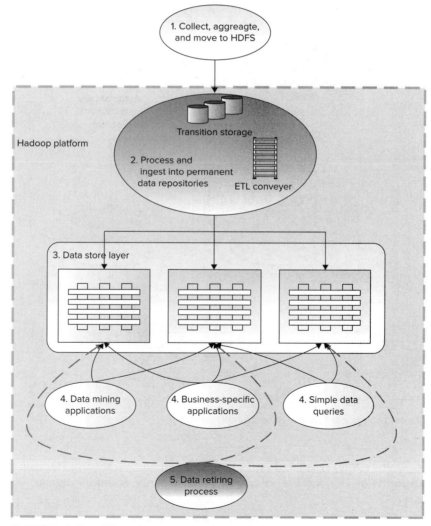

FIGURE 8-4: Data life cycle on the Hadoop platform

For this discussion, let's consider the second step — processing data that arrived onto HDFS up to the point where data is ingested into the data repositories. Consider the case where new data of a different nature can constantly arrive in the form of files sent to the temporary data storage (that is, a set of directories on HDFS). Data should be filtered, validated, transformed, grouped, and eventually distributed into permanent data repositories.

Because Hadoop does not have a transactional mechanism, to prevent the loss of valuable data, the whole process should leverage the failover and scalability offered by the Hadoop platform. Because the amount of constantly arriving data can't be handled without automation, that's where Oozie comes into the picture.

As an illustration of using Oozie and applying some of the described techniques, let's develop a generic Oozie-based design pattern for a general-purpose Hadoop data ingestion process. Let's call this a *data ingestion conveyer*. Figure 8-5 shows the high-level components of the data ingestion conveyer pattern.

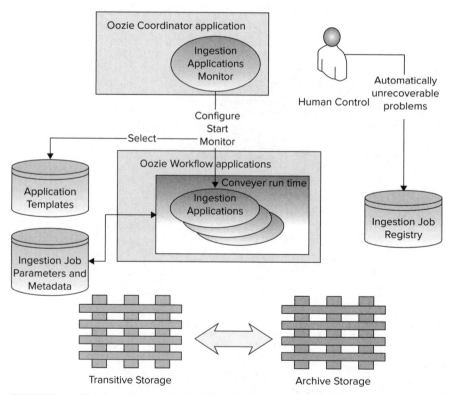

FIGURE 8-5: High-level components of the data ingestion conveyer

The incoming data units (files) are placed into a temporary storage (Transitive Storage), which is a collection of directories on HDFS. That process is out of the scope of this discussion, so no more detail is necessary.

When a new data unit is discovered, the Ingestion Applications Monitor creates a new ingestion job, and registers that job in the Ingestion Jobs Registry.

Each data unit is unique, and the Application Template Storage should contain a Workflow template for that data type. The template is identified using the Ingestion Job Parameters and Metadata database. If such a template is missing, an error occurs that can't be recovered automatically and requires human intervention. In such a case, the data unit is moved from Transitive Storage to the Archive Storage, and the ingestion job is suspended.

The Ingestion Jobs Registry contains the current state and reports for all present ingestion jobs. An operator can resolve a data conflict (for example, add a template, or change the unit data nature), or instruct the Ingestion Applications Monitor to cancel the ingestion job. The data unit stays in the Archive Storage.

If an ingestion template for the data unit is successfully identified, the Ingestion Applications Monitor can group new data units by template, configure a Workflow, create an Oozie job configuration, and submit a new ingestion job to the Oozie server using the Oozie Java API.

The Workflow for the ingestion job would normally contain several Oozie actions. For simplicity, this example includes only `java` actions. Each `java` action is executed as a step in an ingestion pattern context. That context includes additional actions in the Workflow, and the creation of a runtime context for each action.

Before any "actual" action Workflow executes in the ingestion pattern context, an additional decision node checks to determine if the action should be invoked or skipped. If the action is invoked, it will be invoked though the `UberLauncher`. After the `UberLauncher` makes available all resources from the specified uber `jar`, it invokes a `StepRunner` class. As shown in Figure 8-6, that class provides the following:

1. Configuration enrichment (reading parameters from the Ingestion Job Parameters and Metadata database).

2. Parameters validation.

3. Data availability check.

4. External services availability check (and optionally resources allocation).

5. Initialization of a worker step.

6. Invocation of step worker, which is a class that is specified for a conventional Oozie `java` action, such as clustering, ranging by density, and so on.

7. Validation of action result with specified acceptance criteria (for example, the percentage of successfully processed records exceeds the specified threshold).

> **NOTE** *In general, this corresponds to post-conditions in a design-by-contract method, while Steps 3 and 4 are essentially preconditions.*

8. Saving parameters for use in the following steps into the Ingestion Job Parameters and Metadata database.

9. Saving the current ingestion application state and report in the Ingestion Job Registry (including job status after every step, and optional parameters such as the location of temporary output data that can be used to configure the next step).

If a step fails or an acceptance criterion is not satisfied, the ingestion application is suspended, and current working data is moved into Archive Storage. The Ingestion Applications Monitor periodically reviews the status of every job. If the problem is recoverable, the Ingestion Applications Monitor will rerun the job from the last successive step. For example, that could happen in the case where external services were not available, but could be available later. In that case, `StepRunner` would suspend the application with the `REPEAT` status.

If the problem does not enable automatic recovery, the Ingestion Applications Monitor waits for operator intervention. The operator would communicate his or her decision to the Ingestion Applications Monitor by modifying the application status and parameters in the Ingestion Jobs Registry.

Listing 8-22 shows an example of some simplified code for the `StepRunner` class. This code uses methods from other classes, which are not shown here. However, the taxonomy (naming) should explain the logic.

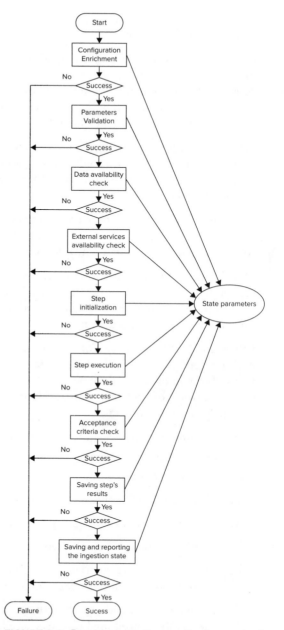

FIGURE 8-6: Runtime ingestion application context

LISTING 8-22: Example StepRunner class

```java
public static void main(String[] args) {
    StepRunner stepRunner = new StepRunner();
    stepRunner.run(args);
}
```

```
    StepWorker worker;
    String stepName;
    StepArchon stepArchon;

    private void run(String[] args) {
        stepArchon = StepArchon.createStepArchon("AWS_STEP_CONFIG");
        PropertyMngr propMngr = PropertyMngr.create(args);
        propMngr.setJvmProperties();
        stepName = propMngr.getValueProgParam(STEP_NAME_WFKEY);
        StepConfig stepConf = stepArchon.getStepConfig(stepName);

        Runnable myHook = StepRunnerShutdownHook.create(this);
        Thread hookThr = new Thread(myHook);
        Runtime.getRuntime().addShutdownHook(hookThr);

        long startTime = System.currentTimeMillis();

        DaoFactory daoFactory = DaoFactory.create(propMngr);
        JobBaseReport report = null;
        boolean bError = true;
        String sErrMsg = "undefined";

        _blok_label: try {
            PrecondArchon precondArchon = PrecondArchon.create(propMngr, args,
    stepArchon);
            if (!precondArchon.check()) {
                sErrMsg = "StepRunner.run(): FATAL ERROR step properties are
                    UNVALID";
                report = ReportFactory.createReport(propMngr,
                    JobStatusEnum.PRECONDITION_FAILED,
                            sErrMsg, null, startTime, System.currentTimeMillis());
                break _blok_label;
            }
            args = precondArchon.setStepParams(args);


            AvailabilityEsTask avaiExTask = new AvailabilityEsTask(propMngr);
            Boolean bExtSys = avaiExTask.checkPrecondition();
            if (!bExtSys) {
                sErrMsg = "StepRunner.run(): FATAL ERROR : ext system not
                    available";
                String failDesk = avaiExTask.getFailureDescription();
                String state = avaiExTask.getCheckAvailState();
                report = ReportFactory.createReport(propMngr,
                JobStatusEnum.EXT_SYS_UNAVAILABLE,
                    failDesk, state, startTime, System.currentTimeMillis());
                break _blok_label;
            }

            AvailabilityDataTask avaiDataTask = new AvailabilityDataTask(propMngr);
            Boolean bDataAvail = avaiDataTask.checkPrecondition();
            if (!bDataAvail) {
                sErrMsg = "StepRunner.run(): FATAL ERROR : data are not available";
```

continues

LISTING 8-22 *(continued)*

```
            String failDesk = avaiDataTask.getFailureDescription();
            String state = avaiDataTask.getCheckAvailState();
            report = ReportFactory.createReport(propMngr,
        JobStatusEnum.DATA_UNAVAILABLE,
                failDesk, state, startTime, System.currentTimeMillis());
            break _blok_label;
        }

        worker = WorkerFactory.create(stepConf);

        int workerExitCode = 0;
        try {
            workerExitCode = worker.go(args);
        }
        catch (Exception ex)
        {
            sErrMsg = "StepRunner.run(): FATAL ERROR - worker exception " + ex;
            sErrMsg = ex.getMessage() + " : worker error - " +
            worker.getJobFailureMsg();
            break _blok_label;
        }

        if(workerExitCode != 0) {
            sErrMsg = worker.getJobFailureMsg();
            break _blok_label;
        }

        OutcomeManager outcomeMngr = OutcomeManager.create(propMngr);
        Boolean bOutcome = outcomeMngr.getOutcome(worker);
        if (!bOutcome) {
            String failMsg = outcomeMngr.getFailureMsg();
            sErrMsg = "StepRunner.run(): FATAL ERROR - bOutcome false " +
                failMsg;
            report = ReportFactory.createReport(propMngr,
        JobStatusEnum.DATA_UNAVAILABLE,
                failMsg, failMsg, startTime, System.currentTimeMillis());
            break _blok_label;
        }

        addParamsForTestWorkers();

        String sProcessUID =
            propMngr.getJvmProperty(INGESTION_TRANSACTION_ID_WFKEY);
        ActionParamExchanger exchanger = ActionParamExcangerFactory.create(
                stepArchon,
                ActionParamExchangerFactory.ActionParameterExcangerEnum.RDB);
        if (exchanger.saveParameters(worker.getConfiguration(), sProcessUID,
            stepName) == false) {
            String failDesk = exchanger.getFailureDescription();
            sErrMsg = "StepRunner.run(): FATAL ERROR - bOutcome false " +
            failDesk;
```

```
            report = ReportFactory.createReport(propMngr,
        JobStatusEnum.DATA_UNAVAILABLE,
                failDesk, failDesk, startTime, System.currentTimeMillis());
            break _blok_label;
        }

    bError = false;
    report = ReportFactory.createReport(propMngr, worker, null, bOutcome,
        startTime,
            System.currentTimeMillis());
}
catch (Throwable thr) {
    StringWriter sw = new StringWriter();
    PrintWriter pw = new PrintWriter(sw);
    thr.printStackTrace(pw);
    sErrMsg = "StepRunner.run() FATAL ERROR - \n" + sw.toString();
    throw new RuntimeException(thr);
}

if (bError == true)
    throw new RuntimeException(sErrMsg);

try   {
    daoFactory.createReportDao().save(report);

    JobStatus status = JobBaseStatus.create(report);
    daoFactory.createStatusDao().save(status);
}
catch (Exception ioe) {
    throw new RuntimeException("StepRunner.saving report and status:
        failed",
        ioe);
}
}
```

SUMMARY

This chapter concludes an extensive (three-chapter) examination of Oozie. This chapter showed you several advanced Oozie use cases, and showed several Oozie customization and extension techniques.

In a real-life application, you always experience problems that are not described in manuals and examples. The main purpose of this chapter has been to show you how to work around certain limitations of Oozie to build real-life automation processes on the Hadoop platform. These techniques include building a custom Oozie action, just-in-time generation of Oozie Workflows, using Oozie Java APIs, and using uber jar files with Oozie.

In Chapter 9, you learn about ways to build real-time Hadoop applications.

9

Real-Time Hadoop

WHAT'S IN THIS CHAPTER?

➤ Getting to know different types of real-time Hadoop applications

➤ Dissecting examples of HBase-based real-time applications

➤ Understanding new approaches for building Hadoop real-time applications

WROX.COM CODE DOWNLOADS FOR THIS CHAPTER

The wrox.com code downloads for this chapter are found at www.wiley.com/go/ prohadoopsolutions on the Download Code tab. The code is in the Chapter 9 download and individually named according to the names throughout the chapter.

So far in this the book, you have learned about how to use Hadoop for batch processing, which is very useful, but limited with regard to the number and types of problems that companies are trying to solve. Real-time access to Hadoop's massive data storage and processing power will lead to an even more expanded use of this ecosystem.

> **NOTE** *The term "real time" derives from its use in early simulation techniques, which simulated real-world processes at a rate that matched the rate of the real process. Typically, a system is considered to be real-time if the correctness of its functionality is defined by both its logical correctness, and the amount of time in which its operations are performed.*

"Real time" is one of those terms that means different things to different people and has different applications. It largely depends on the timing requirement imposed by the system's consumers. In the context of this chapter, "real-time Hadoop" describes any Hadoop-based implementation that can respond to a user's requests in a timeframe that is acceptable for the user. Depending on the use case, this timeframe can range from seconds to several minutes, but not hours.

In this chapter, you learn about the main types of Hadoop real-time applications, and about the basic components that make up such applications. You also learn how to build HBase-based real-time applications.

REAL-TIME APPLICATIONS IN THE REAL WORLD

Hadoop real-time applications are not new. Following are a couple of examples:

➤ **OpenTSDB** — One of the first real-time Hadoop applications was OpenTSDB — a common-purpose implementation of a distributed, scalable Time Series Database (TSDB) that supported storing, indexing, and serving metrics collected from computer systems (for example, network gear, operating systems, and applications) on a large scale. OpenTSDB then made this data easily accessible and graphable.

➤ **HStreaming** — The real-time platform of HStreaming enables the running of advanced analytics on Hadoop in real time to create live dashboards, to identify and recognize patterns within (or across) multiple data streams, and to trigger actions based on predefined rules or heuristics using real-time MapReduce.

A mainstream example of using real-time Hadoop can be seen on the popular social networking site, Facebook, which utilizes several real-time Hadoop applications, including the following:

➤ **Facebook Messaging** — This is a unified system that combines all communication capabilities (including Facebook messages, e-mail, chat, and SMS). In addition to storing all of these messages, the system also indexes (and consequently supports searching and retrieving) every message from a given user, time, or conversation thread.

➤ **Facebook Insights** — This provides real-time analytics for Facebook websites, pages, and advertisements. It enables developers to capture information about website visits, impressions, click-throughs, and so on. It also allows developers to come up with insights on how people interact with them.

➤ **Facebook Metrics System** or **Operational Data Store (ODS)** — This supports the collection, storage, and analysis of Facebook hardware and software utilization.

Currently, both the popularity and number of real-time Hadoop applications are steadily growing. All of these applications are based on the same *architectural principle* — having a processing engine that is always running and ready to execute a required action.

Following are the three most popular directions for real-time Hadoop implementations:

➤ Using HBase for implementing real-time Hadoop applications

➤ Using specialized real-time Hadoop query systems

➤ Using Hadoop-based event-processing systems

The chapter begins with a discussion about HBase usage for implementation of real-time applications.

USING HBASE FOR IMPLEMENTING REAL-TIME APPLICATIONS

As you learned in Chapter 2, an HBase implementation is based on region servers that provide all the HBase functionality. Those servers run all the time, which means that they fulfill a prerequisite for a real-time Hadoop implementation — having a constantly running processing engine ready to execute a required action.

As described in Chapter 2, the main functionality of HBase is scalable, high-performance access to large amounts of data. Although this serves as a foundation for many real-time applications, it is rarely a real-time application itself. (Note that even faster access and more stability is provided by a MapR implementation of HBase, which is part of the M7 distribution.) This typically requires a set of services that, in the most simplistic case, provides access to this data. In more complex cases, such services combine data access with business functionality, and, optionally, access to the additional data required for such data processing.

CONSIDERATIONS FOR USING HBASE TO IMPLEMENT REAL-TIME APPLICATIONS

Although HBase provides fast read and write operations, the write performance of HBase can be seriously impacted by compactions and region splits (see Chapter 2 for more details). When using HBase to implement real-time applications, compactions and region splits must be considered and dealt with.

The following techniques can help to alleviate the impact of region splits:

➤ You can pre-split the tables during creation, which allows for better utilization of region servers. (Remember that, by default, a single region will be created for a table.) This is especially effective in the case of even keys distribution (see Chapter 2 for recommendations on the primary keys design).

➤ You can increase the region's file sizes (`hbase.hregion.max.filesize`) to allow a region to store more data before it must be split. The limitation of this approach is HFile format v1 (see Chapter 2 for more details), which will cause slower read operations as the HFile size grows. The introduction of the HFile v2 format alleviates this problem and allows you to further increase region size.

➤ You can manually split HBase based on the application's activity schedule and the load/capacity of the regions.

You can control major compaction by configuring `HConstants.MAJOR_COMPACTION_PERIOD` to set the desired frequency. It is also possible to turn off automatic compactions completely by setting the value of `HConstants.MAJOR_COMPACTION_PERIOD` to 0.

As shown in Figure 9-1, a common architecture for this type of implementation is very similar to a traditional database-based architecture, where HBase plays the role of traditional database(s). It is comprised of multiple load-balanced service implementations and a load balancer, which directs the client's traffic to these implementations. A service implementation translates a client request into a sequence of read/write operations for HBase (and potentially additional data sources), combines and processes the data, and returns results back to the client.

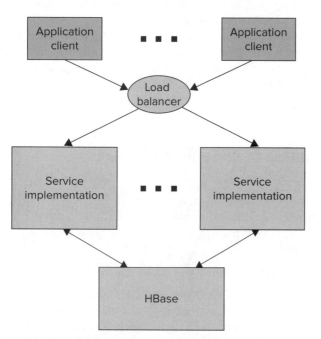

FIGURE 9-1: Typical architecture for HBase-based application services

> **NOTE** *The architecture shown in Figure 9-1 is very similar to the architecture of the remote HBase APIs (including REST APIs, Thrift APIs, and Avro APIs). Despite these similarities, remote HBase APIs are rarely used for real-time Hadoop implementations. Those APIs are implementing HBase semantics — that is, they provide access to HBase tables, column families, and columns, which are typically of no interest to the application user. The user is interested in the application-level semantics, which is very different. Moreover, in a well-designed application, data access (that is, HBase data schemas) must be hidden from the APIs. This enables you to evolve the implementation without directly impacting existing client APIs.*

The main responsibilities of the service implementations in HBase-based real-time applications are similar to traditional service implementations, and include the following:

➤ **Custom processing** — A service provides a convenient place for custom data-processing logic, thus leveraging HBase-based (and potentially additional) data and application functionality.

➤ **Semantic alignment** — The implementation of service APIs enables you to align data in both content and granularity between what (and how) data is actually stored, and what an application is interested in. This provides a decoupling layer between an application's semantics and the actual data storage.

➤ **Performance improvements** — The introduction of the services often improves overall performance because of the capability to implement multiple HBase gets/scans/puts locally, combine results, and send a single reply to the API consumer. (This assumes that the service implementation is co-located with the Hadoop cluster. Typically, these implementations are deployed either directly on Hadoop edge nodes, or, at least, on the same network segment as the Hadoop cluster itself.)

> **NOTE** *When you use HBase coprocessors (see Chapter 2 for more details), you can slightly change the balance between HBase-based services and HBase data access by pushing more processing into HBase regions. This can improve the locality of an execution (compare this to MapReduce data locality discussed in Chapter 4) and simplify overall programming logic.*

For the APIs exposed via the public Internet, you can implement an HBase-based real-time application by using REST APIs and leveraging one of the JAX-RS frameworks (for example, RestEasy or Jersey). If the APIs are used internally (say, within a company's firewall), using the Avro RPC may be a more appropriate solution. In the case of REST (especially for large data sizes), you should still use Avro and binary payloads, which will often lead to better performance and better network utilization.

The remainder of this section examines two examples (using a picture-management system and using HBase as a Lucene back end) that demonstrate how you can build such real-time services while leveraging HBase. These examples show both the design approach to building such applications, and the implementation of the applications.

Using HBase as a Picture Management System

For the first example of a real-time Hadoop implementation, let's take a look at a fictitious picture-management system. This system allows users to upload their pictures (along with the date when the pictures were taken), and then look up the pictures and download them based on the date.

Designing the System

Let's start by designing data storage. Chapter 2 describes two basic data storage mechanisms provided by Hadoop:

➤ **HDFS** — This is used for storing large amounts of data while providing write, read, and append functionality with mostly sequential access.

➤ **HBase** — This is used for providing a full CRUD operations and random gets/scans/puts.

Chapter 2 also describes an approach for combining HDFS and HBase aimed at providing some of the HBase properties to large-sized data items. As shown in Figure 9-2, this is the approach used for this picture-management implementation.

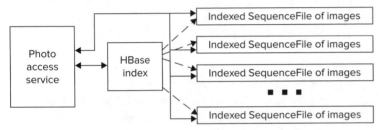

FIGURE 9-2: Architecture for picture management system

For this example, let's assume that every user is identified by a globally unique identifier (GUID), which is assigned to a user once he or she registers with the system. For each user, the system creates a directory containing SequenceFiles, which house the actual images uploaded by user. To simplify the overall design, let's also assume that users are uploading their photos in bulk, and every bulk upload creates a new SequenceFile containing photographs that are part of this upload. Because different uploads can have radically different sizes, this approach can create a lot of "small" HDFS files, so it is necessary to implement a process that periodically combines smaller SequenceFiles into larger ones.

With this SequenceFile in place, the system will be able to store data fast. However, it will not provide a fast random access to pictures, which is typically required for picture-retrieval APIs. The APIs should support the return of a set of images for a given user for a given time interval.

To support the required access functionality, you must add an HBase-based index to the user's pictures. You can do this by indexing all pictures for all users in a specialized HBase table — a picture index table. As shown in Listing 9-1, this table will have a key that contains a concatenation of the user's Universally Unique Identification (UUID) and a timestamp for a picture that shows when the picture was taken.

LISTING 9-1: Picture management table key

```
UserUUID|Year|Mon|Day|Hour|Min|Sec
```

> **NOTE** *To simplify the design of this example implementation, let's assume that no two pictures have been taken by the same user at the same time. This will guarantee the uniqueness of the key. If this condition were not true, you could either increase the precision of the timestamp, or add a counter at the end of the key.*

Such a key design allows for a very efficient search for pictures for a given user for a given time interval, which is required for simple picture-retrieval APIs. A more complex, attribute-based search could be implemented by using a Lucene-based search, which is described later in this chapter.

The picture index table will contain one column family with one column name. Following the recommendations from Chapter 2 to keep these names short, you can use A as a column family name and B as a column name. The content of the column is the name of the SequenceFile (where the picture is stored), along with the byte offset from the beginning of the file.

With this high-level data design in place, the implementation is fairly straightforward. For an upload operation, a list of photographs from a given user is in the form of a timestamp, along with the byte array containing the image itself. At this point, a new SequenceFile is created and populated with the timestamp as a key, and the picture's content as a value. When a new image is written to the file, its starting location (and the filename) are stored in the picture index table.

The read operations are initiated as a picture index table scan operation (for a given user and a date range). For every index found in the picture index table, an image is read from HDFS, based on the filename and offset. A list of pictures is then returned to the user.

You can also delete photographs by deleting a photograph from the index.

Finally, you can implement file compaction as a MapReduce job that is run periodically using an Oozie Coordinator (see Chapters 6 and 7 for more details on how to use Oozie Workflows and Coordinators), such as at midnight. For every user, this job scans the photograph's index and rewrites the user's photographs into a combined, sorted SequenceFile. This operation removes small files to improve HDFS utilization and overall system performance. (Pictures are stored in the timestamp order, thus avoiding additional seeks.) The operation also reclaims disk space by removing (not copying) deleted photographs.

Now, with the high-level design in place, let's take a look at some of the actual implementation code.

Implementing the System

The implementation starts with the creation of a helper class shown in Listing 9-2 (code file: class DatedPhoto), which defines information that is used to send/receive a photo. Every image is accompanied by an epoch timestamp — that is, the number of milliseconds since January 1, 1970, 00:00:00.

LISTING 9-2: DatedPhoto class

```
public class DatedPhoto {

    long _date;
    byte[] _image;

    public DatedPhoto(){
        ..................... .
    }
    public DatedPhoto(long date, byte[] image){
        ..................... .
    }
    ..................................................... .
    public static String timeToString(long time){
        ..................... .
    }
}
```

This is a fairly simple data container class. Not shown here are setters/getters. An additional method — timeToString — enables you to convert time from an epoch representation into a string representation, which is used in the table's row key.

Another helper class shown in Listing 9-3 (code file: class PhotoLocation) defines index information saved for each image in HBase. This class also defines two additional methods — toBytes and fromBytes (remember, HBase stores all the values as byte arrays).

LISTING 9-3: PhotoLocation class

```
public class PhotoLocation implements Serializable{

    private long _pos;
    private long _time;
    private String _file;

    public PhotoLocation(){}

    public PhotoLocation(long time, String file, long pos){
        ..................... .
    }
    ..................................................... .

    public byte[] toBytes(){
        ..................... .
        System.arraycopy(_pos, 0, _buffer, 0, 8);
        System.arraycopy(_time, 0, _buffer, 8, 8);
        System.arraycopy(_file, 0, _buffer, 16, _file.length());
        return _buffer;
    }

    public void fromBytes(byte[] buffer){
        System.arraycopy(buffer, 0, _pos, 0, 8);
```

```
        System.arraycopy(buffer, 8, _time, 0, 8);
        System.arraycopy(buffer, 16, _file, 0, buffer.length - 8);
    }
}
```

This is another data container class (getters/setters methods are omitted for brevity). `toBytes()`/
`fromBytes()` methods in this class use a custom serialization/deserialization implementation. The
custom implementation typically leads to a smallest size of binary data, but the creation of many
custom implementations like this does not scale well as the number of classes grows.

With these two classes in place, you use a `PhotoWriter` class that is responsible for storage of the
actual data to the `SequenceFile`. Then, index information for HBase can look like what is shown
in Listing 9-4 (code file: class `PhotoWriter`).

LISTING 9-4: PhotoWriter class

```java
public class PhotoWriter {

    private PhotoWriter(){}

    public static void writePhotos(UUID user, List<DatedPhoto> photos,
            String tName, Configuration conf) throws IOException{
        String uString = user.toString();
        Path rootPath = new Path(_root);
        FileSystem fs = rootPath.getFileSystem(conf);
        Path userPath = new Path(rootPath, uString);
        String fName = null;
        if(fs.getFileStatus(userPath).isDirectory()){
            FileStatus[] photofiles = fs.listStatus(userPath);
            fName = Integer.toString(photofiles.length);
        }
        SequenceFile.Writer fWriter = SequenceFile.createWriter(conf,............);
        HTable index = new HTable(conf, tName);
        PhotoLocation location = new PhotoLocation();
        location.setFile(fName);
        LongWritable sKey = new LongWritable();
        for(DatedPhoto photo : photos){
            long pos = fWriter.getLength();
            location.setPos(pos);
            location.setTime(photo.getLongDate());
            String key = uString + photo.getDate();
            sKey.set(photo.getLongDate());
            fWriter.append(sKey, new BytesWritable(photo.getPicture()));
            Put put = new Put(Bytes.toBytes(key));
            put.add(Bytes.toBytes("A"), Bytes.toBytes("B"), location.toBytes());
            index.put(put);
        }
        fWriter.close();
        index.close();
    }

}
```

The writePhotos method first determines a new filename by querying a directory for a given user, calculating the number of files, and creating a name as a current length of this directory. It then creates a new SequenceFile writer and connects to a picture index (HBase) table. Once this is done, for every photo, a current file position is returned, and an image is added to the SequenceFile. Once an image is written, its index is added to the HBase table.

Listing 9-5 (code file: class PhotoDataReader) shows a helper class used for reading a specific photo (defined by an offset in the file) from a given file.

LISTING 9-5: PhotoDataReader class

```
public class PhotoDataReader {

    public PhotoDataReader(String file, UUID user, Configuration conf)
            throws IOException{

        _file = file;
        _conf = conf;
        _user = user.toString();
        _value = new BytesWritable();
        Path rootPath = new Path(PhotoWriter.getRoot());
        FileSystem fs = rootPath.getFileSystem(_conf);
        Path userPath = new Path(rootPath, _user);
        _fReader = new SequenceFile.Reader(fs, new Path(userPath, _file), _conf);
        _position = 0;
    }

    public byte[] getPicture(long pos) throws IOException{
        if(pos != _position)
            _fReader.seek(pos);
        boolean fresult = _fReader.next(_header, _value);
        if(!fresult)
            throw new IOException("EOF");
        _position = _fReader.getPosition();
        return _value.getBytes();
    }

    public void close() throws IOException{

        _fReader.close();
    }
}
```

The constructor of this class opens a SequenceFile reader for a given file, and positions the cursor at the beginning of the file. A getPicture method retrieves a picture, given its position in a file. To minimize the number of seeks, you first check if the file is in the right position (there is a high probability that pictures with adjacent indexes are located one after another), and seek only if the file is currently not at the required position. Once the file is at the right position, the method's implementation reads the content of images, remembers the current position, and then returns an image.

Finally, Listing 9-6 (code file: class `PhotoReader`) shows a class that can be used to read either an individual photo, or a set of photos for a given time interval. This class also has an additional method to delete a picture with a given timestamp.

LISTING 9-6: PhotoReader class

```java
public class PhotoReader {

    private PhotoReader(){}

    public static List<DatedPhoto> getPictures(UUID user, long startTime,
            long endTime, String tName,Configuration conf) throws IOException{

        List<DatedPhoto> result = new LinkedList<DatedPhoto>();
        HTable index = new HTable(conf, tName);
        String uString = user.toString();
        byte[] family = Bytes.toBytes("A");
        PhotoLocation location = new PhotoLocation();
        if(endTime < 0)
            endTime = startTime + 1;
        Map<String, PhotoDataReader> readers = new HashMap<String,
            PhotoDataReader>();
        Scan scan = new Scan(Bytes.toBytes(uString +
            DatedPhoto.timeToString(startTime)),
                Bytes.toBytes(uString + DatedPhoto.timeToString(endTime)));
        scan.addColumn(family, family);
        Iterator<Result> rIterator = index.getScanner(scan).iterator();
        while(rIterator.hasNext()){
            Result r = rIterator.next();
            location.fromBytes(r.getBytes().get());
            PhotoDataReader dr = readers.get(location.getFile());
            if(dr == null){
                dr = new PhotoDataReader(location.getFile(), user, conf);
                readers.put(location.getFile(), dr);
            }
            DatedPhoto df = new DatedPhoto(location.getTime(),
                    dr.getPicture(location.getPos())));
            result.add(df);
        }
        for(PhotoDataReader dr : readers.values())
            dr.close();
        return result;
    }

    public static void deletePicture(UUID user, long startTime, String tName,
            Configuration conf) throws IOException{

        Delete delete = new Delete(Bytes.toBytes(user.toString() +
    DatedPhoto.timeToString(startTime)));
        HTable index = new HTable(conf, tName);
        index.delete(delete);
    }
}
```

The implementation of the read method first connects to the HBase table and creates a scan based on the input parameters. For every record returned by the scan, it first checks whether a `PhotoDataReader` for this filename already exists. If it does not, a new `PhotoDataReader` is created and added to the readers list. The reader is then used to obtain an image itself.

The implementation of the `delete` method just deletes photo information from the index table.

The solution presented here (in Listing 9-2 through Listing 9-6) provides a very rudimentary implementation of photo-management implementation, showing only a bare-bones Hadoop implementation. An actual implementation would be significantly more complex, but the code presented here illustrates a basic approach for building an HBase-based real-time system that could easily be extended for a real implementation.

The next example shows how to build an HBase-based back end for an inverted index, which can be used for an Hadoop-based real-time search.

Using HBase as a Lucene Back End

This significantly more realistic example describes an implementation of Lucene with an HBase back end that can be leveraged for real-time Hadoop-based search applications.

> **NOTE** *Search plays a pivotal role in many modern applications ranging from shopping sites to social networks to points of interest. The Lucene search library is today's de facto standard for implementing search engines. It is used in real-life search applications by a wide variety of companies, including Apple, IBM, Attlassian (Jira), Wolfram, and others.*

Overall Design

Before delving into HBase-based implementation, let's start with a quick Lucene refresher. Lucene operates on searchable documents, which are collections of fields, each having a value. A field's value is further comprised of one or more searchable elements — in other words, *terms*. Lucene search is based on an inverted index (refer to Chapter 3 for more about an inverted index and the algorithms for its calculations) that contains information about searchable documents. This inverted index allows for a fast look-up of a field's term to find all the documents in which this term appears.

As shown in Figure 9-3, the following are the main components of the Lucene architecture:

➤ `IndexWriter` calculates the reverse indexes for each inserted document and writes them out.

➤ `IndexSearcher` leverages `IndexReader` to read the inverted index and implement the search logic.

➤ `Directory` abstracts out the implementation of index data set access, and provides APIs (directly mimicking a file system API) for manipulating them. Both `IndexReader` and `IndexWriter` leverage `Directory` for access to this data.

At a very high level, Lucene operates on two distinct data sets, both of which are accessed based on an implementation of a `Directory` interface:

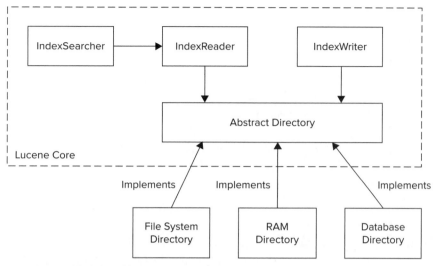

FIGURE 9-3: High-level Lucene architecture

➤ The *index data set* keeps all the field/term pairs (with additional information such as term frequency, position, and so on), as well as the documents containing these terms, in appropriate fields.

➤ The *document data set* stores all the documents (including stored fields, and so on).

The standard Lucene distribution contains several `Directory` implementations, including filesystem-based and memory-based, Berkeley DB-based (in the Lucene `contrib` module), and several others.

The main drawback of a standard filesystem-based back end (`Directory` implementation) is a performance degradation caused by the index growth. Different techniques have been used to overcome this problem, including load balancing and index sharding (that is, splitting indexes between multiple Lucene instances). Although powerful, the use of sharding complicates the overall implementation architecture, and requires a certain amount of an a priori knowledge about expected documents before you can properly partition the Lucene indexes.

A different approach is to allow an index back end itself to shard data correctly, and then build an implementation based on such a back end. As described in Chapter 2, one such back-end storage implementation is HBase.

Because Lucene's `Directory` APIs expose filesystem semantics, a "standard" way to implement a new Lucene back end is to impose such semantics on every new back end, which is not always the simplest (most convenient) approach to porting Lucene. As a result, several Lucene ports (including limited memory index support from the Lucene `contrib` module, Lucandra, and HBasene) took a different approach. As shown in Figure 9-4, these overwrote not a directory, but higher-level Lucene classes — `IndexReader` and `IndexWriter` — thus bypassing the `Directory` APIs.

Although such an approach often requires more work, it also enables you to fully leverage the native capabilities of a particular back end. Consequently, it leads to significantly more powerful implementations. The implementation presented here follows this approach.

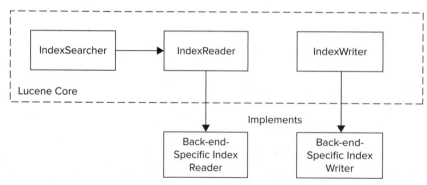

FIGURE 9-4: Integrating Lucene with a back end without filesystem semantics

> **NOTE** *The idea of using a NoSQL database as a Lucene back end is not new. Several open source projects are based on this approach, including Lucandra (based on Cassandra), HBasene (based on HBase), and Solandra (based on Cassandra).*

The overall implementation shown in Figure 9-5 is based on a memory-based back end that is used as an in-memory cache, along with a mechanism for synchronizing this cache with the HBase back end.

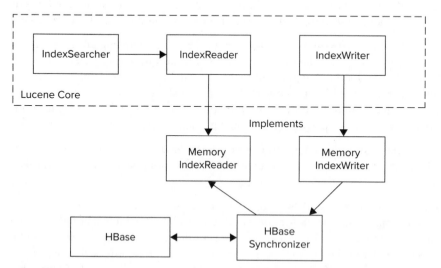

FIGURE 9-5: Overall architecture of HBase-based Lucene implementation

This implementation tries to balance two conflicting requirements — *performance* (the in-memory cache can drastically improve performance by minimizing the number of HBase reads for search and document retrieval) and *scalability* (the capability to run as many Lucene instances as required to support a growing population of search clients). The latter requires minimizing the cache lifetime to synchronize content with the HBase instance (that is, a single copy of truth). A compromise is achieved by implementing a configurable cache time-to-live (TTL) parameter, thus limiting cache presence in each Lucene instance.

CACHE IMPLEMENTATION APPROACHES

A common approach to improving performance of real-time applications is to use an in-memory cache. Two common approaches used to implement this cache are through a separate cache layer, and by using an in-process implementation. Only the in-process implementation is discussed here.

For cases when the amount of data is significantly larger than the amount of available memory, following are the two prevalent approaches:

➤ **Sharded cache** — Every CPU is dedicated to a specific portion of data. A given request is routed to a specific CPU, which is responsible for a portion of data that is cached locally. A cache eviction policy (if any) is least recently used (LRU).

➤ **Random cache** — Any CPU can service any request. The cache stores the results of the most recent requests. An eviction policy is necessary, and is typically least recently used (LRU) based on the amount of memory dedicated to the cache.

Both approaches have their advantages and drawbacks.

A sharding approach usually provides a better probability of reuse of data already in memory. It also supports both read and write (inserts or updates) equally well. Because CPUs are dedicated to a certain data portion, writes can be done directly to memory, and the underlying store can be updated asynchronously. Data is typically available immediately after it was written.

Drawbacks of the sharding approach typically include the necessity to choose an appropriate sharding mechanism (it's not always trivial) and complexity of implementing failover and load balancing for such an implementation. Failover solutions typically require cache synchronization, which is never simple and cheap. Load balancing might require data resharding, which is never a cheap proposition. Additional sharding approaches typically require a specialized, shard-aware load balancer, which shards incoming requests and forwards them to a specific CPU.

On the other hand, random cache provides a cheap and simple failover and scalability capability (just add more computers), but it has its own drawbacks as well.

The biggest typical drawback is the fact that the same data item can simultaneously exist in multiple caches, which makes writes (inserts or updates) significantly more complex. In this case, when an overall system can cope with eventual consistency (writes might appear delayed), you can use a time-expiring cache to provide a very simple implementation for this problem. In this case, writes can bypass the cache and update the back end directly.

Both reads and writes (`IndexReader`/`IndexWriter`) are done through the memory cache, but their implementation is very different.

For reads, the cache first checks to see if the required data is in memory, and it is not stale (that is, has been in memory for too long). If both conditions are fulfilled, in-memory data is used. Otherwise, the cache reads/refreshes data from HBase, and then returns it to the `IndexReader`.

For writes, the data is written directly to HBase without storing it in memory. Although this might create a delay in actual data availability, it makes implementation significantly simpler — the writes can go to any Lucene instance without regard for the instance that might have a specific index value cached. To adhere to business requirements, the delay can be controlled by setting an appropriate cache expiration time.

This implementation is based on two main HBase tables — an *index table* and a *document table*.

As shown in Figure 9-6, the HBase index table, which is responsible for storing an inverse index, is the foundation of the implementation. This table has an entry (row) for every field/term combination (inverse key) known to a Lucene instance. Every row contains one column family (a "Documents family"). This column family contains a column (named as a document ID) for every document containing this field/term.

FIGURE 9-6: HBase index table

The content of each column is a value of `TermDocument`. The Avro schema for it is shown in Listing 9-7. (Chapter 2 provides more information about Avro.)

LISTING 9-7: TermDocument definition

```
{
  "type" : "record",
  "name" : "TermDocument",
  "namespace" : " com.practicalHadoop.lucene.document",
  "fields" : [ {
    "name" : "docFrequency",
    "type" : "int"
  }, {
    "name" : "docPositions",
    "type" : ["null", {
      "type" : "array",
      "items" : "int"
    }]
  } ]
}
```

As shown in Figure 9-7, the HBase document table stores documents themselves, back references to the indexes/norms, references to these documents, and some additional bookkeeping information used by Lucene for document processing. It has an entry (row) for every document known to a Lucene instance.

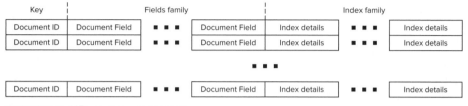

FIGURE 9-7: HBase document table

Each document is uniquely identified by a document ID (key) and contains two column families — the "Fields family" and the "Index family." The Fields column family contains a column (named as a field name) for every field stored for a document. The column value shown in Listing 9-8 is comprised of the value type (string or byte array) and the value itself.

LISTING 9-8: Field definition

```
{
  "type" : "record",
  "name" : "FieldsData",
  "namespace" : " com.practicalHadoop.lucene.document",
  "fields" : [ {
    "name" : "fieldsArray",
    "type" : {
      "type" : "array",
      "items" : {
        "type" : "record",
        "name" : "singleField",
        "fields" : [ {
          "name" : "binary",
          "type" : "boolean"
        }, {
          "name" : "data",
          "type" : [ "string", "bytes" ]
        } ]
      }
    }
  } ]
}
```

The Index column family contains a column (named as a field/term) for every index referencing this document. The column value includes document frequency, positions, and offsets for a given field/term, as shown in Listing 9-9.

LISTING 9-9: TermDocumentFrequency

```
{
  "type" : "record",
  "name" : "TermDocumentFrequency",
  "namespace" : " com.practicalHadoop.lucene.document",
  "fields" : [ {
    "name" : "docFrequency",
    "type" : "int"
  }, {
    "name" : "docPositions",
    "type" : ["null",{
      "type" : "array",
      "items" : "int"
    }]
  }, {
    "name" : "docOffsets",
    "type" : ["null",{
      "type" : "array",
      "items" : {
        "type" : "record",
        "name" : "TermsOffset",
        "fields" : [ {
          "name" : "startOffset",
          "type" : "int"
        }, {
          "name" : "endOffset",
          "type" : "int"
        } ]
      }
    }]
  } ]
}
```

> **NOTE** *Lucene allows you to influence search results by "boosting" calculations on different levels. Boosting is supported at both Indexing time (at document and field level) and at Query time. By default, a field in Lucene is indexed with its norm, a product of the document's boost, the field's boost, and the field's length normalization factor. If you do not use norms, your documents are scored based on the exact number of terms matched, rather than the number of terms in proportion to the document length.*

As shown in Figure 9-8, an optional third table can be implemented if Lucene norms must be supported. The HBase norm table has an entry (row) for every field (key) known to the Lucene instance. Each row contains a single column family — the "Documents norms family." This family has a column (named as document ID) for every document for which a given field's norm must be stored.

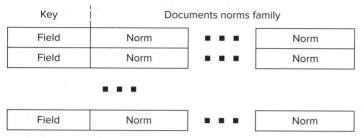

FIGURE 9-8: HBase norm table

One of Lucene's weakest points is spatial search. Although the Lucene spatial contribution package provides powerful support for spatial search, it is limited to finding the closest point. In reality, spatial search often has significantly more requirements, such as which points belong to a given shape (circle, bounding box, polygon), which shapes intersect with a given shape, and so on. As a result, the implementation presented here extends Lucene to solve such problems.

Geospatial Search

The geospatial search implementation for this example is based on a two-level search implementation:

➤ The first-level search is based on a Cartesian Grid search.

➤ The second level implements shape-specific spatial calculations.

For the Cartesian Grid search, the whole world is tiled at some zoom level. (Chapter 7 provides more about tiling and zoom levels.) In this case, a geometric shape is defined by the set of IDs of tiles that contain the complete shape. The calculation of these tile IDs is trivial for any shape type, and can be implemented in several lines of code.

> **NOTE** *In reality, this calculation can be a little bit more complex (for example, for polygons with holes). However, for all practical purposes, the straightforward enclosure is the bounding box, and then mapping of the bounding box in tiles is good enough for implementation of a first-level search as described here.*

In this case, both the document (referring to a certain shape) and the search shape can be represented by the list of tile IDs. This means that the first-level search implementation is just finding the intersection between tile IDs of the search shape and the document's shape.

> **NOTE** *This, of course, is an oversimplification to explain a principle. The real implementation contains IDs for the multiple zoom levels, and selects the most appropriate zoom level based on the size and shape of the search criteria.*

This can be implemented as a "standard" text search operation, which Lucene is very good at. Once the initial selection is done, geometrical arithmetic can be used to attain more precision by filtering the results of the first-level search. Such calculations can be as complex as they need to be to improve the precision of the search. These calculations are technically not part of the base implementation.

Figure 9-9 shows a concrete example. Here, only a limited number of tiles (1 through 12) and four documents ("a" through "e") are shown.

Based on its location and shape, each document can be described as a set of tile IDs — for

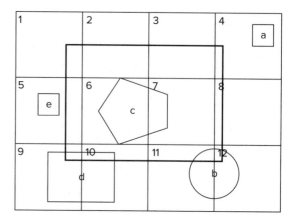

FIGURE 9-9: Two-level search

example, "b" is contained in tiles 11 and 12. Now, let's assume that you are searching for every document that intersects with a bounding box (represented by a wide line in Figure 9-9). As you can see, a search bounding box can be represented as a set of tiles with IDs 1 through 12. All shapes "a" through "e" will be found as a result of the first-level search. The second-level search will throw away shapes "a" and "e," which do not intersect with the result bounding box. The overall search will return back shapes "b," "c," and "d."

Incorporating this two-level algorithm into Lucene is fairly straightforward. The responsibility of Lucene's engine is to support a first-level search — tile matching. The second-level search can be accomplished with external filtering, which does not necessarily need to be incorporated into Lucene.

To support both search levels, the Lucene document must be extended with the following additional fields:

➤ **Shape field** — This describes the shape associated with the document. (The current implementation is based on the serializable shape super class, and several specific shape implementations, including point, bounding box, circle, and polygon.) This can be used by the filter to obtain the shape with which the document is associated to perform explicit filtering.

➤ **Tile ID field** — This contains a field (or fields) describing the tile (or tiles) in which the shape is contained for different zoom levels.

Putting geospatial information directly into the document fields is the most simplistic approach for storing the geospatial information in a Lucene index. The drawback of such an approach is that it leads to the "explosion" of the index size (a new term/value must be created for every tile ID/zoom level combination), which will negatively impact HBase performance because of large row sizes.

As shown in Figure 9-10, a better approach is to store the document's information for a given field/term value as multilevel hash tables.

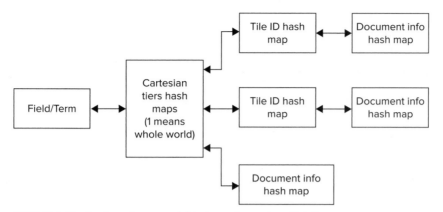

FIGURE 9-10: Storing of geospatial indexes for a given field/term

The first level of this hash is determined by zoom level. For Level 1, the whole world is reserved for the requests without spatial information. This contains document information for all documents containing a given value for a given term. All other levels contain a hash map with document information for every document containing a given value for a given term, and located in a given tile ID. Because the number of documents contained in a given tile is always significantly smaller compared to the number of documents for the whole world, the search based on such an index organization is significantly faster than searches containing geospatial components, while preserving roughly the same search time for searches without them.

Although such an index organization can increase the required memory footprint, this increase will be relatively small because the overall implementation is based on the expiring lazy cache.

Technically, by introducing an additional keys structure, the original HBase table design shown in Figure 9-6 through Figure 9-8 can be used for storing multilevel hash tables.

Alternatively, as shown in Figure 9-11, to better cope with the significantly increased number of rows, and to further improve search scalability, instead of using a single HBase index table, N+1 index tables are introduced — one for global data, and one for every zoom level.

The whole world table shown in Figure 9-10 is exactly the same as an original index table shown in Figure 9-5, whereas tables for every zoom level have the same content, but a different key structure. For them, a key is a concatenation of not two, but three values — tile ID, field name, and term value.

In addition to the fact that splitting tables by zoom level enables you to make each table smaller (which simplifies overall HBase management), you can also add a parallelization of searches — requests for different zoom levels will read from different tables. The keys definition allows for natural support of scanning on the field/term level for a given zoom level/tile ID that is required by this Lucene implementation.

Now that you understand the overall design approach, let's look at some of the implementation approaches — more specifically, the portion of implementation that is specific to Hadoop/HBase.

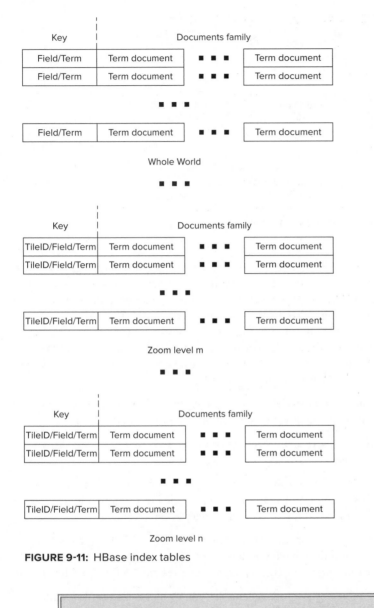

FIGURE 9-11: HBase index tables

> **NOTE** *The complete code is available on this book's companion website at* www.wrox.com.

HBase Implementation Code

The example Lucene implementation requires access by multiple HBase tables several times during a search. Instead of creating and destroying a specific HTable class every time a table access is required (remember HTable class is not thread safe), the implementation leverages an HTablePool class (compare to database connection pooling). Listing 9-10 (code file: class `TableManager`) shows the class encapsulating `HTablePool` (`TableManager`), which additionally provides all configuration information (table names, family names, and so on).

LISTING 9-10: TableManager class

```
public class TableManager {

    // Levels
    private static final int _minLevel = 10;
    private static final int _maxLevel = 24;


    ...........................................................
    // Tables
    private static byte[] _indexTable;
    private static byte[][] _indexLevelTable;
    private static byte[] _documentsTable;
    private static byte[] _normsTable;

    //Families
    private static byte[] _indexTableDocuments;
    private static byte[] _documentsTableFields;
    private static byte[] _documentsTableTerms;
    private static byte[] _normsTableNorms;

    // Pool
    private HTablePool _tPool = null;
    private Configuration _config = null;
    private int _poolSize = Integer.MAX_VALUE;

    // Instance
    private static TableManager _instance = null;

    // Static initializer
    static{
        int nlevels = _maxLevel - _minLevel + 1;
        _indexLevelTable = new byte[nlevels][];
        _indexLevelTablePurpose = new String[nlevels];
        .............................................................. . .

    }


    ..........................................................
    public static void setIndexTable(String indexTable, int level) {
        if(level < 0)
            _indexTable = Bytes.toBytes(indexTable);
        else{
            if((level >= _minLevel) && (level <= _maxLevel)){
                int i = level - _minLevel;
                _indexLevelTable[i] = Bytes.toBytes(indexTable);
            }
```

continues

LISTING 9-10 *(continued)*

```
        }
    }

    .................................................

    public static synchronized TableManager getInstance()
                                    throws NotInitializedException{
        if(_instance == null)
            throw new NotInitializedException();
        return _instance;
    }


    private TableManager(Configuration config, int poolSize){

        if(poolSize > 0)
            _poolSize = poolSize;
        _config = config;
        _tPool = new HTablePool(_config, _poolSize);
    }

    public HTableInterface getIndexTable(int level) {

        if(level == 1)
            return _tPool.getTable(_indexTable);
        else
            return _tPool.getTable(_indexLevelTable[level-_minLevel]);
    }

    public HTableInterface getDocumentsTable(){

        return _tPool.getTable(_documentsTable);
    }

    public HTableInterface getNormsTable(){

        return _tPool.getTable(_normsTable);
    }

    public void releaseTable(HTableInterface t){

        try {
            t.close();
        } catch (IOException e) {}
    }
}
```

Because this class can support different numbers of levels, its static method allocates an array for table names for every level. The getTable methods in this class just get tables from the pool, while the releaseTable method returns tables back to the pool.

This example Lucene implementation uses several tables. A `TableCreator` class shown in Listing 9-11 (code file: class `TableCreator`) is based on `HbaseAdmin` APIs. It ensures that corresponding tables exist and are properly defined.

LISTING 9-11: TableCreator class

```
public class TableCreator {

    public static List<HTable> getTables(TablesType tables, Configuration
            conf) throws Exception{

        HBaseAdmin hBaseAdmin = new HBaseAdmin(conf);
        List<HTable> result = new LinkedList<HTable>();
        for (TableType table : tables.getTable()) {
            HTableDescriptor desc = null;
            if (hBaseAdmin.tableExists(table.getName())) {
                if (tables.isRebuild()) {
                    hBaseAdmin.disableTable(table.getName());
                    hBaseAdmin.deleteTable(table.getName());
                    createTable(hBaseAdmin, table);
                }
                else{
                    byte[] tBytes = Bytes.toBytes(table.getName());
                    desc = hBaseAdmin.getTableDescriptor(tBytes);
                    List<ColumnFamily> columns = table.getColumnFamily();
                    for(ColumnFamily family : columns){
                        boolean exists = false;
                        String name = family.getName();
                        for(HColumnDescriptor fm : desc.getFamilies()){
                            String fmName = Bytes.toString(fm.getName());
                            if(name.equals(fmName)){
                                exists = true;
                                break;
                            }
                        }
                        if(!exists){
                            System.out.println("Adding Famoly " + name + "
                                to the table " + table.getName());
                            hBaseAdmin.addColumn(tBytes,
                                buildDescriptor(family));
                        }
                    }
                }
            } else {
                createTable(hBaseAdmin, table);
            }
            result.add( new HTable(conf, Bytes.toBytes(table.getName())) );
        }
        return result;
    }

    private static void createTable(HBaseAdmin hBaseAdmin,TableType table)
```

continues

LISTING 9-11 *(continued)*

```
        throws Exception{
    HTableDescriptor desc = new HTableDescriptor(table.getName());
    if(table.getMaxFileSize() != null){
        Long fs = 10241 * 10241 *  table.getMaxFileSize();
        desc.setValue(HTableDescriptor.MAX_FILESIZE, fs.toString());
    }
    List<ColumnFamily> columns = table.getColumnFamily();
    for(ColumnFamily family : columns){
        desc.addFamily(buildDescriptor(family));
    }
    hBaseAdmin.createTable(desc);
}

private static HColumnDescriptor buildDescriptor(ColumnFamily family){

    HColumnDescriptor col = new HColumnDescriptor(family.getName());
    if(family.isBlockCacheEnabled() != null)
        col.setBlockCacheEnabled(family.isBlockCacheEnabled());
    if(family.isInMemory() != null)
        col.setInMemory(family.isInMemory());
    if(family.isBloomFilter() != null)
        col.setBloomFilterType(BloomType.ROWCOL);
    if(family.getMaxBlockSize() != null){
        int bs = 1024 * 1024 * family.getMaxBlockSize();
        col.setBlocksize(bs);
    }
    if(family.getMaxVersions() != null)
        col.setMaxVersions(family.getMaxVersions().intValue());
    if(family.getTimeToLive() != null)
        col.setTimeToLive(family.getTimeToLive());
    return col;
}
}
```

This class is driven by an XML document that defines the required tables.

The helper method `buildDescriptor` builds an `HColumnDescriptor` based on the information provided by the XML configuration. The `createTable` method leverages the `buildDescriptor` method to build a table. Finally, the `getTables` method first checks whether the table exists. If it does, the method either deletes and re-creates it (if the `rebuild` flag is `true`), or adjusts it to the required configuration. If the table does not exist, then it just builds the table using the `createTable` method.

As discussed earlier, the two main table types used for implementation are `IndexTable` (as shown in Figure 9-10) and `DocumentTable` (as shown in Figure 9-6). Support for each type of table is implemented as a separate class providing all required APIs for manipulating data stored in the table.

Let's start by looking at the `IndexTableSupport` class shown in Listing 9-12 (code file: class `IndexTableSupport`). As a reminder, this set of tables (one for each zoom level) stores all of the index information. Consequently, the IndexTableSupport class supports all index-related operations, including adding and removing a document to and from a given index, reading all documents for a given index, and removing the whole index.

LISTING 9-12: IndexTableSupport class

```java
public class IndexTableSupport {

    private static TableManager _tManager = null;

    private IndexTableSupport(){}

    public static void init() throws NotInitializedException{
        _tManager = TableManager.getInstance();
    }

    public static void addMultiDocuments(Map<MultiTableIndexKey,
            Map<String,TermDocument>> rows, int level){

        HTableInterface index = null;

        List<Put> puts = new ArrayList<Put>(rows.size());
        try {
            for (Map.Entry<MultiTableIndexKey,
                    Map<String, TermDocument>> row : rows.entrySet()) {
                byte[] bkey = Bytes.toBytes(row.getKey().getKey());
                Put put = new Put(bkey);
                put.setWriteToWAL(false);
                for (Map.Entry<String, TermDocument> entry :
                        row.getValue().entrySet()) {
                    String docID = entry.getKey();
                    TermDocument td = entry.getValue();
                    put.add(TableManager.getIndexTableDocumentsFamily(),
                            Bytes.toBytes(docID),
                                AVRODataConverter.toBytes(td));
                }
                puts.add(put);
            }
            for(int i = 0; i < 2; i++){
                try {
                    index = _tManager.getIndexTable(level);
                    index.put(puts);
                    break;
                } catch (Exception e) {
                    System.out.println("Index Table support. Resetting pool
                        due to the multiput exception ");
                    e.printStackTrace();
                    _tManager.resetTPool();
                }
            }
        }
```

continues

LISTING 9-12 *(continued)*

```java
        } catch (Exception e) {
            e.printStackTrace();
        }
        finally{
            _tManager.releaseTable(index);
        }
    }

    public static void deleteDocument(IndexKey key, String docID)throws Exception{

        if(_tManager == null)
            throw new NotInitializedException();
        HTableInterface index = _tManager.getIndexTable(key.getLevel());
        if(index == null)
            throw new Exception("no Table");
        byte[] bkey = Bytes.toBytes(new MultiTableIndexKey(key).getKey());
        byte[] bID = Bytes.toBytes(docID);
        Delete delete = new Delete(bkey);
        delete.deleteColumn(TableManager.getIndexTableDocumentsFamily(), bID);
        try {
            index.delete(delete);
        } catch (Exception e) {
            throw new Exception(e);
        }
        finally{
            _tManager.releaseTable(index);
        }
    }

    public static void deleteIndex(IndexKey key)throws Exception{

        if(_tManager == null)
            throw new NotInitializedException();
        HTableInterface index = _tManager.getIndexTable(key.getLevel());
        if(index == null)
            throw new Exception("no Table");
        byte[] bkey = Bytes.toBytes(new MultiTableIndexKey(key).getKey());
        Delete delete = new Delete(bkey);
        try {
            index.delete(delete);
        } catch (Exception e) {
            throw new Exception(e);
        }
        finally{
            _tManager.releaseTable(index);
        }
    }

    public static TermDocuments getIndex(IndexKey key)throws Exception{

        if(_tManager == null)
            throw new NotInitializedException();
        HTableInterface index = _tManager.getIndexTable(key.getLevel());
```

```
        if(index == null)
            throw new Exception("no Table");
        byte[] bkey = Bytes.toBytes(new MultiTableIndexKey(key).getKey());
        try {
            Get get = new Get(bkey);
            Result result = index.get(get);
            return processResult(result);
        } catch (Exception e) {
            throw new Exception(e);
        }
        finally{
            _tManager.releaseTable(index);
        }
    }
```

```
    private static TermDocuments processResult(Result result)throws Exception{

        if((result == null) || (result.isEmpty())){
            return null;
        }

        Map<String, TermDocument> docs = null;
        NavigableMap<byte[], byte[]> documents =
            result.getFamilyMap
            (TableManager.getIndexTableDocumentsFamily());
        if((documents != null) && (!documents.isEmpty())){
            docs = Collections.synchronizedMap(new HashMap<String,
                TermDocument>(50, .7f));
            for(Map.Entry<byte[], byte[]> entry : documents.entrySet()){
                TermDocument std = null;
                try {
                    std = AVRODataConverter.unmarshallTermDocument
                        (entry.getValue());
                } catch (Exception e) {
                    System.out.println("Barfed in Avro conversion");
                    e.printStackTrace();
                    throw new Exception(e);
                }
                docs.put(Bytes.toString(entry.getKey()), std);
            }
        }
        return docs == null ? null : new TermDocuments(docs);
    }
}
```

The implementation of the addMultiDocuments method is fairly straightforward. To optimize HBase write performance, it is leveraging multi-PUTs (see the discussion on the HBase PUT performance in Chapter 2). So, it is first building a list of PUTs for all documents that must be added to the index, and then writing all of them to HBase. Note the retry mechanism used in this method. The implementation tries to retry several times, each time resetting the pool to ensure that no stale HBase connections exist.

The `deleteDocument` and `deleteIndex` methods are using the HBase `delete` command for a given column and a complete row, respectively.

Finally, the `getIndex` method is reading information about all the documents for a given index. It is using a simple HBase `Get` command to get the complete row, and then uses the `processResult` method to convert the result to a map of `TermDocument` objects. Both `addMultiDocuments` and `getIndex` methods are leveraging Avro to convert data to and from a binary representation.

The `DocumentTableSupport` class shown in Listing 9-13 (code file: class `DocumentTableSupport`) supports all document-related operations, including adding, retrieving, and removing documents.

LISTING 9-13: DocumentTableSupport class

```java
public class DocumentsTableSupport {

    private static TableManager _tManager = null;

    private DocumentsTableSupport(){}

    public static void init() throws NotInitializedException{
        _tManager = TableManager.getInstance();
    }

    ..................................... . .
    public static void addMultiDocuments(DocumentCollector collector){

        HTableInterface documents = null;
        Map<String, DocumentInfo> rows = collector.getRows();
        List<Put> puts = new ArrayList<Put>(rows.size());
        try {
            for(Map.Entry<String, DocumentInfo> row : rows.entrySet()){
                byte[] bkey = Bytes.toBytes(row.getKey());
                Put put = new Put(bkey);
                put.setWriteToWAL(false);
                for(Map.Entry<String, FieldsData> field :
                        row.getValue().getFields().entrySet())
                    put.add(TableManager.getDocumentsTableFieldsFamily(),
                        Bytes.toBytes(field.getKey()),
                        AVRODataConverter.toBytes(field.getValue()));
                for(Map.Entry<IndexKey, TermDocumentFrequency> term :
                        row.getValue().getTerms().entrySet())
                    put.add(TableManager.getDocumentsTableTermsFamily(),
                        Bytes.toBytes(term.getKey().getKey()),
                        AVRODataConverter.toBytes(term.getValue()));
                puts.add(put);
            }
            for(int i = 0; i < 2; i++){
                try {
                    documents = _tManager.getDocumentsTable();
                    documents.put(puts);
                    break;
                } catch (Exception e) {
```

```
                        System.out.println("Documents Table support. Reseting
                            pool due to the multiput exception ");
                        e.printStackTrace();
                        _tManager.resetTPool();
                    }
                }
        } catch (Exception e) {
            e.printStackTrace();
        }
        finally{
            _tManager.releaseTable(documents);
        }
}

public static List<IndexKey> deleteDocument(String docID) throws Exception{

    if(_tManager == null)
        throw new NotInitializedException();
    HTableInterface documents = _tManager.getDocumentsTable();
    byte[] bkey = Bytes.toBytes(docID);

    List<IndexKey> terms;
    try {
        Get get = new Get(bkey);
        Result result = documents.get(get);
        if(result == null){        // Does not exist
            _tManager.releaseTable(documents);
            return null;
        }
        NavigableMap<byte[], byte[]> data =
            result.getFamilyMap
            (TableManager.getDocumentsTableTermsFamily());
        terms = null;
        if((data != null) && (!data.isEmpty())){
            terms = new LinkedList<IndexKey>();
            for(Map.Entry<byte[], byte[]> term : data.entrySet())
                terms.add(new IndexKey(term.getKey()));
        }
        Delete delete = new Delete(bkey);
        documents.delete(delete);
        return terms;
    } catch (Exception e) {
        throw new Exception(e);
    }
    finally{
        _tManager.releaseTable(documents);
    }
}

..............................................................................

public static List<DocumentInfo> getDocuments(List<String> docIDs) throws
```

continues

LISTING 9-13 *(continued)*

```
            Exception{

    if(_tManager == null)
        throw new NotInitializedException();
    HTableInterface documents = _tManager.getDocumentsTable();
    List<Get> gets = new ArrayList<Get>(docIDs.size());
    for(String docID : docIDs)
        gets.add(new Get(Bytes.toBytes(docID)));
    List<DocumentInfo> results = new ArrayList<DocumentInfo>(docIDs.size());
    try {
        Result[] result = documents.get(gets);
        if((result == null) || (result.length < 1)){
            for(int i = 0; i < docIDs.size(); i++)
                results.add(null);
        }
        else{
            for(Result r : result)
                results.add(processResult(r));
        }
        return results;
    } catch (Exception e) {
        throw new Exception(e);
    }
    finally{
        _tManager.releaseTable(documents);
    }
}

private static DocumentInfo processResult(Result result) throws Exception{

    if((result == null) || (result.isEmpty())){
        return null;
    }
    Map<String, FieldsData> fields = null;
    Map<IndexKey, TermDocumentFrequency> terms = null;
    NavigableMap<byte[], byte[]> data =
            result.getFamilyMap
            (TableManager.getDocumentsTableFieldsFamily());
    if((data != null) && (!data.isEmpty())){
        fields = Collections.synchronizedMap(new HashMap<String,
                FieldsData>(50, .7f));
        for(Map.Entry<byte[], byte[]> field : data.entrySet()){
            fields.put(Bytes.toString(field.getKey()),
                    AVRODataConverter.unmarshallFieldData
                    (field.getValue()));
        }
    }
    data = result.getFamilyMap(TableManager.getDocumentsTableTermsFamily());
    if((data != null) && (!data.isEmpty())){
        terms = Collections.synchronizedMap(new HashMap<IndexKey,
            TermDocumentFrequency>());
```

```
      for(Map.Entry<byte[], byte[]> term : data.entrySet()){
          IndexKey key = new IndexKey(term.getKey());
          byte[] value = term.getValue();
          TermDocumentFrequency tdf =
              AVRODataConverter.unmarshallTermDocumentFrequency
              (value);
          terms.put(key, tdf);
      }
  }
  return new DocumentInfo(terms, fields);
}
```

Implementation of this class is similar to the implementation of the `IndexTableSupport` class. It implements similar methods and employs the same optimization techniques.

Now that you know how to use HBase for building real-time Hadoop implementations, let's take a look at a new growing class of specialized Hadoop applications — specialized real-time Hadoop queries.

USING SPECIALIZED REAL-TIME HADOOP QUERY SYSTEMS

One of the first real-time Big Data query implementations was introduced by Google in 2010. Dremel is a scalable, interactive, ad-hoc query system used to analyze read-only nested data. The foundation of Dremel is as follows:

➤   Dremel represents an implementation of a novel columnar storage format for nested relational data/data with nested structures that was largely introduced in the article, "Column Oriented Storage Techniques for MapReduce" by Avrilia Floratou, Jignesh M. Patel, Eugene J. Shekita, and Sandeep Tata (published by Very Large Data Base Endowment, also known as VLDB, in 2011). The article introduced a format itself, its integration with HDFS, and a "skip list" approach to reading only required data, thus allowing you to significantly improve the performance of conditional reads.

➤   Dremel uses distributed scalable aggregation algorithms, which allow the results of a query to be computed on thousands of machines in parallel.

A columnar storage model shown in Figure 9-12 originates from flat relational data, and is extended to support nested data model. This model contains several fields — A, B, C, D, and E. Fields C, D, and E each have records r1 and r2, while fields A and B have no records, but contain related fields. In this model, all nested fields (B, C, D, and E) are stored continuously. Two main techniques can then be used to optimize read performance:

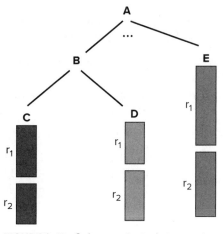

FIGURE 9-12: Column-oriented storage in Dremel

➤ *Skip lists* (for example, if sequential layout is A, B, C, D, E, and only A and E are required, after reading A, you can skip B, C, and D, and jump directly to E)

➤ *Lazy deserialization* (that is, keeping data as a binary blob until serialization is required)

Figure 9-13 shows the implementation of a distributed scalable query that leverages Dremel's multilevel serving tree architecture. The incoming client requests come to the root server, which routes requests to the intermediate servers based on request types. There can be several layers of intermediate servers with their own routing rules. The leaf servers use a storage layer (based on the columnar storage model described earlier) to read the required data (which is bubbling up for aggregation), and the final result is returned to the user.

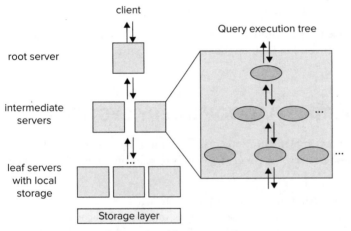

FIGURE 9-13: Dremel overall architecture

Overall, Dremel combines parallel query execution with the columnar format, thus supporting high-performance data access.

As Hadoop's popularity and adoption grow, more people will be using its storage capabilities. As a result, specialized real-time query engines are currently a source of competition among Hadoop vendors and specialized companies. As of this writing, there are several Hadoop projects that have been inspired by Dremel:

➤ Open Dremel is currently part of Apache Drill (an Apache Incubator project since 2012).

➤ Cloudera introduced Impala (currently in beta state), which is part of the Cloudera Hadoop distribution (CDH 4.1). (There are also plans to either move this to Apache, or use an Apache license and make it available as a GitHub project.)

➤ The Stinger Initiative was introduced by Hortonworks in 2013 (real-time Hive). It has been submitted to Apache's incubation process.

➤ HAWQ is part of a version of Greenplum's Hadoop distribution — Pivotal HD.

> **NOTE** *There are also entirely new players in this space, including JethroData (which is a fully indexed columnar database that supports a flexible schema and ACID access), Hadapt's Adaptive Analytical Platform (which combines Postgre's SQL query with Hadoop and introduces a hybrid data storage), and Spire from Drawn to Scale (which provides real-time SQL query based on MapR's implementation of HBase).*

Currently, real-time Hadoop queries represent a "bleeding edge" of Hadoop development. Many believe that such implementations will be new "killer" Hadoop applications by combining the power of Hadoop storage with the pervasive use of SQL. Such systems can also provide an easy path for integration between Hadoop and modern business intelligence (BI) tools, thus simplifying the bringing of Hadoop-based data to a wider audience.

All implementations are in various stages of maturity. For this discussion, let's take a look at the two that have been around the longest — Drill and Impala.

Apache Drill

As of this writing, Drill is a very active Apache incubating project led by MapR with six to seven companies actively participating, and more than 250 people currently on the Drill mailing list.

The goal of Drill is to create an interactive analysis platform for Big Data using a standard SQL-supporting relational database management system (RDBMS), Hadoop, and other NoSQL implementations (including Cassandra and MongoDB).

As shown in Figure 9-14, the foundation of the Drill architecture is a set of Drillbits processes — that is, Drill executables running on Hadoop's DataNodes to provide data locality and parallel query execution.

An individual query request can be delivered to any of the Drillbits. It is first processed by a SQL query parser, which parses the incoming query and passes it to the co-located query planner.

The SQL query planner provides query optimization. A default optimizer is a cost-based optimizer, but additional custom optimizers can be introduced, based on the open APIs provided by Drill.

Once a query plan is ready, it is processed by a set of distributed executors. A query execution is spread between multiple DataNodes in order to support data locality. Execution of a query on a particular data set is done on the node where the data is located. Additionally, to improve the overall performance, results of queries for local data sets are aggregated locally, and only combined query results are returned back to the executor that started a query.

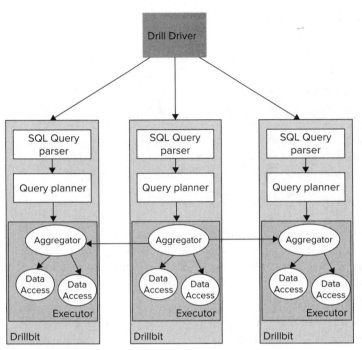

FIGURE 9-14: Overall Drill architecture

Drill's query parser supports full SQL (ANSI SQL:2003), including correlated sub-query, analytics functions, and so on. In addition to standard relational data, Drill supports (using ANSI SQL extensions) hierarchical data, including XML, JavaScript Object Notation (JSON), Binary JSON (BSON), Avro, protocol buffers, and so on.

Drill also supports dynamic data schema discovery (schema-less queries). This feature is especially important when dealing with NoSQL databases, including HBase, Cassandra, MongoDB, and so on, where every record can effectively have a different schema. It also simplifies support for schema evolution.

Finally, the SQL parser supports custom domain-specific SQL extensions based on User Defined Functions (UDFs), User Defined Table Functions (UDTFs), and custom operators (for example, Mahout's k-means operator).

Whereas Drill is, for the most part, still in a development state, the other specialized Hadoop query language implementation — Impala — is currently available for initial experimentation and testing. Let's take a closer look at the details of Impala implementation.

Impala

Impala (which was in beta version at the time of this writing) is one of the first open source implementations of real-time Hadoop query systems. Although technically an open source (GitHub) project, Impala currently requires a specific Hadoop installation (CDH4.2 for the latest Impala version).

An Impala implementation makes use of some of the existing Hadoop infrastructure, namely the Hive metastore and Hive ODBC driver. Impala operates on Hive tables and uses HiveQL as a query language.

HIVEQL SUPPORT IN IMPALA

As of this writing, the following HiveQL functionality is *not* supported by Impala:

➤ Data Definition Language (DDL) such as CREATE, ALTER, and DROP (although it can be implemented using a Hive shell)

➤ LOAD DATA to load raw files (although it can be implemented using a Hive shell)

➤ Non-scalar data types such as maps, arrays, and structs

➤ XML and JSON functions

➤ Extensibility mechanisms such as TRANSFORM, custom UDFs, custom file formats, or custom serialization/deserealization (SerDes)

➤ User Defined Aggregate Functions (UDAFs)

➤ User Defined Table Generating Functions (UDTFs)

➤ Sampling

Also keep in mind that, in the current version, implementation of joins is in memory. Considering that Impala implementation uses the C programming language with no limitation on process memory, joining larger tables may cause a crash of Impala and of a particular node (or nodes).

Figure 9-15 shows Impala's architecture. As shown in the figure, the process is as follows:

1. An Impala client (Impala shell or ODBC driver) connects to an Impala server. Because there is no centralized Impala node, a particular client connects to a specific node that is running an Impala server. (A better option is to use a network switch for load balancing.)

2. Once the request reaches an Impala server, it is first processed by a query planner. The query planner calculates an execution plan, based on the table location information from the data store, and passes it to the query coordinator.

3. Based on this plan and data location, the query coordinator orchestrates a partial query execution between multiple query execution engines running on multiple nodes. It then combines results and passes them back to the query planner (and, consequently, to the original requester).

4. Distribution of the requests to the query execution engines is based on data locality (compare this with MapReduce map jobs distribution). The query execution engine is responsible for both data access and partial query execution.

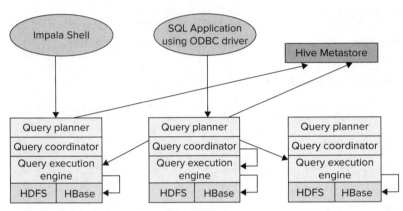

FIGURE 9-15: Impala overall architecture

The current version of Impala supports both HDFS and HBase data storage. File formats currently supported for HDFS include `TextFile`, `SequenceFile`, `RCFile`, and Avro. Support for a new columnar format (Trevini) has been advertised by Cloudera.

HBase support is based on mapping a Hive table to HBase. This mapping can be done either based on a primary key (for best performance), or any other column (using a full table to scan with `SingleColumnValueFilter`, which can cause a significant performance degradation, especially for large tables).

Access for both HDFS and HBase supports several compression codecs, including Snappy, `GZIP`, Deflate, and `BZIP`.

In addition to its own shell, Impala supports Hive's user interface (Hue Beeswax).

Now that you are familiar with Hadoop's real-time queries and some of their implementations, let's see how the real-time query system stacks up against MapReduce.

Comparing Real-Time Queries to MapReduce

Table 9-1 summarizes the main differences between real-time query systems and MapReduce. This table can help you decide on which type of system you should base your implementation.

TABLE 9-1: Key Differences between Real-Time Query System and MapReduce

KEY DIFFERENCES	REAL-TIME QUERY ENGINES	MAPREDUCE
Purpose	Query service for large data sets	Programming model for processing large data sets
Usage	Ad hoc and trial-and-error interactive query of large data sets for quick analysis and troubleshooting	Batch processing of large data sets for time-consuming data conversion or aggregation
OLAP/BI use case	Yes	No
Data mining use case	Limited	Yes
Programming complex data processing logic	No	Yes
Processing unstructured data	Limited (regular expression matching on text)	Yes
Handling large results/join large table	No	Yes

Now that you know about specialized real-time Hadoop query systems, let's look at another fast-growing set of real-time Hadoop-based applications — event processing.

USING HADOOP-BASED EVENT-PROCESSING SYSTEMS

Event processing (EP) systems enable you to track (in real time) and process continuous streams of data. Complex event processing (CEP) systems support holistic processing of data from multiple sources.

Considering Hadoop's capability to store massive amounts of data such as what can be produced by CEP systems, Hadoop seems like a good fit for large-scale CEP implementations.

A common implementation architecture for a CEP system is known as an *actor model*. In this case, every actor is responsible for partial processing of a certain event. (Mapping events to actors can be implemented in different ways, based on the event types, a combination of event types, and some additional attributes.) When an actor is finished with the processing of incoming events, it can send results for further processing to other actors. Such an architecture provides for a very clean componentization of the overall processing, and encapsulates certain processing logic.

THE ACTOR MODEL

The *actor model* is a general model of concurrent computation developed by Carl Hewitt, Henry Baker, and Gul Agha. The foundation of this model is the *actor*, which is a universal primitive of concurrent computation. In response to a message that it receives, an actor can concurrently do the following:

➤ Make local decisions

➤ Create more actors

➤ Send messages

➤ Determine how to respond to the next received message

The actor model is characterized by inherent concurrency of computation within and among actors. A fundamental characteristic of the actor model is the decoupling of a sender from the communications sent. This allows the actor model to represent asynchronous communication, and control structures as patterns of passing messages.

In the actor model, recipients of messages are identified by address. This means that an actor can communicate only with actors whose addresses are available to it. These addresses can be a part of an actor definition, obtained from an incoming message, or based on a lookup in a centralized actor registry.

Once the actor's implementation is in place, the overall system's responsibility is to manage the actor's life cycle and communications between actors.

Although CEP in general is a fairly mature architecture with quite a few established implementations, usage of Hadoop for CEP is relatively new and is not quite mature enough. Two different approaches to implementing CEP-based Hadoop systems exist:

➤ Modifying a MapReduce execution to accommodate event-processing needs. Examples of such systems include HStreaming and HFlame.

➤ "Hadoop-like" CEP implementations, which use a range of Hadoop technologies and can be integrated with Hadoop to leverage its data storing capabilities. Examples of such systems include Storm, S4, and so on.

HFlame

As explained in Chapter 3, MapReduce operates on key/value pairs, as shown in Figure 9-16. A mapper takes input in the form of key/value pairs (k_1, v_1) and transforms them into another key/value pair (k_2, v_2). The framework sorts the mapper's output key/value pairs and combines each unique key with all its values $(k_2, \{v_2, v_2, ...\})$. These key/value combinations are delivered to reducers, which translate them into yet another key/value pair (k_3, v_3).

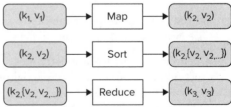

FIGURE 9-16: MapReduce processing

The basic difference between MapReduce processing and the actor model is the fact that the actor model operates on "live" data streams, whereas MapReduce operates on data already stored in Hadoop. Additionally, MapReduce mappers and reducers are instantiated specifically for executing a specific job, which makes MapReduce too slow for real-time event processing.

HFlame is an Hadoop's extension that attempts to improve basic MapReduce performance by providing support for long-running mappers and reducers, which processes the new contents as soon as they are stored in HDFS.

Figure 9-17 shows the overall architecture of HFlame working in this mode.

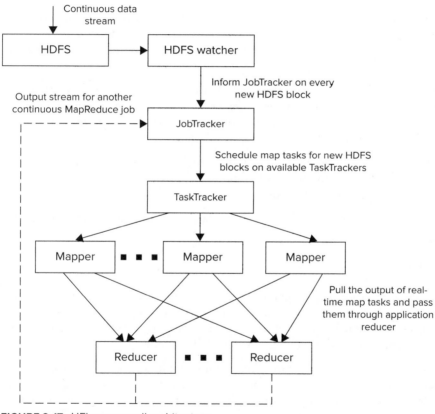

FIGURE 9-17: HFlame overall architecture

In this case, once the data is written to HDFS, a data watcher (HDFS watcher) invokes a MapReduce JobTracker, informing it about the availability of a new data. A JobTracker checks with the TaskTrackers to find an available map task, and passes data to it. Once the map method is complete, the data is sent to the appropriate reducer.

An output of an HFlame continuous job can be further represented as a continuous stream of data, which can be consumed by another MapReduce job running in continuous mode. This execution chaining mechanism allows pipelines of arbitrary complexity to be built (similar to chaining MapReduce jobs, described in Chapter 3).

Although implementation of the actor model in HFlame is quite simple, it often violates one of the principles of functional programming, which is a base MapReduce execution model. The problem is that the majority of implementations of actors are stateful (compared to the in-memory combiner pattern, described in Chapter 4). This means that every actor keeps internal memory for its execution, and you should carefully choose the number of reducers to ensure that a reducer process has enough memory to accommodate all active actors.

Another issue is the fact that, in the case of a reducer's failure, Hadoop will restart the process, but the state of the actors (kept in memory) disappears. This typically is not a problem for a large-scale CEP system that is processing millions of requests, but something that requires careful designing and planning.

The way to get around these problems is to create a persistence layer for an actor's state that can, for example, leverage HBase. However, such an implementation adds latency (with an HBase read prior to actor execution, and one write immediately after) and complexity. But this can make the overall implementation significantly more robust.

The HFlame distribution comes with several CEP examples, including fraud detection for the financial industry, failure/fault detection for the telecommunications and energy industries, continuous insights for Facebook and Twitter, and so on.

Now let's take a look at an Hadoop-like CEP system using Storm as an example, and see how it works.

Storm

Storm is a new real-time event processing system that is distributed, reliable, and fault-tolerant. Storm (sometimes called "Hadoop for stream processing") is not really Hadoop, but leverages many Hadoop ideas, principles, and some Hadoop sub-projects. You can integrate it with Hadoop for storing processing results that can later be analyzed using Hadoop tools.

Figure 9-18 shows the overall Storm architecture. You will notice a lot of commonalities between MapReduce and Storm architectures. Storm's overall execution is controlled by a master process — Nimbus. It is responsible for distributing code around the cluster, assigning tasks to machines, and monitoring for failures. A lot of commonalities exist between the functionality of Nimbus and of the MapReduce JobTracker. Similar to the JobTracker, Nimbus is running on a separate control node, which is called a *master* in Storm.

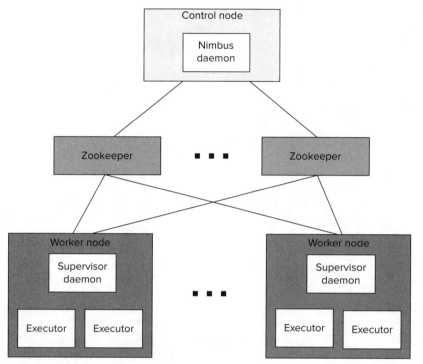

FIGURE 9-18: Storm high-level architecture

All other nodes in the Storm cluster are worker nodes that run one specialized process — Supervisor. The role of the Supervisor is to manage resources on a particular machine (compared to the MapReduce TaskTracker). Supervisor accepts requests for work from Nimbus. It starts and stops local worker processes based on these requests.

Unlike a MapReduce implementation where TaskTrackers monitor a heartbeat directly to the JobTracker (which directly keeps track of the cluster topology), Storm uses a Zookeeper cluster (see Chapter 2 for additional information on Zookeeper) for coordination between master and worker nodes. An additional role of Zookeeper in Storm is to keep state for both Nimbus and Supervisor. This allows both to be stateless, which leads to a very fast recovery of any Storm node. Both Nimbus and Supervisor are implemented to fail fast, which, coupled with fast recovery, leads to a high stability of Storm clusters.

Unlike MapReduce (which operates on a finite number of key/value pairs), Storm operates on *streams of events* — or an unbounded sequence of tuples. As shown in Figure 9-19, Storm applications (or topologies) are defined in the form of input streams (called *spouts*) and a connected graph of processing nodes (called *bolts*).

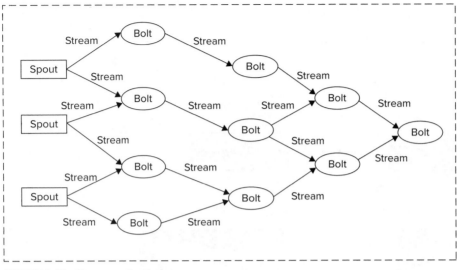

FIGURE 9-19: Storm application

> **NOTE** *In mathematics and computer science, a* tuple *is an ordered list of elements. The term "tuple" originated as an abstraction of the numbering sequence — single, double, triple, quadruple, quintuple, sextuple, septuple, octuple, ..., n-tuple.*

Spouts typically read data tuples from the external source, and emit them into a topology. Spouts can be reliable (for example, replaying a tuple that failed to be processed) and unreliable. A single spout can produce more than one stream.

Bolts are processing workhorses of Storm. They are similar to actors in the actor model. Bolts can do anything from filtering, functions, aggregations, joins, talking to databases, to emitting streams, and more. Bolts can do simple data transformations. Doing complex stream transformations often requires multiple steps, and, thus, chaining bolts (compare this with MapReduce jobs chaining).

The bolt chaining-processing dependency execution (compare this with DAG of MapReduce jobs defined by Oozie) is defined by Storm's topology — that is, a Storm application. The topology is created in Storm using a topology builder.

The routing of tuples between bolts in Storm is accomplished by using stream grouping. Stream grouping defines how specific tuples are sent from one bolt to another. Storm comes with several prebuilt stream groupings, including the following:

➤ **Shuffle grouping** — This provides a random distribution of tuples between the bolts in a way that guarantees that each bolt will get an equal number of tuples. This type of grouping is useful for load balancing between identical stateless bolts.

➤ **Fields grouping** — This provides a partitioning of a stream based on fields specified in the grouping. This type of grouping guarantees that the tuples with the same field(s) value will always go to the same bolt, while tuples with different field value(s) may go to different bolts. This grouping is similar to MapReduce's shuffle and sort processing, guaranteeing that a map's outputs with the same keys will always go to the same reducer. This type of grouping is useful for implementation of stateful bolts, such as counters, aggregators, joins, and so on.

➤ **All grouping** — This replicates stream values across all participating bolt tasks.

➤ **Global grouping** — This allows an entire stream to go to a single bolt (a bolt with the lowest ID is used in this case). This type of grouping is equivalent to a MapReduce job with a single reducer, and is useful for implementing global counters, top N, and so on.

➤ **Direct grouping** — This allows a tuple producer to explicitly pick a tuple's destination. This type of grouping requires a tuple emitter to know the IDs of participating bolts, and is restricted to a special type of streams — *direct streams*.

➤ **Local or shuffle grouping** — This ensures that, if possible, a tuple will be delivered within a local process. If the target bolt does not exist in the current process, this acts as a normal shuffle grouping. This type of grouping is often used for optimizing execution performance.

Additionally, Storm enables developers to implement custom stream grouping.

A topology is packaged in a single `jar` file that is submitted to a Storm cluster. This `jar` contains a class with `main` function that defines the topology to be submitted to Nimbus. Nimbus analyzes the topology and distributes parts of it to the Supervisors, which are responsible for starting, executing, and stopping worker processes, as necessary, for execution of the given topology.

Storm provides a very powerful framework for execution of various real-time applications. Similar to MapReduce, Storm provides a simplified programming model, which hides the complexity of implementing a long-running distributed application, and allows developers to concentrate on a business-processing implementation, while providing all complex infrastructure plumbing.

Now that you are familiar with Hadoop-based event processing and some implementations, let's see how it stacks up against MapReduce.

Comparing Event Processing to MapReduce

Table 9-2 summarizes the main differences between event-processing systems and MapReduce. This can serve as a guide to help you decide on which type of system to base your implementation.

TABLE 9-2: Key Differences between Event-Processing System and MapReduce

KEY DIFFERENCES	EVENT PROCESSING	MAPREDUCE
Purpose	Filter, correlate, and process events in real time	Programming model for processing large data sets
Usage	An environment for development and deployment of event-processing applications that can process and act on hundreds or thousands of events per second	Batch processing of large data sets for time-consuming data conversion or aggregation
Deployment	Separate (predefined)	Just in time (in code)
Real-time, event-driven applications	Yes	No
Programming complex data processing logic	Yes	Yes
Processing unstructured data	Limited	Yes

SUMMARY

In this chapter, you have learned about different approaches to implementing Hadoop-based real-time applications, and the underlying architectural principles behind such implementations.

You also learned how HBase can be leveraged for building Hadoop-based real-time applications. You learned about the design and implementation of two sample applications — a picture-management system, and an HBase-based Lucene back end. Both applications demonstrate how such implementations can be designed, and the role HBase plays in the overall implementation.

This chapter also introduced you to two very active areas of Hadoop development — real-time SQL query systems and Hadoop-based event-processing systems. You learned about the base architecture of such systems, and their overall capabilities. You also learned how such systems can be compared to MapReduce, and what you should consider when choosing a particular implementation.

Now that you have learned different techniques and technologies for development of Hadoop-based applications, Chapter 10 shows you how to secure these applications.

10

Hadoop Security

WHAT'S IN THIS CHAPTER?

- ➤ Understanding Hadoop security challenges and history
- ➤ Understanding authentication
- ➤ Understanding authorization
- ➤ Getting to know network encryption
- ➤ Getting to know Hadoop ecosystem security
- ➤ Taking a look at upcoming changes and enhancements with Project Rhino
- ➤ Reviewing best practices for securing Hadoop

One of the biggest growing concerns in today's Big Data environments revolves around information security. Specifically, organizations must be able to meet access control restrictions, confidentiality rules, privacy restrictions, and may need to support legal mandates related to the use and protection of their data and their analysis of large data sets. Because Hadoop was designed for formatting large amounts of unstructured data on commodity servers in an environment of de facto trust, security was never a driver for its design or development.

Over the past five years, many organizations using Hadoop have been challenged to meet stricter security requirements. As Hadoop's popularity has increased, its security architecture has been exposed to intense scrutiny by security professionals. At the same time, in this era of Big Data, researchers are documenting challenges related to privacy and access control related to the processing of large data sets. These concerns have challenged the Hadoop community to introduce security mechanisms for satisfying requirements for authentication, access control, and privacy. Security mechanisms are in place for Hadoop, and work is ongoing to improve the security of Hadoop and its ecosystem components.

Following are some of the security questions that arise related to the use of Hadoop:

➤ How does Hadoop security work?

➤ How do you enforce access control to your data?

➤ How can you control who is authorized to access, modify, and stop Hadoop MapReduce jobs?

➤ How do you get your (insert application here) to integrate with Hadoop security controls?

➤ How do you enforce authentication for users on all types of Hadoop clients (for example, web consoles and processes)?

➤ How can you ensure that rogue services don't impersonate real services (for example, rogue TaskTrackers and tasks, unauthorized processes presenting block IDs to DataNodes to get access to data blocks, and so on)?

➤ Can you tie in your organization's Lightweight Directory Access Protocol (LDAP) directory and user groups to Hadoop's permissions structure?

➤ Can you encrypt data in transit in Hadoop?

➤ Can your data be encrypted at rest on HDFS?

➤ How can you apply consistent security controls to your Hadoop cluster?

➤ What are the best practices for security in Hadoop today?

➤ Are there proposed changes to Hadoop's security model? What are they?

This book dedicates two chapters to security that will help you answer these questions. This chapter focuses on the security mechanisms that Hadoop natively provides, along with some upcoming security changes and enhancements. Chapter 12 focuses on enterprise security with Hadoop, and that chapter shows how *other* mechanisms can be used with Hadoop to provide the security controls that Hadoop currently does not provide. Chapter 12 also provides more of a holistic (not Hadoop-centric) view of enterprise security for the security professional.

This chapter begins with a brief background of the history of Hadoop security, and focuses on the requirements that projects using Hadoop may need to address. You learn how Hadoop provides authentication, with a focus on the details of Hadoop's use of Kerberos. You also learn how Hadoop uses authentication between processes. This chapter focuses on Hadoop's authorization model, and discusses mechanisms for network encryption in Hadoop. You learn about ongoing security enhancements that are currently being worked on for Hadoop (Project Rhino). Finally, this chapter provides an overview of best practices for securing Hadoop, and provides a "cheat sheet" for authentication and authorization.

A BRIEF HISTORY: UNDERSTANDING HADOOP SECURITY CHALLENGES

It is a well-known fact that security was not a factor when Hadoop was initially developed. Because the initial use of Hadoop revolved around managing large amounts of public web data, data security and privacy were not factors in the initial design. It was always assumed that Hadoop clusters would consist of cooperating, trusted machines used by trusted users in a trusted environment.

Initially, there was no security model — Hadoop didn't authenticate users or services, there was no data privacy, and, because Hadoop was designed to execute code over a distributed cluster of machines, anyone could submit code and it would be executed. Although auditing and authorization controls (HDFS file permissions) were implemented in earlier distributions, such access control was easily circumvented because any user could impersonate any other user with a command-line switch! Because impersonation was prevalent and done by most users, the security controls that did exist were not really effective.

Back then, organizations concerned about security segregated Hadoop clusters onto private networks, and restricted access to authorized users. However, because there were few security controls within Hadoop, many accidents and security incidents happened in such environments. Well-intended users can make mistakes, such as deleting data — and not just their own (a distributed delete can destroy massive amounts of data within seconds). All users and programmers had the same level of access to all of the data in the cluster, any job could access any data in the cluster, and any user could potentially read any data set, which caused concerns related to confidentiality. Because MapReduce had no concept of authentication or authorization, a mischievous user could lower the priorities of other Hadoop jobs to make his or her job complete faster — or worse, kill the other jobs.

As Hadoop became a more popular platform for data analytics, security professionals began to express concerns about the insider threat of malicious users in an Hadoop cluster. A malicious developer could easily write code to impersonate other users' Hadoop services (for example, writing a new TaskTracker and registering itself as an Hadoop service, or impersonating the `hdfs` or `mapred` users, deleting everything in HDFS, and so on). Because DataNodes enforced no access control, a malicious user could read arbitrary data blocks from DataNodes, bypassing access control restrictions, or writing garbage data to DataNodes, undermining the integrity of the data to be analyzed. Anyone could submit a job to a JobTracker and it could be arbitrarily executed.

As Hadoop matured, the community realized that more robust security controls needed to be added to Hadoop. Security professionals identified the need for *authentication*, allowing users, client programs, and servers within an Hadoop cluster to prove their identity to each other. Authorization was also identified as a requirement, along with other security concerns such as confidentiality, integrity, privacy, and auditing. However, other security concerns could not be addressed without authentication, so authentication was the initial focus area that led to a security re-design of Hadoop. With authentication being the weakest link, a team at Yahoo! chose Kerberos as the authentication mechanism for Hadoop in 2009, and developed the following high-level requirements, documented in their initial white paper released that same year:

➤ Users should only be allowed to access HDFS files that they have permission to access.

➤ Users should only be allowed to access or modify their own MapReduce jobs.

➤ Users and services should be mutually authenticated to prevent unauthorized NameNodes, DataNodes, JobTrackers, and TaskTrackers.

➤ Services should be mutually authenticated to prevent unauthorized services from joining a cluster.

➤ Use of Kerberos credentials and tickets should be transparent to the users and applications.

Kerberos was then integrated into Hadoop in order to implement secure network authentication, and other controls were put in place between the various Hadoop processes. Since then, Hadoop and other tools in the Hadoop ecosystem have made good strides to provide security mechanisms that meet the requirements of today's users, and more work is continuing. Let's take a look at what is provided.

AUTHENTICATION

This section focuses on authentication in Hadoop. The first subsection, "Kerberos Authentication," describes the Kerberos protocol, and discusses how Hadoop uses Kerberos authentication for Remote Procedure Calls (RPCs), and how Hadoop web consoles can be protected with Kerberos authentication using HTTP Simple and Protected Negotiation Mechanism (SPNEGO). In the second subsection, "Delegated Security Credentials," you learn how cooperating processes authenticate to each other, initially using Kerberos as a basis, but using other mechanisms to delegate credentials. Both subsections highlight how these mechanisms should be implemented.

Kerberos Authentication

Kerberos became the basis of Hadoop's security model, and this was released in the .20.20x distributions of Hadoop. Developed at MIT in the 1980s, Kerberos is a secret-key–based authentication system used for providing authentication and Single-Sign-On (SSO) of users and servers in an open network. Hadoop uses the Kerberos protocol to authenticate users to Hadoop, and to authenticate Hadoop services to each other. This alleviates the threat of impersonation that was possible in earlier versions of Hadoop, and it provides the foundation to allow Hadoop to ensure that MapReduce and HDFS requests are being executed with the appropriate authorization levels.

> **WHAT VERSIONS OF HADOOP HAVE KERBEROS SECURITY AVAILABLE?**
>
> It is important that you understand what versions of Hadoop actually have Kerberos RPC authentication implemented. The .20.20X releases of Hadoop were the first versions of Hadoop to have Kerberos authentication support. This was later labeled Hadoop version 1.0, which was built from the .20.205 release. Hadoop 2.0 also includes Kerberos security. It is important to know that certain older versions (such as the .21 and .22 branches) don't have full Kerberos security enabled. The distributions of Hadoop from other sources such as Cloudera's CDH3, CDH4, and Hortonworks' HDP all have Kerberos security available to configure.

Kerberos relies on the concept of "tickets" in order to work. In Kerberos, three parties are involved:

➤ A *client* (which can be a user or service) that requests access to a resource.

➤ A *requested resource* (which is typically a service).

➤ The *Kerberos Key Distribution Center (KDC)*, which includes an *Authentication Service (AS)* and a *Ticket Granting Service (TGS)*. The KDC is the main hub of all communications.

In Kerberos, each client or service is called a *principal*, and has a secret key used to negotiate authentication. The Kerberos KDC also has copies of everyone's secret key, and facilitates all communications. Figure 10-1 shows a very high-level functional overview of how it works. You can learn more detail in this chapter's sidebar, "The Bitter Details: How the Kerberos Protocol Works."

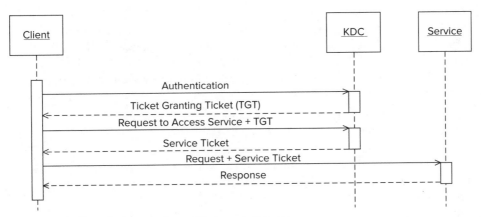

FIGURE 10-1: Functional overview of Kerberos protocol

To begin a session, a client first authenticates to the AS of the KDC. (For Hadoop users, this is done via the `kinit` command.) The KDC responds with something called a *Ticket Granting Ticket (TGT)*, which is simply a ticket used for requesting tickets to communicate to other servers and services. The client uses the TGT to request a service ticket to communicate with a service, and later presents that service ticket to the requested service, which returns a response. Because of the cryptography involved, based on the contents of the TGT, the service ticket, and the Kerberos protocol, the end result is mutual authentication with each party having a high degree of assurance of each other's identity. Simply put, when Kerberos is enabled for clients and Hadoop services, you have a degree of confidence that clients and services are who they say they are.

When Hadoop security is implemented to utilize Kerberos, users authenticate to the edge of the cluster via *Kerberos RPC*, and web consoles utilize *HTTP SPNEGO Kerberos authentication*. All Hadoop services mutually authenticate each other using Kerberos RPC. You learn more about that in the next subsection.

THE BITTER DETAILS: HOW THE KERBEROS PROTOCOL WORKS

Although you have seen a functional overview of Kerberos for simplicity, many people find it helpful to understand exactly how Kerberos works. Kerberos is a simple, effective, and stateless protocol that uses symmetric, or secret key cryptography. Because the Kerberos KDC knows the secret keys of all principals (sometimes called "Kerberized parties"), it can participate in encrypted exchanges with them in a way that the KDC and all of the principals involved are assured that everyone is who they say they are.

In Hadoop, much of the details of Kerberos are abstracted from the user (especially if you are using the `kinit` command line). The following figure shows this amount of abstraction, followed by a walkthrough of the details.

1. A client identifies itself and requests a Ticket Granting Ticket (TGT) from the KDC.

2. The KDC, acting on the response, creates the TGT containing the client's name, the KDC name, the client's IP address, and the session key. This TGT is then encrypted with the KDC's key (so only the KDC can read it). The KDC then responds to the client with the TGT, along with a newly generated session key encrypted with the client's key.

3. The client decrypts the KDC's response with its own key, finding the session key to use in its next request to the KDC. It then creates an authenticator consisting of its name, its IP address, and the time, and encrypts this authenticator with the new session key. It sends this encrypted authenticator, along with the TGT it received from the KDC and the name of a service it wants to request.

4. The KDC decrypts the client's authenticator with the session key, validating the client's identity. The KDC then decrypts the TGT that it encrypted to itself, comparing the information with that in the client's authenticator for validity.

5. The KDC creates a new session key to be used by the client and the requested service. The KDC then creates a service ticket for the requested service, which includes the client's name, the service name, the IP address from the client, and the new session key. This is encrypted with the requested service's key. The KDC then encrypts this service ticket and the new session key with the client's key.

6. The client decrypts the response from the KDC with its key, finding the new session key to use with the service, and the service ticket. The client creates a new authenticator (its name, its IP address, the time) and encrypts it with the new session key, and sends this authenticator and the service ticket to the requested service.

7. The service decrypts the service ticket with its key, and sees the client's name, the client's IP address, its own name, and the session key to use with the client.

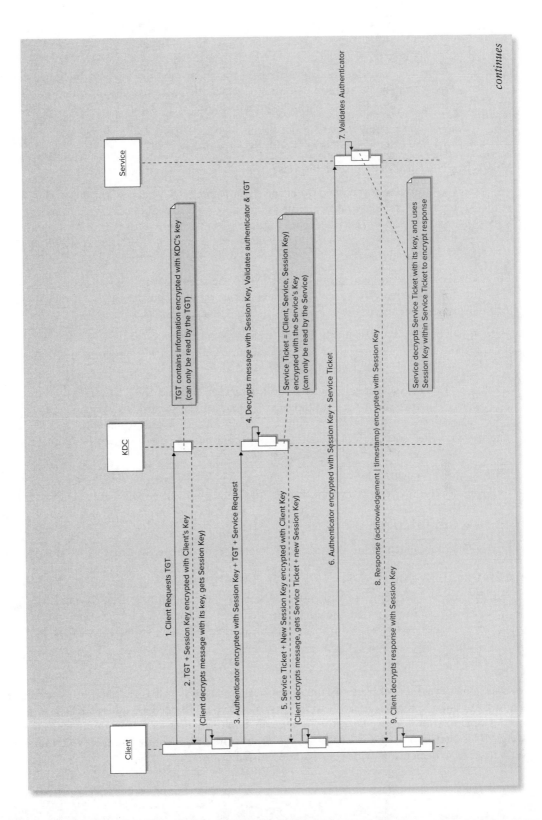

continues

continued

It then uses the session key to decrypt the client's authenticator, which includes the client's name, IP address, and the time, and compares the information from the service ticket with the authenticator.

8. The service now has assurance of the client's identity, and responds with an acknowledgment, encrypted with the session key.

9. The client decrypts the response from the service using the session key.

Steps 1–3 provide authentication of the client to the KDC, because the client must use its own secret key to decrypt the session key used to request a service ticket. When the KDC decrypts the client's authenticator in step 4 with that same session key, and when it compares information in that authenticator with the TGT, which the KDC created in step 2, it has assurance of the client's identity.

Step 2 provides authentication of the KDC to the client, because in Kerberos, only the client and the KDC can know the client's secret key. Because the KDC uses the client's key to encrypt the session key, the client has assurance of the KDC's identity.

In step 5, the KDC sets up the building blocks of authentication between the client and the service, because the KDC encrypts information with the requested service's key, and sets up a new session key for both the client and service to use.

Steps 6 and 7 authenticate the client to the service. Because the KDC encrypted the service ticket to the service containing the client's information, and because the client created an authenticator with the same information encrypted with the session key (also included in the service ticket), this contains enough information to give the service assurance of the client's identity.

Finally, in steps 8 and 9, the service's response provides assurance of the service's identity to the client. Now that the negotiation is finalized between the client and the service, this session key can be used to encrypt other information (for example, tokens).

In Hadoop, much of this process is abstracted from the user, because `kinit` does the interaction and negotiation with the KDC for the user, acting as the "client." All users typically have to do is authenticate once, and `kinit` takes over from there. For services that must be authenticated, `keytab` files containing the encrypted passwords of the services must be generated for the protocol, and the underlying system uses that password information for exchanges.

For users and developers of Hadoop, the use of Kerberos is mostly transparent once your cluster is set up to utilize Kerberos authentication. First of all, you will need a Kerberos KDC — this can be your organization's Active Directory (AD), which natively uses Kerberos, or you can set one up using MIT's distribution of Kerberos 5. However, it is important that you know which versions of Kerberos 5 have been tested with your Hadoop distribution.

> **NOTE** *Distributions of Hadoop, such as Cloudera's distributions of Hadoop (CDH 3 and 4) and Hortonworks' distribution (HDP), have extensive documentation with step-by-step directions and instructions for using and configuring Kerberos.*

Your Hadoop administrator will have to add Kerberos principals for users and all the Hadoop services in your cluster. To ensure that services are not impersonated, an administrator must initially set up all of the services to work with Kerberos, storing service passwords in encrypted keytab files. Different distributions may require different configurations of how exactly these keytab files are stored and where they are stored.

Although this book is geared toward developers and isn't necessarily for administrators, it is helpful to know that the kadmin tool is used for adding Kerberos principals and their keytab files. There is quite a bit of work to install and configure Kerberos security if you have a large cluster of machines, because configuration files and keytabs must be on every machine. Other high-level tools can help with the installation of Kerberos security on your cluster. For example, Cloudera Manager is a tool on Cloudera distributions that helps installation and configuration of your cluster, and can make this a lot easier. Other distributions of Hadoop may have similar tools.

For most developers and users of Hadoop, the use of Kerberos is mostly transparent. Once administrators have set up a Kerberos KDC, Kerberos principals (users, Hadoop services) can be added with the kadmin command. As a developer, you should know that you sign in once using kinit. You initiate the process with this command, and this process facilitates negotiation with the Kerberos KDC. Once you get a TGT, it lasts for ten hours, and is renewable for seven days by default. Once you authenticate, Hadoop commands work exactly as they did before, and it should be seamless to the user.

Underneath the covers, kinit puts your tickets in a Ticket Cache for your processes to use. Table 10-1 provides a list of some of the commands that are used.

TABLE 10-1: Shell Utilities for Kerberos Administration

COMMAND	USE
kadmin	Add, modify, and delete Kerberos principals (Hadoop services and users).
kinit	Obtain credentials from Kerberos (initial authentication). Used on the command line by users.
klist	List tickets held in the Ticket Cache.
kdestroy	Destroy active tickets and delete the Ticket Cache.

Hadoop uses two types of Kerberos Authentication mechanisms — one is used for authentication in remote procedure calls (Kerberos RPC) and another is used for authentication to web-based consoles (HTTP SPNEGO).

Kerberos RPC

Hadoop uses Kerberos version 5, utilizing the Simple Authentication and Security Layer (SASL) that uses the Generic Security Service Application Program Interface (GSSAPI) — referred to interchangeably as "Kerberos RPC" or "SASL/GSSAPI." SASL is an abstraction that allows an authentication protocol to be negotiated, and GSSAPI is a high-level API that implements Kerberos. SASL is used to abstract the authentication layer above Kerberos, and it was also implemented so that, beyond the initial Kerberos authentication, SASL can be used to negotiate other protocols.

Users authenticate themselves to the edge of the cluster, and Hadoop services (NameNode, DataNode, Secondary NameNode, JobTracker, TaskTracker, and so on) authenticate themselves to each other in this way. Kerberos RPC must be configured for the machines in your cluster utilizing Hadoop's configuration files of `core-site.xml`, `hdfs-site.xml`, and `mapred-site.xml`. Table 10-2 provides a list of files, configuration properties, and a detailed explanation of why and how they are used. Depending on your distribution of Hadoop, your configuration may vary, so see your administrator's guide for further clarification.

TABLE 10-2: Kerberos Configuration Parameters

FILE	CONFIGURATION PROPERTY	EXPLANATION
`core-site.xml`	`hadoop.security` `.authentication`	Set to `kerberos` on every machine in the cluster to enable Kerberos. (If set to `simple`, there would be no security.)
`hdfs-site.xml`	`dfs.namenode.keytab.file`	`keytab` file for NameNode.
`hdfs-site.xml`	`dfs.namenode.kerberos` `.principal`	Principal name for NameNode (for example, `nn/_host@domain`).
`hdfs-site.xml`	`dfs.secondary.namenode` `.keytab.file`	`keytab` file for secondary NameNode.
`hdfs-site.xml`	`dfs.secondary.namenode.` `kerberos.principal`	Principal name for secondary NameNode (for example, `nn/_host@domain`).
`hdfs-site.xml`	`dfs.datanode.keytab.file`	`keytab` file for DataNode.
`hdfs-site.xml`	`dfs.datanode.kerberos` `.principal`	Principal name for NameNode (for example, `dn/_host@domain`).
`mapred-site` `.xml`	`mapreduce.jobtracker` `.kerberos.principal`	Principal name for JobTracker (for example, `jt/_host@domain`).
`mapred-site` `.xml`	`mapreduce.tasktracker` `.kerberos.principal`	Principal name for TaskTracker (for example, `/tt/_host@domain`).
`mapred-site` `.xml`	`mapreduce.jobtracker` `.keytab.file`	`keytab` file for JobTracker.
`mapred-site` `.xml`	`mapreduce.tasktracker` `.keytab.file`	`keytab` file for TaskTracker.

As you can see, most of the configuration for your hosts will be straightforward, and involves listing the `keytab` files and the Kerberos principal name for each service. Setting `hadoop.security.authentication` to `kerberos` tells Hadoop to use Kerberos, and it looks for the appropriate principals and `keytabs` in the configuration files. If you use other Hadoop ecosystem components such as Oozie, HBase, and Hive, you must also configure `keytab` files and principals in the same way using the configuration files in `oozie-site.xml`, `hbase-site.xml`, and `hive-site.xml`.

Kerberos for Web-Based Consoles

Many Hadoop HTTP web consoles exist (JobTracker, NameNode, TaskTracker, DataNode, Oozie, Sqoop). Originally, these were not protected by security. When Hadoop security was initially developed, it was decided that security for such web consoles could be "pluggable HTTP authentication," leaving the web authentication mechanism and approach up to the implementer to develop. But this led to some inconsistencies in Hadoop deployments.

Implementers soon realized that it was important to utilize Kerberos consistently for all tools in the Hadoop ecosystem, and so implementations of HTTP SPNEGO (a browser-based mechanism that allows for Kerberos 5 authentication) were created and are now used consistently. Cloudera developed an open source package called Alfredo to implement HTTP SPNEGO, and this was later placed into Hadoop as "Hadoop Auth." Today, Hadoop's web user interfaces (`WebHDFS` and `HttpFS`) can be configured to be protected by Hadoop Auth.

WHAT ABOUT KERBERIZED SSL (KSSL)?

For a while, Kerberos implementations had the option of using Kerberized SSL (KSSL) for HTTP authentication — and it is still an option in many distributions. In earlier versions of the JDK, the implementation of KSSL disallowed strong encryption, and even allowed the option for setting an `hadoop.security.use-weak-http-crypto` flag, which concerned security professionals. As SPNEGO began to be used more consistently throughout the Hadoop ecosystem, and as developers had difficulty with KSSL configurations, developers on the Hadoop core project decided to utilize SPNEGO for web consoles for consistency.

Hadoop Auth provides HTTP SPNEGO authentication for protected web application resources, and sets a signed HTTP cookie that contains a Kerberos authentication token (which can be used until the cookie expires). Once a web application is configured to use HTTP Kerberos SPNEGO, any browser that supports it will be prompted for authentication. You can also use the command-line utility `curl`, which can go directly to the protected URL resource and will enforce authentication with your Kerberos credentials.

If you write a Java client that consumes a web app protected with Hadoop Auth, you simply need to do the following to get the Kerberos from the user's shell, using the `AuthenticatedURL` class, as shown in the following code snippet:

```
URL url = new URL("http://professionalHadoop.com/example");
AuthenticatedURL.Token = new AuthenticatedURL.Token();
HttpURLConnection httpConnection = new AuthenticatedURL().openConnection(url,
    token);
```

In a servlet or JavaServer Page (JSP) that you write in a SPNEGO-protected web application, you can get the user information passed in the HTTP Kerberos SPNEGO simply by calling getUserPrincipal() and getRemoteUser() on the HttpRequest object in the same way that you would get the principal information if the user used username/password authentication, or even digital certificate authentication.

If you want to write a servlet or a web application that uses Hadoop Auth, this is straightforward as well. Hadoop Auth must be configured for Hadoop in configuration files and for web apps using an AuthenticationFilter. To set up Hadoop Auth, you must set up a keytab and a principal to use to protect a resource, and you can configure this in your web app's WEB-INF/web.xml file, as shown in Listing 10-1.

LISTING 10-1: Example web app configuration for Kerberos SPNEGO

```xml
<web-app version="2.5" xmlns="http://java.sun.com/xml/ns/javaee">

  <servlet>
    <servlet-name>exampleServlet</servlet-name>
    <servlet-class>com.professionalHadoop.ExampleServlet</servlet-class>
  </servlet>

  <servlet-mapping>
    <servlet-name>exampleServlet</servlet-name>
    <url-pattern>/kerberos/example</url-pattern>
  </servlet-mapping>

  <filter>
    <filter-name>kerberosFilter</filter-name>
      <filter-class> <!--This is the filter that makes HTTP SPNEGO work-->
        org.apache.hadoop.security.authentication.server.AuthenticationFilter
      </filter-class>

      <init-param> <!--Needs to be type "kerberos"-->
        <param-name>type</param-name>
        <param-value>kerberos</param-value>
      </init-param>

      <init-param> <!-- Validity of token in secs (default 3600) -->
        <param-name>token.validity</param-name>
        <param-value>30</param-value>
      </init-param>

      <init-param> <!-- Domain to use that stores the auth token -->
        <param-name>cookie.domain</param-name>
        <param-value>.professionalHadoop.com</param-value>
      </init-param>
```

```
            <init-param> <!— Path to use for cookie that stores token -->
                <param-name>cookie.path</param-name>
                <param-value>/</param-value>
            </init-param>

            <init-param> <!-- The Web App Principal Name -->
                <param-name>kerberos.principal</param-name>
                <param-value>HTTP/localhost@LOCALHOST</param-value>
            </init-param>

            <init-param> <!—Name of the Kerberos Principal-->
                <param-name>kerberos.keytab</param-name>
                <param-value>/home/keytabs/HTTPauth.keytab</param-value>
            </init-param>
        </filter>
        <filter-mapping>
            <filter-name>kerberosFilter</filter-name>
            <url-pattern>/kerberos/*</url-pattern>
        </filter-mapping>
    </web-app>
```

As you can see in Listing 10-1, a filter that uses the `AuthenticationFilter` class must be configured and associated with a servlet. The listing also shows that you must configure the parameter "type" value to `kerberos`, and you must configure other options, including the token validity duration, cookie parameters, the `keytab` file, and the principal name.

To secure Hadoop web consoles to use HTTP SPNEGO, you must set up an HTTP principal and `keytab` file that is used by all of them, and each web console will need to be separately configured with the principal and `keytab` file. This was shown in Table 10-2 in the web app configuration for an example web application, but it is also shown in Table 10-3 for securing web authentication to the HDFS web interface in the `hdfs-site.xml` file. You will have to do this separately for all web consoles, and you'll see how this is done for Oozie's web console later in the chapter.

TABLE 10-3: hdfs-site.xml Configuration Parameters for Hadoop Auth

FILE	PROPERTY	EXPLANATION
hdfs-site.xml	dfs.web.authentication .kerberos.principal	HTTP Kerberos principal used by Hadoop Auth — must start with "HTTP/" (for example, HTTP/_host@domain)
hdfs-site.xml	dfs.web.authentication .kerberos.keytab	Kerberos `keytab` file for the HTTP Kerberos principal (for example, /keytabs/spnego .keytab)

Now that you understand how Hadoop Kerberos authentication works and how it is configured, let's delve a little deeper to show how authentication is delegated from users to their clients, and from their clients to HDFS and MapReduce processes.

Delegated Security Credentials

Once clients and services have been authenticated to each other via Kerberos, it is important to understand that many more security controls must be implemented beyond this initial authentication. What goes on behind the scenes is a little more complex because of all of the processes and hosts involved. Because developers write applications, and applications access HDFS and execute MapReduce jobs over data stored in HDFS, more security controls are needed to ensure that applications and the various services involved are actually acting *on behalf of the users* executing them. This means "connecting the dots" between the user, the user's process, and all aspects of the internal services of Hadoop, as the following list describes:

➤ Authenticated user's clients must be authenticated to the cluster and all Hadoop services.

➤ Even though Hadoop services authenticate to each other via Kerberos, they must prove that they are authorized to act on behalf of the clients for whom they are performing a task (for example, a client submits a job to a JobTracker, which will assign TaskTrackers to perform that job on behalf of the client).

➤ Clients must be authorized to access data on HDFS, but any service working on behalf of the client must also be able to access the data that the client has permission to see.

To do this, there must be *delegated authentication and authorization*. This means that authenticated users delegate their security credentials to their clients, processes, and the Hadoop services that use them. Because of the delegated aspect of this authentication and authorization, a lot of data flows in Hadoop are beyond the initial Kerberos authentication mechanisms discussed so far in this chapter.

Figure 10-2 shows some of these data flows, and is a subset of a similar diagram in the original 2009 Hadoop Security white paper. It provides a sense of some (but not all) of the data flows in Hadoop where authentication and cryptography are involved in communications for authentication.

As you can see in Figure 10-2 (and as has been discussed in this chapter), HTTP web consoles can be configured to perform Kerberos authentication using the HTTP SPNEGO protocol, which enforces user authentication at the browser level. You have seen how users, Hadoop services, and many projects within the Hadoop ecosystem (for example, Oozie and HBase) authenticate via Kerberos via the SASL/GSSAPI, often referred to as *Kerberos RPC*. What has not been discussed is that other communications exist beyond initial authentication, which include RPC Digest mechanisms. This has been added because of the delegated aspect of services working on behalf of clients.

After a client has authenticated via Kerberos (Kerberos RPC or HTTP SPNEGO authentication), you know that access to HDFS will involve communications between the client, the NameNode, and the DataNode. You also know that for MapReduce jobs to run, this involves submitting a job to the JobTracker, which pushes out work to available TaskTracker nodes in the cluster, which instantiate tasks to do the units of work.

Because all of these services must perform tasks on behalf of the client, more security controls are needed to ensure that all of these services doing the work on behalf of the client are authorized to perform work on behalf of the client. If this were not the case, you can imagine that rogue jobs could be created that read or delete data to which they shouldn't have access. Hadoop's security model uses initial authentication with Kerberos, with subsequent authentication for service interaction utilizing *tokens*, which are described in Table 10-4.

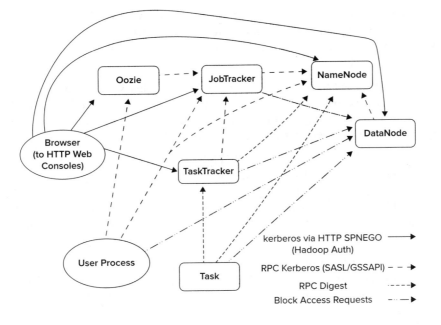

FIGURE 10-2: Subset of Hadoop authentication data flow

TABLE 10-4: Tokens Used in Hadoop Authentication

TOKEN	USED FOR
Kerberos TGT	Kerberos initial authentication to KDC.
Kerberos service ticket	Kerberos initial authentication between users, client processes, and services.
Delegation token	Token issued by the NameNode to the client, used by the client or any services working on the client's behalf to authenticate them to the NameNode.
Block Access token	Token issued by the NameNode after validating authorization to a particular block of data, based on a shared secret with the DataNode. Clients (and services working on the client's behalf) use the Block Access token to request blocks from the DataNode.
Job token	This is issued by the JobTracker to TaskTrackers. Tasks communicating with TaskTrackers for a particular job use this token to prove they are associated with the job.

Because clients must delegate access to other Hadoop services working on the client's behalf, *Delegation tokens* are utilized between the client and the NameNode. To reduce the performance overhead and load on the Kerberos KDC after the initial user authentication, these Delegation tokens are used in SASL/DIGEST MD-5 exchanges for subsequent authenticated access without using the Kerberos servers. Because each Hadoop job can be broken into many tasks, and because simple read operations across HDFS can include many calls to the NameNode and many DataNodes, you can see how enforcing mutual authentication with each call could potentially bring performance to a crawl, and potentially act as a denial-of-service (DoS) attack on your organization's Kerberos KDC.

After a client initially authenticates itself to the NameNode, the NameNode issues the client a Delegation token, which is a shared secret between the client and the NameNode. This has a validity time period for which it can be reused. This Delegation token is used for HDFS access, and it can be periodically renewed by the client and by services working on behalf of the client.

When a client must perform read or write operations on HDFS blocks, another type of token is used. Because DataNodes only speak "blocks" and not "files" or filesystem permissions for filesystem access operations, a token called a *Block Access token* is used to enforce access control to the blocks of data on HDFS. Before Hadoop security, if any client knew a block ID of a data block, it could read it from the DataNode, or write arbitrary data to a data block on HDFS. As you can imagine, this could completely bypass the security described so far.

To prevent this, lightweight and short-lived Block Access tokens using HMAC-SHA1 for authentication are issued by NameNodes for authorized filesystem requests, and they are validated by DataNodes. These tokens are used by client processes and the jobs kicked off by the client processes to verify access to a particular data block.

For MapReduce operations, a client's Delegation token is used in the submission process of a new job, and it can be renewed by the JobTracker for that job. To ensure that only tasks associated with a specific job are involved, the JobTracker creates another type of token — a *Job token* — and distributes those tokens to the TaskTrackers via RPC. Tasks utilize this Job token (which utilizes SASL/DIGEST MD-5) when the tasks communicate with TaskTrackers. Tasks of the job also use the Delegation token when authenticating to NameNode, and they utilize Block Access tokens to enable them to perform the necessary operations on the data block.

Let's walk through an example of the execution of a MapReduce task. Figure 10-3 shows a high-level example of a user authenticating via Kerberos RPC using `kinit` and executing a MapReduce program.

> **NOTE** *To make this example simpler to understand, some of the details have been abstracted. Because so much detail was provided when describing the Kerberos protocol earlier in this chapter, this example simply describes the multi-step protocol as "Kerberos authentication." It is important to know that once the user authenticates via* `kinit`*, the software stack handles all Kerberos communications and stores relevant tickets in the user's Ticket Cache in the filesystem along the way.*
>
> *Some of the details related to inter-service communication have also been abstracted for clarity. Kerberos authentication between the services themselves is mentioned only briefly, and for the purpose of this example, the authentication has already occurred. Because this example is focused on MapReduce, and it shows how JobTrackers assign tasks to TaskTrackers that spawn tasks and access the data, for the sake of simplicity, every service's request to a NameNode and DataNode is also not mentioned.*

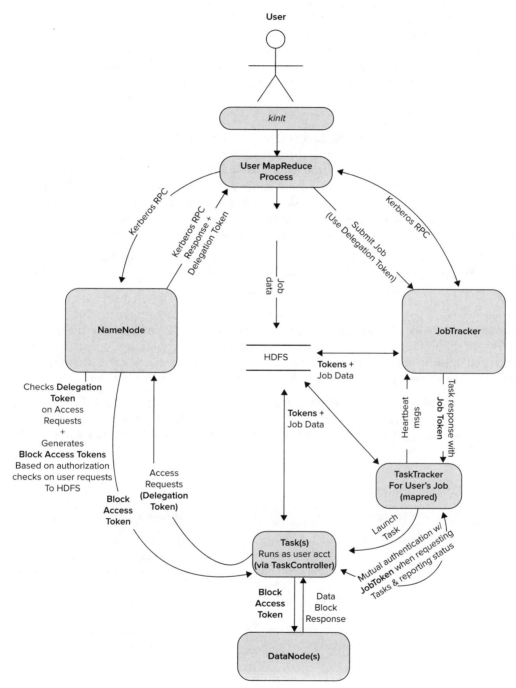

FIGURE 10-3: MapReduce authentication example

In Figure 10-3, a user authenticates via the `kinit` command, which does the work to authenticate the user to the KDC. The user then runs a MapReduce job, which is referred to as the *client* in this example. When the client authenticates itself to the NameNode via Kerberos RPC, the NameNode returns a Delegation token for subsequent calls to the NameNode. The client authenticates to the JobTracker via Kerberos RPC, and passes the Delegation token to the JobTracker when it submits the job, authorizing the JobTracker to be able to renew that Delegation token on the client's behalf. The JobTracker then creates a Job token associated with the job, and stores both tokens in the user's private directory in HDFS.

Next, the JobTracker looks for available TaskTracker nodes in the cluster. (For this example, all Hadoop services have already authenticated themselves to each other via Kerberos RPC.) When the JobTracker receives a heartbeat message from an available TaskTracker to which it chooses to assign the job, it responds, assigning the job and passing on the Job token for the job. The TaskTracker loads the token in memory and instantiates tasks, which should be run as the user that initiated the MapReduce process (you will need to configure that). As the tasks continue, they communicate status information with the TaskTracker, utilizing the Job token for mutual authentication.

When tasks need access to HDFS, they use the Delegation token issued by the NameNode to the client to authenticate to the NameNode. The NameNode provides authorization and issues Block Access tokens, which tasks use for requests to the DataNode.

This should give you a good idea of how authentication *within* an Hadoop cluster works, and how these mechanisms provide security related to the authentication of the end user, the authentication of services, and the authorization checks of various Hadoop processes. However, there are some things that you must ensure that you configure, because it is possible that you could configure *some*, but not all of these security mechanisms (which will lead to potential security vulnerabilities).

For example, it is possible that you could implement Kerberos RPC and HTTP SPNEGO authentication for your consoles as addressed earlier in this chapter, but you might not configure the use of Delegation tokens and Block Access tokens. Table 10-5 addresses the configuration details to set these into place.

TABLE 10-5: Configuring Credential Delegation

FILE	PROPERTY	EXPLANATION
`hdfs-site.xml`	`dfs.block.access.token.enable`	If set to `true`, Block Access tokens are checked when requesting I/O to blocks of data to the DataNode. If this is set to `false`, no checking is done.
`hdfs-site.xml`	`dfs.namenode.delegation.key.update-interval`	This is the update interval for a master key for Delegation tokens in the NameNode (in milliseconds).
`hdfs-site.xml`	`dfs.namenode.delegation.token.renew-interval`	This is the Delegation token renew interval (in milliseconds).

hdfs-site.xml	dfs.namenode.delegation.token.max-lifetime	This is the maximum lifetime (in milliseconds) for which a Delegation token is valid.
mapred-site.xml	mapreduce.job.complete.cancel.delegation.tokens	If true, Delegation tokens are canceled when jobs are complete.
mapred-site.xml	mapreduce.tasktracker.taskcontroller	org.apache.hadoop.mapred.LinuxTaskController Setting the property to the LinuxTaskController allows your tasks to run as the user who submitted the job, and this is important. It is not the default value, so by default, tasks will not run as the user. (You'll learn more about this in the next section, "Configuring the Task Controller.")
mapred-site.xml	mapreduce.tasktracker.group	This value is the group that the TaskTracker will run as (typically mapred).

For the most part, the values in Table 10-5 are fairly self-explanatory. There is a property for enabling the Block Access token, and there are values for configuring the intervals for use of the Delegation token key. The last two properties deal with tasks and how they are executed.

Configuring the Task Controller

By default, tasks are not run as the end user, which can be problematic from a security perspective. For this reason, Hadoop has a LinuxTaskController, which utilizes a setuid program called task-controller that ensures that tasks run as the user who initiated the job. This program has a setuid bit, is owned by root, and runs as the group mapred (as configured in Table 10-5).

For this to work, you must configure a few things. First of all, you will need users to have accounts on all the machines in your cluster if tasks are going to run as the user initiating the job. Next, the last two properties in Table 10-5 must be set, and a taskcontroller.cfg file must be created in a configuration directory that is two directories up from the task controller binary (typically /etc/hadoop/conf/taskcontroller.cfg — but it will depend on your distribution).

The task controller configuration file should look like Listing 10-2, where the Hadoop log directory is specified, and where you list "banned" users that shouldn't submit jobs. For example, the mapred and hdfs accounts should never submit a job.

LISTING 10-2: taskcontroller.cfg

```
hadoop.log.dir=<Path to Hadoop log directory>
mapreduce.tasktracker.group=mapred
banned.users=mapred,hdfs,bin
min.user.id=1000
```

Once you configure Kerberos, the rest is much easier, as you will see in the next section.

AUTHORIZATION

Hadoop provides authorization controls to authenticated users via the use of HDFS file permissions and service-level authorization.

➤ *HDFS* uses a permissions model for files and directories that is similar to the UNIX model. Each file and directory is associated with an owner and a group, and has associated read and write permissions. Based on those file permissions and the user's identity and group membership, HDFS controls access to reads and writes to the distributed filesystem. Unlike the UNIX model, there is no concept of an "executable" permission.

➤ *Service-level authorization* is a capability that provides access control lists (ACLs) of which users have permission to access particular services. A cluster can use this mechanism to control which users and groups have permission to submit jobs.

➤ *Job authorization* is enforced to allow users to only be able to view and modify their own jobs, which is enforced by setting MapReduce parameters.

This section discusses how you can configure these in Hadoop.

HDFS File Permissions

In the previous discussion about delegated security credentials, you learned that the NameNode checks to see if a client has permission to access a particular file, and enforces access control. To configure this, you must set the dfs.permissions property to true in hdfs-site .xml — otherwise, permissions are not checked!

Beyond setting this flag, you may want to set some other properties. First of all, as mentioned previously, you will have to have user accounts on all of the machines in your cluster, and you will have to determine how to map Kerberos credentials to operating system users. Next, you may want to map LDAP group permissions to the group accounts in your cluster. The following discussions walk you through these.

Mapping Kerberos Principals to Operating System Users

Earlier in this chapter, you learned that the core-site.xml file has a configuration parameter called hadoop.security.auth_to-local that maps Kerberos identities to operating system identities to determine group permissions. By default, it takes the first component of the Kerberos principal — for example, if your principal name is carson/admin@domain.com, it is translated to carson — so it will look for an operating system account for carson and determine file permissions based on carson's operating system identity.

Many organizations stick with the default rules, but there are some reasons why you may want to change them — especially if you work with partner organizations of multiple domains. For example, someone with admin privileges in another domain may want to be treated as a special user in your domain with particular privileges. You may want to assign all users from another particular domain to one user with particular privileges.

To do this, you will have to build custom rules, which involves regular expressions and string substitutions. Three components of building these rules are specified in the `hadoop.security` `.auth_to_local` property:

➤ **Principal** — The principal is the string to be translated and filtered, using variables `$0` for the Realm, `$1` for the first component of the principal name, and `$2` for the second component of the principal name. Each principal starts with the rule number. So, `[1:$1@$0]` would translate the principal `jeff@teamManera.com` to `jeff@teamManera.com`, (since `jeff` is the first component of the principal name and `teamManera.com` is the Realm). `[2:$1%$2]` would translate `jeff/admin@teamManera.com` to `jeff%admin` (because `jeff` is the first component of the principal name, and `admin` is the second component of the principal name).

➤ **Acceptance filter** — The acceptance filter is a regular expression in parentheses that must be matched in the principal section of the rule for the rule to apply. For example, looking at the principals set up in the previous example, `(.*@teamManera.com)` would match any principal in the domain `teamManera.com` (the first one in the previous example), and `(.*%admin)` will take any string that ends in `%admin`, such as the second principal set up in the previous example, where `jeff/admin@teamManera.com` was mapped to `jeff%admin`.

➤ **Substitution** — Once the principal and acceptance filter are set up, the substitution is a `sed` rule that translates the regular expression to a fixed string using string substitutions. For example, the `sed` expression `s/@teamManera\.com//` would delete the `@teamManera.com` from a principal matched by an acceptance filter.

Listing 10-3 provides some examples of these rules in action. Here, you want to keep the default rule where, if it is in your own domain, it takes the first part of the Kerberos principal and maps it to an operating system name of the same user. However, you do want to add other rules. For example, if you have a partnership with the TRUMANTRUCK.COM domain, you may want to map all users in this domain to the `truckuser` account. If you have administrators from the `teamManera.com` domain, you want to map them to the `admin` account.

LISTING 10-3: Property values for hadoop.security.auth_to_local

```
<!--from file core-site.xml-->
<property>
  <name>hadoop.security.auth_to_local</name>
  <value>
  <!-- RULE:[#:<principal>](<acceptance filter>)<substitution sed rule>-->
  <!-- Rule 1 take all users from TRUMANTRUCK.COM and maps to a truckuser account
       (1)Principal takes "username@domain"
       (2)the filter matches any string that ends in "@TRUMANTRUCK.COM"
       (3)the substitution rule maps it to the "truckuser" account"
  -->
```

continues

LISTING 10-3 *(continued)*

```
RULE:[1:$1@$0](.@TRUMANTRUCK.COM)s/./truckuser/

<!-- RULE 2: all principals with admin from teamManera.org treated as admin user
     (1)The principal maps names like user/admin@domain to "user%admin@domain"
     (2)The filter matches anything with admin in the domain teamManera.com
     (3)Finally, the sed rule replaces everything to the "admin" user.
 -->
RULE:[2:$1%$2@$0](.%admin@teamManera.COM)s/./admin/
<!—Leave the default rule -->
DEFAULT
</value>
</property>
```

As shown Listing 10-3, the first rule has a principal that takes the first and second component of the Kerberos principal and places an @ sign between them — for example, `jeff@teamManera.com`. The filter then only matches entities from the TRUMANTRUCK.COM domain. Finally, the substitution rule takes what has matched and maps it to the `truckuser` account.

The second rule is different. The principal takes a Kerberos principal like `kevin/admin@mydomain.com` and maps it to `kevin%admin@mydomain.com`. The acceptance filter only matches anything from the resulting principal ending with `%admin@teamManera.com`.

Finally, the `sed` rule changes anything matched by the acceptance filter, and changes it to the `admin` user.

Mapping Kerberos Principals to Hadoop Groups

Once the Kerberos principal has been mapped to a username, the list of groups for the principal is determined by a group mapping service, which is configured by the `hadoop.security.group.mapping` property. By default, it is a shell implementation that simply looks for the user's groups on the operating system. If your accounts are set up on your operating system with the proper groups, this may be all that you need.

However, there is another way that you can get your groups from an LDAP directory, and this is sometimes less administratively intense than setting up large numbers of group entries for every user on every machine in your cluster.

To do this, you will use the approach shown in Listing 10-4. As you can see, you set the `hadoop.security.group.mapping` property to the `LdapGroupsMapping` class, and with the other properties, you configure how this class pulls groups for your Hadoop users.

LISTING 10-4: Customizing group mappings in core-site.xml

```
<property>
    <!-- This goes to an LDAP directory to look for groups -->
    <name>hadoop.security.group.mapping</name>
    <value>org.apache.hadoop.security.LdapGroupsMapping</value>
</property>
<property>
```

```
        <!—LDAP directory to use -->
      <name>hadoop.security.group.mapping.ldap.url</name>
      <value>ldap://ldap.teamManera.com/</value>
</property>
<property>
      <name>hadoop.security.group.mapping.ldap.bind.user</name>
      <value>admin</value>
</property>
<property>
      <name>hadoop.security.group.mapping.ldap.bind.password</name>
      <value>*********</value>
</property>
<property> <!--If you will use SSL-protected LDAP-->
      <name>hadoop.security.group.mapping.ldap.ssl</name>
      <value>true</value>
</property>
<property> <!-- If use SSL, you will need to point to your keystore-->
      <name>hadoop.security.group.mapping.ldap.ssl.keystore</name>
      <value>/mykeystoredirectory/keystore.jks</value>
</property>
 <property><!—-If use SSL to connect to LDAP, point to passwd file to
      keystore-->
      <name>hadoop.security.group.mapping.ldap.ssl.keystore.password.file</name>
      <value>/mykeystoredirectory/passwordToKeystoreFile</value>
</property>
<property> <!—- base search for users-->
      <name>hadoop.security.group.mapping.ldap.base</name>
      <value>DC=ldaptest,DC=local</value>
</property>
<property> <!-- additional search filter for finding users
                below is typical value for Active Directory
              -->
      <name>hadoop.security.group.mapping.ldap.search.filter.user</name>
      <value>(&amp;(objectClass=user)(sAMAccountName={0}))</value>
</property>
<property> <!-- additional filter for finding groups.
                Below is typical value for Active Directory..
              -->
      <name>hadoop.security.group.mapping.ldap.search.filter.group</name>
      <value>(objectClass=group)</value>
</property>
<property><!-- attribute that identifies members of a group..
                Below is typical value for most LDAP implementations
              -->
      <name>hadoop.security.group.mapping.ldap.search.attr.member</name>
      <value>member</value>
</property>
<property>
      <!-- Attribute that is used for finding group name. Below is
         Typical value for most LDAP implementations
         -->
      <name>
        hadoop.security.group.mapping.ldap.search.attr.group.name
      </name>
      <value>cn</value>
</property>
```

It should be noted that not all of the properties shown in Listing 10-4 are always needed. For example, the properties related to SSL and the keystore are only used if you are using LDAP over SSL. It should also be mentioned that although most of the values of the properties for searching users and groups are common to many installations, various LDAP installations differ, and so you may have to configure these properties based on your own installation. Using the `LDAPGroupsMapping` can simplify group management in your Hadoop cluster—allowing you to handle management in a central location.

Service-Level Authorization

Hadoop provides the capability of enabling service-level authorization, which controls which users have permission to access particular services. This ensures that clients that connect to HDFS have necessary permissions to access HDFS, and you can control which users have permissions to submit MapReduce jobs.

To enable service-level authorization in `core-site.xml`, you must set `hadoop.security .authorization` to be `true`, because it is not enabled by default. The `hadoop-policy.xml` file controls ACLs for the services in your cluster, with an example shown in Listing 10-5. The ACLs are at the protocol level, and, by default, everyone is granted access to everything.

LISTING 10-5: Configuring hadoop-policy.xml

```xml
<!-- property values are either * (for everything), or
     Comma-delimited users and groups.
     Examples "alice,bob,hadoopusers", "*", or "hdfs" are possible values.
-->
<configuration>
  <property>
    <name>security.client.protocol.acl</name>
    <value>*</value>
    <description>ACL for ClientProtocol, which is used by user code
    via the DistributedFileSystem to talk to the HDFS cluster.
  </property>

  <property>
    <name>security.client.datanode.protocol.acl</name>
    <value>*</value>
    <description>ACL for client-to-datanode protocol for block recovery.
    </description>
  </property>

  <property>
    <name>security.datanode.protocol.acl</name>
    <value>datanodes</value>
    <description>This should be restricted to the datanode's user
        name</description>
  </property>

  <property>
    <name>security.inter.datanode.protocol.acl</name>
```

```
    <value>datanodes</value>
    <description>ACL for InterDatanodeProtocol, the inter-datanode protocol
    description>
  </property>

  <property>
    <name>security.namenode.protocol.acl</name>
    <value>namenodes</value>
    <description>ACL for NamenodeProtocol, the protocol used by the secondary
    namenode to communicate with the namenode.
    </description>
  </property>

  <property>
    <name>security.inter.tracker.protocol.acl</name>
    <value>tasktrackers</value>
    <description>ACL for InterTrackerProtocol, used by the tasktrackers to
    communicate with the jobtracker.
    </description>
  </property>

  <property>
    <name>security.job.submission.protocol.acl</name>
    <value>*</value>
    <description>ACL for JobSubmissionProtocol, used by job clients to
    communciate with the jobtracker for job submission, querying job status etc.
    </description>
  </property>

  <property>
    <name>security.task.umbilical.protocol.acl</name>
    <value>*</value>
    <description>ACL for TaskUmbilicalProtocol, used by the map and reduce
    tasks to communicate with the parent tasktracker.
    </description>
  </property>

  <property>
    <name>security.refresh.policy.protocol.acl</name>
    <value>*</value>
    <description>ACL for RefreshAuthorizationPolicyProtocol, used by the
    dfsadmin and mradmin commands to refresh the security policy
    </description>
  </property>

  <property>
    <name>security.admin.operations.protocol.acl</name>
    <value>*</value>
    <description>ACL for AdminOperationsProtocol, used by the mradmins commands
    to refresh queues and nodes at JobTracker.  </description>
  </property>
</configuration>
```

In practice, you will want to restrict these ACLs to only the users who need to access the protocols. For example, the ACL that DataNodes use in communicating with the NameNode (`security .datanode.protocol.acl`) should be restricted to the user running the DataNode process (typically `hdfs`). Your Hadoop administrator will need to configure this carefully. You can refresh the service-level authorization for the NameNode and JobTracker without restarting the Hadoop daemons using the `-refreshServiceAcl` command switch on the `dsfadmin` (for NameNode) and `mradmin` (for JobTracker) executables.

Job Authorization

To control access to job operations, you should set the following configuration properties in the `mapred-site.xml` file (and they are disabled by default):

➤ The `mapred.acls.enabled` property specifies whether ACLs should be checked for authorization of users for doing various job operations. If this is set to `true`, access control checks are made by the JobTracker and TaskTracker when requests are made by users for submitting jobs, killing jobs, and viewing job details.

➤ The `mapreduce.job.acl-view-job` property specifies a list of users and/or groups who can view private details about the job. By default, no one else besides the job owner, the user who started the cluster, cluster administrators, and queue administrators can perform view operations on a job.

➤ The `mapreduce.job.acl-modify-job` property specifies a list of users and/or groups who can perform modification operations on the job. By default, only the job owner, the user who started the cluster, cluster administrators, and queue administrators can perform modification operations on a job.

OOZIE AUTHENTICATION AND AUTHORIZATION

In addition to Hadoop itself, services in the Hadoop ecosystem interact with Hadoop and can be configured to provide a level of security. Projects in the Hadoop ecosystem are fairly consistent in their approach of utilizing Kerberos authentication and the way they are configured. Such is the case with Oozie.

As discussed in Chapters 6 through 8, Oozie is a Workflow manager that accepts Workflows and submits them to HDFS and MapReduce. It accepts these Workflows via a web interface, and interacts with the components of Hadoop on behalf of the user that submitted the task. It is a higher-level service in the Hadoop ecosystem that is then trusted to act as other users. Because of this fact, you should take care to secure it — failure to do so has the potential to bypass all the other security controls that you have set up in Hadoop!

Like other services in Hadoop, Oozie can be configured to support Kerberos RPC and HTTP SPNEGO authentication. For Kerberos RPC, the Oozie service user principal must be created and added to your Kerberos Realm. Because Oozie also has a web console that supports Kerberos HTTP SPNEGO authentication, it should also be configured to use the same HTTP principal and `keytab` file used for other HTTP endpoints. Much like the other services in Hadoop, Oozie has a configuration file, `oozie-site.xml`, where these can be set up, with the example file shown in Listing 10-6.

LISTING 10-6: Security configuration in Oozie-site.xml

```
<property>
    <name>oozie.service.AuthorizationService.security.enabled</name>
    <value>true</value>
</property>
<property>
    <name>oozie.service.HadoopAccessorService.kerberos.enabled</name>
    <value>true</value>
</property>
<property>
    <name>local.realm</name>
    <value>EXAMPLE.COM</value>
    <description>Kerberos Realm used by Oozie and Hadoop. Using 'local.realm'
        to be aligned with Hadoop configuration</description>
</property>
<property>
    <name>oozie.service.HadoopAccessorService.keytab.file </name>
    <value>/keytabs/oozie.service.keytab</value>
    <description>The keytab for the Oozie service principal.</description>
</property>
<property>
    <name>oozie.service.HadoopAccessorService.kerberos.principal</name>
    <value>oozie/_HOST1@EXAMPLE.COM</value>
    <description>Kerberos principal for Oozie service</description>
</property>
<property>
    <name>oozie.authentication.type</name>
    <value>kerberos</value>
    <description>Authentication type</description>
</property>
<property>
    <name>oozie.authentication.kerberos.principal</name>
    <value>HTTP/_HOST@EXAMPLE.COM</value>
    <description>SPNEGO HTTP Principal</description>
</property>
<property>
    <name>oozie.authentication.kerberos.keytab</name>
    <value>/keytabs/spnego.service.keytab</value>
    <description>Location of the Oozie SPNEGO keytab file.</description>
</property>
<property>
    <name>oozie.authentication.kerberos.name.rules</name>
    <value><value>
        RULE:[2:$1@$0]([jt]t@.*EXAMPLE.COM)s/.*/$MAPRED_USER/
        RULE:[2:$1@$0]([nd]n@.*EXAMPLE.COM)s/.*/$HDFS_USER/
        RULE:[2:$1@$0](hbase@.*EXAMPLE.COM)s/.*/$HBASE_USER/
        RULE:[2:$1@$0](hbase@.*EXAMPLE.COM)s/.*/$HBASE_USER/
        DEFAULT</value>
</property>
```

As you can see in Listing 10-6, most of these values are similar to the configurations previously explained in configuring the rest of Hadoop. Like the other configurations, you must specify the proper principals and `keytabs`. The last property in that file, `oozie.authentication.kerberos.name.rules`, should have the same configuration as `hadoop.security.auth_to_local`, as was explained earlier in this chapter in the section entitled, "Mapping Kerberos Principals to Operating System Users." Once Oozie has been configured to use Kerberos RPC and SPNEGO authentication, you can also configure Oozie to use SSL with its Tomcat configuration for network encryption.

NETWORK ENCRYPTION

Many organizations concerned about security and privacy have requirements for encryption. Hadoop provides mechanisms for encryption *in transit* on the network. As mentioned earlier in this chapter, Kerberos is used for authentication in two different ways — Kerberos RPC using SASL/GSSAPI, and Kerberos HTTP SPNEGO for Hadoop Web UIs. Although these mechanisms provide authentication, they do not provide encryption or confidentiality — everything is passed in the clear. Furthermore, clients and DataNodes transmit data using the Hadoop Data Transfer Protocol, and this is unencrypted as well. If you have sensitive data on your network and you have a requirement to protect your cluster from eavesdroppers and network sniffers, you will most likely want to encrypt these exchanges.

WHAT ABOUT ENCRYPTED DATA AT REST?

Many people with significant confidentiality requirements are concerned about having data being encrypted in transit over the network, and they are also interested in encrypted data at rest. Hadoop does not currently provide this capability natively, but some distributions come with third-party tools for providing such functionality, as is discussed in Chapter 12. Hadoop is currently working on natively building that functionality, as is discussed later in this chapter in the section, "Security Enhancements with Project Rhino."

Luckily, Hadoop provides the capability for network encryption for all communications on the network — RPC encryption, HDFS data transfer, and HTTP, as described here:

➤ **RPC encryption** — When you utilize Kerberos RPC, you utilize SASL using Kerberos GSSAPI. Earlier you learned that the use of SASL provides flexibility in protocol negotiation. Part of this flexibility is the capability to provide Quality of Protection (QoP), which can either be authentication only (`auth`), authentication and message integrity (`auth-int`), or authentication, integrity, and confidentiality (`auth-conf`). These values can be set in the `hadoop.rpc.protection` configuration in the `core-site.xml` configuration file. When this property is set to `privacy`, this corresponds to the SASL `auth-conf` QoP, ensuring that all transmissions in the SASL connections are encrypted.

➤ **HDFS data transfer encryption** — As discussed earlier, clients (or tasks working on behalf of clients) are issued Block Access tokens by NameNodes, and these tokens are presented to DataNodes with a request for blocks of data. This can be set to be encrypted by setting `dfs.encrypt.data.transfer` configuration property to `true`. If you enable HDFS data transfer encryption, you should also ensure that RPC encryption is enabled, because key exchanges happen using Hadoop RPC. (If you encrypt the data, but pass the encryption keys in the clear, you may be making things slower by encrypting everything, but you would be defeating the purpose of encrypting your data. This is something that can easily be overlooked!)

➤ **Web encryption** — To secure all communications using HTTP (Hadoop web user interfaces, MapReduce Shuffle, and FSImage operations), the Hadoop web server must be configured to use SSL, setting up the proper keystores. This involves configuring many properties in the `core-site.xml` file.

To provide full network encryption for all of these mechanisms, the properties listed in Table 10-6 must be configured and set for your Hadoop cluster. Table 10-6 provides the configuration property, the file the property is in, and an explanation (including the values for enabling network encryption).

TABLE 10-6: Configuration Parameters for Network Encryption

CONFIGURATION PROPERTY	FILE	EXPLANATION
`hadoop.rpc.protection`	`core-site.xml`	Set to `privacy`, it ensures authentication and encrypted transport. This value defaults to `authentication`, which means that only Kerberos mutual authentication is used without encryption. The value of `integrity` means that it guarantees authentication and integrity between client and server. The value of `privacy` ensures authentication, integrity, and privacy.
`dfs.encrypt.data .transfer`	`hdfs-site.xml`	Set to `true`, it ensures HDFS data transfer encryption. Because keys are transferred via Hadoop RPC, it is important that the `hadoop.rpc .protection` is set to `privacy` — otherwise, you won't be accomplishing much by encrypting the data, but sending the keys in the clear.
`hadoop.ssl.enabled`	`core-site.xml`	Setting this value to `true` enables encrypted HTTP for web user interfaces and web transport.

continues

TABLE 10-6 *(continued)*

CONFIGURATION PROPERTY	FILE	EXPLANATION
`hadoop.ssl.require` `.client.cert`	`core-site.xml`	Setting this value to `true` requires client certificate (mutual) authentication for SSL, but this is not needed if you only want network encryption. This may add some complexity to your solution — and if you use SPNEGO authentication, you are already authenticating — so chances are, it will not provide a lot of value.
`hadoop.ssl.hostname` `.verifier`	`core-site.xml`	This is the verifier for `HttpsURLConnections`. Valid values are `ALLOW_ALL`, `DEFAULT_AND_` `LOCALHOST`, `STRICT`, and `DEFAULT`.
`hadoop.ssl.keystores` `.factory.class`	`core-site.xml`	This value is always set to one class that reads keystore files: `org.apache.hadoop.ssl.` `FileBasedKeyStoresFactory`.
`hadoop.ssl.server.conf`	`core-site.xml`	`ssl-server.xml` (the resource file including SSL server keystore info used by the Shuffle server and web user interface) includes information about the keystores and truststores for use by the server, including location and password.
`hadoop.ssl.client.conf`	`core-site.xml`	`ssl-client.xml` (the resource file that includes client keystore info used by the Reducer/Fetcher) includes information about the keystores and truststores for use by the server, including location and password.

SECURITY ENHANCEMENTS WITH PROJECT RHINO

At the beginning of 2013, Intel launched a new Hadoop distribution with security improvements. With its distribution, it also launched an open source effort to improve the security capabilities of Hadoop and the Hadoop ecosystem, contributing code to Apache. As of this writing, these are not yet implemented in releases, but promise to enhance Hadoop's current offering. The overall goals for this open source effort are as follows:

➤ Support for encryption and key management

➤ A common authorization framework beyond ACLs of users and groups that Hadoop currently provides

➤ A common token-based authentication framework

➤ Security improvements to HBase

➤ Improved security auditing

This next section covers some — but not all — of the major tasks being developed that are associated with JIRA tasks for Apache projects for these new capabilities. These changes to Hadoop should greatly improve the security posture of enterprise deployments.

> **NOTE** *See Project Rhino's main web page at* `https://github.com/intel-hadoop/project-rhino/` *to keep track of the current progress.*

HDFS Disk-Level Encryption

JIRA Tasks HADOOP-9331 (Hadoop Crypto Codec Framework and Crypto Codec Implementation) and MAPREDUCE-5025 (Key Distribution and Management for Supporting Crypto Codec in MapReduce) are directly related. The first focuses on creating a cryptography framework and implementation for the capability to support encryption and decryption of files on HDFS. The second focuses on a key distribution and management framework for MapReduce to be able to encrypt and decrypt data during MapReduce operations.

To achieve this, a splittable Advanced Encryption Standard (AES) codec implementation is being introduced to Hadoop, allowing distributed data to be encrypted and decrypted from disk. The key distribution and management framework will allow the resolution of key contexts during MapReduce operations so that MapReduce jobs can perform encryption and decryption. The requirements that they have developed include different options for the different stages of MapReduce jobs, and support a flexible way of retrieving keys.

As you might expect, this can get complicated, and will most likely have a notable impact on performance. Because Intel is contributing code, its implementation of on-disk encryption takes advantage of special Intel processors uniquely suited for AES encryption and decryption. Time will tell how this plays out for other commodity hardware.

Token-Based Authentication and Unified Authorization Framework

JIRA Tasks HADOOP-9392 (Token-Based Authentication and Single Sign-On) and HADOOP-9466 (Unified Authorization Framework) are also related. The first task presents a token-based authentication framework that is not tightly coupled to Kerberos. The second task utilizes the token-based framework to support a flexible authorization enforcement engine that aims to replace (but be backward compatible with) the current ACL approaches for access control.

These will be significant enhancements to Hadoop security. As you have seen in this chapter, Hadoop evolved from "no security" to the addition of Kerberos. Though this works well with organizations that have Kerberos implementations, Hadoop's current model is a challenge to other organizations that use other authentication approaches. The current Hadoop approach for using ACLs for authorization based on users and group permissions can certainly be used for meeting some requirements, but the current approach does not meet the needs for some organizations that need to control access based on Attribute-Based Access Control (ABAC) using attributes such as roles, classification levels, and organizational identity for determining level of access, based on policies.

For the token-based authentication framework, the first JIRA Task plans to support tokens for many authentication mechanisms such as LDAP username/password authentication, Kerberos, X.509 Certificate authentication, SQL authentication (based on username/password combinations in SQL databases), and SAML. The second JIRA Task aims to support an advanced authorization model, focusing on ABAC and the XACML standard.

HBase Cell-Level Security

Project Rhino also focuses on enhancing HBase authorization. HBase is a popular, distributed, and scalable column-oriented data store built on top of Hadoop. Modeled after Google's BigTable, it is a NoSQL database that provides fast and real-time random access to data. Much like other Hadoop services, HBase can be configured to do Kerberos authentication, and it provides access controls based on its data model. Based on Google's BigTable, it is a column-oriented database that includes a Row (consisting of a Table Name), a Column Family, a Column Qualifier, a Timestamp, and a Value, as shown in Figure 10-4. Administrators can set up access control lists based on the table, column family, and column-qualifier level.

Row ID (Table Name)	Column		Timestamp	Value
	Family	Qualifier		

FIGURE 10-4: HBase data model

Providing column and table-level authorization works well for situations that require column-based security, but it does not does address fine-grained access controls at the cell level, such as what is provided by Apache Accumulo (discussed in Chapter 12). Because of much demand for this level of access control, one of Project Rhino's JIRA Tasks adds cell-level security. The JIRA Task HBASE-6222 (Add Per-KeyValue Security) adds cell-level authorization for HBase, which is promising for the number of HBase users out there.

PUTTING IT ALL TOGETHER — BEST PRACTICES FOR SECURING HADOOP

This chapter has provided a brief tour of what is involved in authentication, authorization, and network encryption in Hadoop, and some of the current work that is progressing. It is important that you understand your security requirements before you begin implementing some of these security mechanisms. It is possible to build Hadoop solutions that do not achieve your security requirements, but it is also possible to overengineer security for your Hadoop cluster by adding security controls that you may not need.

When using any security mechanism, there is typically a trade-off between security and performance — making network calls involving a Kerberos KDC to support authentication, cryptography involved in the authentication process, and cryptography will certainly have effects on performance. Therefore, it is important that you know your organization's security requirements, and make certain that you are meeting them with the controls discussed in this chapter. It is also important to architect security from a "big picture" enterprise perspective, and it may be necessary to couple Hadoop security mechanisms with others. (The "big picture" approach to enterprise security for Hadoop is discussed in more detail in Chapter 12.)

This chapter has covered a lot of ground, and because of the complexity of Hadoop and its configuration, it is sometimes possible to unintentionally leave out some steps. For that reason, what follows is a synopsis of the steps that you will need to configure to provide Hadoop security in your enterprise. These steps have been ordered in sections that correspond to the sections of this chapter, so that you can refer back to the proper section for more information.

> **NOTE** *This section is intended to be a high-level guide that covers most of the basics and can be used as a "cheat sheet" for covering the essentials of securing your Hadoop cluster. Distributions can differ, and Hadoop releases change over time, so it is also very important to consult your distribution's security configuration notes in addition to this book!*

Authentication

First of all, it is important to understand your authentication requirements. Now that you understand how Kerberos authentication works from earlier in this chapter, determine if Hadoop's Kerberos authentication mechanism meets your organization's needs. If so, it is important to be consistent — if you Kerberize some of your communications mechanisms (Kerberos RPC), it's best to also Kerberize your web consoles and HTTP transports with Kerberos SPNEGO — otherwise, you would be providing a hole for bypassing security with web consoles when you are securing your RPC mechanisms.

Follow these steps:

1. Generate principals and `keytabs` for all of your services.

2. Generate the HTTP principal and `keytab` for use by all of your web consoles.

3. Set the proper Kerberos properties in your main Hadoop files as described in Table 10-2.

4. For other Hadoop ecosystem components (Oozie, HBase, Hive, and so on), follow a similar pattern of configuring them — that is, similar to the way you configure Oozie authentication shown in Table 10-6. Based on the component, more steps may be needed. Consult your distribution's security guide.

5. Configure Kerberos HTTP SPNEGO authentication on all of your web consoles, as shown in the earlier section, "Kerberos for Web-Based Consoles."

6. Set the properties for credential tokens to be used within Hadoop (Delegation tokens, Block Access tokens), as shown in Table 10-5.

7. Configure the task controller as shown in Table 10-5 and as explained in the section, "Configuring the Task Controller."

Authorization

For authorization, it is important to understand that your cluster will do authorization checking based on users and their group permissions. You may have users coming in from multiple domains, which means that you may want to do some inventive mapping of Kerberos principals to usernames. You may not want to manage lots of user and group accounts throughout every machine in the cluster, which means you may want to use group management via your LDAP instance or Active Directory. (If you are already using Active Directory for Kerberos authentication, it might make sense to do this as well.)

Follow these steps:

1. Enable HDFS file permission checking by setting the `dfs.permissions` property to `true` in `hdfs-site.xml` as discussed in the "Authorization" section of this chapter.

2. Determine whether or not you need to map Kerberos principals to operating system users other than taking the first component of the Kerberos principal name and mapping it to the user. If so, configure `hadoop.security.auth_to-local` as described in the section, "Mapping Kerberos Principals to Operating System Users."

3. Determine how you are going to manage groups. If you are going to use the default approach of using operating system groups for your users, you don't have to do anything. Otherwise, configure your cluster to use LDAP Mappings — see the section, "Mapping Kerberos Principals to Hadoop Groups."

4. Enable service-level authorization by setting `hadoop.security.authorization` to `true` and configure `hadoop-policy.xml` as described in the section, "Service-Level Authorization."

5. Control who has permission to modify, view, and stop jobs by configuring `mapred-site .xml` as described in the "Job Authorization" section.

6. For other Hadoop ecosystem components, review their configuration manuals for performing authorization checks.

Network Encryption

It is important to understand your confidentiality requirements before you enable network encryption for Hadoop. If all data transmitted needs to be encrypted, you will need to perform the following steps:

1. Configure the security properties in Table 10-6, which should cover Kerberos RPC encryption, HDFS transfer encryption, and HTTP encryption.

2. Configure individual Hadoop ecosystem components for network encryption. Because most of them utilize Kerberos SASL/GSSAPI for RPC authentication, they have the capability of using the Quality of Protection that allows encryption, and are configured in a similar way in the component's configuration file.

Stay Tuned for Hadoop Enhancements

As Hadoop continues to evolve, it is important to stay tuned. As noted in the "Security Enhancements with Project Rhino" section, a lot of new developments will impact Hadoop's security in the very near future.

Now that you understand Hadoop's native security controls, Chapter 12 provides an enterprise view of security, which includes Hadoop, but also focuses on some areas that this chapter didn't cover — and talks about how other tools and approaches can complement Hadoop security.

SUMMARY

This chapter has provided an overview of Hadoop's security model. You first learned about authentication, focusing on how Hadoop can be configured to use Kerberos RPC and HTTP SPNEGO. You then learned how the security delegation model works within the components of Hadoop. You saw how network encryption can be enabled, and how tools in the Hadoop ecosystem are configured for security. Finally, this chapter provided a look at the upcoming changes for Hadoop security, and provided a summary of the steps that should be taken when configuring Hadoop security.

Chapter 11 discusses how you can run Hadoop in the Cloud as an alternative to building and configuring in-house clusters of Hadoop servers. Specifically, you learn how to configure, set up, and run Hadoop jobs on Amazon Web Services (AWS).

11

Running Hadoop Applications on AWS

WHAT'S IN THIS CHAPTER?

➤ Understanding options for running Hadoop on AWS

➤ Understanding Elastic MapReduce and its capabilities

➤ Understanding Simple Storage Service and its capabilities

➤ Programming for S3

➤ Programmatically configuring EMR

➤ Understanding the options for orchestrating job execution in EMR

WROX.COM CODE DOWNLOADS FOR THIS CHAPTER

The wrox.com code downloads for this chapter are found at `www.wiley.com/go/` `prohadoopsolutions` on the Download Code tab. The code is in the Chapter 11 download and individually named according to the names throughout the chapter.

Amazon Web Services (AWS) is becoming a more and more popular alternative to an on-premises hardware deployment. The advantages of AWS include (but are not limited to) the following:

➤ Fast and flexible on-demand deployment options enable you to provision only what is required when you need it. It also enables you to ramp up your hardware and software as your needs grow.

➤ Depending on your requirements, AWS provides a wide variety of flexible pricing options.

➤ AWS provides metered billing, which means that you know exactly how many resources you are using at any time, and how much you have to pay for them.

With the growing popularity of both Hadoop and AWS, the use of AWS for running Hadoop applications is rapidly becoming a hot topic.

Now that you know about the main Hadoop architecture and functionality, in this chapter you learn different approaches to running Hadoop on AWS, and major AWS services used for such implementations. You learn how to configure and run the Hadoop cluster on AWS (both using the AWS console and programmatically), how to set up and use Amazon's Simple Storage Service (S3) as Hadoop's storage, and how to programmatically upload and download data from local disk or HDFS to S3. Finally, you learn approaches to orchestrating Hadoop jobs in AWS.

GETTING TO KNOW AWS

AWS started as *infrastructure as a service (IAAS)*, providing basic services such as networking and storage. It has morphed into a *platform as a service (PAAS)* that can be used to develop and run virtually anything from enterprise and Big Data applications to social games and mobile apps. Currently, AWS provides a rich ecosystem of services comprised of the following main components:

> **NOTE** *In the case of AWS, "services" mean significantly more then Web services. In this case, "services" represent deployed application/infrastructure functional units accessible through the well-defined interface (set of the APIs).*

➤ **EC2** — Amazon Elastic Compute Cloud (EC2) is a web service that provides compute capacity in the cloud on demand. It is a foundation of a majority of other Amazon services.

➤ **EMR** — Amazon Elastic MapReduce (EMR) is a web service that provides access to a hosted Hadoop framework utilizing EC2 and S3.

➤ **S3** — Amazon Simple Storage Service (S3) is a web service that can be used to store and retrieve data. It provides highly scalable, reliable, secure, fast, inexpensive infrastructure for storing necessary data.

➤ **DynamoDB** — Amazon DynamoDB is a fully managed NoSQL database that allows scaling up or down an individual table's request capacity without downtime or performance degradation. With it, you can gain visibility into resource utilization and performance metrics.

➤ **IAM** — AWS Identity and Access Management (IAM) is a web service that enables you to control access to AWS services and resources for users in a given account. IAM supports the creation and management of AWS users and groups, and uses policies to allow/deny permissions to AWS resources or resource operations.

➤ **RDS** — Amazon Relational Database Service (RDS) is a web service that enables you to set up, operate, and scale a relational database in the cloud. It supports MySQL, Oracle, or Microsoft SQL Server database engines.

➤ **ElasticCache** — Amazon ElasticCache is a web service that makes it easy to deploy, operate, and scale an in-memory cache in the cloud. ElastiCache is protocol-compliant with memcached, a widely adopted memory object caching system that allows many memcached-enabled tools and applications to work with it.

Additional AWS services include the following:

➤ **CloudWatch** — This provides resource and application monitoring.

➤ **Redshift** — This is a petabyte-scale data warehouse service.

➤ **CloudSearch** — This is a managed search service.

➤ **SQS** — This is a managed simple queue service.

➤ **SNS** — This is a managed simple notification service.

➤ **SWF** — This is a managed workflow service for coordinating application components.

➤ **Data Pipeline** — This is a managed integration for data-driven workflows.

> **NOTE** *Amazon releases new AWS services (while reducing their prices) on a regular basis.*

Now that you know what AWS is and a bit about its major services, in the next section you learn about different options for installing and running Hadoop in AWS.

OPTIONS FOR RUNNING HADOOP ON AWS

When it comes to Hadoop deployment on AWS, you have two distinct options:

➤ Using a custom installation on EC2 instances

➤ Using a managed Hadoop version (such as EMR)

Custom Installation using EC2 Instances

The first option is essentially leveraging Amazon as IAAS-EC2 instances to deploy an Hadoop cluster exactly the same way as you would install your cluster on-premises. To make this install even simpler, you can use plenty of preconfigured public Amazon Machine Image (AMI) images containing a preinstalled instance of Hadoop. Alternatively, it is possible to build a custom image for Hadoop installation. *Apache Whirr* allows you to simplify install even further.

> **NOTE** *An Amazon Machine Image (AMI) is a virtual appliance that is used to create a virtual machine within the Amazon EC2. It serves as the basic unit of deployment for services delivered using EC2.*

Although there are advantages to using EC2 instead of physical hardware (such as lower initial capital expenses, faster time to market, and so on), this approach still requires you to maintain and manage the Hadoop cluster, install patches, and so on. Although this approach enables you to significantly reduce hardware maintenance, it still requires the same amount of software maintenance as the local cluster.

Elastic MapReduce

A managed Hadoop version provided by Amazon — EMR — enables you to completely remove the maintenance burden. In this case, Amazon provides both hardware and software maintenance of the requested Hadoop cluster, and your responsibility is limited to just using it.

Unfortunately, nothing comes for free. There are serious architectural implications that you must deal with if you decide to switch from a local Hadoop installation to EMR.

Additional Considerations before Making Your Choice

Following are some additional things to consider when you are choosing between utilizing a custom install on EC2 instances and using EMR:

➤ **Specific Hadoop version** — When using EMR, you are at the mercy of Amazon. You can use only the provided versions (more on this later), whereas a custom install enables you to use any of the existing Hadoop versions.

➤ **Using additional AWS resources for storage and processing data** — If you are storing some of your data in AWS already using S3 or DynamoDB, your use of EMR can be better integrated with those resources, and provide a better option.

➤ **Tooling** — Your decision may be influenced by the tools provided by EMR or your favorite distribution. Keep in mind that installing additional tools on EMR is fairly simple (which you will learn more about later in the chapter).

➤ **Additional functionality provided by EMR implementation** — This includes simple and robust cluster launching, as well as an easy-to-use web UI. The capability to scale the cluster up or down, integrate it with CloudWatch, and so on, can further impact your decision about whether to use EMR.

The rest of this chapter assumes that you have made a decision to use EMR, and further discusses some of the details regarding EMR usage. In the next section, you learn more detail about EMR.

UNDERSTANDING THE EMR-HADOOP RELATIONSHIP

As shown in Figure 11-1, a local Hadoop cluster is essentially a PAAS cloud that provides a platform for many users to run many applications. It provides all relevant data locally, which allows for high-performance data access. A local Hadoop cluster is a capital expense. Once it is created, payment for its usage is typically small compared to the initial investment, which is why local Hadoop is always up, running, and available.

As shown in Figure 11-2, in the case of AWS, the architecture is different. Here, AWS represents a shared resource, at which a user has an individual account. (In general, using IAM, multiple users can share an account.)

An EMR cluster is just one of the resources available to a user (or group of users). It is a *pay-as-you-go resource*, so having it running all the time typically is not cost-effective. Consequently, similar to other AWS resources, it is typically started to solve a specific problem and then shut down. The implication of such usage is the fact that the actual data must be stored outside of the cluster.

In the case of Amazon, such a storage mechanism is typically S3, which is well integrated with EMR. (In addition to S3, other AWS storage systems such as DynamoDB can be used to store data processed by Hadoop.) So, for all practical purposes, EMR is an Hadoop-based data processing (not data storage) platform supporting MapReduce, Pig, Hive, and so on.

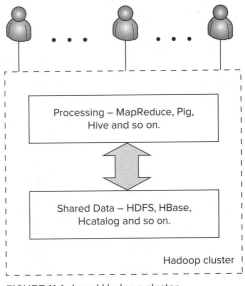

FIGURE 11-1: Local Hadoop cluster

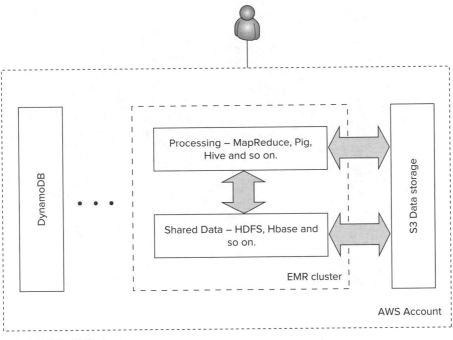

FIGURE 11-2: EMR cluster

EMR Architecture

Amazon EMR software includes enhancements to Hadoop and other open source applications to work seamlessly with AWS, including integration with EC2 to run Hadoop nodes, S3 data storage, and CloudWatch (to monitor the cluster and raise alarms). Figure 11-3 shows the overall EMR architecture. An EMR Hadoop cluster (called *job flow* in EMR) is comprised of the following three instance groups:

➤ **Master Instance Group** — This instance group manages a single master node. The master node runs Hadoop master processes, including HDFS NameNode, JobTracker, HBase master, Zookeeper, and so on.

➤ **Core Instance Group** — This instance group manages a set of core nodes. A core node is an Amazon EC2 instance that runs Hadoop MapReduce map tasks (the `TaskTracker` daemon) and stores data using HDFS (the `DataNode` daemon). If you must use HDFS, you must have at least one or more core nodes. The number of core nodes on the existing job flow can be increased (but not decreased, because it can cause data loss).

➤ **Task Instance Group** — This instance group is managing a set of task nodes. A task node is an Amazon EC2 instance that runs Hadoop MapReduce map tasks (the `TaskTracker` daemon), but does not store data using HDFS (the `DataNode` daemon). Task nodes can be added and removed while running MapReduce jobs, and can be used to manage EC2 instance capacity during task execution. A Task Instance Group is optional for an EMR job flow.

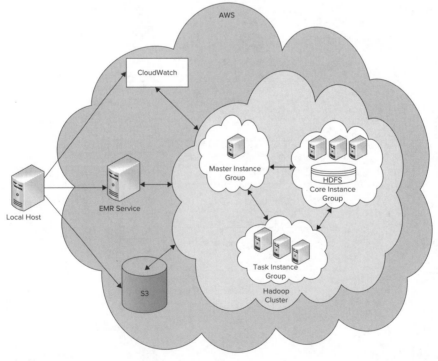

FIGURE 11-3: Overall EMR architecture

As shown in Figure 11-3, EMR Service provides communications with a user's Local Host (either local or inside AWS), and is responsible for user commands sent via the Command-Line Interface (CLI), APIs, or the EMR console. Among these commands are the creation and destruction of the job flow.

EMR provides default job flow startup and configuration, which can be overwritten by the user using default or custom *bootstrap actions* — scripts that are executed on all nodes of a cluster before Hadoop starts. Bootstrap actions can be used to load additional software, change Hadoop configuration, change Java and Hadoop daemon settings, and so on. The predefined bootstrap actions include Hadoop (and the Hadoop daemon configuration). Custom bootstrap actions can be written in any language available on the Hadoop cluster, including Ruby, Python, Perl, or `bash`.

In addition to HDFS and MapReduce, EMR also enables you to run HBase, Hive, and Pig. To use HBase, you should use large enough EC2 instances (`m1.large` or larger) within the Core Instance Group.

> **NOTE** *When running HBase on EMR, you should run a Core Instance Group containing at least three servers. This ensures that none of the HBase region servers will run on the master node, which will make HBase much more stable overall.*
>
> *Additionally, a current HBase limitation is that programmatic access to HBase using the Java APIs is supported only from within AWS. This is because Zookeeper resolves region server IP addresses to the ones that are visible only inside AWS.*

Using S3 Storage

At first glance, it seems like the use of S3-based HDFS should lead to performance degradation for the data access. Two questions that arise in that regard are how significant it is, and what impact it has on specific MapReduce jobs. Although the answer to the second question depends on the job itself, the first one can be answered using the TestDFSIO benchmark tool from Apache. The benchmark reads and writes data to HDFS.

As an example, the authors (with the help of a Nokia colleague, Timur Perelmitov) ran a benchmark test on a 10-node AWS EMR cluster with instances of type `m1.large` used for both master and slave nodes. The cluster was configured with 54 map slots and 1 reducer slot. Table 11-1 shows the results of test execution (including the writing and reading of 100 files, 1 GB each).

TABLE 11-1: I/O Comparison Native and S3-Based HDFS

OPERATION	NATIVE HDFS	HDFS OVER S3
Write throughput (mb/sec)	9.343005461734133	7.731297816627378
Write average I/O rate (mb/sec)	12.117674827575684	12.861650466918945

continues

TABLE 11-1 *(continued)*

OPERATION	NATIVE HDFS	HDFS OVER S3
Write I/O rate standard deviation	5.7651896313176625	9.956230775307425
Read throughput (mb/sec)	24.512070623051336	6.544165130751111
Read average I/O rate (mb/sec)	27.211841583251953	15.739026069641113
Read I/O rate standard deviation	9.856340728198452	12.065322159347629

Based on the benchmark results, the write throughput is very close, whereas read throughput in the case of local HDFS is about four times greater. It also shows that the I/O rate in the case of local HDFS is more consistent (that is, I/O rate standard deviation is lower).

Although the benchmark is showing that S3 I/O is slower, its performance is actually quite good, and it can be used with fairly little impact for most MapReduce implementations.

Maximizing Your Use of EMR

In addition to normal HBase features (described in Chapter 2), EMR provides backup and recovery of HBase directly to S3. Backup can either be done on demand or periodically, based on a timer.

EMR Hadoop publishes the Hadoop user interfaces as websites hosted on the master node. In order for you to access these interfaces, you must either open the port for public access to the master node, or do SSH tunneling to AWS. Table 11-2 lists all available interfaces.

TABLE 11-2: Hadoop Web Interfaces on Master Node

INTERFACE	URL
Hadoop MapReduce JobTracker	`http://master-public-dns-name:9100/`
Hadoop HDFS NameNode	`http://master-public-dns-name:9101/`
Hadoop MapReduce TaskTracker	`http://master-public-dns-name:9103/`
Ganglia Metrics Reports (if installed)	`http://master-public-dns-name/ganglia/`
HBase Interface (if installed)	`http://master-public-dns-name:60010/` `master-status`

> **NOTE** *In Table 11-2,* `master-public-dns-name` *represents an actual public DNS name of the master node.*

Several popular Big Data applications can be used on Amazon EMR with utility pricing. Table 11-3 list those applications.

TABLE 11-3: Big Data Applications Available on EMR

PRODUCT DESCRIPTION	PRODUCT DESCRIPTION
HParser	A tool that can be used to parse heterogeneous data formats and convert them into a form that is easy to process and analyze. In addition to text and XML, HParser can parse proprietary formats such as PDF and Word documents.
Karmasphere	Graphical data mining desktop tools for working with large structured and unstructured data sets on Amazon EMR. Karmasphere Analytics can build new Hive queries, launch new Amazon EMR job flows, or interact with job flows launched with Karmasphere Analytics enabled.
MapR Hadoop distribution	This is an open, enterprise-grade distribution that makes Hadoop easier and more dependable. For ease of use, MapR provides Network File System (NFS) and Open Database Connectivity (ODBC) interfaces. It also provides a comprehensive management suite and automatic compression. For dependability, MapR provides high availability with a self-healing architecture, which eliminates NameNode as a single point of failure, provides data protection with snapshots and disaster recovery, and cross-cluster mirroring.

EMR job flow can execute one or more steps (MapReduce jobs, Pig or Hive scripts, and so on). Steps for job flow can be defined during job flow creation and/or added to a job flow at any time. When a step defines a MapReduce job, its definition includes a `jar` file containing executable code (`main` class), an execution driver, and a set of parameters that are passed to a driver. If any step in the sequence fails, all the steps that are specified behind this step will be canceled by the job flow.

As with all AWS components, EMR is integrated with IAM. IAM policy enables you to control what a given user can do with EMR. The access policy for a given user can range from no access to full access, with a lot of combinations of partial permissions. When a new job flow is started, by default it inherits the identity of the user that started the job flow. Additionally, by specifying the `jobflow-role` role parameter during job flow startup, it is possible to start a job flow in a specific IAM role. If a job flow is started in a role, temporary account credentials can be obtained from any participating EC2 instance metadata using the following command:

```
GET http://169.254.169.254/latest/meta-data/iam/security-credentials/roleName
```

> **NOTE** *The previous command works only when executed from within EC2 node. In addition to users and groups, IAM supports roles. Similar to users, roles support permissions, that (in addition to controlling access to account's resources) enables you to specify access outside of a given account (that is, cross-account permissions). IAM users or AWS services can assume a role to obtain temporary security credentials that can be used to make AWS API calls. The advantage of roles is that they enable you to avoid sharing long-term credentials or defining permissions for each entity that requires access to a resource.*

Additionally, MapReduce execution context contains both a current `AccessKeyId` and `Secret` key. They can be accessed using the following: `fs.s3.awsAccessKeyId` and `fs.s3.awsSecretAccessKey` (Hadoop properties in the Hadoop configuration) using the code shown in Listing 11-1.

LISTING 11-1: Accessing AWS credentials

```
String accessID = conf.get("fs.s3.awsAccessKeyId");
String key = conf.get("fs.s3.awsSecretAccessKey")
```

Utilizing CloudWatch and Other AWS Components

EMR reports an execution metric to CloudWatch, which enables you to simplify the monitoring of EMR job flow and MapReduce job execution. You can also set alarms to warn personnel if a metric goes outside specified ranges. Metrics are updated every five minutes and are archived for two weeks. Data older than two weeks is discarded. The CloudWatch metric enables you to do the following:

➤ Track the progress of MapReduce jobs by examining `RunningMapTasks`, `RemainingMapTasks`, `RunningReduceTasks`, and `RemainingReduceTasks` metrics

➤ Detect idle job flows by examining the `IsIdle` metric that tracks inactivity of a job flow

➤ Detect when a node is running out of storage by examining the `HDFSUtilization` metric representing the percentage of currently used HDFS space

An additional CloudWatch metric is available in the case of HBase usage, and supports HBase backup statistics (including a count of failed HBase backup attempts, backup duration, and time since last backup).

Integration is also provided between EMR and DynamoDB. EMR's extension to Hive enables you to treat DynamoDB as a Hive table. Although integration with DynamoDB seems like a trivial implementation (just implement a custom `InputFormat` and reader classes, similar to ones described in Chapter 4), EMR Hive's implementation optimizes split calculations by leveraging knowledge of Dynamo internals. As a result, EMR's recommendation for using Dynamo-based data is to leverage Hive to move data between DynamoDB and HDFS, and then use HDFS-resident data copy for additional calculations.

Finally, an AWS Data Pipeline (discussed later in this chapter) provides integration with EMR, which simplifies leveraging of EMR in ETL processes.

In addition to integration provided by AWS, integration can also be built that leverages APIs provided by all AWS components, including EMR itself.

EMR provides multiple ways of creating a job flow and running MapReduce steps. Let's take a look at how to use the EMR console to work with EMR job flows.

Accessing and Using EMR

The simplest way to access EMR is by using the EMR console, which provides a set of screens for configuring an Hadoop cluster, and running and debugging Hadoop applications. This discussion walks you through the sequence of screens that support these operations.

Creating a New Job Flow

The creation of the job flow starts by defining base information about it, as shown in the Define Job Flow screen in Figure 11-4.

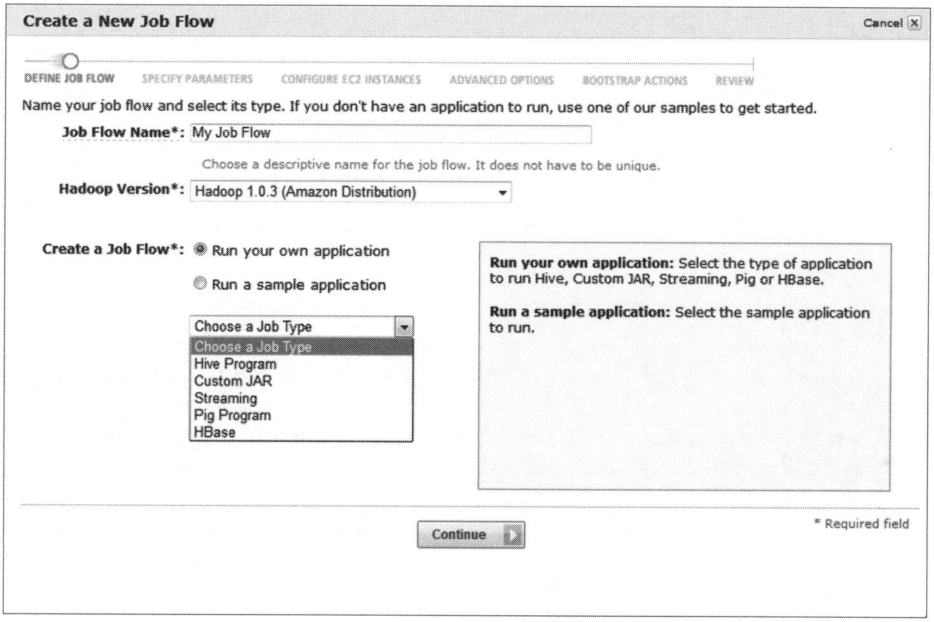

FIGURE 11-4: Using the AWS console to start an Hadoop job flow

This initial screen enables you to define the job flow name and Hadoop version. (Currently supported versions are Amazon Hadoop distribution 1.03, MapR M3, and MapR M5). Additionally, EMR enables you to configure specific applications (including Hive applications, Pig applications, Streaming applications, HBase applications, and a custom `jar` file). The choice of application specifies additional bootstrap actions that are executed by EMR before the first step is executed.

Because HBase has been chosen in this example as an application type, the next screen, the Specify Parameters screen shown in Figure 11-5, enables you to specify whether to restore HBase during a job flow startup, as well as a location of an existing HBase backup. (If a restore is not specified, an empty HBase instance is created.)

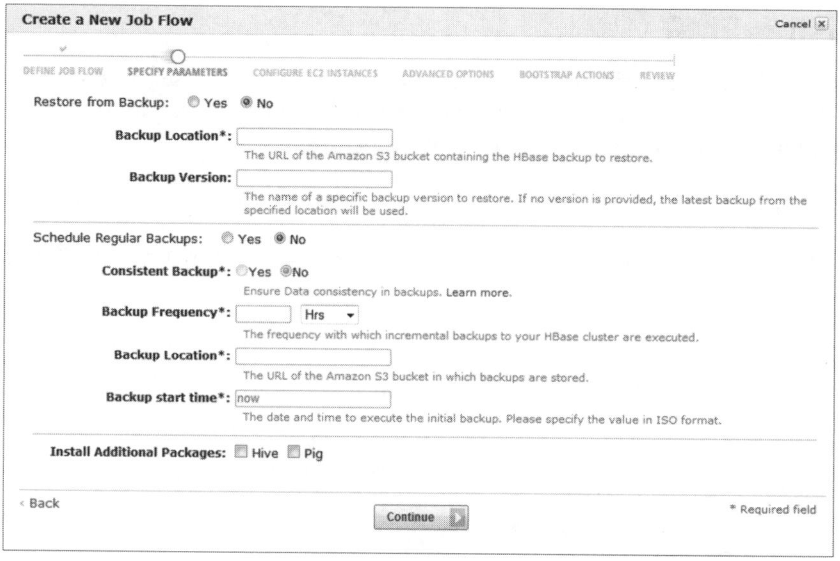

FIGURE 11-5: Using the AWS console to specify backup and recovery for an Hadoop job flow

---

NOTE *The capability of EMR to save and restore HBase content provides a foundation for a common HBase usage pattern. Writing to HBase often requires a significantly larger cluster than reading data. In this case, a larger job flow (EMR cluster) is often created to populate an HBase instance and back it up. Then, this job flow is deleted, and a new smaller job flow is created, which restores an HBase instance and serves data.*

Additionally, this screen enables you to set periodic HBase backups and install additional packages (Hive or Pig).

The next screen, the Configure EC2 Instances screen shown in Figure 11-6, enables you to specify EC2 machines used for job flow execution.

For every one of the EMR instance groups, this screen enables you to specify the type of instance and the number of instances in the group. It also enables you to require spot instances for group instances.

NOTE Spot instances *enable you to name your own price for Amazon EC2 computing capacity. Depending on the utilization, the Spot Price for the spare instances fluctuates. Usage of the spot instance is effectively bidding on spare Amazon EC2 instances based on the spot price. The spot instance pricing model complements other Amazon pricing models, providing potentially the most cost-effective option for obtaining compute capacity.*

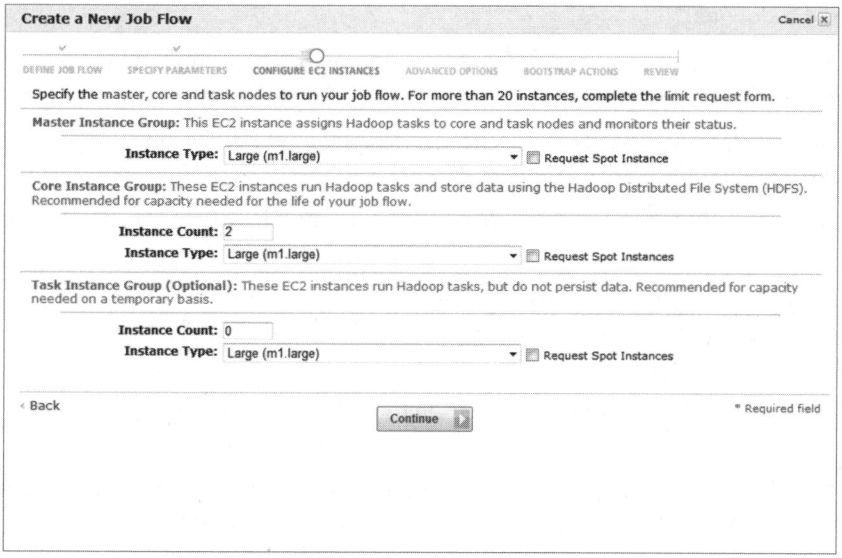

FIGURE 11-6: Using the AWS console to choose nodes for an Hadoop job flow

The next screen, the Advanced Options screen shown in Figure 11-7, is used for specifying advanced options for the job flow.

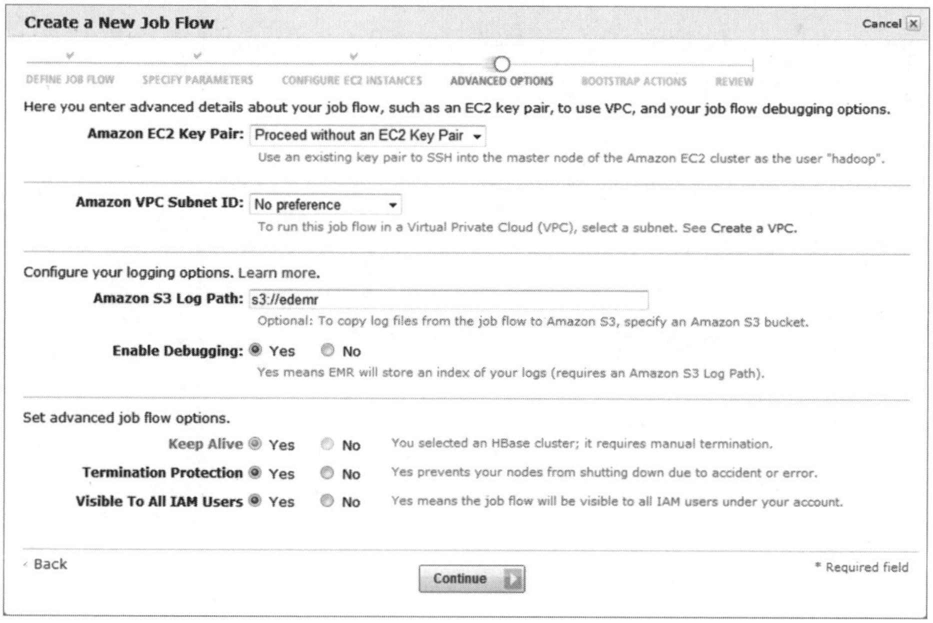

FIGURE 11-7: Using the AWS console to specify advanced options for an Hadoop job flow

These actions include the following:

➤ **Amazon EC2 Key Pair** — You must specify a key pair if you are planning to SSH into one or more of a job flow's (cluster) machine. This key pair is used for authenticating `ssh` login.

➤ **Amazon VPC Subnet ID** — By specifying a Virtual Private Cloud (VPC) subnet, you can place a newly created job flow into a specific VPC.

➤ **Amazon S3 Log Path** — By specifying an S3 log path, you direct EMR to store all the log files in S3.

➤ **Keep Alive** — By specifying the Keep Alive option, you instruct the job flow not to terminate after all execution steps have been completed. This option is useful if you are planning to add additional steps dynamically.

➤ **Termination Protection** — By specifying the Termination Protection option, you instruct the job flow not to terminate because of accidental operator error.

➤ **Visible to All IAM Users** — By specifying the Visible To All IAM Users option, you instruct EMR to make a job flow's execution visible to all members of your account.

> **NOTE** *Amazon Virtual Private Cloud (Amazon VPC) supports provisioning of a logically isolated section of the Amazon Web Services (AWS) Cloud. Creation of VPC enables you to create a virtual network over which you have complete control. When working in a virtual network, you can select your own IP address range, create subnets, and configure route tables and network gateways.*

The final configuration screen, the Bootstrap Actions screen shown in Figure 11-8, enables you to specify additional bootstrap actions that are executed during the job flow startup.

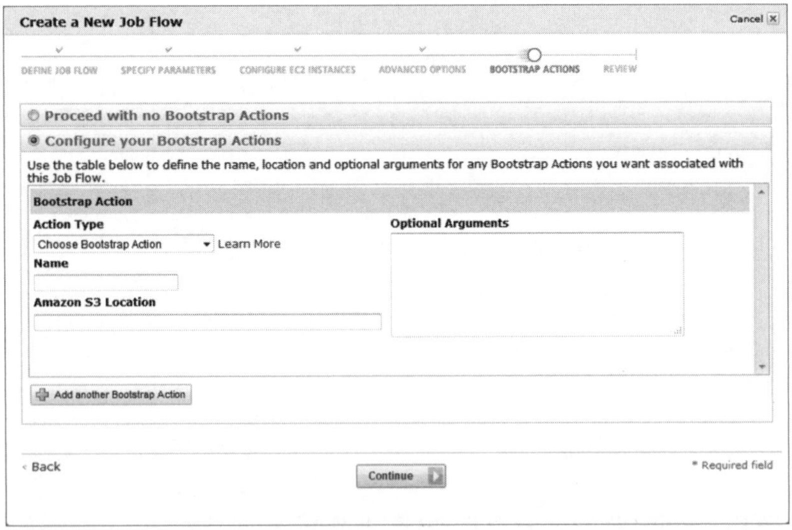

FIGURE 11-8: Using the AWS console to specify bootstrap actions for an Hadoop job flow

Here you can either pick a predefined bootstrap action with a set of arguments, or add a custom action by specifying its location and optional arguments.

Once all parameters for the job flow are specified, an additional screen (the Review screen, not shown here) enables you to look at the parameters summary and confirm a job flow startup.

The AWS console provides support for the monitoring of job flow execution, as shown in Figure 11-9. The monitoring screen has two panes. The upper pane shows the list of all job flows that are visible to you. For every job flow, this pane shows its name, state, creation time, elapsed time, and normalized instance time.

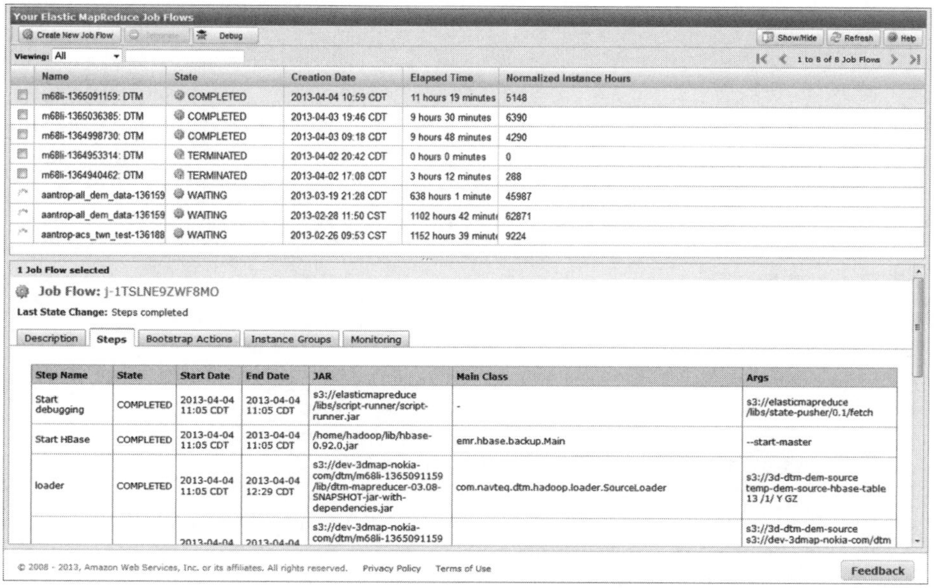

FIGURE 11-9: Using the AWS console to monitor EMR job flow execution

> **NOTE** *The Normalized Instance Hours column shown in the upper pane of Figure 11-9 reflects hours of compute time based on the standard of 1 hour of* `m1.small` *= 1 hour. Usage of normalized instance hours provides utilization numbers, regardless of the instance used.*

By checking a specific job flow in the far left column of Figure 11-9, you can bring up the lower pane, which provides more details on job flow execution. It contains several tabs:

➤ **Description** — The first tab shows the description of the flow, including the master node's public DNS name, which can be used to access a master instance (either through SSH or HTTP).

➤ **Steps** — This tab enables you to see information about every step, including its name, state, start and end date, `jar` that contains the code for this step, the step's `main` class, and additional steps arguments.

➤ **Bootstrap Actions** — This tab enables you to see information about all bootstrap actions, including an action's name, an action's script location, and the parameters that are set.

➤ **Instance Groups** — The content of this tab enables you to see all Instance IDs used by the job flow. For every instance, you can see the role (master, core, or task) that this instance plays in the job flow, instance type, state, market (on demand or spot), running (for terminated job flows, a running count will always be 0), request count, and creation date.

➤ **Monitoring** — This tab shows CloudWatch information for this job flow.

Debugging

Clicking the Debug button at the top-left side of the AWS console brings up a debug view, as you can see in the Debug a Job Flow screen shown in Figure 11-10.

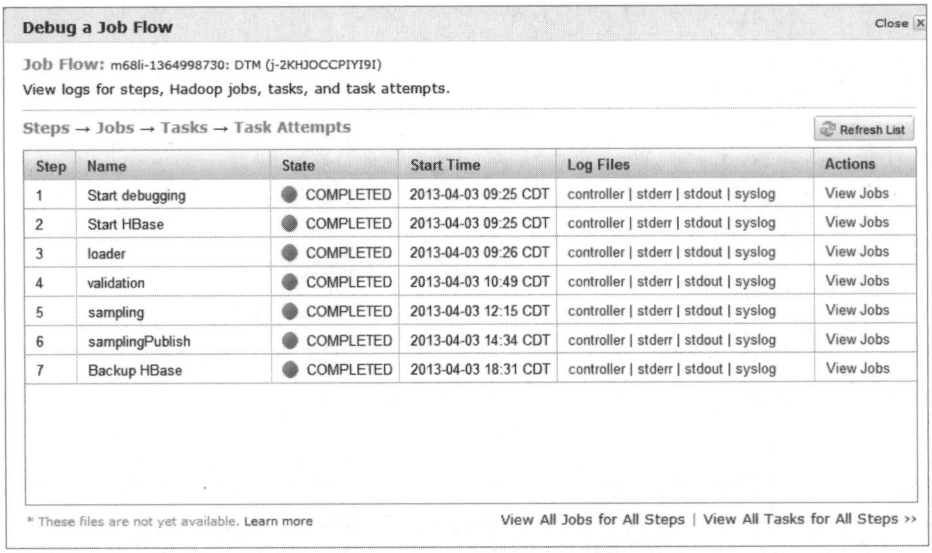

Step	Name	State	Start Time	Log Files	Actions
1	Start debugging	● COMPLETED	2013-04-03 09:25 CDT	controller | stderr | stdout | syslog	View Jobs
2	Start HBase	● COMPLETED	2013-04-03 09:25 CDT	controller | stderr | stdout | syslog	View Jobs
3	loader	● COMPLETED	2013-04-03 09:26 CDT	controller | stderr | stdout | syslog	View Jobs
4	validation	● COMPLETED	2013-04-03 10:49 CDT	controller | stderr | stdout | syslog	View Jobs
5	sampling	● COMPLETED	2013-04-03 12:15 CDT	controller | stderr | stdout | syslog	View Jobs
6	samplingPublish	● COMPLETED	2013-04-03 14:34 CDT	controller | stderr | stdout | syslog	View Jobs
7	Backup HBase	● COMPLETED	2013-04-03 18:31 CDT	controller | stderr | stdout | syslog	View Jobs

Debug a Job Flow   Close ✕

Job Flow: m68li-1364998730: DTM (j-2KHJOCCPIYI9I)
View logs for steps, Hadoop jobs, tasks, and task attempts.

Steps → Jobs → Tasks → Task Attempts   ⟳ Refresh List

* These files are not yet available. Learn more   View All Jobs for All Steps | View All Tasks for All Steps »

FIGURE 11-10: Using the AWS console to debug EMR execution

For every step inside the job flow, this screen shows a step's number, its name, its state, start time links to the log files, and a link to a step's jobs. (Every step that uses MapReduce has a job associated with it — a Pig and Hive step can have several jobs associated with them.) For every job, the screen enables you to view the Hadoop job ID, the parent step number, the job's state, the start time, and a link to the job's tasks.

The Task view is somewhat similar to the task view in the TaskTracker (described in Chapter 5). For every task, the screen enables you to see the task name and type (map or reduce), name of the parent job, the task's state, the start time and elapsed time, as well as a link to a task's attempts.

For every task, this screen shows all task execution attempts. For every attempt, you can see an attempt number, a parent task ID, a task's name and type (map or reduce), an attempt's state, start time, and links to the attempt's logs.

In addition to an EMR console, EMR also provides a CLI. You should read the EMR documentation for more detail about installing and using the CLI.

> **NOTE** *EMR also provides a very powerful set of Java APIs, which are examined later in this chapter.*

Now that you know about the EMR architecture and the ways to interact with EMR, let's take a closer look at S3, which is fundamental for EMR usage.

USING AWS S3

One of the most notable characteristics of EMR is its tight integration with S3, a web service that provides access to a highly scalable and reliable key/object store. (EMR implementation is a rewrite of the original Hadoop implementation of HDFS over S3.) Because EMR execution is ephemeral, it supports storing any information that must survive job flow restarts in S3. This includes the following:

➤ **Storage of the executable code** — All of the user's implementation code executed on the EMR job flow (including Java `jars`, and Hive and Pig scripts) is loaded from S3.

➤ **Storage of configuration files** — This includes some of the specific Hadoop configuration files. For example, `Hive-site.xml` (which is used for configuring Hive execution information) can be located in S3.

➤ **Any data accessed by MapReduce using HDFS (including Hive tables)** — This can reside either on the local HDFS, or at any S3 location. In the latter case, S3 objects are treated as HDFS files.

➤ **Log files storage** — All MapReduce execution log files are stored at an S3 location, which is specified as a parameter to the EMR job flow. This parameter is optional, and if not specified, logs of job flow execution are not available.

➤ **Backup and recovery** — Some of the Hadoop components (for example, HBase) enable you to back up and restore data to and from S3.

Understanding the Use of Buckets

S3 data is organized in *buckets*, which are containers for S3 objects. Buckets serve several purposes, including the following:

➤ They organize the Amazon S3 namespace at the highest level.

➤ They identify the account responsible for storage and data-transfer charges.

➤ They specify the physical location of the data. A bucket can be configured to reside in a specific region.

➤ They specify an object's versioning. Versioning policies can be configured on the bucket level.

➤ They specify an object's expiration. Life-cycle policies can be configured on the bucket level.

➤ They play a role in access control. Many data access permissions can be specified on the bucket level.

➤ They serve as the unit of aggregation for usage statistics and reporting.

USING BUCKETS EFFECTIVELY

Keep in mind that bucket names must be globally unique across S3. This means that when picking a bucket name, try to ensure that there is a certain uniqueness in the name — for example, a company name, application, and so on. Never try to create buckets with generic names — for example, "Bucket 1."

Also be aware that using the Java API for accessing objects will silently create a bucket if one does not already exist, or use an existing one. This behavior can lead to surprising errors. When you try to write an S3 object to the bucket that you think does not exist, but actually does in some other account, the error that you will get is "access denied." This really does make sense, because the bucket is owned by another account.

To avoid these confusing errors, you should consider creating buckets prior to their usage by leveraging, for example, the AWS console. The console will tell you if the bucket already exists.

As mentioned, a bucket is a container of objects. An *object* is a unit of storage and access of data in S3. It consists of data and *metadata*. (Technically, similar to HDFS, S3 objects can be split into parts, similar to an HDFS file, but logically they are viewed as a single entity.) The data portion of an object is opaque to S3 (just a byte array), whereas metadata is a set of key/value pairs that can be used by S3. The default metadata includes some useful system parameters (for example, content type, date last modified, and so on). Additionally, developers can specify custom metadata fields that can be used by a specific application. When using custom metadata, try to keep it small. Metadata is not meant to be used as custom storage.

S3 supports object *expiration*. This means that it is possible to specify how long S3 will keep a given object. By default, objects will live in S3 indefinitely (until explicitly deleted), but you can specify (on a bucket level) an object's *life-cycle configuration*. The life-cycle configuration contains rules that identify an object key prefix and a lifetime (the number of days after creation after which the object will be removed) for objects that begin with this prefix. A bucket can have one life-cycle configuration, which can contain up to 100 rules.

Within a given bucket, an object is uniquely identified by a key (name). Although people often try to view a bucket's content as a filesystem, in reality, S3 has no notion of the filesystem itself — it interprets concatenation of the folder(s) name and the object name as a unique key.

In addition to a key, an object can contain a *version*. Versioning is enabled on the bucket level. If versions are not used, an object is uniquely identified by a key; otherwise, it is a combination of key and version. Unique version IDs are randomly generated by S3 during put operations and cannot be overwritten. A get operation that does not specify a version will always get the latest version. Alternatively, you can do a get for a specified version.

S3 supports get, put, copy, list, and delete operations on objects.

➤ A get operation enables you to retrieve objects directly from S3. There are two flavors of a get operation — retrieve a whole object, and retrieve a portion of an object based on the byte range.

➤ A put operation enables you to upload objects to S3. There are two flavors of a put operation — a single upload and a multipart upload. A single put operation enables you to upload objects up to 5 GB in size. Using the Multipart Upload API enables you to upload large objects up to 5 TB in size. The multipart upload enables you to upload larger objects in parts. Each part can be uploaded independently, in any order, and in parallel. The part size must be at least 5 MB (unless this is the last part of the object, in which case it can be of any required size).

➤ A copy operation enables you to create a copy of an object that is already stored in Amazon S3. An atomic copy operation enables you to copy an object with a size of up to 5 GB. For the larger objects, a multipart upload must be used for copying an object. A copy operation is useful for creating additional copies of objects, renaming an object by copying it (with a new name) and deleting the original one, as well as moving (replicating) objects across S3 locations.

➤ A list operation enables you to list keys in a given bucket. Keys can be listed by prefix. By choosing the appropriate prefixes, this operation enables you to browse keys hierarchically, similar to browsing directories within a filesystem.

➤ A delete operation enables you to delete one or more objects located on S3.

S3 supports the following three access control approaches:

➤ **IAM policies** — As with all other components of AWS, an IAM policy enables you to control what a given user can do with specific objects and buckets. IAM policies enable you to specify a set of operations (get, put, list, delete) that a given user is authorized to execute on a given resource (where a resource can be a bucket, a bucket and a key prefix, or a bucket and a full key).

➤ **Bucket policies** — Bucket policies define access rights for Amazon S3 objects located in a given bucket, and can be defined only by a bucket owner. A bucket policy can do the following:

  ➤ Allow/deny bucket-level permissions.

  ➤ Deny permission on any objects in the bucket.

➤ Grant permission on objects in the bucket only if the bucket owner is the object owner. For objects owned by other accounts, the object owner must manage permissions using ACLs.

➤ **S3 access control lists (ACLs)** — These ACLs enable you to assign access permissions directly to buckets and objects. (Compare this to a filesystem's ACLs.) Each bucket and object has an ACL attached to it as a sub-resource. It defines which AWS accounts or groups are granted access, as well as the type of access. When a request is received against a resource, Amazon S3 checks the corresponding ACL to verify the requester has the necessary access permissions.

Content Browsing with the Console

You can browse S3 at the account level by using the AWS console, as shown in Figure 11-11. The console enables you to browse buckets associated with the account and/or content of the individual bucket based on the key hierarchy. (A standard delimiter "/" is used to split a key name.)

FIGURE 11-11: Interacting with S3 using the AWS console

The left-hand side of the screen shows content of a directory of a bucket. The name of the bucket and the directory are displayed above the list in the top-left corner. The content is comprised of both individual files and directories. Directories are clickable, so that you can drill down into the bucket's content.

The right pane has three tabs. Clicking the None tab removes the right pane and extends the left one to a full-screen view. The Properties tab enables you to view and modify S3 properties described earlier in this chapter. Finally, the Transfers tab enables you to see transfers currently in progress.

Quite a few third-party tools also support interaction with S3. As you can see in Figure 11-12, S3Fox is a browser plug-in that works with Firefox and Chrome, enabling you to view, upload and download (using drag and drop), and delete files from S3. Additionally, S3Fox supports the viewing and modifying of object-level and bucket-level ACLs.

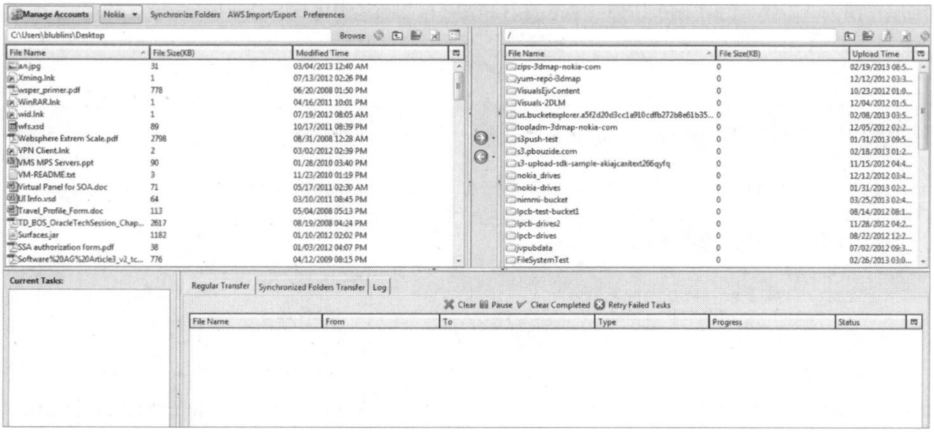

FIGURE 11-12: Interacting with S3 using S3Fox

S3Fox does not support viewing all the bucket/object properties, but does provide handy drag-and-drop support between the local filesystem and S3.

With all the third-party S3 tools available, it is still often advantageous to write code supporting the programmatic upload/download/listing of S3 objects.

Programmatically Accessing Files in S3

AWS provides several SDKs for working with S3, including Java, .NET (C#), PHP, and Ruby. The examples presented here use the Java SDK to show how to implement S3 data manipulation.

> **NOTE** *The bulk of the code for this subsection was produced by Lei Wang and Michael Spicuzza, colleagues of the authors at Nokia and used here with permission.*

Any application that is using AWS requires AWS credentials. As mentioned previously, IAM provides two basic approaches to do this. Credentials can be specified either as an access key/secret pair for a specific user, or, if executed inside AWS, as a role. An individual user's credentials are specified in a properties file, which is similar to what is shown in Listing 11-2.

LISTING 11-2: Credentials properties file

```
accessKey=yourkey
secretKey=yourSecretkey
```

In the case of the role-based security, an EC2 instance that is running in a specific role dynamically generates the key. In this case, AWS provides a specific API that enables you to obtain credentials directly from the instance. When obtaining credentials (as shown in Listing 11-3), it is often advantageous to support a programmatic decision of the way the credentials are obtained.

(This listing shows only individual methods; the full code is available via the book's website, in the project Chapter11, class AWSResource.)

LISTING 11-3: Obtaining AWS credentials

```
public static AWSCredentials getAWSCredentials() throws IOException{
    InputStream is = AWSResource.class.getClassLoader().getResourceAsStream
    ("AwsCredentials.properties");
    if(is != null)
        return new PropertiesCredentials(is);
    return new InstanceProfileCredentialsProvider().getCredentials();
}
```

In this code snippet, you are first trying to get credentials properties, and if a file exists, you are using it to create credentials. Otherwise, you are trying to obtain credentials from an EC2 instance that is hosting execution. AWSCredentials obtained using this code can be used to communicate with AWS services.

Let's first take a look at how to upload data to S3. The code shown in Listing 11-4 is a method that enables you to upload one or more files to S3. (The full code for this implementation is available from the book's website, in the project Chapter11, class GenericS3ClientImpl.)

LISTING 11-4: uploadData method

```
public FileLoadResult uploadData(String s3Path, List<File> sourceFiles)
throws IOException{
    FileLoadResult uploadResult = uploaderInit(s3Path, 0);
    for (File file : sourceFiles){
        if (file.isDirectory()){
            uploadFolderData(s3Path, file, true, uploadResult);
        }
        else{
            uploadResult.setNumberFilesRequested(1);
            uploadDataStream(S3FileUtils.appendFileNameToS3Path(
s3Path, file.getParent()), file.getName(),
            file.getAbsolutePath(),
            new FileInputStream(file), file.length(), uploadResult);
        }
    }

    uploadResult.setEndTime(System.currentTimeMillis());

    return uploadResult;
}
```

This code does not do much. For every file in the sourceFiles list, it checks whether it is a single file or a directory, and invokes an appropriate method for uploading either a directory or an individual file.

Depending on whether an executor (from the java.util.concurrent package) was defined during class initialization, the upload file folder method shown in Listing 11-5 will upload individual files sequentially (executor is null), or in parallel. (The full code for this implementation is available from the book's website, in the project Chapter11, class GenericS3ClientImpl.)

LISTING 11-5: uploadFolderData method

```
private int uploadFolderData(String s3Path, File sourceFile,
    boolean keepSourceFileDirectory, FileLoadResult uploadResult)throws
        IOException{
    Collection<File> sourceFileList = FileUtils.listFiles(sourceFile, null, true);
    uploadResult.addNumberFilesRequested(sourceFileList.size());

    List<Future> completed = null;
    if (executor != null){
        completed = new ArrayList<Future>(sourceFileList.size());
    }
    for (File file : sourceFileList){
        if (executor == null){
            if (!keepSourceFileDirectory){
                uploadDataStream(s3Path, convertFileName(file),
                    file.getAbsolutePath(),
                    new FileInputStream(file),
                    file.length(),
                        uploadResult);
            }
            else{
                    uploadDataStream(S3FileUtils.appendFileNameToS3Path
                        (s3Path, file.getParent()),
                        file.getName(),file.getAbsolutePath(),
                        new FileInputStream(file), file.length(),
                            uploadResult);
            }
        }
        else{
            FileUploadRunnable l = new FileUploadRunnable(s3Path, file,
                            this, keepSourceFileDirectory, uploadResult);
            completed.add(submit(executor, l));
        }
    }

    if (executor != null){
        waitForCompletion(completed);
    }

    return sourceFileList.size();
}
```

In the case of parallel files upload, for every file in the directory, a new runnable class is created and is submitted to the executor. Additionally, in the case of parallel execution, an implementation waits for all of the parallel uploads to complete.

In the case of sequential processing, an uploadDataStream method such as the one shown in Listing 11-6 is used to upload individual files. (The same method is used by Runnable in the case of parallel upload.) (The full code for this implementation is available from the book's website, in the project `Chapter11`, class `GenericS3ClientImpl`.)

LISTING 11-6: uploadDataStream method

```
void uploadDataStream(String s3Path, String sourceFileName, String
        sourceFileFullPath,
    InputStream data, long size, FileLoadResult uploadResult){
    String s3FullPath = S3FileUtils.appendFileNameToS3Path(s3Path,
        sourceFileName);
    S3Location s3Location = S3FileUtils.getS3Location(s3FullPath);
    if (size > PARTSIZE){
        multiPartUploader(sourceFileFullPath, s3Location, data, uploadResult);
    }
    else{
        singlePartUploader(sourceFileFullPath, s3Location, data,
            size, uploadResult);
    }
    System.out.println("Upload file: "
                + S3FileUtils.getS3FullPath(s3Location)
                + ", number files loaded: "
                + uploadResult.getNumberFilesLoaded());
}
```

> **NOTE** *According to S3 documentation, the minimal part size for a multipart upload is 5 MB and the largest is 5 GB. Selection of the optimal part size for a specific implementation is a balancing act between the cost (a smaller part size requires more puts, and is consequently more expensive) and reliability (a larger part size has a higher probability of network failure). A choice of a specific part size depends on many factors, and it also depends on the application, network quality, and so on.*

As described earlier, S3 provides two types of upload — a single-part upload and multipart upload. The upload data stream method makes a decision based on the size of the uploading file. It uses a single-part upload for smaller files, and multipart for larger files. In this particular implementation, a part size of 50 MB is chosen.

The single-part upload method shown in Listing 11-7 first creates object metadata and populates it with an object length. It then uses the `PutObjectRequest` class to send the file upload data (`InputStream`) to S3. (The full code for this implementation is available from the book's website, in the project `Chapter11`, class `GenericS3ClientImpl`.)

LISTING 11-7: singlePartUploader method

```
private void singlePartUploader(String sourceFileFullPath, S3Location s3Location,
    InputStream data, long size,FileLoadResult uploadResult){
    ObjectMetadata om = new ObjectMetadata();
    om.setContentLength(size);
```

```
PutObjectRequest request = new PutObjectRequest(s3Location.getS3Bucket(),
    s3Location.getS3Key(), data, om);
// re-try 3 times when uploading fails
for (int i = 1; i <= RETRY_TIMES; i++){
    try{
        s3Client.putObject(request);
        uploadResult.addNumberFilesLoaded(1);
        break;
    }
    catch (AmazonServiceException ase){
        if (i >= RETRY_TIMES){
            amazonServiceException("putObject", ase,
                s3Location.getS3Key(), sourceFileFullPath,
                uploadResult);
        }
    }
    catch (AmazonClientException ace){
        if (i >= RETRY_TIMES){
            amazonClientException("putObject", ace,
                s3Location.getS3Key(),
                sourceFileFullPath, uploadResult);
        }
    }
}

try{
    data.close();
}
catch (IOException e){
    e.printStackTrace();
}
}
```

This implementation uses a simple retry mechanism (that is, try three times) to deal with potential network issues.

The multiPartUploader method presented in Listing 11-8 first initializes a multipart upload, and then goes through every part of the data. Depending on whether a multipart executor (from java.util.concurrent package) was defined during class initialization, the parts upload happens sequentially or in parallel. (The full code for this implementation is available from the book's website, in the project Chapter11, class GenericS3ClientImpl.)

LISTING 11-8: multiPartUploader method

```
private void multiPartUploader(String sourceFileFullPath, S3Location
        s3Location, InputStream is, FileLoadResult uploadResult){
    List<PartETag> partETags = new ArrayList<PartETag>();
    InitiateMultipartUploadRequest initRequest =
        new InitiateMultipartUploadRequest(s3Location.getS3Bucket(),
        s3Location.getS3Key());
    InitiateMultipartUploadResult initResponse =
```

continues

LISTING 11-8 *(continued)*

```
            s3Client.initiateMultipartUpload(initRequest);
    List<Future> completed = null;
    if (multiPartExecutor != null){
        completed = new ArrayList<Future>();
    }

    int uploadPart = 1;
    try{
        while (true){
            byte[] data = new byte[PARTSIZE];
            int read = is.read(data);
            if (read > 0){
                if (multiPartExecutor == null){
                    partUpload(data, read, uploadPart++, initResponse,
                        partETags);
                }
                else{
                    PartUploadRunnable pl = new PartUploadRunnable(data,
                        uploadPart++, read, this, initResponse,
                        partETags, sourceFileFullPath,uploadResult);
                    completed.add(submit(multiPartExecutor, pl));
                }
            }
            else
                break;
        }
    }
    catch (Throwable e){
        uploadResult.addFile(sourceFileFullPath);
        System.out.println("Unexpected error in multi part upload " +
            initResponse.getKey());
        e.printStackTrace(System.out);
    }

    if (multiPartExecutor != null)
        waitForCompletion(completed);

    // If any part is failed, call abortMultipartUploadRequest to free resources
    if (uploadResult.getFailedFileAbsolutePathList().contains(sourceFileFullPath))
        abortMultipartUploadRequest(initResponse, s3Location.getS3Key());
    else
        completeMultipartUpload(initResponse, partETags,
            s3Location.getS3Key(), sourceFileFullPath, uploadResult);

    try{
        is.close();
    }
    catch (IOException e){
        e.printStackTrace();
    }
}
```

> **NOTE** *To avoid deadlocks, the examples presented here use two different execu-*
> *tors — one for parallelization of the files upload, and another one for paralleliza-*
> *tion of the parts upload.*

In the case of a parallel parts upload, a new `Runnable` class is created for every part, and is submitted to the `executor`. Additionally, in the case of parallel execution, an implementation waits for all of the parallel parts uploads to complete.

In the case of sequential processing, the `partUpload` method presented at Listing 11-9 is used to upload an individual part. (The same method is used by `runnable` in the case of parallel upload.) (The full code for this implementation is available from the book's website, in the project `Chapter11`, class `GenericS3ClientImpl`.)

LISTING 11-9: partUpload method

```
void partUpload(byte[] data, int size, int part,
        InitiateMultipartUploadResult initResponse, List<PartETag> partETags){
    UploadPartRequest uploadRequest = new UploadPartRequest()
        .withBucketName(initResponse.getBucketName())
        .withKey(initResponse.getKey())
    .withUploadId(initResponse.getUploadId()).withPartNumber(part)
    .withInputStream(new ByteArrayInputStream(data))
    .withPartSize(size);
    // Upload part and add response to our list.
    partETags.add(s3Client.uploadPart(uploadRequest).getPartETag());
}
```

If any of the parts uploads fail, the method will abort the whole multipart upload. Otherwise, it will complete the multipart upload.

The `partUpload` method shown in Listing 11-9 uses S3 APIs to upload an individual part. It stores an `Etag` of this part to the overall upload `Etags` list that is used by a `completeMultipartUpload` method shown in Listing 11-10 to report to S3 that the upload is complete, and which parts belong to the file. (The full code for this implementation is available from the book's website, in the project `Chapter11`, class `GenericS3ClientImpl`.)

LISTING 11-10: completeMultipartUpload method

```
private void completeMultipartUpload(InitiateMultipartUploadResult
        initResponse, List<PartETag> partETags, String file,String
        sourceFileFullPath,FileLoadResult uploadResult){
    CompleteMultipartUploadRequest compRequest = new
    CompleteMultipartUploadRequest(initResponse.getBucketName(),
            initResponse.getKey(),initResponse.getUploadId(),partETags);

    // re-try 3 times when uploading fails
    for (int i = 1; i <= RETRY_TIMES; i++){
```

continues

LISTING 11-10 *(continued)*

```
                try{
                    s3Client.completeMultipartUpload(compRequest);
                    uploadResult.addNumberFilesLoaded(1);
                    break;
                }
                catch (AmazonServiceException ase){
                    if (i >= RETRY_TIMES){
                        amazonServiceException("completeMultipartUpload", ase,
                            file, sourceFileFullPath, uploadResult);
                        abortMultipartUploadRequest(initResponse, file);
                    }
                }
                catch (AmazonClientException ace){
                    if (i >= RETRY_TIMES){
                        amazonClientException("completeMultipartUpload", ace, file,
                            sourceFileFullPath, uploadResult);
                        abortMultipartUploadRequest(initResponse, file);
                    }
                }
            }
        }
    }
```

Similar to a single-part upload, this implementation uses a simple retry mechanism (that is, try three times) to deal with potential network issues.

Finally, because S3 does not time-out uncompleted multipart uploads, it is necessary to implement an explicit `abortMultipartUploadRequest` method (shown in Listing 11-11) to clean up failed multipart upload executions. (The full code for this implementation is available from the book's website, in the project `Chapter11`, class `GenericS3ClientImpl`.)

LISTING 11-11: abortMultiPartUploadRequest method

```
    private void abortMultipartUploadRequest(InitiateMultipartUploadResult result,
            String fname){
        AbortMultipartUploadRequest abortRequest =
            new AbortMultipartUploadRequest(result.getBucketName(),
            result.getKey(), result.getUploadId());

        for (int i = 1; i <= RETRY_TIMES; i++){
            try{
                s3Client.abortMultipartUpload(abortRequest);
                break;
            }
            catch (AmazonServiceException ase){
                if (i >= RETRY_TIMES){
                    amazonServiceException("abortMultipartUpload", ase, fname,
                        null, null);
                }
            }
            catch (AmazonClientException ace){
```

```
                    if (i >= RETRY_TIMES){
                        amazonClientException("abortMultipartUpload", ace, fname,
                            null, null);
                    }
                }
            }
        }
```

Execution of this method cleans up the file itself and all temporary S3 parts associated with the file.

S3 provides two methods for getting data from S3 (both are presented in Listing 11-12) — getting the full S3 object content, and getting the object's content in the byte range. (The full code for this implementation is available from the book's website, in the project Chapter11, class GenericS3ClientImpl.)

LISTING 11-12: Reading data from S3

```
public byte[] getData(String s3Path) throws IOException{
    S3Location s3Location = S3FileUtils.getS3Location(checkNotNull(s3Path, "S3
        path must be provided"));
    return getS3ObjectContent(s3Location,
            new GetObjectRequest(s3Location.getS3Bucket(),
                s3Location.getS3Key())));
}
public byte[] getPartialData(String s3Path, long start, long len) throws
        IOException{
    S3Location s3Location = S3FileUtils.getS3Location(checkNotNull(s3Path, "S3
        path must be provided"));
    return getS3ObjectContent(s3Location,
        new GetObjectRequest(s3Location.getS3Bucket(),s3Location.
            getS3Key()).withRange(start, start + len - 1));
}
private byte[] getS3ObjectContent(S3Location s3Location, GetObjectRequest
        getObjectRequest) throws IOException{
    if (s3Location.getS3Key().isEmpty()){
        throw new IllegalArgumentException("S3 file must be provided");
    }
    byte[] bytes = null;
    S3Object object = null;
    try{
        object = s3Client.getObject(getObjectRequest);
    }
    catch (AmazonServiceException ase){
        if (ase.getErrorCode().equalsIgnoreCase("NoSuchBucket")){
                            throw new IllegalArgumentException("Bucket " +
                            s3Location.getS3Bucket() + " doesn't exist");
        }
        if (ase.getErrorCode().equalsIgnoreCase("NoSuchKey")){
            throw new IllegalArgumentException(S3FileUtils.getS3FullPath
                (s3Location) + " is not a valid S3 file path");
        }
        throw new RuntimeException(ase);
    }
```

continues

LISTING 11-12 *(continued)*

```
            if (object != null){
                InputStream ois = object.getObjectContent();
                try{
                        bytes = IOUtils.toByteArray(ois);
                }
                finally{
                        if (ois != null){
                                ois.close();
                        }
                }
            }
        }
        return bytes;
    }
```

The implementation shown here reads the complete InputStream content from the object to the byte array, which is returned to the user. An alternative approach is to return InputStream to the user and allow the user to read data from it. If the user (code) is capable of partial reading of the object data, the latter is the better implementation approach.

S3 provides a specialized copy operation that enables you to copy data within S3, as shown in Listing 11-13. (The full code for this implementation is available from the book's website, in the project Chapter11, class GenericS3ClientImpl.)

LISTING 11-13: Copying S3 data

```
    public void copyFile(String sourceBucket, String sourceKey, String destBucket,
            String destKey){
        CopyObjectRequest request = new CopyObjectRequest(sourceBucket, sourceKey,
                destBucket, destKey);

        try{
                s3Client.copyObject(request);
        }
        catch (AmazonClientException ex){
                System.err.println("error while copying a file in S3");
                ex.printStackTrace();
        }
    }
```

This operation is useful for creating a copy of an existing S3 object, or for modifying an object's metadata.

Deletion of S3 objects is also fairly straightforward, as shown in Listing 11-14. (The full code for this implementation is available from the book's website, in the project Chapter11, class GenericS3ClientImpl.)

LISTING 11-14: Deleting S3 objects

```java
public int deleteMultiObjects(String bucket, List<KeyVersion> keys){
    DeleteObjectsRequest multiObjectDeleteRequest =
                            new DeleteObjectsRequest(bucket);
    multiObjectDeleteRequest.setKeys(keys);
    try{
        DeleteObjectsResult delObjRes =
                    s3Client.deleteObjects(multiObjectDeleteRequest);
        System.out.format("Successfully deleted all the %s items.\n",
                        delObjRes.getDeletedObjects().size());
        return delObjRes.getDeletedObjects().size();
    }
    catch (MultiObjectDeleteException e){
        System.out.format("%s \n", e.getMessage());
        System.out.format("No. of objects successfully deleted = %s\n",
                                e.getDeletedObjects().size());
        System.out.format("No. of objects failed to delete = %s\n",
                                e.getErrors().size());
        System.out.format("Printing error data...\n");
        for (DeleteError deleteError : e.getErrors()){
            System.out.format("Object Key: %s\t%s\t%s\n",
         deleteError.getKey(), deleteError.getCode(), deleteError.getMessage());
        }
    }

    return 0;
}
```

This code uses an S3 API method that enables you to delete multiple S3 objects simultaneously. If you are looking for multiple deletes, a batch delete method provides slightly better performance.

> **NOTE** *Additional classes used for S3 uploading are available from the book's website, in the project* Chapter11, *packages* com.practicalHadoop.s3client *and* com.practicalHadoop.s3client.util.

You have now learned how to write standalone applications with highly parallelized support for the main S3 operations (including put, get, copy, and delete). But what if you have data that you want to move to S3 in your local Hadoop cluster?

Using MapReduce to Upload Multiple Files to S3

EMR Hadoop installation includes S3DistCp, which is an extension of Apache's DistCp optimized to work with S3. S3DistCp enables you to efficiently copy large amounts of data from Amazon S3 into HDFS. You can also use S3DistCp to copy data between Amazon S3 buckets, or from HDFS to Amazon S3. Unfortunately, S3DistCP is not supported on a local Hadoop cluster.

> **NOTE** *This implementation was developed with the help of Gene Kalmens, a Nokia colleague of the authors.*

An implementation presented here leverages the S3 client implementation presented earlier in this chapter, and the `FileListQueueInputFormat` presented in Chapter 4. Listing 11-15 shows the mapper for this implementation. (The full code for this implementation is available from the book's website, in the project `Chapter11`, class `S3CopyMapper`.)

LISTING 11-15: S3CopyMapper class

```
public class S3CopyMapper extends Mapper<Text, Text, NullWritable, NullWritable> {

    @Override
    protected void setup(Context context) throws IOException,
                InterruptedException{

        Configuration configuration = context.getConfiguration();
        AWSPath = configuration.get(Constants.S3_PATH_PROPERTY, "");

        fs = FileSystem.get(configuration);
        int threads = Integer.parseInt(
                        configuration.get(Constants.THREADS_PROPERTY));
        ExecutorService executor = new ThreadPoolExecutor(threads, threads,
        100l, TimeUnit.MILLISECONDS,
            newLinkedBlockingQueue<Runnable>(threads));
        _S3Client = new GenericS3ClientImpl(AWSResource.getAWSCredentials(),
                                            null, executor);
        //attach the shutdown hook for clean exit and retries from the mapper
        queue = HdQueue.getQueue(configuration.get(Constants.QUEUE_PROPERTY));
        files = new ArrayList<String>();
        sHook = new CacheShutdownHook(queue, files);
        sHook.attachShutDownHook();
    }

    @Override
    public void map(Text key, Text value, Context context)
                                throws IOException, InterruptedException {
        String fname = value.toString();
        Path p = new Path(fname);
        FSDataInputStream in = fs.open(p);
        if (in != null) {
            if (files != null)
                files.add(fname);
            _S3Client.uploadData(AWSPath, p.getName(), in,
                            fs.getFileStatus(p).getLen());
            if (files != null)
                files.remove(fname);
            context.setStatus("Copy to S3 Completed for file: "+key);
        }
    }
}
```

```
        @Override
        protected void cleanup(Context context)
                                throws IOException, InterruptedException {
            if (sHook != null) {
                files.clear(); // normal exit, don't roll-back any input key.
            }
        }
    }
}
```

The `setup` method first gets the execution parameters from the execution context, and then creates an `S3Client` that is used by the `map` method to upload data to S3. Because HDFS files can be quite large, `ThreadPoolExecutor` is used with a queue of a fixed size. This will ensure that there is only a limited number of parts in memory at the same time (two times the number of threads), and that the size required for a mapper execution is limited.

`setup` also starts a shutdown hook (see Chapter 4 for more details on shutdown hooks) that restores the state of the queue in the case of mapper failure.

The `map` method gets the next file to be uploaded as a next value, and uses `S3Client` to upload the file. It stores the filename to the list of processed files so that an upload can be retried if the mapper fails. Once the file is uploaded, its name is removed from the retry list so that it will not be uploaded twice.

Finally, a cleanup method ensures that there are no files on the retry list.

> **NOTE** *Additional classes used for the S3 upload MapReduce implementation are available from the book's website, in the project* `Chapter11`, *package* `com.prac-ticalHadoop.s3copytool`.

Now that you know how S3 works, and how it can be used in support of EMR, let's take a look at how you can programmatically configure EMR job flow and submit MapReduce jobs for execution.

AUTOMATING EMR JOB FLOW CREATION AND JOB EXECUTION

As shown earlier in this chapter, many EMR operations can be executed using the EMR console. Although this approach is very good when you are learning how to use EMR, you typically need automated startup, execution, and shutdown of the EMR cluster for production purposes.

Let's take a look at one of the approaches you can use to automate EMR operations.

> **NOTE** *The majority of code for this section was developed with the help of Natalia Zelenskaya, Lei Wang, and Michael Spicuzza, who are Nokia colleagues of the authors.*

Let's assume that you have placed a configuration file into S3 that describes an EMR cluster and steps that you want to execute, as shown in Listing 11-16.

LISTING 11-16: EMR configuration file

```
# Job Flow Description
#-----------------------------------------------------------------
Name=Geometry Alignment
LogUri=s3://3d-geometry-mapreduce/log
SecurityKeyPair=geometry

# Debug Configuration
#-----------------------------------------------------------------
Debug.Start=true
DebugConf.Jar=overwrite_Debug_Default.jar

# Hadoop Configuration
#-----------------------------------------------------------------
HadoopConf.Args.M1=mapred.map.child.env=LD_LIBRARY_PATH=/home/hadoop/geometry,G
     EOID_PATH=/home/hadoop/geometry/geoids
HadoopConf.Args.M2=mapred.task.timeout=172800000
HadoopConf.Args.M3=dfs.namenode.handler.count=66
# HBase Configuration
#-----------------------------------------------------------------
HBase.Start=true
HBaseConf.Args.M1=hbase.rpc.timeout=720001
HBaseDaemondsConf.Args.M1=--hbase-master-opts=-Xmx6140M -XX:NewSize=64m -
     XX:MaxNewSize=64m -XX:+HeapDumpOnOutOfMemoryError -XX:+UseParNewGC -
     XX:+UseConcMarkSweepGC -XX:ParallelGCThreads=8
HBaseDaemondsConf.Args.M2= --regionserver-opts=-Xmx6140M -XX:NewSize=64m -
     XX:MaxNewSize=64m -XX:+HeapDumpOnOutOfMemoryError -XX:+UseParNewGC -
     XX:+UseConcMarkSweepGC -XX:ParallelGCThreads=8
# Bootstrap Actions Descr Section
#-----------------------------------------------------------------
BootstrapActions.M1.Name=Upload libraries
BootstrapActions.M1.Path=s3://3d-geometry-mapreduce/bootstrap/UploadLibraries.sh
BootstrapActions.M1.Args.M1=arg1
# Steps Descr Section
#-----------------------------------------------------------------
Steps.M1.RestoreHBasePath=s3://3d-geometry-mapreduce/resotrePath
Steps.M2.Name=Local Alignment
Steps.M2.ActionOnFailure= CANCEL_AND_WAIT
Steps.M2.MainClass=com.navteq.registration.mapreduce.driver.RegistrationDriver
Steps.M2.Jar=s3://3d-geometry-mapreduce/jar/DriveRegistration-with-
     dependencies1.jar
Steps.M2.Args.M1=s3://3d-geometry-mapreduce/input/part-m-00000
Steps.M2.Args.M2=s3://3d-geometry-mapreduce/output/{jobInstanceName}
Steps.M3.BackupHBasePath=s3://3d-geometry-mapreduce/backupPath
Steps.M4.Name=Outlier Detection
Steps.M4.Jar=s3://3d-geometry-mapreduce/jar/DriveRegistration-with-
     dependencies3.jar
```

This configuration file has several sections:

➤ **Job Flow Description** — This is the main configuration, which includes its name and log location (both required)and (optionally) Hadoop version, description of master, core, and task machine groups (including number of machines and their types), termination protection, and security group. (Optional parameters are not shown in Listing 11-16.)

➤ **Debug Configuration** — This includes the debug flag and debug script.

➤ **Hadoop Configuration** — This enables you to specify the number of mappers and reducers per node, and other Hadoop configuration parameters.

➤ **HBase configuration** — This enables you to specify whether HBase is used by the cluster, and other HBase-specific settings.

➤ **Bootstrap actions** — This a list of bootstrap actions. As described earlier, bootstrap actions are the scripts that are executed on all nodes of a cluster before Hadoop starts.

➤ **Steps** — This is a list of sequential steps executed as part of the job flow in a specified order.

With the properties file in place, a simple JobInvoker class such as the one shown in Listing 11-17 can start the required cluster and optionally wait for its completion. (The full code for this implementation is available from the book's website, in the project Chapter11 JobInvoker class)

LISTING 11-17: JobInvoker class

```
public final class JobInvoker
{
    public static boolean waitForCompletion(File awsCredentialsPropFile,
            String jobInstanceName, Properties jobFlowConfig)throws IOException
    {
        return waitForCompletion(new
            PropertiesCredentials(awsCredentialsPropFile),
            jobInstanceName, jobFlowConfig);
    }

    public static boolean waitForCompletion(AWSCredentials awsCredential,
            String jobInstanceName, Properties jobFlowConfig)throws IOException
    {
        String jobFlowID = submitJob(awsCredential, jobInstanceName,
            jobFlowConfig);

        System.out.println("Job Flow Id: " + jobFlowID);

        int ret = new JobStatus(awsCredential).checkStatus(jobFlowID);
        return (ret == 0);
    }

    public static String submitJob(AWSCredentials awsCredential,
            String jobInstanceName, Properties jobFlowConfig)throws IOException
    {
        // build job flow request
        RunJobFlowRequest request = (new JobFlowBuilder(jobInstanceName,
            jobFlowConfig)).build();

        // Start job flow
        return startJobFlow(request, new
```

continues

LISTING 11-17 *(continued)*

```
                    AmazonElasticMapReduceClient(awsCredential));
    }

    private static String startJobFlow(RunJobFlowRequest request,
        AmazonElasticMapReduce emr)
    {
        // Start job flow
        String jobFlowID = null;
        try
        {
            // Run the job flow
            RunJobFlowResult result = emr.runJobFlow(request);
            jobFlowID = result.getJobFlowId();
        }
        catch (AmazonServiceException ase)
        {
            throw new RuntimeException("Caught Exception: "
                    + ase.getMessage()
                    + " Response Status Code: "
                    + ase.getStatusCode()
                    + " Error Code: "
                    + ase.getErrorCode()
                    + " Request ID: "
                    + ase.getRequestId(), ase);
        }

        return jobFlowID;
    }
}
```

The most important method in this class is submitJob, which takes AWS credentials, a job flow name, and configuration properties (as defined in Listing 11-16). It starts the EMR cluster and steps execution, and returns a job flow ID. This method first builds a job flow request (based on configuration properties), and then submits this request to the EMR web service for cluster creation and execution. This method returns (asynchronously) once the request for cluster creation is accepted by EMR. A synchronous job invocation method — waitForCompletion — enables you to not only invoke the cluster, but also to wait for the job completion.

The submitJob method is using a build method on the JobFlowBuilder class shown in Listing 11-18 to build an EMR request for creation of the cluster. (The full code for this implementation is available from the book's website, in the project Chapter11, class JobFlowBuilder.)

LISTING 11-18: Build RunJobFlowRequest method

```
    public build()
    {
        System.out.println("--------------- Job Flow ---------------");

        String name = this.getValueOrError("Name", "Missing property
```

```
      \"Name\". This property describes jobflow name. Example:
      MyJobFlowName")
            + ": " + JobFlowContext.getInstanceName();
System.out.println(String.format("JobFlow Name: %s", name));

String logUri = this.getValueOrError("LogUri", "Missing property
      \"LogUri\". This property describes where to write jobflow logs.
      Example: s3://mapreduceBucket/log");
System.out.println(String.format("JobFlow LogUri: %s", logUri));

// Instance groups
InstanceGroupConfig master = new InstanceGroupConfig();
master.setInstanceRole(InstanceRoleType.MASTER);
master.setInstanceCount(1);
String masterType = this.getValueOrLoadDefault("MasterType");
master.setInstanceType(masterType);
System.out.println(String.format("Master Group, type %s, count %d",
      masterType, 1));

InstanceGroupConfig core = new InstanceGroupConfig();
core.setInstanceRole(InstanceRoleType.CORE);
String coreType = this.getValueOrLoadDefault("CoreType");
core.setInstanceType(coreType);
int coreCount = Integer.parseInt
      (this.getValueOrLoadDefault("CoreCount"));
core.setInstanceCount(coreCount);
System.out.println(String.format("Core Group, type %s, count %d",
      coreType, coreCount));

List<InstanceGroupConfig> instanceGroups = new
      ArrayList<InstanceGroupConfig>();
instanceGroups.add(master);
instanceGroups.add(core);

// Get keepJobFlowAlive value from input parms
String keepJobFlowAliveStr =
      this.getValueOrLoadDefault("KeepJobflowAliveWhenNoSteps");
boolean keepJobFlowAlive =
      (keepJobFlowAliveStr.toLowerCase().equals("true"));

// Get TerminationProtected value from input parms
String terminationProtectedStr =
      this.getValueOrLoadDefault("TerminationProtected");
boolean terminationProtected =
      (terminationProtectedStr.toLowerCase().equals("true"));

// Instances
JobFlowInstancesConfig instances = new JobFlowInstancesConfig();
instances.setInstanceGroups(instanceGroups);
instances.setEc2KeyName(this.getValueOrLoadDefault("SecurityKeyPair"));
instances.setKeepJobFlowAliveWhenNoSteps(keepJobFlowAlive);
instances.setTerminationProtected(terminationProtected);
instances.setHadoopVersion(this.getValueOrLoadDefault("HadoopVersion"));

RunJobFlowRequest result = new RunJobFlowRequest(name, instances);
```

continues

LISTING 11-18 *(continued)*

```
        result.setLogUri(logUri);
        result.setAmiVersion("latest");
        result.setVisibleToAllUsers(true);
        result.setBootstrapActions(this.buildBootstrapActions());
        result.setSteps(this.buildSteps());

        return result;
    }
```

This method examines configuration properties and overwrites default values with the parameters submitted by the user. This method further uses `BootstrapActionBuilder` and `StepBuilder` classes (available from the book's download website) to complete job flow creation requests.

With this code in place, creation and execution of EMR jobs can be fully automated. (Additional classes used for EMR automation implementation are available from the book's website, in the project `Chapter11`, packages `com.practicalHadoop.emr`, `com.practicalHadoop.emr.builders`, and `com.practicalHadoop.emr.builders.utils`.) Moreover, such an approach effectively creates Java APIs for starting the EMR cluster, which can be used for integrating this operation into a larger enterprise workflow. Additional APIs for obtaining job flow status (class `JobStatus`) and killing a job flow (class `JobKill`) are available from the book's download page. You can create additional APIs, as required, using the provided ones as examples.

Now that you are familiar with the programmatic invocation of the EMR operations, let's take a look at possible approaches for orchestrating EMR-based job execution.

ORCHESTRATING JOB EXECUTION IN EMR

Earlier in this book, you learned about the importance of the orchestration and scheduling of MapReduce jobs and the ways Oozie can be used for this purpose. Unfortunately, the standard EMR distribution does not include Oozie. Instead, it provides the capability to organize MapReduce execution as a set of sequential steps. In some cases, this simple sequential execution paradigm is good enough. But often it is necessary to implement a more complex execution strategy, including parallelization of execution (forks, joins), conditional execution, events coordination, and so on.

In this section, you learn how to install Oozie on your EMR cluster, and about alternatives to Oozie that are provided by AWS.

Using Oozie on an EMR Cluster

The simplest way to use Oozie with EMR is to install Oozie on the master node of the EMR cluster during cluster creation. You can do this with a custom bootstrap action, as suggested in Karan Bhatia's `emr-oozie-sample` GitHub project at `https://github.com/lila/emr-oozie-sample`.

Listing 11-19 shows a slightly modified (from the GitHub project) version of the Oozie configuration script (bootstrap action).

LISTING 11-19: Oozie configuration script

```
OOZIE-DIST=http://archive.apache.org/dist/incubator/oozie/oozie-3.1.3-
    incubating/oozie-3.1.3-incubating-distro.tar.gz
EXT-DIST=http://extjs.com/deploy/ext-2.2.zip
HADOOP-OOZIE-VER=0.20.200
OOZIE_DIR=/opt/oozie-3.1.3-incubating/

sudo useradd oozie -m

# download files
cd /tmp
wget $OOZIE-DIST
wget $EXT-DIST

# unpack oozie and setup
sudo sh -c "mkdir /opt"
sudo sh -c "cd /opt; tar -zxvf /tmp/oozie-3.1.3-incubating-distro.tar.gz"
sudo sh -c "cd /opt/oozie-3.1.3-incubating/; ./bin/oozie-setup.sh -extjs /tmp/ext-
    2.2.zip -hadoop $HADOOP-OOZIE-VER /home/hadoop/"

# add config
sudo sh -c "grep -v '/configuration' $OOZIE_DIR/conf/oozie-site.xml >
    $OOZIE_DIR/conf/oozie-site.xml.new;
    echo '<property>
      <name>oozie.services.ext</name>
      <value>org.apache.oozie.service.HadoopAccessorService</value>
    </property>' >> $OOZIE_DIR/conf/oozie-site.xml.new; echo '
    <property>
      <name>hadoop.proxyuser.oozie.hosts</name>
      <value>*</value>
      </property>
      <property>
      <name>hadoop.proxyuser.oozie.groups</name>
        <value>*</value>
      </property>
    </configuration>' >> $OOZIE_DIR/conf/oozie-site.xml.new"
sudo sh -c "mv $OOZIE_DIR/conf/oozie-site.xml $OOZIE_DIR/conf/oozie-site.xml.orig"
sudo sh -c "mv $OOZIE_DIR/conf/oozie-site.xml.new $OOZIE_DIR/conf/oozie-site.xml"
sudo sh -c "chown -R oozie $OOZIE_DIR"

# copy emr jars to oozie webapp
sudo sh -c "sudo -u oozie sh -c 'cp /home/hadoop/lib/*
    $OOZIE_DIR/oozie-server/lib'"
sudo sh -c "sudo -u oozie sh -c 'cp /home/hadoop/*.jar
    $OOZIE_DIR/oozie-server/lib'"

# startup oozie
sudo sh -c "sudo -u oozie sh -c $OOZIE_DIR/bin/oozie-start.sh"
```

Skipping technical details of shell programming, the script contains the following steps:

1. Create user `oozie`.

2. Download the Oozie Apache archive and `Sencha` JavaScript application framework (`etjs`) archive. The version and URLs can change.

3. Unpack the archives.

4. Run the `oozie-setup.sh` script and configure Oozie.

5. Unpack and configure the `etjs` framework.

6. Fix permissions for Oozie files.

7. Add Hadoop (EMR) `jar` files to the Oozie web application.

8. Start the Oozie web application (with an internal Tomcat web server and Derby database).

To use this bootstrap action, you must copy the `./config` directory from the GitHub project to some S3 location (for example, `s3://boris.oozie.emr/`). Once this is done, you can execute the bootstrap actions shown in Listing 11-20 to install Oozie on the EMR cluster.

LISTING 11-20: Oozie bootstrap actions

```
--bootstrap-action s3://elasticmapreduce/bootstrap-actions/configure-hadoop
\--args "-c,hadoop.proxyuser.oozie.hosts=*,-c,hadoop.proxyuser.oozie.groups=*,-
    h,dfs.permissions=false" \
--bootstrap-action s3://boris.oozie.emr/config/config-oozie.sh
```

Here, the first bootstrap action is used to configure Hadoop with Oozie-specific configurations, and the second one does the actual Oozie installation.

Note that, in this installation, both the Oozie server and Oozie web application are running on the master node of the EMR cluster, which might require you to use a more powerful machine for a master node.

To invoke an Oozie Workflow job, you can open an SSH terminal session on the EMR master node, change the user to `oozie`, and issue the command shown in Listing 11-21.

LISTING 11-21: Staring an Oozie job on an EMR cluster

```
% ./bin/oozie job  -oozie http://localhost:11000/oozie -config
./examples/apps/map-reduce/job.properties -run

job: 0000001-120927170547709-oozie-oozi-W
```

Now you can use the Oozie web console on port 11000 of the EMR cluster master node to monitor the Oozie application. You must use SSH tunneling to connect with the Oozie console from outside of AWS. If you run a browser on an EC2 server, you must use an internal AWS IP address for the EMR master node. With SSH tunneling set up, you can navigate from the Oozie console to the EMR MapReduce Administration console, and log files for each task.

If you run an Oozie Workflow on EMR, you do not see steps in the AWS EMR console.

Because of these shortcomings of Oozie support in EMR, you might consider different tooling that is natively supported by AWS, as described in the following sections.

AWS Simple Workflow

The *Amazon Simple Workflow Service (SWF)* is a web service that can be used for developing asynchronous and distributed applications. It provides a programming model and infrastructure for coordinating distributed components, and maintaining their execution state.

The fundamental concept in Amazon SWF is the *workflow*, which is a set of *activities* that carry out some objective based on the logic that coordinates the activities.

Actual execution of an SWF activity is called an *activity task*. Activity tasks are carried out by *activity workers* — software programs that receive activity tasks, perform them, and return execution results back. An activity worker can either perform a task by itself, or serve as conduit to a person who executes the actual task. Activity tasks participating in SWF can be executed synchronously or asynchronously. Activity workers that perform activity tasks can be distributed across multiple computers (potentially in different geographic regions both inside and outside of AWS), or they can all run on the same computer. Different activity workers can be written in different programming languages, and run on different operating systems.

The coordination logic in a workflow is contained in a software program called a *decider* (that is, an implementation of a workflow itself). The decider schedules activity tasks, provides input data to the activity workers, processes events that arrive while the workflow is in progress, and ends (or closes) the workflow when the objective has been completed.

Amazon also provides the *AWS Flow Framework*, a programming framework that simplifies implementation of both activities and workflow logic in Java.

Although there is nothing in SWF or the AWS Flow Framework that directly supports EMR, it is quite simple to leverage them for controlling both the creation and destruction of EMR job flows, as well as controlling steps execution inside the cluster.

The overall approach for such an implementation is quite simple:

1. Create a job flow with no steps in the beginning of the workflow using the `JobInvoker` class.
2. Wait for the cluster to start up using the `JobStatus` class.
3. Use workflow logic to decide on the next job that must be executed on the cluster.
4. Add a step to the cluster.
5. Wait for step completion using `JobStatus` class.
6. When the workflow is complete, use a `JobKill` class to terminate a workflow.

This simple approach allows for creation of the workflows of any complexity that can leverage both EMR execution and any other AWS resources.

An AWS Data Pipeline framework is built on similar principles, and enables you to hide some of the complexities of interacting between multiple AWS resources in the same workflow.

AWS Data Pipeline

AWS Data Pipeline is a web service that can be used to automate the ETL processes — movement and transformation of data. It supports definition and execution of data-driven workflows, comprised of the tasks that can be dependent on the successful completion of previous tasks.

Three main components of AWS Data Pipeline work together to manage your data:

➤ A *pipeline definition* specifies the business logic of a pipeline, and can contain the following types of components:

> ➤ **DataNode** — This is the location of input data for a task, or the location where output data is to be stored. Currently supported DataNodes include an Amazon S3 bucket, a MySQL database, Amazon DynamoDB, and a local DataNode.

> ➤ **Activity** — This is an interaction with the data. Currently supported activities include data copy, launching an Amazon EMR job flow, running a custom `bash` script from the command line (requires a UNIX environment to run the script), a database query, and a Hive query.

> ➤ **Precondition** — This is a conditional statement that must be true before an action can run. Currently supported preconditions include successful completion of a `bash` script, existence of data, reaching of a specific time or a time interval relative to another event, and existence of an S3 object or DynamoDB or RDS table.

> ➤ **Scheduling** — Currently supported scheduling options include defining a time at which an action should start and stop, as well as how often it should run.

➤ The AWS Data Pipeline web service provides *user interaction* (through the AWS console and APIs), interprets the pipeline definition, and assigns tasks to workers to move and transform data.

➤ *Task Runners* (similar to activity runners in SWF) are processes responsible for execution of Data Pipeline tasks. Task Runners are installed and run automatically on resources created by a pipeline definition. Data Pipeline provides several "standard" Task Runner implementations, and provides the capability for users to create custom Task Runners.

As shown in Figure 11-13, the AWS console provides a graphical Data Pipeline designer that simplifies the creation of a data pipeline.

The left pane of the designer provides a graphical representation of the pipeline. Buttons on the top of the pane enable you to add activities and DataNodes. The right pane enables you to configure created activities and DataNodes, including connections between them. It also enables you to configure the other elements of Data Pipeline, including schedules, resources, preconditions, and so on. Once a pipeline is created, it can be saved and activated using the buttons on the left side of the screen.

There are a lot of commonalities between Oozie Coordinator functionality and Data Pipeline, and there are a lot of use cases where either can be used to coordinate EMR-based processes.

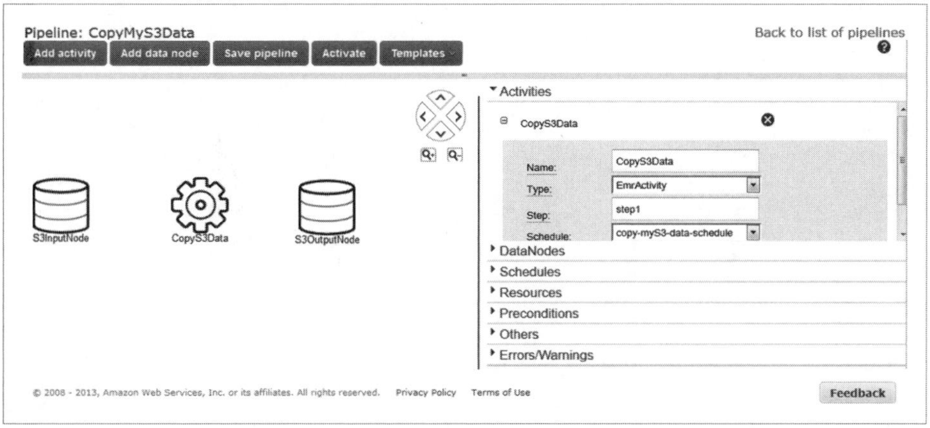

FIGURE 11-13: Data Pipeline designer

In addition, Data Pipeline enables you to coordinate execution between EMR and other AWS-based execution.

As both Data Pipeline and SWF mature, they represent a valuable AWS-specific alternative to using Oozie.

SUMMARY

This chapter discussed the ways that you can leverage cloud computing — specifically, Amazon Web Services (AWS) — to run Hadoop. You have learned about the rich AWS ecosystem, and the ways you can leverage AWS for running Hadoop clusters. You have learned about Elastic MapReduce (EMR) service fundamentals, and the way EMR implements Hadoop functionality. The chapter covered both the use of the AWS console and the use of programmatic approaches for creating an EMR cluster, as well as execution of MapReduce jobs.

You have also learned about S3 — Amazon's supplement to EMR HDFS — as well as administrative (through the AWS console and third-party tools) and programmatic access to it.

Finally, you learned about different approaches to orchestrating MapReduce job execution on EMR, including the installation of Oozie on EMR, the use of an AWS simple workflow, and the Data Pipeline framework.

In Chapter 12, you learn about building secure enterprise solutions with Hadoop.

12

Building Enterprise Security Solutions for Hadoop Implementations

WHAT'S IN THIS CHAPTER?

➤ Understanding security concerns for enterprise applications

➤ Understanding what Hadoop security does not provide for enterprise applications

➤ Looking at approaches for building enterprise security solutions

Chapter 10 discussed Hadoop security and the mechanisms within Hadoop that are used to provide security controls. When building enterprise security solutions (which may encompass many applications and enterprise services that interact with Hadoop data sets), securing Hadoop itself is only one aspect of the security solution. Organizations struggle with applying consistent security mechanisms on data that is extracted from heterogeneous data sources with different security policies. When organizations take data from multiple sources, and then extract, transform, and load that data into Hadoop, the security challenges become even more complicated as the resulting data sets are imported into enterprise applications. For example, how do you enforce the access control policies from the initial data sets, when the data sets produced from Hadoop jobs represent a combination of multiple data sets?

To complicate matters, many organizations are finding that the level of security that Hadoop provides does not meet all of their security and compliance requirements, and they must complement Hadoop's security model. For example, some organizations are required to encrypt data at rest in order to meet their compliance regulations — functionality that Hadoop does not natively provide. Still, other organizations require that Hadoop queries provide a level of granular, attribute-based access control for data scientists performing analytical queries. Although this is certainly on the road map and in Hadoop security's future (as discussed in Chapter 10), such functionality currently requires more than what Hadoop itself can provide.

Because of these challenges, enterprise solutions must be developed with a holistic (and not an Hadoop-centric) security approach. Certainly, you can use native security mechanisms in Hadoop to satisfy some of your security requirements, but in many organizations, you will find that Hadoop's security mechanisms will not solve all of them. Enterprise applications that make use of Hadoop must be planned for, designed, and complemented with other security mechanisms, looking at the enterprise "big picture."

As discussed in Chapter 10, Hadoop was designed and developed without security in mind, and for quite a while there was little to no security for Hadoop implementations. An early assumption adopted by the community was that Hadoop clusters would consist of cooperating, trusted machines used by trusted users in a trusted environment. Since those early days, the Hadoop community adopted a new security architecture with new security controls (as discussed in Chapter 10), but many organizations with significant access control restrictions, confidentiality rules, privacy restrictions, and compliance mandates have still not been able to use the basic tools in the Hadoop ecosystem to meet their security requirements. Because they want to leverage Hadoop's capabilities, they have had to build security into other tools, or design solutions using Hadoop in different ways.

This chapter is written for developers of enterprise applications who want to utilize Hadoop, but who also must "answer the mail" on security. It is important to understand that most enterprise applications are required to adhere to an organization's security requirements. This may include integrating with identity and access management infrastructure, other network infrastructure, and it may also mean applying other security controls that are not integrated with Hadoop "out of the box." This chapter provides a methodology and potential solutions for meeting such requirements.

This chapter begins with a brief overview of security concerns for developing enterprise applications that utilize Hadoop. It then discusses what Hadoop security does not provide out of the box, and provides a number of approaches for building enterprise security solutions with Hadoop, including real-world examples. Finally, this chapter briefly covers security provided by another tool that you can use with Hadoop distributions — Apache Accumulo, which is a highly secure data storage and retrieval system originally built on top of Hadoop by the National Security Agency (NSA) for the purpose of fine-grained access control.

SECURITY CONCERNS FOR ENTERPRISE APPLICATIONS

When building Hadoop solutions, it is not only important that you think about securing Hadoop itself (as discussed in Chapter 10), but it is also important that you understand the big picture from a security policy and a data-centric perspective.

As you can see in Figure 12-1, there is an Hadoop data life cycle that must be understood. When building Hadoop solutions, there is a process of retrieving data sets from information sources, loading them into an Hadoop cluster, running queries and analytics, and utilizing the result sets. As this data travels, it is the goal of the security architect to ensure that all policies are enforced throughout that life cycle.

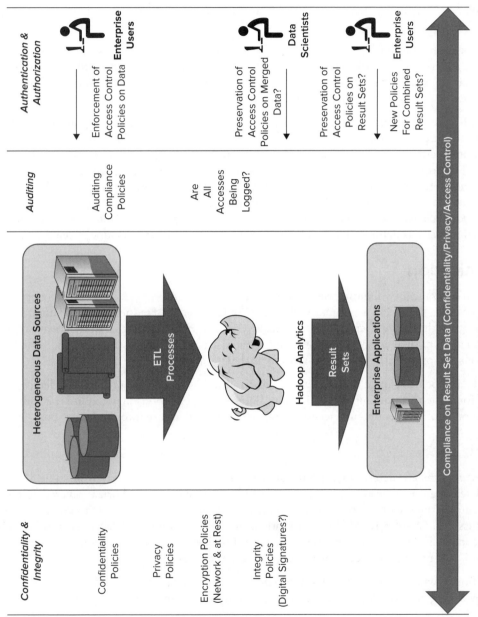

FIGURE 12-1: Security concerns in the data life cycle of Hadoop

Regardless of the tools involved, data is extracted from a wide variety of data sources, transformed into a common format, and loaded into an Hadoop cluster onto HDFS, in what is typically referred to as an Extract, Transform, and Load (ETL) process. Data analysts then run a series of MapReduce jobs, and perform queries that produce result sets, which are, in turn, typically used by enterprise applications.

The challenge here is multifaceted. You must be able to protect the data as it transitions through this life cycle, adhering to the original security policies. As data is extracted, loaded, and combined with other data sets on a cluster of machines, and as result sets are used by other applications, this can be a challenge.

Figure 12-1 should provide a good overview of some of the concerns examined in this chapter. To build secure enterprise solutions that involve Hadoop, architects must have an understanding of information security fundamentals, and how they can be applied. Many security goals for solutions utilizing Hadoop require some explanation, and understanding best practices is dependent on understanding security concerns and the terminology associated with those terms. This discussion is not intended to be an exhaustive list or explanation of every security concern, but it provides a brief information security vocabulary for the security goals that enterprise architects need to know. For each goal the term is defined, and you learn why it is important in the Hadoop context.

Authentication

Authentication means validating the identity of a subject. A *subject* can be a user, an application, a task, or other "actor" in a system. As discussed in Chapter 10, Hadoop can be configured to use Kerberos to authenticate users, services, and servers in an Hadoop cluster. Authentication provides a certain amount of assurance that users and services are who they say they are, and thwarts the impersonation of users, tasks, and services by malicious systems.

It should also be mentioned that not every organization has an enterprise Kerberos deployment that is used for authentication outside of Hadoop. Enterprise applications may require the additional integration of other identity and access management infrastructure into their solutions.

Authorization

Authorization means determining what a subject has permission to do. After the subject's identity is validated in authentication, systems must determine the subject's authorization credentials, and must compare them with an expressed authorization policy to provide access to requested resources. As discussed in Chapter 10, Hadoop currently provides a certain level of access control by utilizing access control lists (ACLs) to express access control policy for certain aspects of Hadoop, and UNIX-like file permissions for owner and group user permissions.

In addition to what Hadoop provides, most enterprise organizations have additional controls for authorization. For example, an organization may have one or more of the following:

➤ Lightweight Directory Access Protocol (LDAP) directories or Active Directory (AD) instances that store groups, roles, and permissions for subjects

➤ Attribute Services that use attributes as authorization credentials for subjects

➤ Security Token Services (STS) that are used for issuing tokens related to a subject's authorization credentials, and for issuing authorization decisions in transactions

➤ Policy Services that use standards such as the eXtensible Access Control Markup Language (XACML) and the Security Assertion Markup Language (SAML) to express access control policy for resources, and provide access control decisions for subjects

Enterprise solutions utilizing Hadoop may need to control access to data sets based on their organization's enterprise access control policies, which typically means complementing Hadoop's native authorization controls with other mechanisms.

Remember that it is important for authorization to be consistently addressed throughout the data life cycle. If your original data sources have access control policies on their data, it may be important for you to provide the same access control to the data scientists running queries on that data. It may be even more important for any result sets that are later imported into enterprise applications to also be properly controlled. This is indeed a challenge.

Confidentiality

Confidentiality is the security goal for restricting sensitive information so that only authorized parties can see it. When sensitive information is transmitted on the network, it may be a requirement that this information is not seen in transit by eavesdroppers. This is accomplished by network encryption. Some organizations require on-disk encryption, or "data at rest" encryption, where cryptography is used on the data where it is stored, reducing the risk of theft of unprotected data.

As you learned in Chapter 10, Hadoop provides the capability and the mechanisms for providing network encryption. However, it does not provide the capabilities for encrypting data at rest. You learn more about strategies for achieving this goal later in this chapter.

Integrity

Integrity means providing the assurance that data has not been altered in transit or at rest. This is typically achieved via cryptography through the use of message digests, hash codes, or as a side effect of a digital signature. When Hadoop is configured to implement network encryption, it applies data integrity in transit.

Integrity at rest is another matter, and luckily, much data integrity is built into Hadoop because of the duplication of data for reliability. An intended side effect of Hadoop's robust, distributed architecture was data integrity and reliability. Because HDFS was designed to run on commodity hardware, it provides duplication of data onto multiple nodes to provide fault tolerance. Because of the amount of replication, and because of the mechanisms of checksum checking and corruption detection, it provides a robust mechanism for the integrity of data sets stored in HDFS.

However, security architects sometimes voice a concern that if a node in an Hadoop cluster is compromised, a malicious user could potentially modify the data, resulting in skewed data analysis. This is certainly a possibility, but by complementing Hadoop's security mechanisms (server/service authentication, integrity checks, and so on) with a defense-in-depth strategy for security, enterprise solution architects can reduce such risks.

Auditing

Most companies rely on security *auditing* to provide assurance of compliance issues, and to identify potential security breaches. Hadoop can certainly be configured to log all access — the NameNode stores a local log, and an audit log can be configured to write to a secured volume to ensure log integrity. Organizations may have further audit requirements related to authentication and authorization.

> **NOTE** *Although most descriptions of the classical security goals are typically focused on "confidentiality," "integrity," and "availability," the focus here has been on authentication, authorization, confidentiality, integrity, and auditing because these are key aspects of security for enterprise applications. Availability (assuring access to Hadoop) is certainly important — and this has been a concern because of the way it was designed. Hadoop clusters are highly reliable, have a great track record for availability, and can be complemented by other security mechanisms in your enterprise (such as Intrusion Detection Systems) to protect against Denial-of-Service (DoS) attacks. That is not covered in this chapter because this discussion is geared toward the enterprise application developer.*

WHAT HADOOP SECURITY DOESN'T NATIVELY PROVIDE FOR ENTERPRISE APPLICATIONS

With some context and security terminology now in place for the rest of this chapter, it is important that you understand some aspects of enterprise security that Hadoop doesn't natively provide. Certainly, Hadoop does provide a level of authentication (Kerberos), a certain amount of authorization (ACLs and UNIX-level file permissions), and capabilities to support network encryption and integrity. However, there are some aspects of security that Hadoop simply does not provide.

Data-Oriented Access Control

Other than ACLs and POSIX-based file permissions (read and write) for users and groups on HDFS, Hadoop does not natively keep track of the access control policies for its data. As you have learned in this chapter, many organizations restrict access based on policies that may be quite complex. There could be situations in which an Hadoop implementation may contain data sets from data that must be protected from data analysts who may not have permission to see the results of MapReduce jobs and queries.

Following are a few good examples of this:

➤ A health care organization may have an access control requirement that a physician can only access data related to his own patients, during normal business hours (9 a.m. to 5 p.m.). This means that to provide access control to patient data, a system providing access to that data must restrict data based on the user's role (physician), the time of day (normal business hours), and whether or not the data is a record belonging to the physician's patient.

➤ A government document may restrict access based on a user's citizenship and/or security clearance by requiring what is known as Mandatory Access Control (MAC).

➤ A financial advisor who advises a particular company should not have access to plans and advice for that company's competitors. This is typically known as a "conflict of interest" or "Chinese wall" policy.

➤ A university may collect student data from all of its divisions and sub-organizations, ranging from finance, medical records, and campus police. The university may be required to control access to that data based on the division or role (medical, police, financial).

In each of these cases, Hadoop's native security mechanisms cannot easily be used to enforce these access control policies. Some of these challenges are architectural, based on the way that the MapReduce algorithm was designed. Imported data may initially be associated with access control policies (in examples where data is "marked up" with the security policies). However, there is a split of this association between the policies and the data as the data is distributed over HDFS, and later combined with other data sets as jobs are run. This may result in new, combined data sets where access control policies are not completely clear.

This is a challenging problem for organizations needing to provide this level of access control, and one that will be examined later in this chapter.

Differential Privacy

For nearly 40 years, research has been conducted on the topic of unintentionally disclosing information from statistical databases, as well as security and privacy concerns related to data mining. In 2006, Dr. Cynthia Dwork of Microsoft Research defined this area of data science as *differential privacy.*

Differential privacy focuses on the protection against disclosure of information from multiple data sets and databases. As Hadoop and other data analytics platforms have brought together the capability to process multiple, large data sets with a large amount of computing power, differential privacy has become a very hot topic with serious privacy and legal implications. This has been especially true with regulations like the Health Insurance Portability and Accountability Act (HIPAA) and other privacy-preserving digital laws.

Even if it is "anonymized" with privacy information stripped out, an Hadoop data set may contain (or may be coupled with) other seemingly harmless information that may be used to disclose the identity of an individual or other sensitive information, resulting in a violation of privacy policies. It may be possible to combine information derived from multiple Hadoop jobs in such a way that the data scientist or the Hadoop user is not allowed to see the exposed information. However, Hadoop itself does not provide differential privacy. Certainly, this has access control implications for internal users, but also has serious implications for organizations sharing statistics and data sets with other organizations.

Because Hadoop is a powerful analytic platform used by many organizations, it can be used to discover information that you may not want discovered. An organization should think twice before releasing its data sets into the public or to its business partners. There may also be internal controls on your data — depending on your environment, be aware that some of your Hadoop users may not be authorized to see certain results of their analytical queries. This was one of the concerns of the NSA, which developed and later released Accumulo to Apache as open source, providing cell-level security.

EXAMPLES OF THE "DIFFERENTIAL PRIVACY" PROBLEM

One of the most publicized examples of differential privacy happened at Netflix. In 2006, Netflix offered a $1 million prize for a 10 percent improvement in its movie recommendation system, and released an "anonymized" training data set of the movie viewing history of half a million subscribers so that developers participating in the contest would have some data to use for the contest. This data set had the ratings of movies that the Netflix subscribers had watched, with all personally identifying information removed.

Two researchers, Dr. Arvind Narayanan and Dr. Vitaly Shmatikov from the University of Texas at Austin, linked together the Netflix data set with the Internet Movie Database (IMDB) review database, applying a new "de-anonymization algorithm." They published a research paper showing that they could mathematically identify many of the users in the released Netflix data set. Based on a user's IMDB ratings of just a few movies, the researchers showed that their algorithm could personally identify the same individuals in the Netflix data set to find the Netflix subscriber's entire movie viewing history prior to 2005, resulting in potential revelations related to the subscriber's religious beliefs, sexuality, and political leanings. As a result, a Netflix subscriber filed a lawsuit against Netflix, claiming that its release of their data violated the Video Protection Privacy Act (VPPA) and "outed" her as a lesbian. Netflix settled the lawsuit for $9 million in 2010.

During that same time, AOL released a set of "anonymized" search engine logs for research purposes, and a *New York Times* reporter was able to cross-reference this data set with phonebook listings to personally identify users. This exposed three months of AOL users' search histories — some of which were quite embarrassing. This resulted in the resignation of AOL's Chief Technology Officer (CTO), the firing of two AOL employees, and a class-action lawsuit against the company.

There are countless other examples of note — one researcher at MIT was able to identify her governor's medical records from an "anonymized" state insurance database when she analyzed that data set with publicly available state voter registration records.

These examples demonstrate the issue at hand, and show how information in data sets can be used together to potentially violate privacy laws, regulations, and bypass access control restrictions on users. By applying these same principles, your internal Hadoop users may be able to bypass security restrictions if you do not set the proper controls in place.

Encrypted Data at Rest

Because of the many threats to the confidentiality of information stored on disks and end-user devices, many organizations with sensitive information have policies that require the encryption of data at rest. Many of the reasons for such a policy relate to the threat of malware, the sensitivity or confidentiality of the data, or legal regulations. HIPAA, for example, has guidance related to encrypting data at rest related to Electronic Protected Health Information (EPHI), and other laws protecting Personally Identifiable Information (PII) come into play.

Some organizations are pushing for encrypting data at rest on HDFS, which Hadoop does not natively provide. However, third-party libraries and other products can be used along with Hadoop to satisfy these requirements, and Project Rhino (as discussed in Chapter 10) is working to address this issue in Hadoop.

Enterprise Security Integration

Most businesses have all sorts of security infrastructure in their enterprises, ranging from Public Key Infrastructure (PKI) components for authentication, Active Directory instances, Security Token Services, Attribute Services, and Policy Servers used for authenticating users, providing authorization credentials, and making and enforcing access control decisions. Hadoop's native security capabilities will not always allow you to "fit it" into or integrate with the security infrastructure of every organization. When security requirements dictate that enterprise applications integrate with an organization's security infrastructure, it is therefore the security architect's job to design a solution that uses other tools to integrate with that security infrastructure while utilizing Hadoop.

APPROACHES FOR SECURING ENTERPRISE APPLICATIONS USING HADOOP

Recently, a significant number of projects, Hadoop add-ons, and proprietary Hadoop distributions have promised to enhance the security of Hadoop. Hortonworks' Knox Gateway, Intel's security-enhanced distribution of Hadoop, and open source projects such as Project Rhino have been released and hold much promise for helping the enterprise application developer satisfy security requirements. Regardless, it is important to remember that every enterprise application is different, and requirements for security in every deployment will be different.

Before getting into the nuts and bolts, it is important that you understand some general basics and guidelines for providing secure enterprise applications that make use of Hadoop. A lot of projects run off the rails when they jump into focusing on specific security mechanisms and don't follow some of these common-sense guidelines that apply to any project.

Each project's enterprise security strategy may be different, based on the customer's mission and requirements, but will follow these common-sense rules:

> ➤ **Determine your security requirements** — Understanding your security requirements is crucial. Requirements for authentication, access control, auditing, encryption, integrity, and privacy will be dictated by your organization. Some of the questions that you might have to ask may revolve around the security of the resulting data sets from Hadoop MapReduce

jobs, versus the security of the Hadoop run time itself (providing access control to the applications/users doing the queries and running the jobs). Meet with the proper decision makers to understand what is needed, so that you can plan accordingly.

➤ **Design for security from the beginning** — One of the biggest problems with these types of projects is trying to retrofit security at the end — such practices lead to a short-lived and brittle architecture, and they typically leave a project doomed for failure. If your project has the security requirements discussed in this chapter, and you think you will focus only on data analytics and try to worry about securing the solution later, then you run a great risk of failure. Focus on developing an initial high-level security architecture that can be discussed with the proper authorities for concept approval.

➤ **Don't secure what you don't need to** — If you don't have the security requirements to achieve some of the goals discussed in this chapter, then don't! Don't add the complexity or the performance overhead by implementing what you don't need.

➤ **Use a "defense-in-depth" approach** — It should never be assumed that an individual security approach or mechanism that you employ will thwart or prevent an attack or a violation of security policy. A defense-in-depth strategy involves multiple layers of defense.

➤ **Keep the big picture in mind** — Understand your data's life cycle, such as the one shown earlier in Figure 12-1. Understand that providing security may mean controlling access, as well as preserving and enforcing policies throughout this life cycle — from the data in the original data sources, to data loaded onto an Hadoop cluster, to the result set data.

The following sections delve into concrete approaches for meeting some of the security requirements, and complementing the security that Hadoop natively provides. The discussion focuses on three main approaches, which provide the building blocks of enterprise security when coupled with Hadoop's native mechanisms. In these next sections, the discussion focuses on Apache Accumulo.

Access Control Protection with Accumulo

Apache Accumulo is a sparse, distributed, sorted, and multidimensional key/value store that has the property of fine-grained access control at the cell level. Developed by the NSA in 2008 and based on Google's design of BigTable, it was released into the Apache open source community in 2011, and now it is a top-level Apache project. It is a highly scalable NoSQL database that is built on top of Hadoop and Zookeeper. Part of the reason that it was developed was to solve Big Data security problems.

Accumulo extended BigTable's data model, but added an element that provided cell-level, mandatory Attribute-Based Access Control (ABAC). All data that is imported into Accumulo can be marked with visibility controls, and as data analysts query the data, they will see only what they are supposed to see, based on the visibility controls in the access control policy. Accumulo's API provides the capability for you to write clients to authenticate users and integrate with enterprise attribute services to pull down authorization credentials of users to provide a level of access control. It also provides the capability for user and authorization information to be stored in Accumulo itself.

As you can see in Figure 12-2, Accumulo is a key/value store whose key is a 5-tuple. A key in Accumulo is a combination of a Row ID, Column Family, Column Qualifier, Column Visibility, and a Timestamp. This 5-element key is associated with a Value.

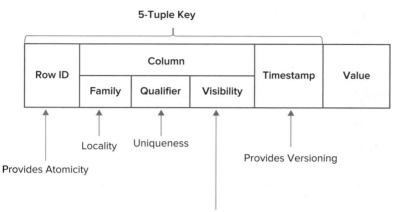

FIGURE 12-2: Accumulo data model

This 5-tuple key provides atomicity, locality, uniqueness, access control, and versioning. It is important to note that the Timestamp aspect of the key contains the capability to provide multiple versions of the same data, based on different times and days. For the most part, Accumulo's data model borrowed much of the data model of BigTable, but added the Visibility element to provide data-oriented security — it will return only cells whose visibility labels are satisfied by the credentials of the user/application running a query.

THE DIFFERENCE BETWEEN THE DATA-LEVEL SECURITY IN ACCUMULO AND HBASE

HBase and Accumulo are similar — they are both Apache projects running implementations of BigTable over Hadoop. The security in HBase and the security in Accumulo provide data-level security in similar, but different, ways. As discussed in Chapter 10, HBase can provide access control to data on a per-table or per-column basis. At this point, it does not provide the cell security that Accumulo does, but there is currently work in Intel's distribution of Project Rhino, where HBase may soon offer cell-based security.

HBase easily integrates with Hadoop's security model (using Kerberos), and this approach is consistent with the rest of the Hadoop ecosystem. Accumulo, on the other hand, is newer as a top-level Apache project, and it includes an internal access control database, and it does not approach security in the same manner as the other tools in the Hadoop ecosystem.

Both HBase and Accumulo are popular. Because of its access control security features at the cell level, Accumulo is most popular in highly secure environments, and promises to offer solutions related to Mandatory Access Control (MAC) and differential security.

Most developers who are more familiar with relational databases are typically used to seeing tables that look like Table 12-1, which is a two-dimensional model.

TABLE 12-1: Example Data in Relational Data Model

NAME	UNIVERSITY	BIRTH STATE	SIGNATURE PHRASE
Billy	UCLA	West Virginia	"Brutal"
Jeff	UVA	New Jersey	"C'Mon Man"

In Accumulo's structure, the same data would look similar to Table 12-2, where data is stored with a fine degree of granularity, including visibility and a timestamp that enables you to track data that changes over time.

TABLE 12-2: Data in Accumulo Data Model

ROW ID	FAMILY	QUALIFIER	VISIBILITY	TIMESTAMP	VALUE
Billy	School	University	Public	20130503	UCLA
Billy	Birth Record	State of Birth	Admin	20120503	West Virginia
Billy	Greeting	Signature Phrase	Public	20120503	"Brutal"
Jeff	School	University	Public	20120503	UVA
Jeff	Birth Record	State of Birth	Admin	20120503	New Jersey
Jeff	Greeting	Signature Phrase	Public	20120503	"C'Mon Man"

Note that in Table 12-2, visibility is marked up with security labels. These labels can be added to a record, using AND/OR boolean logic. For example, you can come up with authorization policies similar to Table 12-3, where authorization credentials can be created and associated with users, restricting access to each cell in the table.

TABLE 12-3: Example Security Policies and Their Security Label Syntax

EXAMPLE POLICY FOR ACCESS TO A RECORD	SECURITY LABEL SYNTAX
Must be a Republican and a U.S. Citizen	Republican & USCitizen
Must either be a Police Officer, or must be both a U.S. Citizen and in the Armed Forces	Police Officer | (USCitizen & ArmedForces)
Must be a Project Manager and must be either in the FGM or White Oak organizations	ProjectManager & (FGM | White Oak)
Over 17 years old or parental consent	Over17 | parentalConsent

In the security model for Accumulo, users authenticate to trusted clients (which you, as a developer, can write), and the clients have the responsibility of authenticating the users and passing the proper authorization credentials to Accumulo. You have the option of integrating with your own authentication and authorization system, or you can use Accumulo's internal authentication/authorization component, where users and their authorization credentials can be stored. This section provides an example of each.

A Simple Example

Let's consider a university database example, where a university collects data from various departments and sub-organizations about their students. In this example, you have data coming from campus medical centers, the finance center, university administration, the sports facility, and the campus police. A wide variety of information is collected, and can be queried by the entire organization. You have a requirement to protect certain information, such as the following:

➤ Student medical test records should be seen only by medical personnel or the university administration.

➤ Students in college athletics have records related to sports records that should be visible only to their coaches, and sometimes also medical personnel.

➤ Payment records, grades, and sensitive information such as Social Security numbers should be visible only to university administration.

➤ Campus police records for students should be visible only to campus police or university administration.

For this example, let's load some sample data into an Accumulo database, as shown in Table 12-4. In this simple example, you have a student named Kirk Rest, who has a variety of information collected from a number of data sources in the university.

TABLE 12-4: Key/Values for University Data Example

ROW ID	FAMILY	QUALIFIER	VISIBILITY	TIMESTAMP	VALUE
Kirk Rest	SSN	999999999	ADMIN	20050612	
Kirk Rest	Phone	804-555-0005	ADMIN	20050612	
Kirk Rest	Address	111 Carson Ave, Richmond VA	ADMIN	20050612	
Kirk Rest	Weight	170	MEDICAL | COACH	20110711	
Kirk Rest	Running Test	10K	COACH	20110812	56
Kirk Rest	Running Test	10K	COACH	20110517	58
Kirk Rest	Running Test	5K	COACH	20110716	24

continues

TABLE 12-4 *(continued)*

ROW ID	FAMILY	QUALIFIER	VISIBILITY	TIMESTAMP	VALUE
Kirk Rest	Running Test	5K	COACH	20110612	27
Kirk Rest	Payment	Semester Payment	ADMIN	20111223	1000
Kirk Rest	Medical Test Report	Cholesterol	MEDICAL	20111222	200
Kirk Rest	Medical Test Report	Biopsy	MEDICAL	20111012	Negative
Kirk Rest	Grade	Organic Chem	ADMIN	20111201	A
Kirk Rest	Grade	Calculus 1	ADMIN	20111201	B
Kirk Rest	Grade	Radical Presbyterianism	ADMIN	20100612	D
Kirk Rest	Police Charge	Curfew Violation	ADMIN | POLICE	20071103	Pending Hearing
Kirk Rest	Police Charge	DUI Arrest	ADMIN | POLICE	20091104	Guilty

Let's say that this information is loaded into an Accumulo store that you have set up on a test Hadoop instance. To do this, you would use the Accumulo shell, which is a simple client that can be used to create and modify tables, as well as create users and assign authorization credentials to those users. Because this chapter is focused on security and not the finer details of Accumulo, this discussion won't address the details of loading the data.

> **NOTE** *Because different Accumulo versions work with different versions of Hadoop and Zookeeper, it is sometimes a challenge to set up! An easy way to get started with Accumulo is to work with an already configured virtual machine (VM). The Sqrrl company's website provides an Amazon Machine Instance (AMI) standalone as a quick start for Apache Accumulo, and the company also provides a preconfigured VM on Oracle VirtualBox. For more details, see their website at* `http://www.sqrrl.com/`, *and the VM at* `http://blog.sqrrl.com/post/40578606670/quick-accumulo-install/`.

Accumulo is optimized to quickly retrieve values for keys. To do this, an Accumulo client that you develop (or, in this case, the client is the Accumulo shell) creates a *scanner* that iterates over values. As you can see in Listing 12-1, the `scan` command enables you to iterate over the values in the new table you created — `universitydata` (as root, who was assigned blanket access to everything in the table).

LISTING 12-1: Viewing the data

```
root@accumulo universitydata> scan

Kirk Rest Address:111 Carson Ave, Richmond VA [ADMIN]
Kirk Rest Grade:Calculus 1 [ADMIN]     B
Kirk Rest Grade:Organic Chem [ADMIN]     A
Kirk Rest Grade:Radical Presbyterianism [ADMIN]     D
Kirk Rest Medical Test Report:Cholesterol [MEDICAL]     200
Kirk Rest Nedical Test Report:Biopsy [MEDICAL]     Negative
Kirk Rest Payment:Semester Payment [ADMIN]     1000
Kirk Rest Phone:8045550005 [ADMIN]
Kirk Rest Police Charge:Curfew Violation [ADMIN|POLICE]     Pending Hearing
Kirk Rest Police Charge:DUI Arrest [ADMIN|POLICE]     Guilty
Kirk Rest Running Test:10K [COACH]     56
Kirk Rest Running Test:5K [COACH]     27
Kirk Rest SSN:99999999 [ADMIN]
Kirk Rest Weight:170 [MEDICAL|COACH]
```

To demonstrate an example of cell visibility, you create the following users:

➤ A doctor (drhouse), to whom you assign the MEDICAL role

➤ An administrator (denyseAccountant), to whom you assign the ADMIN role

➤ A coach (coachTark), to whom you assign the COACH role

➤ A police chief (chiefDoug), to whom you assign the POLICE role

As shown in Listing 12-2, you use the shell to assign permissions for all of these users to be able to read the table (granting them each the Table.READ privilege), and assign them each the appropriate roles for visibility using the setauths command.

LISTING 12-2: Assigning permissions and user views

```
root@accumulo universitydata> grant Table.READ -t universitydata -u drhouse
root@accumulo universitydata> setauths -s MEDICAL -user drhouse

root@accumulo universitydata> grant Table.READ -t universitydata -u
    denyseAccountant
root@accumulo universitydata> setauths -s ADMIN -user denyseAccountant

root@accumulo universitydata> grant Table.READ -t universitydata -u coachTark
root@accumulo universitydata> setauths -s COACH -user coachTark

root@accumulo universitydata> grant Table.READ -t universitydata -u chiefDoug
root@accumulo universitydata> setauths -s POLICE -user chiefDoug
```

Finally, to show that Accumulo will now protect access to the table, you log in as each user using the Accumulo shell. You scan (or iterate) over the universitydata table. Listing 12-3 shows how you might have logged in as the users coachTark, drHouse, denyseAccountant, and chiefDoug, iterated over the table, and the table provided access control based on the privileges of each user.

LISTING 12-3: Demonstrating roles and visibility for users

```
root@accumulo universitydata> user coachTark
Enter password for user coachTark: *********

coachTark@accumulo universitydata> scan
Kirk Rest Running Test:10K [COACH]      56
Kirk Rest Running Test:5K [COACH]       27
Kirk Rest Weight:170 [MEDICAL|COACH]


root@accumulo universitydata> user drhouse

Enter password for user drhouse: *******
drhouse@accumulo universitydata> scan

Kirk Rest Medical Test Report:Cholesterol [MEDICAL]     200
Kirk Rest Nedical Test Report:Biopsy [MEDICAL]      Negative
Kirk Rest Weight:170 [MEDICAL|COACH]

drhouse@accumulo universitydata> user denyseAccountant

Enter password for user denyseAccountant: ******
denyseAccountant@accumulo universitydata> scan

Kirk Rest Address:111 Carson [ADMIN]
Kirk Rest Grade:Calculus 1 [ADMIN]      B
Kirk Rest Grade:Organic Chem [ADMIN]      A
Kirk Rest Grade:Radical Presbyterianism [ADMIN]      D
Kirk Rest Payment:Semester Payment [ADMIN]      1000
Kirk Rest Phone:8045550005 [ADMIN]
Kirk Rest Police Charge:Curfew Violation [ADMIN|POLICE]      Pending Hearing
Kirk Rest Police Charge:DUI Arrest [ADMIN|POLICE]      Guilty
Kirk Rest SSN:999999999 [ADMIN]

denyseAccountant@accumulo universitydata> user chiefDoug
Enter password for user chiefDoug: *********
chiefDoug@accumulo universitydata> scan

Kirk Rest Police Charge:Curfew Violation [ADMIN|POLICE]      Pending Hearing
Kirk Rest Police Charge:DUI Arrest [ADMIN|POLICE]      Guilty
```

As you can see from Listing 12-3, Accumulo is able to restrict access based on the authorization controls of each user, which has been demonstrated by using the Accumulo shell. Now, let's build an Accumulo client in Java that will demonstrate the same level of access control for this example, integrating with identity and access management infrastructure in the enterprise.

As it pertains to integrating with enterprise infrastructure, Accumulo has a flexible model. As previously mentioned, it is the Accumulo client's responsibility to authenticate the user and retrieve the authorization credentials of the users, presenting this to Accumulo for processing. As long as the visibility of the data in tables in Accumulo is marked with the same attributes or roles in your enterprise attribute store, it will work nicely. If not, you will most likely need to do some processing of the attributes you pull from your attribute store in your client to ensure that they are exactly the same characters.

To demonstrate this, let's go through a simple example of how you would be able to write a very simple client that authenticates the user through the authentication mechanism of your choice, and pulls authorization credentials from the Attribute Service or LDAP directory of your choice.

Listing 12-4 shows an example of writing a Java class that connects to Accumulo. In order to connect, you must establish an Accumulo connection using the `Connector` class. To do that, you must first connect to the Zookeeper instance keeping track of Accumulo by instantiating a `ZookeeperInstance` class, which will return a connector.

LISTING 12-4: Example Accumulo client code

```java
import java.util.Collection;
import java.util.Collections;
import java.util.Map.Entry;

import org.apache.accumulo.core.client.Connector;
import org.apache.accumulo.core.client.ZooKeeperInstance;

import org.apache.accumulo.core.client.Scanner;
import org.apache.accumulo.core.data.Key;
import org.apache.accumulo.core.data.Range;
import org.apache.accumulo.core.data.Value;
import org.apache.accumulo.core.security.Authorizations;

public class QueryExample
{
  public static void main(String[] args) throws Exception
  {

    //Simple Example of the name of your accumulo instance & zookeeper
    ZooKeeperInstance inst = new ZooKeeperInstance("accumulo", "localhost");

    //Obviously this is just an example
    Connector connector = inst.getConnector("root", "secret");

    //Scan in the username and password for this simple example

    java.util.Scanner in = new java.util.Scanner(System.in);
    System.out.println("Username:");
    String username = in.nextLine();
    System.out.println("Password:");
    String password = in.nextLine();

    Authorizations auths = null;

    try
    {
        //An example of how you can interact with other systems (LDAP,etc)

        CustomAuthenticator authenticator = new CustomAuthenticator();
```

continues

LISTING 12-4 *(continued)*

```
            authenticator.authenticate(username,password);

            //Retrieve credentials from external system
            auths = authenticator.getAuthorizationInfo(username);
        }
        catch (Exception authenticationException)
        {
            System.out.println("Authentication Failure.");
            System.exit(-1);
        }

        // Search our university data example & print out everything

        Scanner scanner = connector.createScanner("universitydata", auths);
        for (Entry<Key,Value> entry : scanner) {
            System.out.println( entry.getKey().toString());
        }
    }
}
```

Once you establish a connection, you want to authenticate the user. In this case, for such a simple example, you grab it from the command line, and pass it to an external class called `CustomAuthenticator`, written simply to show that you can use another authentication mechanism and authorization mechanism outside of Accumulo. In that class, you pass the username and password you scanned in from the command line in that class's `authenticate()` method. If the user was successful in authenticating, you then pull the user's authorization credentials from an external store, returning the value in Accumulo's expected `org.apache.accumulo.core.security.Authorizations` class. Finally, you create a scanner to iterate over the values in the same table as shown in the earlier example, and simply print the results.

Listing 12-5 shows the results on the command line. In this example, you set up an external LDAP directory with a user called `joeUser` in the `ADMIN` role.

LISTING 12-5: Results of Accumulo client

```
Script started on Fri 03 May 2013 12:45:09 AM EDT
$ java QueryExample
13/05/03 00:45:16 INFO zookeeper.ZooKeeper:
    Client environment:zookeeper.version=3.4.3--1,
    built on 03/20/2012 16:15 GMT
13/05/03 00:45:16 INFO zookeeper.ZooKeeper: Client environment:host.name=ubuntu
13/05/03 00:45:16 INFO zookeeper.ZooKeeper:
    Client environment:java.version=1.6.0_27
13/05/03 00:45:16 INFO zookeeper.ZooKeeper:
    Client environment:java.vendor=Sun Microsystems Inc.
13/05/03 00:45:16 INFO zookeeper.ZooKeeper:
    Client environment:java.home=/usr/lib/jvm/java-6-openjdk-amd64/jre
13/05/03 00:45:16 INFO zookeeper.ZooKeeper: Client environment:java.class.path=.
```

```
13/05/03 00:45:16 INFO zookeeper.ZooKeeper:
    Client environment:java.library.path=/usr/lib/jvm/java-6-openjdk-
    amd64/jre/lib/amd64/server:/usr/lib/jvm/java-6-openjdk-
    amd64/jre/lib/amd64:/usr/lib/jvm/java-6-openjdk-
    amd64/jre/../lib/amd64:/usr/java/packages/lib/amd64:/usr/lib/x86_64-linux-
    gnu/jni:/lib/x86_64-linux-gnu:/usr/lib/x86_64-linux-
    gnu:/usr/lib/jni:/lib:/usr/lib
13/05/03 00:45:16 INFO zookeeper.ZooKeeper: Client environment:java.io.tmpdir=/tmp
13/05/03 00:45:16 INFO zookeeper.ZooKeeper: Client environment:java.compiler=<NA>
13/05/03 00:45:16 INFO zookeeper.ZooKeeper: Client environment:os.name=Linux
13/05/03 00:45:16 INFO zookeeper.ZooKeeper: Client environment:os.arch=amd64
13/05/03 00:45:16 INFO zookeeper.ZooKeeper:
    Client environment:os.version=3.2.0-29-generic
13/05/03 00:45:16 INFO zookeeper.ZooKeeper: Client environment:user.name=accumulo
13/05/03 00:45:16 INFO zookeeper.ZooKeeper:
    Client environment:user.home=/usr/lib/accumulo
13/05/03 00:45:16 INFO zookeeper.ZooKeeper:
    Client environment:user.dir=/usr/lib/accumulo/classes
13/05/03 00:45:16 INFO zookeeper.ZooKeeper: Initiating client connection,
    connectString=localhost sessionTimeout=30000
    watcher=org.apache.accumulo.core.zookeeper
    .ZooSession$AccumuloWatcher@6791d8c1
13/05/03 00:45:16 INFO zookeeper.ClientCnxn:
    Opening socket connection to server /127.0.0.1:2181
13/05/03 00:45:16 INFO client.ZooKeeperSaslClient:
    Client will not SASL-authenticate because the default JAAS
    configuration section 'Client' could not be found. If you are not
    using SASL, you may ignore this. On the other hand,
    if you expected SASL to work, please fix your JAAS configuration.
13/05/03 00:45:16 INFO zookeeper.ClientCnxn:
    Socket connection established to localhost/127.0.0.1:2181,
    initiating session
13/05/03 00:45:16 INFO zookeeper.ClientCnxn:
    Session establishment complete on server localhost/127.0.0.1:2181,
    sessionid = 0x13e6757677611f1, negotiated timeout = 30000
Username:
joeAdmin
Password:
******
Kirk Rest Address:111 Carson [ADMIN] 20050612 false
Kirk Rest Grade:Calculus 1 [ADMIN] 20111201 false
Kirk Rest Grade:Organic Chem [ADMIN] 20111201 false
Kirk Rest Grade:Radical Presbyterianism [ADMIN] 20100612 false
Kirk Rest Payment:Semester Payment [ADMIN] 20111223 false
Kirk Rest Phone:804 [ADMIN] 20050612 false
Kirk Rest Police Charge:Curfew Violation [ADMIN|POLICE] 20071103 false
Kirk Rest Police Charge:DUI Arrest [ADMIN|POLICE] 20091104 false
Kirk Rest SSN:99 [ADMIN] 20050612 false
```

The user that authenticated in this example, joeAdmin, was not stored in Accumulo like the users in earlier examples. As shown here, you could write a Java client to authenticate a user, pull authorization credentials from an enterprise store, and query Accumulo.

There is much more to Apache Accumulo — much more than has been covered in this section of this chapter. However, it is important to realize that for organizations that use Accumulo for data security, Accumulo is only one aspect of an enterprise security solution. Enterprise security requires defense-in-depth, and must cover the security of the entire data life cycle — not just when the data is stored in Hadoop.

Encryption at Rest

Encrypted data at rest in Hadoop is a topic that is being worked on in many different projects — some open source, and some commercial. Hadoop does not natively provide such functionality. Currently, a number of companies are protecting sensitive data in different distributions of Hadoop not only to protect the sensitive information, but also to comply with laws such as HIPAA and other security regulations. Many organizations want to use encryption at rest to protect against malicious users who might attempt to obtain unauthorized access to DataNodes.

Some of the solutions currently provided include Gazzang zNcrypt, which provides data security for Cloudera CDH distributions. Intel's distribution of Hadoop, released in early 2013, has been optimized to do encryption at rest when using their company's Xeon processors. There seem to be new solutions coming out every day — but so far, all of them are currently proprietary, or promise to tie you to a particular distribution of Hadoop. As mentioned in Chapter 10, Project Rhino (contributed by Intel to Apache) contains enhancements that include distributed key management and the capability to do encryption at rest. The Hadoop developer community is currently reviewing this for the inclusion in a future Hadoop distribution.

Regardless of the mechanisms that you can use to achieve encryption at rest for Hadoop, it is very important to also understand the unintentional effects of such functionality. If you need a solution for encryption at rest, keep in mind the impact that encryption will have on your performance. If you think your MapReduce jobs might be slower than desired now, imagine what encryption at rest will do to your performance. Intel's distribution of Hadoop is optimized to do encryption and decryption for use on machines with specific Intel processors that are optimized to do the encryption and decryption. Just as Intel's distribution was developed with its hardware accelerators in mind, it is also important for enterprise architects to weigh the cost of encryption at rest for their applications — if you indeed need such functionality, plan accordingly for performance.

For now, unless you are in dire need of encryption at rest, at this point you may want to avoid it for a few reasons. First of all, this is a functionality area that is very complex because of the distributed data and key management challenges. Secondly, enhancements in this area from Project Rhino may be forthcoming, and until then, there is the potential for you to be locked into a particular distribution or vendor. Finally, as mentioned, there are performance ramifications related to encryption at rest. If your data is so sensitive that you are exploring the possibility of encryption at rest, the next section may be a potential solution.

Network Isolation and Separation Approaches

As mentioned previously, organizations with confidential and sensitive data have traditionally used network isolation of their Hadoop clusters as an approach for meeting their security requirements. These organizations often control access to the individual clusters based on the authorization levels of the user, often using physical security as one protection mechanism. Others utilize a less-restrictive approach, separating the network, but allowing some transmissions from trusted servers and workstations to travel between the two networks.

Such approaches are still very viable options for a number of reasons:

➤ **Complexity of security integration** — If your security policies are so strict and your data is so sensitive that you will have to integrate an immense amount of non-native security controls into your Hadoop cluster, consider using network isolation, separating it from your other networks, and restricting access to only authorized users. If you do that, you will only have to worry about the releasability of resulting Hadoop data sets — and not your runtime Hadoop security. This will minimize your overall risk, and will most likely reduce costs.

➤ **Performance** — It is often said that "security is the enemy of performance." The more security mechanisms you throw at a solution, the slower it will often become. This is true with securing Hadoop, especially if you are considering using third-party tools to encrypt and decrypt data on HDFS at rest. Many people will choose a network isolation approach to simply avoid the performance penalty.

➤ **Data levels of differing sensitivity** — Some data in your organization may only be releasable to certain groups of people. If this is the case, the result sets of Hadoop jobs will be sensitive as well. Although some tools used with Hadoop (such as HBase and Accumulo) can provide a way of filtering access at the column level (HBase) and cell level (Accumulo), other tools used with Hadoop will not provide that level of security. If you are running Java MapReduce applications for building result sets, and are using a variety of different tools, it may be smart to consider separating clusters based on who can see them.

➤ **The evolving Hadoop security landscape** — A number of new products, releases, and distributions for Hadoop are providing new security features. As mentioned in Chapter 10, security enhancements for Hadoop may be forthcoming within the next year. These upcoming changes will affect enterprise applications using Hadoop, and so many organizations are choosing the network isolation model until they understand the ramifications of such changes.

➤ **Data security review before integration** — Because a network isolation approach does not provide real-time access to the data by enterprise applications on other networks, it would allow review and filtering of the material before it is used by enterprise applications, minimizing potential confidentiality and privacy breaches. (This is certainly a "double-edged sword" in that network isolation is typically a barrier to real-time Hadoop, and requires a process for releasing data sets for use by enterprise applications.)

Network isolation can be used in a number of ways in the security of enterprise applications. Figure 12-3 shows one way to achieve this. An organization creates a "data analytics" network, separate from the organization's enterprise network with a physical "air gap" that prevents any data from being transferred between the two networks. Data scientists with the appropriate access controls perform queries and MapReduce operations on the Hadoop cluster(s) in the data analytics network, and access to this network is controlled by physical security and/or authentication to the client machines used to perform queries.

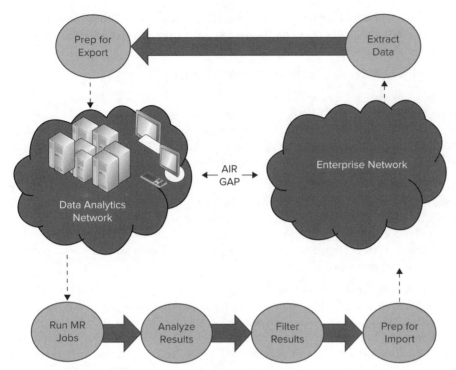

FIGURE 12-3: "Air gap" network isolation with import/export workflow

To support enterprise applications that utilize the results of these data sets, there is a significant workflow process that must be developed and utilized:

1. First, any data to be analyzed must be extracted from the proper databases and applications in the enterprise network, written to media, and brought into the separate network.

2. Once the data is prepared for analysis and loaded onto the cluster, Hadoop MapReduce jobs can be run until the results are reviewed.

3. Based on the results, the results must either be marked up with an authorization policy that can be controlled by an external enterprise application, or the results must be filtered so that sensitive, confidential, or privacy-protected data is removed.

4. Once this data set is filtered or marked up with an access control policy, the data set is written to media and imported into the enterprise application.

For many organizations, this is a cumbersome process because it involves a physical separation between the two networks, and it requires a workflow of exporting data from the original network, importing it into the data analytics network, and analyzing, filtering, and preparing the result set data for loading into an enterprise application. However, when the data is extremely sensitive, many organizations are taking this approach.

Because of the complexity involved, some organizations are moving to a similar model, but one that restricts traffic from trusted hosts in the enterprise network to the data analytics network, as shown in Figure 12-4. In this situation, the ETL process can be done over the network, removing the first step in the process described earlier.

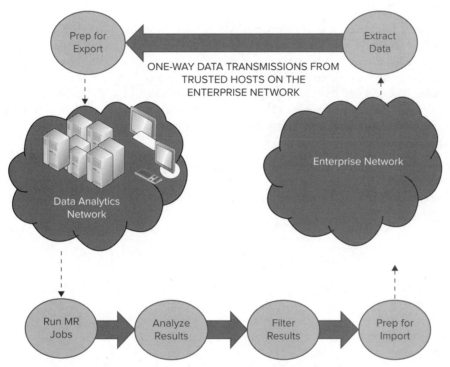

FIGURE 12-4: Network isolation with one-way transmissions

Some organizations that primarily utilize Apache Accumulo for controlling access to data perform the data-filtering results for the result sets that can be released to the enterprise network — for example, creating the "Enterprise Network User, who has credentials equal to the lowest authorization level of the network. Filtering data to be released based on such a user often makes the result set easier to post internally without fear of the unintentional release of information.

Network isolation can be used in countless other ways — these are just a few of them. Others involve isolating Hadoop clusters based on the type of data that they use, and some less-restrictive approaches involve allowing connections to and from machines in the enterprise network, utilizing ACLs to restrict access to only trusted hosts.

Each part of your solution for enterprise security will depend on your organization's security requirements — two organizations are seldom the same. Regardless, the examples and the guidance provided in this chapter should help you as you build your enterprise security solution.

SUMMARY

This chapter provided you with an enterprise view of security, focusing on the data life cycle from a security-policy and a data-centric perspective. It is important that security architects understand this big picture, while being able to address different aspects of enterprise security that Hadoop and complementary security tools provide.

This chapter began with a brief overview of security concerns for developing enterprise applications that utilize Hadoop. You learned about some security challenges that Hadoop itself does not address — including data-oriented security, differential privacy, and encryption at rest. You saw a number of approaches for building enterprise security solutions with Hadoop, and worked through some guidance and examples. You learned how to use Apache Accumulo for cell-level security, and gained some insight into encryption at rest and some of the offerings that are currently available. You also learned about some approaches related to network isolation used by many organizations that are concerned with exposing sensitive data.

Security is certainly an evolving topic for Hadoop, and an area where Hadoop will be growing in the next few years. Chapter 13 focuses on some other enhancements that are forthcoming for Hadoop, and discusses trends that are emerging today, and will continue to grow in the future.

13

Hadoop's Future

WHAT'S IN THIS CHAPTER?

- ➤ Learning about current and emerging DSLs for MapReduce
- ➤ Learning about faster and more scalable processing changes
- ➤ Reviewing security enhancements
- ➤ Understanding emerging trends

Hadoop is rapidly evolving. It seems that every week, news items appear telling about new Hadoop distributions being released that offer enhanced functionality, and new open source projects are released that utilize Hadoop. If you look at the JIRA enhancement requests for Hadoop at Apache (some of which were discussed in Chapter 10), you will see that the Hadoop of tomorrow will have much more functionality.

Over the past few years, new Domain Specific Languages (DSLs) have been developed for the simplification of Hadoop MapReduce programming, and this is a growth area of Hadoop — especially in the area of graph processing. Real-time Hadoop (as discussed at length in Chapter 9) is a growing trend that is here today, and something that will continue to grow in the future. As mentioned in Chapters 10 and 12, security is something that will continue to change and evolve. Although this book has touched on many of the things that will change and will continue to grow into the future, you should know about some additional areas covered in this chapter.

This chapter begins by highlighting the current trends of simplifying MapReduce programming with the use of DSLs. This approach typically shortens code development by operating on higher-level concepts suitable to particular problem domains, and by utilizing an easy-to-use API. You learn about the newer implementations of MapReduce run time introduced in Hadoop 2, which provides better scalability and performance for MapReduce execution.

In this chapter, you also learn about Tez — a new Hadoop run time that combines the power of MapReduce and Oozie into a single framework aimed at supporting general real-time implementation. This chapter also briefly highlights upcoming security changes. Finally, you learn about emerging trends in the use of Hadoop. As has been shown throughout this book, Hadoop can be used to solve many different problems. In this chapter, the focus is on growing trends of how organizations are using Hadoop now, and how organizations will be using it in the future.

Let's start by discussing DSLs and the role they play in Hadoop programming.

SIMPLIFYING MAPREDUCE PROGRAMMING WITH DSLs

So far, this book has concentrated on MapReduce — the main Hadoop programming model allowing you to split a task's execution across a cluster of machines. MapReduce enables the developer to fully utilize Hadoop's power, and even customize execution (as shown in Chapter 4) to better utilize Hadoop's capabilities. With all the power that MapReduce provides, it is a fairly low-level model, and it can often be challenging to implement for new Hadoop developers. One of the ways to simplify Hadoop development is to use DSLs developed for Hadoop.

Although entire books could be written about every DSL for Hadoop, this section gives you a quick "taste" of some of them to show how this growing area of Hadoop can lower the barriers to the learning curve of Hadoop for its users. This section highlights some DSLs that have been around for a long time (HiveQL and PigLatin, for example), and also features others that are new and emerging for Hadoop.

What Are DSLs?

A DSL is a programming language designed specifically to express solutions to problems in a specific domain. DSLs mimic the terminology and concepts used by experts in a domain. For example, the Structured Query Language (SQL) can be considered a DSL for the relational model. DSLs try to minimize the gap between the domain concepts that must be implemented and the underlying runtime system.

Some well-designed DSLs enable non-programmers to write their own "programs." Many casual SQL users know very little about the details of the underlying structure of a relational database, yet they are capable of using SQL queries to get the information they need. Another great example of a widely used DSL is the scripting language in Microsoft Excel, called Visual Basic for Applications (VBA). Although DSLs are geared toward non-programmers, they can still be an asset for developers, because DSLs enable developers to think in the same language as the domain experts. In practice, DSLs should make programmers far more productive compared to working with lower-level programming constructs.

DSLs are often not *Turing complete*, which effectively means that they can't be used to write arbitrarily complex algorithms in the same way as general-purpose programming languages. Instead, they are usually *declarative*, where the user expresses the desired outcome, and the implementation decides how to achieve that outcome. In SQL, for example, you declare the schemas of your data in tables and what operations to perform on that data through queries. In most relational databases, the runtime system decides how to store the data and how to satisfy your queries.

DSLs are also categorized by whether they are external or internal:

➤ An *external DSL* is implemented using the same tools used for other programming languages. A unique grammar is defined for an external DSL, and a custom compiler is written to parse programs in the language.

➤ An *internal DSL* (sometimes called an *embedded DSL*) is "hosted" in another, more general-purpose programming language (or DSL), meaning that it uses a stylized form of the host language's syntax, rather than having a unique grammar of its own.

Early adopters of Hadoop started inventing DSLs rather quickly. You may have heard of some of them — Hive, Pig, Clojure-Hadoop, Grumpy (Groovy Hadoop), Sawzall, Scoobi, Lingual, Pattern, Crunch, Scrunch — and the list keeps growing every day.

DSLs for Hadoop

Hadoop DSLs typically fall into several main categories:

➤ **SQL-based DSLs** — DSLs based on SQL (which may be loosely based on SQL and are "SQL-like") are most useable to non-programmers who have a database background. Using these DSLs, people who "think" in database language can accomplish data analytics tasks without having to think about MapReduce.

➤ **Data flow DSLs** — These DSLs expose the metaphor of data pipelines to filter, transform, and aggregate data as it flows through the pipeline.

➤ **Problem-specific programming languages** — These DSLs focus on a certain problem domain, and sometimes use different models for processing data. Graph processing is an example that models data as a graph (for example, friend connections in social networks), and performs computations over the graph.

Hive and SQL-based DSLs

You may already be familiar with Hive, which utilizes HiveQL, one of the first SQL-like DSLs on Hadoop. This is just one example of a SQL-oriented DSL that makes MapReduce easy to use for non-programmers. A SQL-like query tool for data on HDFS, it enables users to define tables with schemas for the data, and write queries that are implemented internally using MapReduce. Hive is not a relational database management system (RDBMS), because it has no concept of transactions or record-level CRUD (Create, Read, Update, and Delete). But it does provides a language (called HiveQL) that is easy for database users to understand. It puts the emphasis on querying — asking questions about data, and performing aggregations.

Although users new to Hadoop might be tempted to use Hive as a relational database, it is important to know that HiveQL commands are translated into MapReduce batch jobs. This makes Hive unsuitable for queries that need to be fast (although, there is work underway to make Hive much faster by decoupling it from MapReduce, as discussed later in this chapter). Hive was never meant to be a replacement for an enterprise data warehouse, but as a way to simplify working with the sets of data so that a person doesn't have to be a Java developer to process data sets and gain value from the data.

Facebook invented Hive and open-sourced it as an Apache project in 2008. Facebook's data analysts needed user-friendly, productive tools to work with the data Facebook was accumulating in Hadoop clusters. Because SQL knowledge was so widespread, a SQL-based tool was a logical choice. Hive is perhaps the most important tool driving Hadoop adoption, because it typically provides the lowest entry barrier for Hadoop newcomers.

Hive uses an external DSL (as classified previously). HiveQL has its own grammar, compiler, and run time. Most Hive queries are implemented as MapReduce jobs, but data definition language (DDL) statements that are used to create and modify databases, tables, and views don't require MapReduce. Hive stores this metadata information in a separate relational database (such as MySQL). Most queries trigger one or more MapReduce jobs to read and process the data in HDFS or another data store, via Hive's plug-in support for different data formats.

Let's explore the concept of Hive as a DSL with an example of server log data ingested into HDFS and partitioned by the year, month, and day. All the specific details of what's happening won't be addressed here, but just the highlights that illustrate the value of a powerful DSL. Listing 13-1 provides an example DDL table definition for server log data.

LISTING 13-1: Logs table definition

```
CREATE TABLE logs (
   severity    STRING,      -- e.g., FATAL, ERROR, ...
   server      STRING,      -- DNS name for the server
   processid   SMALLINT,    -- 2-byte integer
   message     STRING,      -- text of the actual message
   hour        TINYINT,     -- hour from the timestamp
   min         TINYINT,     -- minute from ...
   sec         TINYINT,     -- second ...
   msec        INT)         -- microseconds ...
PARTITIONED BY (            -- Also considered columns:
   year        SMALLINT,    -- year from the timestamp
   month       TINYINT,     -- month ...
   day         TINYINT)     -- day ...
STORED AS SEQUENCEFILE;     -- file format
```

The Table definition shown in Listing 13-1 is comprised of three main parts. The first part contains field definitions and their types (similar to an ordinary database table). The second part is specific to Hive, and specifies *data partitioning*. The data partitioning statement in Listing 13-1 says that the table will be comprised of several files — one for every day of logs. Finally, the third part of the table definition in Listing 13-1 specifies that every partition is stored as a separate sequence file.

Hive organizes the partitioned data into separate directories. If the "warehouse" directory is configured to be a warehouse in HDFS, then the directory structure for this partitioned table looks like what is shown in Listing 13-2.

LISTING 13-2: Partitions directory

```
. . .
/warehouse/logs/year=2013/month=4/day=13
/warehouse/logs/year=2013/month=4/day=14
/warehouse/logs/year=2013/month=4/day=15
. . .
```

As shown here, all the data for April 13 will be in the first directory shown. Now, consider an example query (Listing 13-3), which looks at what happened between noon and 1 p.m. on April 13.

LISTING 13-3: Example query

```
SELECT hour, min, sec, msec, severity, message
FROM logs
WHERE year = 2013 AND month = 4 AND day = 13 AND
      hour >= 12 AND hour <= 13
ORDER BY severity DESC, hour, min, sec, msec;
```

The HiveQL statement in Listing 13-3 should be fairly intuitive to anyone familiar with SQL. In contrast, writing this query in the Java MapReduce API is challenging, because implementation of the ORDER BY clause might require knowledge of the specialized programming idioms.

From this example, note that queries of logs will almost always be range-bound, as shown here with the WHERE clause that bounds the range of timestamps of interest. Because the data is already partitioned by year, month, and day, Hive knows it only needs to scan the files in the subset of directories (the one for the April 13, in this example), thus providing relatively fast results, even over a logs data set that could contain terabytes of data covering many years.

HiveQL does several essential things that a good DSL must do:

➤ It provides a concise, declarative way to state the structure of the information and how to work with it.

➤ The language is intuitive to domain experts (that is, data analysts). Hive hides the complexity of implementing storage and queries.

➤ It makes it easy to specify data organization hints (partitioning by timestamp, in this case) that improve query speeds.

➤ HiveQL imposes relatively little overhead compared to handwritten Java MapReduce code.

➤ It provides *extension hooks*, enabling you to plug in different formats and capabilities.

Hive enables you to extend its capabilities in many different ways:

➤ It allows you to specify different input formats and output formats.

➤ It allows you to use a custom serializer and deserializer (known as *SerDe*) for different file formats.

➤ It allows you to create user-defined functions (UDFs) that can be written in Java and called from a HiveQL statement.

➤ It also allows you to create custom mappers and reducers that you can put into your query.

Let's look at some examples of how Hive can be extended. If you look back at the DDL statement shown in Listing 13-1, it instructs Hive to store the data in the sequence file, and, by default, this uses the SequenceFile input format. For flexibility and extensibility, Hive enables a developer to easily plug in his or her own input format, which allows the reading of records that are stored in various formats and proprietary files. It also enables you to plug in your own output format, which formats query results. This hook has been used to integrate Hive with data stored in HBase, Cassandra, and other data stores.

As mentioned, Hive also enables you to support unique record formats by specifying a SerDe (serializer/deserializer) that knows how to parse an input record into columns, and optionally write output columns in the same format. Note that Hive makes a clean distinction between the input and output formats that understand how records are stored in files (or byte streams in general), and the SerDe understands how each record is parsed into columns.

A popular example of a record format is JavaScript Object Notation (JSON). Listing 13-4 provides a modification to the previous logs DDL statement for the data stored as JSON in plaintext files, where each JSON document is stored on a single line in the file.

LISTING 13-4: Table definition with JSON records

```
CREATE TABLE logs ( -- the
  severity    STRING,
  ...,
  hour        TINYINT,
  ...)
PARTITIONED BY (...)
STORED AS ROW FORMAT SERDE
  'org.apache.hadoop.hive.contrib.serde2.JsonSerde'
WITH SERDEPROPERTIES (
  "severity"="$.severity",
  ...,
  "hour"="$.timestamp.hour",
  ...);
```

In this table definition example, a JsonSerde class implements the Hive SerDe API, which is an important Hive feature that enables you to instruct Hive exactly how to process the record. In this example, Hive will call the JSON SerDe to parse each JSON record into columns using the mapping defined in the SERDEPROPERTIES specified in the table definition. SERDEPROPERTIES is a Hive feature that passes the specified key-value definitions to the specified SerDe interface. In this case, the $ references the JSON document, so $.timestamp.hour means "use the hour field inside the timestamp object inside the record," which will be used as the hour "column."

Finally, Hive also supports UDFs to extend the available operations on individual records and columns, or aggregations over them. With UDFs, you can write a Java function and it can be evaluated by a HiveQL statement. This can be helpful when Hive itself doesn't provide certain functionality that you need. For example, Hive does not provide "windowing" functions for doing aggregations over a moving "window" of the records — something that most RDBMS SQLs provide. A classic calculation used by stock traders is the moving average of a stock's closing price over a number of days, which reveals current and emerging trends more clearly. This is something that can be provided by a custom UDF.

Hive represents a great example of an Hadoop DSL that hides the complexity of MapReduce, and provides a widely understood language for working with data in Hadoop. For most scenarios, it imposes minimal overhead over handwritten Java MapReduce code, and it provides extension points for custom code to address most requirements not already covered by Hive. This approach abstracts the concepts of MapReduce from database engineers, enabling them to focus on their data problems and not programming.

Other SQL-based DSLs usage exists. Specialized Hadoop real-time query engines discussed in Chapter 9 (Cloudera Impala and Apache Drill) use SQL-based DSLs as their programming language.

Data Flow and Related DSLs

Data flow DSLs enable developers to represent data processing of large data sets in the form of *pipelines* comprised of filtering, transforming, and aggregating components. The best known example of such DSLs is used by Pig — a tool that is bundled with most Hadoop distributions. Pig uses a procedural data flow language that abstracts the MapReduce framework, but uses MapReduce underneath the covers.

Pig

Whereas Facebook invented Hive to enable analysts to work with Hadoop data using a familiar SQL DSL, Yahoo! invented Pig to make it easier to transform, filter, and aggregate data. Pig has a custom language called *PigLatin* that is not SQL-based, which means the learning curve is higher for experienced SQL users, and is best suited for developers.

Although Hive was mainly introduced for querying data, Pig was initially introduced for *Extract, Transform, and Load (ETL) processing.* With PigLatin, developers can specify how the data is loaded and where to checkpoint data in the pipeline, and it is highly customizable. However, the features of Pig and Hive overlap so much that you can actually use both languages for querying and ETL.

To demonstrate the common functionality between Pig and Hive let's consider an example query that groups daily stock records for AAPL (Apple) by year, and then averages over the closing price, suggesting how AAPL's stock trends year-over-year. Listing 13-5 shows a Hive query for this example. It's fairly straightforward SQL.

LISTING 13-5: Hive implementation of Apple query

```
SELECT year(s. YYYY-MM-DD), avg(s.close)
FROM stocks s
WHERE s.symbol = 'AAPL'
GROUP BY year(s. YYYY-MM-DD);
```

Unlike Hive, Pig does not have a DDL. As a result, the equivalent Pig version shown in Listing 13-6 starts by reading the data from a tab-delimited file.

LISTING 13-6: Pig implementation of Apple query

```
aapl = load '/path/to/AAPL.tsv' as (
YYYY-MM-DD:        chararray,
  ...,
  close:        float,
  ...);
by_year = group aapl by SUBSTRING(YYYY-MM-DD, 0, 4);
year_avg = foreach by_year generate
            group, AVG(aapl.close);
-- Dump to console:
dump year_avg;
```

In Listing 13-6, you can see the familiar GROUP BY operation from SQL, while foreach a generate b is the projection operator, equivalent to SELECT b FROM a in SQL. Note that when you grouped over aapl, generating a new relation called by_year, Pig named the first field group, which contains the year values over which you grouped. Pig named the second field aapl (the name of the relation you grouped over), which holds the grouped records. So, the expression foreach by_year generate group, AVG(aapl.close) really means, "iterate over the records in by_year, and project the year (group field) and the average of the group for each year."

Pig is informally described as a data flow language, because you define a sequence of statements that describe each step in the processing of the data, from its source and original schema to the final output.

Listing 13-7 shows an example of the Word Count program implementation, written in Pig.

LISTING 13-7: Pig implementation of Word Count

```
inpt = LOAD '/path/to/input' using TextLoader  AS (line:chararray);
words = FOREACH inpt GENERATE flatten(TOKENIZE(line)) AS word;
grpd = GROUP words BY word;
cntd = FOREACH grpd GENERATE group, COUNT(words);
STORE cntd INTO '/path/to/output';
```

It looks like this implementation contains a sequence of "variable = value" statements, but in reality, each line defines a relation (in the relational model sense of the word) on the right-hand side, and an alias (or name) for the relation on the left-hand side.

This implementation first loads the data, treating each line of text as a record with a single field named line of type chararray (that is, a string) in the schema for input. Next, it iterates over each record, tokenizing the text into words and "flattening" the words into individual records. Then, it groups the words, so that each group contains all the occurrences for a given word. Finally, it projects out each word (the field holding the word is now named group) and the size of each group (the field holding the group's contents is given the name of the grouped-over relation, namely words). You store the results to an output path.

Pig is a natural fit for data flows like this, but it also has all the conventional relational operations that Hive contains (with some exceptions), including GROUP BY, JOIN, PROJECTION, FILTERING (that is, WHERE clauses), limiting, and so on.

Like Hive, Pig is an external DSL with its own grammar and compiler. It is also not a Turing-complete language — so, for example, general looping is not supported (apart from iteration through the records). Also, like Hive, Pig supports *plug-in file formats* and UDFs, but Pig supports writing UDFs in several languages, including Python, Ruby, and JavaScript, in addition to Java.

Pig's main benefit over Hive is the greater flexibility of the step-by-step specification of the data flow. Whereas database users prefer Hive, programmers often prefer Pig because it looks and feels more like a conventional programming language.

Now let's turn to DSLs based on a Java virtual machine (JVM) that expose higher-level abstractions than Hadoop's Java API for MapReduce. Note that a JVM is being used here rather than Java, because, as you'll see, some DSLs use other languages running on the JVM besides Java.

Cascading and Scalding

Cascading is the most popular Java DSL on top of the low-level MapReduce API. It was introduced in late 2007 as a DSL to implement functional programming for large-scale data workflows. Cascading provides a Turing-complete, internal or embedded DSL for MapReduce programming, with explicit metaphors for sequencing pipes together into data flows. Cascading hides many of the details of the lower-level API, enabling the developer to focus on the problem at hand.

Cascading is based on a "plumbing" metaphor to assemble pipelines to split, merge, and join streams of data, performing operations on them. With Cascading, a data record is called a *tuple*, a pipeline is called a *pipe assembly*, and the records going through the pipeline is called a *tuple stream*. Using the plumbing analogy, Cascading defines workflows out of familiar plumbing elements, such as pipes, taps, and traps.

➤ A *pipe* connects the main elements of the workflow (or pipeline), and defines what work should be done against the tuple stream passing through it. Pipes consist of types Each (applying a function or filter), GroupBy (which groups streams on tuple fields), CoGroup (which joins a common set of values), Every (which applies an aggregator or sliding window operation), and SubAssembly (which combines other pipe assemblies).

➤ A *tap* represents a resource, or a connection to a physical data source in a data flow. A source tap is typically the *input tap* (where you are reading data from), and a sink tap is the *output tap* (where you are writing data).

➤ A *trap* is like a sink tap — it is a place to write data that results in a failed operation, enabling you to continue processing your data without losing track of the data that caused a fault.

Figure 13-1 shows an example of a Cascading pipeline, representing the familiar Word Count example.

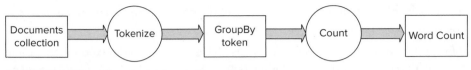

FIGURE 13-1: Word Count workflow in Cascading

The workflow in Figure 13-1 has two taps — an input tap (receiving a collection of documents) and an output tap (which produces word counts). The pipeline also has two functions — a tokenize and a count function (which is an aggregator), and the workflow has a `GroupBy` pipe assembly. Listing 13-8 shows a version of a Word Count implementation written using Cascading.

LISTING 13-8: Cascading implementation of Word Count

```
import org.cascading.*;
// other imports...
public class WordCount {
  public static void main(String[] args) {
    // Set up app properties.
    Properties properties = new Properties();
    FlowConnector.setApplicationJarClass(properties, WordCount.class);

    // Define the input and output "taps".
    Scheme sourceScheme = new TextLine(new Fields("line"));
    Scheme sinkScheme = new TextLine(new Fields("word", "count"));
    String inputPath  = args[0];
    String outputPath = args[1];
    Tap source = new Hfs(sourceScheme, inputPath);
    Tap sink   = new Hfs(sinkScheme, outputPath, SinkMode.REPLACE);

    // Connect the pipes for the data flow.
    Pipe assembly = new Pipe("wordcount");
    // Regular expression to tokenize into words.
    String regex = "(?<!\\pL)(?=\\pL)[^ ]*(?<=\\pL)(?!\\pL)";
    Function function = new RegexGenerator(new Fields("word"), regex);
    assembly = new Each(assembly, new Fields("line"), function);
    assembly = new GroupBy( assembly, new Fields("word"));
    Aggregator count = new Count(new Fields("count"));
    assembly = new Every(assembly, count);

    FlowConnector flowConnector = new FlowConnector( properties );
    Flow flow = flowConnector.connect( "word-count", source, sink, assembly);
    flow.complete();
  }
}
```

The code begins by setting up the application properties and source. It then sinks "taps." The pipes are joined together to create the data flow. Note that where SQL has keywords for operations like group by and projection, and functions for counting, Cascading encapsulates these operations as Java classes. Like the previous Pig script (Listing 13-7), you loop over "each" line, tokenizing into words (using a regular expression this time), then grouping over the words, counting the group sizes, and finally writing the results to the output tap.

This example shows how Cascading focuses on the relational operations required for the algorithm. There is much less framework boilerplate here than you have seen in the typical MapReduce "word count" examples that are used to demonstrate how MapReduce works.

> **NOTE** *For an example of a much more complex data flow, see the "CMU Workshop on CoPA (Cascading + City of Palo Alto Open Data)," available at* https://github.com/Cascading/CoPA/wiki, *which shows how to use Cascading and Hadoop to clean up raw, unstructured open data for parks, streets, and tree data. Workshop suggests several applications that could be built with this data, and provides an example application.*

Although Cascading is a Java API, APIs are now available for other languages that use Cascading. The list includes Scalding for Scala, Cascalog for Clojure, PyCascading for Python, and others. Some of these APIs add enhancements not found in the Java API. For example, Cascalog adds a logic-based query capability inspired by Datalog, while Scalding adds math libraries that are useful for graph-traversal problems and many machine-learning algorithms.

Listing 13-9 shows a version of Word Count written in Scalding.

LISTING 13-9: Scalding implementation of Word Count

```
import com.twitter.scalding._
class WordCountJob(args: Args) extends Job(args) {
  TextLine(args("input"))
    .read
    .flatMap('line -> 'word) {
      line: String =>
          line.trim.toLowerCase.split("\\W+")
    }
    .groupBy('word) { group => group.size('count) }
  }
  .write(Tsv(args("output"))) // tab-delim. output
}
```

As the `import` suggests in Listing 13-9, Scalding was developed at Twitter. Without explaining all the details of Scala syntax, let's note a few important things.

First, the code is terse — and dramatically smaller than the Java counterparts. With some exceptions, this code looks like typical Scala code for working with the built-in API for smaller, in-memory data collections.

Next, the relational operations (like grouping) are now function calls, not classes. The line `.groupBy('word) { group => group.size('count)` means call the `groupBy` function on the output of the previous function (pipeline step). Grouping, in this case, is done over the field-named word. Additionally, an anonymous function is passed to `groupBy` that takes each group as an argument and returns the size of the group, labeling that value as a field-named count. The schema of the data output from this step (and written in tab-delimited format to the output) contains each word and its count.

What does `flatMap` do in Listing 13-9? It represents the map phase of a MapReduce job. In mathematics, mapping is actually always one-to-one, meaning one output element for each input element. MapReduce relaxes this constraint, allowing zero-to-many output elements per input element. This is exactly what `flatMap` actually means, too. The anonymous function passed to `flatMap` outputs a collection of zero-to-many elements for each input element from the original collection, and then `flatMap` "flattens" the nested collections into one "flat" collection. Hence, you have really been working with `FlatmapReduce` all along.

Crunch and Scrunch

Another MapReduce DSL for MapReduce is called Crunch, and was modeled after Google's FlumeJava, using a number of small primitive operations for working on pipelines of enormous amounts of data. Crunch is based on three data abstractions: `PCollection<T>` (for parallelized collections of data having a certain type `T`), `PTable<K,V>` (for parallelized tables of key-value data of types `K` and `V`, respectively), and `PGroupedTable<K,V>` (for the output of group-by operations). Parallel implementations of operations for working with records in these structures across a cluster also exist.

Listing 13-10 shows a Word Count implementation written in Crunch.

LISTING 13-10: Crunch implementation of Word Count

```
// import statements...
public class WordCount {
  public static void main(String[] args) throws Exception {
    // Setup the pipeline and the input.
    Pipeline pipeline = new MRPipeline(WordCount.class);
    PCollection<String> lines =
      pipeline.readTextFile(args[0]);

    // Tokenize the lines into words in parallel.
    PCollection<String> words = lines.parallelDo(
      "my splitter", new DoFn<String, String>() {
      public void process(
        String line, Emitter<String> emitter) {
        for (String word : line.split("\\s+")) {
          emitter.emit(word);
        }
      }
    }, Writables.strings());

    // Count the words.
    PTable<String, Long> counts = Aggregate.count(words);

    pipeline.writeTextFile(counts, args[1]);
    pipeline.run();
  }
}
```

As you can see from the example in Listing 13-10, Crunch enables the developer to explicitly use more of the low-level Java Hadoop APIs (see, for example, the use of `Writables`). It also provides the capability to write data using the Avro type. It is simple to use, and for developers who know Java, it is easy to learn.

The Scala version of Crunch is called Scrunch. Listing 13-11 shows a Word Count implementation in Scrunch.

LISTING 13-11: Scrunch implementation of Word Count

```
// imports...
class WordCountExample {
  val pipeline = new Pipeline[WordCountExample]

  def wordCount(fileName: String) = {
    pipeline.read(from.textFile(fileName))
      .flatMap(_.toLowerCase.split("\\W+"))
      .filter(!_.isEmpty())
      .count
  }
}
```

Listing 13-11 shows the same sort of elegant, concise expression of the data flow as it was for the Scalding DSL. The group by example shown for Cascading and Scalding would be similar in size and complexity.

As mentioned, Crunch and Scrunch place greater emphasis on statically typing the fields in the schemas, compared to Cascading. It's not clear that either static or dynamic typing offers demonstrable advantages over the other, but the differences might influence your tool selection, based on your own preferences.

Graph Processing

The final DSL category to discuss is less widely used today, but you will see more of these over time — DSLs that model data as a graph and run parallel algorithms over the graph. The number of use cases is huge.

Online social graphs are rapidly growing in size, and there is a growing demand to analyze them. Online social networking sites such as Facebook, LinkedIn, Google+, and Twitter, and even e-mail sites like Yahoo! and Google, have hundreds of millions of users, and analyzing people and their connections plays a big role in advertising and personalization. Google was one of the first to capitalize on the importance of analyzing graphs, using an algorithm called PageRank for their search engine. Invented by Larry Page and Sergey Brin (the founders of Google), the algorithm orders search results by "link popularity" — the more sites that are linked to a web page, the more relevant the result. Although one of the many factors in determining relevance rankings, the algorithm is used in all of Google's web search tools.

A lot of other problems require link, graph, and network analysis, and today, Facebook seems to be leading the way for Hadoop in this area. Using graph-based DSLs will be a growing area for Hadoop in the future.

So far, graph processing systems for Hadoop are fairly new because scalable graph processing across a cluster of computers is closer to the bleeding edge of research, where a number of problems such as the following are the subject of active investigation:

➤ How do you partition a potentially dense graph across a cluster?

➤ How can you cut the graph for distribution across the cluster so that the number of arcs bridging machines is minimized?

➤ How do you communicate updates efficiently across those links that span machines?

There is currently much active work and a growing amount of interest in the practical applications of graph processing in Hadoop. This section just briefly mentions the approaches and projects in this sector of the "DSL space," and you should investigate further on your own.

As usual, Google research papers are leading the way, and Apache is following. *Pregel* (http://googleresearch.blogspot.com/2009/06/large-scale-graph-computing-at-google.html) is a large-scale graph system in use at Google that is used for graph data analysis. One of Apache's projects, *Giraph* (which is discussed later in this section), is the open source counterpart to Pregel that uses Hadoop. It is used by Facebook to analyze social graphs formed by users, and their various connections with friends and groups.

Graph processing systems such as Pregel and Giraph are based on a parallel processing model called *Bulk Synchronous Parallel* (BSP), where communications between graph nodes are processed currently in lock-step. To demonstrate how BSP works, at time t0, all nodes send messages to other connected nodes at the same time. All nodes update their states, as needed, followed by another round of messages at time t1, and so on. Barrier synchronization occurs after each sending of a message.

Based on this concurrent communications model, you might think that MapReduce would be a poor fit for this highly iterative model — and you would be correct. Natively implementing BSP in MapReduce alone would require a separate MapReduce job per iteration of BSP with terrible overhead!

However, graph processing systems are beginning to utilize Hadoop's data storage and some MapReduce operations in parallel with their own BSP calculations. A number of graph processing systems exist, but let's focus on two open source systems that work with Hadoop in one way or another:

➤ *Giraph* is an Apache project that is an implementation of Google's Pregel, and implements BSP on top of HDFS. In Giraph, you launch a conventional MapReduce job, but Giraph internally handles the iteration steps using the context of a Vertex, keeping the graph state in memory without chaining together inefficient MapReduce jobs. Giraph leverages the resource management infrastructure of Hadoop and HDFS for data storage, but it works around the inefficiencies of using MapReduce for BSP. Giraph also incorporates Zookeeper to provide a fault-tolerant, centralized coordination service.

➤ *Hama* is also an Apache project. Like Giraph, it is a BSP computing framework that runs over the top of HDFS. However, Hama bypasses MapReduce altogether, spinning up its own set of computing processes across the cluster. Hama avoids the limitations of fitting within the Hadoop resource scheduling approach and MapReduce job model. But organizations may be reluctant to introduce an additional set of cluster processes that compete with MapReduce for resources, rather than attempting to work within that framework. For that reason, clusters doing this type of analysis are typically dedicated to the use of Hama.

There is definitely future growth potential for graph DSLs using Hadoop.

This brief summary of DSLs for Hadoop demonstrates that, in addition to the base MapReduce framework, there is a rich set of DSLs available to write Hadoop jobs more productively using tools that best suit the needs of the user. New Hadoop DSLs are created on a regular basis. Cascading, for example, just introduced two new DSLs:

➤ **Lingual** — A new SQL DSL

➤ **Pattern** — A new machine-learning DSL

Now that you know how DSLs enable you to simplify MapReduce usage, the next section takes a look at advances of MapReduce itself, allowing it to utilize Hadoop resources more efficiently.

FASTER, MORE SCALABLE PROCESSING

As discussed throughout this book, the MapReduce infrastructure implementation is effectively a monolithic one, and a major component of this implementation is the JobTracker (see Chapter 3 for more details), which is responsible for both resource management and job scheduling and monitoring. Among other things, implementers have found that the JobTracker implementation is very complex and can suffer from some drawbacks, including increased memory consumption, a rigid threading model, and problems related to scalability, reliability, and performance.

As a result of this analysis, the Hadoop community did a complete overhaul of MapReduce — sometimes called "NextGen MapReduce," "MapReduce 2.0" (MRv2), or Yet Another Resource Negotiator (YARN), which is covered in this section. After this overhaul was introduced, a new project called "Tez" (which is Hindi for "speed") was introduced into Apache Incubation, and it promises to dramatically speed performance in Hadoop. You learn more about both of these later in this chapter.

> **NOTE** *It is important to note that although what is described in the next section is sometimes called "MapReduce 2," the changes described do not change the actual MapReduce programming model, or the APIs that developers use as described throughout this book!*

Apache YARN

The Hadoop developer committee decided that the solution for some deficiencies in the original MapReduce was to split up resource management and job scheduling into separate daemons. A new global resource manager called YARN splits the functionality of a JobTracker into two separate daemons:

➤ A global *Resource Manager (RM)* that consists of a Scheduler and an Applications Manager.

➤ An *Application Master (AM)* that provides support for a specific application, where an application is either a single job in the classical sense of MapReduce jobs, or a Directed Acyclic Graph (DAG) of jobs. (Compare this to Oozie, described in Chapters 6 through 8.)

Splitting up the functionality of the JobTracker provides more flexibility and better performance.

YARN's resource management is based on a very general resource model for applications. Resources are organized in the containers that provide a specific number of resources (memory, CPU, and so on). As with everything else in Hadoop, YARN's resource management and execution framework is implemented by leveraging the master/slave architecture. Slaves, or Node Managers (NMs), run on every node. They manage containers on a specific node, they monitor a node's execution, and they report resource availability to the Master — called the Resource Manager. The Master is responsible for arbitrating resources among all the applications in the system. (Compare this to the HDFS architecture described in Chapter 2.)

Execution of the specific application is controlled by the Application Master. An Application Master is fully distributed — there is an instance of an Application Master running on every node. The Application Master is responsible for splitting an application into multiple tasks and negotiating with the Resource Manager for execution resources (containers). Once resources are allocated, the Application Master interacts with the Node Manager(s) to place, execute, and monitor an individual application's tasks.

The overall application flow is shown in Figure 13-2.

It contains the following steps:

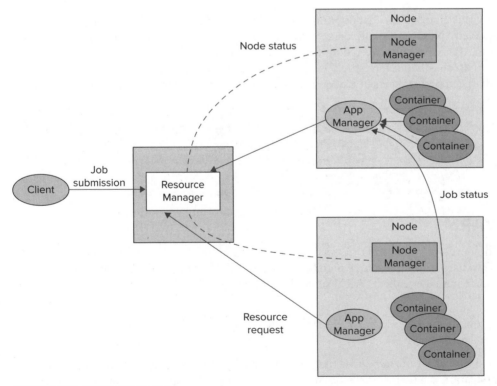

FIGURE 13-2: YARN architecture

1. A client program submits the application, including the necessary specifications to launch the application-specific Application Master. As part of the application submission, the client must provide sufficient information to the Resource Manager to launch the application's first container — the Application Master. The required information (application submission context) includes local files/jars that must be available for an application to run, the actual command that must be executed (with the necessary command-line arguments), any UNIX environment settings (optional), and so on. Effectively, it is necessary to describe the UNIX process(es) that must be launched by an Application Master.

2. The Resource Manager allocates a required container for an Application Master, and then launches the Application Master.

3. During the startup, the Application Master registers with the Resource Manager. This allows the client program to query the Resource Manager for Application Master details, including its address. After getting these details, a client can directly communicate with its own Application Master.

4. Once the Application Master is up and running, it examines an application request and negotiates appropriate resource containers required for application execution.

5. Once the required container(s) is allocated, the Application Master launches it by providing the container launch specification to the Node Manager.

6. During execution, application code provides necessary information (progress, status, and so on) to its Application Master. This information is also available to the client, which communicates directly with the Application Master.

7. Once the application is complete, the Application Master releases resources, deregisters itself, and shuts down, releasing its own container.

The important thing to notice about YARN is that it does not change the actual MapReduce programming model (the name MapReduce 2, used for YARN, is an unfortunate and misleading name) or the APIs that are used by developers. It simply provides a new resource management model and implementation that is used to execute MapReduce jobs. As a result, in the most simplistic case, existing MapReduce applications will work as is, but will require recompiling.

YARN can be used for the creation of new frameworks and execution models (in addition to MapReduce) that can leverage both the compute power of an Hadoop cluster and its rich data storage models to solve specific new classes of problems. Such new frameworks can leverage YARN resource management, but provide a new implementation of the Application Manager. As of this writing, the following projects have either ported or are in the process of porting their implementation to YARN:

➤ Spark (an open source cluster computing system)

➤ Apache Hama (the graph analytic framework described earlier in this chapter)

➤ Apache Giraph (the graph analysis framework described earlier in this chapter)

➤ Open MPI (an open source project for high-performance computing)

➤ Storm (an open source, distributed, real-time computation system described in Chapter 9)

➤ Apache S4 (an Apache project similar to Storm that provides real-time events processing)

The YARN architecture allows for the coexistence of multiple Application Managers sharing the same Hadoop cluster, as well as the data residing on this cluster. This simplifies data-level integration between multiple frameworks residing on the same Hadoop cluster.

Executing MapReduce applications using YARN improves scalability, but the MapReduce programming model does not fully utilize YARN capabilities, especially the built-in DAG support. The use of MapReduce is typically supplemented by Oozie for the orchestration of individual MapReduce jobs. Although this approach works well for batch applications, it suffers from the overhead of passing data through HDFS and the application's start-up time for real-time Hadoop applications.

Some of these shortcomings are eliminated in the new Hadoop execution framework called Tez.

Tez

Tez provides a general-purpose, highly customizable framework, which natively supports the orchestration of individual jobs into DAG. Tez doesn't just execute resources for individual MapReduce jobs, but does so for the whole graph of jobs, resulting in much faster performance than Oozie-orchestrated MapReduce jobs. The faster performance using Tez is achieved by the elimination of the overhead involved with launching multiple jobs, and it can meet requirements for human-interactive response times and high throughput at petabyte scale. (Compare this to the definition of real-time processing provided in Chapter 9.)

Originally created in support of the Stinger initiative, with the goal of making Apache Hive 100 times faster, Tez provides a single underlying framework to support both latency and throughput-sensitive applications. Consequently, it eliminates the necessity for multiple frameworks and systems to be installed, maintained, and supported, thus providing significant cost savings for the enterprise.

Tez was contributed to Apache in early 2013 by Hortonworks, and entered the Incubation stage. It is a very active project with many involved developers working on issues. Tez has a bright future for real-time applications for Hadoop.

SECURITY ENHANCEMENTS

As described in Chapter 10, the Hadoop community is working on many security enhancements. With the addition of new cryptographic codecs, a new token-based authentication mechanism that supports more authentication protocols, a unified authorization system that supports Attribute Based Access Control (ABAC) and supports policy enforcement using open standards and XACML, and changes to HBase to allow cell-level authorization, Hadoop will be able to move from isolated cluster environments with perimeter-level security to very secure deployments that can meet the requirements of highly secure environments.

> **NOTE** *For more information, see the "Security Enhancements with Project Rhino" section in Chapter 10.*

EMERGING TRENDS

This book has certainly covered many trends in Hadoop. Though the authors certainly don't have a crystal ball, they do see the following as key areas that will grow in the future:

➤ **Real-time Hadoop** — This trend is obviously here today, and it will continue. As mindsets shift from viewing Hadoop as a batch-mode processing system, Hadoop's use in the future (especially with some of the recent and emerging performance and scalability improvements) will be real-time analytics with human-response times. Jobs that you may be accustomed to taking a long time will be capable of being performed rapidly. This will play out on several different fronts — fraud detection and analysis for transactions, security vulnerability analysis and anomaly detection for real-time events, and on-demand analytics processing with other tools in the Hadoop ecosystem.

➤ **Graph analytics and new algorithms beyond MapReduce** — If you follow the brief history of Hadoop's beginnings, you can certainly see Google's influence. Google's use of new graph algorithms for highly scalable and distributed graph analysis has triggered more interest in distributed algorithms other than MapReduce. Because Apache Giraph (discussed earlier in this chapter) is an open source implementation of Google's high-performance graph analytics platform (Pregel), and because Facebook is using Giraph for graph analytics on its social network, there is no question that this will be a major growth area for Hadoop. Apache Hama (also discussed earlier in this chapter), utilizes HDFS storage, but uses other graph algorithms with Hadoop. This trend will continue.

➤ **Machine learning** — Although you didn't read much about it in this book, this is a growing topic. With projects like Apache Mahout and Pattern, a Cascading DSL for machine learning, predictive modeling and machine learning will be used more and more with Hadoop for common use cases like recommendations, fraud detection, and security vulnerability detections.

➤ **Higher-level abstractions and DSLs** — Earlier in this chapter, you learned about the power of DSLs for Hadoop, and how they simplify programming. The learning curve for using MapReduce and Hadoop is greatly reduced with the use of such languages and tools, and this trend will continue to grow. Although there can certainly be a performance penalty related to the use of some of these tools, as Hadoop's processing gets faster, more data scientists and domain experts will be able to perform data analytics with tools focused specifically to their domains, removing the barrier to entry. It could be that this will be so common that data scientists might not even know that they are using Hadoop!

Hadoop is evolving quickly and has a bright future. With the ongoing enhancements shown in the proliferation of new projects, performance improvements, security, and DSLs, new directions are quickly approaching, and it is an exciting time to be an Hadoop developer!

SUMMARY

This chapter highlighted the growing trend of using DSLs to simplify MapReduce programming. You learned about YARN and Tez, which will drastically improve the scalability and performance of Hadoop. You also learned about upcoming security changes, and emerging trends seen in Hadoop's future.

APPENDIX

Useful Reading

No matter how much the authors have tried, it is virtually impossible to cover the Hadoop ecosystem in a single book. This appendix provides additional reading recommendations that you might find useful. They are organized by the main topics covered in the book.

STORING AND ACCESSING HADOOP DATA

"Apache HBase Book." http://hbase.apache.org/book.html.

"Bloom Filter." http://en.wikipedia.org/wiki/Bloom_filter.

"BloomMapFile — Fail-Fast Version of MapFile for Sparsely Populated Key Space." https://issues.apache.org/jira/browse/HADOOP-3063.

Borthakur, Dhruba. "Hadoop AvatarNode High Availability." http://hadoopblog .blogspot.com/2010/02/hadoop-namenode-high-availability.html.

Chang, Fay; Dean, Jeffrey; Ghemawat, Sanjay; Hsieh, Wilson C.; Wallach, Deborah A.; Burrows, Mike; Chandra, Tushar; Fikes, Andrew; and Gruber, Robert E. "BigTable: A Distributed Storage System for Structured Data." http://static.googleusercontent .com/external_content/untrusted_dlcp/research.google.com/en/us/archive/ bigtable-osdi06.pdf.

Chen, Yanpei; Ganapathi, Archana Sulochana; and Katz, Randy H. "To Compress or not to Compress — Compute vs. I/O Tradeoffs for MapReduce Energy Efficiency." http://www .eecs.berkeley.edu/Pubs/TechRpts/2010/EECS-2010-36.pdf.

Dikant, Peter. "Storing Log Messages in Hadoop." http://blog.mgm-tp.com/2010/04/ hadoop-log-management-part2/.

Dimiduk, Nick, and Khurana, Amandeep. HBase in Action (Shelter Island, NY: Manning Publications, 2012). http://www.amazon.com/HBase-Action-Nick-Dimiduk/ dp/1617290521/.

George, Lars. *HBase: The Definitive Guide* (Sebastopol, CA:O'Reilly Media, 2011). http://www.amazon.com/HBase-Definitive-Guide-Lars-George/dp/1449396100.

Ghemawat, Sanjay; Gobioff, Howard; and Leung, Shun-Tak. "The Google File System." http://www.cs.brown.edu/courses/cs295-11/2006/gfs.pdf.

"HDFS Architecture Guide." http://hadoop.apache.org/docs/stable/hdfs_design.html.

"HDFS High Availability with NFS." http://hadoop.apache.org/docs/current/hadoop-yarn/hadoop-yarn-site/HDFSHighAvailabilityWithNFS.html.

"HDFS High Availability Using the Quorum Journal Manager." http://hadoop.apache.org/docs/current/hadoop-yarn/hadoop-yarn-site/HDFSHighAvailabilityWithQJM.html.

Radia, Sanjay. "HA Namenode for HDFS with Hadoop 1.0." http://hortonworks.com/blog/ha-namenode-for-hdfs-with-hadoop-1-0-part-1/.

"Simple Example to Read and Write Files from Hadoop DFS." http://wiki.apache.org/hadoop/HadoopDfsReadWriteExample.

Srinivas, Suresh. "An Introduction to HDFS Federation." http://hortonworks.com/blog/an-introduction-to-hdfs-federation/.

"The Hadoop Distributed File System." http://developer.yahoo.com/hadoop/tutorial/module2.html.

White, Tom. *Hadoop: The Definitive Guide* (Sebastopol, CA:O'Reilly Media, 2012). http://www.amazon.com/Hadoop-Definitive-Guide-Tom-White/dp/1449311520/.

White, Tom. "HDFS Reliability." http://www.cloudera.com/wp-content/uploads/2010/03/HDFS_Reliability.pdf.

Zuanich, Jon. "Hadoop I/O: Sequence, Map, Set, Array, BloomMap Files." http://www.cloudera.com/blog/2011/01/hadoop-io-sequence-map-set-array-bloommap-files/.

MAPREDUCE

Adjiman, Philippe. "Hadoop Tutorial Series, Issue #4: To Use or not to Use a Combiner." http://philippeadjiman.com/blog/2010/01/14/hadoop-tutorial-series-issue-4-to-use-or-not-to-use-a-combiner/.

"Apache Hadoop NextGen MapReduce (YARN)." http://hadoop.apache.org/docs/current/hadoop-yarn/hadoop-yarn-site/YARN.html.

Blomo, Jim. "Exploring Hadoop OutputFormat." http://www.infoq.com/articles/HadoopOutputFormat.

Brumitt, Barry. "MapReduce Design Patterns." http://www.cs.washington.edu/education/courses/cse490h/11wi/CSE490H_files/mapr-design.pdf.

"C++ World Count." http://wiki.apache.org/hadoop/C%2B%2BWordCount.

Cohen, Jonathan. "Graph Twiddling in a MapReduce World." http://www.adjoint-functors.net/su/web/354/references/graph-processing-w-mapreduce.pdf.

"Configuring Eclipse for Hadoop Development (a Screencast)." http://www.cloudera.com/blog/2009/04/configuring-eclipse-for-hadoop-development-a-screencast/.

Dean, Jeffrey, and Ghemawat, Sanjay. "MapReduce: Simplified Data Processing on Large Clusters." http://www.usenix.org/event/osdi04/tech/full_papers/dean/dean.pdf.

Ghosh, Pranab. "Map Reduce Secondary Sort Does it All." http://pkghosh.wordpress.com/2011/04/13/map-reduce-secondary-sort-does-it-all/.

Grigorik, Ilya. "Easy Map-Reduce with Hadoop Streaming." http://www.igvita.com/2009/06/01/easy-map-reduce-with-hadoop-streaming/.

"Hadoop MapReduce Next Generation — Writing YARN Applications." http://hadoop.apache.org/docs/current/hadoop-yarn/hadoop-yarn-site/WritingYarnApplications.html.

"Hadoop Tutorial." http://archive.cloudera.com/cdh/3/hadoop/mapred_tutorial.html#Partitioner.

"How to Include Third-Party Libraries in Your Map-Reduce Job." `http://www.cloudera.com/blog/2011/01/how-to-include-third-party-libraries-in-your-map-reduce-job/`.

Katsov, Ilya. "MapReduce Patterns, Algorithms, and Use Cases." `http://highlyscalable.wordpress.com/2012/02/01/mapreduce-patterns/`.

Lin, Jimmy, and Dyer, Chris. *Data-Intensive Text Processing with MapReduce* (San Francisco: Morgan & Claypool, 2010). `http://www.amazon.com/Data-Intensive-Processing-MapReduce-Synthesis-Technologies/dp/1608453421`.

Mamtani, Vinod. "Design Patterns in Map-Reduce." `http://nimbledais.com/?p=66`.

MapReduce website. `http://www.mapreduce.org/`.

Mathew, Ashwin J. "Design Patterns in the Wild." `http://courses.ischool.berkeley.edu/i290-1/s08/presentations/Day6.pdf`.

Murthy, Arun C. "Apache Hadoop: Best Practices and Anti-Patterns." `http://developer.yahoo.com/blogs/hadoop/posts/2010/08/apache_hadoop_best_practices_a/`.

Murthy, Arun C.; Douglas, Chris; Konar, Mahadev; O'Malley, Owen; Radia, Sanjay; Agarwal, Sharad; Vinod; K V. "Architecture of Next Generation Apache Hadoop MapReduce Framework." `https://issues.apache.org/jira/secure/attachment/12486023/MapReduce_NextGen_Architecture.pdf`.

Noll, Michael G. "Writing an Hadoop MapReduce Program in Python." `http://www.michael-noll.com/tutorials/writing-an-hadoop-mapreduce-program-in-python/`.

Owen, Sean; Anil, Robin; Dunning, Ted; and Friedman, Ellen. *Mahout in Action* (Shelter Island, NY: Manning Publications, 2011). `http://www.amazon.com/Mahout-Action-Sean-Owen/dp/1935182684/ref=sr_1_1?s=books&ie=UTF8&qid=1327246973&sr=1-1`.

Rehman, Shuja. "XML Processing in Hadoop." `http://xmlandhadoop.blogspot.com/`.

Riccomini, Chris. "Tutorial: Sort Reducer Input Values in Hadoop." `http://riccomini.name/posts/hadoop/2009-11-13-sort-reducer-input-value-hadoop/`.

Shewchuk, Richard. "An Introduction to the Conjugate Gradient Method Without the Agonizing Pain." `http://www.cs.cmu.edu/~quake-papers/painless-conjugate-gradient.pdf`.

"Splunk App for HadoopOps." `http://www.splunk.com/web_assets/pdfs/secure/Splunk_for_HadoopOps.pdf`.

Thiebaut, Dominique. "Hadoop Tutorial 2.2 — Running C++ Programs on Hadoop." `http://cs.smith.edu/dftwiki/index.php/Hadoop_Tutorial_2.2_--_Running_C%2B%2B_Programs_on_Hadoop`.

"When to Use a Combiner." `http://lucene.472066.n3.nabble.com/When-to-use-a-combiner-td3685452.html`.

Winkels, Maarten. "Thinking MapReduce with Hadoop." `http://blog.xebia.com/2009/07/02/thinking-mapreduce-with-hadoop/`.

"Working with Hadoop under Eclipse." `http://wiki.apache.org/hadoop/EclipseEnvironment`.

"Hadoop Streaming with Ruby and Wukong." `http://labs.paradigmatecnologico.com/2011/04/29/howto-hadoop-streaming-with-ruby-and-wukong/`.

"Yahoo! Hadoop Tutorial." `http://developer.yahoo.com/hadoop/tutorial/`.

Zaharia, Matei; Borthakur, Dhruba; Sarma, Joydeep Sen; Elmeleegy, Khaled; Shenker, Scott; and Stoica, Ion. "Delay Scheduling: A Simple Technique for Achieving Locality and Fairness in Cluster Scheduling." `http://www.cs.berkeley.edu/~matei/papers/2010/eurosys_delay_scheduling.pdf`.

OOZIE

"Oozie Bundle Specification." http://oozie.apache.org/docs/3.1.3-incubating/BundleFunctionalSpec.html.

"Oozie Client javadocs." http://archive.cloudera.com/cdh/3/oozie/client/apidocs/index.html.

"Oozie Command Line Utility." http://rvs.github.io/oozie/releases/1.6.0/DG_CommandLineTool.html.

"Oozie Coordinator Specification." http://archive.cloudera.com/cdh/3/oozie/CoordinatorFunctionalSpec.html.

"Oozie Custom Action Nodes." http://oozie.apache.org/docs/3.3.0/DG_CustomActionExecutor.html.

"Oozie Source Code." https://github.com/apache/oozie.

"Oozie Specification, a Hadoop Workflow System." http://oozie.apache.org/.

"Oozie Web Services APIs." http://archive.cloudera.com/cdh4/cdh/4/oozie/WebServicesAPI.html.

"xjc Binding Compiler." http://docs.oracle.com/javase/6/docs/technotes/tools/share/xjc.html.

REAL-TIME HADOOP

"Actors Model." http://c2.com/cgi/wiki?ActorsModel.

"Add Search to HBASE." https://issues.apache.org/jira/browse/HBASE-3529.

"Apache Solr." http://lucene.apache.org/solr/.

Bienvenido, David, III. "Twitter Storm: Open Source Real-Time Hadoop." http://www.infoq.com/news/2011/09/twitter-storm-real-time-hadoop.

Borthakur, Dhruba; Muthukkaruppan, Kannan; Ranganathan, Karthik; Rash, Samuel; Sarma; Joydeep Sen, Spiegelberg, Nicolas; Molkov, Dmytro; Schmidt, Rodrigo; Gray, Jonathan; Kuang, Hairong; Menon, Aravind; and Aiyer, Amitanand. "Apache Hadoop Goes Realtime at Facebook." http://borthakur.com/ftp/RealtimeHadoopSigmod2011.pdf.

"Cassandra." http://cassandra.apache.org/.

Haller, Mike. "Spatial Search with Lucene." http://www.mhaller.de/archives/156-Spatial-search-with-Lucene.html.

"HBase Avro Server." http://hbase.apache.org/0.94/apidocs/org/apache/hadoop/hbase/avro/AvroServer.HBaseImpl.html.

"HBasene." https://github.com/akkumar/hbasene.

"HBasePS." https://github.com/sentric/HBasePS.

"HStreaming." http://www.hstreaming.com/.

Ingersoll, Grant. "Location-Aware Search with Apache Lucene and Solr." http://www.ibm.com/developerworks/opensource/library/j-spatial/.

Kumar, Animesh. "Apache Lucene and Cassandra." http://anismiles.wordpress.com/2010/05/19/apache-lucene-and-cassandra/.

Kumar, Animesh. "Lucandra — An Inside Story!" http://anismiles.wordpress.com/2010/05/27/lucandra-an-inside-story/.

Lawson, Loraine. "Exploring Hadoop's Real-Time Potential." http://www.itbusinessedge.com/cm/blogs/lawson/exploring-hadoops-real-time-potential/?cs=49692.

"Local Lucene Geographical Search." http://www.nsshutdown.com/projects/lucene/whitepaper/locallucene_v2.html.

"Lucandra." https://github.com/tjake/Lucandra.

Marz, Nathan. "A Storm Is Coming: More Details and Plans for Release." http://engineering.twitter.com/2011/08/storm-is-coming-more-details-and-plans.html.

Marz, Nathan. "Preview of Storm: The Hadoop of Realtime Processing." https://www.memonic.com/user/pneff/folder/queue/id/1qSgf.

McCandless, Michael; Hatcher, Erik; and Gospodnetic, Otis. *Lucene in Action, Second Edition* (Shelter Island, NY: Manning Publications, 2010). http://www.amazon.com/Lucene-Action-Second-Covers-Apache/dp/1933988177/ref=sr_1_1?ie=UTF8&qid=1292717735&sr=8-1.

"OpenTSDB." http://opentsdb.net/.

"Powered by Lucene." http://wiki.apache.org/lucene-java/PoweredBy.

"Stargate." http://wiki.apache.org/hadoop/Hbase/Stargate.

"Thrift APIs." http://wiki.apache.org/hadoop/Hbase/ThriftApi.

AWS

"Amazon CloudWatch." http://aws.amazon.com/cloudwatch/.

"Amazon Elastic MapReduce." http://aws.amazon.com/elasticmapreduce/.

"Amazon Simple Storage Service." http://aws.amazon.com/s3/.

"Amazon Simple Workflow Service." http://aws.amazon.com/swf/.

"Apache Whirr." http://whirr.apache.org/.

"AWS Data Pipeline." http://aws.amazon.com/datapipeline/.

"How-to: Set Up an Apache Hadoop/Apache HBase Cluster on EC2." http://blog.cloudera.com/blog/2012/10/set-up-a-hadoophbase-cluster-on-ec2-in-about-an-hour/.

Linton, Rob. *Amazon Web Services: Migrating Your .NET Enterprise Application* (Olton, Birmingham, United Kingdom: Packt Publishing, 2011). http://www.amazon.com/Amazon-Web-Services-Enterprise-Application/dp/1849681945.

"What Are the Advantages of Amazon EMR, Vs. Your Own EC2 Instances, Vs. Running Hadoop Locally?" http://www.quora.com/What-are-the-advantages-of-Amazon-EMR-vs-your-own-EC2-instances-vs-running-Hadoop-locally. (quora account required).

HADOOP DSLS

"Apache Hama." http://hama.apache.org/.

Capriolo, Edward; Wampler, Dean; and Jason Rutherglen. *Programming Hive* (Sebastopol, CA: O'Reilly Media, 2012). http://www.amazon.com/Programming-Hive-Edward-Capriolo/dp/1449319335/ref=sr_1_1?s=books&ie=UTF8&qid=1368408335&sr=1-1&keywords=hive.

"Cascading/CoPA." https://github.com/Cascading/CoPA.

"Cascading Lingual." http://www.cascading.org/lingual/.

"Cascading Pattern." http://www.cascading.org/pattern/.

Cascading website. http://www.cascading.org/.

Cascalog website. https://github.com/nathanmarz/cascalog.

Crunch website. `https://github.com/cloudera/crunch/tree/master/scrunch`.

Czajkowski, Grzegorz. "Large-Scale Graph Computing at Google." `http://googleresearch.blogspot.com/2009/06/large-scale-graph-computing-at-google.html`.

"Domain Specific Language." `http://c2.com/cgi/wiki?DomainSpecificLanguage`.

Gates, Alan. *Programming Pig* (Sebastopol, CA: O'Reilly Media, 2011). `http://www.amazon.com/Programming-Pig-Alan-Gates/dp/1449302645/ref=sr_1_1?ie=UTF8&qid=1375109835&sr=8-1&keywords=Gates%2C+Alan.+Programming+Pig`.

"Introduction to Apache Crunch." `http://crunch.apache.org/intro.html`.

Fowler, Martin. *Domain-Specific Languages* (Boston: Addison-Wesley, 2010). `http://www.amazon.com/Domain-Specific-Languages-Addison-Wesley-Signature-Fowler/dp/0321712943`.

Scalding website. `https://github.com/twitter/scalding`.

"Welcome to Apache Giraph!" `http://giraph.apache.org/`.

"What Are the Differences between Crunch and Cascading?" `http://www.quora.com/Apache-Hadoop/What-are-the-differences-between-Crunch-and-Cascading`.

Wills, Josh. "Apache Crunch: A Java Library for Easier MapReduce Programming." `http://www.infoq.com/articles/ApacheCrunch`.

HADOOP AND BIG DATA SECURITY

"Accumulo User Manual — Security." `http://accumulo.apache.org/1.4/user_manual/Security.html`.

"Apache Accumulo." `http://accumulo.apache.org/`.

"Authentication for Hadoop Web-Based Consoles." `http://hadoop.apache.org/docs/stable/HttpAuthentication.html`.

Becherer, Andrew. "Hadoop Security Design – Just Add Kerberos? Really?" `https://media.blackhat.com/bh-us-10/whitepapers/Becherer/BlackHat-USA-2010-Becherer-Andrew-Hadoop-Security-wp.pdf`.

Dwork, Cynthia. "Differential Privacy", from 33rd International Colloquium on Automata, Languages, and Programming, Part II (ICALP 2006) (Springer Verlag, 2007), available at `http://research.microsoft.com/apps/pubs/default.aspx?id=64346`.

"Hadoop Service Level Authorization Guide." `http://hadoop.apache.org/docs/stable/service_level_auth.html`.

"HDFS Permissions Guide." `http://hadoop.apache.org/docs/stable/hdfs_permissions_guide.html`.

IETF. "Simple Authentication and Security Layer (SASL)." `http://www.ietf.org/rfc/rfc2222.txt`.

IETF. "The Kerberos Version 5 Generic Service Application Program Interface (GSS-API) Mechanism: Version 2." `http://tools.ietf.org/html/rfc4121`.

IETF. "The Simple and Protected GSS-API Negotiation (SPNEGO) Mechanism." `http://tools.ietf.org/html/rfc4178`.

"Kerberos: The Network Authentication Protocol." `http://web.mit.edu/kerberos/`.

Naryanan, Shmatikov, "Robust De-Anonymization of Large Sparse Datasets." `http://www.cs.utexas.edu/~shmat/shmat_oak08netflix.pdf`.

O'Malley, Owen; Zhang, Kan; Radia, Sanjay; Marti, Ram; and Harrell, Christopher. "Hadoop Security Design", October 2009, available at `https://issues.apache.org/jira/secure/attachment/12428537/security-design.pdf`.

"Project Rhino." `https://github.com/intel-hadoop/project-rhino/`.

"Security Features for Hadoop", JIRA HADOOP-4487, `https://issues.apache.org/jira/browse/HADOOP-4487`.

Williams, Alex. "Intel Releases Hadoop Distribution and Project Rhino — An Effort to Bring Better Security to Big Data." `http://techcrunch.com/2013/02/26/intel-launches-hadoop-distribution-and-project-rhino-an-effort-to-bring-better-security-to-big-data/`.

INDEX

N

O

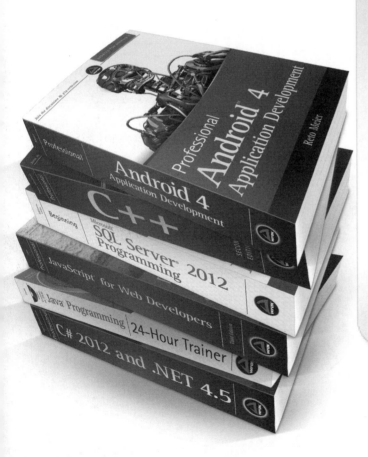